STRUGGLE FOR THE LAND

Other Books by Ward Churchill

Authored:

Fantasies of the Master Race:
Literature, Cinema and the Colonization of
American Indians
(Revised, expanded edition published by City Lights, 1998)

A Little Matter of Genocide:
Holocaust and Denial in the Americas, 1492 to the Present
(Published by City Lights, 1997)

Indians Are Us?
Culture and Genocide in Native North America (1994)

Since Predator Came:
Notes from the Struggle for American Indian Liberation (1995)

From a Native Son:
Selected Essays in Indigenism, 1985-1995 (1996)

Coauthored:

Pacifism as Pathology:
Reflections on the Role of Armed Struggle in North America
With Mike Ryan (1998)

Culture versus Economism:
Essays on Marxism in the Multicultural Arena
with Elisabeth R. Lloyd (1984)

Agents of Repression:
The FBI's Secret Wars Against the Black Panther Party
and the American Indian Movement
with Jim Vander Wall (1988)

The COINTELPRO Papers:
Documents from the FBI's Secret Wars
Against Dissent in the United States
with Jim Vander Wall (1990)

Edited:

Marxism and Native Americans (1983)

Critical Issues in Native North America (2 vols., 1989-90)

Coedited:

Cages of Steel:
The Politics of Imprisonment in the United States
with J.J. Vander Wall (1992)

STRUGGLE FOR THE LAND

NATIVE NORTH AMERICAN RESISTANCE TO GENOCIDE, ECOCIDE AND COLONIZATION

BY WARD CHURCHILL

CITY LIGHTS
SAN FRANCISCO

Cover design by Rex Ray

Library of Congress Cataloging-in-Publication Data

Churchill, Ward.
   Struggle for the land : Native North American resistance to genocide, ecocide, and
colonization / by Ward Churchill.
       p.   cm.
   Includes bibliographical references and index.
   ISBN 0-87286-414-6 / 978-0-87286-414-6 (pbk.)
       1. Indians of North America—Land tenure.   2. Indians of North America—Claims.
       3. Indians of North America—Government relations.   I. Title.
   E98.L3 .C48 2002   2002073846

Visit our website: http://www.citylights.com

CITY LIGHTS BOOKS are edited by Lawrence Ferlinghetti and Nancy J. Peters and
published at the City Lights Bookstore, 261 Columbus Avenue, San Francisco, CA 94133

for my mother

CONTENTS

FOREWORD

Buying Time

With the money they made by stealing our land
They have bought themselves some time—
Air time
Water time
War time
And underground time.
By that they believe that they have bought history.

But when I look back, past the hundreds of years
Of history they claim to own,
Through our own thousands of years,

And when I think of the millions of red flowers
That opened each Spring of those thousands of years
No matter how white the winters,

I see hours like stars in the eyes of our children.

—Jimmie Durham

INDIAN LAND CLAIMS & TREATY AREAS OF NORTH AMERICA

SUCCEEDING INTO NATIVE NORTH AMERICA
A Secessionist View

THE map on the facing page could be called the indigenous North American view of bioregional secession. Although the scale in which it is presented prevents the details from being clear, the treaty and land claim areas involved are not exactly how it was B.C. (Before Columbus). They are instead the basic outlines of the *legally* defined land areas of native nations.[1] The map, even through its general contours, may help correct some of the basic miseducation with which most non-Indian residents of the continent have been afflicted.

First, the map shows how North America's indigenous peoples lived in what amounted to natural, bioregional configurations. Second, it shows that North America's reigning nation-state governments—those of the United States and Canada—are, according to the indigenous "host" nations, on shaky grounds, both legally and environmentally. Very little land in North America should not rightly be under native jurisdiction, administered under indigenous rather than immigrant values.

Back to the first point. When I was in grade school, I was taught there were Plains Indians (warlike), Woodland Indians (democratic), and Pueblo Indians (pacifistic), and that's about all. What was left out was that the treaty areas and treaty rights of indigenous people in North America are *ongoing*, and that they accrue to recognized *nations*, demonstrating distinct sociocultural and linguistic patterns. Also omitted from my education was the fact that these nations had lived quite well within these defined territories since time immemorial; there was/is trade between each of the indigenous areas, but each was also essentially self-sufficient.

Today, a lot of people question the necessity and utility of centralized nation-state governances and economics.[2] They find the status quo to be increasingly absurd and are seeking alternatives to the values and patterns of

Notes

1. For fuller details, see Charles C. Royce, *Eighteenth Annual Report of the American Bureau of Ethnography: Indian Land Cessions in the United States* (Washington, D.C.: Smithsonian Institution, 1899).

2. A good reading in this regard is Pierre Clastres, *Society Against the State* (New York: Urizen Books, 1977).

3. For orientation to the principles at issue within the rubric of "bioregionalism," see Alexandra Hart, ed., *North American Bioregional Congress II: Proceedings, August 25-29, 1986* (Forestville, CA: Hart Publishing, 1987).

4. Leopold Kohr, *The Breakdown of Nations* (New York: E.P. Dutton, 1957) and *The Overdeveloped Nations: The Diseconomies of Scale* (New York: Schoken Books, 1978). On the struggles of the indigenous peoples of Iberia, see Kenneth Medhurst, *The Basques and Catalans*, Minority Rights Group Report No. 9, Sept. 1977.

5. For parallel analysis centered in a practical contemporary application, see Gudmundur Alfredson, "Greenland and the Law of Political Decolonization" (Bonn: *German Yearbook on International Law*, 1982).

6. See Zed Nanda, "Self-Determination Under International Law: Validity of Claims to Secede," *Case Western Reserve Journal of International Law*, No. 13, 1981.

THE INDIGENOUS PEOPLES OF NORTH AMERICA
A Struggle Against Internal Colonialism

> The Europeans who began taking over the New World in the sixteenth and seventeenth centuries were not ecologists. Although they were compelled to realize that the Americas were not quite *un*inhabited, they were not prepared to recognize that these new lands were, in an ecological sense, much more than "sparsely" inhabited. This second hemisphere was, in fact, essentially "full."

> —William Catton
> *Overshoot*

THE standard Euroamerican depiction of "precontact" Native North Americans has long been that the relative handful of us who existed wandered about perpetually in scattered bands, grubbing out the most marginal subsistence by hunting and gathering, never developing writing or serious appreciations of art, science, mathematics, governance, and so on. Aside from our utilization of furs and hides for clothing, the manufacture of stone implements, use of fire, and domestication of the dog, there is little in this view to distinguish us from the higher orders of mammalian life surrounding us in the "American wilderness."[1]

The conclusions reached by those who claim to idealize "Indianness" are little different at base from the findings of those who openly denigrate it: Native people were able to inhabit the hemisphere for tens of thousands of years without causing appreciable ecological disruption only because we lacked the intellectual capacity to create social forms and technologies that would substantially alter our physical environment. In effect, a sort of sociocultural retardation on the part of Indians is typically held to be responsible for the pristine quality of the Americas at the point of their "discovery" by Europeans.[2]

In contrast to this perspective, it has recently been demonstrated that, far from living hand-to-mouth, "Stone Age" Indians adhered to an economic structure that not only met their immediate needs but provided considerable surpluses of both material goods and leisure time.[3] It has also been established that most traditional native economies were based in agriculture rather than hunting and gathering—a clear indication of a stationary, not nomadic, way of life—until the European invasion dislocated the indigenous populations of North America.[4]

It is also argued that native peoples' long-term coexistence with our environment was possible only because of our extremely low population density. Serious historians and demographers have lately documented how estimates of precontact indigenous population levels were deliberately lowered during the nineteenth and early twentieth centuries in order to lessen the implications of genocide bound up in the policies of the U.S., Canada and their colonial antecedents.[5] A noted ecologist has also recently determined that, rather than being dramatically underpopulated, North America was in fact saturated with people in 1500. The feasible carrying capacity of the continent was, moreover, outstripped by the European influx by 1840, despite massive reductions of native populations and numerous species of large mammals.[6]

Another myth is contained in the suggestion that indigenous forms of government were less refined than those of their European counterparts. The lie is put to this notion, however, when it is considered that the enlightened republicanism established by the United States during the late 1700s—usually considered an advance over then-prevailing European norms—was lifted directly from the model of the currently still functioning Haudenosaunee (Iroquois) confederacy.[7] In many ways the Haudenosaunee were indicative of political arrangements throughout Native North America.[8] American Indians evidenced similar achievements in preventative medicine, mathematics, astronomy, architecture and engineering, all without engendering appreciable environmental disruption.[9] Such a juxtaposition of advanced sociocultural matrices and sustained ecological equilibrium is inexplicable from the vantage point of conventional Euroderivative assumptions.

Unlike Europeans, Native Americans long ago attained a profound intellectual apprehension that human progress must be measured as an integral aspect of the natural order rather than as something apart from and superior to it. Within this body of knowledge, elaborated and perfected through oral tradition and codified as "law" in ceremonial/ritual forms, the indigenous peoples of this hemisphere lived comfortably and in harmony with the environment, the health of which was recognized as an absolute requirement for our continued existence.[10]

In simplest terms, the American Indian world view may be this: Human beings are free—indeed, encouraged—to develop our innate capabilities, but only in ways that do not infringe upon other elements—called "relations," in the fullest dialectical sense of the word—of nature. Any activity going beyond this is considered as "imbalance," a transgression, and is strictly prohibited. Engineering, for example, was and is permissible, but only insofar as it does not permanently alter the earth itself. Similarly, agriculture was widespread, but only within parameters that did not supplant natural vegetation.[11]

Key to the indigenous American outlook is a firm acknowledgment that the human population may expand only to the point, determined by natural geographic and environmental circumstances, where it begins to displace other animal species and requires the permanent substitution of cropland for normal vegetation in any area. North America's aboriginal populations never entered into a trajectory of excessive growth, and, even today, many native societies practice a self-regulation of population size that allows the substance of our traditional world views with their interactive environmental relationships to remain viable.[12]

Cultural Imperialism

> They came for our land, for what grew or could be grown on it, for the resources in it, and for our clean air and pure water. They stole these things from us, and in the taking they also stole our free ways and the best of our leaders, killed in battle or assassinated. And now, after all that, they've come for the very last of our possessions; now they want our pride, our history, our spiritual traditions. They want to rewrite and remake these things, to claim them for themselves. The lies and thefts just never end.
>
> —Margo Thunderbird, 1988

Within the industrial wasteland of the late twentieth century, such traditional perspectives are deformed right along with the physical dimensions of indigenous culture. Trivialized and co-opted, they have been reduced to the stuff of the settler society's self-serving pop mythology, commercialized and exploited endlessly by everyone from the Hollywood moguls and hippie filmmakers who over the past 75 years have produced literally thousands of celluloid parodies not merely of our histories, but of our most sacred beliefs, to New Age yuppie airheads like Lynne Andrews who pen lucrative "feminist" fables of our spirituality, to the flabbily overprivileged denizens of the "Men's Movement" indulging themselves in their "Wildman Weekends," to psuedoacademic frauds like Carlos Castaneda who fabricate our traditions out of whole cloth, to "well-intentioned friends" like Jerry Mander who simply appropriate the real thing for their own purposes. The list might easily be extended for pages.[13]

Representative of the mentality is an oft-televised public service announcement featuring an aging Indian, clad in beads and buckskins, framed against a backdrop of smoking factory chimneys while picking his way carefully among the mounds of rusting junk along a well-polluted river. He concludes his walk through the modern world by shedding a tragic tear induced by the panorama of rampant devastation surrounding him. The use of an archaic Indian image in this connection is intended to stir the settler population's subliminal craving for absolution. "Having obliterated Native North America as a means of expropriating its landbase," the subtext reads, "Euroamerica is now obliged to 'make things right' by preserving and protecting what was stolen." Should it meet the challenge, presumably, not only will its forebears' unparalleled aggression at last be in some sense redeemed, but so too will the blood-drenched inheritance they bequeathed to their posterity be in that sense legitimated. The whole thing is of course a sham, a glib contrivance designed by and for the conquerors to promote their sense of psychic reconciliation with the facts and fruits of the conquest.[14]

A primary purpose of this book is to disturb—better yet, to destroy altogether—such self-serving and -satisfied tranquillity. In doing so, its aim is to participate in restoring things Indian to the realm of reality. My hope is that it helps in the process to heal the disjuncture between the past, present and future of Native North American peoples which has been imposed by nearly four centuries of unrelenting conquest, subjugation and dispossession on the part of Euroamerica's multitudinous invaders. This does not make for pleasant reading, nor should it, for my message is that there can be no absolution, no redemption of past crimes unless the outcomes are changed. So long as the aggressors' posterity continue to reap the benefits of that aggression, the crimes are merely replicated in the present. In effect, the aggression remains ongoing and, in that, there can be no legitimacy. Not now, not ever.

Contemporary Circumstances

> We are not ethnic groups. Ethnic groups run restaurants serving "exotic" foods. We are *nations.*

> —Brooklyn Rivera, 1986

The current situation of the indigenous peoples of the United States and Canada is generally miscast as being that of ethnic/racial minorities. This is a fundamental misrepresentation in at least two ways. First, there is no given ethnicity which encompasses those who are indigenous to North America. Rather, there are several hundred distinctly different cultures—"ethnicities," in anthropological parlance—lumped together under the catch-all classification of "Native Americans" (and/or "Aboriginals" in Canada). Similarly, at least three noticeably different "gene stocks"—the nomenclature of "race"—are encompassed by such designators. Biologically, "Amerinds" like the Cherokees and Ojibwes are as different from Inuits ("Eskimo-Aleuts") and such "Athabascan" ("Na-Dene") types as the Apaches and Navajos as Mongolians are from Swedes or Bantus.[15]

Secondly, all concepts of ethnic or racial minority status fail conspicuously to convey the sense of *national* identity by which most or all North American indigenous populations define ourselves. Nationality, not race or ethnicity, is the most important single factor in understanding the reality of Native North America today.[16] It is this sense of ourselves as comprising coherent and viable nations which lends substance and logic to the forms of struggle in which we have engaged over the past third of a century and more.[17]

It is imperative when considering this point to realize that there is nothing rhetorical, metaphorical or symbolic at issue. On the contrary, a concrete and precise meaning is intended. The indigenous peoples of North America—indeed, everywhere in the hemisphere—not only constituted but continue to constitute nations according to even the strictest definitions of the term. This can be asserted on the basis of two major legal premises, as well as a range of more material considerations. Let's take them in order:

- To begin with, there is a doctrine in modern international law known as the "right of inherent sovereignty" holding that a people constitutes

19

a nation, and is thus entitled to exercise the rights of such, simply because it has done so "since time immemorial." That is, from the moment of its earliest contact with other nations the people in question have been known to possess a given territory, a means of providing their own subsistence (economy), a common language, a structure of governance and corresponding form of legality, and a means of determining membership/social composition. As was to some extent shown above, there can be no question but that Native North American peoples met each of these criteria at the point of initial contact with Europeans.[18]

- Second, it is a given of international law, custom and convention that treatymaking and treaty relations are entered into *only* by nations. This principle is constitutionally enshrined in both U.S. and Canadian domestic law. Article 1 of the U.S. Constitution, for instance, clearly restricts treatymaking prerogatives to the federal rather than state, local or individual levels. In turn, the federal government itself is forbidden to enter into a treaty relationship with any entity aside from another fully sovereign nation (i.e., it is specifically *dis*empowered from treating with provincial, state or local governments, or with corporations and individuals). It follows that the U.S. government's entry into some 400 ratified treaty relationships with North America's indigenous peoples—an even greater number prevail in Canada—abundantly corroborates our various claims to sovereign national standing.[19]

Officials in both North American nation-states, as well as the bulk of the settler intelligentsia aligned with them, presently contend that, while native peoples may present an impeccable argument on moral grounds, and a technically valid legal case as well, pragmatic considerations in "the real world at the dawn of the twenty-first century" precludes actualization of our national independence, autonomy, or any other manifestation of genuine self-determination. By their lights, indigenous peoples are too small, both in terms of our respective landbases/attendant resources and in population size(s), to survive either militarily or economically in the contemporary international context.[20]

At first glance, such thinking seems plausible enough, even humane. Delving a bit deeper, however, we find that it conveniently ignores the examples of such tiny European nations as San Marino, Monaco and Liechtenstein, which have survived for centuries amidst the greediest and most warlike continental setting in the history of the world. Further, it blinks the matter of comparably sized nations in the Caribbean and Pacific Basins whose sovereignty is not only acknowledged, but whose recent admissions to the United Nations have been endorsed by both Canada and the U.S. (See charts on following pages.) Plainly, each of these countries is at least as militarily vulnerable as any North American Indian people. The contradictions attending U.S./Canadian Indian policy are thus readily apparent to anyone willing to view the situation honestly. The truth is that the nation-states' "humanitarianism" is in this connection no more than a gloss meant to disguise a very different set of goals, objectives and sensibilities.

Nor do arguments to the "intrinsic insolvency" of indigenous economies hold up to even minimal scrutiny. The Navajo Nation, for instance, possesses a landbase larger than those of Monaco, Fiji and Grenada combined. Within this area lies an estimated 150 billion tons of low sulfur coal, about forty percent of "U.S." uranium reserves and significant deposits of oil, natural gas, gold, silver, copper and gypsum, among other minerals. This is aside from a limited but very real grazing and agricultural capacity.[21] By any standard of conventional economic measure, the Navajos—or Diné, as they call themselves—have a relatively wealthy resource base as compared to many Third World nations and more than a few "developed" ones. To hold that the Navajo Nation could not survive economically in the modern world while admitting that Grenada, Monaco and Fiji *can* is to indulge in sheer absurdity (or duplicity).

While Navajo is probably the best illustration of the material basis for assertions of complete autonomy by Native North American nations, it is by no means the only one. The combined Lakota reservations in North and South Dakota yield an aggregate landbase even larger than that of the Diné and, while it exhibits a somewhat less spectacular range of mineral assets, this is largely offset by a greater agricultural/grazing capacity and smaller population size.[22] Other, smaller, indigenous nations possess landbases entirely adequate to support their populations and many are endowed with rich economic potentials which vary from minerals to timbering to ranching and farming to fishing and aquaculture. Small-scale manufacturing and even tourism also offer viable options in many instances.[23]

All this natural wealth exists within the currently held native landbase ("reserves" in Canada, "reservations" in the U.S.). Nothing has been said thus far about the possibility that something approximating a just resolution

Table 1 Comparative National Landbases

Nation	Square Miles	Indian Tribe	Square Miles	Nation	Square Miles	Indian Tribe	Square Miles
1. Costa Rica	19,575	Navajo	21,838			Fort Belknap	1,027
2. Dominican Republic	18,816					Flathead Tribe	969
3. Bhutan	18,147					Red Lake Chippewa	882
4. Denmark	16,619					Warm Springs Tribe	881
5. Switzerland	15,941					Fort Hall Shoshone	817
6. Netherlands	14,125					Pyramid Lake Paiute	742
7. Taiwan	13,886						
8. Belgium	11,781					Mescalero Apache	719
9. Lesotho	11,716					Northern Cheyenne	678
10. Albania	11,100					Laguna Pueblo	652
11. Equatorial Guinea	10,852					Fort Berthold	651
12. Burundi	10,747					Zuni Pueblo	636
13. Haiti	10,714					Sisseton	629
14. Rwanda	10,166					Pima	582
15. El Salvador	8,260					Walker River	500
16. Israel	7,993					Duck Valley	452
17. Fiji	7,055					Kiowa, Comanche, Apache	370
18. Swaziland	6,704					Osage	340
19. Kuwait	6,178					Spokane	300
20. Qatar	6,000			28. Mauritius	720		
21. Jamaica	4,411	Papago	4,460	29. Tonga	269		
22. Lebanon	4,015			30. Bahrain	231		
23. Gambia	4,005			31. Singapore	226	Quinault	200
24. Cyprus	3,572	Hopi	3,862			Kaibab Piute	188
		Wind River Tribes	2,947	32. Andorra	179		
		White Mountain Apache	2,898	33. Barbados	166	Rocky Boys	162
		San Carlos Apache	2,855			Chippewa-Cree	
		Pine Ridge Sioux	2,600			Nez Percé	137
		Crow Tribe	2,434			Hoopa Valley	134
		Cheyenne River Sioux	2,210	34. Malta	122		
25. Trinidad and Tobago	1,979			35. Maldives	112		
		Yakima Tribe	1,711			Couer d'Alene	108
		Uintah and Ouray	1,581				
		Colville Tribe	1,569	36. Liechtenstein	62		
		Hualapai Tribe	1,551	37. San Marino	23.5		
		Fort Peck Sioux	1,534	38. Nauru	8		
		Rosebud Sioux	1,526	39. Monaco	0.6		
		Blackfeet Tribe	1,420	40. Vatican City	0.17		
		Standing Rock Sioux	1,320				
		Jicarilla Apache Tribe	1,159				
26. Western Samoa	1,130						
27. Luxembourg	999						

Source: Vine Deloria, Jr., "The Size and Status of Nations," in Susan Lobo and Steve Talbot, eds., *Native American Voices: A Reader* (New York: Longman, 1998) pp.460-1.

Table 2

Countries with Fewer than 1,000,000 Population

1.	Vatican City	1,000
2.	Nauru	7,000
3.	San Marino	20,000
4.	Andorra	20,550
5.	Liechtenstein	21,550
6.	Monaco	23,000
7.	Tonga	90,000
8.	Maldives	110,000
9.	Qatar	115,000
10.	Western Samoa	146,000
11.	United Arab Emirates	200,000
12.	Sikkim	200,000
13.	Iceland	210,000
14.	Bahrain	220,000
15.	Barbados	240,000
16.	Equatorial Guinea	290,000
17.	Malta	330,000
18.	Luxembourg	340,000
19.	Gambia	380,000
20.	Swaziland	420,000
21.	Gabon	500,000
22.	Fiji	533,000
23.	Cyprus	640,000
24.	Botswana	670,000
25.	Oman	680,000
26.	Guyana	740,000
27.	Kuwait	830,000
28.	Mauritius	840,000
29.	Lesotho	930,000
30.	Congo (Brazzaville)	960,000

Source: Vine Deloria, Jr., "The Size and Status of Nations," in Susan Lobo and Steve Talbot, eds., *Native American Voices: A Reader* (New York: Longman, 1998) p.463.

might be effected concerning indigenous claims to vast territories retained by treaty—or to which title is held through unextinguished aboriginal right—all of which has been unlawfully expropriated by the two North American settler-states.[24] Here, the Lakota Nation alone would stand to recover, on the basis of the still-binding 1868 Fort Laramie Treaty, some five percent of the U.S. 48 contiguous states area. The region includes the Black Hills, reputedly the 100 most mineral-rich square miles on the entire planet.[25] All told, naturalization of persons residing within the treaty areas— or those who might wish to relocate there for purposes of placing themselves under native rather than U.S./Canadian jurisdiction—would likely increase the citizenry of Native North America by several millions.[26]

In sum, just as the indigenous peoples of North America "once" possessed the requisite ingredients of nationhood, so too do we continue to possess them. This is true whether one uses as one's point(s) of reference the dimension of our territories, the basis of our economies, the size of our populations, or any other reasonable criteria. Perhaps most important in a legal sense, as well as in terms of ethics and morality, we continue to hold our inherent rights and standing as nations because, quite simply and undeniably, we have never voluntarily relinquished them. To argue otherwise, as so many settler officials and "scholars" are prone to do, is to argue the invalidity of the Laws of Nations.[27]

Internal Colonialism

> The sea, O the sea, *a ghrádh-gheal mo chrí*,
> Long may it roll between England and me;
> God help the poor Scotsmen, they'll never be free
> But we are surrounded by water!
>
> —Traditional Irish Song

One of the major problems confronting those seeking to articulate the situation of indigenous nations on this continent has to do with the form of imperialism imposed upon us: "internal colonialism." Admittedly, the idea is a bit unorthodox. The conventional analysis of colonization ranges from that adopted by the United Nations under Resolution 1514 (XV) in 1960— which requires by strict definition that at least thirty miles of open "blue water" separate colonizer from colonized for a condition of "true" colonialism to exist[28]—to that of typical socialist thinking, which, with certain

24

exceptions, adheres to a somewhat less rigid but nonetheless similar interpretation.[29]

Internal colonialism, on the other hand, is the result of an especially virulent and totalizing socioeconomic and political penetration whereby the colonizing power quite literally swallows up contiguous areas and peoples, incorporating them directly into itself.[30] In a closely related variation known as "settler-state colonialism," the colonizing power exports a sufficient portion of its own population ("settlers"), to supplant rather than simply subordinate the indigenous people(s) of the colony.[31] Often, under such conditions, the settler population itself eventually revolts against the Mother Country and establishes itself as an independent or quasi-independent sovereignty. Indigenous peoples/nations are consequently encapsulated *within* the resulting "settler-state's" claimed territory rather than being subject to the more classic formula of domination from abroad.[32]

Aside from the U.S. and Canada, the modern world witnesses numerous other examples of this phenomenon. Among these are Australia, New Zealand, Northern Ireland, Israel, Kurdistan, and most of South and Central America.[33] Until their transformations by African liberation forces, both Zimbabwe (formerly Rhodesia) and South Africa (Azania) fell into this category.[34] The same could be said of the host of nationalities encapsulated within the former Soviet Union, as well as those within present-day China.[35] Additionally, a variant form of internal colonialism may be seen as prevailing in many of the old compartments of the classic European empires: Zaire vis-à-vis Katanga, for instance, or India vis-à-vis Nagaland.[36] By the same token, it is possible to view a number of peoples in Europe itself—the Welsh and Scots in the United Kingdom, for example, or the Basques and Catalans in Spain—as being internally colonized nations.[37]

Plainly, the magnitude of the problem represented by internal colonialism has been vastly underestimated, or rather arbitrarily discounted, by analysts of virtually every ideological persuasion. One solid indication may be found, however, in a survey conducted during the late 1980s. Conducted by cultural geographer Bernard Neitschmann, it revealed that of the more than 100 armed conflicts then raging around the world, about 85 percent were between indigenous peoples and one or more nation-states presuming to exercise jurisdictional authority over them and/or their traditional territories.[38] Little has transpired since then to change things for the better. On the contrary, indications are that escalation has occurred in many quarters.[39]

This, then, is the context in which the native liberation struggle in North America should be viewed. The agendas of the American Indian Movement (AIM) and the more organic warrior societies which have lately (re)emerged in several indigenous nations—as well as armed confrontations at places like Wounded Knee, Oka and Gunnison Lake—have nothing to do with attaining civil rights and other forms of "equality" for native people within the U.S. and Canadian systems.[40] Nor are they meant to foster some "revolutionary" reorganization of either. Rather, the purpose is, quite specifically, to reassert the genuinely sovereign and self-determining status to which our nations are and have always been entitled.[41]

Hence, while we share a common oppressor with our relatives of African, Asian and "Latin" origins—as well as poor whites, whether they realize it or not—the goals, objectives and many of the means of our struggle must be understood in terms necessarily different from theirs.[42] We, the "Indians" of the North and the "Indios" of the South, alone among the peoples now resident to the Americas, struggle for the liberation of our homelands rather than for the liberation of land on which to build our homes. We, alone among the peoples of the Americas, engage in such struggles on the basis of our cultures—our freely collective societies, born in and thus always indigenous to this hemisphere—rather than struggling to create liberatory cultures allowing the expression of human freedom.

Ours, in a word, is a struggle to achieve *decolonization*. We seek neither to better our "place" within settler-state societies nor to seize the reigns of power over them. Instead, for us, liberation can be found nowhere but in our ultimate ability to detach ourselves from the corpus of the states themselves, dismantling their purported geographic integrity and, to that extent, radically diminishing the basis upon which they wield economic, political and military power. In this, there lies the potential of liberation not simply for American Indians, but for everyone.

Struggle for the Land

> We believe that the conscious and organized undertaking by a colonized people to reestablish the sovereignty of that nation constitutes the most complete and obvious cultural manifestation that exists.
>
> —Frantz Fanon
> *The Wretched of the Earth*

The present volume, comprising a considerable updating and revision of the edition originally published by Common Courage Press in 1993, is intended mainly to elaborate upon and amplify certain of the themes raised above. Beginning with a new essay, "The Tragedy and the Travesty," which traces the convoluted and often untenable legal doctrines through which the U.S. and Canada have sought to rationalize their colonization of Native North America, the book goes on to explore the impacts of such sophistry when applied to the real world.

This is undertaken through a series of case studies ranging from that of the Haudenosaunee in upstate New York ("Struggle to Regain a Stolen Homeland") to that of the Lakotas on the northern Plains ("The Black Hills Are Not For Sale"), from that of the Lubicon Cree in northern Alberta ("Last Stand of the Lubicon Cree") to that of the Diné and Newe (Western Shoshone) in the upper Sonoran and Intermountain desert regions of the U.S. ("Genocide in Arizona" and "The Struggle for Newe Segobia"). Numerous other examples might of course have been selected, but those chosen seemed indicative of the rest at the time the book was conceived, and they still seem so.

Each essay was written not only with an eye towards illuminating the motives underlying the various modalities of domination visited by North America's settler-states upon indigenous nations, but the physical/material, cultural and political effects of this upon the targeted peoples. Here, I have paid close attention not only to Sartre's famous dictum that colonialism equals genocide—a proposition to which I not only subscribe, but which I seek to validate throughout my work—but to a lesser-known formulation holding that colonialism also equals ecocide.[43] The latter idea is taken up most directly in a pair of essays dealing with uranium mining in Canada and the U.S. ("Geographies of Sacrifice") and water diversion projects in the Canadian north ("The Water Plot").

A new essay on another of internal colonialism's more debilitating effects, the systematic displacement of indigenous people from their homelands ("Like Sand in the Wind"), is also included before *Struggle for the Land* wraps up with a piece ("I Am Indigenist") offering a scenario of what an alternative future for the U.S. portion of North America might look like. It should be borne in mind that this "utopian vision"—commonly described as "dystopian" by statists and white supremacists alike—was/is meant as a discussion paper rather than as a blueprint, and that it might be as readily applied to Canada (perhaps more so). Much the same can be said of the newly attached appendix ("TREATY: The Platform of Russell Means' Campaign for President of the Oglala Lakota People, 1982").

It should also be noted that earlier versions of much of the material contained herein have been published elsewhere. Winona LaDuke's "Succeeding Into Native North America," which is included as a preface, first saw the light of day in *CoEvolution Quarterly* (No. 32, 1981). Jimmie Durham's poem "Buying Time," which serves as a foreword, is taken from his *Columbus Day* (Minneapolis: West End Press, 1983). John Trudell's poetry, which appears as preludes to each section of the book, is excerpted from his *Living In Reality: Songs Called Poems* (Minneapolis: Society of People Struggling to Be Free, 1982). Appreciation is due to the authors and their publishers for permission to use the work in its present capacities.

Of my own essays, "The Tragedy and the Travesty" initially appeared in the *American Indian Culture and Research Journal* (Vol. 22, No. 2, 1998). "The Black Hills Are Not For Sale" came out in its original form in *Journal of Ethnic Studies* (Vol. 18, No. 1, 1990). Iterations of "Last Stand at Lubicon Lake" and "The Water Plot" were first published in *Z Magazine* (Sept. 1989 and Apr. 1991 respectively). Portions of "Radioactive Colonization" appeared in *Environment* (Vol. 28, No. 6, 1986) and *Akwesasne Notes* (Vol. 18, No. 6, 1986). "I Am Indigenist" made its debut in *The Z Papers* (Vol. 1, No. 3, 1992). Two sections of this introduction were originally presented at the II Seminario sobre la situation de las negras, chicanas, cubana, nativa norteamericanas, puertorriquena, caribena y asiatica en los Estadas Unidas in Habana, Cuba during December of 1984 and subsequently published in *Black Scholar* (Vol. 16, No. 1, 1985). Thanks to all publishers for permission to reprint.

A number of people have provided invaluable advice and criticism over the years, much of it finding its way into this book. Among the more cogent have been Faith Attaguile, Nilak Butler, Bobby Castillo, Shelly Davis, Vine Deloria, Jr., Jimmie Durham, the late Lew Gurwitz, Moana Jackson, Lilikala Kame'eleihiwa, the Kelly brothers—John, Fred and Peter, Winona LaDuke, Russ Means, John Mohawk, Nick Meinhart, Glenn Morris, Jim Page, Bob Robideau, Chief John Ross, the late Robert K. Thomas, Madonna Thunderhawk, George Tinker, Mililani and Haunani-Kay Trask, John Trudell, Jim Vander Wall, Sharon Venne, Deward E. Walker, Jr., Troy Lynne Yellow Wood and Phyllis Young. And, to be sure, I have learned much from the elders, the people of the land themselves. Probably most influential in this regard have been Thomas Banyacya, Roberta Blackgoat, Shorty Blacksmith, Carrie Dann, the late Philip Deer, the late Chief Frank Fools Crow, the late Matthew King (Noble Red Man), Joe and Vivian Locust, the late David Monongye, Momacita, Kee Shay, Katherine Smith, the late David Sohappy, and Chief Raymond Yowell. Certainly, while each has contributed significantly in his/her way, none of these individuals bears the least responsibility for whatever errors, either of fact or in emphasis, I may have made.

My thanks to Jeff Holland, former staff cartographer in the Department of Geography at the University of Colorado, for his help in preparing the maps. Gratitude is also extended to Todd Scarth and John Samson at Arbeiter Ring Publishing for their able efforts in editing and preparing this second edition, to Elaine Katzenberger of City Lights for her comparable role with the copublisher, and to the Saxifrage Group for its assistance with indexing and proofing. Colorado AIM provided all the support, spiritual and material, anyone might have asked in a project of this sort. The Department of Ethnic Studies at UC/Boulder provided the necessary environment of collegiality. And, of course, there was Leah to see me through…

—*Ward Churchill*
Boulder, Colorado
June 1998

Notes

1. References in this regard are legion. In a canonical sense, the perfect representation may be found in a lengthy selection essays assembled by Margaret Mead and Ruth L. Bunzel and entitled *The Golden Age of American Anthropology: The Growth of the Science of Man on the North American Continent as Told by Those Who Laid the Foundations* (New York: George Braziller, 1960)

2. This was certainly true during the nineteenth century; see, e.g., Francis Paul Prucha, ed., *Americanizing the American Indian: Writings of the "Friends of the Indian," 1800-1900* (Lincoln: University of Nebraska Press, 1973). For contemporary counterpoint, see, e.g., Jerry Mander, *In the Absence of the Sacred: The Failure of Technology and Survival of the Indian Nations* (San Francisco: Sierra Club Books, 1991).

3. Marshall Sahlins, *Stone Age Economics* (Chicago: Aldine, 1972) pp. 1-40.

4. With respect to the approximately two-thirds of all vegetal foodstuffs currently consumed by humanity, and which were under cultivation in this hemisphere alone as of 1492, see Jack Weatherford's *Indian Givers: How the Indians of the Americas Transformed the World* (New York: Crown, 1988). Concerning agricultural forms and techniques, see the deeply flawed but nonetheless useful study by R. Douglas Hurt entitled *Indian Agriculture in America: Prehistory to the Present* (Lawrence: University Press of Kansas, 1987).

5. The apparently willful reductionist manipulation of demographic data pertaining to Native North America by historians such as John Gorman Palfrey and, subsequently, by anthropologists like James Mooney and Alfred L. Kroeber, is well-covered by Francis Jennings in his *The Invasion of America: Indians, Colonialism and the Cant of Conquest* (New York: W.W. Norton, 1976) pp. 15-31. As compared to the Mooney/Kroeber estimates of approximately one million people north of the Río Grande in 1492, a figure long enshrined as "truth" by the Smithsonian Institution, more reasonable/realistic assessments suggest a population of 12.5-18.5 million. See, e.g., Henry F. Dobyns, *Their Number Become Thinned: Native American Population Dynamics on the Eastern Seaboard* (Knoxville: University of Tennessee Press, 1976) p. 42; Russell Thornton, "American Indian Historical Demography: A Review Essay with Recommendations for the Future," *American Indian Culture and Research Journal*, No. 3, 1979; Russell Thornton, *American Indian Holocaust and Survival: A Population History Since 1492* (Norman: University of Oklahoma Press, 1987) pp. xvii, 242. A best guess among responsible scholars at this point is that there were about fifteen million people residing in North America at the time of the Columbian landfall; Kirkpatrick Sale, *The Conquest of Paradise: Christopher Columbus and the Columbian Legacy* (New York: Alfred A. Knopf, 1990) p. 316.

6. William R. Catton, Jr., *Overshoot: The Ecological Basis for Revolutionary Change* (Urbana: University of Illinois Press, 1981).

7. For a detailed accounting of the Haudenosaunee influence on the Founding Fathers' construction of the U.S. Constitution, see Donald A. Grinde, Jr., and Bruce Johansen, *Exemplar of Liberty: Native America and the Founding of American Democracy* (Los Angeles: UCLA American Indian Studies Center, 1991). Also see Donald A. Grinde, Jr., *The Iroquois and the Founding of the American Nation* (San Francisco: Indian Historian Press, 1977) and Bruce Johansen, *Forgotten Founders: How the American Indians Helped Shape Democracy* (Boston: Harvard Common Press, 1982).

8. A good survey of traditional indigenous forms of governance will be found in Rebecca Robbins' "Self-Determination and Subordination: The Past, Present and Future of American Indian Self-Governance," in M. Annette Jaimes, ed., *The State of Native America: Genocide, Colonization and Resistance* (Boston: South End Press, 1992).

9. The Maya of the Yucatan and present-day Guatemala, for example, had developed the concepts of zero and prime number extraction long before they were known in Europe; Charles Gallenkamp, *Maya: The Riddle and Rediscovery of a Lost Civilization* (New York: Viking, [3rd ed.], 1985) pp. 79-80. An hemispheric overview is provided in Michael P. Closs, ed., *Native American Mathematics* (Austin: University of Texas Press, 1986). On the sophistication of indigenous medical practices, which included brain surgery at a time when Europe's doctors still believed that drawing off "bad blood" would cure illness, see Virgil Vogel, *American Indian Medicine* (Norman: University of Oklahoma Press, 1970) and Miguel Guzmá Peredo, *Medical Practices in Ancient America* (Mexico City: Ediciones Euroamericanas, 1985). Aspects of indigenous astronomy are well-covered in Guillermo Céspedes, *América Indigena* (Madrid: Alianza, 1985). On architecture, see Peter Nabokov and Robert Easton, *American Indian Architecture* (New York: Oxford

University Press, 1988). Buddy Mays' *Ancient Cities of the Southwest* (San Francisco: Chronicle Books, 1982) covers the latter topic as well as engineering marvels such as the 400 miles of Hohokam irrigation canals which are still used by the city of Phoenix.

10. One example of this practice, that of the Haudenosaunee, is delineated in Paul A.W. Wallace's *The White Roots of Peace* (Philadelphia: University of Philadelphia Press, 1946).

11. For analysis and discussion, see the essays contained in Christopher Vecsey and Robert W. Venables, eds., *Native American Environments: Ecological Issues in American Indian History* (Syracuse, NY: Syracuse University Press, 1980).

12. See, e.g., Frank Waters, *The Book of the Hopi* (New York: Viking, 1963).

13. The examples listed, as well as a number of others, are discussed at length in my *Fantasies of the Master Race: Literature, Cinema and the Colonization of American Indians* (San Francisco: City Lights, [2nd ed.] 1998) and *Indians "R" Us: Culture and Genocide in Native North America* (Winnipeg: Arbeiter Ring, 2nd [ed., forthcoming]2000).

14. Such propagandistic manipulation of native imagery by the settler society has ample historical precedent; see, e.g., Robert F. Berkhofer, Jr., *The White Man's Indian: Images of the American Indian from Columbus to the Present* (New York: Alfred A. Knopf, 1978). On the specific image referenced, see the memoirs of the actor depicted; Iron Eyes Cody, *Iron Eyes: My Life as a Hollywood Indian* (New York: Everest House, 1982).

15. The three groupings are recognized by linguists and geneticists alike; Joseph H. Greenberg, *Language in the Americas* (Stanford, CA: Stanford University Press, 1988). Of the trio, Amerind is by far the oldest and most extensive, demonstrating a continuous presence in the hemisphere for at least 40,000 years—perhaps 70,000 years or longer—and encompassing most of the area from central Canada to Tierra del Fuego; L.S. Cressman, *Prehistory of the Far West: Homes of Vanquished Peoples* (Salt Lake City: University of Utah Press, 1977); Richard Wolkomir, "New Find Could Rewrite the Start of American History," *Smithsonian*, No. 21, Mar. 1991. The current argument that there may have been a fourth stock is well-made in Theodore Schurr, et al., "Amerindian Mitochondrial DNAs Have Rare Asian Mutations at High Frequencies, Suggesting They Derived from Four Primary Maternal Lineages," *American Journal of Human Genetics*, No. 46, 1990; also see Satoshi Harai, et al., "Peopling of the Americas: Founded by Four Major Lineages of Mitochondrial DNA," *Molecular Biology of Evolution*, Vol. 10, No. 1, 1993.

16. The distinction is handled well in L. Mandell, "Indians Nations: Not Minorities," *Les Cahiers de Droit*, No. 27, 1983.

17. For an interesting overview, see Troy Johnson, Joane Nagel and Duane Champagne, eds., *American Indian Activism: Alcatraz to the Longest Walk* (Urbana: University of Illinois Press, 1997). Also see Peter Matthiessen, *In the Spirit of Crazy Horse: The Story of Leonard Peltier* (New York: Viking, [2nd ed.] 1991); Rex Wyler, *Blood of the Land: The U.S. Government and Corporate War Against the American Indian Movement* (Philadelphia: New Society, [2nd ed.] 1992).

18. See, e.g., Felix S. Cohen, "Original Indian Title," in Lucy Cohen, ed., *The Legal Conscience: Selected Papers of Felix S. Cohen* (New Haven, CT: Yale University Press, 1960) pp. 273-304; Michael Asch, ed., *Aboriginal and Treaty Rights in Canada: Essays on Law, Equality, and Respect for Difference* (Vancouver: UBC Press, 1997). More broadly, see Gordon Bennett, *Aboriginal Rights in International Law* (London: Royal Institute, 1978). Oddly complimentary views are expressed in *Selections from V.I. Lenin and J.V. Stalin on the National Colonial Question* (Calcutta: Calcutta Book House, [2nd ed.] 1975).

19. The texts of 371 treaties with indigenous peoples ratified by the U.S. Senate between 1787 and 1871 are compiled in Charles J. Kappler's *Indian Treaties, 1778-1883* (New York: Interland, 1973). Lakota scholar Vine Deloria, Jr., has collected more than a dozen other such instruments, although they remain unpublished at present. As concerns Canada, the texts of some 480 treaties are compiled in *Canada: Indian Treaties and Surrenders from 1680 to 1890*, 3 vols. (Ottawa: Queen's Printer, 1891; reprinted by Coles [Toronto], 1971; reprinted by Fifth House [Saskatoon], 1992). The implications of formal recognition of indigenous nations are codified as law in the U.N. Charter and elsewhere; Cristeau Aurelieu, *The Historical and Current Development of the Right to Self-Determination on the Basis of the Charter of the United Nations and Other Instruments adopted by United Nations Organs, With Particular Reference to the Protection of Human Rights and Fundamental Freedoms* (U.N. Doc. E/CN.4/Sub.2/404, 2 June 1978). Also see Michla Pomerance, *Self-Determination in Law and Practice* (The Hague: Marinus Nijhoff, 1982).

20. For illustrative expression of such sentiments, see the quotations of various U.S. officials

PART 1: THE LAW

American "Justice"
At times
They were kind
They were polite
in their sophistication
smiling but never too loudly
acting in a civilized manner
an illusion of gentleness
always fighting to get their way
While the people see
   the people know
   the people wait
   the people say
The closing of your doors
will never shut us out
The closing of your doors
can only shut you in
We know the predator
we see them feed
on us
We are aware
to starve the beast
is our destiny
At times
they were kind
they were polite
but never honest.

          —John Trudell
          from *Living in Reality*

THE TRAGEDY AND THE TRAVESTY

The Subversion of Indigenous Sovereignty in North America

> Much ink has been spilled during the late twentieth century explaining that
> the rights of indigenous peoples are a matter of internal, "domestic" consid-
> eration on the part of the various States in which we reside, as if our status
> was merely that of "ethnic minorities" integral and subordinate to these
> larger politicoeconomic entities. Such an interpretation is inaccurate, invalid,
> and in fact illegal under international law. We are *nations*, and, at least in
> North America, we have the treaties to prove it. We are thus entitled—mor-
> ally, ethically and legally entitled—to exercise the same sovereign and self-
> determining rights as the States themselves. This cannot be lawfully taken
> from us. Our entitlement to conduct our affairs as sovereigns will remain in
> effect until such time as we ourselves voluntarily modify or relinquish it.
>
> —Glenn T. Morris, 1997

QUESTIONS concerning the rights and legal/political standing of
indigenous peoples have assumed a peculiar prominence in the world's
juridical debates over the past quarter-century.[1] Nowhere is this more
pronounced than in North America, a continent presided over by a pair of
Anglo-European settler powers, the United States and Canada,[2] both of
which purport to have resolved such issues—or to being very close to
resolving them—in a manner which is not only legally consistent, but so
intrinsically just as to serve as a "humanitarian model" deserving of emula-
tion on a planetary basis.[3] Indeed, the U.S. in particular has long been prone
to asserting that it has already implemented the programs necessary to guarantee self-determination, including genuine self-governance, to the native
peoples residing within its borders.[4] Most recently, its representatives to the
United Nations announced that it would therefore act to prevent the
promulgation of an international convention on the rights of indigenous
peoples if the proposed instrument contradicted U.S. domestic law in any
significant way.[5]

While it is true that the treatment presently accorded Native North

Americans is far less harsh than that visited upon our counterparts in many other regions—by the government of Guatemala upon Mayas, for instance, or of Indonesia upon East Timorese—it is equally true that this has not always been the case, and that the material conditions to which indigenous peoples in the U.S. and Canada are subjected remain abysmal.[6] Moreover, there are firm indications that whatever relative physical advantages may be enjoyed by North America's native peoples vis-à-vis those in Third World nation-states accrue simply and directly from the extent to which we are seen as being more thoroughly pacified than they. The governments of both North American settler-states have recently demonstrated a marked willingness to engage in low intensity warfare against us whenever this impression has proven, however tentatively, to be erroneous.[7]

Such circumstances hardly bespeak the realization, by any reasonable definition, of indigenous self-determination. Rather, they are more immediately suggestive of internal colonial structures along the lines of those effected in England and Spain during the final phases of their consolidation.[8] It is thus necessary to separate fact from fable in this respect, before the latter is foisted off and codified as an element of international law supposedly assuring the former.[9] The present essay attempts to accomplish this, briefly but clearly, by advancing an historical overview of the process predicating the contemporary situation in which North America's native peoples find ourselves and, thus, determining with some degree of precision what this situation actually is. From there, it will be possible to offer an assessment of what must be changed, and the basis on which such change might be approached, if indigenous self-determination is ever to be (re)attained on this continent.[10]

Along the way, we will be at pains to explain the nature and origin of the customary and conventional international legal entitlements possessed by North American Indians, and the manner in which these have been systematically abridged by the U.S. and Canada. Emphasis will be placed on U.S. practice throughout, if only because Canada has become something of a junior partner in the enterprise at issue, implicitly—yet sometimes with remarkable explicitness—resorting to an outright mimicry of the "doctrinal innovations" by which its more substantial southern neighbor has sought to rationalize and justify its Indian policies.[11]

The Question of Inherent Sovereignty

It is important to bear in mind that there is a distinction to be drawn between nations and states. There is a rough consensus among analysts of virtually all ideological persuasions that a nation consists of any body of people, independent of its size, who are bound together by a common language and set of cultural beliefs, possessed of a defined or definable landbase sufficient to provide an economy, and evidencing the capacity to govern themselves.[12] A state, on the other hand, is a particular form of centralized and authoritarian sociopolitical organization.[13] Many or perhaps most nations are not and have never been organized in accordance with the statist model. Conversely, only a handful the world's states are or have ever really been nations in their own right (most came into being and are maintained through the coerced amalgamation of several nations).[14] Hence, although the term "state" has come to be employed as a virtual synonym for "nation" in popular usage—the membership of the "United Nations," for example, is composed entirely of states—the two are not interchangeable.[15]

Regardless of the manner in which they are organized, all nations are legally construed as being imbued with a sovereignty which is inherent and consequently inalienable.[16] While the sovereign rights of any nation can be violated—i.e., its territory can be occupied through encroachment or military conquest, its government usurped or deposed altogether, its laws deformed or supplanted, and so forth—it is never extinguished by such actions.[17] Just as a woman retains an absolute right not to be raped even as she is subjected to it, a nation continues to possess its full range of sovereign rights even as their violation occurs. The only means by which the sovereignty of any nation can be legitimately diminished is in cases where the nation itself *voluntarily* relinquishes it.[18]

There can be no question but that the indigenous peoples of North America existed as fully self-sufficient, self-governing and independent nations prior to commencement of the European invasions.[19] Nor can there be any real doubt as to whether the European powers were aware of this from the outset. Beginning almost the moment Columbus set foot in this hemisphere, Spanish jurists like Franciscus de Vitoria were set to hammering out theories describing the status of those peoples encountered in the course of Iberian expeditions to the "New World," the upshot being a conclusion that "the aborigines undoubtedly had dominion in both public

their territories are inviolable by any other sovereignty... They are entirely self-governed, self-directed. They treat, or refuse to treat, at their pleasure; and there is no human power that can rightly control their discretion in this respect.[40]

So clear were such pronouncements that, more than 150 years later, even such habitual unapologetic Euroamerican triumphalists as the late historian Wilcomb Washburn have been forced to concede that the "treaty system, which governed American Indian relations [with the United States and Canada], explicitly recognizes the fact that [both] governments ... acknowledged the independent and national character of the Indian peoples with whom [they] dealt."[41] Insofar as "recognition once given is irrevocable unless the recognized [nation] ceases to exist or ceases to have the elements of nationhood," it is accurate to observe that the effect of the treaties is as forceful and binding now as when they were signed.[42] Legally speaking, it is the treaties rather than settler-state statutory codes which continue to define the nature of the relationship between most American Indian peoples, Canada and the United States.[43]

This is and will remain unequivocally the case, absent an ability on the part of the U.S. and/or Canada to demonstrate that the indigenous nations with which they entered into treaties have either undergone some legitimate diminishment in their status or gone out of existence altogether. To quote Attorney General Wirt again:

> So long as a tribe exists and remains in possession of its lands, its title and possession are sovereign and exclusive. We treat with them as separate sovereignties, and while an Indian nation continues to exist within its acknowledged limits, we have no more right to enter upon their territory than we have to enter upon the territory of [any] foreign prince.[44]

There are of course arguments, typically advanced by officials and other advocates of settler-state hegemony, that literal extinction applies in certain cases, and that the requisite sorts of diminishment in standing has in any event occurred across-the-board through processes ranging from discovery and conquest to the voluntarily sociopolitical and economic merger of once distinct indigenous polities with the "broader" settler societies which now engulf us.[45] Since any of these contentions, if true, would serve to erode native claims to inherent sovereignty as well as treaty rights, it is worth examining each of them in turn.

Discovery Doctrine

It has been considered something of a truism in the United States since its inception that America's vestiture of title in and jurisdiction over its pretended landbase accrues "by right of discovery."[46] This is a rather curious proposition since, unlike Canada, which has always maintained a certain fealty to the British Crown, the U.S. can make no pretense that its own citizenry ever "discovered" any portion of North America. Nor, the claims of several of the country's "Founding Fathers" and many of their descendants notwithstanding, did Great Britain transfer its own discovery rights to the insurgent Continental Congress at the conclusion of America's decolonization struggle.[47] Rather, under the 1783 Treaty of Paris, England simply quit-claimed its interest in what is now the U.S. portion of the continent lying eastward of the Mississippi River.[48]

Moreover, even had the American republic somehow inherited its former colonizer's standing as a bona fide discovering power, this would not in itself have conveyed title to the territory in question. Contrary to much popular—and preposterous—contemporary mythology, the medieval "Doctrine of Discovery," originating in a series of interpretations of earlier papal bulls advanced by Innocent IV during the mid-thirteenth century and perfected by Vitoria and others three hundred years later, did nothing to bestow ownership of new found territory upon Europeans other than in cases where it was found to be *territorium res nullius* (genuinely uninhabited).[49] In all other instances, the Doctrine confirmed the collective title of indigenous peoples to our land—in essence, our sovereignty over it—and, thus, our right to retain it.[50]

> [N]otwithstanding whatever may have been or may be said to the contrary, the said Indians and all other peoples who may later be discovered by Christians, are by no means to be deprived of their liberty or the possession of their property, even though they may be outside the faith of Jesus Christ; and that they may and should, freely and legitimately, enjoy their liberty and the possession of their property; nor should they be in any way enslaved; should the contrary happen, it shall be null and of no effect.[51]

What the discovering power actually obtained was a monopolistic right vis-à-vis other European powers to acquire the property in question, should its native owners ever willingly consent to its alienation.[52] As John Marshall correctly observed in 1832, discovery "could not affect the rights of those already in possession, either as aboriginal occupants, or by virtue of a

43

discovery made before the memory of man. It gave the exclusive right to purchase, but did not found that right on a denial of the right of the possessor to sell."[53] In substance, the Doctrine was little more than an expedient to regulate relations among the European powers, intended to prevent them from squandering the Old World's limited assets by engaging in bidding wars—or, worse, outright military conflicts among themselves—over New World territories.

> [Since the Crowns of Europe] were all in pursuit of nearly the same object, it was necessary, in order to avoid conflicting settlements, and consequent war with each other, to establish a principle, which all should acknowledge as the law by which the right of acquisition, which they all asserted, should be regulated, as between themselves. This principle was, that discovery gave title to the government by whose subjects, or by whose authority, it was made, against other governments, which title might be consummated by possession. The exclusion of all other Europeans, necessarily gave to the nation making the discovery the sole right of acquiring the soil from the natives, and establishing settlements upon it. It was a right with which no Europeans could interfere.[54]

That such understandings were hardly unique to Marshall, is witnessed in a 1792 missive from then Secretary of State Thomas Jefferson to the British foreign ministry, in which he acknowledged that the Treaty of Paris had left the U.S., not with clear title to lands west of the Appalachian Mountains, but rather with an ability to replace England in asserting what he called a "right of preemption."[55]

> [T]hat is to say, the sole and exclusive right of purchasing from [indigenous peoples] whenever they should be willing to sell... We consider it as established by the usage of different nations into a kind of *Jus gentium* for America, that a white nation settling down and declaring such and such are their limits, makes an invasion of those limits by any other white nation an act of war, but gives no right of soil against the native possessors."[56]

So plain was the pattern of law and historical precedent in Marshall's mind that he openly scoffed at notions, prevalent among his countrymen, that the Doctrine of Discovery did, or could have done, more.

> The extravagant and absurd idea, that feeble settlements made along the seacoast ... acquired legitimate power to govern [native] people, or occupy the lands from sea to sea, did not enter into the mind of any man. [Crown charters] were well understood to convey the title which, according to the common law of European sovereigns respecting America, they might rightly convey, and no more. This was the exclusive right of purchasing such lands as the natives were willing to sell. The crown could not

undertake to grant what the crown could not affect to claim; nor was it so understood.[57]

The same problems afflicting arguments that title to unceded Indian land advocates claim was passed to the U.S. via the Treaty of Paris also besets other acquisitions from European/Euroamerican powers. This is most notably true with respect to the 1803 Louisiana Purchase and the 1848 cession of the northern half of Mexico under the Treaty of Guadalupe Hidalgo, but also pertains to the 1845 admission of Texas to the Union, the 1846 purchase of Oregon Territory from Russia, and so on.[58] As concerns the largest single annexation ever made by the U.S., encompassing the entire Transmississippi West:

> What [the United States] acquired from Napoleon in the Louisiana Purchase was not real estate, for practically all of the ceded territory that was not privately owned by Spanish and French settlers was still owned by the Indians, and the property rights of all the inhabitants were safeguarded by the terms of the treaty of cession. What we did acquire from Napoleon was not the land, which was not his to sell, but simply the right [to purchase the land].[59]

Similarly, the Treaty of Guadalupe Hidalgo, by which the U.S. war against Mexico was concluded, made express provision that already-existing property rights, including those of the region's indigenous peoples, be respected within the vast area ceded by the Mexican government.[60] In no instance is there evidence to support assertions that the U.S. obtained anything resembling valid title to its presently claimed continental territoriality through interaction with non-indigenous governments, whether European or Euroamerican. Less, can such contentions be sustained with regard to Hawai'i.[61] The matter is confirmed by the 1928 *Island of Palmas* case, in which the International Court of Justice (ICJ, or "World Court") found that title supposedly deriving from discovery cannot prevail over a title based in a prior and continuing display of sovereignty.[62]

Territorium res Nullius

Although John Marshall himself, while readily conceding many of its implications, would ultimately pervert the Doctrine of Discovery in a relatively sophisticated fashion as he attempted to rationalize and legitimate his country's territorial ambitions (this will be taken up below), many of his peers operated much more crudely. Hence, in the 1842 *Martin v. Waddell* case,

45

decided only seven years after Marshall's death, the Supreme Court set down the following opinion (despite the clear exposition of the Doctrine's actual contents the late Chief Justice had so recently bequeathed).

> The English possessions in America were not claimed by right of conquest, but by right of discovery. For, according to the principles of international law, as understood by the then civilized powers of Europe, the Indian tribes in the new world were regarded as mere temporary occupants of the soil, and the absolute rights of property and dominion were held to belong to the European nation by which any particular portion of the country was first discovered. Whatever forbearance may have been practiced towards the unfortunate aborigines, either from humanity or policy, yet the territory they occupied was disposed of by the governments of Europe, at their pleasure, as if it had been found without inhabitants.[63]

In so thoroughly misconstruing extant law, rewriting history in the process, what the good Justices were about was devising a legal loophole. Through it, they intended to pour a veneer of false legitimacy over U.S. plans, by now openly and officially announced as the country's "Manifest Destiny," of rapidly extending its reach from the Mississippi to the Pacific and beyond, ignoring indigenous rights, not only to land but to liberty and often life itself, at every step along the way.[64] The mechanism they seized upon for this purpose was the principle of *Territorium res Nullius*, the element of Discovery Doctrine providing that uninhabited territory might be claimed outright by whoever first found it.[65]

It's not that the Supreme Court of the United States or anyone else ever really argued that North America was completely unoccupied at the time of the initial European arrivals. Instead, they fell back on the concept of the "Norman Yoke," an ancient doctrine particularly well developed in English legal philosophy, stipulating that to be truly owned it was necessary that land be "improved."[66] Whomever failed within some "reasonable" period to build upon, cultivate or otherwise transform their property from its natural "state of wilderness" forfeited title to it. The land was then simply declared to be "vacant" and subject to claim by anyone professing a willingness to "put it to use."[67]

The Puritans of Plymouth Plantation and Massachusetts Bay Colony had experimented with the idea during the 1620s—arguing that while native property rights might well be vested in our townsites and fields, the remainder of our territories, since it was uncultivated, should be considered *terra nullius* and thus unowned—but their precedent never evolved into a more generalized English practice.[68] Indeed, the Puritans themselves abandoned such presumption in 1629.[69]

> Whatever theoretical disagreements existed concerning the nature of the respective ownership rights of Indians and Europeans to land in America, practical realities shaped legal relations between the Indians and colonists. The necessity of getting along with powerful Indian [peoples], who outnumbered the European settlers for several decades, dictated that as a matter of prudence, the settlers buy lands that the Indians were willing to sell, rather than displace them by other methods. The result was that the English and Dutch colonial governments obtained most of their lands by purchase. For all practical purposes, the Indians were treated as sovereigns possessing full ownership of [all] the lands of America.[70]

By the early nineteenth century, the demographic/military balance had shifted dramatically in favor of settler populations.[71] One result was that the potential of invoking the Norman Yoke in combination with the broader principle of *res Nullius* began to be rethought. In terms of international law, the principle eventually found expression in the observation of jurist Emmerich de Vattel that no nation holds a right to "exclusively appropriate to themselves more land than they have occasion for, or more than they are able to settle and cultivate."[72] For all practical intents and purposes, John Marshall himself employed such reasoning in an 1810 opinion holding that portions of Indian Country not literally occupied or cultivated by indigenous peoples might, at least in certain instances, be construed as unowned and therefore open to claims by settlers.[73]

Over the next 75 years, the principle was brought to bear in the continuously evolving formation of U.S. Indian policy—as well as judicial interpretation of indigenous property entitlements—with the size of an ever greater number of the areas set aside (reserved) for native use and occupancy demonstrating no relationship at all to the extent of aboriginal holdings or to more recent treaty guarantees of territoriality. Rather, federal policymakers, judges and bureaucrats alike increasingly took to multiplying the number of Indians believed to belong to any given people by the number of acres it was thought each individual might use "productively." The aggregate figure arrived at would then be assigned as that people's reserved landbase.[74] By the latter part of the nineteenth century, the process in Canada was much the same.[75]

In the U.S., the trend culminated in passage of the 1887 General Allotment Act, a measure by which the government authorized itself to impose such terms upon every indigenous nation encompassed within the country's claimed boundaries.[76] At the stroke of the congressional pen, traditional native modes of collective landholding were unilaterally abolished in favor of the self-anointedly more "advanced" or "civilized" Euroamerican system of individual ownership.[77] The methods by which the Act was implemented began with the compilation of official "rolls" of the members of each "tribe" in accordance with criteria sanctioned by the federal Bureau of Indian Affairs (BIA).[78] When this task was completed, each individual listed on a roll was allotted a parcel of land, according to the following formula.

1. To each head of a family, one-quarter section [160 acres].

2. To each single person over eighteen years of age, one-eighth section.

3. To each orphan child under eighteen years of age, one-eighth section.

4. To each other single person under eighteen years of age living, or who may be born prior to the date of the order … directing allotment of the lands, one-sixteenth section.[79]

Once each native person had received his or her allotment, the balance of each reserved territory was declared "surplus" and made available to non-Indian settlers, parceled out to railroads and other corporations and/or converted into federal parks, forests and military compounds.[80] In this manner, the indigenous landbase, which had still amounted to an aggregate of 150 million acres at the time the Act went into effect, was reduced by approximately two-thirds before it was finally repealed in 1934.[81] Additionally, under provision of the 1906 Burke Act, which vested authority in the Secretary of Interior to administer all remaining native property in trust, a further "27,000,000 acres or two-thirds of the land allotted to individual Indians was also lost to sale" by the latter year.[82] What little territory was left to indigenous nations at that point was thus radically insufficient to afford economic sustenance, much less to accommodate future population growth.[83]

Needless to say, native people agreed to none of this. On the contrary, we have continuously resisted it through a variety of means, including efforts to secure some just resolution through U.S. courts. Our refusal to participate in allotment and similar processes has often resulted in our being left effectively landless, defined as "non–Indians" and worse.[84] The response of the Supreme Court to our "due process" initiatives has been to declare, in the 1903 case *Lonewolf v. Hitchcock*, that the United States enjoys a permanent "trustee relationship" to its native "wards," affording it a "plenary power" over our affairs which frees it to "change the form of" our property—from land, say, to cash or other "benefits"—at its own discretion. As a concomitant, the court argued that the U.S. holds a unilateral right, based in no discernible legal doctrine at all, to abrogate such terms and provisions of its treaties with indigenous nations as it may come to find inconvenient while still binding us to the remainder.[85]

By 1955, things had reached such a pass that native peoples were required for the first time to demonstrate that we had acquired title to our lands from a European/Euroamerican power rather than the other way around.[88] Even in cases where such recognition of title was/is clear and apparent—the Rainbow Bridge and G–O Road cases of the 1980s, to name two prime examples—U.S. courts have consistently ruled that the "broader interests" of North America's settler society outweighs the right of indigenous owners to make use of our property in a manner consistent with our own values, customs and traditions.[87] In other instances, such as *U.S. v. Dann*, treaty land has been declared vacant even though native people were obviously living on it.[88]

Canadian courts, although not necessarily citing specific U.S. precedents, has followed much the same trajectory. This has been perhaps most notable in the 1984 *Bear Island* case, in which it was concluded that, Crown law to the contrary notwithstanding, federal law allowed provincial extinguishment of aboriginal title claims to "unoccupied" territories.[89] Relatedly, opinions have been rendered in several other instances— the 1973 *Calder* case, for example, and the *Cardinal* case a year later—holding that federal Canadian law functions independently of any historical guarantees extended to native people by Great Britain, a position essentially duplicating the effect of *Lonewolf*.[90] Indeed, Canada has recently gone so far as to claim the kind of permanent trust authority over indigenous nations within its ostensible boundaries earlier asserted by the U.S.[91] The rights of native people in Canada have of course suffered accordingly.[92]

Whatever merit may once have attended such legalistic maneuvering by the United States and Canada—and it was always dubious in the extreme—it has long since evaporated. The Charter of the United Nations has effectively outlawed the assertion of perpetual and nonconsensual trust relationships between nations since 1945, a circumstance reaffirmed and amplified by the 1960 Declaration on the Granting of Independence to Colonial Countries and Peoples.[93] The *Lonewolf* court's grotesque interpretation of

U.S. prerogatives to exercise a "line item veto" over its treaties with indigenous nations has been thoroughly repudiated by the 1967 Vienna Convention on the Law Treaties.[94] And, since the World Court's 1977 advisory opinion in the *Western Sahara* case, claims to primacy based in the notion of *Territorium res Nullius* have been legally nullified.[95]

Rights of Conquest

It has become rather fashionable in many quarters of North America's settler societies to refer to indigenous peoples as having been "conquered."[96] The basic idea has perhaps been expressed best and most forcefully by the U.S. Supreme Court in its 1955 *Tee-Hit-Ton* opinion.

> Every American schoolboy knows that the savage tribes of this continent were deprived of their ancestral ranges by force and that, even when the Indians ceded millions of acres by treaty in return for blankets, food and trinkets, it was not a sale but the conquerors' will that deprived them of their land.[97]

"After the conquest," the court went on, Indians "were permitted to occupy portions of the territory over which they had previously exercised 'sovereignty,' as we use the term. This is not a property right but amounts to a right of occupancy which the sovereign grants and protects against intrusion by third parties but which right of occupancy may be terminated and such lands fully disposed of by the sovereign itself without any legally enforceable obligation to compensate the Indians."[98] This curiously bellicose pontification, advanced a scant few years after U.S. jurists had presided over the conviction at Nuremberg of several German officials—including judges—in no small part for having vomited up an almost identical rhetoric,[99] is all the more peculiar in that it appears to bear virtually no connection to the case supposedly at hand.

> The Alaska natives [who had pressed a land claim in *Tee-Hit-Ton*] had never fought a skirmish with Russia [which claimed their territories before the U.S.] or the United States... To say that the Alaska natives were subjugated by conquest stretches the imagination too far. The only sovereign act that can be said to have conquered the Alaska native was the *Tee-Hit-Ton* opinion itself.[100]

If it may be taken as a rudiment that any conquest entails the waging of war by the conqueror against the conquered, then the sweeping universalism evident in the high court's pronouncement goes from the realm of the oddly erroneous to that of the truly bizarre. While the U.S. officially acknowledges the existence of well over 400 indigenous nations within its borders, it admits to having fought fewer than fifty "Indian Wars" in the entirety of its history.[101] Assuming that it was victorious in all of these—in actuality, it lost at least one[102]—and could on this basis argue that it had conquered each of its opponents, the United States would still have to account for the nature of its contemporary relationship to several hundred *un*conquered indigenous nations by some other means.

Lumping the native peoples of Canada into the bargain, as the language of *Tee-Hit-Ton* plainly suggests was its intent, renders the court's reading of history even more blatantly absurd. North of the border, with the exception of two campaigns mounted to quell Louis Riel's rebellious Métis during the mid-nineteenth century, nothing that might rightly be termed an Indian war was fought after 1763.[103] On the contrary, it was explicit and successfully enforced Crown policy from that point onward to avoid military conflicts with North America's indigenous nations by every available means.[104] Of all imaginable descriptions of what might constitute a basis for Britain's assertion of rights in Canada, then, "conquest" is without doubt among the most wildly inaccurate.[105]

Benighted as was the *Tee-Hit-Ton* court's knowledge of historical fact, its ignorance of relevant law appears to have been even worse. The difficulties begin with the court's interpretation of the ancient notion of the "Rights of Conquest," which it erroneously construed as asserting that any nation possessed of the power to seize the assets of another holds a "natural" right to do so ("might makes right," in other words).[106] In reality, if the doctrine had ever embodied such a principle—and no evidence has been produced to show that it did—it had not done so for some 900 years.[107] By the sixteenth century, Vitoria, Matías de Pas and others had codified conquest rights as an adjunct or subset of Discovery Doctrine, constraining them within very tight limits.[108]

Such rights might be invoked by a discovering power, they wrote, only on occasions where circumstances necessitated the waging of a Just War. With respect to the New World, the bases for the latter were delineated as falling into three categories: first, instances in which, without provocation, a native people physically attacked representatives of the discovering Crown; second, instances in which the natives arbitrarily refused to engage in trade with Crown representatives; and, third, instances in which native people refused to admit Christian missionaries among them. Should any or all of these circumstances be present, the jurists agreed, discoverers held the right to use whatever force was necessary to compel compliance with international law.[109] Having done so, they were then entitled to compensate themselves from the property of the vanquished for the costs of having waged the war.[110] In all other instances, however, legitimate acquisition of property could occur only by consent of its indigenous owners.[111]

The problem is that in the entire history of Indian–white relations in North America, there is not a single instance in which any of the three criteria can be documented.[112] Hence, contra the *Tee-Hit-Ton* court's all-encompassing declaration that Euroamerican title to the continent derives from conquest, such a result does not obtain, legally at least, even with regard to the relatively few instances in which wars were actually fought.[113] It follows that the only valid land title presently held by either the U.S. or Canada is that accruing from bilateral and mutually consensual treaties through which certain native lands were ceded to those countries or predecessor powers like England and France.[114]

Earlier U.S. jurists and legislators understood the law, even if the *Tee-Hit-Ton* court did not. One consequence was the 1787 Northwest Ordinance, in which the Congress foreswore all wars of conquest against native peoples and pledged the country to conducting its relations on the basis of treaties negotiated in "utmost good faith."[115] As has been mentioned, John Marshall classified contentions that North America's indigenous nations had been conquered as "extravagant and absurd."[116] Elsewhere, he observed that "law which regulates, and ought to regulate in general, the relations between the conqueror and conquered, [is] incapable of application" to American Indians.[117] Even the *Martin* court, hostile to native interests by any estimation, was at pains to state that "English [and, by extension, U.S.] rights in America were *not* claimed by right of conquest (emphasis added)."[118] Probably the most definitive assessment was that offered by Indian Commissioner Thomas Jefferson Morgan in 1890, after the Indian Wars had run their course.

> From the execution of the first treaty made between the United States and the Indian tribes residing within its limits … the United States has pursued a uniform course of extinguishing Indian title only with the consent of those tribes which were recognized as having claim to the soil by reason of occupancy, such consent being expressed by treaties.[119]

In light of all this, it is fair to say that there is not a scintilla of validity attending the *Tee-Hit-Ton* opinion, either legally or in any other way. The same holds true for the dominant society's academic and popular discourse of conquest, perhaps best represented by the 2,000-odd "Cowboys and Indians" movies produced by Hollywood over the past 75 years.[120] To pretend otherwise, as the *Tee-Hit-Ton* court did, does nothing to legitimate Euroamerican claims of primacy over native territories. Rather, it is to enter a tacit admission that, in the U.S. at least, much land has been acquired in the most illegitimate fashion of all—the waging of aggressive war—and that a considerable part of the continent constitutes what one analyst has termed "occupied America."[121]

Extinction

Although both the United States and Canada officially maintain that genocide has never been perpetrated against the indigenous peoples within their borders,[122] both have been equally prone to claim validation of their title to native lands on the basis that "group extinction" has run its course in a number of cases. Where there are no survivors or descendants of preinvasion populations, the argument goes, there can be no question of continuing aboriginal title. Thus, in such instances, the land—vacated by the literal die-off of its owners—must surely have become open to legitimate claims by the settler-states under even the most rigid constructions of *Territorium res Nullius*.[123]

While the reasoning underpinning this position is essentially sound, and in conformity with accepted legal principles, the factual basis upon which it is asserted is not. With the exception of the Beothuks of Newfoundland, whose total extermination was complete at some point in the 1820s, it has never been demonstrated that any of the peoples native to North America, *circa* 1500, has ever been completely eradicated.[124] Take the Pequots as a case in point. In 1637, they were so decimated by a war of extermination waged against them by English colonists that they were believed to have gone out of existence altogether. Even their name was abolished under colonial law.[125] For three centuries, Pequots were officially designated as being extinct. Yet, today, the federal government has been forced, grudgingly, to admit that several hundred people in Connecticut are directly descended from this "extirpated" nation.[126]

Similar examples abound. The Wampanoags of Massachusetts were declared extinct in the aftermath of the 1675 "King Philip's War," but managed to force recognition of their continuing existence during the 1970s.[127] More-or-less the same principle applies to a number of other peoples of the Northeast,[128] the Piscataways, Yamasees, Catawbas and others of the Southeast, all of whom were reportedly extinct by 1800,[129] the Yuki, Yahi and others of northern California, largely annihilated through the "cruelties of the original settlers" prior to 1900,[130] and so on around the country. James Fenimore Cooper's "Last of the Mohicans" wasn't, nor was Alfred Kroeber's Ishi really the "last of his tribe."[131] In sum, the fabled "Vanishing Red Man," alternately bemoaned and celebrated with a great deal of glee in turn-of-the-century literature, didn't.[132]

By-and-large, "extinction" is and has always been more a classification bestowed for the administrative convenience of the settler-states than a description of physical or even cultural reality. The classic example occurred when, during the decade following the adoption of House Resolution 108 in 1953, the U.S. Congress systematically terminated its recognition of more than 100 indigenous peoples.[133] Some, like the Menominees of Wisconsin, were eventually able to obtain formal "reinstatement."[134] The majority, however, like the Klamaths of Oregon and an array of smaller peoples in southern California, have been unsuccessful in such efforts. They remain officially "dissolved," whatever remained of their reserved territories absorbed by the surrounding settler-state.[135]

In other instances, the U.S. has simply refused ever to admit the existence of indigenous peoples. Notably, this pertains to the Abenakis of Vermont, who, having never signed a treaty of cession, actually hold title to very nearly the entire state.[136] Other examples include the Lumbees of North Carolina, perhaps the most populous indigenous people in all of North America, and a number of fragmentary groups like the Miamis of Ohio scattered across the Midwestern states.[137] While not following precisely the same pattern, Canada has also utilized policies of declining to acknowledge native status and/or refusing to recognize the existence of entire groups as a means of manipulating or denying altogether indigenous rights to land and sovereign standing.[138]

While neither such official subterfuges nor the popular misconceptions attending them have the least effect in terms of diminishing the actual rights of the peoples in question, they do place the settler-states in positions of patent illegality. Among other things, it is readily arguable that official declarations that still-viable human groups have gone out of existence, coupled to policies designed and intended to bring this about, constitute the Crime of Genocide, not only within the definition of the term as originally advanced by Raphaël Lemkin during the Second World War, but as it is now codified in international law.[139]

Merger with Settler Society

A final line of argument extended by the United States and Canada to justify their denials of indigenous rights to self-determination is that most native peoples have "long since" commingled with the settler societies of both countries to the point, in many if not most cases, of rendering our sovereignty self-nullifying.[140] Although it is true that international law recognizes the "voluntary merger" of one nation into another as the sole sure and acceptable means by which national identity and concomitant national rights can be extinguished, it is dubious whether the description actually applies to any but a handful of North America's indigenous nations (if at all).[141]

> In many instances there is simply no evidence of a voluntary merger by treaty agreements or in any manner. One will search the treaties of the Six Nations Confederacy and no doubt many other Indian nations in vain for such evidence... Very few treaties, perhaps none, include provisions even remotely suggesting voluntary merger or voluntary surrender of sovereignty [although a] few treaties contain provisions subjecting the Indian parties to United States law... Many Indian nations such as the Hopi have never made a treaty or agreement with the United States and [therefore] cannot be said to have assented to a merger.[142]

The state contended in *Worcester v. Georgia* that, since, under Article III of the Treaty of Hopewell, the Cherokee Nation had voluntarily placed itself under the military protection of the U.S., it had effectively relinquished its national sovereignty, merging with "the stronger power."[143] Chief Justice Marshall rejected this argument unequivocally and in terms which encompass all indigenous nations finding themselves in a comparable situation.

> [T]he settled doctrine of the law of nations is that a weaker power does not surrender its independence—its right of self-government—by associating with a stronger, and taking its protection. A weak state, in order to provide for its safety, may place itself under the protection of one more powerful, without stripping itself of the right of government, and ceasing to be a state.[144]

That Marshall's 1832 opinion yields a continuing validity is amply borne out in the status accorded such tiny "protectorates" as Liechtenstein,

San Marino and Monaco in Europe itself, examples which, along with Luxembourg, Grenada, the Marshall Islands and a number of other small nations around the world whose right to sovereignty is not open to serious challenge, also preempt questions of scale.[145] As Onondaga leader Oren Lyons has aptly put it, "Nations are not according to size. Nations are according to culture. If there are twenty people left who are representing their nation … they are a nation. Who are we to say less?"[146]

Other mainstays of the merger argument are the facts that native peoples both north and south of the border have become increasingly assimilated into settler culture, accepted citizenship in both the U.S. and Canada, adopted forms of governance explicitly subordinated to those of the settler-states and are now thoroughly encompassed by the statutory codes of the latter.[147] Even the most casual examination of the record reveals, however, that none of this has occurred in anything resembling a "voluntary" manner on the part of the indigenous nations involved. Indeed, native resistance to all four aspects of the process has been, and in many cases continues to be, substantial.

For starters, the kind and degree of cultural assimilation among native people evident today in both countries results, not from any choice made by Indians to "fit in," whether collectively or individually, but from extraordinarily draconian conditions imposed upon them by the settler-state governments. From at least as early as the last quarter of the nineteenth century, the United States and Canada alike implemented policies of compulsory assimilation involving direct intervention in the domestic affairs of all indigenous nations within their respective spheres.[148] Among the techniques employed was the systematic subversion of traditional native governments through the creation, underwriting and other support for oppositional factions, and routine disruption of customary social/spiritual practices.[149] Most especially in the U.S., but also to a considerable extent in Canada, the early phases of such initiatives were coupled to the previously discussed program of land allotment and manipulation of "tribal" membership.[150] Meanwhile, the traditional economies of an ever increasing number of native peoples throughout North America were undermined and in many cases obliterated altogether.[151]

While all of this was obviously devastating to the ability of indigenous nations to maintain their cohesion and cultural integrity, the real linchpin of assimilation policy on both sides of the border was the imposition of universal compulsory "education" upon native children.[152] Between 1880 and 1930, up to eighty percent of all American Indian youngsters were sent, almost always coercively, often forcibly, to remote boarding schools, far from family, friends, community, nation and culture. Thus isolated, shorn of their hair, compelled to dress in Euroamerican attire, forbidden to speak their native languages or follow their spiritual beliefs, subjected to severe corporal punishment and/or confinement for the slightest breach of "discipline," the students were typically held for years, systematically indoctrinated all the while to accept Christianity, speak "proper" English and generally adopt Western values and perspectives.[153]

The express objective of the boarding school system was, according to U.S. Superintendent of Indian Schools Richard H. Pratt, to "kill the Indian" in each pupil, converting them into psychological/intellectual replications of non-Indians.[154] The broader goal, articulated repeatedly by the administrators of U.S. assimilation policy as a whole, was to bring about the functional disappearance of indigenous societies, as such, by some point in the mid-1930s.[155] The intent in Canada was no different, albeit geared to a somewhat slower pace.[156] While such a process of sociocultural "merger" can by no conceivable definition be described as "voluntary," it is glaringly genocidal under even the strictest legal definition of the term.[157]

Citizenship fares little better as a justification for statist presumption. Indians, as a rule, sought to become citizens of neither the U.S. nor Canada. On the contrary, the record demonstrates conclusively that in the latter country we began to be treated as "subjects" at a time when we were strongly and all but unanimously asserting the exact opposite. Consider, for example, the following observation, drawn from opinion of a twentieth century Canadian court.

> It is well-known that claims have been made from the time of Joseph Brant [Thayendanegea, a Mohawk who led a faction of his people to fight on the British side during the U.S. War of Independence, and afterwards into Canada] that the Indians were not really subjects of the King but an independent people—allies of His Majesty—and in a measure at least exempt from the civil laws governing the true subject. "Treaties" had been made in which they were called "faithful allies" and the like... As to the so-called treaties, John Beverly Robinson, Attorney-General for Upper Canada, in an official letter to Robert Wilmot Horton, Under Secretary of State for War and Colonies, March 14, 1824, said: "To talk of treaties with the Mohawk Indians, residing in the heart of one of the most populous districts of Upper Canada ... is much the same, in my humble opinion, as to talk of making a treaty of alliance with the Jews of Duke Street ..."[158]

More formally, in the sense of enfranchisement and the like, citizenship was not extended to indigenous people until An Act to Encourage the Gradual Civilization of the Indian Tribes was effected by the Province of Canada in 1857.[159] Since the law made acceptance voluntary—Indians had to apply, and were declared legally "white" upon acceptance—there were relatively few takers.[160] Hence, pursuant to the 1867 British North American Act ("Constitution Act"), native citizenship in Canada was simply made declarative, irrespective of objections raised by its alleged beneficiaries.[161] As Prime Minister Sir John A. MacDonald put it in 1887, "the great aim of [such] legislation has been to do away with the tribal system and assimilate the Indian people in all respects with the other inhabitants of the dominion, as speedily as they are fit for the change."[162]

In the United States, citizenship was first imposed upon native people in a large-scale fashion during the 1880s, as a *quid pro quo* in the release of individually allotted land parcels from trust status.[163] In 1924, an act was passed unilaterally conferring citizenship upon all Indians who had been overlooked in earlier processes, or who had proven resistant to accepting it.[164] As in Canada, "The grant of citizenship was not sought by the Indian population, and many Indian nations have consistently and vigorously denied United States citizenship. The Six Nations Confederacy, to use a now familiar example, has repeatedly gone on public record to reject United States citizenship and deny the federal government's power to make them citizens."[165]

> It has never been held by any court, national or international, that the unilateral conferral of citizenship upon a population deprives them of their separate nationhood. The ultimate question is, after all, whether Congress [or the Canadian parliament] has the right or the legal power under international law to legislate over Indian nations without their consent.[166]

As to the fact that indigenous governments are presently considered as parts of the settler-state governmental hierarchies themselves, native people no more chose this status than they did U.S./Canadian citizenship or any other aspect of assimilation.[167] Traditional forms of governance throughout the United States were systematically supplanted, nation by nation, under the 1934 Indian Reorganization Act (IRA) with a constitutional structure designed by the BIA.[168] In the great majority of cases, the resulting "tribal councils" were patterned more after corporate boards than actual governing bodies, while all of them derived their authority from and were underwritten by the U.S. rather than their own ostensible constituents.[169]

Although superficially democratic in its implementation—referenda were conducted on each reservation prior to its being reorganized—the record is replete with instances in which federal officials misrepresented what was happening in order to convince native voters to cast affirmative ballots.[170] In certain instances—among the Lakota, for example, where a sufficient number of dead persons to swing the outcome were later shown to have "voted"—outright electoral fraud prevailed.[171] Hopi provides another useful illustration.

> [Indian Commissioner John] Collier reported to the Secretary of Interior in 1936 that [in 1935] the Hopis had accepted the IRA by a vote of 519 to 299, the total votes cast representing 45 percent of the eligible voters, [yet he] came up with a figure of 50 percent for the percentage of voters coming to the polls a year later, in 1936, to vote on the constitution, in his annual report for 1937. [But] according to the statistics contained in the ratified and Interior-approved constitution itself, only 755 people voted in the constitutional referendum. This is 63 fewer people than voted in the 1935 referendum on the Indian Reorganization Act. How can 818 voters constitute 45 percent of the eligible voters in 1935 and, a year later, 755 voters constitute 50 percent?... Clearly, Collier made up his own statistics, and perpetrated a good deal of deception in order to make it seem the Hopis [embraced the IRA], when they did not.[172]

Moreover, a "number of Hopis assert today that voters were told they were voting for retention of their land, not for reorganization; that registration papers were falsified; and that votes were fabricated."[173] In reality, voter turnout was less than thirty percent.[174] Even this does not tell the whole story, since, as was made clear to BIA representatives at the time, the bulk of eligible voters did not "abstain." Instead, they opted to exercise their traditional right of signifying "no" by actively boycotting the proceeding.[175] Tabulated in this fashion, the best contemporary estimate is that fewer than fifteen percent of all eligible Hopis actually voted for reorganization, while more than 85 percent voted against it.[176] Nonetheless, it remains the official position of the United States that the IRA council is the "legitimate" government of the Hopi people.

In Canada, meanwhile, provision was first made in the 1876 Indian Act to establish a system of "band governments" under federal rather than native authority.[177] In 1880, the law was amended to deprive traditional "chiefs" (i.e., leaders) of their authority as rapidly as elected officials became available.[178] In 1884, the Indian Advancement Act was passed for, among other things, the specific purpose of preparing federally-created and -funded band councils to assume functions roughly analogous to municipal governments.[179] In 1920, an amendment to the then-prevailing Indian Act of 1906 empowered the councils, by simple majority vote, to make Canadian citizens of their constituency as a whole.[180] And so it has gone, right up through the 1982 rewriting of the Canadian Constitution, a document which explicitly delineates the location and prerogatives of native governments *within* the settler-state corpus.[181]

Under the circumstances already described in this section, suggestions that other unilaterally imposed "accommodations of" native people within U.S. and Canadian statutory codes might somehow imply the legitimate merger of indigenous nations with the settler-states are too ludicrous to warrant serious response.[182] On balance, both the arrangement and the duplicitous nature of the arguments used to rationalize and defend such ideas are entirely comparable to those employed by France with respect to Algeria during the early 1950s.[183] As such, they are frankly colonialist and therefore in violation of black letter international law.[184]

No mere adjustments to the status quo—the enactment of another statute here, a constitutional amendment there—can rectify a situation which is so fundamentally at odds with legality. The only possible course by which either Canada or the United States can redeem its posture as an outlaw state is to recall and act upon the 1832 observation of John Marshall that "Indian nations [have] always been considered as distinct, independent political communities, retaining their original natural rights... The very term 'nation,' so generally applied to them, means 'a people distinct from others'... The words 'treaty' and 'nation' are words of our own language, selected in our diplomatic and legislative proceedings, by ourselves, having a definite and well-understood meaning. We have applied them to other nations of the earth. They are applied to all in the same sense."[185]

The Marshall Innovation

It will undoubtedly be argued that there is yet another way out of the box of illegality in which the settler-states would otherwise appear to be trapped, and that Marshall himself supplied it a year before he made the above-quoted statement. This is found in a formulation extended by the Chief Justice in an 1831 opinion, *Cherokee v. Georgia*, as he struggled with the impossible task of reconciling the legal realities of indigenous sovereignty to the insistence of his own country upon asserting its dominion over them.[186] After conceding that argumentation "intended to prove the character of the Cherokees as a state, as a distinct political society, separated from others, capable of governing itself, has ... been completely success-ful,"[187] he went on to observe:

> [Y]et it may well be doubted whether those tribes which reside within the acknowledged boundaries of the United States can, with strict accuracy, be denominated foreign nations. They may, more correctly, perhaps be denominated domestic dependent nations.[188]

There were several bases upon which Marshall rested this idea, prob-ably most importantly the element of Discovery Doctrine vesting sole rights of territorial acquisition in discovering Crowns he had previously explored in his *McIntosh* opinion.[189] While, as has been mentioned, the intent of this proviso was to regulate affairs among the European powers, not Indians, Marshall reconfigured it as a kind of restraint of trade measure imposed upon the indigenous nations themselves. From there, he was able to extrapolate that, insofar as discovering powers enjoyed a legitimate right to constrain native peoples in the alienation of their property, to that extent at least the sovereignty of the discover stood at a level higher than that of the discovered. Ultimately, from a juridical perspective, this was the logical loophole employed to recast the relations between the United States and indigenous nations not as an association of peers, but in terms of supremacy and subordination.[190]

Although Marshall's interpretation stood the accepted meaning of international law squarely on its head—and there is ample indication he was fully aware of this[191]—it served the purpose of rationalizing U.S. expansion-ism quite admirably.[192] From the foundation laid in *Cherokee*, it was possible for American jurists and policymakers alike to argue that indigenous nations were always sovereign enough to validate U.S. territorial ambitions through treaties of cession, never sovereign enough to decline them (indeed, after 1831, native refusals to comply with U.S. demands were often enough construed as "acts of aggression" requiring military response).[193] Here too, lay the groundwork for the eventual assertion of perpetual trust discussed above in relation to *Lonewolf*, allotment, reorganization and all the rest.[194]

So useful has the doctrine emanating from Marshall's quartet of "Indian Cases"—*Peck, McIntosh, Cherokee* and *Worcester*—proven in enabling the U.S. judiciary to justify, or at least to obfuscate its Indian policy that Canadian courts have openly and increasingly embraced it. This began as early as 1867, when a Québec court quoted an entire passage from *Worcester* in the landmark case, *Connolly v. Woolrich*.[195] In its 1973 *Calder* opinion, the Supreme Court of Canada lavished praise on the *McIntosh* opinion as "the *locus classicus* of the principles governing aboriginal title."[196] By 1989, in determining the outcome of the *Bear Island* case, a Canadian appellate court simply abandoned its country's legal code altogether, adopting as precedents what it deemed to be the relevant aspects of U.S. common law. Most especially, these included the "domestic dependent nation" formulation advanced by Marshall in *Cherokee*.[197] Canadian policymakers have, of course, trotted dutifully down the same path.[198]

Whatever its utility for settler-states, however, the Marshall doctrine does not add up to internationally valid law. On the contrary, the *Cherokee* opinion in particular cannot be said to stand muster even in terms of its adherence to U.S. constitutional requirements. This is because, irrespective of the nomenclature he applied to us, when the Chief Justice held that indigenous nations occupy both a position within the federal dominion and a level of sovereignty below that of the central government, he was effectively placing us on the same legal footing as the individual States of the Union.[199] This he could not do, by virtue of the earlier-mentioned constitutional prohibition against treatymaking by and with such subordinate sovereignties, while simultaneously arguing that we should be treated as fully independent nations for purposes of conveying land title through treaties.[200]

The matter cannot be had both ways. Either we were/are sovereign for purposes of treating, or we were/are not. In the first instance, we could not have been and thus are not now legally subordinated to any other entity. In the second, we could not have been considered eligible to enter into treaties with the federal government in the first place, a matter which would serve to void all pretense that the U.S. holds legitimate title to any but a tiny fraction of its claimed territoriality outside the original thirteen Atlantic Coast states.[201]

By insisting upon playing both ends against the middle as he did, Marshall effected no reconciliation of conflicting legal principles whatsoever. Rather, he enshrined an utterly irreconcilable contradiction as the very core of federal Indian law and policy. In the process, he conjured up the fiction of "quasi-sovereign nations"—aptly described by one indigenous leader as "the judicial equivalent of the biological impossibility that a female can be partly pregnant"—a concept which has been firmly repudiated in international law.[202] As a consequence, so long as the U.S. continues to rely upon the Marshall doctrine in defining its relationship to native peoples, it will remain in a legally untenable posture. No less does this hold true for Canada

Subversion of International Law

The second half of the 1960s saw the growth of a strong and steadily more effective movement toward national liberation among the native peoples of North America. In the U.S., traditional elders joined forces with younger militants to engage in an extended series of confrontations, some of them armed, with federal authorities.[203] These were highlighted by a protracted fishing rights campaign in Washington State (1964-69), the thirteen-month occupation of government facilities on Alcatraz Island (1969-70), the seizure of BIA headquarters in Washington, D.C. (1972), and the 71-day siege of the Wounded Knee hamlet, on the Pine Ridge Reservation (1973).[204] Initially concentrated south of the border, such initiatives had become noticeably more evident in Canada as well by the mid-70s.[205]

By that point, an organization calling itself the American Indian Movement (AIM) had emerged as the galvanizing force within the liberation struggle and had become the target of severe physical repression by the federal government.[206] It was in this context, with world attention drawn to U.S.-Indian relations by the extraordinary pattern of events, that Lakota elders convened a meeting on the Standing Rock Reservation for purposes of establishing an organization to bring the question of indigenous treaty rights before the United Nations. Charged with responsibility for carrying out this task was AIM leader Russell Means, who, in turn, named Cherokee activist Jimmie Durham to direct the day-to-day operations of what was dubbed the International Indian Treaty Council (IITC).[207]

Within months, Durham had established the presence of "AIM's international diplomatic arm" at both the U.N. headquarters in New York and the Palace of Nations in Geneva, Switzerland, and had begun lobbying for hearings on settler-state denial of self-determination to indigenous nations and other abuses. This agenda dovetailed neatly with investigations already underway in several U.N. agencies and led to an unprecedented conference on discrimination against native peoples in Geneva during the summer of 1977, attended by representatives of some 98 indigenous nations of the Western Hemisphere.[208] In some ways prefiguring a special session of the Russell Tribunal convened in Rotterdam to consider the same matters two years later,[209] the 1977 "Indian Summer in Geneva" sparked serious discussion within the United Nations concerning the need for a more regularized body to consider indigenous issues.[210]

Meanwhile, undoubtedly in part to preempt just such developments, the U.S. Congress came forth in 1975 with a statue bearing the supremely unlikely title of "American Indian Self-Determination and Educational Assistance Act."[211] While the Act did nothing at all to meet the requirements of international legal definition—quite the opposite, it offers little more than a hiring preference to native people in programs attending policies implemented "in their behalf" by the federal government[212]—U.S. representatives at the U.N. were quick to use it in asserting that questions of indigenous self-determination in the United States were "superfluous" since it was the only country in the world to specifically guarantee such rights within its own statutory code.[213]

This in itself was insufficient to halt the international process, given that a U.S. domestic law, no matter how it was presented, could hardly be argued as bearing upon the circumstances of native peoples elsewhere. Thus, after much maneuvering, the United Nations Working Group on Indigenous Populations, a subpart of the Economic and Social Council (ECOSOC), was established in 1981.[214] Its mission was to conduct twice-annual sessions at the Palace of Nations during which native delegations would present information, and to submit regular reports to ECOSOC's Commission on Human Rights, with the preliminary goal of completing a then ongoing global study of the conditions imposed upon native peoples.[215] After 1984, although Durham and others had hoped to see a direct application of existing law to native circumstance, the Working Group was also mandated to produce a whole new draft declaration of indigenous rights for endorsement by the U.N. General Assembly.[216]

There followed a lengthy period of procrastination and outright obstruction on the part of various nation-state delegations. Those of Canada and the United States, to take notable examples, tied things up for several *years* while arguing that the draft document, like the name of the Working

Group itself, should be couched in terms of "populations" rather than "peoples."[217] This was because the former term, used interchangeably with "minorities," is employed with reference to demographic subsets of given polities, a classification automatically placing them within the parameters of their respective countries' "internal" affairs.[218] "Peoples," on the other hand, are construed as distinct polities on their own merit, and, as such, are universally guaranteed the unfettered right of self-determination under international law.[219]

It was not until 1989 that the two North American settler–states abandoned their terminological objections, and then only with the caveat that they were doing so with the specific understanding that use of the word "peoples" would not be construed as conveying legal connotations.[220] By then, their joint bottleneck had stalled the formulating procedure to the point that the Draft Declaration, originally intended for consideration by the General Assembly during the U.N.'s 1992 "Year of Indigenous Peoples," could not be completed on that schedule.[221] Another year was required before the document was reviewed and tentatively approved by native delegations, a further eighteen months before it had been signed off by the Working Group and its immediate parent, ECOSOC's Sub-Commission on Prevention of Discrimination and Protection of Minorities.[222]

Matters finally came to a head in October 1996, when, prior to its submission to ECOSOC's main body, and thence the General Assembly, a subgroup of the Commission on Human Rights convened in Geneva to review the draft. When the panel, composed exclusively of nation-state representatives, set out to "revise" the document in a manner intended quite literally to gut it, a unified body of indigenous delegates demanded that it be sent forward unchanged. U.S. representatives, who had for the most part remained a bit more circumspect in their approach over the preceding twenty years, then at last openly announced that the function of the proposed declaration was, in their view, to confirm rather than challenge the convoluted doctrines through which their country purportedly legitimates settler hegemony.[223] The United States, they made clear, would reject anything else, a position quickly seconded by Canada's representatives. This affront precipitated a mass walkout by native delegates, thereby bringing the entire process to a temporary halt.[224]

Prospects and Potentials

The recent events in Geneva represent something of a crossroads in the struggle for native sovereignty and self-determination, not only in North America, but globally. The sheer audacity with which the U.S. and Canada have moved to convert a supposed universal declaration of indigenous rights into little more than an extrapolation of their own mutual foreclosure upon the most meaningful of these clearly describes one direction in which things are moving. If the North American settler-states are successful in pushing through their agenda, indigenous rights the world over will be formally defined in much the same truncated and subordinative fashion as is presently the case here. Native peoples everywhere will then be permanently consigned to suffer the same lack of recourse before the ICJ and other international adjudicating bodies that we have long experienced in U.S./Canadian courts.[225]

In the alternative, if the all but unanimous indigenous refusal to contine-nence substantive alteration of the draft document they themselves endorsed proves inadequate to compel its eventual acceptance by the General Assem-bly, other options must be found. The most promising of these would appear to reside in a generalized native repudiation of any statist version of the proposed declaration of indigenous rights combined with a return to the strategy advocated by Durham and others during the late 1970s.[226] This, quite simply, devolves upon the devising of ways to force acknowledgment of indigenous rights under existing law rather than the creation of a new instrument.[227]

There are numerous routes to this end, beginning with the seeking of ICJ advisory opinions on the broader applicability of its interpretations in the *Island of Palmas* and *Western Sahara* cases.[228] Perhaps more important are a range of possibilities by which the ICJ and/or appropriate U.N. organs might be compelled to advance concrete interpretations of the meaning inherent to assorted declarations, covenants and conventions—the 1966 International Covenant on Economic, Social and Cultural Rights, for example, and the 1966 International Covenant on Civil and Political Rights—vis-à-vis indigenous peoples.[229] Probably salient in this regard is the 1960 Declaration on the Granting of Independence to Colonial Countries and Peoples (General Assembly Resolution 1514 (XV)), the fifth point of which stipulates that:

Immediate steps shall be taken, in Trust and Non-Self-Governing Territories or all other territories which have not yet attained independence, to transfer all powers to the peoples of those territories, without conditions or reservations, in accordance with their freely expressed will or desire, without any distinction as to race, creed or colour, to enable them to enjoy complete independence and freedom.[230]

The nature of the "immediate steps" to be taken are neither mysterious nor left to the interpretive discretion of colonizing states. Rather, they are spelled out clearly in Articles 73-91 of the United Nations Charter.[231] In essence, all such territories/peoples must be inscribed by the colonizer on a list maintained by the U.N. Trusteeship Council, which then must approve a plan, including a timetable, by which complete decolonization will occur at the earliest feasible date.[232] The colonizer is then required to submit regular reports to the Council on progress made in fulfillment of the plan.[233] The process culminates in a referendum or comparable procedure, monitored by the U.N. and sometimes conducted under its direct supervision, by which the colonized people determine for themselves exactly what they wish their political status to be, and what, if any, relationship they wish to maintain with their former colonizers.[234]

One significant hurdle which must be cleared in the course of bringing such elements of black letter law to bear on the question of native rights are the provisions contained in Article 1 (4) of the United Nations Charter and Point 7 of General Assembly Resolution 1514 (XV) guaranteeing the territorial integrity of all states.[235] By and large, the meaning of these clauses has been interpreted in accordance with the so-called "Blue Water Principle" of the 1960s, a doctrine holding that in order to be eligible for decolonization, a territory must be physically separated from its colonizer by at least thirty miles of open ocean.[236] By this standard, most indigenous peoples are obviously not and will never be entitled to exercise genuine self-determining rights.

There are, however, substantial problems attending the Blue Water formulation, not just for indigenous peoples but for everyone. It would not, for instance, admit to the fact that Germany colonized contiguous Poland during World War II, or that the Poles possessed a legitimate right to decolonization. Plainly, then, a basic reformulation is in order, starting perhaps from the basic premise that "integrity" is not so much a matter of geography as it is a question of whether a given territory can be shown to have been legitimately acquired in the first place. Thus, the definitional obstacle at hand readily lends itself to being rendered far less "insurmountable" than it might now appear.[237]

Ultimately, such issues can be resolved only on the basis of a logically consistent determination of whether indigenous peoples actually constitute "peoples" in a legal sense. While the deliberately obfuscatory arguments entered on the matter by the U.S., Canada and several other settler-states during the 1980s have by this point thoroughly muddied the situation with respect to a host of untreatied peoples throughout the world, the same cannot be said of treatied peoples in North America. As has been discussed in this essay, we have long since been formally recognized by our colonizers not only as peoples, but as nations, and are thereby entitled in existing law to exercise the rights of such *regardless* of our geographic disposition.[238]

The path leading to an alternative destiny for indigenous peoples is thus just as clear as that the settler-states would prescribe for us. By relentless and undeviating assertion of the basic rights of treatied peoples—at all levels, through every available venue and excluding no conceivable means of doing so—we can begin to (re)secure them, restoring to ourselves and our posterity our/their rightful status as sovereign and coequal members of the community of nations, free of such pretense as IRA-style "self-governance" and subterfuges like the "Self-Determination" Act. In achieving success in this endeavor, we will eventually position ourselves to tangibly assist our relatives in other parts of the world, untreatied and thus unrecognized as being imbued with the same self-determining rights as we, to overcome the juridical/diplomatic quandary in which this circumstance places them.

Notes

1. See generally, see Douglas Sanders, "The Re-Emergence of Indigenous Questions in International Law," *Canadian Human Rights Yearbook*, No. 3, 1983; S. James Anaya, "The Rights of Indigenous Peoples and International Law in Historical and Contemporary Perspective," in Robert N. Clinton, Nell Jessup Newton and Monroe E. Price, eds., *American Indian Law: Cases and Materials* (Charlottesville, VA: Michie Co., 1991).

2. It is of course true that Mexico is geographically part of the North American continent. Since its colonial/legal tradition is Iberian rather than Angloamerican, however, it is excluded from the present analysis (which is thus restricted to the area north of the Río Grande). Those interested in the circumstances pertaining to Iberoamerica would do well to reference Greg Urban and Joel Sherzer, eds., *Nation-States and Indians in Latin America* (Austin: University of Texas Press, 1991). Of additional interest is Roxanne Dunbar Ortiz, *Indians of the Americas: Human Rights and Self-Determination* (London: Zed Books, 1984).

3. Perhaps the most coherent articulation of the thinking embodied in this claim will be found in Charles F. Wilkinson's *Indians, Time and Law* (New Haven, CT: Yale University Press, 1987). For more analyses specific to Canada, see Russel Barsh and James Youngblood Henderson, "Aboriginal Rights, Treaty Rights, and Human Rights: Indian Tribes and Constitutional Renewal," *Journal of Canadian Studies*, Vol. 17, No. 2, 1982; Paul Williams, "Canada's Laws About Aboriginal Peoples: A Brief Overview," *Law & Anthropology*, No. 1, 1986; Sharon H. Venne, "Treaty and Constitution in Canada," in Ward Churchill, ed., *Critical Issues in Native North America* (Copenhagen: IWGIA Doc. 62, 1989).

4. See, e.g., the statements quoted by Jimmie Durham in his *Columbus Day* (Minneapolis: West End Press, 1983). For detailed analysis of the actualities involved, see Carol J. Minugh, Glenn T. Morris and Rudolph C. Ryser, eds., *Indian Self-Governance: Perspectives on the Political Status of Indian Nations in the United States of America* (Kenmore, WA: World Center for Indigenous Studies, 1989).

5. For further details, see my "Subterfuge and Self-Determination: Suppression of Indigenous Sovereignty in the 20th Century United States," in *Z Magazine*, May 1997.

6. See, e.g., Robert M. Carmack, ed., *Harvest of Violence: The Maya Indians and the Guatemala Crisis* (Norman: University of Oklahoma Press, 1988); John G. Taylor, *Indonesia's Forgotten War: The Hidden History of East Timor* (London: Zed Books, 1991). On the historical treatment of native peoples both north of the Río Grande and south, see David E. Stannard, *American Holocaust: Columbus and the Conquest of the New World* (New York: Oxford University Press, 1992). For particular emphasis on the U.S. portion of North America, including current data on health, life expectancy and so forth, see Ward Churchill, *A Little Matter of Genocide: Holocaust and Denial in the Americas* (Winnipeg: Arbeiter Ring, 1998).

7. Most notably, this applies to the counterinsurgency campaign waged during the 1970s against the American Indian Movement by U.S. civil authorities, backed up by the military, and, to a lesser extent, actions undertaken against the Mohawk Warriors Society by Canadian military/police units twenty years later; see Bruce Johansen and Roberto Maestas, *Wasi'chu: The Continuing Indian Wars* (New York: Monthly Review Press, 1978); Ward Churchill and Jim Vander Wall, *Agents of Repression: The FBI's Secret Wars Against the Black Panther Party and the American Indian Movement* (Boston: South End Press, 1988); Geoffrey York and Loreen Pindera, *People of the Pines: The Warriors and the Legacy of Oka* (Boston: Little, Brown, 1991).

8. On England, see Michael Hecter, *Internal Colonialism: The Celtic Fringe in British National Development, 1536-1966* (Berkeley: University of California Press, 1975); Peter Berresford Ellis, *The Celtic Revolution: A Study in Anti-Imperialism* (Talybont, U.K.: Y Lolfa Cyf., 1985). On Spain, see Robert P. Clark, *Negotiating with ETA: Obstacles to Peace in the Basque Country, 1975-1988* (Reno: University of Nevada Press, 1990); Cyrus Ernesto Zirakzadeh, *A Rebellious People: Basques, Protests, and Politics* (Reno: University of Nevada Press, 1991).

9. There is much theoretical precedent for such an outcome with respect to enunciating principles of self-determination, not least within such ostensibly liberatory perspectives as marxism–leninism; see Walker Connor, *The National Question in Marxist-Leninist Theory and Strategy* (Princeton, NJ: Princeton University Press, 1984). For a concrete example of the U.S., and Canada secondarily, manipulating the codification of international law in such fashion as to protect their own prerogatives to engage in certain

of the practices ostensibly proscribed, see Lawrence J. LeBlanc, *The United States and the Genocide Convention* (Durham, NC: Duke University Press, 1991).

10. It might be useful for some readers at this point to offer a reference addressing the meaning of the term "self-determination" in not only its theoretical but also its legal and practical applications; see generally, Michla Pomerance, *Self-Determination in Law and Practice* (The Hague: Marinus Nijhoff, 1982).

11. The first indication that this is so may be found in the 1867 Québec case *Connolly v. Woolrich* (11 LCJ 197) in which a Canadian court considering the validity of a marriage effected under native tradition for purposes of determining inheritance rights repeated verbatim a lengthy passage from Chief Justice of the U.S. Supreme Court John Marshall's opinion in *Worcester v. Georgia* (6 Peters 515 (1832)). For a comprehensive overview of this phenomenon, see Bruce Clark, *Indian Land Title in Canada* (Toronto: Carswell, 1987).

12. See, e.g., J.V. Stalin, *Marxism and the National and Colonial Questions* (New York: International, 1935); V.I. Lenin, *The Right of Nations to Self-Determination: Selected Writings* (New York: International, 1951); Louis L. Snyder, *The Meaning of Nationalism* (New Brunswick, NJ: Rutgers University Press, 1954); Ernst Gellner, *Nations and Nationalism* (Ithaca, NY: Cornell University Press, 1983).

13. For a variety of viewpoints, all arriving at more-or-less the same conclusion, see Ernst Cassirer, *The Myth of the State* (New Haven: Yale University Press, 1946); Perry Anderson, *Lineages of the Absolute State* (London: New Left Books, 1974); L. Tivey, ed., *The Nation-State* (New York: St. Martin's Press, 1981); J. Frank Harrison, *The Modern State: An Anarchist Analysis* (Montréal: Black Rose Books, 1984)

14. For further clarification, see Hugh Seton-Watson, *Nations and States: An Inquiry into the Origins of Nations and the Politics of Nationalism* (Boulder, CO: Westview Press, 1977); Anthony D. Smith, *State and Nation in the Third World* (Brighton, U.K.: Harvester Press, 1983).

15. As American Indian Movement leader Russell Means quipped during a talk delivered in Denver on October 9, 1996 U.N., "to be accurate, the United Nations should really have been called the United States. But the name was already taken" (tape on file).

16. Sovereignty is a theological concept originally associated with the transcendent power of the deity. It was secularized during the sixteenth century when the French theorist Jean Bodin used it to describe the authority of the Crown, beyond which no worldly authority was seen to exist (monarchs, ruling by "divine right," were in his view accountable only to natural and supernatural law). Eventually, during the era of the American and French revolutions, the idea was reworked so that sovereignty might be understood as something vested in the people themselves, or, most recently, in the states supposedly embodying their "will"; L. Oppenheim, *International Law* (London: Longman's, Green, [8th ed.] 1955) pp. 120-2; Carl Schmidt, *Political Theology: Four Chapters on the Concept of Sovereignty* (Cambridge: MIT Press, 1985).

17. This is not to say that the actions themselves bear an intrinsic illegitimacy, simply that they do not represent a negation of sovereignty. Even in the most extreme instances—the unconditional surrenders and subsequent occupations of Germany and Japan at the end of World War II, for example—it is understood that such outcomes are of a temporary nature, that the sovereignty of the defeated nations remains intact, and that their self-determining existence will resume at the earliest possible date. For elaboration of the legal and other principles involved, see Michael Walzer, *Just and Unjust Wars: A Moral Argument with Illustrations* (New York: Basic Books, 1977).

18. For an interesting array of perspectives on, and especially sensitive handling of, this matter, see R.B.J. Walker and Saul H. Mendlovitz, eds., *Contending Sovereignties: Redefining Political Community* (Boulder, CO: Lynne Rienner, 1990).

19. For a good summary, see Jack Weatherford, *Indian Givers: How the Indians of the Americas Transformed the World* (New York: Fawcett Columbine, 1988).

20. Felix S. Cohen, "Original Indian Title," *Minnesota Law Review*, No. 32, 1947, p. 44, n. 34. Vitoria's *De Indis et de Ivre Belli Reflectiones* (Washington, D.C.: Carnegie Institution, 1917 reprint of 1557 original), a compilation of meditations begun in 1532, was more-or-less definitive and endorsed as legal doctrine by both the Iberian monarch and the Pope. Among other things, Vitoria—and, by extension, the Vatican and the Spanish Crown—acknowledged indigenous peoples' ownership of their lands and other property, right to govern themselves within these territories, and to convey citizenship; Felix S. Cohen, "The Spanish Origin of Indian Rights in the United States," *Georgetown Law Journal*, Vol. 31, No. 1, 1942; Lewis Hanke, *The Spanish Struggle for Justice in the Conquest of America* (Philadelphia: University of

Pennsylvania Press, 1947); Etienne Grisel, "The Beginnings of International Law and General Public Law Doctrine: Francisco de Vitoria's *De Indis prior*," in Fredi Chiapelli, ed., *First Images of America*, 2 vols. (Berkeley: University of California Press, 1976) Vol 1. More broadly, see Robert A. Williams, Jr., *The American Indian in Western Legal Thought: The Discourses of Conquest* (New York: Oxford University Press, 1990).

21. See Howard Peckham and Charles Gibson, eds., *Attitudes of the Colonial Powers Toward the American Indian* (Salt Lake City: University of Utah Press, 1969).

22. Quoted in Francis Paul Prucha, *American Indian Policy in the Formative Years: The Trade and Intercourse Acts, 1790-1834* (Lincoln: University of Nebraska Press, 1970) p. 141.

23. Quoted in George Dewey Harmon, *Sixty Years of Indian Affairs: Political, Economic, and Diplomatic, 1789-1850* (Chapel Hill: University of North Carolina Press, 1941) p. 16.

24. *Worcester v. Georgia*, at p. 559. For further amplification, see Howard Berman, "The Concept of Aboriginal Rights in the Early History of the United States," *Buffalo Law Review*, No. 27, Fall 1978.

25. Edwin de Witt Dickenson, *The Equality of States in International Law* (Cambridge, MA: Harvard University Press, 1920). The principle at issue was consistently recognized by the U.S. judiciary with respect to American Indians as late as the 1883 case *Ex Parte Crow Dog* (109 U.S. 556), in which the court held that the United States lacked a jurisdictional standing to prosecute criminal offenses committed in Indian Country. Congress responded by passing the 1885 Major Crimes Act (ch. 120, 16 Stat. 544, 566, now codified at 25 U.S.C. 71), unilaterally extending the reach of U.S. courts into reserved territories with regard to seven felonious offenses. Hence, it was not until *U.S. v. Kagama* (118 U.S. 375 (1886)) that the Supreme Court began to speak of the federal government possessing an "incontrovertible right" to exercise jurisdiction over native lands; see Sidney L. Harring, *Crow Dog's Case: American Indian Sovereignty, Tribal Law, and United States Law in the Nineteenth Century* (Cambridge, U.K.: Cambridge University Press, 1994). Usurpation of native jurisdiction in Canada began earlier, with the 1803 Act for Extending Jurisdiction of the Courts of Justice in the Provinces of Upper and Lower Canada, to the Trial and Punishment of Persons Guilty of Crimes and Offenses within Certain Parts of North America Adjoining to Said Provinces (43 Geo. III, c. 138), amplified and extended into the civil domain by the 1821 Act for Regulating the Fur Trade and Establishing a Criminal and Civil Jurisdiction within Certain Parts of North America (1 & 2 Geo. IV, c. 66); Bruce Clark, *Native Liberty, Crown Sovereignty: The Existing Aboriginal Right of Self-Government in Canada* (Montréal: McGill-Queens University Press, 1990) pp. 124-7. For a strongly articulated native repudiation of the U.S. performance, see the testimony of Vine Deloria, Jr., during the 1974 "Sioux Sovereignty Hearing" conducted before a federal court in Lincoln, Nebraska; Roxanne Dunbar Ortiz, ed., *The Great Sioux Nation: Sitting in Judgment on America* (New York/San Francisco: International Indian Treaty Council/Moon Books, 1977) pp. 141-6. On Canada, see the positions advanced by Ontario Region Chief Gordon Peters, John Amagolik, Doris Ronnenberg and others in Frank Cassidy, ed., *Aboriginal Self-Determination: Proceedings of a Conference held September 30-October 3, 1990* (Lantzville, B.C.: Oolichan Books, 1991) pp. 33-60.

26. This prescription for the interaction of nations was worked out very well by the time of Dutch jurist Hugo Grotius' *De Jure Belli ac Pacis Libri Tres: In quibus ius naturae & Gentium, item iuris publicipraecipua explicantur* (Paris: Buon, 1625). For interpretation, see, Hidemi Suganami, "Grotius and International Equality," in Hedley Bull, Benedict Kingsbury and Adam Roberts, eds., *Hugo Grotius and International Law* (Oxford, U.K.: Clarendon Press, 1990).

27. A particularly astute rendering of this principle will be found in John Howard Clinebell and Jim Thompson, "Sovereignty and Self-Determination: The Rights of Native Americans Under International Law," *Buffalo Law Review*, No. 27, Fall 1978.

28. Suganami, "Grotius and International Equity," op. cit. Also see Hedley Bull, "The Grotian Conception of International Relations," in Herbert Butterfield and Martin Wright, eds., *Diplomatic Investigations: Essays in the Theory of International Politics* (London: Allen & Unwin, 1966); Cornelius J. Murphy, "Grotius and the Peaceful Settlement of Disputes," *Grotiana*, No. 4, 1983. For translation of Grotian thought into the relatively more concrete terms of contemporary legal/diplomatic practice, see Martin Lachs, "The Grotian Heritage, the International Community and Changing Dimensions of International Law," in *International Law and the Grotian Heritage* (The Hague: T.M.C. Asser Instituut, 1985).

29. See generally, Vitoria, "On the Law of War," in *De Indis et De Jure Belli Relaciones*, op. cit. More particularly, see Walzer *Just Wars*, op. cit., pp. 51-3; and *Report of the Special Committee on the Question of*

Defining Aggression (Gen. Ass. Off. Rec. No. A/9619, 29 sess. 19 (1974)) pp. 10–13. On the military dimension of U.S./Indian relations, see, e.g., Alan Axelrod, *Chronicle of the Indian Wars from Colonial Times to Wounded Knee* (New York: Prentice Hall, 1993).

30. As the point is delineated in the United Nations Resolution on the Definition of Aggression (U,N.G.A. Res. 3314 (XXIX), 29 U.N. GAOR, Supp. (N0. 31) 142, U.N. Doc. A/9631 (1975)), "No territorial acquisition or special advantage resulting from aggression is or shall be recognized as lawful." This is an element of what has come to be known as the "Nuremberg Doctrine"; see, e.g., Quincy Wright, "The Law of the Nuremberg Trials," *American Journal of International Law*, No. 41, Jan. 1947. For the text of the instrument by which the international community accepted this doctrine, see "Agreement for the Prosecution and Punishment of the Major War Criminals of the European Axis Powers and Charter of the International Military Tribunal" ("London Agreement," Aug. 8, 1945) in Burns H. Weston, Richard A. Falk and Anthony D'Amato, eds., *Basic Documents in International Law and World Order* (St. Paul, MN: West Publishing, [2nd ed.] 1990) pp. 138–9. On the role of the United States in articulation of the Nuremberg principles, and its endorsement of them, see Bradley F. Smith, *The Road to Nuremberg* (New York: Basic Books, 1981); *The American Road to Nuremberg: The Documentary Record, 1944-1945* (Stanford, CA: Hoover Institution Press, 1982). With respect to the crimes for which the German leadership was tried in this connection, see Office of United States Chief Council for Prosecution of Axis Criminality, *Nazi Conspiracy and Aggression*, 8 vols. (Washington, D.C.: U.S. Government Printing Office, 1946).

31. The point is exceedingly well-established; see, Pomerance, *Self-Determination*, op. cit.; W. Ofuatey-Kodjoe, *The Principle of Self-Determination in International Law* (Hamden, CT: Archon Books, 1972); A. Rigo Sureda, *The Evolution of the Right to Self-Determination: A Study of United Nations Practice* (Leyden, Netherlands: A.W. Sijhoff, 1973); Lee C. Buchheit, *Secession: The Legitimacy of Self-Determination* (New Haven: Yale University Press, 1978); Ved Nanda, "Self-Determination Under International Law: Validity of Claims to Secede," *Case Western Journal of International Law*, No. 13, 1981.

32. This principle was enunciated by Supreme Court Justice Robert H. Jackson, at the time serving as lead prosecutor for the United States, in his opening statement to the court at Nuremberg on November 21, 1945; International Military Tribunal, *Trial of the Major War Criminals before the International Military Tribunal*, 42 vols. (Nuremberg: Allied Control Authority, 1949) Vol. 2, pp. 98-155. Also see Jackson's *The Nürnberg Case* (New York: Alfred A. Knopf, 1947).

33. On the contrary, instruments such as the Universal Declaration of the Rights of Peoples ("Algiers Declaration," July 4, 1976), go in precisely the opposite direction; for text, see Richard Falk, *Human Rights and State Sovereignty* (New York: Holmes & Meier, 1981) pp. 225–8.

34. This has been so since at least as early as publication of Grotius' 1625 *De Jure Belli* (op. cit.), and was reconfirmed quite forcefully by the renowned jurist Emmerich de Vattel in his massive three volume *The Laws of Nations* (Philadelphia: T. & J.W. Joseph, 1883 reprint of 1758 original; Washington, D.C.: Carnegie Institution, 1925 reprint). Most definitively, the Vienna Convention on the Law of Treaties (U.N. Doc. A/CONF.39/27 at 289 (1969), 1155 U.N.T.S. 331, reprinted in 8 I.L.M. 679 (1969)) is explicit in positing that a "'treaty' means an agreement concluded *between States* in a written form and governed by international law (emphasis added)." It was agreed by those who met to formulate the Convention that its contents are "merely expressive of rules which existed under customary international law"; *United Nations Conference on the Law of Treaties, Official Records, Second Session* (A Conf.39/11 Add.1 (1969)). See generally, Shabati Rosenne, *The Law of Treaties: A Guide to the Legislative History of the Vienna Convention* (Leyden: A.W. Sijhoff, 1970); Sir Ian Sinclair, *The Vienna Convention on the Law of Treaties* (Manchester, U.K.: Manchester University Press, 1984). With particular reference to the fact that the Vienna Convention merely codified existing custom rather than creating new law, see Samuel Benjamin Crandell, *Treaties: Their Making and Enforcement* (New York: Columbia University Press, [2nd. ed.] 1916).

35. Oppenheim, *International Law*, op. cit., pp. 146, 148; H. Chen, *International Law of Recognition* (Leyden, Netherlands: A.W. Sijhoff, 1951) p. 194. It is crucial to emphasize that one nation does not "create" another by entering into a treaty with it. Sovereignty is not *imparted* through treaty recognition. Rather, a treaty represents the acknowledgment by each party of the other's *preexisting* standing as a sovereign nation. In effect, then, the hundreds of European and Euroamerican treaties with North America's indigenous peoples are all reiterations of the involved states' formal recognition that the natives were and had always been inherently sovereign. For a good sampling of instruments deriving from the colonial era, see Alden T. Vaughan, *Early American Indian Documents: Treaties and Laws, 1607-1789*

(Washington, D.C.: University Publications of America, 1979).

36. Art. I, § 10 of the U.S. Constitution precludes any private concern or level of government below that of the federal authority itself from entering into a treaty. The courts have interpreted this in terms of a "rule of reciprocity": since lesser entities are prohibited from treating, the federal government is equally prohibited from treating with them. It follows that any entity with which the government treats must be, by definition, another sovereign national entity. This being true, Article VI, Cl. 2—the so-called "Supremacy Clause"—stipulates that ratified treaties "are superior to any conflicting state laws or constitutional provisions"; Rennard Strickland, et al., eds., *Felix S. Cohen's Handbook on Federal Indian Law* (Charlottesville, VA: Michie Co., 1982) pp. 62-3.

37. A notable example is to be found in George III's Royal Proclamation of 1763 (RSC 1970, App. II, No. 1, at 127) and subsequent legislation; Jack Stagg, *Anglo-Indian Relations in North America to 1763 and an Analysis of the Royal Proclamation of 7 October 1763* (Ottawa: Carlton University Press, 1981). A useful summary and assessment of implications will be found in Clark, *Native Liberty, Crown Sovereignty*, op. cit., esp. pp. 134-46. Also see the opening chapter of Dorothy V. Jones, *License for Empire: Colonialism by Treaty in Early America* (Chicago: University of Chicago Press, 1982).

38. Under Art. II, Cl. 2 of the U.S. Constitution, treaties are negotiated by the president or his delegate(s), but do not become law until confirmed by two-thirds vote of the Senate. The standard count on ratified treaties has until recently been 371, the complete texts of which are collected in Charles J. Kappler, ed., *Indian Treaties, 1778-1885* (New York: Interland, 1973). Lakota scholar Vine Deloria, Jr., has, however, collected a further dozen such instruments overlooked by Kappler (these are to be included in an as yet unpublished study). As concerns unratified treaties, it should be noted that U.S. courts have in numerous instances opted to view them as binding upon Indians while exempting the United States from even a pretense of compliance with terms delineating reciprocal obligations. An especially egregious example concerns the more than forty unratified treaties with California's native peoples used by the federal judiciary to impose the so-called "Pit River Land Settlement" during the late 1960s; see generally, Florence Connolly Shipeck, *Pushed into the Rocks: Southern California Indian Land Tenure, 1769-1986* (Lincoln: University of Nebraska Press, 1988).

39. *Canada: Indian Treaties and Surrenders from 1680 to 1890*, 3 vols. (Ottawa: Queen's Printer, 1891; reprinted by Coles [Toronto], 1971; reprinted by Fifth House [Saskatoon], 1992). A useful interpretation will be found in John Leonard Taylor's "Canada's North-West Indian Policy in the 1870s: Traditional Premises and Necessary Innovations," in J.R. Miller, *Sweet Promises: A Reader on Indian-White Relations in Canada* (Toronto: University of Toronto Press, 1991).

40. *Opinions of the Attorney General* (Washington, D.C.: U.S. Government Printing Office, 1828) pp. 613-8, 623-33. The validity of Wirt's equating the legal standing of indigenous nations to that of "any other nation" has been repeatedly conceded by the Supreme Court: e.g., *Holden v. Joy* (84 U.S. (17 Wall.) 211 (1872)); *United States v. 43 Gallons of Whiskey* (93 U.S. 188 (1876)); *Washington v. Fishing Vessel Association* (443 U.S. 675 (1979))

41. Wilcomb E. Washburn, *Red Man's Land, White Man's Law: The Past and Present Status of the American Indian* (Norman: University of Oklahoma Press, [2nd. ed.] 1995) p. 57. It is worth noting, to reinforce the point, that under provision of the 1796 Trade and Intercourse Act (Ch. 30, 1 Stat. 469) all U.S. nationals intending to travel into Indian Country were required to obtain a passport.

42. Robert T. Coulter, "Contemporary Indian Sovereignty," in National Lawyers Guild, Committee on Native American Struggles, *Rethinking Indian Law* (New Haven, CT: Advocate Press, 1982) p. 117. He cites M. Whitman, *Digest of International Law* §1 at 2 (1963) on this point.

43. This is all but axiomatic; see, e.g., Wilfred C. Jencks, *Law in the World Community* (New York: Oxford University Press, 1967) pp. 31, 83-7.

44. *Opinions of the Attorney General* (Washington, D.C.: U.S. Government Printing Office, 1821) p. 345.

45. For a prime example of such argumentation, see Wilcomb E. Washburn, *The Indian in America* (New York: Harper & Row, 1975).

46. For good surveys of such contentions, see Reginald Horsman, *Expansion and American Policy, 1783-1812* (Lansing: Michigan State University Press, 1967); Richard Drinnon, *Facing West: The Metaphysics of Indian Hating and Empire Building* (Minneapolis: University of Minnesota Press, 1980). Also see Richard E. Buel, Jr., *Securing the Revolution: Ideology in American Politics, 1789-1815* (Ithaca, NY: Cornell University Press, 1972).

47. To be fair about it, the U.S. founders and their heirs are by no means the only parties to advance this sort of spurious argument. The English themselves, for example, claimed to have inherited discovery rights to Mikmakik (Nova Scotia) from France under the 1713 Treaty of Utrecht, despite a firm French denial that they held title to what was in fact acknowledged Mi'kmaq territory. To further complicate matters, Canadian courts now contend that their country has inherited title from Great Britain, although they, no more than anyone else, can say exactly when or how Mi'kmaq title was ever extinguished; W.E. Daugherty, *The Maritime Indian Treaties in Perspective* (Ottawa: Indian and Northern Affairs Canada, 1981) pp. 45-7; Peter A. Cumming and Neil H. Mickenberg, *Native Rights in Canada* (Toronto: General Publishing/Indian-Eskimo Association of Canada, 1972) p. 95.

48. The complete text of the Treaty of Paris (Sept. 3, 1783) is included in Ruhl J. Bartlett, ed., *The Record of American Diplomacy: Documents and Readings in the History of U.S. Foreign Relations* (New York: Alfred A. Knopf, [4th ed.] 1964) pp. 39-42. Under both British common law and relevant international law, to quit a claim of interest in a property/territory means that unclouded title reverts to the original owners. In this case, other than in those relatively small areas to which the Crown had acquired an outright title through purchase or other agreement, this would be the indigenous nations whose lands were/are at issue.

49. Most important was Innocent III's bull *Quod super his*, promulgated in 1210 to legitimate the Crusades. Relying on the intervening theoretical work of Thomas Aquinas and others, Innocent IV subjected his predecessor's bull to the question of whether it was "licit to invade a land which infidels possess, or which belongs to them?" He ultimately answered in the affirmative, but only under specific circumstances and in recognition of the "natural rights" of those invaded to their property; James Muldoon, *The Expansion of Europe: The First Phase* (Philadelphia: University of Pennsylvania Press, 1977) pp. 191-2. Also see Brian Tierney, *The Crisis of Church and State, 1050-1300* (Engelwood Cliffs, NJ: Prentice-Hall, 1964) pp. 155-6. On development of the Innocentian position by Vitoria, et al., see Hanke, *Spanish Struggle for Justice*, op. cit.; Williams, *American Indian in Western Legal Thought*, op. cit.; John Taylor, *Spanish Law Concerning Discoveries, Pacifications, and Settlements Among the Indians* (Salt Lake City: University of Utah Press, 1980); L.C. Green and Olive P. Dickason, *The Law of Nations in the New World* (Edmonton: University of Alberta Press, 1989).

50. See generally, Mark Frank Lindsey, *The Acquisition and Government of Backward Country in International Law: A Treatise on the Law and Practice Relating to Colonial Expansion* (London: Longman's, Green, 1926); W.J. Mommsen and J.A. de Moor, *European Expansion and the Law: The Encounter of European and Indigenous Law in 19th and 20th Century Africa and Asia* (Oxford: Berg, 1992).

51. Bull *Sublimis Duis*, promulgated by Pope Paul III in 1537; quoted in Frank MacNutt, *Bartholomew de Las Casas* (Cleveland: Arthur H. Clark, 1909) p. 429. It is worth noting that understanding of the principle involved was still demonstrated by U.S. courts well into the twentieth century. In *Deere v. St. Lawrence River Power Company* (32 F.2d 550 (2d Cir. 1929)), for example, it was admitted that, "The source of [native] title is no letters patent or other form of grant by the federal government... Indians claim immemorial rights, arising prior to white occupation, and recognized and protected by treaties between Great Britain and the United States and the United States and the Indians [under which] the right of occupation of [their] lands...was not granted, but recognized and affirmed."

52. This amounted to a universalization of the principle expounded by Pope Alexander VI in his bull *Inter Caetera* of May 4, 1493, dividing interests in the southern hemisphere of the New World between Spain and Portugal; Paul Gottschalk, *The Earliest Diplomatic Documents of America* (Albany: New York State Historical Society, 1978) p. 21.

53. *Worcester v. Georgia* at 544.

54. *Johnson & Graham's Lessee v. McIntosh*, 21 U.S. (8 Wheat.) 543 (1823) at 572.

55. Quoted in Washburn, *Red Man's Land*, op. cit., p. 56. Precisely the same understanding continued to be demonstrated by the federal judiciary, however occasionally, throughout the nineteenth century. In *Jones v. Meehan* (175 U.S. 1 (1899)), for instance, the court admitted that the "United States had [by a 1785 Treaty with the Wiandots, Delawares, Chippewas and Ottawas] relinquished and quitclaimed to said nations respectively all the lands lying within certain limits, to live and hunt upon, and otherwise occupy as they saw fit; but the said nations, or either of them, were not at liberty to dispose of those lands, except to the United States."

56. Washburn, *Red Man's Land*, op. cit., p. 56. For an almost identical statement, this one made in a

legal opinion rendered on May 3, 1790, see Andrew A. Lipscomb and Albert Ellery Bergh, eds., *The Writings of Thomas Jefferson*, 20 vols. (Washington, D.C.: Thomas Jefferson Memorial Association, 1903-1904) Vol. VII, pp. 467-9. Further comments will be found in Merrill D. Peterson's *Thomas Jefferson and the New Nation* (New York: Oxford University Press, 1970) pp. 771, 820-1.

57. *Worcester v. Georgia* at 545.

58. See generally, David M. Pelcher, *The Diplomacy of Annexation: Texas, Oregon and the Mexican War* (Columbia: University of Missouri Press, 1973).

59. Cohen, "Original Indian Title," op. cit., p. 35; for the text of the Treaty Between the United States and France for the Cession of Louisiana (Apr. 30, 1803), see Bartlett, *Record of American Diplomacy*, op. cit., pp. 116-7. Also see Alexander de Conde, *This Affair of Louisiana* (New York: Charles Scribner's Sons, 1976).

60. Treaty of Peace, Friendship, Limits, and Settlement Between the United States and Mexico, Feb. 2, 1848; for text, see Bartlett, *Record of American Diplomacy*, op. cit., pp. 214-6. On the causes of the conflict preceding the treaty, see Gene M. Brack, *Mexico Views Manifest Destiny: An Essay on the Origins of the Mexican War* (Albuquerque: University of New Mexico Press, 1975).

61. The Hawaiian Archipelago was annexed by the United States in 1898, following an 1893 *coup d'etat* carried out by American nationals—supported by U.S. troops—against its indigenous government, a constitutional monarchy. In 1959, following a referendum conducted in a manner violating the most basic requirements of the United Nations Charter (the settler population as well as the much smaller native population was allowed to vote), it was incorporated into the U.S. as its fiftieth state; Michael Kioni Dudley and Keoni Kealoha Agard, *A Call for Hawaiian Sovereignty* (Honolulu: Na Kane O Ka Malo Press, 1990); Haunani-Kay Trask, *From a Native Daughter: Colonialism and Sovereignty in Hawai'i* (Monroe, ME: Common Courage Press, 1993).

62. *American Journal of International Law*, No. 22, 1928, p. 1928; reporting the *Island of Palmas* case (*U.S. v. Netherlands*, Perm. Ct. Arb., Hague, 1928).

63. 41 U.S. (6 Pet.) 367 (1842) at 409.

64. U.S. ambitions in North America were hardly confined to the 48 contiguous states and Alaska. There was, for example, serious consideration given during the late 1860s to the idea of seizing all of what is now Canada west of Ontario. The idea of gobbling up what remained of Mexico after 1848 was also a perennial favorite. For varying perspectives, see Albert K. Weinberg, *Manifest Destiny: A Study of National Expansionism in American History* (Baltimore: Johns Hopkins University Press, 1935); Frederick Merk, *Manifest Destiny and Mission in American History: A Reinterpretation* (New York: Alfred A. Knopf, 1963); Sidney Lens, *The Forging of the American Empire* (New York: Thomas Y. Crowell, 1971); Reginald Horsman, *Race and Manifest Destiny: The Origins of American Racial Anglo-Saxonism* (Cambridge, MA: Harvard University Press, 1981).

65. A point worth making is that, given the realities of global demography, the whole idea of *Territorium res Nullius* has always lacked applicability anywhere outside Antarctica and a few remote sandspits scattered across the seven seas. There were an estimated billion people on the planet when the Supreme Court penned its *Martin* opinion in 1842—upwards of three-quarters that number in 1492—less than twenty percent of them of European derivation; see, e.g., Kenneth C. Davis, *Don't Know Much About Geography: Everything You Ever Wanted to Know About the World but Never Learned* (New York: William Morrow, 1992) p. 300.

66. The idea found form in 1066, when Pope Alexander recognized the conquest of Saxon England, vesting underlying fee title to English land in the Norman invaders. Thereafter, as a part of their policy of abolishing the preexisting system of collective land tenure, the Normans established an evolving structure of rules to individuate Saxon property titles on the basis of certain forms of utilization or "development"; Carl Erdmann, *The Origin of the Idea of the Crusade* (Princeton, NJ: Princeton University Press, 1977) pp. 150-60. More broadly, see Otto Freidrich von Gierke, *Political Theories of the Middle Ages* (Boston: Beacon Press, 1958). By the time of the American War of Independence, philosopher John Locke had discovered what he believed to be a liberatory usage of the Norman system, arguing that individual developmental usage of given tracts of land bestowed upon those who engaged in it a "natural right" to ownership which transcended all state prerogatives to preempt title; Crawford Brough Macpherson, *The Political Theory of Possessive Individualism: Hobbes to Locke* (Oxford, UK: Clarendon Press, 1962). For application of all this specifically to North America, see Williams, *American Indian in Western Legal Thought*, op. cit., esp. pp. 233-80.

67. This is the premise underlying the 1862 Homestead Act (*U.S. Statures at Large*, Vol. XII, at p. 392) by which any U.S. citizen could claim a quarter-section (160 acres) of "undeveloped" land merely by paying an extremely nominal "patent fee" to offset the expense of registering it. He or she then had a specified period of time, usually five years, to build fell trees, build a house, plow fields, etc. If these requirements were met within the time allowed, the homesteader was issued a deed to the property. For background, see Robert A. Williams, Jr., "Jefferson, the Norman Yoke, and American Indian Lands," *Arizona Law Review*, No. 29, 1987.

68. For analysis, see Alden T, Vaughan, *The New England Frontier* (Boston: Little, Brown, 1965) pp. 113-21; Francis Jennings, "Virgin Land and Savage People," *American Quarterly*, No. 23, 1971.

69. Letter from the Massachusetts Bay Company to Governor John Endicott, Apr. 17, 1629; N. Shurtleff, ed., *Records of the Governor and the Company of the Massachusetts Bay in New England* (Boston: William White, 1853). At p. 100 of Vattel's *Laws of Nations, Book I* (op. cit.), the Puritans are praised for their "moderation" in adopting this posture, as are William Penn's Quakers in Pennsylvania.

70. *Cohen's Handbook*, op. cit., p. 55.

71. The U.S. invocation of *Territorium res Nullius* has proceeded along a number of tracks, not all judicial. An especially glaring illustration has been the deliberate and systematic falsification of indigenous historical demography to make it appear that the preinvasion population of North America was not more than a million when, in fact, the best available evidence suggests that it was at least 12.5 million and perhaps as large as 18.5 million. The methods used by major Euroamerican historians and anthropologists in "undercounting" native people are covered very well by Francis Jennings in the chapter entitled "The Widowed Land" in his *The Invasion of America: Indians, Colonialism and the Cant of Conquest* (New York: W.W. Norton, 1975). More credible estimates of the indigenous population, circa 1500, will be found in Henry F. Dobyns, *Their Number Become Thinned: Native American Population Dynamics in Eastern North America* (Knoxville: University of Tennessee Press, 1983). In any event, the aggregate native population has been reliably estimated as having been reduced to something less than a million by 1800. The settler population, meanwhile, had burgeoned to approximately fifteen million. For regional breakouts, see Russell Thornton, *American Indian Holocaust and Survival: A Population History Since 1492* (Norman: University of Oklahoma Press, 1987).

72. Vattel, *The Laws of Nations*, op. cit., Book I, p. 99. This was not one of Vattel's more tenable positions. If settlement and cultivation were actually employed to determine the quantity of land nations "have occasion for," the territoriality of Canada, Australia, Brazil, Russia and several other countries would be immediately diminished by more than half. Nothing in the formulation admits to the legitimacy of speculative acquisition such as the U.S. engaged in during the nineteenth century, or of current policies "banking" land against anticipated future needs. By the same token, no nation would be able to maintain commons such as national wilderness areas, wildlife preserves, military training areas and so forth, on pain of losing the right to possess them. Nor does Vattel's overall system of legal equity allow for the application of one set of standards to indigenous nations, another to settler-states.

73. *Fletcher v. Peck*, 10 U.S. (6 Cranch.) 87 (1810). By all indications, this aspect of Marshall's opinion was an expediency designed to facilitate redemption of scrip issued to troops during the American decolonization struggle in lieu of cash. These vouchers were to be exchanged for land parcels in Indian Country once victory had been achieved (Marshall and his father received instruments entitling them 10,000 acres apiece in what is now Kentucky, part of the more than 200,000 acres they jointly amassed there). The question was how to validate title to such parcels, a matter belatedly addressed by *Peck*. Having thus solved his and his country's immediate problem, all indications are that the Chief Justice promptly dropped Vattel's dubious premise—see note 72, above—in favor of a more subtle approach in his efforts to validate U.S. title to native lands. For details on the Marshalls' Kentucky land transactions, see Jean Edward Smith, *John Marshall: Definer of a Nation* (New York: Henry Holt, 1996) pp. 74-5. On the case itself, see C. Peter McGrath, *Yazoo: The Case of* Fletcher v. Peck (New York: W.W. Norton, 1966).

74. Although there were obvious antecedents in New York State and elsewhere, the clearest early formal indication of this policy comes in the 1854 Treaty with the Omahas, Article 6 of which specifies that the Indians will accept a survey of their land and assignment of individual allotments at some future date; Vine Deloria, Jr., and Clifford M. Lytle, *American Indians, American Justice* (Austin: University of Texas Press, 1983) p. 8. On the New York precedents, see Franklin B. Hough, ed., *Proceedings of the Commission of*

Indian Affairs, Appointed by Law for Extinguishment of Indian Title in the State of New York, 2 vols. (Albany, NY: John Munsell, 1861); Helen M. Upton, *The Everett Report in Historical Perspective: The Indians of New York* (Albany, NY: New York State Bicentennial Commission, 1980).

75. For an overview of Canadian practice, see, e.g., the description offered in George F.G. Stanley's *The Birth of Western Canada* (Toronto: University of Toronto Press, 1975); George Brown and Ron McGuire, *Indian Treaties in Historical Perspective* (Ottawa: Indian and Northern Affairs Canada, 1979). Perhaps the main distinction to be drawn between Canada and the U.S. in terms of setting aside reserved areas was that, in the latter, priority was given to concentrating all of a given people—sometimes several peoples—in one locality. This had the effect of creating vast expanses of "native-free" territory, but often left indigenous nations with relatively large blocks of land on which we were able to hold ourselves together, socially and politically, at least for a while. Canada opted to reverse this emphasis, preferring a strategy of divide and rule which has resulted in an amazing proliferation of tiny "band" reserves scattered across the map; see generally, Boyce Richardson, *People of* Terra Nullius: *Betrayal and Rebirth of Aboriginal Canada* (Vancouver/Seattle: Douglas & McIntyre/University of Washington Press, 1993).

76. 25 U.S.C.A. § 331, also known as the "Dawes Act" in recognition of its primary congressional sponsor, Massachusetts Senator Henry Dawes; see generally, D.S. Otis, *The Dawes Act and the Allotment of American Indian Land* (Norman: University of Oklahoma Press, 1973).

77. The purpose of the Act was sometimes framed in superficially noble-sounding terms, as when, in 1881, President Chester A. Arthur described an early draft a means to "introduce among the Indians the customs and pursuits of civilized life"; quoted in Deloria and Lytle, *American Indians, American Justice*, op. cit., p. 8. At other times, it has been officially referenced with far more accuracy, as when Indian Commissioner Francis Leupp called it "a great pulverizing engine to grind down the tribal mass"; Francis A. Leupp, *The Indian and His Problem* (New York: Scribner's, 1910) p. 93.

78. This in itself constituted a gross violation of native sovereignty insofar as it was a direct intervention by the United States in the internal affairs of each indigenous nation for purposes of defining its citizenry. Insofar as the means employed to determine native identity was explicitly racial—the use of a "blood quantum" system—this U.S. aggression was doubly sinister, representing as it did a prefiguration of apartheid; for analysis, see George M. Frederickson, *White Supremacy: A Comparative Study in American and South African History* (New York: Oxford University Press, 1981). Canada effected similar interventions, albeit without the U.S. larding of scientific racism, creating categories of "status" and "non-status" Indians; see, e.g., Bill Wilson, "Aboriginal Rights: A Non-Status Indian View," in Menno Boldt and J. Anthony Long, *The Quest for Justice: Aboriginal People and Aboriginal Rights* (Toronto: University of Toronto Press, 1985). On the problematic nature of the term "tribe"—as opposed to "nation" or "people"—see the essay, "Naming Our Destiny: Toward a Language of American Indian Liberation," in my *Indians "R" Us: Culture and Genocide in Native North America* (Winnipeg: Arbeiter Ring,[2nd ed., forthcoming] 2000). Of related interest, see Robert A. Williams, Jr., "Documents of Barbarism: The Contemporary Legacy of European Racism and Colonialism in the Narrative Traditions of Federal Indian Law," *Arizona Law Review*, Vol. 31, No. 2, 1989.

79. Deloria and Lytle, *American Indians, American Justice*, op. cit., p. 9.

80. See generally, Janet A. McDonnell, *The Dispossession of the American Indian, 1887-1934* (Bloomington: University Press of Indiana, 1991). On railroads, etc., see, e.g., H. Craig Miner, *The Corporation and the Indian: Tribal Sovereignty and Industrial Civilization in Indian Territory, 1865-1907* (Columbia: University of Missouri Press, 1976).

81. Kirk Kicking Bird and Karen Ducheneaux, *One Hundred Million Acres* (New York: Macmillan, 1973); Otis, *Dawes Act and Allotment*, op. cit.; McDonnell, *Dispossession of the American Indian*, op. cit.

82. 34 Stat. 182. All told, only about eleven million acres actually remained reserved for native usage by 1973; Washburn, *Red Man's Land*, op. cit., pp. 145, 150.

83. Leaving aside property alienated as a result of the Burke Act, land was allotted in correspondence to the number of Indians surviving, *circa* 1890, the nadir point of indigenous population decline in North America; Thornton, *American Indian Holocaust and Survival*, op. cit., pp. 159-85. The native population has by now "rebounded" to at least ten times its turn-of-the-century size. For implications, see Ward Shepard, "Land Problems of an Expanding Indian Population," in Oliver La Farge, ed., *The Changing Indian* (Norman: University of Oklahoma Press, 1943); Ethel J. Williams, "Too Little Land, Too Many Heirs: The Indian Heirship Land Problem," *Washington Law Review*, No. 46, 1971.

84. A good example is that of the traditionalist Cherokees who refused even to enroll as such with the Dawes Commission during the early twentieth century. Not only were they accorded no land rights whatsoever, they were ultimately disenfranchised as Cherokees; Emmett Starr, *A History of the Cherokee Indians* (Oklahoma City: Warden, 1922).

85. 187 U.S. 553. For analysis, see Ann Laquer Estin, "*Lonewolf v. Hitchcock*: The long Shadow," in Sandra L. Cadwalader and Vine Deloria, Jr., eds., *The Aggressions of Civilization: Federal Indian Policy Since the 1880s* (Philadelphia: Temple University Press, 1984).

86. *Tee-Hit-Ton v. United States*, 348 U.S. 272, (1955).

87. Most especially see *Badoni v. Higginson*, 638 F.2d (10th Cir. 1980), *cert. denied*, 452 U.S. 954 (1981), otherwise known as the "Rainbow Bridge Case"; *Lyng v. Northwest Indian Cemetery Protective Association*, 485 U.S. 439 (1988), otherwise known as the "G-O Road Case." Related opinions will be found in *Montana v. United States*, 450 U.S. 544 (1981); *Brendale v. Confederated Tribes and Bands of the Yakima Nation*, 109 S.Ct. 2994 (1989).

88. See, e.g., *United States v. Dann*, 470 U.S. 39 (1985).

89. *Attorney General of Ontario v. Bear Island Foundation*, 49 OR 353 (HC), affirmed (1989) 68 OR 394 (CA).

90. *Calder v. Attorney General for British Columbia*, SCR 313, 333, 344 (1973); *Cardinal v. Attorney General Alta*, 2 SCR 695 (1974). In substance, Canada wishes to have it both ways, claiming simultaneously that the legitimacy of its land title accrues from cessions made by native peoples in their treaties with the Crown *and* that, since the Canadian government itself never negotiated or ratified the instruments, it is not obligated to honor the range of reciprocal commitments the Crown made to native people. A good overview of such thinking is provided in Peter Hogg, *The Liability of the Crown* (Toronto: Carswell, 1989).

91. For a fairly exhaustive overview of the official position, see Canada, *Lands, Revenues and Trust Review* (Ottawa: Supplies and Services, 1988-90).

92. See, e.g., *Isaac v. Davey*, 5 OR 92d) 610 (1974); *Sandy v. Sandy*, 27 OR (2d) 248 (1979); *Four B. Manufacturing v. United Garment Workers of America*, 1 S.C.R. 1031 (1980). For interpretation and analysis, see Clark, *Indian Title*, op. cit.; Richardson, *People of* Terra Nullius, op. cit.

93. 59 Stat. 1031, T.S. No. 933, 3 Bevans 1153m 1976 Y.B.U.N. 1043 (June 26, 1945); U.N.G.A. Res. 1514 (XV), 15 U.N. GAOR, Supp. (No. 16) 66, U.N. Doc. A/4684 (1961). For texts, see Weston, Falk, and D'Amato, *Documents in International Law*, op. cit., pp. 16-32, 343-4.

94. It is important to reiterate that the Vienna Convention merely codified existing, customary treaty law. In other words, the Supreme Court's opinion in *Lonewolf* was legally invalid at the time it was rendered; Rosenne, *Law of Treaties*, op. cit.; Sinclair, *Vienna Convention on the Law of Treaties*, op. cit.

95. International Court of Justice, *Advisory Opinion on Western Sahara* (The Hague: International Court of Justice, 1975) p. 46. For analysis, see Robert Vance, "Questions Concerning Western Sahara: Advisory Opinion of the International Court of Justice, October 16, 1975," *International Lawyer*, No. 10, 1976; "Sovereignty Over Unoccupied Territories: The Western Sahara Decision," *Case Western Reserve Journal of International Law*, No. 9, 1977.

96. Aside from the several books already cited, see, as examples of academic usage, William H. Leckie's *The Military Conquest of the Southern Plains* (Norman: University of Oklahoma Press, 1963); Dan Thrapp's *The Conquest of Apacheria* (Norman: University of Oklahoma Press, 1967); Harry A. Stroud's *The Conquest of the Prairies* (Waco, TX: Texian Press, 1968); Patricia Nelson Limerick's more recent and much-touted *The Legacy of Conquest: The Unbroken Past of the American West* (New York: W.W. Norton, 1987).

97. *Tee-Hit-Ton v. U.S.* at 291.

98. Ibid. at 289-90.

99. There were two primary levels to this. The first was the "Trial of the Major Nazi War Criminals," in which both Supreme Court Justice Robert H. Jackson and former Attorney General Francis Biddle assumed leading roles—Jackson as lead U.S. prosecutor, Biddle as a member of the tribunal itself—in which diplomats Joachim von Ribbentrop and Constantin von Neurath were convicted of conspiring to wage aggressive war, largely on the basis of having pursued policies framed in terms precisely like those articulated in *Tee-Hit-Ton*. Ribbentrop was executed as a result, while Neurath was sentenced to fifteen years imprisonment, serving eight; Eugene Davidson, *The Trial of the Germans, 1945-1946* (New York: Macmillan, 1966) pp. 147-76. The second was the so-called "Justice Case" of 1947, in

which former Ohio Supreme Court Justice Carrington T. Marshall served as a tribunal member. In this case, fourteen highranking members of the German judiciary were tried and convicted of having committed Crimes Against Humanity, mainly because of the various legalistic rationalizations they had advanced in justification of nazism's pattern of aggression; John Alan Appleman, *Military Tribunals and International Crimes* (Westport, CT: Greenwood Press, 1971 reprint of 1954 original) pp. 157-62.

100. Nell Jessup Newton, "At the Whim of the Sovereign: Aboriginal Title Reconsidered," *Hastings Law Journal*, No. 31, 1980, pp. 1215, 1244. The Pacific coast of North America, as far south as California, was claimed by Russia during the early 1740s; William Cortez Abbott, *The Expansion of Europe: A History of the Foundations of the Modern World*, 2 vols. (London: G. Bell & Sons, 1919) Vol. 1, pp. 193-4. As has been mentioned, the U.S. purchased Russia's rights in what are now the states of Oregon, Washington and Idaho in 1846. In 1867, with passage of the British North American Act making Canada a dominion of the Commonwealth, Russian claims to present-day British Columbia were also extinguished by purchase. The United States followed up the same year, buying out Russia's rights in Alaska; Samuel Eliot Morrison, *The Oxford History of the American People* (New York: Oxford University Press, 1965) pp. 706, 765, 806.

101. "The Indian wars under the United States government have been more than 40"; U.S. Bureau of the Census, *Report on Indians Taxed and Not Taxed (1890)* (Washington, D.C.: U.S. Government Printing Office, 1894) p. 638. It should be noted that the term used is entirely inappropriate. Given that all the conflicts in question were precipitated by invasions of Indian Country rather than Indian invasions of someone else's domain, they should be referred to as "White Man's Wars," "Settlers' Wars" or, most accurately, "U.S. Wars of Aggression against Indians."

102. This was "Red Cloud's War" in present-day Wyoming, 1866-68; see the relevant chapter in Dee Brown's *Bury My Heart at Wounded Knee: An Indian History of the American West* (New York: Holt, Rinehart & Winston, 1970). On U.S. failure to comply with the terms and provisions of the treaty by which peace was temporarily restored, see Edward Lazarus, *Black Hills, White Justice: The Sioux Nation versus the United States, 1775 to the Present* (New York: HarperCollins, 1991).

103. On the "Riel Rebellions" of 1868 and 1885, see D. Bruce Sealey and Antoine S. Lussier, *The Métis: Canada's Forgotten People* (Winnipeg: Manitoba Métis Association Press, 1975).

104. As an example, when Governor Frederick Seymor of British Columbia observed in a December 1864 letter to the Colonial Office in London that he "might find [himself] compelled to follow in the footsteps of the Governor of Colorado…and invite every white man to shoot each Indian he may meet," he was firmly rebuked by Secretary of State Edward Cardwell and reminded that the "imperial government's policy was to quite the opposite effect"; quoted in Clark, *Native Liberty, Crown Sovereignty*, op. cit., p. 61. Seymor's reference was to Colorado Territorial Governor David Evans, who had not only issued the statements indicated, but who had been complicit in the wholesale massacre of noncombatant Cheyennes and Arapahos at Sand Creek a month before Seymor's missive was written; David Svaldi, *Sand Creek and the Rhetoric of Extermination: A Case-Study in Indian White Relations* (Washington, D.C.: University Press of America,, 1989).

105. Indeed, Canadian courts have themselves been exceedingly careful to avoid constructions based on notions of conquest. This has been so since at least as early as the 1773 case, *Mohegan Indians v. Connecticut*, in which the Privy Council opined that "the medieval concept" of conquest was simply "inadequate" to meet Crown needs in much of the New World. The "realities of colonial administration" in North America dictated, the Council affirmed, a more "prudent" course of recognizing the status of indigenous nations and guaranteeing our rights; J.H. Smith, *Appeals to the Privy Council from the American Plantations* (New York: Columbia University Press, 1950) p. 417. With this said, however, it is important to note that such policy by no means prevailed throughout the British Empire; see, e.g., Byron Farwell, *Queen Victoria's Little Wars* (New York: W.W. Norton, 1972).

106. This, again, is very close to—indeed, interchangeable with—the Hitlerian conception of the rights of the stronger over the weaker; see, e.g., the explanations of "*Lebensraumpolitik*" (politics of living space) offered in *Mein Kampf* (Boston: Houghton-Mifflin, 1962 reprint of 1925 original); *Hitler's Secret Book* (New York: Grove Press, 1961); *Hitler's Secret Conversations* (New York: Signet, 1961).

107. The Greek and Roman imperial systems, for example, manifested no conception of conquest rights remotely comparable to that voiced in *Tee-Hit-Ton*; see, e.g., William Scott Ferguson, *Greek Imperialism* (New York: Houghton-Mifflin, 1913); Earl of Cromer, *Ancient and Modern Imperialism* (New

York: Longman's, Green, 1910). By the time of the Norman Conquest of 1066, it was articulated canon law that such seizures were valid only when occurring under the divine authority of the Church: see Erdmann, *Origin of the Idea of the Crusade*, op. cit., pp. 150-60; Walter Ullmann, *Medieval Papalism: The Political Theories of the Medieval Canonists* (London: Methuen, 1949); James Muldoon, "The Contributions of the Medieval Canon Lawyers to the Foundations of International Law," *Traditio*, No. 28, 1972. Accepted notions of "natural law" also run directly counter to that argued by the Supreme Court in *Tee-Hit-Ton*; see, e.g., Otto Frederick von Gierke, *Natural Law and the Theory of Society, 1500-1800* (Cambridge, UK: Cambridge University Press, 1934); Lloyd Weinreb, *Natural Law and Justice* (Cambridge, MA: Harvard University Press, 1987).

108. These ideas were tentatively codified in the 1512 Laws of Burgos; see generally, Hanke, *Spanish Struggle*, op. cit.; James Muldoon, *Popes, Lawyers and Infidels: The Church and the Non-Christian World, 1250-1550* (Philadelphia: University of Pennsylvania Press, 1979).

109. Vitoria, "On the Law of War," op. cit.; Jorge Díaz, "Los Doctrinas de Palacios Rubios y Matías de Paz ante la Conquista America," in *Memoria de El Colegio Nacional* (Burgos: Colegio Nacional, 1950). Overall, see Williams, *American Indian in Western Legal Thought*, op. cit., pp. 85-108.

110. "[W]hatever is done in the right of war receives the construction most favorable to the claims of those engaged in a just war"; Vitoria, "On the Law of War," op. cit., p. 180.

111. Cohen, "Spanish Origins," op. cit., p. 44; Robert A. Williams, Jr., "The Medieval and Renaissance Origins of the Status of American Indians in Western Legal Thought," *Southern California Law Review*, Vol. 57, No. 1, 1983.

112. Nothing in international law precluded indigenous peoples from defending themselves when attacked or invaded. Nor did it prevent them from expelling or otherwise punishing missionaries who violated native law while residing in Indian Country, or from breaking off trade relations with entities which could be shown to have cheated them. In every instance, without exception, in which bona fide Indian-white warfare is known to have occurred the requisite provocation to legitimate native resort to arms is abundantly evident. *Ipso facto*, European/Euroamerican claims to having engaged in Just Wars against the indigenous peoples of North America are invalidated. For a succinct overview of the presumptive right of any nation to defend its territorial integrity and political sovereignty against violation by other nations, see Walzer, *Just and Unjust Wars*, op. cit., pp. 53-5.

113. This goes back to the point made in note 30, above, and accompanying text.

114. This is essentially the conclusion drawn by the U.S. government's Indian Claims Commission, which, despite thirty years of exhaustive study, concluded in its final report that it had been unable to find any sort of title by which to validate the country's claims to approximately 35 percent of its purported territoriality; Indian Claims Commission, *Final Report* (Washington, D.C.: U.S. Government Printing Office, 1978). For analysis, see Russel Barsh, "Indian Land Claims Policy in the United States," *North Dakota Law Review*, No. 58, 1982; "Behind Land Claims: Rationalizing Dispossession in Anglo-American Law," *Law & Anthropology*, No. 1, 1986.

115. 1 Stat. 50. The British/Canadian counterpart—or, more accurately, precursor—is the Royal Proclamation of 1763 which specifies, among other things, that North America's indigenous peoples should remain "unmolested and undisturbed" by the Crown and its subjects; Stagg, *Anglo-American Relations*, op. cit.

116. Note 57, above.

117. *Johnson v. McIntosh* at 591.

118. Note 63, above.

119. U.S. Department of Interior, *Report of the Commissioner of Indian Affairs for 1890* (Washington, D.C.: U.S. Government Printing Office, 1891) p. xxix.

120. For academic articulations of the theme, see note 96, above. On the films, see Ralph and Natasha Friar, *The Only Good Indian... The Hollywood Gospel* (New York: Drama Book Specialists, 1972); William Raymond Stedman, *Shadows of the Indian : Stereotypes in American Culture* (Norman: University of Oklahoma Press, 1982). On cinematic counterparts north of the border, see Daniel Francis, *The Imaginary Indian: The Image of the Indian in Canadian Culture* (Vancouver: Arsenal Pulp Press, 1992). On the capacity of such a disinformational onslaught to indoctrinate the general populace to accept sheer falsity as truth, see Jacques Ellul, *Propaganda: The Formation of Men's Attitudes* (New York: Alfred A. Knopf, 1965).

121. This brings the principle delineated in note 30 into play. More broadly, see C.A. Pompe,

Aggressive War: An International Crime (The Hague: Martinus Nijhoff, 1953). For use of the referenced term, see Rudolfo Acuña, *Occupied America: The Chicano's Struggle for Liberation* (San Francisco: Canfield Press, 1972).

122. For excellent samples of rhetoric, see LeBlanc, *United States and the Genocide Convention*, op. cit.; Robert Davis and Mark Zannis, *The Genocide Machine in Canada: The Pacification of the North* (Montréal: Black Rose Books, 1973); Terrance Nelson, et al., *Genocide in Canada* (Ginew, Manitoba: Roseau River First Nation, 1997).

123. Questions as to when extinction occurred are largely academic, since, whenever the final die-out transpired—even if only in the past fifteen minutes—it remains presumptive that there are no heirs to contest title or receive compensation.

124. L.F.S. Lupton, "The Extermination of the Beothuks of Newfoundland," *Canadian Historical Review*, Vol. 58, No. 2, 1977.

125. The colonists sought "'to cut off the Remembrance of them from the Earth.' After the war, the General Assembly of Connecticut declared the name extinct. No survivors should be called Pequots. The Pequot River became the Thames, and the village known as Pequot became New London"; Drinnon, *Facing West*, op. cit., p. 55.

126. Mashantucket Pequot Indian Claims Settlement Act (S.1499; signed Oct. 18, 1983). At least one analyst has seized upon this fact to "prove" that what was done to Pequots was never really genocide in the first place; Steven T. Katz, "The Pequot War Reconsidered," *New England Quarterly*, No. 64, 1991.

127. See generally, Paul Brodeur, *Restitution: The Land Claims of the Mashpee, Passamaquoddy, and Pennobscot Indians of New England* (Boston: Northeastern University Press, 1985).

128. Road Island Indian Claims Settlement Act of 1978 (94 Stat. 3498). More broadly, see Harry B. Wallace, "Indian Sovereignty and the Eastern Indian Land Claims," *New York University Law School Review*, No. 27, 1982.

129. See, e.g., Charles M. Hudson, "The Catawba Indians of South Carolina: A Question of Ethnic Survival," in Walter L. William, ed., *Southeastern Indians Since the Removal Era* (Athens: University of Georgia Press, 1979).

130. More broadly, see Lynwood Carranco and Estle Beard, *Genocide and Vendetta: The Round Valley Wars of Northern California* (Norman: University of Oklahoma Press, 1981).

131. James Fenimore Cooper, *The Last of the Mohicans* (New York: Barnes and Noble, 1992 reprint of 1826 original), Robert F. Heizer and Theodora Kroeber, eds., *Ishi the Last Yahi: A Documentary History* (Berkeley: University of California Press, 1979). For the record, the Mohicans were administratively amalgamated with the fragments of several other peoples under the heading "Stockbridge-Munsee" during the nineteenth century and now reside in Wisconsin. On Ishi's people, see Virginia P. Miller, "Whatever Happened to the Yuki?" *Indian Historian*, No. 8, 1975.

132. See, as examples, B.O. Flower, "An Interesting Representative of a Vanishing Race," *Arena*, July 1896; Simon Pokagon, "The Future of the Red Man," *Forum*, Aug. 1897; William R. Draper, "The Last of the Red Race," *Cosmopolitan*, Jan. 1902; Charles M. Harvey, "The Last Race Rally of Indians," *World's Work*, May 1904; E. S. Curtis, "Vanishing Indian Types: The Tribes of the Northwest Plains," *Scribner's*, June 1906; James Mooney, "The Passing of the Indian," *Proceedings of the Second Pan American Scientific Congress, Sec. 1: Anthropology* (Washington, D.C.: Smithsonian Institution, 1909-1910); Joseph K. Dixon, *The Vanishing Race: The Last Great Indian Council* (Garden City, NY: Doubleday, 1913); Stanton Elliot, "The End of the Trail," *Overland Monthly*, July 1915; Ella Higginson, "The Vanishing Race," *Red Man*, Feb. 1916; Ales Hrdlicka, "The Vanishing Indian," *Science*, No. 46, 1917; J.L. Hill, *The Passing of the Indian and the Buffalo* (Long Beach, CA: n.p., 1917); John Collier, "The Vanishing American," *Nation*, Jan. 11, 1928. For implications of this literary barrage, see Ellul, *Propaganda*, op. cit.

133. Larry W. Burt, *Tribalism in Crisis: Federal Indian Policy, 1953-1961* (Albuquerque: University of New Mexico Press, 1982); Donald L. Fixico, *Termination and Relocation: Federal Indian Policy, 1945-1960* (Albuquerque: University of New Mexico Press, 1986). It is worth mentioning that termination of recognition flies directly in the face of the international legal principle delineated in note 42 and accompanying text.

134. Nicholis Peroff, *Menominee DRUMS; Tribal Termination and Restoration, 1954-1974* (Norman: University of Oklahoma Press, 1982).

135. Theodore Stern, *The Klamath Tribe: The People and Their Reservation* (Seattle: University of

Washington Press, 1965); Shipeck, *Pushed Into the Rocks*, op. cit.

136. The U.S. position is that any surviving Abenakis fled to Canada after they were subjected to wholesale massacre by George Rogers Clark's Ranger Company in 1759; Collin G. Calloway, *The Western Abenaki of Vermont, 1600-1800: War, Migration, and the Survival of an Indian People* (Norman: University of Oklahoma Press, 1991).

137. See generally, L. Weatherhead, "What is an Indian Tribe? The Question of Tribal Existence," *American Indian Law Review*, No. 8, 1980; David Rotenberg, "American Indian Tribal Death: A Centennial Remembrance," *University of Miami Law Review*, No. 41, 1986.

138. Wilson, "Aboriginal Rights," op. cit.; B. Morris and R. Groves, "Canada's Forgotten Peoples: The Aboriginal Rights of Metis and Non-Status Peoples," *Law & Anthropology*, No. 2, 1987. A prime example of Canadian-style non recognition concerns the Lubicon Cree, a group overlooked in the process of negotiating Treaty 8. When the Ottawa government realized its error, it attempted to lump the Lubicons in with an entirely different, albeit related, group, and has yet to acknowledge the full extent of Lubicon rights; John Goddard, *Last Stand of the Lubicon Cree* (Vancouver: Douglas & McIntyre, 1991).

139. For the original definition, see Raphaël Lemkin, *Axis Rule in Occupied Europe* (Washington, D.C.: Carnegie Institution, 1944) p. 79. With respect to black letter law, Article II of the 1948 Convention on the Prevention and Punishment of the Crime of Genocide (U.S.T._____, T.I.A.S. No. _____, U.N.T.S. 277) makes it illegal to cause "serious bodily or *mental* harm ...with intent to destroy, in whole or in part, a national, ethnical, racial or religious group, as such (emphasis added)" or deliberately inflict "conditions of life calculated to bring about its physical destruction in whole or in part." Article III makes it a crime not only to commit such acts, but to conspire to commit them, to attempt to commit them, to incite others to do so, or to be in any way complicit in their perpetration; Weston, et al., *Documents in International Law*, op. cit., p. 297. For further analysis, see Rennard Strickland, "Genocide at Law: An Historic and Contemporary View of the American Indian Experience," *University of Kansas Law Review*, No. 34, 1986.

140. On the U.S., see, e.g., American Indian Policy Review Commission, "Separate and Dissenting Views," *Final Report* (Washington, D.C.: U.S. Government Printing Office, 1976) p. 574. For analysis, see F. Martone, "American Indian Tribal Government in the Federal System: Inherent Right or Congressional License?" *Notre Dame Law Review*, No. 51, 1976. On Canada, see, e.g., *Report of the Special Committee of the House of Commons on Indian Self-Government* (Ottawa: Supplies and Services, 1983); *Response of the Government to the Report of the Special Committee on Indian Self-Government* (Ottawa: Indian Affairs and Supplies and Services, 1984).

141. Oppenheim, *International Law*, op. cit., p. 120.

142. Coulter, "Contemporary Indian Sovereignty," op. cit., p. 118.

143. 7 Stat. 18, 19 (1785).

144. *Worcester v. Georgia* at 560-1.

145. Such comparisons are made by Vine Deloria, Jr., in his *Behind the Trail of Broken Treaties: An Indian Declaration of Independence* (Austin: University of Texas Press, [2nd. ed.] 1984) pp. 161-86.

146. Oren Lyons, "Introduction: When You Talk About Client Relationships, You are Talking About the Future of Nations," in *Rethinking Indian Law*, op. cit., p. iv. Lyons is correct. There is nothing in international law establishing a minimum population level, below which a group loses its nationhood. Grenada, it should be remembered, has a total population of only 120,000, and, although it has recently suffered gross violation at the hands of the United States, is recognized as enjoying the same sovereign rights as any other nation.

147. Policy Review Commission, *Final Report*, op. cit.; *Response of the Government*, op. cit.

148. See generally, Henry E. Fritz, *The Movement for Indian Assimilation, 1860-1890* (Philadelphia: University of Pennsylvania Press, 1963); Fred Hoxie, *A Final Promise: The Campaign to Assimilate the Indians, 1880-1920* (Lincoln: University of Nebraska Press, 1984).

149. See, e.g., William Hagan, *Indian Police and Judges: Experiments in Acculturation and Control* (New Haven, CT: Yale University Press, 1966); Curtis E. Jackson and Marcia J. Galli, *A History of the Bureau of Indian Affairs and Its Activities Among the Indians* (San Francisco: R&E Associates, 1977); Douglas Cole and Ira Chaikan, *An Iron Hand Upon the People: The Law Against the Potlatch on the Northwest Coast* (Vancouver,: Douglas & McIntyre, 1990); Katherine Pettitpas, *Severing the Ties That Bind: Government Repression of Indigenous Religious Ceremonies on the Prairies* (Winnipeg: University of Manitoba Press, 1994).

150. Otis, *Dawes Act*, op. cit.; McDonnell, *Dispossession of the American Indian*, op. cit. Good readings with respect to Canada will be found in Brian Slattery's *Ancestral Lands, Alien Laws: Judicial Perspectives on Aboriginal Title* (Saskatoon: University of Saskatchewan Native Law Center, 1983), and the early chapters of Michael Asch's *Home and Native Land: Aboriginal Rights and the Canadian Constitution* (Toronto: Methuen, 1984).

151. Perhaps the most striking example was when, in 1873, General Phil Sheridan called for the deliberate extermination of an entire species of large mammals, the North American Bison ("Buffalo"), in order to "destroy the commissary" of the Plains Indians; General Philip Sheridan to Commanding General William Tecumseh Sherman, May 2, 1873; quoted in Paul Andrew Hutton, *Phil Sheridan and His Army* (Lincoln: University of Nebraska Press, 1985) p. 246. At one point in the mid-1870s, Congress considered legislation to preserve what was left of the dwindling herds. Sheridan vociferously opposed it, suggesting that the legislators instead "strike a medal, with a dead buffalo pictured on one side and a discouraged Indian on the other," and present it to the buffalo hunters; John R. Cook, *The Border and the Buffalo: An Untold Story of the Southwest Plains* (New York: Citadel Press, 1976) pp. 163-5. Also see William T. Hornaday, *Exterminating the American Bison* (Washington, D.C.: Smithsonian Institution, 1899); Tom McHugh and Victoria Hobson, *The Time of the Buffalo* (New York: Alfred A. Knopf, 1972).

152. For a contemporaneous and quite glowing affirmation of the centrality of "instruction" to the entire Canadian assimilation process, see Thompson Ferrier, *Our Indians and Their Training for Citizenship* (Toronto: Methods Mission Rooms, 1991). For a bit longer view on its role in the U.S., see Evelyn C. Adams, *American Indian Education: Government Schools and Economic Progress* (New York: King's Crown Press, 1946). Appropriate contextualization will be found in Martin Carnoy's *Education as Cultural Imperialism* (New York: David McKay, 1974).

153. The time-period indicated represents only the most intensive phase of the process. It actually began earlier and lasted much longer in both countries. On the U.S., see Michael C. Coleman, *American Indian Children at School, 1850-1930* (Jackson: University Press of Mississippi, 1993); David Wallace Adams, *Education for Extinction: American Indians and the Boarding School Experience, 1875-1928* (Lawrence: University Press of Kansas, 1995). On Canada, see Celia Haig-Brown, *Resistance and Renewal: Surviving the Indian Residential School* (Vancouver: Tillacum Library, 1988); J.R. Miller, *Shingwauk's Vision: A History of Native Residential Schools* (Toronto: University of Toronto Press, 1996).

154. Col. Richard H. Pratt, *Battlefield and Classroom: Four Decades with the American Indian, 1867-1904* (New Haven, CT: Yale University Press, 1993 reprint of 1906 original) p. 293.

155. See, e.g., Leupp, *Indian and His Problem*, op. cit.

156. See generally, Jean Barman with Yves Hébert and D. McCaskill, eds., *Indian Education in Canada: The Legacy* (Vancouver: Nakoda Institute and University of British Columbia Press, 1986); Noel Dyck, *What is the Indian "Problem"? Tutelage and Resistance in Canadian Indian Administration* (St. John's: Institute of Social and Economic Research, Memorial University of Newfoundland, 1991).

157. Not only do the criteria of the Genocide Convention delineated in note 139 apply here, but also the provision under Article II making it a Crime of Genocide to systematically transfer children from targeted racial, ethnical, national or religious groups with intent to bring about destruction of the group as such.

158. *Sero v. Gault*, 50 OLR 27 (1921). Robinson's position, adopted by the *Sero* court, completely ignores the fact that the treaties in question already existed and that the Crown had long maintained a formal diplomatic mission to the Mohawks and others of the Six Nations; James Thomas Flexner, *Lord of the Mohawks: A Biography of Sir William Johnson* (Boston: little, Brown, 1979). On the service rendered to the Crown by Brant and the Mohawks, see Barbara Greymount, *The Iroquois in the American Revolution* (Syracuse, NY: Syracuse University Press, 1975).

159. S Prov. c 1857, c. 26. For analysis, see J. Tobias, "Protection, Civilization, Assimilation: An Outline of Canada's Indian Policy," *Western Canadian Journal of Anthropology*, Vol. 4, No. 2, 1976.

160. The racially idiosyncratic aspects of the law are hardly unparalleled; see, e.g., Noel Ignatiev, *How the Irish Became White* (New York: Routledge, 1995). More broadly, see Theodore W. Allen, *The Invention of the White Race: Racial Oppression and Social Control* (London: Verso, 1994).

161. In statutory terms, Canada's national policy was first given form by An Act for the Gradual Enfranchisement of the Indians, the Better Management of Indian Affairs, and the extend Provisions of the Act (31 Vict. c. 42, SC 1869, c. 6) and An Act to Amend and Consolidate the Laws Respecting Indians

(SC 1880, c. 28). Despite Canada's supplanting of its original 1871 Constitution Act with another in 1982, evolution of its policy on native citizenship has been consistent from start to finish: see, e.g., The Indian Advancement Act (1884, SC 1884, c. 28), the Indian Act (RSC 1886, c. 43), the second Indian Act (RSC 1906, c. 81), An Act to Amend the Indian Act (SC 1919-1920, c. 50), the third Indian Act (RSC 1927, c. 98), An Act to Amend the Indian Act (SC 1932-33, c. 42), the fourth and fifth generations of Indian Acts (SC 1951, c. 29; RSC 1952, c. 149; RSC 1970, c. 1-16), as well as 1988 amendments to the 1970 Indian Act; Indian and Northern Affairs Canada, *Indian Acts and Amendments, 1868-1850* (Ottawa: Treaties and Historical Research Center, 1981). For interpretation, see J. Leighton, *The Development of Federal Indian Policy in Canada, 1840-1890* (London, Ont.: University of Western Ontario, 1975); Bernard Schwartz, *First Principles: Constitutional Reform with Respect to the Aboriginal Peoples of Canada, 1982-1984* (Kingston, Ont.: Institute of Intergovernmental Relations, Queen's University, 1986).

162. Quoted in M. Montgomery, "The Six Nations and the MacDonald Franchise," *Ontario History*, Vol. 57, No. 1, 1965, p. 37. Although it was not until 1933 that a supplemental amendment to the Indian Act formally authorized the government to naturalize even non-applying natives at its own discretion, this had been de facto policy for more than fifty years; Clark, *Native Liberty, Crown Sovereignty*, op. cit., pp. 156-7.

163. Deloria and Lytle, *American Indian, American Justice*, op. cit., pp. 9-10.

164. Indian Citizenship Act, ch. 233, 43 Stat. 253 (1924), now codified at 8 U.S.C. § 1401 (a) (2).

165. Coulter, "Contemporary Indian Sovereignty," op. cit., p. 118. Also see Deloria, *Trail of Broken Treaties*, op. cit., p. 18.

166. Coulter, "Contemporary Indian Sovereignty," op. cit., p. 118.

167. Indigenous governments are now officially described as being a "third level of governance" in the U.S., below that of the federal and state governments, but generally above those of counties and municipalities; U.S. Senate, Select Committee on Indian Affairs, *Final Report and Legislative Recommendations: A Report of the Special Committee on Investigations* (Washington, D.C.: 101st Cong., 2d Sess., U.S. Government Printing Office, Nov. 20, 1989). In Canada, it is also official policy to view "federal and provincial governments as at a higher level than aboriginal governments"; Clark, *Native Liberty, Crown Sovereignty*, op. cit., p. 154; J. Anthony Long and Menno J. Boldt, eds., *Governments in Conflict? Provinces and Indian Nations in Canada* (Toronto: University of Toronto Press, 1988).

168. Ch. 576, 48 Stat. 948; now codified at 25 U.S.C. 461-279; also referred to as the "Wheeler-Howard Act," in recognition of its congressional sponsors. For an overly sympathetic overview, see Vine Deloria, Jr., and Clifford M. Lytle, *The Nations Within: The Past and Future of American Indian Sovereignty* (New York: Pantheon, 1984).

169. The constitutions were boilerplate documents hammered out by technicians at the BIA headquarters in Washington, D.C.: see generally, Graham D. Taylor, *The New Deal and American Indian Tribalism: Administration of the Indian Reorganization Act, 1934-1935* (Lincoln: University of Nebraska Press, 1980).

170. See, e.g., the accounts of Rupert Costo and others in Ken Philp, ed., *Indian Self-Rule: First-Hand Accounts of Indian/White Relations from Roosevelt to Reagan* (Salt Lake City: Howe Bros., 1986).

171. On this and other sorts of fraud perpetrated in the "Sioux Complex" of reservations, see Thomas Biolosi, *Organizing the Lakota: The Political Economy of the New Deal on the Pine Ridge and Rosebud Reservations* (Tucson: University of Arizona Press, 1992).

172. Richard O. Clemmer, *Continuities of Hopi Culture Change* (Albuquerque: Acoma Books, 1978) pp. 60-1. Also see Charles Lummis, *Bullying the Hopi* (Prescott, AZ: Prescott College Press, 1968).

173. Clemmer, *Continuities*, op. cit., p. 61.

174. Steven M. Tullberg, "The Creation and Decline of the Hopi Tribal Council," in *Rethinking Indian Law*, op. cit., p. 37.

175. The BIA official assigned responsibility for reorganizing Hopi was Oliver LaFarge. He compiled what he called a "running narrative" of the process which confirms all points raised herein, communicating his concerns to Indian Commissioner Collier as he went along. In the manuscript, which unfortunately remains unpublished (it is lodged in the LaFarge collection at the University of Texas, Austin), he remarks at p. 8: "[I]t is alien to [the Hopis] to settle matters out of hand by majority vote. Such a vote leaves a dissatisfied minority, which makes them very uneasy. Their natural way of doing is to discuss among themselves at great length and group by group until public opinion as a whole has settled

overwhelmingly in one direction... *Opposition is expressed by abstention.* Those who are against something stay away from meetings at which it is discussed and *generally refuse to vote on it* (emphasis added)."

176. Frank Waters, *Book of the Hopi* (New York: Ballantine, 1969) p. 386.

177. David C. Hawkes, *Aboriginal Self-Government: What Does It Mean?* (Kingston: Ont.: Institute for Intergovernmental Relations, Queen's University, 1983) p. 9.

178. This was subjected to legal challenge in the 1977 case of *Davey v. Isaac* (77 DLR (3d) 481 (SSC)). Predictably, the courts confirmed the "right" of the federal government to effect such interventions in the internal affairs of indigenous nations.

179. *Special Report on Indian Self-Government*, op. cit.; *Response of the Government*, op. cit.;

180. Noel Lyon, *Aboriginal Self-Government: Rights of Citizenship and Access to Government Services* (Kingston, Ont.: Institute for Intergovernmental Relations, Queen's University, 1986) p. 15.

181. For analysis, see Asch, *Home and Native Land*, op. cit.; Schwartz, *First Principles*, op. cit.; E. Robinson and H. Quinney, *The Infested Blanket: Canada's Constitution: Genocide of Indian Nations* (Winnipeg: Queenston House, 1985).

182. One example of what is at issue here is Public Law 280 (ch. 505, 67 Stat. 588 (1953); now codified at 18 U.S.C. § 1162, 25 U.S.C. §§ 1321-1326, 28 U.S.C. §§ 1360, 1360 note), placing American Indian reservations in a dozen U.S. states under state rather than federal criminal jurisdiction. While the Indians involved ostensibly "consented" to this diminishment of their standing to essentially the level of counties, their alternative was outright termination. In California, the process has gone further, with the placement of many reservations under county jurisdiction as well; Carol Goldberg, "Public Law 280: The Limits of State Jurisdiction Over Reservation Indians," *UCLA Law Review*, No. 22, 1975; "The Extension of County Jurisdiction Over Indian Reservations in California: Public Law 280 and the Ninth Circuit," *Hastings Law Journal*, No. 25, 1974. More recently, under the 1988 Indian Gaming Act (Public Law 100-497), a number of peoples have been coerced into placing themselves under state regulatory authority for purposes of engaging in gambling operations. In the alternative, they faced continuing destitution; see generally, William R. Eadington, ed., *Indian Gaming and the Law* (Reno: Institute for the Study of Gaming and Commercial Gambling, University of Nevada, 1990). Suffice it to say that such impositions do not conform to international legal definitions of "voluntary merger."

183. The French sought to circumvent the U.N. Charter requirement that they decolonize all "non-self-governing territories" under their control by declaring Algeria to be an integral part of the "Home Department" (i.e., France itself) pursuant to its 1834 annexation of the entire Maghrib region. Such sophistry was rejected by the international community; see, e.g., J.L. Miège, "Legal Developments in the Maghrib, 1830-1930," in *European Expansion and the Law*, op. cit.; Joseph Kraft, *The Battle for Algeria* (Garden City, NY: Doubleday, 1961).

184. See note 93, above, and accompanying text.

185. *Worcester v. Georgia* at 559-60.

186. 30 U.S. (5 Pet.) 1. For background, see Starr, *History of the Cherokee Indians*, op. cit.; Thurman Wilkins, *Cherokee Tragedy: The Ridge Family and the Destruction of a People* (New York: Macmillan, 1970). On the case itself, see J. Burke, "The Cherokee Cases: A Study in Law, Politics, and Morality," *Stanford Law Review*, No. 21, 1969.

187. *Cherokee v. Georgia* at 16.

188. Ibid. at 17.

189. A good overview of the flow and interrelationship of Marshall's "Indian cases," as well as their implications for both native and Euroamerican societies will be found in G. Edward White, *The Marshall Court and Cultural Change, 1815-1835* (New York: Macmillan, 1988) esp. Chap. 10. Also see Robert A. Williams, Jr., "The Algebra of Federal Indian Law: The Hard Trail of Decolonizing the White Man's Jurisprudence," *Wisconsin Law Review*, No. 31, 1986.

190. For a fuller exposition, see Williams, *American Indian in Western Legal Thought*, op. cit., pp. 312-7, 321-3.

191. A year later, in *Worcester* (at 559), Marshall again remarked upon how the Doctrine "excluded [native peoples] from intercourse with any other European potentate than the first discoverer of the coast of the particular region claimed" as being the "single exception" to the fullness of our sovereignty under international law. This time he framed the matter more correctly, however, by going on to observe that "this was a restriction which those European potentates imposed upon themselves, as well as upon the

Indians." In other words, all parties being equal, there was no implication of supremacy or subordination involved. Even at that, Marshall overstated the case. Under the law, absent a treaty or agreement to the contrary indigenous nations were free to trade with anyone they wished. It was the European powers themselves which were constrained from trading with natives in one another's discovery domains; aside from the citations contained in note 52, above, see generally, Gordon Bennett, *Aboriginal Rights in International Law* (London: Royal Anthropological Association, 1978).

192. While Marshall was ostensibly writing about the specific circumstances of the Cherokee Nation, he couched his opinion in terms of all native peoples within claimed U.S. boundaries. At the time, this already included the vast Louisiana Territory, to which the Jefferson Administration had purchased French acquisition rights but in which there was virtually no U.S. settlement. Hence, while Marshall's characterization of the "domestic dependency" of indigenous nations might have borne a certain resemblance to the situation of Cherokee, encapsulated as it was within the already settled corpus of the United States, the same can hardly be said of more westerly peoples like the Cheyennes, Comanches, Navajos and Lakotas. In this sense, the views expressed in *Cherokee* were not so much an attempt to apprehend extant reality as they were an effort to forge a sort of judicial license for future U.S. aggression. There is thus considerable merit to the observation of Glenn T. Morris, offered during a 1987 lecture at the University of Colorado, that, far from constituting an affirmation of indigenous rights, as is commonly argued (e.g., Wilkinson, *Indians, Time and Law*, op. cit.), the Marshall doctrine is "fundamentally a sophisticated juridical blueprint for colonization."

193. A good illustration is that of the U.S. military campaign against the Lakota and allied peoples in 1876-77. During the late fall of 1875, the administration of President Ulysses S. Grant issued instructions that all Lakotas residing within their own territories, recognized by treaty in both 1851 and 1868, should assemble at specific locations therein by a given date in January 1876. When the Indians failed to comply, Grant termed their refusal of his presumption an "act of war" and sent in the army to "restore order"; for details, see John E. Gray, *Centennial Campaign: The Sioux War of 1876* (Norman: University of Oklahoma Press, 1988).

194. For elaboration, see my "Perversions of Justice: Examining the Doctrine of U.S. Rights to Occupancy in North America," in David S. Caudill and Steven Jay Gold, eds., *Radical Philosophy of Law: Contemporary Challenges to Mainstream Legal Theory and Practice* (Atlantic Highlands, NJ: Humanities Press, 1995).

195. On the nature of the Canadian case, see note 11, above.

196. SCR 313 at 380. Contextually, see John Hurley, "Aboriginal Rights, the Constitution and the Marshall Court," *Revue Juridique Themis*, No. 17, 1983.

197. In concluding that the federal government of Canada enjoys a unilateral prerogative to extinguish indigenous rights, the court noted that it had been "unable to find a Canadian case dealing with precisely the same subject" and that it would therefore rely on a U.S. judicial interpretation found in *State of Idaho v. Coffee* (56 P 2d 1185 (1976)); 68 OR (2d) 353 (HC), 438 at 412-3.

198. In general, see Slattery, *Ancestral Lands, Alien Laws*, op. cit.; and "Understanding Aboriginal Rights," *Canadian Bar Review*, No. 91, 1987.

199. At the point Great Britain abandoned its struggle to retain the thirteen insurgent American colonies, each became an independent state in its own right. Their subsequent relinquishment of sovereignty/consensual subordination to federal authority was exactly comparable to that imposed by the U.S. as a result of the *Cherokee* opinion upon indigenous nations; see generally, Peter S. Onuf, *The Origins of the Federal Republic: Jurisdictional Controversies in the United States, 1775-1787* (Philadelphia: University of Pennsylvania Press, 1983).

200. See note 36 and accompanying text. Incidentally, the explanation offered by Bruce Clark of the difference between U.S. and Canadian approaches to Indian relations—that the native right to sovereignty is protected in the Canadian Constitution but not in that of the U.S.—is erroneous; *Native Liberty, Crown Sovereignty*, op. cit., pp. 56-7. Indigenous sovereignty *is* protected under Article I of the U.S. Constitution for reasons indicated herein. That the southern settler-state government ignores this fact as a matter of policy hardly negates its existence.

201. For a sustained but unsuccessful effort by several scholars to get around this problem, see Imre Sutton, ed., *Irredeemable America: The Indians' Estate and Land Tenure* (Albuquerque: University of New Mexico Press, 1986).

202. The description comes from Russell Means, in a lecture delivered at the University of Colorado, July 1986. With respect to formal repudiation, see note 93 and accompanying text.

203. It is important to note that resort to armed struggle by bona fide National Liberation Movements is entirely legitimate. United Nations Resolution 3103 (XXVII; Dec. 12, 1972) declares that "the struggle of people under colonial and alien domination and racist régimes for the implementation of their rights to self-determination and independence is legitimate and in full accordance with the principles of international law." Accordingly, Section I, Clause 4 of Protocol I Additional to the Geneva Conventions of August 12, 1949, and Relating to the Protection of Victims of International Armed Conflicts, done at Geneva on June 10, 1977, expressly includes "armed conflicts in which peoples are fighting against colonial domination or alien occupation and against racist régimes in the exercise of their right to self-determination, as enshrined in the Charter of the United Nations..." Resolution 3103 goes on to state that "any attempt to suppress the struggle against colonial and alien domination and racist régimes is incompatible with the Charter of the United Nations...and constitutes a threat to international peace and security"; Weston, et al., *Documents in International Law*, op. cit., pp. 230-46. In effect, resort to arms in order to restore inherent sovereignty is lawful, while use of armed force to suppress or deny it is not.

204. On the fishing rights struggle, see American Friends Service Committee, *Uncommon Controversy: Fishing Rights of the Muckleshoot, Puyallup, and Nisqually Indians* (Seattle: University of Washington Press, 1970). On Alcatraz, see Troy R. Johnson, *The Occupation of Alcatraz Island: Indian Self-Determination and the Rise of Indian Activism* (Urbana: University of Illinois Press, 1996). On the BIA building takeover, see Deloria, *Behind the Trail of Broken Treaties*, op. cit. On Wounded Knee, see Robert Burnette and John Koster, *The Road to Wounded Knee* (New York: Bantam, 1974).

205. On the early phases, see, e.g., Stan Steiner, *The New Indians* (New York: Harper & Row, 1968); Alvin M. Josephy, Jr., *Red Power: The American Indians' Fight for Freedom* (New York: McGraw-Hill, 1971). On the Anicinabe Park occupation in northwestern Ontario and other subsequent events in Canada, see the various issues of *Akwesasne Notes*, 1970-75, inclusive.

206. On the growth of AIM, see Paul Chaat Smith and Robert Allen Warrior, *Like a Hurricane: The American Indian Movement from Alcatraz to Wounded Knee* (New York: New Press, 1996). On the repression, see Johansen and Maestas, *Wasi'chu*, op. cit.; Churchill and Vander Wall, *Agents of Repression*, op. cit.; Peter Matthiessen, *In the Spirit of Crazy Horse* (New York: Viking, [2nd. ed.] 1991).

207. Deloria, *Behind the Trail of Broken Treaties*, op. cit.

208. On the famous "Indian Summer in Geneva," see "The United Nations Conference on Indians" in Jimmie Durham, *A Certain Lack of Coherence: Writings on Art and Cultural Politics* (London: Kala Press, 1993).

209. Russell Tribunal, *The Rights of the Indians of the Americas* (Rotterdam: Fourth Russell Tribunal, 1980).

210. Sanders, "Re-Emergence of Indigenous Questions," op. cit. Also see Gordon Bennett, "The Developing Law of Aboriginal Rights," *The Review*, No. 22, 1979.

211. 88 Stat. 2203; now codified at 25 U.S.C. 450a and elsewhere in Titles 25, 42 and 50, U.S.C.A. It is worth noting that in 1984 Canada made an abortive attempt to come up with its own version of this handy statute. Entitled "An Act Relating to Self-Government for Indian Nations" (Federal Bill c-52), the measure dissolved in the mists of transition from liberal to conservative government; Clark, *Native Liberty, Crown Sovereignty*, op. cit., p. 169. As it stands, Canada relies upon the Section 35 (1) of the 1982 Constitution Act, a component of the so-called "Charter of Rights and Freedoms" specifically enumerating the "Rights of the Aboriginal Peoples of Canada." The provisions found therein seem clear enough—among other things, it states unequivocally that the "existing aboriginal and treaty rights of the aboriginal peoples of Canada are hereby recognized and confirmed"—to assure indigenous self-determination in a genuine sense; L.C. Green, "Aboriginal Peoples, International Law, and the Canadian Charter of Rights and Freedoms," *Canadian Bar Review*, No. 61, 1983; K. McNeil, "The Constitution Act, 1982, Sections 25 and 35," *Canadian Native Law Reporter*, No. 1, 1988. It should be noted, however, that in practice the courts of Canada have quietly voided these apparent guarantees by subjecting them to "reasonability tests" during a pair of 1989 cases. In *R. v. Dick* (1 CNLR 132 (BC Prov. Ct.)), the Provincial Court of British Columbia found the exercise of aboriginal rights to be unreasonable insofar as it conflicted with provincial statutes. In *R. v. Agawa* (65 OR 92d) 505 (CA)), the Ontario Court of

Appeal reached the same conclusion with respect to treaty rights; see generally, Venne, "Treaty and Constitution in Canada," op. cit.; Thomas Berger, "Native Rights and Self-Determination," *The Canadian Journal of Native Studies*, Vol. 3, No. 2, 1983.

212. Michael D. Gross, "Indian Self-Determination and Tribal Sovereignty: An Analysis of Recent Federal Policy," *Texas Law Review*, No. 56, 1978. For background, see Jack D. Forbes, *Native Americans and Nixon: Presidential Politics and Minority Self-Determination* (Los Angeles: UCLA American Indian Studies Center, 1981).

213. Samples of the rhetoric indulged in at the U.N. by U.S. representatives is laced throughout Jimmie Durham's *Columbus Day* (Minneapolis: West End Press, 1983). For responses, see Alexander Ewen, ed., *Voices of Indigenous Peoples: Native People Address the United Nations* (Santa Fe, NM: Clear Light, 1994).

214. Douglas Sanders, "The U.N. Working Group on Indigenous Peoples," *Human Rights Quarterly*, No. 11, 1989; Jimmie Durham, "American Indians and Carter's Human Rights Sermons," in *A Certain Lack of Coherence*, op. cit.

215. José R. Martinez Cobo, *Study of the Problem of Discrimination of Indigenous Populations* (U.N. Doc. E/CN.4/Sub.2/1983/21/Ass.83, Sept. 1983). For context and amplification, see Independent Commission on Humanitarian Issues, *Indigenous Peoples: A Global Quest for Justice* (London: Zed Books, 1987).

216. On the decision to draft a new instrument, see Anaya, "The Rights of Indigenous Peoples and International Law," op. cit. For further background, see Dunbar Ortiz, *Indians of the Americas*, op. cit.; Sanders, "Re-Emergence of Indigenous Questions," op. cit.

217. Sanders, "U.N. Working Group," op. cit.

218. Article 1 (7) of the United Nations Charter specifically excludes intervention "in matters which are essentially within the jurisdiction of any state" and exempts member states from having "to submit such matters to settlement" by the community of nations; Weston, et al., *Documents in International Law*, op. cit., p. 17. For analysis, see generally, Joseph B. Kelly, "National Minorities in International Law," *Denver Journal of International Law and Politics*, No. 3, 1973; L. Mandell, "Indians Nations: Not Minorities," *Les Cahiers de Droit*, No. 27, 1983.

219. Article 1 (2) of the United Nations Charter has required since 1945 that all member states "respect...the principle of equal rights and self-determination of peoples." Since then, it has become almost pro forma to incorporate the following sentence into international legal instruments: "All peoples have the right to self-determination; by virtue of that right they freely determine their political status and freely pursue their economic, social and cultural development"; see, e.g., Article 1 (1) of the 1967 International Covenant on Economic, Social and Cultural Rights (U.N.G.A. Res 2200 (XXI), 21 U.N. GAOR, Supp. (No. 16) 49, A/6316 (1967), reprinted in 6 I.L.M. 360 (1967); Article 1 (1) of the 1967 International Declaration on Civil and Political Rights (U.N.G.A. Res. 2200 (XXI), 21 U.N. GAOR, Supp. (No. 16) 52, U.N. Doc. A/6316 (1967 reprinted in 6 I.L.M. 368 (1967); and the Preamble to the 1986 Declaration on the Right to Development (U.N.G.A. Res. 41/128, 41 U.N. GAOR, Supp. (No. 53) U.N. Doc. A/41/925 (1986). The 1960 Declaration on the Granting of Independence to Colonial Countries and Peoples (op. cit.) not only includes the same language as Point 2, but obviously incorporates the concept into its very title. Moreover, as point 1, it states that the "subjection of peoples to alien subjugation, domination and exploitation constitutes a denial of fundamental human rights, is contrary to the Charter of the United Nations and is an impediment to world peace and cooperation"; Weston, et al., *Documents in International Law*, op. cit., pp. 17, 371, 376, 485, 343-4. See generally, Pomerance, *Self-Determination in Law and Practice*, op. cit.; Ofuatey-Kodjoe, *Principles of Self-Determination*, op. cit.; Rigo-Sureta, *Evolution of the Right to Self-Determination*, op. cit.

220. See, e.g., Article 1 (3) of the International Labor Organization Convention (No. 169) Concerning Indigenous and Tribal Peoples in Independent Countries; International Labor Conference, *The Indigenous and Tribal Peoples Convention* (76th Sess., Prov. Rec. 25, 1989).

221. The timing, corresponding with the quincentenniary of the Columbian landfall in America, was selected as optimal for obtaining speedy passage of the proposed declaration by the General Assembly.

222. See generally, Isabelle Schulte-Tenckhoff, "The Irresistible Ascension of the UN Draft Declaration on the Rights of Indigenous Peoples: Stopped Dead in Its Tracks?" *European Review of Native American Studies*, Vol. 9, No. 2, 1995.

223. It should be noted that the U.S. has conducted itself in a similar fashion throughout the history of the United Nations, beginning with the 1946 deliberations over the content of a draft convention on prevention and punishment of genocide. In that instance, U.S. representatives acted decisively to delete an entire article on cultural genocide, which they correctly interpreted as describing much of their own country's Indian policy. Even then, the United States refused to ratify the law for forty years, until it felt it could exempt itself from aspects it found inconvenient; LeBlanc, *United States and the Genocide Convention,* op. cit. The same pattern of obstructing and subverting the formation of international law has continuously marked the U.S. performance over the years, most recently with respect to its refusal to accept a universal prohibition against the use of antipersonnel mines unless it—alone among nations—could be formally exempted from full compliance.

224. The substance of this paragraph has been confirmed by several of the indigenous delegates in attendance, notably Sharon H. Venne, Moana Jackson, Glenn T. Morris, Josh Dillabaugh, Mona Roy, Troy Lynn Yellow Wood, Phyllis Young and Russell Means.

225. Aside from the many references already made which bear on this point, see Robert T. Coulter, "The Denial of Legal Remedies to Indian Nations Under U.S. Law," in *Rethinking Indian Law,* op. cit.

226. It is unlikely that, absent at least some pretense of genuine native endorsement, any form of declaration will be passed by the General Assembly at all. From an indigenous perspective, this would be an entirely acceptable outcome since, at least in this instance, "something" is definitely *not* "better than nothing." From the settler-state perspective, of course, the precise opposite pertains. Hence, the U.S. in particular has set out to coopt key indigenous organizations into accepting some "compromise" formulation. Ironically, it appears that the once militantly principled IITC—which has by now drifted *very* far from its roots, having long since incorporated itself (shedding control by the elders, original trustees and grassroots supporters in the process)—has proven one of the more receptive in this regard; Churchill, "Subterfuge and Self-Determination," op. cit. The seeds for this ugly development were noted by some observers as far back as 1979; Jimmie Durham, "An Open Letter to the Movement," in *A Certain Lack of Coherence,* op. cit.

227. This is the route implicitly suggested in A. Kienetz, "Decolonization in the North: Canada and the United States," *Canadian Review of Studies in Nationalism,* Vol. 8, No. 1, 1986. Also see S. Powderface, "Self-Government Means Biting the Hand that Feeds Us," in Leroy Little Bear, Menno Boldt and Jonathan Long, eds., *Pathways to Self-Determination: Canadian Indians and the Canadian State* (Toronto: University of Toronto Press, 1984).

228. See notes 62 and 95, above, and accompanying text.

229. See 219, above.

230. Weston, et al., *Documents in International Law,* op. cit., p. 344. Both the U.S. and Canada will undoubtedly argue that native territories within their borders are already "self-governing"—as the U.S. at least has claimed they are "self-determining" under its laws—but neither can pretend that indigenous nations presently "enjoy complete independence," or that they have ever been afforded an opportunity to do so.

231. Ibid., pp. 27-30.

232. As is stated at Point 6 of Resolution 1514, "Inadequacy of political, economic, social or educational preparedness should never be used as a pretext for delaying independence"; ibid., p. 344.

233. In cases where the colonizer is found to have falsified reporting data in ways which allowed it to rig outcomes, the colony is reinscribed on the list of non-self-governing territories and the entire process starts over under direct U.N. supervision (rather than monitoring). Witness the recent case of New Caledonia; G.A. Res. 41/41A UN GAOR Supp. (No. 53), UN Doc. A/41/53 (1986) at 49. Also see "Report of the Special Committee on the Situation with regard to the Implementation of the Declaration on the Granting of Independence to Colonial Countries and Peoples," 41 UN GAOR (No. 23), UN Doc A/41/23 (1986). For further background, see Stephen Bates, *The South Pacific Island Countries and France: A Study of Inter-State Relations* (Canberra: Australian National University, 1990) p. 77. Both Hawai'i and Puerto Rico are presently subject to this same procedure. On Hawai'i, see note 61, above, and accompanying text, as well as the essay, "Reinscription: The Right of Hawai'i to be Restored to the United Nations List of Non-Self-Governing Territories," in my *Perversions of Justice: Reflections on Federal Indian Law and Policy* (San Francisco: City Lights, forthcoming). On Puerto Rico, see, e.g., Ronald Fernandez, *Prisoners of Colonialism: The Struggle for Justice in Puerto Rico* (Monroe, ME: Common Courage Press, 1994).

234. A colonized people is not legally required to opt for complete independence and separation from its colonizer in exercising its right to self-determination. Instead, it may elect to limit its own sovereignty to some extent, as in the case of Greenland; Gudmunder Alfredsson, "Greenland and the Law of Political Decolonization," *German Yearbook of International Law*, No. 25, 1982; Nannum Hurst, *Autonomy, Sovereignty and Self-Determination* (Philadelphia: University of Pennsylvania Press, 1990). Colonizing states, however, are legally required to acknowledge without qualification the right of colonial subjects to complete independence/separation and to do nothing at all to orchestrate any other outcome to the process of decolonization. Independence is thus legally presumed to be the outcome of any decolonizing process unless the colonized themselves demonstrate unequivocally that they desire a different result; Nanda, "Self-Determination Under International Law," op. cit.; Buchheit, *Secession*, op. cit.

235. Weston, et al., *Documents in International Law*, op. cit., pp. 17, 344.

236. The principle was adopted in response to the "Belgian Thesis," a proposition put forth by that country as it was being forced to relinquish the Congo, that each of the native peoples within the colony would be at least as entitled to exercise self-determining rights as would the decolonized Congolese state (which Belgium, after all, had itself created); *The Sacred Mission of Civilization: To Which Peoples Should the Benefit be Extended?* (New York: Belgium Government Information Center, 1953). While the Belgian position, that each indigenous nation possessed a right equal to or greater than the state, was essentially correct, it was advanced for transparently neocolonialist purposes and was therefore rebuffed; Roxanne Dunbar Ortiz, "Protection of American Indian Territories in the United States: Applicability of International Law," in *Irredeemable America*, op. cit., esp. pp. 260-1.

237. For discussion, see, e.g., Russel Barsh, "Indigenous North America and International Law," *Oregon Law Review*, No. 62, 1983.

238. For elaboration of this argument, see Catherine J. Jorns, "Indigenous People and Self-Determination: Challenging State Sovereignty," *Case Western Reserve Journal of International Law*, No. 24, 1992. Potentially applicable precedents will be found in Jencks, *Law in the World Community*, op. cit.

PART II: THE LAND

In Struggle for the Land
Wandering amongst the opulence
wondering what not to touch
times not knowing
times getting bit
times of temptation
times of seduction
Wandering in the poverty
touched by everything
knowing the bite
no time for temptation
only time for doing
babylon in terror
world run over by machines
the economics of captured dreams
the rich are poorer
while the poor are waiting
everyone pretending to live
calling exploitation progress
calling submission freedom
calling madness profit
calling earth a planet
plaguing her
with civilization…

—John Trudell
from *Living in Reality*

STRUGGLE TO REGAIN A STOLEN HOMELAND
Iroquois Land Rights in Upstate New York

> The inhabitants of your country districts regard—wrongfully, it is true—Indians and forests as natural enemies which must be exterminated by fire and sword and brandy, in order that they may seize their territory. They regard themselves, themselves and their posterity, as collateral heirs to all the magnificent portion of land which God has created from Cumberland and Ohio to the Pacific Ocean.
>
> —Pierre Samuel Du Pont de Nemours
> Letter to Thomas Jefferson, December 17, 1801

ONE of the longest fought and more complicated land rights struggles in the United States is that of the Haudenosaunee, or Iroquois Six Nations Confederacy. While the 1783 Treaty of Paris ended hostilities between the British Crown and its secessionist subjects in the thirteen colonies, it had no direct effect upon the state of war existing between those subjects and the various indigenous peoples allied with the Crown. Similarly, while by the treaty George III quitclaimed his own country's rights under the Doctrine of Discovery within the affected portion of North America, it was the opinion of Thomas Jefferson and others that this had done nothing to vest title to these lands in the newly born United States.[1]

On both counts, the Continental Congress found it imperative to enter into treaty arrangements with indigenous nations as expeditiously as possible.[2] A very high priority in this regard was accorded the Haudenosaunee, four members of which—the Mohawks, Senecas, Cayugas, and Onondagas—had fought with the British (the remaining two, the Oneidas and Tuscaroras, had remained largely neutral but occasionally provided assistance to the colonists).[3] Hence, during October of 1784, the U.S. conducted extensive negotiations with representatives of the Six Nations at Fort Stanwix, in the State of New York.

The result was a treaty, reinforced with a second negotiated at Fort Harmar in 1789, by which the Indians relinquished their interest in lands lying west of a north-south line running from Niagara to the border of Pennsylvania—that is to say, their territory within the Ohio River Valley—as well as parcels on which certain military posts had been built. In exchange, the U.S. guaranteed three of the four hostile nations the bulk of their traditional homelands. The Oneida and Tuscarora were also "secured in the possession of the lands on which they are now settled." Altogether, the Haudenosaunee reserved some six million acres—about half of the present state of New York—as permanent homelands (see Map 1).[4]

This arrangement, while meeting most of the Indians' needs, was also quite useful to the U.S. central government. As has been observed elsewhere:

> First...in order to sell [land in the Ohio River area] and settle it, the Continental Congress needed to extinguish Indian title, including any claims by the Iroquois [nations] of New York. Second, the commissioners wanted to punish the...Senecas. Thus they forced the Senecas to surrender most of their land in New York [and Pennsylvania] to the United States... Third, the United States...wanted to secure peace by confirming to the [Haudenosaunee] their remaining lands. Fourth, the United States was anxious to protect its frontier from the British in Canada by securing land for forts and roads along lakes Erie and Ontario.[5]

New York State, needless to say, was rather less enthusiastic about the terms of the treaty. Indeed, it had already attempted, unsuccessfully, to obtain additional land cessions from the Iroquois during meetings conducted prior to arrival of the federal delegation at Fort Stanwix.[6] Further such efforts were barred by Article IX of the Articles of Confederation, and subsequently by Article I (Section 10) and the Commerce Clause of the Constitution, all of which combined to render treatymaking and outright purchases of Indian land by states illegal. New York therefore resorted to subterfuge, securing a series of twenty-six "leases," many of them for 999 years, on almost all native territory within its purported boundaries.

The Haudenosaunee initially agreed to these transactions because of Governor George Clinton's duplicitous assurances that the leases represented a way for them to *keep* their land, and for his government to "extend its protection over their property against the dealings of unscrupulous white land speculators" in the private sector. The first such arrangement was forged with the Oneidas in a meeting begun at Fort Schuyler on August 28, 1788.

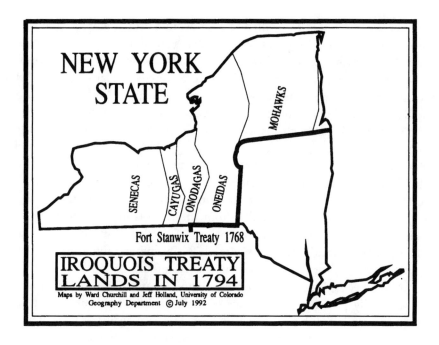

NEW YORK STATE

MOHAWKS

SENECAS

CAYUGAS

ONONDAGAS

ONEIDAS

Fort Stanwix Treaty 1768

IROQUOIS TREATY LANDS IN 1794

Maps by Ward Churchill and Jeff Holland, University of Colorado Geography Department © July 1992

The New York commissioners…led them to believe that they had [already] lost all their land to the New York Genesee Company, and that the commissioners were there to restore title. The Oneidas expressed confusion over this since they had never signed any instruments to that effect, but Governor Clinton just waved that aside… Thus the Oneidas agreed to the lease arrangement with the state because it seemed the only way they could get back their land. The state received some five million acres for $2,000 in cash, $2,000 in clothing, $1,000 in provisions, and $600 in annual rental. So complete was the deception that Good Peter [an Oneida leader] thanked the governor for his efforts.[7]

Leasing of the Tuscaroras' land occurred the same day by a parallel instrument.[8] On September 12, the Onondagas leased almost all their land to New York under virtually identical conditions.[9] The Cayugas followed suit on February 25, 1789, in exchange for payment of $500 in silver, plus an additional $1,625 the next June and a $500 annuity.[10]

New York's flagrant circumvention of constitutional restrictions on non-federal acquisitions of Indian land was a major factor in passage of the first of the so-called Indian Trade and Intercourse Acts in 1790.[11] Clinton, however, simply shifted to a different ruse, avoiding such tightening in the of mechanisms of federal control over his state's manipulations by backdating them. In 1791, for example, he announced that New York would honor a 999-year lease negotiated in 1787 by a private speculator named John Livingston. The lease covered 800,000 acres of mainly Mohawk land, but had been declared null and void by the state legislature in 1788.[12]

Concerned that such maneuvers might push the Iroquois, the largely landless Senecas in particular, into joining Shawnee leader Tecumseh's pan-Indian alliance and physically resisting further U.S. expansion into the Ohio Valley, the federal government sent a new commission to meet with the Haudenosaunee leadership at the principle Seneca town of Canandaigua in 1794. In exchange for a pledge from the Six Nations not to bear arms against the United States, their ownership of the lands guaranteed them at Fort Stanwix was reaffirmed, the state's leases notwithstanding, and the bulk of the Seneca territory in Pennsylvania was restored.[13]

Nonetheless, New York officials, obviously undaunted by this turn of events, rapidly parceled out sections of the leased lands in subleases to the very "unscrupulous whites" it had pledged to guard against. On September 15, 1797, the Holland Land Company, in which many members of the state government had invested, assumed control over all but ten tracts of land, totaling 397 square miles, of the Fort Stanwix Treaty area. The leasing instrument purportedly "extinguished" native title to the land, a process which would be repeated many times over in the coming years (see Map 2).[14]

Expropriation

Given the diminishing military importance of the Six Nations after the Shawnees' 1794 defeat at Fallen Timbers and the eventual vanquishing of Tecumseh at Tippecanoe in 1814, federal authorities ultimately did little or nothing to correct the situation despite continuous Iroquois protests.[15] New York, along with others of the individual states, was thus emboldened to proceed with wholesale appropriations of native territory (albeit an appearance of "free enterprise within the private sector" rather than official policy was usually maintained).

In 1810, for instance, the Holland Company "sold" some 200,000 acres of its holdings in Seneca and Tuscarora land to its own accountant, David A. Ogden, at a price of fifty cents per acre. Ogden then issued shares against development of this land, many of them to Albany politicians who already

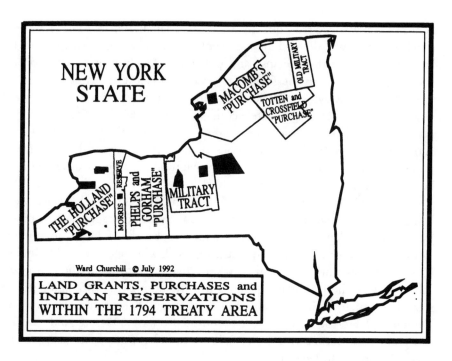

NEW YORK
STATE

MACOMB'S "PURCHASE"

OLD MILITARY TRACT

TOTTEN and CROSSFIELD "PURCHASE"

THE HOLLAND "PURCHASE"

MORRIS RESERVE

PHELPS and GORHAM "PURCHASE"

MILITARY TRACT

Ward Churchill © July 1992

LAND GRANTS, PURCHASES and INDIAN RESERVATIONS WITHIN THE 1794 TREATY AREA

held stock in Holland. Thus (re)capitalized, the "Ogden Land Company" was able to push through a deal in 1826 to buy a further 81,000 acres of previously unleased reservation land at fifty-three cents per acre. A federal investigation into the affair was quashed in 1828 by Secretary of War Peter B. Porter, himself a major stockholder in Ogden.[16]

Under such circumstances, most of the Oneidas requested in 1831 that what was left of their New York holdings, which they were sure they would lose anyway, be exchanged for a 500,000-acre parcel purchased from the Menominees in Wisconsin. President Andrew Jackson, at the time pursuing his policy of general Indian Removal to points west of the Mississippi, readily agreed.[17] In the climate created by Jackson's own posturing, an ever-increasing number of federal officials followed Porter's example, actively colluding with their state-level counterparts and private speculators, thereby erasing altogether whatever meager protection of native rights had previously emanated from Washington, D.C.[18]

One outcome was that on January 15, 1838, federal commissioners oversaw the signing of the Treaty of Buffalo Creek, wherein 102,069 acres of

Seneca land was "ceded" directly to the Ogden Company. The $202,000 purchase price was divided almost evenly between the government (to be held "in trust" for the Indians), and individual non–Indians seeking to buy and "improve" plots in the former reservation area. At the same time, what was left of the Cayuga, Oneida, Onondaga and Tuscarora holdings were wiped out, at an aggregate cost of $400,000 to Ogden.[19] The Haudenosaunee were told they should relocate en mass to Missouri. Although the Six Nations never consented to the treaty, and it was never properly ratified by the Senate, President Martin Van Buren proclaimed it to be the law of the land on April 4, 1840.[20]

By 1841, Iroquois complaints about the Buffalo Creek Treaty were being joined by increasing numbers of non–Indians outraged not so much by the loss of land to Indians it entailed as by the obvious corruption involved in its terms.[21] Consequently, in 1842, a second Treaty of Buffalo Creek was drawn up. Under this new and "better" instrument, the U.S. again acknowledged the Haudenosaunee right to reside in New York and restored small areas such as the Allegany and Cattaraugus Seneca reservations. The Onondaga Reservation was also reconstituted on a 7,300-acre landbase, the Tuscarora Reservation on a paltry 2,500 acres. The Ogden Company, for its part, was allowed to keep the rest.[22]

Although the Tonawanda Band of Senecas immediately filed a formal protest of these terms with the Senate, all they received for their efforts was an 1857 "award" of $256,000 of their own money with which to "buy back" a minor portion of their former territory. [23] Ogden, of course, was thus perfectly positioned to reap an extraordinary profit against what it had originally paid the same unwilling "sellers." And so it went, year after year.

So rich were the rewards to be gleaned from peddling Indian land that, beginning in 1855, the Erie Railway Company entered the picture. While the state legislature quickly approved the company's bids to obtain long-term leases on significant portions of both the Cattaraugus and Allegany Reservations, the state judiciary sensed an even greater opportunity. Playing upon the depth of then-prevailing federal enthusiasm for railroad construction, New York's high court justices engaged in a cynical and rather elaborate ploy meant to "persuade" Congress to open the door of legitimation to the full range of the state's illicit leasing initiatives.

Though the [railroad] leases were ratified by New York, the state's supreme court in 1875 invalidated them. In recognition of this action, the New York legislature passed a concurrent resolution that state action was not sufficient to ratify leases because "Congress alone possesses the power to deal with and for the Indians." Instead of setting aside the leases, Congress in 1875 passed an act authorizing [them]. The state now made [all] leases renewable for twelve years, and by an amendment in 1890 the years were extended to ninety-nine. Later the Supreme Court of New York deemed them perpetual.[24]

As a result, by 1889 eighty percent of all Iroquois reservation land in New York was under lease to non-Indian interests and individuals. The same year, a commission was appointed by Albany to examine the state's "Indian Problem." Rather than "suggesting that the appropriation of four-fifths of their land had deterred Indian welfare, the commission criticized the Indians for not growing enough to feed themselves," thereby placing an "undue burden" on those profiting from their land. Chancellor C. N. Sims of Syracuse University, a commission member, argued strongly that only "obliteration of the tribes, conferral of citizenship, and allotment of lands" would set things right.[25]

Washington duly set out to undertake allotment, but was stunned to discover it was stymied by the "underlying title" to much of the reserved Haudenosaunee land it had allowed the Ogden Company to obtain over the years. In 1895, Congress passed a bill authorizing a buy-out of Ogden's interest, again at taxpayer expense, but the company upped its asking price for the desired acreage from $50,000 to $270,000.[26] The plan thereupon collapsed, and the Six Nations were spared the individual/social/political trauma, and the potential of still further land loss, to which they would have been subjected in the allotment process.[27]

Not that the state did not keep trying. In 1900, after uttering a string of bellicosities concerning "backward savages," Governor Theodore Roosevelt created a commission to reexamine the matter. This led to the introduction in 1902 of another bill (HR 12270) aimed at allotting the Seneca reservations—with fifty thousand acres in all, they were by far the largest remaining Iroquois land areas—by paying Ogden $200,000 of the *Indians'* "trust funds" to abandon its claims on Allegany and Cattaraugus.[28]

The Senecas retained attorney John VanVoorhis to argue that the Ogden claim was invalid because, for more than a hundred years, the company had not been compelled to pay so much as a nickel of tax on the acreage it professed to "own." By this, they contended, both Ogden and the government had all along admitted that, for purposes of federal law, the land was really still the property of "Indians not taxed." Roosevelt's bill was withdrawn in some confusion at this point, and allotment was again averted.[29] In 1905, the Senecas carried the tax issue into court in an attempt to clear their land title once and for all, but the case was dismissed on the premise that Indians held no legal standing upon which to sue non-Indians.[30]

Yet a third attempt to allot the Six Nations reservations (HR 18735) foundered in 1914, as did a New York State constitutional amendment, proposed in 1915, to effectively abolish the reservations. Even worse from New York's viewpoint, in 1919 the U.S. Justice Department for the first time acted in behalf of the Haudenosaunee, filing a suit which (re)established a thirty-two-acre "reservation" near Syracuse for the Oneidas.[31]

The state legislature responded by creating yet another commission, this one headed by attorney Edward A. Everett, a political conservative, to conduct a comprehensive study of land title questions in New York and to make recommendations as to how they might be cleared up across-the-board, once and for all.[32] The fix again seemed to be in. After more than two years of hearings and intensive research, however, Everett arrived at a thoroughly unanticipated conclusion: The Six Nations still possessed legal title to all six million acres of the Fort Stanwix treaty area.

> He cited international law to the effect that there are only two ways to take a country away from a people possessing it—purchase or conquest. The Europeans who came here did recognize that the Indians were in possession and so, in his opinion, thus recognized their status as nations... If then, the Indians did hold fee to the land, how did they lose it?... [T]he Indians were [again] recognized by George Washington as a nation at the Treaty of 1784. Hence, they were as of 1922 owners of all the land [reserved by] them in that treaty unless they had ceded it by a treaty equally valid and binding.[33]

In his final report, Everett reinforced his basic finding with references to the Treaties of Forts Harmar and Canandaigua, discounted both Buffalo Creek Treaties as fraudulent, and rejected not only the leases taken by entities such as the Holland and Ogden Companies but those of New York itself as lacking any legal validity at all.[34] The Albany government quickly shelved the document rather than publishing it, but could not prevent its implications from being discussed throughout the Six Nations.

On August 21, 1922, a council meeting was held at Onondaga for purposes of retaining Mrs. Lulu G. Stillman, Everett's secretary, to do research on the exact boundaries of the Fort Stanwix treaty area.[35] The Iroquois land claim struggle had shifted from dogged resistance to dispossession to the offensive strategy of land recovery, and the first test case, *James Deere v. St. Lawrence River Power Company* (32 F.2d 550), was filed on June 26, 1925, in an attempt to regain a portion of the St. Regis Mohawk Reservation taken by New York. The federal government declined to intervene on the Mohawks' behalf, as it was plainly its "trust responsibility" to do, and the suit was dismissed by a district court judge on October 10, 1927. The dismissal was upheld on appeal in April 1929.[36]

Efforts at Land Recovery

Things remained quiet on the land claims front during the 1930s, as the Haudenosaunee were mainly preoccupied with preventing the supplanting of their traditional Longhouse form of government by "tribal councils" sponsored by the Bureau of Indian Affairs via the Indian Reorganization Act of 1934.[37] Probably as a means of coaxing them into a more favorable view of federal intentions under the IRA, Indian Commissioner John Collier agreed towards the end of the decade that his agency would finally provide at least limited support to Iroquois claims litigation.

This resulted, in 1941, in the Justice Department's filing of *U.S. v. Forness* (125 F.2d 928) on behalf of the Allegany Senecas. The suit, ostensibly aimed at eviction of an individual who had refused to pay his $4-per-year rent to the Indians for eight years, actually sought to enforce a resolution of the Seneca Nation canceling hundreds of low-cost, 99-year leases taken in the City of Salamanca on the reservation in 1892. Intervening for the defendants was the Salamanca Trust Corporation, a mortgage institution holding much of the paper at issue. Although the case was ultimately unsuccessful in its primary objective, it did force a judicial clarification of the fact that, in and of itself, New York law had no bearing on leasing arrangements pertaining to Indian land.[38]

This was partly "corrected," in the state view, on July 2, 1948, and September 13, 1950, when Congress passed bills placing the Six Nations under New York jurisdiction in first criminal and then civil matters.[39] Federal responsibility to assist Indians in pursuing treaty-based land claims was nonetheless explicitly preserved.[40] Washington, of course, elected to treat this obligation in its usual cavalier fashion, plunging ahead during the 1950s— while the Indians were mired in efforts to prevent termination of their federal recognition altogether—with the flooding of 130 acres of the St. Regis Reservation near Messena (and about 1,300 acres of the Caughnawaga Mohawk Reserve in Canada) as part of the St. Lawrence Seaway Project.[41]

The government also proceeded with plans to flood more than nine thousand acres of the Allegany Reservation as a byproduct of constructing the Kinzua Dam. Although studies revealed an alternative site for the dam that would not only spare the Seneca land from flooding but better serve "the greater public good" for which it was supposedly intended, Congress pushed ahead.[42] The Senecas protested the project as a clear violation of the Fort Stanwix guarantees, a position with which lower federal courts agreed, but the Supreme Court ultimately declined to decide the question and the Army Corps of Engineers completed the dam in 1967.[43]

Meanwhile, the New York State Power Authority was attempting to seize more than half (1,383 acres) of the Tuscarora Reservation, near Buffalo, as a reservoir for the Niagara Power Project. In April 1958, the Tuscaroras physically blocked access by construction workers to the site, and several were arrested (charges were later dropped). A federal district judge entered a temporary restraining order against the state, but the appellate court ruled that congressional issuance of a license through the Federal Power Commission constituted sufficient grounds for the state to "exercise eminent domain" over native property.[44] The Supreme Court again refused to hear the resulting Haudenosaunee appeal. A "compromise" was then implemented in which the state flooded "only" 560 acres, or about one-eighth of the remaining Tuscarora land.[45]

Ganiekeh

By the early 1960s, it had become apparent that the Six Nations, because their territory fell "within the boundaries of one of the original thirteen states," would not be allowed to seek redress through the Indian Claims Commission.[46] The decade was largely devoted to a protracted series of discussions between state officials and various sectors of the Iroquois leadership. Agreements were reached in areas related to education, housing, and revenue sharing, but on the issues of land claims and jurisdiction, the position of Longhouse traditionals was unflinching. In their view, the state holds *no* rights over the Haudenosaunee in either sphere.[47]

The point was punctuated on May 13, 1974, when Mohawks from the St. Regis and Caughnawaga Reservations occupied an area at Ganiekeh

(Moss Lake), in the Adirondack Mountains. They proclaimed the site to be sovereign Mohawk territory under the Fort Stanwix Treaty—"[We] represent a cloud of title not only to [this] 612.7 acres in Herkimer County but to all of northeastern N.Y."—and set out to defend it, and themselves, by force of arms.[48] After a pair of local vigilantes engaged in shooting at the Indians were wounded by return gunfire in October, the state filed for eviction in federal court. The matter was bounced back on the premise that it was not a federal issue, and the New York attorney general, undoubtedly discomfited at the publicity prospects entailed in an armed confrontation on the scale of the 1973 Wounded Knee siege, let the case die.[49]

The state next dispatched a negotiating team headed by then future, now ex-, Governor Mario Cuomo. In May 1977, partially as a result of Cuomo's efforts but more importantly because of the Indians' obvious willingness to slug it out with state authorities if need be, the "Moss Lake Agreement" was reached. Under its provisions, the Mohawks assumed permanent possession of a land parcel at Miner Lake, near the town of Altona, and another in the nearby McComb Reforestation Area.[50] Mohawk possession of the sites remains ongoing in 1998, a circumstance which has prompted others among the Six Nations to pursue land recovery through a broader range of tactics and, perhaps, with greater vigor than they might otherwise have employed (e.g., Mohawk actions taken in Canada concerning a land dispute at the Oka Reserve, near Montréal, during 1990).[51]

The Oneida Land Claims

As all this was going on, the Oneidas had, in 1970, filed the first of the really significant Iroquois land claims suits. The case, *Oneida Indian Nation of New York v. County of Oneida* (70-CV-35 (N.D.N.Y.)), charged that the transfer of 100,000 acres of Oneida land to New York via a 1795 lease engineered by Governor Clinton was fraudulent and invalid on both constitutional grounds and because it violated the 1790 Trade and Intercourse Act. It was dismissed because of the usual "Indians lack legal standing" argument but reinstated by the Supreme Court in 1974.[52] Compelled to actually examine the merits of the case for the first time, the U.S. District Court agreed with the Indians (and the Everett Report) that title still rested with the Oneidas.

> The plaintiffs have established a claim for violation of the Nonintercourse Act. Unless the Act is to be considered nugatory, it must be concluded that the plaintiff's right of

occupancy and possession of the land in question was not alienated. By the deed of 1795, the State acquired no rights against the plaintiffs; consequently, its successors, the defendant counties, are in no better position.[53]

Terming the Oneidas a "legal fiction," and the lower courts' rulings "racist," attorney Allan Van Gestel appealed on behalf of the defendants to the Supreme Court.[54] On October 1, 1984, the high court ruled against Van Gestel and ordered his clients to work out an accommodation, indemnified by the state, including land restoration, compensation and rent on unrecovered areas.[55] Van Gestel continued to howl that "the common people" of Oneida and Madison Counties were being "held hostage," but as the Oneidas' attorney, Arlinda Locklear, put it in 1986:

> One final word about responsibility for the Oneida claims. It is true that the original sin here was committed by the United States and the state of New York. It is also no doubt true that there are a number of innocent landowners in the area, i.e., individuals who acquired their land with no knowledge of the Oneida claim to it. But those facts alone do not end the inquiry respecting ultimate responsibility. Whatever the knowledge of the claims before then, the landowners have certainly been aware of the Oneida claims since 1970 when the first suit was filed. Since that time, the landowners have done nothing to seek a speedy and just resolution of the claims. Instead, they have as a point of principle denied the validity of the claims and pursued the litigation, determined to prove the claims to be frivolous. Now that the landowners have failed in that effort, they loudly protest their innocence in the entire matter. The Oneidas, on the other hand, have since 1970 repeatedly expressed their preference for an out-of-court resolution of their claims. Had the landowners joined with the Oneidas sixteen years ago in seeking a just resolution, the claims would no doubt be resolved today. For that reason, the landowners share in the responsibility for the situation in which they find themselves today.[56]

Others would do well to heed these words because, as Locklear pointed out, the Oneida case "paved the legal way for other Indian land claims."[57] Not least of these are other suits by the Oneidas themselves. In 1978, the New York Oneidas filed for adjudication of title to the entirety of their Fort Stanwix claim, about 4.5 million acres, in a case affecting not only Oneida and Madison Counties, but Broome, Chenango, Cortland, Herkimer, Jefferson, Lewis, Onondaga, Oswego, St. Lawrence and Tiago Counties as well (the matter was shelved, pending final disposition of the first Oneida claims litigation).[58] Then, in December 1979, the Oneida Nation of Wisconsin and the Thames Band of Southgold, Ontario, joined in an action pursuing rights in the same claim area, but naming the state rather than individual counties as defendant.[59] The Cayuga Nation, landless throughout the twentieth century, has also filed suit against Cayuga and Seneca Counties for recovery of 64,015 acres taken during Clinton's leasing foray of 1789 (the Cayuga claim may develop into an action overlapping with those of the Oneida; see Map 3).[60]

The Cayuga Land Claims

The latter case, filed on November 19, 1980, resulted from attempts by the Cayugas to negotiate some sort of landbase and compensation for themselves with federal, state and county officials from the mid-70s onward. By August 1979, they had worked out a tentative agreement that would have provided them with the 1,852 acre Sampson Park in southern Seneca County, the 3,629-acre Hector Land Use Area in the same county, and an $8 million trust account established by the Secretary of the Interior (up to $2.5 million of which would be used to buy additional land).[61]

Although not one square inch of their holdings was threatened by the arrangement, the response of the local non-Indian population was rabid. To quote Paul D. Moonan, Sr., president of the local Monroe Title and Abstract Company: "The Cayugas have no moral or legal justification for their claim."[62] Wisner Kinne, a farmer near the town of Ovid, immediately founded the Seneca County Liberation Organization (SCLO), a group defined by nothing so much as its propensity to express the most virulent anti-Indian sentiments. SCLO attracted several hundred highly vocal members from the sparsely populated county.[63]

A bill to authorize the settlement subsequently failed due to this "white backlash," and so the Cayugas went to court to obtain a much larger area, eviction of 7,000 county residents and $350 million in trespass damages. Attempts by attorneys for SCLO to have the suit dismissed failed in 1982, as did a 1984 compromise offer initiated by Representative Frank Horton. The latter, which might well have been accepted by the Cayugas, would have provided them with the 3,200-acre Howland Game Management Reserve along the Seneca River, a 2,850-acre parcel on Lake Ontario possessed by the Rochester Gas and Electric Company, and a 2,000-acre parcel adjoining Sampson State Park. Additionally, the Cayugas would have received "well in excess" of the $8 million they had originally sought.[64]

While SCLO appears by this point to have decided that acquiescence might well be the better part of valor, the proposal came under heavy attack

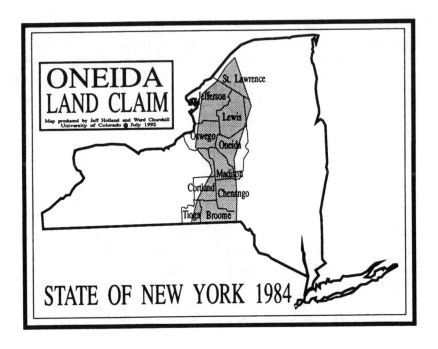

ONEIDA
LAND CLAIM
Map produced by Jeff Holland and Ward Churchill
University of Colorado @ July 1992

St. Lawrence
Jefferson
Lewis
Oswego
Oneida
Madison
Cortland
Chenango
Tioga
Broome

STATE OF NEW YORK 1984

from non-Indian environmentalists and other supposed progressives "concerned about the animals in the Howland Reserve." Ultimately, it was nixed by Ronald Reagan in 1987, not out of concern for local fauna, or even as part of some broader anti-Indian agenda, but because was he angry with Horton for voting against his own proposal to fund the Nicaraguan Contras' low intensity war against that country's Sandinista government.[65] The suit is therefore ongoing.

Salamanca

In the town of Salamanca, to which the leases expired at the end of 1991, the Allegany Senecas also undertook decisive action during the second half of the 1980s. Beginning as early as 1986, they stipulated their intent not only to not renew leasing instruments, but to begin eviction proceedings against non-Indian lease and mortgage holders in the area unless the terms of any new arrangement were considerably recast in their favor. In substance, they demanded clarification of underlying Seneca title to the township, a shorter leasing period, fair rates for property rental, and preeminent jurisdiction over both the land and income derived from it.[66]

A further precondition to lease renewal was that compensation be made for all non-payment and underpayment of fair rental values of Seneca property accruing from the then-existing lease. Although these demands unleashed a storm of protest from local whites, who, as usual, argued vociferously that the Indian owners of the land held no rights to it, the Senecas were successful both in court and in Congress.[67] With passage of the Seneca Nation Settlement Act in 1990, the more essential Seneca demands were met. These included an award of $60 million, with costs borne equally by the federal, state and local governments, to reimburse the Allegany Band for rental monies they should have received in over the past ninety-nine years, but did not.

The Road Ahead

The limited but real gains posted thus far, in both the Oneida land claims and with regard to renegotiation of the Salamanca leases, point to a viable strategy for a gradual recovery of Haudenosaunee land and jurisdictional rights in upstate New York during the years ahead. As of this writing, the second Oneida suit remains in process, as does the Cayuga suit. Based against the sort of settlement achieved in the earlier Oneida win, these seem likely to generate, if not a truly fair resolution of the issues raised, then a marked improvement in the circumstances of both nations.

Also at issue is a long-term lease of Onondaga land upon which the City of Syracuse has been built. Following the pattern evidenced at Salamanca, the Onondagas have been able to secure an agreement in principle with state, local and federal authorities which would both compensate them for lost rental earnings over the past century and generate a much higher level of income in the future. These monies can, in turn, be invested in the restoration of rural areas adjoining the presently tiny Onondaga Reservation to the nation's use and control.

Overall, it seems probable that such efforts at litigation and negotiation will continue over the next ten to twenty years, and thereby serve to enhance the relative positions of the Tuscarora and Mohawk nations as well as their four confederates. The increasing scope of native jurisdiction in New York which such a process would necessarily entail may accomplish a changed sensibility among the state's non-Indian residents, as they discover firsthand that a genuine exercise of indigenous rights does not automatically lead to their disenfranchisement or dispossession of personal property.

Indeed, it may be that at least some sectors of New York's non-Indian population may learn that coming under Indian jurisdiction can be preferable to remaining under the jurisdiction of the state (which has, among other things, one of the highest tax levies in the country). If so, it may be that the ongoing (re)assertion of Haudenosaunee sovereignty within the 1794 treaty territory will develop peacefully and with a reasonably high degree of Indian/white cooperation over the long run, reversing the unrelenting manifestation of Euroamerican avarice, duplicity and racism which has marked this relationship over the past two centuries.

In the alternative, when the methods of litigation and negotiation reach the limit of the state's willingness or ability to give ground—as surely they must, absent a profound alteration in the attitudes of the interloping white populace—conflicts of the sort previewed at Ganiekeh and Oka must be the inevitable result. Something of a crossroads is thus at hand in northern New York State; things could go either way. And in the final analysis, the choice is one which resides with the state and its immigrant citizens. The Haudenosaunee own the land there by all conceivable legal, moral and ethical definitions. They always have, and will continue to until *they* decide otherwise. As a whole, they have demonstrated a remarkable patience with those who have presumed to take what was and is theirs. But such patience cannot last forever.

Notes

1. Jefferson and other "radicals" held that U.S. sovereignty accrued from the country itself and did not "devolve" from the British Crown. Hence, U.S. land title could not devolve from the Crown. Put another way, Jefferson—in contrast to John Marshall—held that Britain's asserted discovery rights in North America had *no* bearing on U.S. rights to occupancy on the continent. See Gordon Wood, *The Creation of the American Republic, 1776-1787* (Chapel Hill: University of North Carolina Press, 1969) pp. 162-96; Merrill D. Peterson, *Thomas Jefferson and the New Nation* (New York: Oxford University Press, 1970) pp. 113-24.

2. The theme is explored by Vine Deloria, Jr., in his essay entitled "Self-Determination and the Concept of Sovereignty," in Roxanne Dunbar Ortiz and Larry Emerson, eds., *Economic Development in American Indian Reservations* (Albuquerque: Native American Studies Center, University of New Mexico, 1979). Also see Walter Harrison Mohr, *Federal Indian Relations, 1774-1788* (Philadelphia: University of Pennsylvania Press, 1933).

3. Barbara Graymont, *The Iroquois in the American Revolution* (Syracuse, NY: Syracuse University Press, 1975). The concern felt by Congress with regard to the Iroquois as a military threat, and the consequent need to reach an accommodation with them, is expressed often in early official correspondence; see Washington C. Ford, et al., eds., *Journals of the Continental Congress, 1774-1789*, 34 vols. (Washington, D.C.: U.S. Government Printing Office, 1904-1937).

4. Henry M. Manley, *The Treaty of Fort Stanwix, 1784* (Rome, NY: Rome Sentinel, 1932). The text of the Fort Stanwix Treaty (7 Stat. 15) as well as that of the Fort Harmar Treaty (7 Stat. 33) will be found in Charles J. Kappler, ed., *Indian Treaties, 1787-1883* (New York: Interland, 1973) pp. 5-6, 23-5.

5. Jack Campisi, "From Fort Stanwix to Canandaigua: National Policy, States' Rights and Indian Land," in Christopher Vescey and William A. Starna, eds., *Iroquois Land Claims* (Syracuse, NY: Syracuse University Press, 1988) pp. 49-65; quote from p. 55.

6. For an account of these meetings, conducted by New York's Governor Clinton during August and September 1784, see Franklin B. Hough, ed., *Proceedings of the Commissioners of Indian Affairs, Appointed by Law for Extinguishment of Indian Titles in the State of New York*, 2 vols. (Albany, NY: John Munsell, 1861) pp. 41-63.

7. Campisi, "Fort Stanwix," op. cit., p. 59. Clinton lied, bold-faced. New York's references to the Genesee Company concerned a bid by that group of land speculators to lease Oneida land which the Indians had not only rejected, but which the state legislature had refused to approve. In effect, the Oneidas had lost *no* land, were unlikely to, and the governor knew it.

8. The leases are covered at various points in *Public Papers of George Clinton: First Governor of New York*, Vol. 8 (Albany, NY: New York State Historical Society, 1904).

9. The price paid by New York for the Onondaga lease was "1,000 French Crowns, 200 pounds in clothing, plus a $500 annuity"; Helen M. Upton, *The Everett Report in Historical Perspective: The Indians of New York* (Albany: New York State Bicentennial Commission, 1980) p. 35.

10. Ibid., p. 38.

11. 1 Stat. 37, also called the "Nonintercourse Act." The relevant portion of the statute reads: "[N]o sale of lands made by any Indians, or any nation or tribe of Indians within the United States, shall be valid to any person or persons, or to any state, whether having the right of pre-emption to such lands or not, unless the same shall be made and duly executed at some public treaty, held under the authority of the United States." See generally, Francis Paul Prucha, *American Indian Policy in the Formative Years: The Trade and Intercourse Acts, 1790-1834* (Lincoln: University of Nebraska Press, 1970).

12. Upton, *The Everett Report*, op. cit., p. 40.

13. For ratification discussion on the meaning of the Treaty of Canandaigua, see *American State Papers: Documents, Legislative and Executive of the Congress of the United States, from the First Session to the Third Session of the Thirteenth Congress, Inclusive*, Vol. 4 (Washington, D.C.: Gales and Seaton, 1832) pp. 545-70. The text of the Canandaiga Treaty (7 Stat. 44) will be found in Kappler, *Indian Treaties*, op. cit., pp. 34-7. On Tecumseh's alliance, see R. David Edmunds, *Tecumseh and the Quest for Indian Leadership* (Boston: Little, Brown, 1984).

14. Paul D. Edwards, *The Holland Company* (Buffalo, NY: Buffalo Historical Society, 1924).

15. For background, see John Sugden, *Tecumseh's Last Stand* (Norman: University of Oklahoma Press, 1985); Allan W. Eckert, *A Sorrow in Our Heart: The Life of Tecumseh* (Boston: Little, Brown, 1992).

16. Henry S. Manley, "Buying Buffalo from the Indians," *New York History*, No. 28, July 1947.

17. For background, see Ronald Satz, *American Indian Policy in the Jacksonian Era* (Lincoln: University of Nebraska Press, 1975); Ernest Downs, "How the East Was Lost," *American Indian Journal*, Vol. 1, No. 2, 1975.

18. A good dose of the rhetoric attending passage of the Removal Act, and thus a glimpse of official sensibilities during the period, will be found in U.S. Congress, *Speeches on the Removal of the Indians, April-May, 1830* (New York: Jonathan Leavitt, 1830; New York: Kraus Reprints, 1973).

19. For text of the Treaty of Buffalo Creek (7 Stat. 550), see Kappler, *Indian Treaties*, op. cit., pp. 502-16. An interesting contemporaneous analysis will be found in Society of Friends (Hicksite), *The Case of the Seneca Indians in the State of New York* (Stanfordville, NY: Earl E. Coleman, 1979 reprint of 1840 original).

20. Most principle leaders of the Six Nations never signed the Buffalo Creek Treaty. Each of the three consecutive votes taken in the Senate on ratification, requiring two-thirds affirmation to be lawful, resulted in a tie, broken only by the "aye" vote of Vice President Richard Johnson; Manley, "Buying Buffalo from the Indians," op. cit.

21. U.S. House of Representatives, H. Doc. 66, 26th Cong., 2d Sess., January 6, 1841.

22. The text of the second Buffalo Creek Treaty (7 Stat. 586) will be found in Kappler, *Indian Treaties*, op. cit., pp. 537-42.

23. The Tonawanda protest appears as U.S. Senate, S. Doc. 273, 29th Cong., 2d Sess., April 2, 1842. On the award, made on November 5, 1857, see *Documents of the Assembly of the State of New York*, 112th Sess., Doc. 51, Albany, 1889, pp. 167-70.

24. Upton, *Everett Report*, op. cit., p. 53. The New York Supreme Court's invalidation of the leases is covered in *U.S. v. Forness*, 125 F.2d 928 (1942). On the court's deeming of the leases to be perpetual, see U.S. House of Representatives, Committee on Indian Affairs, *Hearings in Favor of House Bill No. 12270* (Washington, D.C.: 57th Cong., 2d Sess., 1902).

25 Assembly Doc. 51, op. cit., pp. 43, 408.

26. 28 Stat. 887, Mar. 2, 1895. On the Ogden maneuver, see Upton, *Everett Report*, p. 161.

27. Allotment was a policy designed to supplant the traditional indigenous practice of collective landholding with the supposedly more "civilized" Euroamerican individuated property titles. For a survey of the impacts of the federal government's 1887 General Allotment Act (Ch. 119, 24 Stat. 388) upon native peoples, mostly west of the Mississippi, see Janet A. McDonnell, *Dispossession of the American Indian, 1887-1934* (Bloomington: Indiana University Press, 1991).

28. *Hearings in Favor of House Bill No. 12270*, op. cit. p. 23.

29. Ibid., p. 66.

30. The original case is *Seneca Nation v. Appleby*, 127 AD 770 (1905). It was appealed as *Seneca Nation v, Appleby*, 196 NY 318 (1906).

31. The case, *United States v. Boylan*, 265 Fed. 165 (2d Cir. 1920), is not important because of the negligible quantity of land restored but because it was the first time the federal judiciary formally acknowledged New York had never acquired legal title to Haudenosaunee land. It was also one of the very few times in American history when non-Indians were actually evicted in order that Indians might recover illegally-taken property.

32. New York State Indian Commission Act, Chapter 590, Laws of New York, May 12, 1919.

33. Upton, *Everett Report*, op. cit., p. 99.

34. The final document is Edward A. Everett, *Report of the New York State Indian Commission*, Albany, NY, Mar. 17, 1922 (unpublished). The points mentioned are raised at pp. 308-09, 322-30.

35. Stenographic record of Aug. 21, 1922 meeting, Stillman files; New York State Historical Society, Albany.

36. Upton, *Everett Report*, op. cit., pp. 124-29.

37. Ch. 576, 48 Stat. 948; now codified at 25 U.S.C. 461-279; also referred to as the "Wheeler-Howard Act," in recognition of its congressional sponsors. For a somewhat too sympathetic overview, see Vine Deloria, Jr., and Clifford M. Lytle, *The Nations Within: The Past and Future of American Indian Sovereignty* (New York: Pantheon, 1984).

38. The total amount to be paid the Senecas for rental of their Salamanca property was $6,000 per year, much of which had gone unpaid since the mid-30s. The judges found the federal government to have defaulted on its obligation to regulate state and private leases of Seneca land and instructed it to take an active role in the future. See Hauptman, Laurence M., "The Historical Background to the Present-Day Seneca Nation-Salamanca Lease Controversy," in Vecsey and Starna, *Iroquois Land Claims*, op. cit., pp. 101-22. Also see Arch Merrill, "The Salamanca Lease Settlement," *American Indian*, No. 1, 1944.

39. These laws, which were replicated in Kansas and Iowa during 1952, predate the more general application of state jurisdiction to Indians embodied in Public Law 280, passed in August 1953. U.S. Congress, Joint Legislative Committee, *Report: Leg. Doc. 74* (Washington, D.C.: 83rd Cong., 1st Sess., 1953).

40. This was based on a finding in *United States v. Minnesota* (270 U.S. 181 (1926), s.c. 271 U.S. 648) that state statutes of limitations do not apply to federal action in Indian rights cases.

41. See Jack Campisi, "National Policy, States' Rights, and Indian Sovereignty: The Case of the New York Iroquois," in Michael K. Foster, Jack Campisi and Marianne Mithun, eds., *Extending the Rafters: Interdisciplinary Approaches to Iroquoian Studies* (Albany: State University of New York Press, 1984).

42. For the congressional position and commentary on the independent study of alternative sites undertaken by Dr. Arthur Morgan, see U.S. Senate, Committee on Interior and Insular Affairs, *Hearings Before the Committee on Interior and Insular Affairs: Kinzua Dam Project, Pennsylvania* (Washington, D.C.: 88th Cong., 1st Sess., May-Dec. 1963).

43. For further detail on the struggle around Kinzua Dam, see Lawrence M. Hauptman, *The Iroquois Struggle for Survival: World War II 7o Red Power* (Syracuse, NY: Syracuse University Press, 1986).

44. *Tuscarora Indians v. New York State Power Authority*, 257 F.2d 885 (1958).

45. On the compromise acreage, see Lawrence M. Hauptman, "Iroquois Land Claims Issues: At Odds with the 'Family of New York'," in Vecsey and Starna, *Iroquois Land Claims*, op. cit., pp. 67-86.

46. It took another ten years for this to be spelled out definitively; *Oneida Indian Nation v. United States*, 37 Ind. Cl. Comm. 522 (1971).

47. For a detailed account of the discussions, agreements and various factions within the process, see Upton, *Everett Report*, op. cit., pp. 139-61.

48. Margaret Treur, "Ganiekeh: An Alternative to the Reservation System and Public Trust," *American Indian Journal*, Vol. 5, No. 5, 1979, pp. 22-6. On Wounded Knee, see, e.g., Editors, *Voices from Wounded Knee, 1973* (Mohawk Nation via Rooseveltown, NY: Akwesasne Notes, 1974).

49. *State of New York v. Danny White, et al.*, Civ. No. 74-CV-370 (N.D.N.Y.), April 1976; *State of New York v. Danny White, et al.*, Civ. No. 74-CV-370, Memorandum Decision and Order, 23 Mar. 1977.

50. On the Moss Lake Agreement, see Kwartler, Richard, "'This Is Our Land': Mohawk Indians v. The State of New York," in Robert B. Goldman, ed., *Roundtable Justice: Case Studies in Conflict Resolution* (Boulder, CO: Westview Press, 1980).

51. See Geoffrey York and Loreen Pindera, *People of the Pines: The Warriors and the Legacy of Oka* (Boston: Little, Brown, 1991); Linda Pertusati, *In Defense of Mohawk Land: Ethnopolitical Conflict in Native North America* (Albany: State University of New York Press, 1997).

52. *Oneida Indian Nation of New York v. County of Oneida*, 14 U.S. 661 (1974).

53. *Oneida Indian Nation of New York v. County of Oneida*, 434 F. Supp. 527, 548 (N.D.N.Y. 1979).

54. Allan Van Gestel, "New York Indian Land Claims: The Modern Landowner as Hostage," in Vecsey and Starna, *Iroquois Land Claims*, op. cit., pp. 123-39. Also see the revisions published as "When Fictions Take Hostages," in James E. Clifton, ed., *The Invented Indian: Cultural Fictions and Government Policies* (New Brunswick, NJ: Transaction Books, 1990) pp. 291-312; and "The New York Indian Land Claims: An Overview and a Warning," *New York State Bar Journal*, Apr. 1981.

55. *County of Oneida v. Oneida Indian Nation of New York*, 84 L.Ed.2d 169, 191 (1984).

56. Arlinda Locklear, "The Oneida Land Claims: A Legal Overview," in Vecsey and Starna, *Iroquois Land Claims*, op. cit., pp. 141-53, quote at p. 153.

57. Ibid., p. 148.

58. This suit was later recast to name the state rather than the counties as primary defendant, and enlarged to encompass six million acres. It was challenged, but upheld on appeal; *Oneida Indian Nation of New York v. State of New York*, 691 F.2d 1070 (1982). Dismissed by a district judge four years later (Claire Brennan, "Oneida Claim to 6 Million Acres Voided," *Syracuse Post-Standard*, Nov. 22, 1986), it was

reinstated in by the Second Circuit Court in 1988 (*Oneida Indian Nation of New York v. State of New York*, 860 F.2d 1145), and is ongoing as of this writing.

59. *Oneida Nation of Indians of Wisconsin v. State of New York*, 85 F.D.R. 701, 703 (N.Y.D.C. 1980).

60. New York has attempted various arguments to obtain dismissal of the Cayuga suit. In 1990, the state's contention that it had obtained bona fide land title to the disputed area in leases obtained in 1795 and 1801 was overruled at the district court level (*Cayuga Indian Nation of New York v. Cuomo*, 730 F. Supp. 485). In 1991, an "interpretation" by the state attorney general that reservation of land by the Six Nations in the Fort Stanwix Treaty "did not really" vest recognizable title in them was similarly overruled (*Cayuga Indian Nation of New York v. Cuomo*, 758 F. Supp. 107). Finally, in 1991, a state contention that only a special railroad reorganization would have jurisdiction to litigate claims involving areas leased to railroads was overruled (*Cayuga Indian Nation of New York v. Cuomo*, 762 F. Supp. 30). The suit is ongoing.

61. The terms of the agreement were published in *Finger Lakes Times*, Aug. 18, 1979.

62. Quoted in ibid.

63. Ibid.

64. For further details, see Chris Lavin, "The Cayuga Land Claims," in Vecsey and Starna, *Iroquois Land Claims*, op. cit., pp. 87–100.

65. Ibid.

66. The one jurisdictional exception derives from a 1988 Second Circuit Court ruling that a federal statute passed in 1875 empowers the City of Salamanca, rather than the Senecas, to regulate zoning within the leased area so long as the leases exist (*John v. City of Salamanca*, 845 F.2d 37).

67. The non-Indian city government of Salamanca, a subpart of which is the Salamanca Lease Authority, filed suit in 1990 to block settlement of the Seneca claim as "unconstitutional," and to compel a new 99-year lease on its own terms (*Salamanca Indian Lease Authority v. Seneca Indian Nation*, Civ. No. 1300, Docket 91-7086). They lost and appealed. The lower court decision was affirmed by the Second Circuit Court on Mar 15, 1991, on the basis that the Senecas enjoy "sovereign immunity" from any further such suits.

THE BLACK HILLS ARE NOT FOR SALE
The Lakota Struggle for the 1868 Treaty Territory

> One does not sell the earth upon which the people walk.
>
> —Tesunke Witko (Crazy Horse), 1875

THE defining characteristic of federal-Indian relations since the moment the United States was born has been an insatiable U.S. quest to expropriate native land by any and all means available to it. Prior to the American War of Independence, less than ten percent of the aboriginal land base within what are now the forty-eight contiguous states of the United States had been occupied by the European powers. Between 1787 and 1930, working westward from the original "thirteen colonies" area of the eastern seaboard, the federal government seized approximately ninety percent of all remaining Indian acreage. Much of this land was retained by the government in the form of a sprawling complex of national forests, parks, military bases, and other facilities. The rest was parceled out to a broad variety of corporate clients and the Euroamerican public at large. By 1990, indigenous people inside the United States retained only about two-and-a-half percent of the aggregate land base we enjoyed in 1600. On the basis of such "internal" conquest and ongoing occupation, the United States has projected itself into the posture of a world power.

For our part, American Indians have suffered greatly and consistently in our efforts to hold onto our territories, not infrequently experiencing outright genocide in the process of confronting Euroamerican invaders. Nonetheless, the survivors have persistently sought to recover our homelands, once taken. The pattern has been replicated in hundreds of different settings across the face of North America. Perhaps the best known, and certainly one of the more sustained, of these struggles is that of the Lakota Nation—otherwise known as the "Western Sioux" or "Teton Dakota," composed of the Oglala, Sicungu (Brûlé), Hunkpapa, Minneconjou, Itusipco (Sans Arc), Sihasapa (Blackfeet; not to be confused with the indigenous nation of the same name), and Bohinunpa (Two Kettles) Bands—for the Black Hills Region over the past century. In many ways, the Black Hills Land Claim serves as a lens through which all such Indian-government conflicts can be viewed and more readily understood. Its ultimate outcome will have a wide-ranging impact upon native rights to land and self-determination throughout the United States.

The Treaties of Fort Laramie and the "Great Sioux War"

In 1851, the United States entered into the first Fort Laramie Treaty with the Lakota, Cheyenne, Arapaho, Crow, and other indigenous nations of the northern and central plains regions. In large part, the treaty was an attempt by the federal government to come to grips with the matter of Indian territoriality within the vast "Louisiana Purchase" area it had acquired from France earlier in the century. The Lakota were formally recognized in the 1851 treaty as being entitled to a huge tract centering upon their sacred lands, called Paha Sapa (Black Hills), including virtually all of the present states of South Dakota and Nebraska, as well as appreciable portions of Kansas, North Dakota, Montana, and Wyoming, and a small portion of Colorado. In sum, the U.S. formally recognized Lakota sovereignty and national "ownership" of between six and seven percent of the overall territory now comprising the lower 48 states.[1]

It was not long, however, before gold and silver were discovered in the Virginia City portion of Montana Territory, and a "short route" to these ore fields began to be considered essential to a U.S. economy beset by the demands of the Civil War. Hence, at least as early as 1864, the government entered into open violation of the 1851 treaty, sending troops to construct a series of forts intended to secure what was called the "Bozeman Trail," directly through the western portion of the Lakota homeland. The Lakota, under the political leadership of Red Cloud, an Oglala, responded by forming an alliance with the Cheyenne and Arapaho, bringing their joint military forces to bear upon the trail during the winter of 1866-67. By early 1868, the United States, having suffered several defeats in the field, and finding its troops trapped in their forts, sued for peace.[2]

This led, that same year, to a second Fort Laramie Treaty in which (in exchange for being allowed to withdraw its remaining soldiers in one piece) the federal government once again recognized Lakota sovereignty and national territoriality, this time establishing a "Great Sioux Reservation" encompassing all of contemporary South Dakota west of the east bank of the Missouri River, and acknowledging that the "Greater Sioux Nation" was entitled to permanent use of "Unceded Indian Territory" involving large portions of Nebraska, Wyoming, Montana, and North Dakota.[3] Further, the new treaty committed U.S. troops to prevent non-Indians from trespassing in the Lakota domain, specified that it did nothing to "abrogate or annul" Lakota land rights acknowledged in the 1851 treaty,[4] and provided that:

> No [subsequent] treaty for cession of any portion of the reservation herein described which may be held in common shall be of any validity or force as against said Indians, unless executed and signed by at least three-fourths of all adult male Indians [the gender provision was a U.S., rather than Lakota, stipulation], occupying or interested in the same.[5]

Again, the United States was unwilling to honor the treaty for long. A Catholic priest, Jean de Smet, ventured illegally into the Black Hills and afterwards reported to the *Sioux Falls Times* (South Dakota) that he had discovered gold therein.[6] In short order, this led to the government's reinforcing Lt. Colonel George Armstrong Custer's élite Seventh Cavalry Regiment and violating *both* the 1851 and 1868 treaties by sending this heavy military force directly into the Hills on a "fact-finding" mission. Custer's 1874 report that he too had found gold in the Paha Sapa, much ballyhooed in the eastern press, led to another military foray into the Hills, the Jenny Expedition, during the summer of 1875.[7] The fact that there was gold in the heart of Lakota Territory, in their most holy of places, was thus confirmed to the satisfaction of Washington officials.

With that, the government sent yet another treaty commission to meet with the Lakota leadership, this time in an effort to negotiate purchase of the Black Hills.[8] When the Lakotas refused to sell (as was clearly their right, under either or both treaties), Washington responded by transferring its relations with them from the Bureau of Indian Affairs (BIA) to the Department of War. All Lakotas were ordered to gather at their "assigned agencies" within the Great Sioux Reservation by no later than the end of January 1876, although they plainly had every right to be anywhere they chose within their treaty territory; those who failed to comply with this utterly unlawful federal directive were informed that *they* would be viewed as having "broken the peace" and consequently treated as "hostiles." Meanwhile, President Ulysses S. Grant completed the government's raft of treaty violations by secretly instructing his army commanders to disregard U.S. obligations to prevent the wholesale invasion of the Lakota heartland by non-Indian miners.[9]

Rather than submitting to federal dictates, the Lakotas gathered in the remote Powder River County of southeastern Montana, a part of their unceded territory, to discuss how they should respond. In turn, the army used this "gesture of hostility" as a pretext for launching a massive assault upon them, with the express intent of "crushing Sioux resistance completely, once and for all." The U.S. objective in this was, of course, to simply obliterate any Lakota ability to effectively oppose federal expropriation of the Black Hills. The mechanism chosen to accomplish this task was a three-pronged campaign consisting of some 3,000 troops under Major Generals George Crook (coming into the Powder River Country from the south) and Alfred Terry (from the east). Another thousand men under Colonel John Gibbon were to approach from the west, and the Lakotas (as well as their Cheyenne and Arapaho allies) were to be caught between these powerful forces and destroyed.[10]

The army's plan failed completely. On June 17, 1876, Crook's entire column was met by an approximately equal number of Lakotas led by Crazy Horse, an Oglala. The soldiers were quickly defeated and sent into full retreat.[11] This was followed, on June 25, by the decimation of Custer's Seventh Cavalry, part of Terry's column, in the valley of the Little Big Horn River.[12] For the second time in a decade, the Lakota had successfully defended Paha Sapa, militarily defeating the U.S. Army in what has come to be known as the "Great Sioux War."

On this occasion, however, the victory was to prove bitter. Vengefully licking its wounds after having been unable to best the Indians in open combat, the army imported Colonel Ranald Mackenzie, a specialist who had perfected the craft of "total war" in earlier campaigns against the Kiowas and Comanches on the southern plains of present-day Texas and Oklahoma. The new tactician spent the winter of 1876-77 locating individual Lakota and Cheyenne villages which had been rendered immobile by cold and snow. He then used sheer numbers to overpower each village as it was located, slaughtering women, children, and old people as matter of course.[13] By the

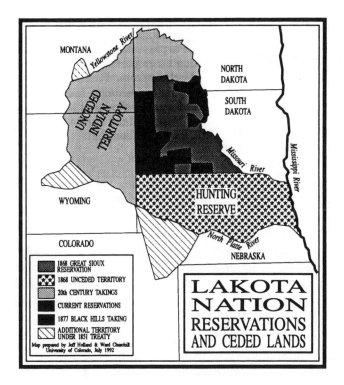

MONTANA

Yellowstone River

NORTH DAKOTA

SOUTH DAKOTA

UNCEDED INDIAN TERRITORY

Missouri River

Mississippi River

WYOMING

HUNTING RESERVE

COLORADO

North Platte River

NEBRASKA

1868 GREAT SIOUX RESERVATION
1868 UNCEDED TERRITORY
20th CENTURY TAKINGS
CURRENT RESERVATIONS
1877 BLACK HILLS TAKING
ADDITIONAL TERRITORY UNDER 1851 TREATY

Map prepared by Jeff Holland & Ward Churchill, University of Colorado, July 1992

LAKOTA NATION RESERVATIONS AND CEDED LANDS

spring of 1877, in order to spare their non–combatants further butchery at the hands of the army, most Lakotas decided it was time to stop fighting. Sitting Bull and Gall, Hunkpapa leaders, took their followers to sanctuary in Canada, not returning until 1881. Having laid down his arms, Crazy Horse, preeminent among Oglala resistance leaders, was assassinated by the military on September 5, 1877, and the era of Lakota defensive warfare was brought to a close.[14]

The Theft of Paha Sapa

Undoubtedly as a result of the military advantage it ultimately gained over the Lakotas during the Great Sioux War, the Congress felt itself empowered to pass an act on February 28, 1877, taking for itself a large portion of the Great Sioux Reservation containing the Black Hills (the Unceded Indian Territory was taken about the same time; see Map I).[15] There is strong evidence that Congress was aware that this act was patently illegal, given that it had effected a slightly earlier measure suspending delivery of subsistence rations, to which the Lakota were entitled, both under their treaties *and* under the Laws of War, until such time as the Indians "gave up their claim over the Black Hills."[16]

In simplest terms, the United States set out deliberately to starve the captive Lakota population into compliance with its plan. Even under these conditions, however, a commission headed up by George Manypenny and sent to obtain the Lakota consent was unable to get the job done. While the 1868 treaty required the agreement of 75 percent of all adult male Lakotas to legitimate any "Sioux Land Cession," Manypenny's commission came away with the signatures of only about ten percent of the Lakota men. Nonetheless, Congress enacted its statute "lawfully" expropriating the Hills.[17]

Over the following two decades, erosion of Lakota sovereignty and land base were exacerbated by imposition of the Major Crimes and General Allotment Acts.[18] The Lakota economy was thus prostrated, and the political process by which the nation had traditionally governed itself was completely subverted. By 1890, despair at such circumstances had reached a level leading to the widespread adoption of the Ghost Dance religion, a belief that the rigorous performance of certain rituals would lead to a return of things as they had been before the Euroamerican invasion. This phenomenon, dubbed an "incipient uprising" by Indian agents, provided the government an excuse to declare a state of military emergency during which Sitting Bull (last of the great recalcitrant leaders) was assassinated at his home near Standing Rock, and some 350 of his followers were massacred along Wounded Knee Creek on what is now the Pine Ridge Reservation.[19] Lakota spiritual practices were then outlawed in general.[20] After that, Washington tended to view the victims as being "thoroughly broken."

During the 1920s and '30s, Lakota sovereignty was diminished even further through imposition, first of the Indian Citizenship Act, and then the Indian Reorganization Act (IRA).[21] The former did much to confuse Lakota national allegiances, engendering a distorted sort of loyalty to the United States among many younger Indians, especially men, desperate to overcome their sense of personal disempowerment. In practice, such "patriotism," common to most colonial systems, has meant Indians being "allowed" to serve in the military of their oppressors, fighting (usually against other peoples of color) and dying as mercenaries and in disproportionate numbers during the Second World War, Korea, and Vietnam. [22]

The IRA was in some ways even more insidious, putting in place a "more democratic and representative" form of "elected council" governance, owing its very existence to federal authority, as a replacement for the popular and consensus-oriented traditional Councils of Elders.[23] As a consequence, divisiveness within Lakota society increased sharply during the 1940s, with "progressives" in the tribal council orbit pitted by Washington directly against the much larger population of grassroots traditionals.[24]

By the mid-1950s, things had deteriorated to such an extent that Congress could seriously consider "termination" (i.e., externally and unilaterally imposed dissolution) of the Lakota Nation altogether.[25] Although, unlike the situation of the Menominees, Klamaths, and a number of other indigenous nations dissolved during the 1950s, the Lakota termination was never ultimately consummated, by 1967 nearly half the "Sioux" population had been removed to city slums—Denver, Minneapolis, Chicago, San Francisco, and Los Angeles were the preferred dumping grounds—through federal relocation programs designed and intended to depopulate the reservations.[26] The degeneration of social cohesion resulting from this policy-generated diaspora has created for the Lakota and other impacted peoples staggering problems that have never been resolved.

Other effects of advanced colonization were almost as devastating: By the contemporary era, the 1868 treaty territory had been reduced to a meager ten percent of its original area and broken up into a "complex" of reservations geographically separating the bands from one another. Of the residual landbase, assertion of BIA leasing prerogatives under a unilaterally assumed federal "trust responsibility" over Lakota property, a matter accommodated within the U.S. doctrine of exercising "plenary [full] power" over Indian affairs, placed more than two-thirds of the most productive reservation acreage in the hands of non-Indian ranchers, farmers, and corporate concerns.[27]

Completely dispossessed of their land and traditional economy, modern Lakotas confront a circumstance on their reservations in which unemployment for Indians has hovered in the ninetieth percentile throughout the past half-century and more.[28] The implications of this situation are both predictable and readily apparent. The poorest county in the United States every year since World War II has been Shannon, on the Pine Ridge Reservation. Todd County, on the adjoining Rosebud Reservation, has kept pace, consistently placing among the ten poorest locales in the federal poverty index.[29]

The Legal Battle

Many Lakotas, of course, never accepted the fact or circumstances of their colonization. Realizing in the wake of the Wounded Knee Massacre that any direct military response to U.S. transgressions would be at best self-defeating, they opted instead to utilize the colonizers' own legal codes—and its pretense of being a "humanitarian power, bound by the laws of civilized conduct"—as a means of recovering what had been stolen from them.[30]

The First Court Case

In 1920, a federal law was passed which "authorized" the Lakotas to sue the government "under treaties, or agreements, or laws of Congress, on the misappropriation of any funds or lands of said tribe or band or bands thereof."[31] The law was hardly altruistic. Realizing that there had been "difficulties" with the manner in which Lakota "consent" had been obtained for the 1877 Black Hills land cession, the government saw the bill as a handy means to buy the now-impoverished Indians off and at last "quiet title" to the Hills. This was amply revealed in 1923 when the Lakotas entered their suit with the federal Court of Claims seeking return of their stolen land rather than the monetary compensation the United States had anticipated would be at issue. Not knowing what to do in the face of this unexpected turn of events, the court stalled for nineteen years, endlessly entertaining motions and countermotions while professing to "study" the matter. Finally, in 1942, when it became absolutely clear the Lakotas would not accept cash in lieu of land, the court dismissed the case, claiming the situation was a "moral issue" rather than a constitutional question over which it held jurisdiction.[32] In 1943, the U.S. Supreme Court refused to even review the claims court decision.[33]

The Claims Commission

The litigational route appeared to be stalemated. But on August 13, 1946, the Indian Claims Commission Act was passed by a Congress anxious to put the best possible face on the government's past dealings with American Indians.[34] Motivation for this accrued from the recently announced U.S. intention of sitting in judgment of the nazi and imperial Japanese leadership for having engaged in "Crimes Against the Peace" (planning and engaging in "aggressive war"), War Crimes, and other "Crimes Against Humanity" (notably, mass forced relocations, slavery, and genocide).[35] Under such circumstances, the federal government wished to present an impeccably moral facade to the world. Section II of the new act defined the bases upon which Indians might sue for lands lost, including:

- Claims in law or equity arising under the Constitution, laws, and treaties of the United States.

- Claims based on fraud, duress, unconscionable consideration, mutual or unilateral mistake, whether of law or of fact, or any other ground recognizable by the court of inquiry.[36]

Recognizing that such language might arguably cover U.S. aquisition of the Black Hills, the Lakotas (re)filed their original Court of Claims case with the Claims Commission in 1950. The Commission, however, opted to view the case as having been "retired" by the 1942 Court of Claims dismissal and subsequent Supreme Court denial of *certiorari*. It likewise dismissed the matter in 1954.[37] The Court of Claims upheld the Commission's decision on appeal from the Lakotas during the same year.[38] Undeterred by this failure of "due process," the Lakotas entered a second (very different) appeal, and in 1958: "[T]he Indian Claims Commission [was] ordered by the Court of Claims to reopen the case on the grounds that the Sioux had previously been represented by inadequate counsel and as a consequence an inadequate record [had] been presented."[39]

In 1961, the U.S. Department of Justice attempted to have the Black Hills case simply set aside, entering a writ of *mandamus* seeking such "extraordinary relief" for the government; the Court of Claims rejected this tactic during the same year. The Claims Commission was thereby forced to actually consider the case. After a long hiatus, the Commission announced that, having "studied the matter," it was reducing the scope of the issue to three elements:

- What land rights were acquired by the U.S. vis-à-vis the Black Hills in 1877?

- What consideration had been given by the U.S. in exchange for these lands?

- If no consideration had been given, had any payment been made by the U.S.?[40]

Proceeding on this basis, the Commission entered a preliminary opinion in 1974 that Congress had been exercising its "power of eminent domain" in 1877, and that it had therefore been "justified" in taking the Black Hills from the Lakotas, although the United States was obligated to pay them "just compensation" for their loss, as provided under the Fifth Amendment to the U.S. Constitution.[41] The opinion denied any right of the Lakotas to recover the land taken from them, and they therefore objected to it quite strongly.

The federal government also took strong exception to the direction things were moving, given its reluctance to pay any large sum of money as compensation for territory it had always enjoyed free of charge. Hence, in 1975, the Justice Department appealed to the Court of Claims, securing a *res judicata* prohibition against the Claims Commission "reaching the merits" of any proposed Lakota compensation package.[42] What this meant, in simplest terms, was that the Commission was to be denied the prerogative of determining and awarding to the Lakotas anything beyond "the value of the land in question *at the time of taking*." The stipulation resulted in the Commission's arriving at an award of $17.5 million for the entire Black Hills, against which the government sought to "offset" $3,484 in rations issued to the Lakotas in 1877.[43]

End Game Moves

The Lakotas attempted to appeal this to the Supreme Court, but the high court of the United States again refused to consider the matter.[44] Meanwhile, arguing that acceptance of compensation would constitute a bona fide land cession, and invoking the 1868 treaty consent clause, the Lakotas themselves conducted a referendum to determine whether three-fourths of the people were willing to relinquish title to Paha Sapa. The answer was a resounding "no."

The unexpected referendum results presented the government with yet another dilemma in its continuing quest to legitimize its theft of Lakota territory; in order to make the best of an increasingly bad situation, Congress passed a bill in 1978 enabling the Court of Claims to "review" the nature and extent of Lakota compensation.[45] This the court did, "revising" the proposed award in 1979 to include five percent simple interest, accruing annually since 1877, adding up to a total of $105 million; added to the original $17.5 million principal award, this made the federal offer $122.5 million.[46]

The Justice Department again attempted unsuccessfully to constrict the amount of compensation the government would be obliged to pay by filing an appeal with the Supreme Court. In 1980, the high court upheld the Claims Court's award of interest.[47] The Lakotas, however, remained entirely unsatisfied. Pointing to a second poll of the reservations conducted in 1979 showing that the people were no more willing to accept $122.5 million than they had been $17.5 million in exchange for the Black Hills, and arguing that return of the land itself had always been the object of their suits, they went back to court. On July 18, 1980, the Oglalas entered a claim naming the United States, the State of South Dakota, and a number of counties, towns, and individuals in the U.S. District Court, seeking recovery of the land per se, as well as $11 *billion* in damages. The case was dismissed by the court on September 12, supposedly because "the issue [had] already been resolved."[48]

In 1981, the U.S. Eighth Circuit Court of Appeals affirmed the district court's dismissal, and, in 1982, the Supreme Court once again declined to hear the resultant Lakota appeal.[49] These decisions opened the way in 1985 for the Court of Claims to finalize its award of monetary compensation as the "exclusive available remedy" for the Black Hills land claim.[50] In sum, further Lakota recourse in U.S. courts had been extinguished by those courts. The game had always been rigged, and the legal strategy had proven quite unsuccessful in terms of either achieving Lakota objectives or even holding the United States accountable to its own professed system of legality.

On the other hand, the legal route did mark solid achievements in other areas: Pursuing it demonstrably kept alive a strong sense of hope, unity, and fighting spirit among many Lakotas that might otherwise have diminished over time. Further, the more than sixty years of litigation had forced a range of admissions from the federal government concerning the real nature of the Black Hills expropriations; the Supreme Court, for example, termed the whole affair a "ripe and rank case of dishonorable dealings" and "a national disgrace." Such admissions went much further toward fostering broad public understanding of Lakota issues than a "one-sided" Indian recounting of the facts could ever have. Cumulatively then, the Lakota legal strategy set the stage for both an ongoing struggle and for public acceptance of a *meaningful* solution to the Black Hills claim.

The Extralegal Battle

It is likely that the limited concessions obtained by the Lakotas from U.S. courts during the 1970s were related to the emergence of strong support for the American Indian Movement (AIM) on Pine Ridge and Rosebud Reservations during the early part of the decade. At the outset, AIM's involvement on Pine Ridge concerned the provision of assistance to local traditional Oglalas attempting to block the illegal transfer of approximately one-eighth of the reservation (the so-called Sheep Mountain Gunnery Range) to the U.S. Forest Service by a corrupt tribal administration headed by Richard Wilson.[51] AIM provided a marked stiffening of the Lakota resolve to pursue land rights by demonstrating a willingness to go toe-to-toe with federal forces on such matters, an attitude largely absent in Indian Country since 1890.

The virulence of the federal response to AIM's "criminal arrogance" in this regard led directly to the dramatic siege of the Wounded Knee hamlet in 1973, a spectacle which riveted international attention on the Black Hills land issue for the first time. In turn, this scrutiny resulted in analysis and an increasingly comprehensive understanding of the vast economic interests underlying federal policy in the region (see Map II). This process steadily raised the level of progressive criticism of the government and garnered further non-Indian support for the Lakota position. Anxious to reassert its customary juridical control over questions of Indian land rights, the government engaged in what amounted to a counterinsurgency war against AIM and its traditional Pine Ridge supporters from 1973 to 1976.[52]

By the latter year, however, it was a bit too late to effectively contain AIM's application of external pressure to the U.S. judicial system. In 1974, the Lakota elders had convened a treaty conference on the Standing Rock Reservation and charged Oglala Lakota AIM leader Russell Means with taking the 1868 Fort Laramie Treaty "before the family of nations."[53] Means therefor formed AIM's "diplomatic arm," the International Indian Treaty Council (IITC) and set about achieving a presence within the United Nations, not only for the Lakotas, but for all the indigenous peoples of the Western Hemisphere. IITC accomplished this in 1977—largely on the basis of the work of its first director, a Cherokee named Jimmie Durham—when delegations from 98 American Indian nations were allowed to make presentations before a subcommission of the U.N. Commission on Human Rights

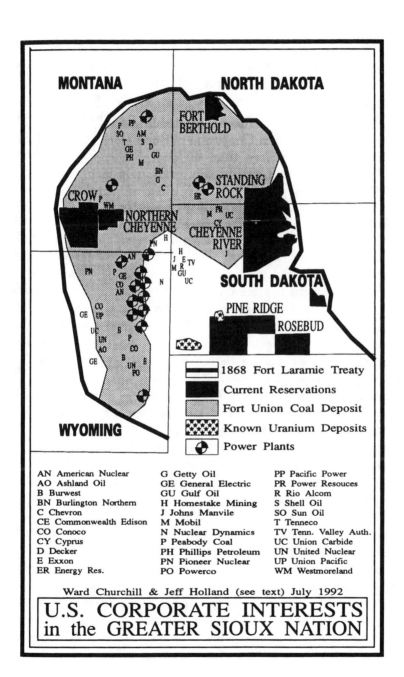

MONTANA

NORTH DAKOTA

FORT BERTHOLD

CROW

NORTHERN CHEYENNE

STANDING ROCK

CHEYENNE RIVER

SOUTH DAKOTA

PINE RIDGE

ROSEBUD

WYOMING

1868 Fort Laramie Treaty

Current Reservations

Fort Union Coal Deposit

Known Uranium Deposits

Power Plants

AN American Nuclear	G Getty Oil	PP Pacific Power
AO Ashland Oil	GE General Electric	PR Power Resouces
B Burwest	GU Gulf Oil	R Rio Alcom
BN Burlington Northern	H Homestake Mining	S Shell Oil
C Chevron	J Johns Manvile	SO Sun Oil
CE Commonwealth Edison	M Mobil	T Tenneco
CO Conoco	N Nuclear Dynamics	TV Tenn. Valley Auth.
CY Cyprus	P Peabody Coal	UC Union Carbide
D Decker	PH Phillips Petroleum	UN United Nuclear
E Exxon	PN Pioneer Nuclear	UP Union Pacific
ER Energy Res.	PO Powerco	WM Westmoreland

Ward Churchill & Jeff Holland (see text) July 1992

U.S. CORPORATE INTERESTS
in the GREATER SIOUX NATION

at the Palace of Nations in Geneva, Switzerland.[54]

In 1981, the United Nations reacted to what it had heard by establishing a Working Group on Indigenous Population, lodged under the United Nations Economic and Social Council (ECOSOC), an entity dedicated to the formulation of international law concerning the rights and status of indigenous nations vis-à-vis the various nation-states which had subsumed them.[55] The regularized series of hearings integral to working group procedure provided an international forum within which American Indians and other indigenous peoples from Australia, New Zealand, Polynesia, and Micronesia could formally articulate the basis of their national rights and the effects of governmental abridgment of these rights.[56]

By the late 1980s, the working group had completed a global study of the conditions under which indigenous peoples were forced to live, and had commissioned a comprehensive study of the treaty relationships existing between nation-states and various native nations.[57] The stated objective of the working group has become the eventual promulgation of a "Universal Declaration of Indigenous Rights" (originally scheduled for submission to the U.N. General Assembly in 1992), holding the same legal and moral force as the Universal Declaration of Human Rights, the 1948 Convention on Prevention and Punishment of the Crime of Genocide, assorted Geneva Conventions, and other elements of international law.[58]

The result of this international approach was to deny the United States the veil of secrecy behind which it had conducted its Indian affairs as a purely "internal matter." Exposed to the light of concentrated international attention, the federal government was repeatedly embarrassed by the realities of its own Indian policies and court decisions. As a consequence, federal courts became somewhat more accommodating in the Black Hills case than they might otherwise have been.

Still, when the Lakotas rejected monetary settlement of their land claim in 1979-80, AIM was instrumental in forging the popular slogan "The Black Hills Are Not For Sale." This was again coupled with direct extralegal action when Russell Means initiated an occupation in 1981 of an 880-acre site near Rapid City in the Black Hills (see Map I). This was couched in terms of being "the first step in the physical reoccupation of Paha Sapa." The AIM action again caused broad public attention to be focused upon the Lakota land claim, and precipitated the potential for another major armed clash with federal forces. The latter possibility was averted at the last moment by a federal district judge who, reflecting the government's concern not to become engaged in another "Wounded Knee-type confrontation," issued an order enjoining the FBI and U.S. Marshals Service from undertaking an assault upon the occupants of what was by then called Yellow Thunder Camp.[59]

Under these conditions, the government was actually placed in the position of having to sue the Indians in order to get them to leave what it claimed was U.S. Forest Service property.[60] AIM countersued on the basis that federal land-use policies in the Black Hills violated not only the 1868 treaty, but also Lakota spiritual freedom under the First Amendment to the U.S. Constitution and the American Indian Religious Freedom Act.[61] In 1986, the government was stunned when U.S. District Judge Robert O'Brien ruled in favor of AIM, finding that the Lakotas had every right to the Yellow Thunder site, and that the United States had clearly discriminated against them by suggesting otherwise. The Yellow Thunder ruling was a potential landmark, bearing broad implications for application in other Indian land claims cases in the United States. However, O'Brien's finding was severely undercut by the Supreme Court's "G-O Road Decision" in 1988 and was consequently nullified by the Eighth Circuit Court.[62]

Like the Lakota legal strategy, AIM's course of largely extralegal action has proven insufficient in itself to resolve the Black Hills land claim. Nonetheless, it can be seen to have had a positive bearing on the evolution of litigation in the matter, and it has accomplished a great deal in terms of bringing public attention to and understanding of the real issues involved. In this sense, the legal and extralegal battles fought by Lakotas for Paha Sapa may be viewed as having been, perhaps inadvertently, mutually reinforcing. And, together, these two efforts may have finally created the context in which a genuine solution can finally be achieved.

The Bradley Bill

By the mid-1980s, the image of the United States regarding its treatment of the Lakotas had suffered so badly that a liberal New Jersey senator, Bill Bradley, took an unprecedented step, introducing legislation to Congress which the Lakotas themselves had proposed.[63] With the goal of finally ending the Black Hills "controversy," the draft bill, S. 1453, was proposed to "re-convey" title to 750,000 acres of the Hills currently held by the federal government, including subsurface (mineral) rights, to the Lakotas. Further, it provided that certain spiritual sites in the area would be similarly retitled. These sites, along with some 50,000 of the reconveyed acres, would be designated a "Sioux Park"; the balance of the land returned would be designated a "Sioux Forest."

Additionally, considerable water rights within the South Dakota portion of the 1868 treaty territory would be reassigned to the Lakotas. A "Sioux National Council," drawn from all existing Lakota reservations, holding increased jurisdiction within the whole 8.5 million acres of the 1868 Great Sioux Reservation, would also be established. Timbering and grazing permits, mineral leasing, etcetera, in the Black Hills would be transferred to Lakota control two years after passage of the bill, thus establishing a viable Lakota economic base for the first time in nearly a century. The $122.5 million awarded by the Court of Claims, plus interest accrued since 1980—a total of nearly $300 million—would be disbursed as compensation for Lakotas' historic loss of use of their land rather than as payment for the land itself. Finally, the draft bill posited that it would resolve the Black Hills claim *only*, having no effect on "subsisting treaties." In other words, with satisfactory settlement of the Hills issue in hand, the Lakotas would remain free to pursue resolution of their claims to the 1868 Unceded Indian Territory and the 1851 treaty territory.[64]

Although the Bradley Bill was obviously less than perfect—compensation remained very low, considering that the Hearst Corporation's Homestake Mine *alone* has extracted more than $18 *billion* in gold from the Black Hills since 1877,[65] and the United States and its citizens are left with considerable land and rights in the area to which they were never legally entitled—it represented a major potential breakthrough not only with regard to the Black Hills land claim, but to U.S.-Indian relations far more generally. Although the full Lakota agenda was not met by the bill, it probably came close enough that the bulk of the people would have endorsed it. That, more than anything, was a testament to their own perseverance in struggle in the face of astronomical odds. The bill, however, foundered during the late eighties in the wake of a campaign to "improve" upon it advanced by a rather mysterious individual named Phil Stevens.

Throughout his life, Stevens functioned as a non-Indian, fashioning for himself a highly profitable defense contracting corporation in Los Angeles. Deciding to retire in 1984, he sold his company for an estimated $60 million. Thereupon, he claimed to have "discovered" he was a direct descendant of a noted Lakota leader and to be consumed with a belated passion to "help" his people. In 1986, he began to approach certain disaffected elements on the reservation, arguing that with his federal contacts and "negotiating expertise," he could better not only the monetary compensation portions of the Bradley Bill, increasing reparations to $3.1 billion, but improve upon its jurisdictional provisions as well.[66] He punctuated his points by spreading relatively small quantities of cash around destitute Lakota communities[67] and stipulated that all he needed was to be provided "proper authority"—that is, to be elevated to the nonexistent position of "Great Chief of All the Sioux"—to get the job done.

Resistance to Stevens' posturing was intense in many quarters, especially among those who had worked most unstintingly to bring Bradley's initiative into being. Nonetheless, interest in Stevens' ideas had reached sufficient proportions by early 1988 that Gerald Clifford, chief negotiator and chair of the steering committee opposing Stevens, was compelled to take him to Washington, D.C., to broach his proposals to various key congresspeople.[68] The timing was most inopportune, given that Bradley had, since introducing his bill for a second time on March 10, 1987, been able to secure support for the legislation even from such notoriously anti-Indian senators as Lloyd Meeds (Washington). The chairs of both the House and Senate Interior Committees—Representative Morris Udall (Arizona) and Senator Daniel Inouye (Hawai'i)—had also agreed to serve as cosponsors.

The baleful consequences of Stevens' Washington tour soon became evident. Bradley had no intention of amending his bill to include Stevens' $3.1 billion compensation package or getting caught in the crossfire between competing Sioux factions. With Clifford's reluctant concurrence, Bradley decided to hold his bill in abeyance until the Sioux settled their internal dispute.[69] With the first significant congressional land return initiative in U.S. history thoroughly in tatters, Stevens quickly quit the field, withdrawing his flow of funds to the Lakota communities as well.

Meanwhile, "liberal" South Dakota Senator Tom Daschle capitalized on the situation, founding what he called the "Open Hills Committee," designed to "counter...the long-term campaign...by those who seek to replace the 1980 Supreme Court settlement with a massive land and even more massive money transfer."[70] The committee is chaired by Daschle's close friend David Miller, reactionary "revisionist historian" at Black Hills State University in Spearfish, South Dakota.

> The Open Hills Committee [mainly] riled up what Miller himself described as South Dakota's considerable redneck population, people who would "just as soon load up shotguns" as return any portion of the Hills to the Sioux. In a part of the country where many people thought of Indians either as dirty drunks or crazed militants, the Open Hills Committee had no difficulty recruiting.[71]

In a context of mounting tension between Indians and whites in South Dakota during 1989, Daschle easily teamed up with his fellow senator from South Dakota, Larry Pressler, to secure an agreement from Inouye, by then chair of the Senate Select Committee on Indian Affairs, that there would be "no hearings, mark-ups, or other action" taken on any Black Hills legislation without the express consent of the "South Dakota senatoral delegation."[72] In 1990, Pressler sought to follow up by introducing a resolution which would have required yet another reservation-by-reservation poll of the increasingly desperate Lakotas with regard to accepting the Supreme Court's 1980 cash award as "final resolution of the Black Hills question."[73]

Small wonder that "Clifford [along with many others who question Stevens' story about his ancestry] view the emergence of Stevens' program as an unmitigated disaster, the work not of a savior but of a 'manipulator and salesman,' a gloryhound whose ties to the tribe were at best attenuated."[74] Russell Means, observing that "no provocateur could have done a better job of screwing up the Black Hills land claim," has openly expressed suspicions that Stevens may have been an outright federal agent of some sort, or at least an individual aligned with the opponents of the Lakota land claims.[75] Uncharacteristically, even arch-conservative editor of the *Lakota Times* Tim Giago agrees with Means, describing Stevens as "a ringer, pure and simple."[76]

A Crossroads

In the end, the question becomes whether some version of the Bradley Bill can ever be passed in anything resembling its original form. If so, the Lakotas' long fight for their land, and for their integrity as a nation, will have been significantly advanced. Moreover, a legislative precedent will have been set which could allow other peoples indigenous to what is now the U.S. to begin the long process of reconstituting themselves. This, in turn, would allow the United States itself to begin a corresponding process of reversing some of the worst aspects of its ugly history of colonization and genocide against American Indians. The prospect remains, but it is now only a feeble glimmer of what it was ten years ago. Likely, only a substantial upsurge of non-Indian support for the concept—unlikely, given the typical priorities manifested by even the most progressive sectors of Euroamerica—would now serve to salvage the legislative remedy.

In the alternative, if comparable legislative remedies are rejected, and thus fail to resolve what by any measure is the best known of all Indian land claims in North America, it will be a clear sign that the United States remains unswervingly committed to its longstanding policy of expropriating Indian assets by whatever means are available to it, and to destroying indigenous societies as an incidental cost of "doing business." In that event, the Lakotas will have no real option but to continue their grim struggle for survival, an indication that the future may prove even worse than the past. The crossroads in this sense has already been reached.

Notes

1. The full text of the "Treaty of Fort Laramie with the Sioux, Etc., 1851" (11 Stat. 749), may be found in Charles J. Kappler, *Indian Treaties, 1778-1883* (New York: Interland, 1973) pp. 594-96. Context is well presented in Remi Nadeau, *Fort Laramie and the Sioux* (Lincoln: University of Nebraska Press, 1967).

2. Dee Brown, *Fort Phil Kearny: An American Saga* (Lincoln: University of Nebraska Press, 1971) pp. 184-90. For further background, see LeRoy R. Hafen and Francis Marion Young, *Fort Laramie and the Pageant of the West, 1834-1890* (Lincoln: University of Nebraska Press, 1938).

3. The full text of the 1868 Fort Laramie Treaty (15 Stat. 635) may be found in Kappler, *Indian Treaties*, op. cit., pp. 998-1007. Lakota territoriality is spelled out under Articles 2 and 16. Additional background information may be obtained in George E. Hyde, *Red Cloud's Folk: A History of the Oglala Sioux Indians* (Norman: University of Oklahoma Press, 1937).

4. *1868 Treaty*, Article 17.

5. Ibid., Article 12.

6. William Ludlow, *Report of a Reconnaissance of the Black Hills of Dakota*, U.S. Government Printing Office, Washington, D.C., 1875. More accessibly, see Donald Jackson, *Custer's Gold: The United States Cavalry Expedition of 1874* (Lincoln: University of Nebraska Press, 1966) p. 8.

7. Ibid. Also see Walter P. Jenny's *Report on the Mineral Wealth, Climate and Rainfall and Natural Resources of the Black Hills of Dakota* (Washington, D.C.: 44th Congress, 1st Session, Exec. Doc. No. 51, 1876).

8. This was the "Allison Commission" of 1875. For the most comprehensive account of the Commission's failed purchase attempt, see U.S. Department of Interior, Bureau of Indian Affairs, *Annual Report of the Commissioner of Indian Affairs*, 1875 (Washington, D.C.: U.S. Government Printing Office, 1875).

9. Frank Pommershein, "The Black Hills Case: On the Cusp of History," *Wicazo Sa Review*, Vol IV, No. 1, Spring 1988, p. 19. The government's secret maneuvering is spelled out in a summary report prepared by E. T. Watkins, 44th Congress, 1st Session, Exec. Doc. No. 184, Washington, D.C., 1876, pp. 8-9.

10. Ralph Andrist, *The Long Death: The Last Days of the Plains Indians* (New York: Collier Books, 1964) pp. 276-292.

11. John Trebbel, *Compact History of the Indian Wars*, (New York: Tower Books, 1966) p. 277. More generally, see Evan S. Connell, *Son of the Morning Star: Custer and the Little Big Horn* (San Francisco: North Point Press, 1984).

12. Dee Brown, *Bury My Heart At Wounded Knee: An Indian History of the American West* (New York: Holt, Rinehart and Winston, 1970) pp. 301-10. Also see Mari Sandoz, *The Battle of the Little Big Horn* (New York: Curtis Books, 1966).

13. On the "total war" policy and its prosecution, see Andrist, *The Long Death*, op. cit., p. 297.

14. Brown, *Bury My Heart*, op. cit., p. 312. Also see Mari Sandoz, *Crazy Horse: Strange Man of the Oglalas* (Lincoln: University of Nebraska Press, 1942).

15. 19 Stat. 254 (1877).

16. Act of August 15, 1876, Ch. 289, 19 Stat. 176, 192; the matter is well covered in "1986 Black Hills Hearings on S. 1453, Introduction" (prepared by the office of Senator Daniel Inouye), reproduced in *Wicazo Sa Review*, op. cit., p. 10.

17. Ibid.

18. 18 U.S.C.A. § 1153 (1885) and 25 U.S.C.A. § 331 (1887), respectively. The Allotment Act is often referred to as the "Dawes Act," after its sponsor, liberal Massachusetts Senator Henry M. Dawes.

19. Andrist, *The Long Death*, op. cit., pp. 351-52.

20. Richard Erdoes, *The Sun Dance People: The Plains Indians, Their Past and Present* (New York: Vintage, 1972) p. 174.

21. 8 U.S.C.A. § 140 (a) (2) (1924) and 25 U.S.C.A. 461 (1934), respectively. The IRA is often called the "Wheeler-Howard Act," after its sponsors, Senator Burton K. Wheeler and Congressman Edgar Howard.

22. Tom Holm, "Patriots and Pawns: State Use of American Indians in the Military and the Process of Nativization in the United States," in M. Annette Jaimes, ed., *The State of Native America: Genocide, Colonization and Resistance* (Boston: South End Press, 1992) pp, 345-70. More broady, see Patrick MacRory, *The Fierce Pawns* (Philadelphia: J.B. Lippencott, 1966); Cynthia Enloe, *Ethnic Soldiers: State Security in a Divided Society* (Baltimore: Penguin, 1980).

23. A detailed examination of the IRA and its passage is to be found in Vine Deloria, Jr., and Clifford M. Lytle, *The Nations Within: The Past and Future of American Indian Sovereignty* (Pantheon: Pantheon, New York, 1984).

24. Analysis of such trends may be found in the Committee on Native American Struggles, *Rethinking Indian Law* (New York: National Lawyers Guild, 1982).

25. This would have occurred under House Concurrent Resolution 108 (67 Stat. B132); Vine Deloria, Jr., and Clifford M. Lytle, *American Indians, American Justice* (Austin: University of Texas Press, 1983) pp. 17-18.

26. On the Menominees, see Nicholas C. Peroff, *Menominee DRUMS: Tribal Termination and Restoration, 1954-1974* (Norman: University of Oklahoma Press, 1982). On the Klamath, see Theodore

Stern, *The Klamath Tribe: The People and Their Reservation* (Seattle: University of Washington Press, 1965). For a more general view of U.S. termination/relocation policies and their place in the broader sweep of federal affairs, see Richard Drinnon, *Keeper of Concentration Camps: Dillon S. Myer and American Racism* (Berkeley: University of California Press, 1987).

27. This occurred as a result of an 1891 amendment (26 Stat. 794) to the General Allotment Act providing that the Secretary of the Interior ("or his delegate," meaning the BIA) might lease out the land of any Indian who, in his opinion, "by reason of age or other disability" could not "personally and with benefit to himself occupy or improve his allotment or any part thereof." As Deloria and Lytle observe (*American Indians, American Justice*, op. cit., p. 10): "In effect this amendment gave the secretary of [the] interior almost dictatorial powers over the use of allotments since, if the local agent disagreed with the use to which [reservation] lands were being put, he could intervene and lease the lands to whomsoever he pleased." Thus, by the 1970s, the bulk of the useful land on many reservations in the U.S.—such as those of the Lakota—had been placed in the use of non-Indian individuals or business enterprises, and at *very* low rates.

28. R. Jones, *American Indian Policy: Selected Issues in the 98th Congress* (Washington, D.C.: Issue Brief No. 1B83083, Library of Congress, Governmental Division, [updated version] 2/6/84) pp. 3-4.

29. Department of Health and Human Services, Indian Health Service, *American Indians: A Statistical Profile* (Washington, D.C.: U.S. Government Printing Office, 1988).

30. The language accrues from one of President Woodrow Wilson's many speeches on the League of Nations in the immediate aftermath of World War I.

31. 41 Stat. 738 (1920)

32. *Sioux Tribe v. United States*, 97 Ct. Cl. 613 (1943); this was a thoroughly spurious argument on the part of the court insofar as treaties are covered quite well under Articles I and VI of the U.S. Constitution.

33. *Sioux Tribe v. United States*, 318 U.S. 789 (1943).

34. Ch. 959, 60 Stat. 1049 (1946). An excellent elaboration of the convoluted nature of the Claims Commission's mandate is to be found in Imre Sutton, ed., *Irredeemable America: The Indians' Estate and Land Claims* (Albuquerque: University of New Mexico Press, 1985).

35. A fine exposition on U.S. governmental sensibilities during the period leading up to the implementation of the post-World War II tribunals may be found in Bradley F. Smith, *The Road to Nuremberg* (New York: Basic Books, 1981).

36. 60 Stat. 1049, 23 U.S.C.§70 *et seq.* (1983).

37. *Sioux Tribe v. United States*, 2 Ind. Cl. Comm. (1956).

38. *Sioux Tribe v. United States*, 146 F. Supp. 229 (1946).

39. Inouye, "Introduction," op. cit., pp. 11-12.

40. *United States v. Sioux Nation*, 448 U.S. 371, 385 (1968).

41. *Sioux Nation v. United States*, 33 Ind. Cl. Comm. 151 (1974); the opinion was/is a legal absurdity insofar as congress holds *no* such "power of eminent domain" over the territoriality of *any* other nation.

42. *United States v. Sioux Nation*, 207 Ct. Cl. 243, 518 F. 2d. 1293 (1975).

43. Inouye, "Introduction," op. cit., p. 12.

44. 423 U.S. 1016 (1975).

45. Public Law 95-243, 92 Stat. 153 (1978).

46. *Sioux Nation v. United States*, 220 Ct. Cl. 442, 601 F. 2d. 1157 (1975).

47. 488 U.S. 371 (1980).

48. *Oglala Sioux v. United States* (Cir. No. 85-062) (W.D.N.D. 1980), Sept. 22, 1980.

49. 455 U.S. 907 (1982).

50. *Sioux Tribe v. United States*, 7 Cl. Ct. 80 (1985).

51. Peter Matthiessen, *In the Spirit of Crazy Horse: The Story of Leonard Peltier* (New York: Viking, [2nd ed.] 1991) pp. 425-28. Also see Johansen and Roberto Maestas, *Wasi'chu: The Continuing Indian Wars* (New York: Monthly Review Press, 1979).

52. See my and Jim Vander Wall's *Agents of Repression: The FBI's Secret Wars Against the Black Panther Party and American Indian Movement* (Boston: South End Press, 1988) and the chapter titled "COINTELPRO-AIM" in our *The COINTELPRO Papers: Documents from the FBI's Secret Wars Against*

Dissent in the United States (Boston: South End Press, 1990).

53. This is well-handled in Rex Weyler's *Blood of the Land: The Government and Corporate War Against the American Indian Movement* (Philadelphia: New Society, [2nd ed.] 1992).

54. Durham's work is covered in Vine Deloria, Jr.'s *Behind the Trail of Broken Treaties: An American Indian Declaration of Independence* (Austin: University of Texas Press, 1984) p. 267 Also see the relevant material in Durham's *A Certain Lack of Coherence: Writings on Art and Cultural Politics* (London: Kala Press, 1993) esp. the essays entitled "United Nations Conference on Indians" and "American Indians and Carter's Human Rights Sermons."

55. The United Nations Sub-Commission on Prevention of Discrimination and Protection of Minorities Resolution 2 (XXXIV) of 8 September 1981; endorsed by the Commission on Human Rights by Resolution 1982/19 of 10 March 1982; authorized by ECOSOC Resolution 1983/34 on May 7, 1982.

56. See, e.g., Sadruddin Aga Khan and Hallin Bin Talal, *Indigenous Peoples: A Global Quest for Justice* (London: Zed Books, 1987).

57. As concerns the study of conditions, this is the so-called "Cobo Report," U.N. Doc. E/CN.4/Sub.2/AC.4/1985/WP.5. Much of the Cobo Report's content also appears in Julian Burger, *Report From the Frontier: The State of the World's Indigenous Peoples* (London: Zed Books, 1987).

58. For an overview of the current status of the drafting process, see my "Subterfuge and Self-Determination: Suppression of Indigenous Sovereignty in the 20th Century United States," *Z Magazine*, May 1997.

59. Perhaps the most comprehensive assessment of the meaning of the AIM action during this period may be found in my "The Extralegal Implications of Yellow Thunder Tiospaye: Misadventure or Watershed Action?" *Policy Perspectives*, Vol. 2, No. 2, 1982. Also see the chapter entitled "Yellow Thunder" in Weyler's *Blood of the Land*, op. cit.

60. *United States v. Means, et al.*, Docket No. Civ. 81-5131 (D.S.D., December 9, 1985).

61. P.L. 95-431, 92 Stat. 153 (1978).

62. *Lyng v. Northwest Indian Cemetery Protective Association*, 56 *U.S. Law Week* 4292. For analysis, see Vine Deloria, Jr.'s "Trouble in High Places: Erosion of American Indian Religious Freedom in the United States," in *The State of Native America*, op. cit., pp. 267-87.

63. The bill was drafted by the Black Hills Sioux National Council, nominally headed by Gerald Clifford and Charlotte Black Elk at Cheyenne River.

64. The full text of S. 1453 may be found at p. 3 of *Wicazo Sa Review*, op. cit.

65. On Homestake, see Weyler, *Blood of the Land*, op. cit., pp. 262-3.

66. The figure was apparently arrived at by computing rent on the Black Hills claim area at a rate of eleven cents per acre for 100 years, interest compounded annually, plus $310 million in accrued mineral royalties. Much of the appeal of Stevens' pitch, of course, was that it came much closer to the actual amount owed the Lakotas than that allowed in the Bradley Bill.

67. For instance, he made a cash donation of $34,000 to the Red Cloud School, on Pine Ridge, in 1987.

68. On Pine Ridge, for example, Stevens had attracted support from the influential elder Oliver Red Cloud and his Grey Eagle Society, as well as then-tribal attorney Mario Gonzales. His "plan" was therefore endorsed by votes of the tribal councils on Pine Ridge, Rosebud, and Cheyenne River.

69. Arthur Lazarus, *Black Hills, White Justice: The Sioux Nation versus the United States, 1775 to the Present* (New York: HarperCollins, 1991) p. 424.

70. Quoted in ibid., p. 425.

71. Ibid. Miller offers his outlandish view of Black Hills regional history in *Wicazo Sa Review*, op. cit.

72. Lazarus, *Black Hills, White Justice*, op. cit., p. 425.

73. Ibid. The resolution failed to pass the Senate by a narrow margin.

74. Ibid., p. 424.

75. Russell Means, conversation with the author, April 1991.

76. Tim Giago, statement on National Public Radio, May 1988.

GENOCIDE IN ARIZONA

The "Navajo-Hopi Land Dispute" in Perspective

> Genocide is always and everywhere a political occurrence.
>
> —Irving Louis Horowitz
> *Genocide*

THERE are an estimated twenty to forty billion tons of high grade, low sulfur coal underlying a stretch of Arizona desert known as Black Mesa. Rich veins of the mineral rest so near the surface that erosion has exposed them to sunlight in many places. A veritable stripminer's delight, the situation presents obviously lucrative potentials for the corporate interests presently profiting from America's spiraling energy consumption. The only fly in the ointment of commerce has been the fact that the land which would be destroyed in extracting the "black gold" was until quite recently inhabited by a sizable number of people who would not—indeed, from their perspective, *could* not—leave. This problem has caused the United States government to engage in one of the more cynical and convoluted processes of legalized expropriation in its long and sordid history of Indian affairs.

It all began in the mid–1860s when the army fought "The Kit Carson Campaign," a vicious war designed to eliminate the Diné (Navajo) people of the Southwest as a threat to ranching and mining concerns. The war featured a scorched earth policy directed against such targets as the Diné sheep herds and the peach orchards which had been carefully established over several generations at the bottom of Cañon de Chelly, in northeastern Arizona. The plan was to starve the Indians into submission, and it worked very well. The whole ugly business culminated in 1864 with the forced march of virtually the entire Diné people to a concentration camp at Bosque Redondo, in eastern New Mexico, a desolate place where about half of them died of disease, exposure and starvation in barely two years.[1]

Finally in 1868, intent upon avoiding a scandal concerning its own treatment of a vanquished foe after having executed officers of the Confederate Army for engaging in comparable atrocities against U.S. troops at such prison camps as Andersonville, the government relented and entered into a treaty with the Diné. The instrument formally acknowledged, among other things, the Indians' right to a huge chunk of relatively barren land, mostly in western New Mexico.[2]

Over the next decade, however, it was discovered that much of the new reservation was usable for cattle grazing. Consequently, the government continually "adjusted" the boundaries westward into Arizona until the territory of the Diné completely engulfed that of another people, the Hopi. Still, there was no particular problem in many ways. The Diné, whose economy was based on sheep herding, lived dispersed across the land, while the Hopi, agriculturalists, remained clustered in permanent villages. Conflict was minimal; the two peoples coexisted in a sort of natural balance, intermarrying frequently enough to create an interethnic entity known as the Tobacco Clan.[3]

This began to change in 1882, when President Chester A. Arthur set out to provide a jurisdictional basis for Indian agent J. H. Fleming to assist Mormon missionaries in kidnapping Hopi children ("to educate them"). Quite literally at the stroke of a pen, Arthur carved out a Hopi Reservation within the area already reserved for the Diné. Arbitrarily designated as being a rectangle of one degree longitude by one degree latitude, the new reservation left Moenkopi, a major Hopi village, outside the boundary. Conversely, much Diné pasturage—and about 600 Diné—were contained within the area, a matter supposedly accommodated by wording that it would henceforth be the territory of the Hopi and "such other Indians as the President may select."[4]

For a generation equilibrium was maintained. Then, in 1919, the Standard Oil Company set out to negotiate mineral leases on Diné land. In 1920, the Diné Council of Elders, a traditional mechanism of governance drawn in equal proportions from each of the clans comprising the nation and holding undisputed power in such matters, unanimously rejected the idea. Standard lobbied, and in 1923 federal authorities unilaterally replaced the existing Diné government with a "Grand Council" composed of individuals of U.S. rather than Navajo choosing. Being made up of men compulsorily educated off the reservation rather than of traditionals, and owing their status to the U.S. rather than to the people they ostensibly represented, the new council promptly signed the leasing instruments. Thereafter, it was the only entity recognized by the United States as "legitimately" representing Diné interests.[5]

This experiment was such a success that an idea was shortly hatched to replace *all* indigenous governing bodies with comparably "modern and democratic" ones, based for the most part on models of corporate management. In 1934, with passage of the so-called Indian Reorganization Act (IRA), this concept became law. Native resistance to the IRA varied from place to place, the rule of thumb being that the more acculturated the people, the greater the ease with which it was accepted.[6]

At Hopi, where the traditional Kikmongwe form of government was and is still very much alive, eighty-five percent of all people eligible to vote on the question of reorganization simply refused to participate, boycotting entirely a referendum required to foster the illusion that they had accepted reorganization. As Bureau of Indian Affairs (BIA) employee Oliver LaFarge observed at the time, "there were only 13 people in the [Hopi village of Hotevilla] willing to go to the polls out of a potential voting population of 250, [a spiritual leader] having announced he would have nothing to do with so un-Hopi a thing as a referendum. Here we also see the Hopi method of opposition... [A]bstention of almost the whole village should be interpreted as a heavy opposition vote."[7]

Although much the same situation prevailed in each of the Hopi villages, Indian Commissioner John Collier, the primary architect of reorganization, overcame this "difficulty" by quietly ordering that all abstentions be considered "yes" votes. While such fraud provided an appearance to the press and general public that the Hopis had all but unanimously embraced implementation of the IRA, it did nothing to change the actual results. The fact is that despite their overwhelming rejection of Collier's script, the Hopi were nonetheless hurriedly reorganized, opening a deep schism within their society that has not only never healed, but is in some ways more acute today than it was fifty years ago.[8]

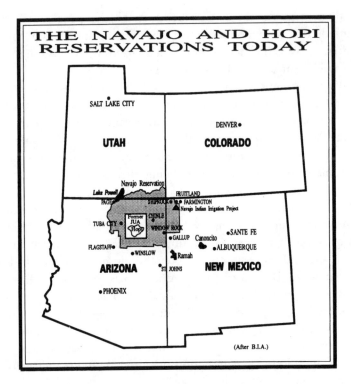

THE NAVAJO AND HOPI
RESERVATIONS TODAY

(After B.I.A.)

Effects of Reorganization

As was noted at the time by La Farge and others, leadership of the ten-to-fifteen percent segment of Hopi society that had been assimilated into non-Hopi values via compulsory education and Mormon indoctrination—this group represented the totality of Hopi voter turnout during reorganization and in all subsequent Hopi "elections"—had long been the station of the Sekaquaptewa family.[9] The men of the family—the brothers Abbott and Emory, later their sons Emory Jr. and Wayne—immediately attained political ascendancy within the new Hopi Tribal Council when it was established in 1936.

As is usually the case where patently imposed forms of governance are utilized by a colonial power to administer a subject people, the new council shortly learned to translate service to the oppressor into personal profit. Correspondingly, by 1938 the Sekaquaptewas had garnered something of a monopoly on incoming U.S. government contracts and concessions, business

138

starts, and the like. Their new wealth was duly invested in a system of patronage among the Mormon Hopis, and this most un-Hopi sector of Hopi society became far and away its richest and most powerful strata. In short order, what had by-and-large remained a remarkably homogeneous and egalitarian culture was thus saddled with the sorts of ideological polarization, class structure and elitism marking Euroamerican "civilization."[10]

Indian Commissioner Collier was meanwhile quite concerned that the concept of reorganization, upon which he had staked his political future and personal credibility, would work in terms of making IRA governments functional, "successful" reflections of mainstream corporate society. The Mormon Hopis were only too happy to oblige in moving Collier's grand scheme along, serving as something of a showpiece in exchange for a quid pro quo arrangement by which they became the only segment of Hopi society with which the U.S. would deal directly. By 1940, the Sekaquaptewas and their followers had converted their alignment with the federal government into control, not only of all Hopi political offices, appointed positions, and budgets, but of the sole Hopi newspaper (*Qua Toqti*), grazing interests, and externally generated cashflow as well. However, they had still bigger plans.

These had emerged clearly by 1943, when the council, in collaboration with the BIA and over strenuous objections from the Kikmongwe, successfully consummated a lobbying effort for the creation of "Grazing District 6," a 650,013-acre area surrounding the main Hopi villages and marked off for "exclusive Hopi use and occupancy." Since nothing in traditional Hopi lifeways had changed to cause them to disperse across the land, the only beneficiaries were the Sekaquaptewa clique, whose grazing revenues were considerably expanded as a result of the establishment of the district. Meanwhile, some one hundred Diné families who had lived on newly defined District 6 land for generations were forced to relocate beyond its boundaries into the remainder of the 1882 Executive Order Area (EOA).[11]

Enter John Boyden

By the early-1950s, with their gains of the forties consolidated and digested, the Sekaquaptewas were once again casting about for ways to expand their clout and income. Following the consolidation of Grazing District 6, they had allowed their council activities to lapse for several years while they pursued personal business enterprises. In 1951, however, they appear to have decided that reconstitution of the IRA government would be an expedient means through which to advance their interests. Given their religious affiliation, it was perhaps natural that they should retain the services of a well-connected Salt Lake City Mormon lawyer named John Boyden to pursue this end in the name of "Hopi self-governance."[12]

Undoubtedly sensing a potential for immense profitability both for himself and for his church in the move, Boyden accepted the position of Hopi Tribal Attorney. At the top of his list of priorities in doing so, by agreement with the Sekaquaptewas, was an initiative to claim *all* of the EOA in the name of the Hopi IRA government. This he pursued through a strategy of first authoring legislation allowing him to do so, and then pursuing lawsuits such as the *Healing v. Jones* cases, initially before the Indian Claims Commission and then in federal district court.[13]

What was at issue was no longer merely the land, concomitant grazing rights, and the like. By 1955, the full extent of mineral deposits in the Four Corners region were being realized by the U.S. government and corporations.[14] Anaconda, Kerr-McGee, and other energy conglomerates were buying leases and opening uranium mining/milling operations, feeding the guaranteed market established by the ore-buying program of the Atomic Energy Commission. Standard, Phillips, Gulf, and Mobil (among others) were moving in on oil and natural gas properties.[15] The "worthless desert" into which the U.S. had shoved the Indians was suddenly emerging as a resource mecca, and it was felt that the EOA might be a particularly rich locale.

Indications are that Boyden and the Sekaquaptewas originally hoped what might be argued in court as constituting Hopi territory would overlie a portion of the Grants Uranium Belt. This did not pan out, however, and royalties (as well as contamination) from the uranium boom continued to accrue only to neighboring peoples such as the Navajo and Laguna Pueblo (see "Geographies of Sacrifice," in this volume). Still, oil exploration proved a more lucrative proposition, and Boyden opened sealed bidding for leasing rights with District 6 during the fall of 1964. The proceeds came to $2.2 million, of which a full million in fees and bonuses was paid to Boyden's Salt Lake City law firm.[16]

The next move was rather more intricate. Enlisting the assistance of a pair of regional politicos—Secretary of the Interior Stewart Udall (a fellow

Mormon) and Colorado Representative Wayne Aspinall, both of whom professed to believe that energy development would be "good for the West"—Boyden was able to set up a triangular mining arrangement between the Navajo and Hopi councils on the one hand, and the Peabody Coal Company (which he also represented) on the other. Not coincidentally, a significant interest in Peabody was held at that time by the Mormon Church, for which he was also serving as legal counsel during the negotiations. Overall, Boyden's personal take on the deal, in which he represented all parties except the Navajos, is said to have again run into seven figures.[17] For him, things were moving right along.

The Nature of the "Land Dispute"

The upshot of the Peabody contract was the company's launching of a massive coal stripping operation on Black Mesa, near the village of Kayenta, along the northern boundary of the EOA. With a long-term moneymaker thus secured for himself and his clients, Boyden returned to his real agenda of locking up their "undivided rights" to both the remaining land and the fossil fuels underlying it. While opening moves in this gambit had been made during the 1950s, the serious campaign really got off the ground during the early seventies. In a major suit, *Hamilton v. Nakai*, he argued that an earlier judicial determination that both the Hopi and Diné were entitled to "equal use and benefit" from the EOA outside of Grazing District 6 meant the Diné had no right to keep livestock in numbers exceeding "their half" of the federally established "carrying capacity" of the land. This held true, he claimed, even if it could be shown that no Hopis were keeping animals in this so-called "Joint Use Area" (JUA).

Boyden was thereby able to obtain court orders requiring a ninety percent reduction in the number of Diné livestock within the JUA.[18] Any such diminishment being tantamount to starvation for a people like the traditional Diné, dependent for subsistence upon a sheep economy, Boyden and the Sekaquaptewas anticipated this courtroom victory would have the effect of driving them out of the area altogether. Then, with virtually no Diné living on the contested land, arguments concerning the exclusivity of Hopi interests and prerogatives would seem much more reasonable.

Here, the Boyden/Sekaquaptewa combination seriously miscalculated the manner in which the Diné would defend themselves. When they simply ignored the court-ordered stock reduction, Boyden was forced into a whole series of related suits, each of them generating additional judicial decrees against the Diné. A "freeze" was placed upon their right to build new homes, corrals, or other structures within the JUA, for example, but none of this in itself accomplished much in terms of forcing them to move.[19] Even more frustrating for Boyden, federal authorities were less than interested in deploying the level of force necessary to implement their courts' various decisions.

And then came the "Energy Crisis" of the 1970s.

Overnight, "energy self-sufficiency" became a national obsession. Shale oil, coal gasification, and other esoteric terminology became household matters of discussion. Congress sat down to do a quick inventory of its known energy assets, and, suddenly, the Black Mesa coal which had barely elicited a yawn from legislators a few months before, became a focus of attention. Arizona superhawks like Senator Barry Goldwater and Representative Sam Steiger in particular saw a way to put their state on the energy map of "national interest" by consummating plans already laid by powerful economic entities such as Western Energy Supply and Transmission (WEST) Associates.[20]

There was only one hitch in the program: it was and is impossible to stripmine land so long as people are living on it. The solution, of course, for the federal government as well as for the Hopi council and the energy corporations, was to remove the people. Hence, as early as 1971, Boyden was successful in offering his services to draft a bill delineating a formal division of the JUA into halves for introduction in the house of representatives.

The plan called for all Hopis living on the Diné side of a partition line to be relocated into Hopi territory and vice versa. Given that virtually no Hopis actually lived in the JUA, the law would serve the purpose of emptying half of the desired acreage of population and thereby open it up for mining.[21] Several scientific studies already suggested that once stripmining and slurry operations began in a substantial portion of Black Mesa, the adjoining areas would be rendered uninhabitable in short order, forcing the Diné off their remaining portion of the EOA.[22] The Boyden/Steiger scheme was thus clearly to use the appearance of an "equitable resolution" of a property rights question as a means to totally dispossess the Diné, accomplishing at last what Boyden and his clients had been trying to do all along.

Steiger dutifully introduced the bill in 1972, but it met with certain public relations problems. After all, the sort of mass forced relocation of indigenous people proposed hadn't occurred in the U.S. since the nineteenth century. While it squeaked through the House by a narrow margin, the bill stalled in the Senate.[23] The fear seems to have been that, energy crisis notwithstanding, the American public might balk at such a policy, a prospect seeming quite likely in the context of the black liberation, antiwar, and other dissident movements then in full flower. Democratic Party presidential nominee George McGovern came out publicly against the idea, and even Goldwater, the archconservative, expressed doubts about its wisdom under such circumstances.[24] A plausible humanitarian cover was needed under which to effect the desired legislation.

Here, Boyden once again proved his mettle. Retaining David Evans & Associates, yet another Mormon-controlled Salt Lake City firm, to handle the "public image of the Hopi Tribe," he oversaw the creation of what was called "the Navajo-Hopi range dispute." Within this scenario, which the Evans public relations people packaged rather sensationally and then fed to the media in massive doses, the Hopis and Diné occupying the JUA were at irreconcilable odds over ownership of the land. The result was a virtual "shooting war" fueled not only by the property rights dispute, but by "deep historical and intercultural animosities." No mention was made of mineral interests or that Evans was simultaneously representing WEST Associates, avid as that consortium was to mine and burn JUA coal. As *Washington Post* reporter Mark Panitch recounted in 1974:

> The relationship between the Hopi council and the power companies became almost symbiotic. On the one hand, [Hopi Tribal Chairman Clarence] Hamilton speeches written by Evans would be distributed through the public relations machinery of 23 major Western utilities [comprising the WEST group]. On the other hand, these utilities would tell their customers, often through local media contacts, that the Hopis were "good Indians" who wouldn't shut off the juice which ran their air conditioners... Because of the efforts by representatives of the Hopi to present the [IRA government's] viewpoint, the Hopi rapidly took on the aura of the underdog who just wanted to help his white brother. Some of the Navajo, on the other hand, were saying threatening things about closing down polluting power plants and requiring expensive reclamation of strip-mined land.[25]

The image of "range war type violence" was carefully reinforced with photographs of out-buildings and junk vehicles abandoned at various locations in the JUA. These were frequently used for target practice by teenaged "plinkers"—a common enough practice throughout rural America—and therefore often riddled with bullet holes. The Evans spin doctors presented their photos to the media as evidence of periodic "firefights" between Hopis and Dinés.

> During 1971-72, few newspapers escaped a Sunday feature on the "range war" about to break out between two hostile tribes. Photos of burned corrals and shot up stock tanks and wells were printed… By calling Evans and Associates, a TV crew could arrange a roundup of trespassing Navajo stock. Occasionally, when a roundup was in progress, Southwestern newsmen would be telephoned and notified of the event.[25]

What real violence there was came mainly from thugs, including a non-Indian named Elmer Randolph, put on the payroll and designated as "Hopi Tribal Rangers" by the IRA régime. Their specialty was beating to a pulp and arresting for trespass any Diné who came to retrieve sheep that had strayed into Grazing District 6.[27] When a group of Diné attempted to erect a fence to keep their livestock off Hopi land, the Sekaquaptewas first called a television crew to the spot and then personally tore the fence down, demanding before the cameras that the Arizona National Guard be dispatched to "restore order" within the JUA. This, too, was passed along by straightfaced news commentators as an indication of "the level of violence existing among the Indians."[28] The federal government was morally obligated, so the argument went, to physically separate the two "warring groups" before there were fatalities.

Predictably, Representative Steiger gave this theme official voice. "There is nothing funny about the violence which has already transpired," he claimed, pointing to "livestock mutilations, corral burnings, fence destruction, water tank burnings, and at least one shooting incident. If we permit ourselves to be seduced into some kind of legal procrastination and someone is killed, I am sure we would assume the responsibility that is patently ours. Let us not wait for that kind of catalyst."[29]

At this juncture, Goldwater, one of the more powerful political figures in the country, decided the time was ripe to weigh in along the Boyden/Sekaquaptewa/Steiger axis. "I have not supported the Steiger approach mostly because it involved money [to relocate the impacted Diné]," the senator announced, "[but now] I do not think we have to pay money to relocate Indians, when in the case of the Navajo they have sixteen million acres [outside the JUA]." He went on to assert with astonishing falsity that the Diné had "literally tens of thousands of acres that are not being used"

144

and therefore available to absorb those displaced by the partition/relocation proposal, ostensibly without significantly altering their way of life.[30]

For his part, Boyden seized the opportunity to draft a new bill, this one to be introduced by Goldwater and Arizona's other senator, Pat Fannin. It called for partition and the rapid, uncompensated and compulsory relocation of all Diné residing within the Hopi portion of the JUA (referred to as "Hopi Partion Lands" or "HPL"). By comparison, the Steiger draft bill, which had called for the federal government to underwrite all costs associated with relocation, including the acquisition of additional lands as needed to resettle those affected, seemed benign.[31]

Relocation Becomes Law

Actually, the Goldwater/Fannin initiative was a PR ruse designed to allow liberal Democrats to counter the bill's harsh proposals with a "gentler" plan of their own. This assumed the form of House Resolution 10337, yet another proposal in which Boyden took a hand, this one introduced by Utah Representative Wayne Owens. It called not only for compensation to the victims of the partition, as the Steiger draft had already done, but a decade-long period during which relocation was to be "phased in" so that those to be moved would not be overly traumatized. Tellingly, when Owens offered his proposition, Steiger promptly abandoned his own and became an endorser of the "Owens Bill." This newly-hatched liberal/conservative coalition was destined to finally produce Boyden's intended result.

Despite a letter sent by Arizona Representative Manuel Lujan that passage of H.R. 10337 might result in "a bloodbath in northern Arizona that would make the My Lai Massacre look like a Sunday School picnic," and that it would in any event be "the most shameful act this government has perpetrated on its citizens since Colonial days," the Owens/Boyden concept was approved by the House Interior Committee by voice vote in February 1974.[32] It was then forwarded to the full house for passage. This was accomplished on May 29, 1974, by a vote of 290 to 38.[33] On the same day, Judge James Walsh issued a contempt of court decree against Chairman Peter McDonald and the Navajo tribal council for having failed to comply with his order to reduce Diné livestock in the JUA.[34]

The bill was passed by the Senate shortly thereafter by a vote of 72 to 0 and in a somewhat different form than it had been approved by the House.

Although this usually precipitates an ad hoc committee meeting involving representatives of both chambers in order to hammer out a mutually acceptable joint version of the legislation, in this instance the House took the extraordinary step of simply approving the Senate's rendering without further discussion.[35] The statute was then routed on an urgent basis to President Gerald R. Ford, who signed it without reading it while enjoying a ski vacation in Vail, Colorado.[36]

Enacted as Public Law 93-531, the statute required a fifty-fifty division of the JUA, with the actual partition boundary to be established by the federal district court in Arizona. It also established a three-member "Navajo-Hopi Relocation Commission," to be appointed by the secretary of the interior. Within two years of the date the court's partition line was defined, the commission was charged with submitting a plan to Congress detailing how relocation was to be accomplished. Thirty days after Congress approved the relocation plan, a five-year period would begin during which relocation would be carried out.[37]

A total of $37 million was initially budgeted, both to underwrite the relocation commission's functioning, and to pay "incentive bonuses" of $5,000 to the head of each Diné family who agreed to relocate voluntarily during the first operational year of the program. Bonuses of $4,000 were slated to be paid to those who agreed to go during the second year, $3,000 during the third, and $2,000 during the fourth. In addition, each family of three or fewer individuals was deemed eligible to receive up to $17,000 with which to acquire "replacement housing." Families of four or more could receive up to $25,000 for this purpose.

Public Law 93-531 also contained several other important provisions. It directed the secretary of the interior to implement Judge Walsh's order for Diné livestock reduction by outright impoundment. It authorized the secretary to sell the Navajo Nation up to 250,000 acres of land under jurisdiction of the Bureau of Land Management at "fair market value," and provided the Navajo tribal council authority to acquire up to 150,000 additional acres of privately held land (this is as opposed to 911,000 acres from which Diné were ordered removed in the JUA).[38] The law also authorized litigation to resolve Hopi claims to land surrounding the village of Moenkopi, left out of the original Executive Order Area.[39]

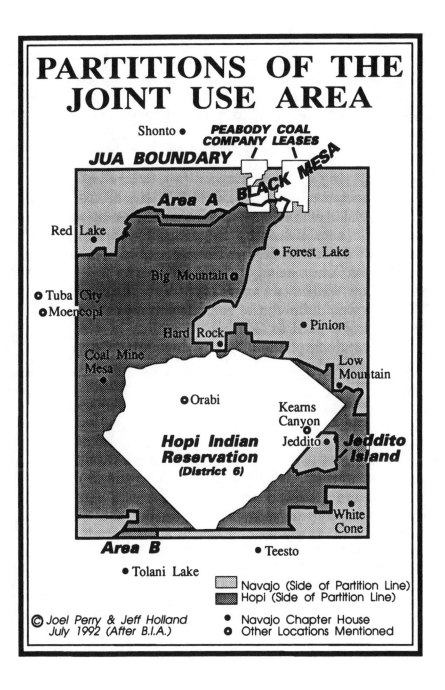

PARTITIONS OF THE JOINT USE AREA

Shonto ●

PEABODY COAL COMPANY LEASES

JUA BOUNDARY

BLACK MESA

Area A

Red Lake ●

● Forest Lake

Big Mountain ⊙

● Tuba City
⊙ Moencopi

● Pinion

Hard Rock ⊙

Low Mountain

Coal Mine Mesa ●

⊙ Orabi

Kearns Canyon

Low Mountain

Jeddito Island

Jeddito ● ⊙

Hopi Indian Reservation
(District 6)

White Cone ●

Area B

● Teesto

● Tolani Lake

☐ Navajo (Side of Partition Line)
■ Hopi (Side of Partition Line)

© *Joel Perry & Jeff Holland*
July 1992 (After B.I.A.)

● Navajo Chapter House
⊙ Other Locations Mentioned

The "Public Law"

The first grit in P.L. 95-531's gears appeared almost immediately, when it became apparent that virtually none of the targeted people were likely to relocate on anything resembling a voluntary basis. The second followed shortly thereafter when it was discovered that the number of Diné subject to relocation had been dramatically underestimated. This was due to language in the act stipulating that the partition would "include the higher density population areas of each tribe within the portion of the lands partitioned to each tribe to minimize and avoid undue social, economic, and cultural disruption insofar as possible." Congress had apparently accepted without question an assertion made by Boyden through Evans and Associates that if this principle were adhered to, the number of impacted Diné would be "about 3,500."[40] There was no reason to assume this information was accurate.

More to the point, when the court's partition line was ultimately finalized on February 10, 1977—this is usually referred to as the "Simkin Line," after federal mediator William Simkin, who actually drew it—it conformed much more closely to coal deposits than to demography.[41] Those areas Peabody preferred to mine first, areas of the northern JUA furthest from the Hopi mesas but adjoining the company's Kayenta operation, were included within the Hopi territory (see map). Consequently, estimates of the number of Diné to be relocated were quickly raised to 9,525 by 1980,[42] and eventually reached 13,500 people overall.[43] Only 109 Hopis were effected, and their relocation was completed in 1976.[44]

Correspondingly, the costs associated with the relocation program escalated wildly. While in 1974, Congress estimated the entire effort could be underwritten through allocation of $28 million in direct costs and another $9 million in "administrative overhead," by 1985 the relocation alone was consuming $4 million per year (having by then cost nearly $21 million in all). With a Diné population vastly larger and more resistant than originally projected, direct costs were by 1985 being projected at a level of "at least $500 million."[45] Similarly, the original 1982 timetable for completing removal of all Diné from the HPL quickly proved impractical. Revised several times, as of 1985 the "wrap-up date" was being projected into 1993.[46]

As all this was coming out, the true magnitude of Goldwater's prevarication about there being "tens of thousands" of idle acres in the Navajo Nation where relocatees could move and continue their traditional lifeways began to emerge. Leaving aside the spiritual significance of specific JUA geography to its Diné residents, it turned out the government's own data indicated the entirety of the reservation, consisting exclusively of arid and semiarid terrain, had been saturated with sheep, and thus with people, since at least as early as the mid-1930s.[47]

Meanwhile, the 400,000 acres of "replacement lands" authorized under P.L. 93-531 for acquisition by the Navajo Nation—"New Lands," as they are now called—as a means of absorbing "surplus" relocatees was blocked by a combination of conflicting congressional interests, a requirement in the law that such land be within eighteen miles of the reservation's boundaries, non-Indian lobbying, and avarice on the part of the Navajo tribal government itself.[48] The result was that relocatees were left with no possible destination other than urban areas representing the very antithesis of their way of life.

Additionally, Congress was forced to concede the inaccuracy of both the "range war" hoax and notions that the Hopis were unified by a desire to see the Diné pushed from any part of the JUA. There was no excuse for its ever having believed otherwise. As early as 1972, Kikmongwe Mina Lansa had come before the House Interior Committee while the Steiger Bill was being considered and made it clear that the traditional Hopi majority wished to see the Diné remain on the land, if for no other reason than because their presence prevented stripmining. She further informed the legislators that:

> The [IRA] council of people, Clarence Hamilton and others say all Hopis are supporting this bill through the newspapers and publicizing to the world that both Hopi and Navajo are going to fight each other. These things are not true, and it makes us very ashamed to see that some of our young people who claim to represent us created much publicity in this way while in this capital lately.[49]

In 1975, Lansa took the unprecedented step, for a Kikmongwe, of openly participating in a largely non-Indian coalition seeking to repeal P.L. 93-531. "We should all work together against Washington to revoke this bill," she said. "The Hopi council favors this bill. But as a Hopi chief, I say no. The Hopis and Navajos can live right where they are."[50] She withdrew her support from the non-Indian group when one of its leaders, Bill Morrall, called for the abolition of both the Hopi and Navajo reservations, per se.[51] However, her opposition to the Hopi IRA government and the re-location law remained outspoken and unswerving. In 1975 and 1976, she and other Hopi spiritual leaders such as David Monongye and Thomas

Banyacya supported suits intended to challenge federal authority to implement policy on the say–so of the Hopi council.[52]

The double-standard of determining "equity" inherent to U.S. legal treatment of indigenous peoples also became increasingly obvious to those scrutinizing the official rationalizations attending relocation policy: Wherever the federal government or its non-Indian citizenry have been shown to be in possession of illegally acquired Indian land, the victims have never been allowed to recover their property. U.S. judicial doctrine has held that they are entitled only to "just compensation," in the form of money, and in an amount determined to be "fair" by those who stole the property in the first place.[53] No white population has ever been relocated in order to satisfy a native land right. Attorney Richard Schifter framed the question plainly and succinctly before the Senate Interior Committee in September 1972.

> Could it be, may I ask, that where the settlers are white, we pay the original owners off in cash; but where the settlers are Indian, we find expulsion and removal an acceptable alternative? Can such a racially discriminatory approach be considered as meeting the constitutional requirement for due process?[54]

Sam Steiger himself made what appears to be the de facto governmental response when he replied that he "would simply tell the gentleman that the distinction between that situation and this one is that in those instances we were dealing with non-Indians occupying and believing they have a right in the lands. Here we are dealing with two Indian tribes. That is the distinction."[55]

Under the circumstances, it should have been manifestly evident to any official willing to look the situation in the face by 1977 that the sort of "minimal" social, economic, and cultural impacts so blithely posited during the hearings leading up to passage of P.L. 93-531 were at best a fiction. Again, there was no excuse for tardy realization. Apart from an abundance of Diné testimony during the congressional deliberation process as to the likely consequences of relocation, anthropologist David Aberle, a consultant retained by the House Subcommittee on Indian Affairs, reported on May 15, 1973, that the outcome would be sociocultural disintegration.

> Remove the sheepherder to a place where he cannot raise stock, remove the herd, and you have removed the foundation on which the family is vested. Demoralization and social disorganization are the inevitable consequences, and the younger people, no longer beneficiaries of a stable home life, become just another addition to the problems of maladjustment and alienation in our society.[56]

Yet the relocation program moved forward.

Impact Upon the Diné

Aberle was hardly the only expert warning that the consequences of P.L. 93-531 would be dire. As early as 1963, sociologists such as Marc Fried had been explaining the high costs of imposed relocation upon various populations.[57] By 1973, anthropologists like Thayer Scudder had also published in-depth studies specifically focusing upon the consequences of forcibly relocating landbased indigenous peoples from rural to urban environments.[58] And, of course, there were the predictions of the Diné themselves. Such augury was coming, not only from the traditionals out on the land, but from younger, college-educated Navajos.[59]

As for the traditionals, they had never been less than unequivocal in their assessment. For instance, Katherine Smith, an elder from the Big Mountain area of the northern JUA, told Senate investigators in 1972 that she would "never leave the land, this sacred place. The land is part of me, and I will one day be part of the land. I could never leave. My people are here, and have been here forever. My sheep are here. All that has meaning is here. I live here and I will die here. That is the way it is, and the way it must be. Otherwise, the people will die, the sheep will die, the land will die. There would be no meaning to life if this happened."[60]

As the relocation program began to come alive, such warnings were borne out. The impact was exacerbated by the tactics used to convince the Diné to "voluntarily" sign up for relocation. High on the list of these was the impoundment of sheep. The day after Judge Walsh signed the order declaring the Simkin Line official, Hopi Tribal Chairman Abbott Sekaquaptewa, who replaced Clarence Hamilton in 1976, ordered a group of his rangers into the HPL to begin seizing every head of Diné livestock they could find. Sekaquaptewa had no legal authority to undertake such action,[61] but a special force of forty SWAT-trained and equipped BIA police were immediately sent in to back him up.[62] This precipitated a crisis in which Walsh formally enjoined the Hopis from going ahead with their stock impoundment program.[63] Sekaquaptewa, seeming "almost eager for a shootout," defied the order and demanded the government "get the army and some machine guns out here, because that's all the Navajos understand."[64]

Rather than arresting Sekaquaptewa for inciting violence and blatant contempt of court, the BIA's operational director in the JUA, Bill Benjamin (Chippewa), attempted to placate him with a plan whereby the Bureau would buy up Diné sheep within the HPL at 150 percent of market rate. This, he argued, would remove many of the offending animals peacefully while providing the Diné with funds to underwrite their move to "their own side of the line." Under provisions of the law, Benjamin had five years in which to complete his stock reduction program; using the buy-out scheme, he was able to secure 67,000 of the estimated 120,000 sheep being herded by Diné on Hopi-partitioned land. At the end of the year, however, the BIA refused to allocate the monies promised to make good on Benjamin's "purchases."

The people who had turned over their animals were, of course, left destitute, while Benjamin was made to appear a liar, destroying the element of trust which the Diné had extended to him. As he himself put it at the time, "Those people are under tremendous strain. They are facing the unknown of relocation, and as their stock is taken away they are losing a way of life. Traditionally, their day was planned around the needs of the flock, and if they needed money they could sell a sheep or two. But as things are now, we can expect a lot of personal and family problems... All I know is that I can't deliver on a promise I made to people in a very difficult situation."[65]

The stock impoundment effort slowed after this, but has been continued at a steady, deliberate and—for the Diné—socially, economically, and psychologically debilitating pace ever since. It has not, however, been the only coercive measure used. Judge Walsh's order making the Simkin Line official also included an instruction renewing the earlier freeze on Diné construction within the HPL, other than with "a permit from the Hopi Tribe."[66] The Hopi council, of course, has issued no such permits and has instead used its rangers to destroy any new structures which have appeared (as well as more than a few older ones). Even repair of existing structures has been attacked as a violation of the building freeze. This has caused a steady deterioration in the living conditions of the targeted Diné, as well as chronic anxiety about whether the very roofs of their hogans might not be simply ripped off from over their heads.[67]

At the same time, those who bowed to the unrelenting pressure and accepted relocation were meeting a fate at least equally as harsh as that being visited upon those who refused. As of March 1984, not a single acre of rural land had been prepared to receive relocatees. For the approximately one-third of all targeted families who had allowed themselves to be moved into cities or towns, "even the Relocation Commission's statistics revealed a problem of tremendous proportions."

> [A]lmost forty percent of those relocated to off-reservation communities no longer owned their government-provided house. In Flagstaff, Arizona, the community which received the largest number of relocatees, nearly half the 120 families who had moved there no longer owned their homes. When county and tribal legal services offices discovered that a disproportionate [number] of the houses had ended up in the hands of a few realtors, allegations of fraud began to surface. Lawsuits were filed by local attorneys; investigations were begun by the United States Attorney's Office, the Federal Bureau of Investigation, the Arizona Department of Real Estate, and the Relocation Commission; and the most in-depth review of the Relocation program which has ever been undertaken by a body of Congress was prepared.[68]

A classic example of what was/is happening is that of Hosteen Nez.

> In 1978, Nez, an 82-year-old relocatee, moved to Flagstaff from Sand Springs. Within a year, Nez suffered a heart attack, could not pay his property taxes or utility bills, lost his $60,000 ranch-style home, and moved back to the reservation [where he also had no home, having relocated from his old one].[69]

By the mid-80s, relocatee reports of increased physical illness, stress, alcoholism, and family breakup were endemic.[70] At least one member of the relocation commission itself had publicly denounced the program as being "as bad as…the concentration camps in World War II," and then resigned his position.[71] A few local editorialists had also begun to denounce the human consequences of P.L. 93-531 in the sharpest terms imaginable.

> [I]f the federal government proceeds with its genocidal relocation of traditional Navajos to alien societies, [the problem] will grow a thousandfold and more… The fact that it is a problem manufactured in Washington does not ease the pain and suffering—nor does it still the anger that fills too many hearts.[72]

Use of the term "genocide" in this connection was by then not uncommon and neither rhetorical nor inaccurate, Scudder and others having already documented the reality of what was being called "the deliberate, systematic, willful destruction of a people."[73] At least two careful legal studies had also arrived at the conclusion that U.S. policy vis-à-vis the JUA Diné violated a broad range of international laws, including the United Nations'

1948 Convention on Prevention and Punishment of the Crime of Genocide.[74]

But still the government moved forward.

Diné Resistance

Resistance to extermination, whether physical or cultural, is a natural and predictable human response. In the case of the JUA Diné, it was foreshadowed in a 1953 statement to Indian Commissioner Philleo Nash by Navajo tribal council member Carl Todacheenie, shortly after the *Healing v. Jones (II)* decision: "The only way the Navajo people are going to move, we know, is they have to have another Bataan Death March. The United States government will have to do that... We're settled out there [in the JUA], and we're not going to advise our people to move, no matter who says. They probably got to chop off our heads. That's the only way we're going to move out of there."[75]

More than two decades later, on March 3, 1977, when Arizona Senator Dennis DeConcini—who had first taken Sam Steiger's seat in the House and then moved up to replace Wayne Owens—attended a meeting of Diné at White Cone, in the southeastern Navajo Partition Area (NPL), he heard exactly the same thing. "Livestock reduction means starvation to us," DeConcini was told by 84-year-old Emma Nelson. "Washington has taken our livestock without replacing it with any other way of making a living." Another area Diné, Chester Morris, was more graphic: "The enforcement of P.L. 93-531 means starvation, homelessness, mentally disturbed [*sic*], alcoholism, family dislocation, crime and even death for many." "This is very emotional," Miller Nez, a local resident, went on, "and at some point I think we're going to resist any further attempt by Washington to take away our only source of support. I think sooner or later there will be killing of individuals."[76]

The Diné were, to be sure, already resisting, and had been for a quarter-century, simply by their refusal to comply with the terms of *Healing v. Jones, Hamilton v. Nakai* and various other judicial decrees. Tension escalated on October 2, 1977, when an elder named Pauline Whitesinger faced down a crew hired by the BIA to erect a barbed wire fence. When the crew began to construct a section of fence bisecting Whitesinger's sheep graze, she told them to stop. When they didn't, she drove her pickup truck straight at them.

They left, but returned the next day and resumed work. This time, she chased them away by throwing handfuls of dirt into their faces. Whitesinger was shortly arrested for "assault," charges, but later acquitted.[77]

Often during the following year-and-a-half, fencing crews showed up for work in the morning only to find the wire and posts they'd laboriously installed the day before had been torn down during the night. During the mid-summer of 1979 a crew set out to fence off the property of elder Katherine Smith, only to find themselves staring into the muzzle of her .22 caliber rifle. She fired over their heads, and, when they scattered, she began dismantling the fence before their eyes. Smith was arrested on serious charges, only to receive a directed verdict of acquittal from a judge responsive to her argument that she had been beside herself with rage in confronting a law she knew to be not only wrong, but immoral.[78]

At about the time Smith was firing her rifle, the American Indian Movement (AIM) was conducting its Fifth International Indian Treaty Council (IITC) at the sacred site of Big Mountain in the northern portion of the HPL. Convened in that location at the request of the Diné elders, the gathering was intended as a means of garnering outside support for what the targeted population expected to be a bitter battle for survival. In the course of the meeting, the elders prepared a statement which read in part, "We do hereby declare total resistance to any effort or influence to be removed from our homes and ancestral lands. We further declare our right to live in peace with our Hopi neighbors."[79]

Traditional Hopi leaders David Monongye and Thomas Banyacya attended the gathering, extending unity and support from the Kikmongwe to the Big Mountain resistance. IITC pledged itself to take the situation before the United Nations.[80] Diné AIM leader Larry Anderson then announced his organization was establishing a permanent survival camp at the council site, located on the property of AIM member Bahe Kadenahe. Anderson also promised to establish a legal defense apparatus to support the resisters as rapidly as possible. This was accomplished by securing the services of Boston attorney Lew Gurwitz to head up what became known as the Big Mountain Legal Defense/Offense Committee (BMLDOC). By 1982, BMLDOC, utilizing funds provided by the National Lawyers Guild (NLG), had opened a headquarters in Flagstaff, the most proximate town of any size to the JUA.[81]

Over the next two years, Gurwitz entered several suits on behalf of individual Diné people suffering the impact of stock impoundment, and began to assemble a legal staff composed primarily of student interns underwritten by the NLG.[82] He also began to organize an external support network for the Big Mountain resistance which at its peak evidenced active chapters in 26 states and several foreign countries.[83] On a related front, BMLDOC put together an independent commission to study the international legal implications of federal relocation policy in the JUA, and collaborated with organizations such as the Washington, D.C.-based Indian Law Resource Center in making presentations to the U.N. Working Group on Indigenous Populations.[84]

The level of physical confrontation also mounted steadily. In 1980, Kadenahe was arrested along with twenty others (dubbed the "Window Rock 21") during a confrontation with BIA police. Charged with several offenses, he was later acquitted on all counts. At about the same time, elder Alice Benally and three of her daughters confronted a fencing crew, were maced, arrested, and each charged with eight federal crimes. They too were eventually acquitted on all counts. The spring of 1981 saw a large demonstration at the Keams Canyon BIA facility which caused Acting Commissioner of Indian Affairs Kenneth Payton to temporarily suspend livestock impoundment operations. In 1983, after livestock reduction had been resumed, Big Mountain elder Mae Tso was severely beaten while physically resisting impoundment of her horses. Arrested and jailed, she suffered two heart attacks while incarcerated. She was ultimately acquitted of having engaged in any criminal offense.[85]

Matters reached a peak during June 1986 as the resisters prepared for the federally established date—July 7 of that year—when outright forced re-location was supposed to begin. The anticipated process involved large units of heavily armed BIA police and U.S. marshals moving into the HPL, physi-cally removing all Diné who had failed to respond to less drastic forms of coercion. BMLDOC managed to bring some 2,000 outside supporters into the contested zone, and AIM made it known that its contribution to defense of the area would likely be "other than pacifistic." The government backed away from the specter of what Gurwitz described as "70-year-old Diné grandmothers publicly engaged in armed combat with the forces of the United States of America."[86]

Rather than suffering the international public relations debacle which would undoubtedly have accompanied an open resort to force of arms, fed-eral authorities opted to engage in a waiting game, utilizing the relentless pressure of stock impoundment, fencing, and the rest to simply wear down the resisters. Their reasoning also seems to have encompassed the likelihood that, absent the sort of head-on government/Indian confrontation implicit to imposition of an absolute deadline, the attention of non-Indian supporters would be difficult or impossible to hold. The defense coalition BMLDOC had so carefully nurtured was thus virtually guaranteed to atrophy over a relatively short term of apparent government inactivity, affording authorities a much greater latitude with which to proceed than they possessed in mid-'86.[87]

In 1988, Big Mountain defense attorney Lee Brooke Phillips, in collaboration with attorneys Roger Finzel and Bruce Ellison, filed a lawsuit, *Manybeads v. United States Government*, in an attempt to take the pressure off the Diné by blocking relocation on the basis of the policy's abridgment of First Amendment guarantees of religious freedom.[88] Although it initially seemed promising, the suit was dismissed by federal District Judge Earl Carroll on October 20, 1989, following the Supreme Court's adverse decision in *Lyng v. Northwest Cemetery Protective Association* (the so-called "G-O Road Case" concerning the rights of indigenous people in northern California to specific geographic areas for spiritual reasons).[89]

Resistance under these conditions adds up more than anything to a continuing refusal to leave the land. By the summer of 1990, approximately half of the Diné originally targeted for relocation under P.L. 93-531 remained where they were at the outset, stubbornly replenishing their flocks despite ongoing impoundments, repairing hogans and corrals in defiance of the building freeze, and conducting periodic forays to dismantle sections of the hated partition line fence.[90]

Liberal Obfuscation

Almost from the moment that it became evident Diné resistance would be a serious reality, the government began a campaign to mask the implications of P.L. 93-531. The first overt attempt along this line occurred in July 1978 when Barry Goldwater responded to a challenge publicly presented by Diné elders Roberta Blackgoat and Violet Ashke during the culmination of AIM's "Longest Walk" in Washington, D.C., the same month. At their invitation, he traveled to Big Mountain to meet with the resisters, but used the occasion to try and confuse the issue by asserting that the relocation act entailed no governmental policy "that says that [the Diné] have to move or what [they] have to do."[91] Even the establishment press responded negatively to such clumsy distortion.[92]

Finding for once that boldfaced lying wouldn't carry him through, Goldwater quietly signaled his colleagues that he would not oppose whatever token gestures might be proposed by congressional liberals to soften the appearance of what was happening. The main weight of this effort fell upon Dennis DeConcini in the Senate and Representative Morris Udall, a Mormon who had already openly sided with the Sekaquaptewas, in the House.[93]

Both lawmakers tendered proposals that would amend P.L. 93-531 to provide "life estates" allowing limited numbers of Diné elders to remain on ninety-acre parcels within the HPL until they died. No provisions were made to allow these selected elders to retain the familial/community context which lent meaning to their lives, to have access to sufficient grazing land to maintain their flocks, or to pass along their holdings to their heirs. In effect, they were simply granted the "right" to live out their lives in impoverished isolation. Not unreasonably, the Diné began in short order to refer to the idea as an offering of "death estates."

Nonetheless, a combination of the DeConcini and Udall initiatives were passed as P.L. 96-305 in 1980.[94] Touted as having "corrected the worst of the problems inherent to P.L. 93-531," the new law immediately became a focus of resistance in its own right. It was generally viewed, as Diné activist Danny Blackgoat put it in 1985, as "a way to divide the unity of the people, setting up struggles between relatives and neighbors over who should receive an 'estate,' and causing those who were offered estates to abandon those who weren't. That way, the resistance would fall apart, and the government would be able to do whatever it wanted." But, as Blackgoat went on to observe, "It didn't work. The people rejected the whole idea, and our struggle actually increased after the 1980 law was passed."[95]

As Diné resistance and outside support mounted with the approach of the government's relocation deadline, the liberals adopted a different strategy. Udall first engineered a February 25, 1986, memorandum of understanding whereby the relocation commission, which was by that point openly admitting it could not meet its goals, would essentially dissolve itself and hand over responsibility for relocation to the BIA. He next secured an agreement from both Ivan Sidney (who had replaced Abbott Sekaquaptewa as Hopi tribal chairman) and Indian Commissioner Ross Swimmer to forego forcible relocation, pending "further legislative remedy of the situation." He then teamed up with Arizona Representative (now Senator) John McCain to introduce "compromise legislation," House Resolution 4281, which would have allowed an exchange of land between Diné and Hopi within the partitioned areas without disturbing the basic premises of P.L. 93-531 in any way at all.[96]

The Udall-McCain bill was already in the process of being rejected by the resistance on the grounds that it accomplished nothing of substance when Goldwater began entering his own objections to the effect that it was time to stop "coddling" the resisters. H.R. 4281 thus died without being put to a vote. This provoked New Mexico Representative Bill Richardson to propose a bill (H.R. 4872) requiring a formal moratorium on forced relocation until the matter might be sorted out. Udall quickly killed this initiative in his capacity as chair of the House Interior and Insular Affairs Committee.[97]

A stalemate of sorts prevailed until 1987 when California Senator Alan Cranston introduced a bill (S. 2452) more-or-less reiterating Richardson's by calling for an eighteen-month moratorium on relocation, pending "further study" and the devising of a resolution "to which all parties might agree." This effort continued in altered form into the early 1990s, officially designated as S. 481, and was cosponsored by Illinois Senator Paul Simon and Colorado Senator Tim Wirth. A lower chamber version of the bill, H.R. 1235, was cosponsored by twenty members of the House.[98]

Meanwhile, with the help of Udall, McCain was able to push through still another different bill (S. 1236) which became P.L. 100-666 in 1989. The statute contained elements of the earlier Udall/McCain land exchange contrivance while requiring that the relocation commission be reactivated and that relocation go forward, to be completed by the end of 1993.[99] In the end, however, this measure proved no more effective in accomplishing the latter objective that had its predecessors.

Finally, in October 1996, Congress approved a so-called Accommodation Agreement, P.L. 104-301, which revamped the 1980 statute's provisions so as to reinstitute "life estates" in the form of long-term leases to much smaller parcels of land.[100] A March 31, 1997, deadline was also stipulated, by which time all Diné remaining in the HPL were either to have signed forms acknowledging Hopi ownership of their property and agreeing to lease it, or indicating their intent to relocate within the near future.

The Hopi Tribe and the U.S. Department of Justice gave the Dineh families remaining on the HPL until March 31 [1997] to sign the Accommodation Agreement in order to stay on what government entities recognize as Hopi Land. By signing the Agreement, the Dineh families are acknowledging Hopi Tribal jurisdiction on the land where they live. They will be subject to provisions of the Agreement as well as Hopi Tribal Ordinances. They may remove their names from the Agreement at any point during a three-year trial period. If they remove their names, they will be told to relocate or face eviction.[101]

On March 26, Ferrell Secakuku, who replaced Ivan Sidney as Hopi Chair, announced that his police, augmented by federal personnel "as need be," would begin forceable removal of any "holdouts" on February 1, 2000.[102] "They have a choice," he said, "to sign a lease to legally stay, or to return to the Navajo Reservation or the New Lands, through the relocation process, or to be considered a trespasser by not signing the Agreement" and, in the latter instance, they will be "dealt with."[103]

The Present Situation

As things stand, it seems unlikely there will be many Diné resisters remaining by the time Secakuku sends out his troops. The cynical federal strategy adopted in 1986 has succeeded all too well. Worn down by the stress, both physical and psychological, attending decades of continuous pressure, and still with no positive outcome anywhere in sight, people had begun to lose hope in droves by 1989.[104] Consequently, the relocation rate has risen sharply during the '90s. By the time the 1997 deadline rolled around, it was estimated that some 12,000 of the original HPL Diné population had already left the area.[105] Of the thousand or so who remained, a number indicated they planned to leave within the year.[106] Among those opting to stay, the heads-of-family at 82 of 96 homesites, including such longtime resisters as Mae Tso, signed the agreement, accepting Hopi ownership of and jurisdiction over their land.[107]

The "hard core" of twenty or so announcing their intention to continue to resist, "no matter what," include Pauline Whitesinger and Roberta Blackgoat. But, like most of the holdouts, both women have reached an age where their ability to sustain such defiance seems doubtful. Indeed, most of their peers among the traditional resisters are already dead, a matter all but precluding any meaningful resurgence of the resistance movement they once galvanized.[108]

As to the recent relocatees, the bulk have ended up in "instant communities" like Nahata Dzil which have been rapidly erected to cluster them on the "New Lands" purchased by the Navajo tribal council along the "I-40 Corridor" in Arizona. There, they have been denied any possibility of reconstructing the way of life they led around Big Mountain. Instead, the old have been systematically marginalized and disemployed while the younger members of their families have been channeled into low-wage menial occupations. As one area activist put it, the latter group now comprises "an indigenous labor force [concentrated by moving it] *en masse* in order to provide cheap labor for industries such as coal, uranium and coal-fired electricity."[109]

By any reasonable estimation, then, those who spoke of genocide during the 1980s have been proven correct. The Big Mountain Diné, who comprised by far the largest remaining enclave of traditional native culture in the U.S. a scant quarter-century ago, have at this point been systematically extinguished as a distinct society.[110] Theirs may have been a "sugar-coated genocide" in comparison to that which has been visited upon other peoples of late—the Aché Indians of Paraguay, for example—but it is genocide nonetheless.[111] Pretending otherwise simply ensures more of the same.[112]

The principle applies equally to ecocide. In early 1989, Peabody Coal requested that the federal Office of Surface Mining (OSM) approve expansion of its mining activities on Black Mesa. Although Peabody had never obtained permits, required by law since 1985, to operate at its already-existing mine sites, the OSM raised no objections to this new application. Instead, it referred the matter for "review" within the framework of an officially commissioned and supposedly objective environmental impact study released on June 2, the same year.[113]

The study is suspect on a number of grounds, not least of which is an assertion that postextraction reclamation of the area to be strip mined will be "100 percent effective." Such a claim is contradicted by the available scientific evidence, although it is customarily advanced by representatives of Peabody Coal.[114] Other problems include inadequate assessments of the effects of water drawdown for increased slurry operations, selenium accumulation, atmospheric pollution, and sociocultural effects. "Lack of available information" is typically cited as a reason for these deficiencies, despite the facts that the missing data are known to exist, and that a number of regional experts were never contacted for their opinions. Although the study allegedly took four years to complete, public response time was restricted by the OSM to sixty days, thus severely limiting the type and quantity of countervailing information submitted.[115]

Hence, while it is true that expanded mining operations in the northern HPL have not yet commenced, all indications are that an official go-ahead for such activity has already been given. This in turn establishes the prospect that the question of residual Diné resistance within the area may ultimately be "resolved" by neither the Hopi rangers nor the resisters' eventual "die out," but by Peabody's simply digging the very ground from beneath their feet. It follows that the whole of Black Mesa will shortly have been converted into what the National Academy of Science has termed "a national sacrifice area in the interests of energy development," an outcome which must foreclose the future of the Hopis as surely as it has the Diné around Big Mountain.[116]

As Roberta Blackgoat put it years ago, "If they come and drag us all away from the land, it will destroy our way of life. That is genocide. If they leave me here, but take away my community, it is still genocide. If they wait until I die and then mine the land, the land will still be destroyed. If there is no land and no community, I have nothing to leave my grandchildren. If I accept this, there can be no Diné, no Hopi, because there will be no land. That is why I will never accept it... I *can* never accept it. I will die fighting this law."[117] Beyond this, there seems nothing left to say.

Notes

1. See Clifford E. Trafzer, *The Kit Carson Campaign: The Last Great Navajo War* (Norman: University of Oklahoma Press, 1982); Gerald Thompson, *The Army and the Navajo: The Bosque Redondo Reservation Experiment, 1863-1868* (Tucson: University of Arizona Press, 1982); Ruth Roessel, ed., *Navajo Stories of the Long Walk* (Tsaile, AZ: Navajo Community College Press, 1973).

2. The full text of the Treaty of 1868, United States-Navajo Nation (15 Stat. 667) will be found in Charles J. Kappler, *Indian Treaties, 1778-1883* (New York: Interland, 1973) pp. 1015-20. For background on the "negotiations" going into this international agreement, see U.S. House of Representatives, Executive Document 263 (Washington, D.C.: 49th Congress, 1st Session, 1868). On Andersonville, see Ovid L. Futch, *The History of Andersonville Prison* (Gainesville: University of Florida Press, 1968).

3. For context, see Clyde Kluckhohn and Dorothea Leighton, *The Navajo* (Cambridge, MA: Harvard University Press, 1948). Also see James F. Downs, *The Navajo* (New York: Holt, Rinehart and Winston, 1972); Frank Waters, *Book of the Hopi* (New York: Viking, 1963). Concerning intermarriage, see *The Tobacco Clan*, a pamphlet circulated by the Big Mountain Legal Defense/Offense Committee, Flagstaff, AZ, *circa* 1984.

4. The Executive Order was signed on Dec. 16, 1882, demarcating an area seventy miles long by fifty-five miles wide, enclosing some 2,472,095 acres. It is estimated that approximately 600 Diné and 1,800 Hopis lived within the demarcated zone at the time the order went into effect. For general history, see Jerry Kammer, *The Second Long Walk: The Navajo-Hopi Land Dispute* (Albuquerque: University of New Mexico Press, 1980). For legal history, see *Healing v. Jones* (II), 210 F. Supp. 125 (D. Ariz 1962); *Hopi Tribe v. United States*, 31 Ind. Cl. Comm. 16 (1973) (Docket 196).

5. See generally, U.S. Department of Justice, Commission on Civil Rights, *The Navajo Nation: An American Colony* (Washington, D.C.: U.S. Government Printing Office, Sept. 1975); R. Allan, "The Navajo Tribal Council: A Study of the American Indian Assimilation Process," unpublished 1983 report available from the *Arizona Law Review*.

6. The Indian Reorganization Act (IRA), 25 U.S.C.A. § 461, is also known as the "Wheeler-Howard Act" after its Senate and House sponsors, Senator Burton K. Wheeler and Representative Edgar Howard. An in-depth analysis of the Act may be found in Vine Deloria, Jr., and Clifford M. Lytle, *The Nations Within: The Past and Future of American Indian Sovereignty* (New York: Pantheon, 1984). Also see Theodore H. Haas, "The Indian Reorganization Act in Historical Perspective," in Lawrence H. Kelly, ed., *Indian Affairs and the Indian Reorganization Act: The Twenty Year Record* (Tucson: University of Arizona Press, 1954).

7. Oliver LaFarge, *Notes for Hopi Administrators* (Washington, D.C.: U.S. Department of Interior, Bureau of Indian Affairs, 1936); quoted in Robert T. Coulter, et al., *Report to the Kikmongwe and Other Traditional Hopi Leaders on Docket 196 and Other Threats to Hopi Land and Sovereignty* (Washington, D.C.: Indian Law Resource Center, 1979) p. 49.

8. The information accrues from Oliver La Farge's *Running Narrative of the Organization of the Hopi Tribe of Indians*, an unpublished study in the La Farge Collection, University of Texas at Austin. Also see Charles Lummis, *Bullying the Hopi* (Prescott, AZ: Prescott College Press, 1968); Jay B. Nash, Oliver La Farge and W. Carson Ryan, *New Day for the Indians: A Survey of the Workings of the Indian Reorganization Act* (New York: Academy Press, 1938).

9. See, e.g., La Farge, *Running Narrative*, op. cit.; Laura Thompson, *A Culture in Crisis: A Study of the Hopi Indians* (New York: Harper, 1950); the relevant chapters in Peter Matthiessen's *Indian Country* (New York: Viking, 1984). For a broader view of the indoctrination process, see David Wallace Adams, *Education for Extinction: American Indians and the Boarding School Experience, 1875-1928* (Lawrence: University Press of Kansas, 1995).

10. Kammer, *Second Long Walk*, op. cit., p. 78. For context, see Helen Sekaquaptewa and Louise Udall, *Me and Mine* (Tucson: University of Arizona Press, 1969); Richard O. Clemmer, *Continuities of Hopi Culture Change* (Ramona, CA: Acoma Books, 1978).

11. Grazing District 6 has an interesting history. It was initially established in 1936 as at the request of the Mormon segment of Hopi society in exchange for their participation in the federally-desired reorganization of Hopi governance. At the time, it was provisionally constituted at 499,248 acres, pending

the results of a U.S. Forest Service study which would fix its "permanent" acreage, based on actual Hopi "need" (210 Fed. Supp. 125 [1962]). In November 1939, the "exclusive Hopi use and occupancy area" was expanded to 520,727 acres, upon the recommendation of Forest Service official C. E. Rachford. This was followed, in 1941, with a plan proposed by Indian Commissioner John Collier, responding to Mormon Hopi demands, to expand the grazing district to 528,823 acres. The Sekaquaptewas rejected the Collier proposal in council, arguing that their continued participation in IRA governance entitled them to more. A second Forest Service study was then commissioned, leading to a recommendation by Forester Willard Centerwall that "final boundaries" be drawn which encompassed what he computed as being 631,194 acres. This was accepted by the Sekaquaptewa faction. A 1965 BIA survey disclosed, however, that Centerwall had noticeably miscalculated; the real acreage encumbered within the final version of Grazing District 6 is actually 650,013; Kammer, *Second Long Walk,* op. cit., pp. 40-1.

12. Boyden was first retained by the Hopi IRA government in 1951 to file a claim for preeminence of Hopi mineral rights over the entirety of the 1882 Executive Order Area. Tellingly, this was done over the direct objections of the traditional Kikmongwe, who had delivered a formal proclamation in 1948 opposing any and all mineral development by their nation. The precipitating factor underlying the traditional position was the earlier issuance of a report by BIA Solicitor General Felix S. Cohen ("Ownership of Mineral Estate in Hopi Executive Order Reservation," U.S. Department of the Interior, Bureau of Indian Affairs, 1946). Very interesting is the fact that Boyden had gone before the Navajo Tribal Council almost as soon as the Cohen report was released, attempting to market his services in securing its interests *against* the Hopis. In late 1951, the Kikmongwe attempted to enter a suit with the Indian Claims Commission which would have blocked Boyden's actions "in their behalf" on the minerals front. The ICC dismissed this suit out of hand in 1955, insofar as the Kikmongwe were not the "federally recognized government" representing the Hopi Nation; Anita Parlow, *Cry, Sacred Land: Big Mountain, U.S.A.* (Washington, D.C.: Christic Institute, 1988) pp. 198-99.

13. The primary initiative was Boyden's authoring of P.L. 85-547, passed by the U.S. Congress in 1958. The statute authorized litigation to resolve conflicting land claims within the 1882 Executive Order Area once and for all. This allowed Boyden to file what is called the *Healing v. Jones* (I) suit (174 F. Supp. 211 [D. Ariz. 1959]), by which he sought to obtain clear title to the entire 1882 parcel for his Mormon Hopi clients. The results of this foray were inconclusive. Hence, Boyden launched the earlier-cited *Healing v. Jones* (II) suit (see Note 4). This failed in 1962 when a special three-judge panel from the U.S. District Court ruled that equal rights applied to both Hopis and Navajos outside of Grazing District 6; the mutually-held territory was proclaimed a "Navajo-Hopi Joint Use Area" (JUA). On appeal, Circuit Judge Frederick Hamley upheld the lower court, observing that, absent a treaty, Hopi held "no special interest" in the disputed area, and that any land rights it might actually possess were subject entirely to the federal "plenary power authority" accruing from the 1903 *Lonewolf v. Hitchcock* decision (187 U.S. 553). Hamley clarified his position as being that both Navajos and Hopis were "no more than tenants" in the Executive Order Area (174 F. Supp. 216). In 1963, the U.S. Supreme Court upheld Hamley's interpretation of the case. For further details, see Richard Schifter and Rick West, "*Healing v. Jones*: Mandate for Another Trail of Tears?" *North Dakota Law Review,* No. 73, 1974; Hollis Whitson, "A Policy Review of the Federal Government's Relocation of Navajo Indians Under P.L. 95-531 and P.L. 96-305," *Arizona Law Review,* Vol. 27, No. 2, 1985.

14. In 1955, the BIA and University of Arizona College of Mines completed a $500,000 joint study of mineral resources on both Diné and Hopi lands, suggesting that extensive coal stripping and concomitant electrical power generation were likely in "the foreseeable future." The three-volume report specifically highlighted Black Mesa in the northern portion of the JUA as holding up to 21 billion tons of low sulfur coal beneath an almost nonexistent overburden of soil. In 1956, an independent study undertaken by geologist G. Kiersch for the Arizona Bureau of Mines (*Metalliferous Minerals and Mineral Fuels, Navajo-Hopi Indian Reservations*) estimated the Black Mesa deposits at nineteen billion tons. By either assessment, the area was seen to hold a rich potential for stripmining.

15. According to the Winter 1965 issue of *Petroleum Today,* there were actually a total of sixteen energy corporations involved at this stage.

16. Oil exploration leases for Grazing District 6 were let by sealed bid during September and October of 1964, generating $984,256 for the top 56 parcels, $2.2 million overall. John Boyden's bill for setting up the leasing procedure was $780,000. The Sekaquaptewas saw to it that he received even more:

a total of $1 million in "fees and bonuses" for "services rendered." Ironically, it turned out there was no oil at all under Grazing District 6; Kammer, *Second Long Walk*, op. cit., pp. 77-8.

17. As a matter of record, John Boyden was a legal representative of Peabody Coal's attempted merger with Kennecott Copper during the very period he was negotiating Peabody's Black Mesa lease on behalf of the Hopi IRA government. The 35-year lease was signed in 1966, giving Peabody access to 58,000 acres sitting atop what the Arizona Bureau of Mines estimated in 1970 were billions of tons of readily accessible low sulfur coal (Note 14). Peabody then opened the Kayenta Mine on the northern edge of the JUA, a location directly impacting only Diné, no Hopis. Its contract allowed the corporation to draw off desert ground water in order to slurry coal 273 miles to Southern California Edison's Mohave Generating Station near Bullhead, Nevada. The Navajo Nation was persuaded by Representative Aspinall, chair of the House Interior Committee and a personal friend of Boyden, to give up rights to some 31,400 acre feet per year in upper Colorado River water—as "compensation" for water used in the Peabody slurry operation—while simultaneously providing right of way for Arizona's Salt River Project to construct a 78 mile rail line from the mine site to its Navajo Power Plant near the town of Page. Udall, whose job as Interior Secretary was to protect *all* Indian interests in the affair, saw to it instead that the complex of agreements were quickly and quietly approved; his motivation may be found in the fact that the Interior Department's Bureau of Reclamation owned a 25 percent interest in the Navajo Power Plant, a matter which figured into the Interior's plan to divert some 178,000 acre feet of the Diné share of Colorado River water to its Central Arizona Project, meeting the needs of the state's non-Indian population. All in all, as an editorial writer in the New Mexico *Gallup Independent* observed on May 14, 1974, the whole thing was "a miserable deal for the Navajo Tribe." The Sekaquaptewas were of course delighted with the transaction and reputedly paid Boyden some $3.5 million from the Hopi share of the Peabody royalties over the years for his skill in "finessing" the situation to their advantage. Meanwhile, the Mormon Church, of which both they and their attorney were members, and for which Boyden was also acting as an attorney, owned an estimated eight percent of Peabody's stock (and a substantial block of Kennecott stock, as well) in 1965. The value of and revenue from the church's Peabody holding nearly doubled during the three years following Boyden's successful participation in the Black Mesa lease initiative. For further information, see Peter Wiley and Robert Gottlieb, *Empires in the Sun: The Rise of the New American West* (New York: Putnam's, 1982). Also see Alvin M. Josephy, Jr., "Murder of the Southwest," *Audubon*, July 1971.

18. *Hamilton v. Nakai* (453 F.2d 152 [9th Cir. 1972]), *cert. denied*, 406 U.S. 945). Boyden introduced a 1964 BIA range-use study indicating that the maximum carrying capacity of the JUA was 22,036 "sheep units." Under provision of the "equal entitlement" stipulations of *Healing v. Jones (II)*, he argued, the Diné were entitled to graze an equivalent of 11,018 sheep units in the JUA. He then introduced a BIA stock enumeration showing that some 1,150 traditional Diné families were grazing approximately 63,000 head of sheep and goats, 8,000 cattle, and 5,000 horses—the equivalent of 120,000 sheep units—a number the court was "compelled" to order reduced by about ninety percent. U.S. District Judge James Walsh concurred and, for reasons which are unclear, established a "cap" on Diné grazing rights at a maximum of 8,139 sheep units. This was/is less than half the land's natural carrying capacity.

19. These suits include *Hamilton v. McDonald* (503 F.2d 1138 [9th Cir. 1974]), *Sekaquaptewa v. McDonald* (544 F. 2d. 396 [9th Cir. 1976]) and *Sidney v. Zah* (718 F.2d 1453 [9th Cir. 1983]).

20. WEST Associates is a consortium of 23 regional utility companies which banded together with the Federal Bureau of Reclamation in 1964 to advance a unified strategy for energy development and profit-making in the Southwest. Members include Arizona Public Service Company, Central Arizona Project, El Paso (TX) Electric, El Paso Natural Gas, Public Service of New Mexico, Southern California Edison, Tucson (AZ) Gas and Electric, the Salt River (AZ) Project, Texas Eastern Transmission Company, Los Angeles (CA) Water and Power, San Diego (CA) Gas and Electric, Nevada Power Company, Utah Power and Light, Public Service Company of Colorado, and Pacific Gas & Electric. The WEST group is closely interlocked with the so-called "Six Companies" which have, since the 1930s, dominated dam construction, mining, and other major development undertakings in the western U.S.; these include Bechtel, Kaiser, Utah International, Utah Construction and Mining, MacDonald-Kahn, and Morrison-Knudson. And, of course, the ripples go much further. For example, in 1977 Bechtel was a key player in a consortium including Newmont Mining, the Williams Company, Boeing, Fluor, and Equitable Life Insurance, which bought Peabody Coal after John Boyden's 1966 attempt to effect a merger between

Peabody and Kennecott Copper was blocked by Congress on antitrust grounds. In any event, by the late 1960s, WEST had developed what it called "The Grand Plan" for rearranging the entirety of the Southwest into a "power grid" involving wholesale coal stripping, dozens of huge slurry-fed coal-fired generating plants, a complex of new dams (including those such as Glen Canyon and Echo Canyon, which have in fact been built) for hydroelectric generation purposes, several nuclear reactors adjoining uranium mining and milling sites, and a fabric of high-voltage transmission lines girdling the entire region. Given the fact that infrastructural development costs were designed to be largely underwritten by tax dollars, the potential profitability of the plan for WEST members and affiliated corporations are absolutely astronomical over the long term; Wiley and Gottlieb, *Empires in the Sun*, op. cit.

21. For further details on the initial bill, see Kevin Tehan, "Of Indians, Land and the Federal Government," *Arizona State Law Journal*, No. 176, 1976.

22. Several such studies are alluded to in the Ralph Nader Congress Project's *The Environmental Committees* (New York: Grossman, 1975). These should be understood in the context of the 1970 Arizona Bureau of Mines Bulletin No. 182 (*Coal, Oil, Natural Gas, Helium and Uranium in Arizona*), which articulated the range of incentives available for massive "energy development" programs in the area. For context, see my "Letter From Big Mountain," *Dollars and Sense*, Dec. 1985.

23. The Senate did not vote the idea down. Rather, it opted to postpone its decision until after the 1972 elections. A pretext was provided when the House, collaborating, scheduled a series of "preliminary" hearings on the relocation issue in Winslow, Arizona; U.S. Senate, Subcommittee on Indian Affairs of the Committee on Interior and Insular Affairs, *Authorizing Partition of Surface Rights of Navajo-Hopi Land: Hearings on H.R. 11128* (Washington, D.C.: 92d Cong., 2d Sess., Sept. 14-15, 1972), hereinafter referred to as *Authorization Hearings*.

24. McGovern wrote in a letter to Navajo Tribal Chairman Peter McDonald that if "there has been no satisfactory agreement reached [between the Hopis and Diné] before next January [1973], I will propose comprehensive new legislation to resolve the problem in such a way that no family is needlessly removed from its home land" (quoted in the *Gallup Independent*, Aug. 3, 1972). On Goldwater, see Kammer, *Second Long Walk*, op. cit., pp. 97-8.

25. Mark Panitch, "Whose Home on the Range? Coal Fuels Indian Dispute," *Washington Post*, July 21, 1974. It is worth noting that before going freelance, Panitch had worked as a reporter for the *Arizona Star* in Tucson covering the land dispute. In this capacity, he had been repeatedly conned into reporting false or distorted information by the Evans public relations effort. His analysis of what happened thus offers a significant degree of firsthand authenticity and credibility.

26. Ibid. Also see Joe Conason, "Homeless on the Range: Greed, Religion, and the Hopi-Navajo Land Dispute," *Village Voice*, July 29, 1986.

27. As Kammer observes (*Second Long Walk*, op. cit., p. 92), "A particularly nasty incident began when Randolph ordered a ninety-seven-year-old Navajo named Tsinijinnie Yazzie to get off his horse and submit to arrest for trespassing with his sheep. Yazzie did not understand English and remained mounted, so Randolph jerked him off his horse, injuring him seriously. Randolph [then] jailed Yazzie on charges of trespassing and resisting arrest."

28. See Panitch's article on the incident in the *Arizona Star*, March 26, 1972.

29. *Authorizing Partition of Surface Rights of Navajo-Hopi Land*, op. cit., p. 23. Perhaps ironically, Navajo Tribal Chairman McDonald played directly into his opponents' script by announcing that unless federal authorities acted to curb the Sekaquaptewas' tactics, the Diné would "get their fill of this and take things into their own hands" (*Arizona Sun*, Mar. 1, 1972).

30. Quoted in Kammer, *Second Long Walk*, op. cit., p. 105.

31. Fannin went on record as having cosponsored the draconian idea, not only to "avoid violence," but because Diné overgrazing was "killing" the JUA (*Navajo Times*, Sept. 27, 1973). That this was a rather interesting concern for a lawmaker whose professed objective was to see the entire area strip mined and depleted of ground water went unremarked at the time.

32. The quote from Lujan is taken from a "dear colleagues" letter he disseminated to Congress on Mar. 16, 1974. In the alternative to what he proposed therein, he had cosponsored, with Arizona Representative John Conlan, a 1973 proposal that the Diné should be allowed to purchase JUA land from the Hopi, or that Congress might appropriate monies for this purpose. These funds could then be used for whatever purpose the Hopis chose, including acquisition of land south of Grazing District 6, upon

which no Diné lived, but under which there was no coal. Mineral rights within the JUA would continue to be shared by both peoples. The idea was that such compensation would serve to satisfy both the "equal interest" provisions of the *Healing v. Jones* (II) decision and elementary justice for the Hopis without committing the United States to engage in human rights violations against the Diné. New Mexico Senator Joseph Montoya carried a version of the Lujan/Conlan initiative into the Senate. It is a testament to the extent to which the "land dispute" was/is really about mining that the enlightened approach offered by the Lujan/Conlan initiative met with vociferous resistance from the entire Boyden/ Sekaquaptewa/Goldwater/Steiger group, as well as WEST Associate lobbyists. The only responsive party turns out to have been the McDonald administration at Navajo, which had been formally offering to buy out Hopi surface interests in the JUA since 1970.

33. The lopsidedness of the House vote is partially accounted for by the fact that influential Arizona Representative Morris "Moe" Udall, brother of former Interior Secretary Stuart Udall, withdrew his opposition to H.R. 10337. He did so, by his own account, at the specific request of Helen Sekaquaptewa, a family friend and fellow Mormon. Udall's articulated position had previously been quite similar to that of Lujan, Conlan, and Montoya (*Congressional Record*, May 29, 1974, p. H4517).

34. *Sekaquaptewa v. McDonald, supra*; it is noted that McDonald was assessed a penalty of $250 per day for each day "excess" stock remained within the JUA.

35. A good portion of the credit for this atypical situation seems due to the effective and sustained lobbying of the Interior Department's Assistant Secretary for Land Management Harrison Loesch, an ardent advocate of mineral development on "public lands" and early supporter of the Steiger draft legislation. It is instructive that less than a year and a half after P.L. 93-531 was passed, Loesch was named vice president of Peabody Coal.

36. Kammer, *Second Long Walk*, op. cit., pp. 128-9.

37. 88 Stat. 1714 (1974), otherwise known as the "Navajo-Hopi Settlement Act."

38. On this point, see Whitson, "Policy Review," op. cit., pp. 379-80.

39. The litigation provision accrued from an effort by Goldwater, et al., to simply assign ownership of a quarter-million acres surrounding Moenkopi to the Hopis. An amendment introduced jointly by South Dakota Senator Abourezk and New Mexico Senator Montoya narrowly averted this outcome, by a vote of 37-35, by authorizing a judicial determination instead.

40. This Boyden/Evans myth was still being repeated as late as 1977 by William Simkin, the federal mediator charged with establishing exact placement of the partition line. Simkin fixed the number of Diné to be relocated at 3,495; *Navajo Times*, Jan. 24, 1977.

41. The Simkin partition line is virtually identical to that originally proposed by Sam Steiger in 1971. The Steiger line had been drawn by John Boyden in consultation with Peabody Coal; Kammer, *Second Long Walk*, op. cit., p. 134.

42. Navajo-Hopi Indian Relocation Commission (NHIRC), *1981 Report and Plan*, Flagstaff, Apr. 1981.

43. This figure is advanced by Whitson ("Policy Review," op. cit., p. 372), using the NHIRC *Statistical Program Report for April 1985* (Flagstaff, May 3, 1985). The commission found that 774 Diné families had been certified and relocated from the Hopi partition zone by that point, while 1,555 families had been certified but not yet relocated. Another 1,707 Diné families had refused both certification and relocation. Using the conventional commission multiplier of 4.5 persons per "family unit," Whitson projected a "conservative estimate of between 10,480 and 17,478 persons, 3,483 of whom had been relocated by May 1985."

44. NHIRC, *1981 Report and Plan*, op. cit.

45. U.S. Department of Interior, Surveys and Investigations Staff, *A Report to the Committee on Appropriations, U.S. House of Representatives, on the Navajo and Hopi Relocation Commission* (Washington, D.C.: 99th Cong., 1st Sess., Jan. 22, 1985) p. 12; hereinafter referred to as *Surveys and Investigations Report.*

46. Ibid.; testimony Relocation Commission Chairman Ralph Watkins, p. 6.

47. U.S. Senate, Committee on Interior and Insular Affairs, Subcommittee on Indian Affairs, *Relocation of Certain Hopi and Navajo Indians* (Washington D.C.: 96th Cong., May 15, 1979).

48. The problem began in July 1975 when Navajo Chairman McDonald announced his government's intent to purchase the full quarter-million acres of BLM replacement lands in House Rock Valley, an area known as the "Arizona Strip" north of the Colorado River. The idea was met first with

furious resistance by non-Indian "environmentalist" and "sporting" organizations such as the Arizona Wildlife Federation and th Save the Arizona Strip Committee (which advocated abolishing Indian reservations altogether). Next, it was discovered that a dozen Mormon families held ranching interests in the valley, and this brought Arizona's Mormon Congressman Moe Udall into the fray. In 1979, Udall introduced legislation, ultimately incorporated into P.L. 96-305, the 1980 amendment to P.L. 93-531, which placed House Rock Valley out-of-bounds for purposes of Diné acquisition. The next selection was the 35,000-acre Paragon Ranch in New Mexico, apparently chosen by the administration of Navajo Chairman Peterson Zah for its energy development potential rather than as a viable relocation site. In 1982, Interior Secretary James Watt blocked this initiative by withdrawing the ranch from public domain, thereby making it unavailable for acquisition (47 *Fed. Reg.* 9290); Zah filed what was to prove an unsuccessful suit, seeking to compel the land transfer (*Zah v. Clark*, Civ. No. 83-1753 BB (D. N.M., filed Nov. 27, 1983)). Meanwhile, in early 1983, the Navajo government indicated it had selected 317,000 acres of public and private lands in western New Mexico, contiguous with the eastern border of the Navajo Nation. The plan met with such fierce reaction from local ranchers that it was soon abandoned (*Surveys and Investigations Report*, op. cit., p. 24). On June 24, 1983, Zah announced the selection had been switched to five parcels in Arizona (*Navajo Times*, June 29, 1983). By May 1985, only the Walker Ranch, a 50,000-acre tract, had actually been acquired. There were and are serious problems with water availability, and the ability of the land to sustain grazing was and is subject to serious question ("Water Rights Become Issue in Acquiring Land for Tribe," *Arizona Daily Sun*, Apr. 7, 1985). Such surface water as is available comes mainly from the Río Puerco, heavily contaminated by the massive July 1979 United Nuclear Corporation Church Rock uranium spill 51 miles upstream at Sanders, Arizona; see "Geographies of Sacrifice," in this volume; also see L.J. Mann, and E. A. Nemecek, "Geohydrology and Water Use in Southern Apache County," *Arizona Department of Water Resources Bulletin*, Jan. 1983). Nonetheless, the first relocatees were moved onto this land in 1987 (Parlow, *Sacred Land*, op. cit., p. 202). As of 1997, there had been no real improvement to the situation.

49. Quoted in the *Arizona Republic*, Feb. 17, 1977.

50. Quoted in the *Arizona Star*, Aug. 13, 1975.

51. Morrall was quoted in the *Arizona Daily Sun* (July 9, 1975) as saying, "[The Indians'] future lies in forgetting their 'Separate Nation' status and become dues paying Americans like the rest of us."

52. *Lomayatewa v. Hathaway*, 52 F.2d 1324, 1327 (9th Cir. 1975), *cert. denied*, and *Suskena v. Kleppe*, 425 U.S. 903 (1976).

53. Examples of this principle are legion. As an illustration, see the U.S. Supreme Court's "resolution" of the Black Hills Land Claim, 448 U.S. 907 (1982); covered in "The Black Hills Are Not For Sale," in this volume.

54. Schifter's query appears in *Authorization Hearings*, op. cit., p. 208. It is possible the Senate Committee might have been swayed by the question. Such logic was, however, more than offset by the efficient and persistent lobbying of the committee's staff director, Jerry Verkler, who appears to have been, among other things, feeding inside information on the committee deliberations directly to Evans and Associates. Shortly after P.L. 93-531 was safely passed in 1974, Verkler left government service. In January 1975, he was named manager of the Washington, D.C. office of Texas Eastern Transmission Company, one of the WEST Associates consortium. By 1980, he had been promoted to fill a position as the corporation's vice president for government affairs; Kammer, *Second Long Walk*, op. cit., pp. 135-6.

55. Steiger's statement appears in the transcript of a meeting of the House Subcommittee on Indian Affairs, Nov. 2, 1973, lodged in the committee files of the National Archives, Washington, D.C., at p. 127.

56. *Relocation of Certain Hopi and Navajo Indians*, op.cit., p. 35.

57. See, e.g., Marc Fried, "Grieving for a Lost Home," in L. J. Dunn, ed., *The Urban Condition* (New York: Basic Books, 1963) pp. 151-71.

58. Thayer Scudder, "The Human Ecology of Big Projects: River Basin Development on Local Populations," *Annual Review of Anthropology*, No. 2, 1973, pp. 45-61.

59. Betty Beetso Gilbert, "Navajo-Hopi Land Dispute: Impact of Forced Relocation on Navajo Families," unpublished Master of Social Work thesis, Arizona State University, 1977.

60. Smith's statement was made to an aid to Massachusetts Senator Ted Kennedy, Wendy Moskop, during a fact-finding trip to the JUA in 1974. Quoted in a flyer distributed by the Big Mountain Legal

Defense/Offense Committee, Flagstaff, *circa* 1982.

61. Walsh's February 10, 1977, order did provide for both Hopi and Navajo jurisdiction on their respective sides of the partition line. However, it also specifically stated that livestock impoundment might proceed only under supervision of the secretary of the interior, who was charged with assuring that "the civil rights of persons within the area are not obstructed" in the process. Sekaquaptewa's approach simply discarded Diné civil rights as an irrelevancy.

62. According to Kammer (*Second Long Walk*, op. cit., p. 157), "[BIA Phoenix Area Office Director John] Artichoker had the police supplied with enough arms to repulse a tank assault. Weapons flow in from a special BIA arsenal in Utah included grenade launchers and automatic rifles."

63. Sekaquaptewa is quoted in the *Gallup Independent* (Mar. 9, 1977) as saying, regardless of the judge's view, his rangers couldn't "have an ordinance around without enforcing it."

64. The "eager for a shootout" phrase will be found in ibid. Abbot Sekaquaptewa is quoted from the *Gallup Independent*, Mar. 18, 1977.

65. The details of Benjamin's plan, and quotation of his remarks, are taken from Kammer, *Second Long Walk*, op. cit., p. 158. For analysis of the impact of the compulsory stock reduction program upon the targeted Diné, see John J. Wood, *Sheep is Life: An Assessment of Livestock Reduction in the Former Navajo-Hopi Joint Use Area* (Flagstaff, AZ: Department of Anthropology Monographs, Northern Arizona University, 1982).

66. The actual order is unpublished. It is quoted in part, however, in *Sekaquaptewa v. McDonald* (II) and *Sidney v. Zah*.

67. For details on the effects of the building freeze, see Whitson, "Policy Review," op. cit., pp. 404-6.

68. Ibid., p. 389. Whitson draws upon several sources in advancing her claims: Memorandum, "Relocatees Sale and Nonownership of Their Replacement Homes," David Shaw (NHIRC staff) to Steve Goodrich (NHIRC executive director); NHIRC *Report and Plan*, June 1983; *Surveys and Investigations Report*; James Schroeder, "U.S. Probing Fraud Claims in Relocation of Navajos," *Arizona Republic*, Mar. 7, 1984; *Monroe v. High Country Homes*, Civ. No. 84-189 PCT CLH (D. Ariz, filed Feb. 9, 1984).

69. *Monroe v. High Country Homes*, p. 388.

70. Thayer Scudder, "Expected Impacts of Compulsory Relocation of Navajos with Special Emphasis on Relocation from the Former Joint Use Area Required by P.L. 93-531," unpublished report, Mar. 1979.

71. "Federal Commissioner says Relocation is like Nazi concentration camps," *Navajo Times*, May 12, 1982.

72. *Big Mountain Support Group Newsletter*, June 14, 1982.

73. Thayer Scudder, et al., *No Place To Go: Effects of Compulsory Relocation on Navajos* (Philadelphia: Institute for the Study of Human Issues, 1982).

74. See my "Examination and Analysis of U.S. Policy Within the Navajo-Hopi Joint Use Area Under Provisions of International Law," *Akwesasne Notes*, Vol. 17, Nos. 3-4, May-Aug. 1985. Also see Note 110.

75. Todacheenie is quoted in Kammer, *Second Long Walk*, op. cit., p. 79.

76. All quotes appear in the *Gallup Independent*, May 5, 1977.

77. Kammer, *Second Long Walk*, op. cit., pp. 1-2; Parlow, *Sacred Land*, op. cit., p. 200.

78. Kammer, *Second Long Walk*, op. cit., pp. 209-10; Parlow, *Sacred Land*, op. cit., p. 201.

79. Quoted in ibid., p. 201.

80. This effort was maintained until 1984, at which point AIM fragmented and IITC virtually collapsed due to the insistence of some elements of the leadership of each organization to support Sandinistas rather than Indians in Nicaragua. Strange as this may seem, IITC mounted what might be called a "flying tribunal," sending it around the country to purge "unreliable individuals" guilty of expressing an "impure political line" by demanding rights of genuine self-determination for the Miskito, Sumu, and Rama peoples of Nicaragua's Atlantic Coast region. Among those discarded was Gurwitz (in late 1986), who had served as the hub of the BMLDOC operation. The national and international support networks he had built up eroded very quickly, leaving the Big Mountain resistance with only a small—and relatively ineffectual—portion of the organized external support base it had once enjoyed. As

for IITC, at last count, it was down to a staff of three operating from an office in San Francisco. While no longer a functional entity, it is, to be sure, "ideologically pure."

81. Anderson contacted Gurwitz during a National Lawyers Guild conference in Santa Fe, New Mexico, during the spring of 1982. Gurwitz responded immediately, opening the Flagstaff office during the fall of the same year.

82. Perhaps most notable among the interns was Lee Brooke Phillips, who ultimately succeeded Gurwitz as head of the legal defense effort. BMLDOC was redesignated as the "Big Mountain Legal Office" (BMLO) in 1987.

83. Parlow, *Sacred Land*, op. cit., p. 117. The foreign countries at issue included Switzerland, West Germany, Austria, Italy, Canada, Great Britain, and Japan.

84. The commission, composed of Joan Price, Loughrienne Nightgoose, Omali Yeshitela and myself, was first convened during the annual Big Mountain Survival Gathering, Apr. 19-22, 1984. Its collective findings were presented to the elders over the following year. The Indian Law Resource Center intervention was presented to the Working Group by staff attorney Joe Ryan on Aug. 31, 1981.

85. For further information on these and other aspects of the physical resistance, see Parlow, *Sacred Land*, op. cit., esp. pp. 115-51 and 201-2; Peter Matthiessen, "Forced Relocation at Big Mountain," *Cultural Survival Quarterly*, Vol. 12, No. 3, 1988.

86. The quote is taken from a speech made by Gurwitz at the University of Colorado, Colorado Springs, Feb. 17, 1986.

87. The federal judgment seems to have been quite sound in this regard, as should be apparent from the events described in Note 80. At present, organized support for the Big Mountain resistance has fallen to less than ten percent of 1986 levels, and continues to decline. As of late 1989, the BMLO facility in Flagstaff, established by Gurwitz in 1982, had to be closed for lack of financial support.

88. The *Manybeads* suit was based in large part upon initially successful litigation of the Yellowthunder case (*United States v. Means, et al.*, Docket No. Civ. 81-5131, Dist. S.D., Dec. 9, 1985), in which attorneys Ellison, Finzel, and Larry Leventhal argued that the entire Black Hills region is of spiritual significance to the Lakota. The same principle was advanced on behalf of the Diné resistance with regard to the Big Mountain area. However, the favorable decision reached by the U.S. District Court in Yellowthunder was overturned by the 8th Circuit Court of Appeals in the wake of the Supreme Court's "G-O Road Decision" (*Lyng v. Northwest Cemetary Protective Association*, 56 U.S. Law Week 4292). This in turn led to the dismissal of *Manybeads*. It was reinstated on a limited basis during the early '90s in order to facilitate negotiations leading to the 1996 "Accomodation Agreement" between the Navajo and Hopi councils (see Note 100).

89. Shortly after the *Manybeads* suit was entered, a second suit—*Attakai v. United States*—was filed, contending that specific sites within the Hopi partition area of the JUA are of particular spiritual significance to the Diné. This case remains active, although the only positive effect it had generated as of the summer of 1990 was a ruling by Judge Carroll that the federal government and/or Hopi tribal council were required to provide seven days prior notification to both the Big Mountain Legal Office and Navajo tribal council of the "development" of such designated sites. In principle, this was to allow the Diné an opportunity to present information as to why targeted sites should not be physically altered. Rather obviously, however, the time period involved was too short to allow for effective response; Phil Diamond, "Big Mountain Update," *Akwesasne Notes*, Vol. 21, No. 6, 1989-90. On *Lyng*, see Vine Deloria, Jr., "Trouble in High Places: Erosion of American Indian Rights to Freedom in the United States," in M. Annette Jaimes, ed., *The State of Native America: Genocide, Colonization and Resistance* (Boston: South End Press, 1992).

90. During the spring of 1990, the Big Mountain Legal Office estimated that as many as 9,000 of the "at least 12,000" Diné subject to relocation under P.L. 93-531 remained on the land. Official government estimates were unavailable; Deborah Lacerenza, "An Historical Overview of the Navajo Relocation," *Cultural Survival Quarterly*, Vol. 12, No. 3, 1988.

91. Quoted from *Navajo Times*, Aug. 31, 1978. At the time Goldwater made this statement, Judge Walsh's order approving the Simkin partition line and requiring relocation of all Dinés within the HPL had been in effect for more than eighteen months.

92. For example, on Aug. 31, 1978, the *Arizona Star* editorialized, under the title "Goldwater's Confusion," that the senator, "who either has uniformed or inaccurate sources on Arizona Indian affairs,

has not spent enough time gathering firsthand information or he has simply lost interest in the subject. If the latter is true, [he] should refrain from public comment."

93. It is instructive to note that Representative Wayne Owens, who sponsored Boyden's successful draft legislation, went to work for Boyden's Salt Lake City law firm after being voted out of office in Arizona. Such apparent conflict of interest situations are normal within the context of U.S. Indian affairs.

94. 94 Stat. 932; 25 U.S.C. §§ 640d-28 (1983). Perhaps one reason this superficial deviation from the P.L. 93-531 hard line was passed with relatively little furor was that John Boyden died in mid-1980. He was replaced as attorney for the Hopi IRA government by John Kennedy, a senior partner in Boyden's law firm. By all accounts, the stance and attitudes adopted by Boyden over nearly thirty years of involvement in the "land dispute" have continued unchanged.

95. Danny Blackgoat, interview on radio station WKOA, Denver, CO, March 13, 1985.

96. Parlow, *Sacred Land*, op. cit., p. 202.

97. Ibid. She quotes Indian Commissioner Ross Swimmer as applauding Udall's action in at least momentarily opening the door for the BIA to begin forced relocation operations. Although Swimmer himself has been replaced as head of the BIA, the sentiments he represented within the Bureau have not changed appreciably.

98. Diamond, "Big Mountain Update," op. cit.

99. Ibid.

100. "Background: The Accommodation Agreement," *Navajo-Hopi Observer*, Apr. 12, 1997 (hereinafter referred to as "Accomodation Agreement"). It should be noted that the "agreement" was reached between attorneys representing the various parties during court-ordered negotiations deriving from attempts to reinstate the *Manybeads* suit during the early '90s (see Note 89). Navajo Nation President Albert Hale consented to the arrangement in its draft form (S. 1973) during the summer of 1996.

101. "Accommodation Agreement," op cit.

102. Quoted in ibid.

103. Quoted in Wendy Young, "The Legal Options: Sign or Move," *Navajo-Hopi Observer*, Apr. 2, 1997.

104. As longtime resister Rena Babbitt Lane put it, "Twenty-two years I've lived in depression. Sleepless nights, not eating a healthy dinner. We live in the harassment [by] the government." Her livestock have been impounded "many times," often abused and sometimes disappearing altogether. In addition, she has been physically assaulted by Hopi Rangers on two occasions, once severely enough that she had to wear a neck brace for severeal months. Her story is typical; Wendy Young, "Signing the Lease: Some HPL residents tell why they signed," *Navajo-Hopi Observer*, Apr. 16, 1997.

105. "Accomodation Agreement," op. cit.

106. Wendy R. Young, "Signing the Agreement: 'We don't want to get in trouble with those Hopis," *Navajo-Hopi Observer*, May 21, 1997.

107. "Overwhelming majority of Navajos on HPL sign Accomodation Agreement," *Navajo-Hopi Observer*, May 21, 1997. Mae Tso's holdings were reduced to three acres, on which she is supposedly to maintain an extended family numbering more than twenty persons; Young, "The Legal Options," op. cit.

108. Ibid.

109. The activist, a Navajo who asked to remain anonymous, points to a 1984 report entitled *Economic Development on the I-40 Corridor*, written by a consultant named Frank Mangin for the Relocation Commission. In the document, it is observed that population dispersal and resulting "commuting distances" serve as "barriers" to a greater Navajo presence in the regional wage labor force. This is described as "retarding industrial development" of the area. Therefore, Mangin argues, relocation should be viewed as an "opportunity" to concentrate Navajos as potential workers in locations close to new/planned industrial facilities. The document specifically references Unit 5 of the Cholla Electrical Power Generating Station at Joseph City, then under construction, which he estimates will need a "stable workforce of 2,000" upon completion. Tellingly, Nahata Dzil was then built with easy access to the new plant and provides the bulk of its unskilled labor; Sandra J. Wilson, "One Local Activist Charges Apartheid," *Navajo-Hopi Observer*, June 11, 1997.

110. Article II of the United Nations Convention on Prevention and Punishment of the Crime of Genocide (U.S.T, , T.I.A.S. , U.N.T.S. 277, 1948) defines genocide as being any policy undertaken with

"intent" (read, "knowledge") to "destroy" (read, "extinguish"), whether "in whole or in part, a national, ethnical, racial or religious group, as such." Among the categories of activity specified as being genocidal are Article II(b): "Causing serious bodily or psychological harm to members of the group" so that they separate themselves from the group in order to avoid further such harm and thus precipitate group dissolution. Another is Article II(c): "Deliberately inflicting on members of the group conditions of life calculated to bring about its physical destruction in whole or in part." For those who may be confused on this point, little things like the building freeze constitute infliction of *precisely* such "conditions," and the resulting geographical dispersal of the targeted group all along enunciated as a U.S. policy objective constitutes *precisely* the sort of "physical destruction" at issue. Coerced dispersal, after all, *is* a physical imposition under which the group, as such, cannot continue to exist. What, emphatically, is *not* meant by the term "physical destruction" is "killing members of the group." The latter phrase is accorded its own separate standing as Article II(a); for Convention text, see Ian Brownlie, ed., *Basic Documents on Human Rights* (Oxford, UK: Clarendon Press, [3rd ed.] 1992) pp. 31-4. Also see Note 74.

111. The term "sugar-coated genocide" is taken from a speech by Colorado AIM leader Glenn T. Morris delivered at the Federal Building, Denver, May 19, 1989. On the extermination of the Aché, see Richard Arens, ed., *Genocide in Paraguay* (Philadelphia: Temple University Press, 1976).

112. "Where scholars deny genocide, in the face of decisive evidence that it has ocurred, they contribute to a false consciousness that can have the most dire revereberations. Their message in effect is: [genocide] requires no confrontation, no reflection, but should be ignored, glossed over. In this way, scholars lend their considerable authority to the acceptance of this ultimate human crime. More than that, they encourage—indeed invite—a repetition of the crime from virtually any source in the immediate or distant future. By closing their minds to the truth, that is, scholars contribute to the deadly psychohistorical dynamic in which unopposed genocide begets new genocides"; Roger F. Smith, Eric Markusen and Robert Jay Lifton, "Professional Ethics and Denial of the Armenian Genocide," *Holocaust and Genocide Studies*, No. 9, 1995. To be sure, the principle is more broadly and appropriately applicable than to scholars alone.

113. Diamond, "Big Mountain Update," op. cit.

114. See, e.g., Thadias Box, et al., *Rehabilitation Potential for Western Coal Lands* (Cambridge: Ballinger, 1974). Based upon this study and others, the National Academy of Science recommended a year later that locales such as Black Mesa be declared "national sacrifice areas in the interests of energy development. This is covered well in Carl L. Burley, "Indian Lands—An Industry Delimma," *Journal of the Rocky Mountain Mineral Law Institute*, No. 28, 1982. With respect to the opposing contentions of Peabody and other mining companies, see Jeff Mayers, "Mining Firms Dig for Support," *Wisconsin State Journal*, Aug. 1, 1991; Terry Anderson, "Q&A: Reclamation Important Part of Mining, Executives Say," *Green Bay Press Gazette*, Aug. 4, 1991.

115. Diamond, "Big Mountain Update," op. cit. Hustles of this sort are analyzed by Thomas C. Meredith in his "Environmental Impact, Cultural Diversity, and Sustainable Rural Development," *Environmental Impact Assessment Review*, Vol. 12, Nos. 1-2, 1992.

116. See Note 114.

117. The quote is taken from a talk given by Roberta Blackgoat at the University of Colorado, Boulder, Mar. 11, 1984. Mrs. Blackgoat, now 82, is one of several elder women who emerged as primary spokespersons for the Big Mountain Resistance during the 1980s. Her son, Danny, served for a period as head of the BMLDOC office in Flagstaff (see Note 95).

THE STRUGGLE FOR NEWE SEGOBIA
The Western Shoshone Battle for Their Homeland

> Of course our whole national history has been one of expansion... That the barbarians recede or are conquered, with the attendant fact that peace follows their retrogression or conquest, is due solely to the power of the mighty civilized races which have not lost their fighting instinct, and which by their expansion are gradually bringing peace into the red wastes where the barbarian peoples of the world hold sway.
>
> —Theodore Roosevelt
> *The Strenuous Life*, 1901

In 1863, the United States entered into the Treaty of Ruby Valley with the Newe (Western Shoshone) Nation, agreeing—in exchange for Indian commitments of peace and friendship, willingness to provide right-of-way through their lands, and the granting of assorted trade licenses—to recognize the boundaries encompassing the approximately 24.5 million acres of the traditional Western Shoshone homeland, known in their language as Newe Segobia (*see* map).[1] The U.S. also agreed to pay the Newes $100,000 in restitution for environmental disruptions anticipated as a result of Euroamerican "commerce" in the area.

As concerns the ultimate disposition of territorial rights within the region, researcher Rudolph C. Ryser has observed that, "Nothing in the Treaty of Ruby Valley ever sold, traded or gave away any part of the Newe Country to the United States of America. Nothing in this treaty said that the United States could establish counties or smaller states within Newe Country. Nothing in this treaty said the United States could establish settlements of U.S. citizens who would be engaged in any activity other than mining, agriculture, milling and ranching."[2]

From the signing of the treaty until the mid-twentieth century, no action was taken by either Congress or federal courts to extinguish native title to Newe Segobia.[3] Essentially, the land was an area in which the United States took little interest. Still, relatively small but steadily growing numbers

of non-Indians did move into Newe territory, a situation which was generally accommodated by the Indians so long as the newcomers did not become overly presumptuous. By the late 1920s, however, conflicts over land use had begun to sharpen. Things worsened after 1934, when the federal government installed a tribal council form of government—desired by Washington but rejected by traditional Newes—under provision of the Indian Reorganization Act (IRA).[4] It was to the IRA council heading one of the Western Shoshone bands, the Temoak, that attorney Ernest Wilkinson went with a proposal in early 1946.

Anatomy of a "Land Dispute Resolution"

Wilkinson was a senior partner in the Washington-based law firm Wilkinson, Cragen, and Barker, commissioned by Congress toward the end of World War II to draft legislation creating the Indian Claims Commission. The idea he presented to the Temoak council was that his firm be retained to "represent their interests" before the Commission.[5] Ostensibly, his objective was to secure the band's title to its portion of the 1863 treaty area. Much more likely, given subsequent events, is that his purpose was to secure title for non-Indian interests in Nevada and to collect the ten percent attorney's fee he and his colleagues had written into the Claims Commission Act as pertaining to any compensation awarded to native clients.[6] In any event, the Temoaks agreed, and a contract between Wilkinson and the council was approved by the Bureau of Indian Affairs in 1947.[7]

Wilkinson followed up in 1951 with a petition to the Claims Commission arguing that his representation of the Temoaks should be construed as representing the interests of the entire Newe Nation. The Commission concurred, despite protests from the bulk of the people involved.[8] While such a ruling may seem contrary to popular notions of "American Justice," it is in fact entirely consistent with the form and function of the Commission, and of federal Indian law more generally. As Dan Bomberry, head of the Seventh Generation Fund, has explained:

> When the U.S. succeeded in forcing the Indian Reorganization Act upon tribes, installing puppet governments, the ultimate U.S. aim was to make Indians a resource colony, like Africa was for Europe. Sometimes the issue is coal or uranium and sometimes it's just open land... The role of the Indian Claims Commission is to get the land of tribes who do not have puppet governments, or where the traditional people are leading a fight to keep land and refuse money.[9]

It follows that from the outset, Wilkinson's pleadings, advanced in court by his partner, Robert W. Barker, led directly away from Newe rights to the Ruby Valley Treaty Territory. The Shoshone objectives in agreeing to go to court have been explained by tribal elder Saggie Williams, a resident of Battle Mountain: "All we wanted was for the white men to honor the treaty. [We] believed the lawyers we hired were to work for the Indians and to do what the Indians asked. But they didn't. They did as they pleased and told us we didn't have any land. At the time, we didn't talk about selling our land with the lawyer because we had the treaty, which settled the land question; it protected [our] lands."[10]

As Glenn Holly, a Temoak leader of the contemporary land claims struggle, puts it, "Most of our people never understood that by filing with the Claims Commission, we'd be agreeing we lost our land. They thought we were just clarifying the title question."[11] However, "Barker filed the claim in 1951, asserting that the Western Shoshones had lost not only their treaty lands, but also their aboriginal land extending into Death Valley, California. He put the date of loss at 1872 (only nine years after the Treaty of Ruby Valley), and he included in the twenty-four million acre claim some sixteen million acres that the Shoshones insist were not occupied by anyone but Indian bands, and that were never in question. But the U.S. Justice Department agreed with Barker's contention. Since opposing attorneys agreed, the Claims Commission did not investigate or seek other viewpoints."[12]

Clarence Blossom, one of the Newe elders who signed the original contract with Wilkinson, and who supported Barker for a time, points out that "[t]he land claim was never explained to the people. The old people do not even understand English. It was years later that I read that once you accept money, you lose your land. The government pulled the wool over our eyes. If I had known what was going on, I never would have accepted the attorney contract."[13]

As Raymond Yowell, a member of the Temoak Band Council and another original signatory, laid it out in a 1978 issue of the *Native Nevadan*: "A majority of the people present [at a 1965 mass meeting called to confront the attorneys] objected to the way Barker was giving up the remaining rights to our lands and walked out... Soon after, at [another such] meeting, about 80 percent of the people showed their opposition by walking out. It is important that at these meetings *Barker insisted we had no choice* as to whether to keep title to some lands or to give them up for claims money. The only choice was whether to approve or disapprove the [compensation package]. And if we disapproved we would get nothing (emphasis added)."[14]

Ultimately, the Wilkinson, Cragen, and Barker firm received a $2.5 million federal subsidy for "services rendered" in its "resolution of the matter" in a fashion which was plainly detrimental to the express interests of its ostensible clients.[15] Shawnee scholar and activist Glenn T. Morris has summarized the matter in what is probably the best article on the Western Shoshone land struggle to date.

> In 1962, the commission conceded that it "was unable to discover any formal extinguishment" of Western Shoshone to lands in Nevada, and could not establish a date of taking, but nonetheless ruled that the lands were taken at some point in the past. It did rule that approximately two million acres of Newe land in California was taken on March 3, 1853 [contrary to the Treaty of Ruby Valley, which would have supplanted any such taking], but without documenting what specific Act of Congress extinguished the title. Without the consent of the Western Shoshone Nation, on

February 11, 1966, Wilkinson and the U.S. lawyers arbitrarily stipulated that the date of valuation for government extinguishment of Western Shoshone title to over 22 million acres of land in Nevada occurred on July 1, 1872. This lawyers' agreement, entered without the knowledge or consent of the Shoshone people, served as the ultimate loophole through which the U.S. would allege that the Newe had lost their land.[16]

By 1872 prices, the award of compensation to the Newe for the "historic loss" of their territory was calculated, in 1972, at $21,350,000, an amount revised upwards to $26,154,600 (against which the government levied an offset of $9,410.11 for "goods" delivered in the 1870s) and certified on December 19, 1979.[17] In the interim, by 1976, even the Temoaks had joined the other Newe bands in maintaining that Wilkinson and Barker did not represent their interests; they fired them, but the BIA continued to renew the firm's contract "on the Indians' behalf" until the Claims Commission itself was dissolved in 1978.[18]

Meanwhile, the Newes retained other counsel and filed a motion to suspend commission proceedings with regard to their case. This was denied on August 15, 1977, appealed, but upheld by the U.S. Court of Claims on the basis that if the Newe desired "to avert extinguishment of their land claims, they should go to Congress" rather than the courts for redress. The amount of $26,145,189.89 was then placed in a trust account with the U.S. Treasury Department in order to absolve the U.S. of further responsibility in the matter.[19]

One analyst of the case suggests that if the United States were honest in its valuation date of the taking of Newe land, the date would be December 19, 1979—the date of the ICC award—since the [commission] could point to no other extinguishment date. The U.S. should thus compensate the Shoshone in 1979 land values and not those of 1872. Consequently, the value of the land "that would be more realistic, assuming the Western Shoshone were prepared to ignore violations of the Ruby Valley Treaty, would be in the neighborhood of $40 billion. On a per capita basis of distribution, the United States would be paying each Shoshone roughly $20 million... The [U.S.] has already received billions of dollars in resources and use from Newe territory in the past 125 years. Despite this obvious benefit, the U.S. government is only prepared to pay the Shoshone less than a penny of actual value for each acre of Newe territory.[20]

The Newes as a whole have refused to accept payment for their land under the premise articulated by Yowell, now Chair of the Western Shoshone Sacred Lands Association: "We entered into the Treaty of Ruby

Valley as co-equal sovereign nations... The land to the traditional Shoshone is sacred. It is the basis of our lives. To take away the land is to take away the lives of the people."[21] Glenn Holly, concurs. "Nothing happened in 1872," he says. "No land was 'taken' by the government. We never lost that land, we never left that land, and we're not selling it. In our religion, it's forbidden to take money for land. What's really happening is that the U.S. government, through this Claims Commission, is stealing the land from us right now."[22] "We should have listened to our old people," Yowell sums up, "They told us Barker was selling out our lands. It took me years to realize it."[23]

The Dann Case

Giving form to this sentiment, were the sisters Mary and Carrie Dann, who not only refused eviction from their homes by the U.S. Bureau of Land Management (BLM)—which claimed at that time to own property that had been in their family for generations—but challenged *all* U.S. title contentions within the Newe treaty area when the Bureau attempted to enforce its position in court.

In 1974, the Dann sisters were herding cattle near their home (a ranch outside Crescent Valley, Utah) when a BLM ranger stopped them and demanded to see their grazing permit. The Danns replied that they did not need a permit since they were not on U.S. land, but the land of the Western Shoshone Nation. They were charged with trespassing. "I have grazed my cattle and horses on that land all my life," says Carrie Dann, "and my mother did before me and her mother before her. Our people have been on this land for thousands of years. We don't need a permit to graze here."[24]

The trespassing case was filed in the U.S. District Court for Reno, where the sisters invoked aboriginal land rights as a defense. The ensuing litigation has caused federal courts to flounder about in disarray ever since. As John O'Connell, an attorney retained by the Newes to replace Barker, and who has served as lead counsel in defending the Danns, has put it, "We have asked the government over and over again in court to show evidence of how it obtained title to Shoshone land. They start groping around and can't find a damn thing. In fact, the relevant documents show the United States never wanted the Nevada desert until recently. There's no doubt in my mind that the Western Shoshones still hold legal title to most of their aboriginal territory. The great majority of them still live there and they don't want money for it. They love that desert. But if the Claims Commission has its way, the United States may succeed in finally stealing the land 'legally.'"[25]

In 1977, the district court ruled that the Danns were indeed "trespassers"—fining them $500 each, an amount they have steadfastly refused to pay—because the Claims Commission had allegedly resolved all title questions. This decision was reversed on appeal to the Ninth Circuit Court in 1978 because, in the higher court's view, the question of land title "had not been litigated, and has not been decided."[26]

On remand, the district court engaged in a conspicuous pattern of stalling, repeatedly delaying its hearing of the case for frivolous reasons. "The judge never wanted [the second] trial," O'Connell recalls. "At one point I accused the government of deliberately delaying the Dann case long enough to get the Indian claims check written, under the theory that once payment was received Indian title would have been extinguished and the Danns would have been prevented from asserting it. The judge admitted on record that he was 'sympathetic with the government's strategy in this regard."[27] In the end, this is exactly what was done.

> In other words, a $26 million payment to Indians who never sought it, tried to stop it, and refused to accept it—payment for lands that were alleged by the payer to have been "taken" in 1872, but which the courts have finally affirmed were never "taken" at all—is now being used as the instrument to extinguish Indian title.[28]

The district court, however, in attempting to reconcile its mutually contradictory determinations on the topic, observed that "Western Shoshone Indians retained unextinguished title to their aboriginal lands *until December of 1979,* when the Indian Claims Commission judgment became final (emphasis added)."[29] This, of course, demolished the articulated basis—that a title transfer had been effected more than a century earlier—for the commission's award amount. It also pointed to the fact that the commission had comported itself illegally in the Western Shoshone case insofar as the Indian Claims Commission Act explicitly disallowed the commissioners (never mind attorneys representing the Indians) from extinguishing previously unextinguished land titles. Thus armed, the Danns went back to the Ninth Circuit and obtained another reversal of the lower court's ruling.[30]

The government appealed to the Supreme Court and, entering yet *another* official (and exceedingly ambiguous) estimation of when Newe title was supposed to have been extinguished, the justices reversed the circuit court's reversal of the district court's last ruling. Having thus served the government's interest on appeal, the high court declined in 1990 to hear an appeal from the Danns concerning the question of whether they might retain individual aboriginal property rights based on continuous occupancy even if the collective rights of the Newe were denied.[31]

Tom Luebben, another of the non-Indian attorneys involved in defending Newe rights, has assessed the methods of litigation employed by the U.S. "It is clear that one of the main strategies the government uses in these cases is simply to wear out the Indians over decades of struggle," he observes. "The government has unlimited resources to litigate. If the Indians win one victory in court, the government just loads up its legal guns, adds a new, bigger crew of fresh lawyers, and comes back harder. It is the legal equivalent of what the cavalry did a hundred years ago. There is simply no interest in justice. It is hardball all the way. The government has all the time in the world to achieve its goals. The Indians run out of money, they get tired of fighting; they get old, and finally, after 10 to 20 years, somebody says, 'The hell with it; let's take what we can. It's really understandable that it worked out that way, but it's disgusting and it's wrong.'"[32]

Thus far, such tactics have proven unsuccessful against the Newe. "A new [resistance] strategy was hatched [in 1990] to sue the government for mineral and trespass fees from 1872 to 1979," says analyst Jerry Mander. "The logic of the argument was that since the courts now recognize that the Shoshones did have legal title until the Claims Commission took it away in 1979, they are entitled to mineral and trespass fees for 109 years. This would amount to billions of dollars due the Shoshones; it was hoped that this amount [would be] sufficient to cause the government to negotiate. But the [district] court rejected this new intervention on the technical grounds that the specific interveners were not parties to the original claim. This suit may yet re-emerge."[33]

The need for it was punctuated in November 1992 which the Dann sisters' brother, Clifford, took direct action to block a BLM impoundment of wild horses and other livestock. Stating that in "taking away our livelihood and our lands, you are taking away our lives," he doused himself with gasoline and attempted to set set himself afire. Quickly sprayed with fire extinguishers by surrounding BLM rangers, Dann was then arrested and, for reasons never adequately explained, charged with assaulting them. On May 17, 1993, he was sentenced to serve nine months in prison, two years probation and a $5,000 fine.[34]

For their part, Mary and Carrie Dann have announced their intent to go back into court with a new suit of their own, contending that the continuous use and occupancy evidenced by Newes on the contested land "prior to the authority of the Bureau of Land management" (which began in 1935) affords them tangible rights to pursue their traditional livelihood. "They hope," Mander notes, "to carve a hole in the earlier [judicial] decisions…which might open a doorway for the rest of the Western Shoshones" to do much the same thing.[35]

The chances were bolstered on March 6, 1998, when the Inter-American Commission on Human Rights of the Organization of American States issued a formal request to the U.S. government that it stay all further action with respect to evictions, impoundment of livestock and the like, "pending an investigation by the Commission" into the historical context of the case, the respective rights of the parties involved, and, consequently, the legal validity of current U.S. policies vis-à-vis the Newes.[36]

Perhaps most important, as of this writing, the Dann sisters remain on their land in defiance of federal authority. Their physical resistance, directly supported by most Newes and an increasing number of non-Indians, forms the core of whatever will come next. Carrie Dann is unequivocal: "We have to be completely clear. We must not allow them to destroy Mother Earth. We've all been assimilated into white society but now we know it's destroying us. We have to get back to our own ways."[37] Corbin Harney, a resistance leader from the Duckwater Shoshone Community in northern Nevada, reinforces her position: "We don't need their money. We need to keep these lands and protect them."[38]

The Most Bombed Nation on Earth

Federal officials tend to be equally straightforward, at least in what they take to be private conversation. Mander quotes one Interior Department bureaucrat, a reputed "Jimmy Carter liberal" responsible for seeing to it that Indians get a "fair shake," as saying in an interview, "[L]et me tell you one goddamn thing. There's no way we're ever letting any of the Indians have title to their lands. If they don't take the money, they'll get nothing."[39]

The accuracy of this anonymous assertion of federal policy is amply borne out by the fact that an offer of compromise extended by a portion of the Shoshone resistance in 1977—that the Newes would drop their major land claim in exchange for the establishment of a three million-acre reservation, guarantee of perpetual access to specified sacred sites outside the reservation, and payment of cash compensation against the remaining 21 million acres—was peremptorily rejected by then Secretary of Interior Cecil Andrus. No explanation of this decision was ever offered by the government other than that the secretary considered their being relegated to a landless condition to be in their "best interests."[40]

Leo Kurlitz, an assistant to Andrus and the Interior Department's chief attorney at the time the compromise offer was rejected, admits that he "didn't give the legal issues much thought."[41] Admitting that he was "uncomfortable" with the very idea that the Shoshones "still seem to possess title" to their land, he acknowledges that "under no circumstances was I going to recommend that we create a reservation... I saw my job as assessing the resource needs of the Shoshones, but I couldn't recommend that we establish a reservation."[42]

Mander's unnamed source says much the same thing, observing that, "These Indian cases make me so damned uncomfortable, I wish I didn't have to work on them at all."[43] He professes a certain bewilderment that at least some indigenous nations refuse to be bought off: "I really can't understand what these people want. Their lawyers get them great settlements—the Shoshones were awarded $26 million, and the Sioux may get [more than $300 million] for the Black Hills—and damn if they don't turn around and start talking about land."[44]

Such uniform and undeviating adamance on the part of diverse Interior Department personnel that not so much as a square inch of the Nevada desert, other than the minor reservations already designated as such, will be committed for Newe use and occupancy may seem somewhat baffling on its face. Their collective willingness to lay out not inconsiderable quantities of tax dollars in order to retain absolute control over such barren and lightly populated territory —with interest, the Western Shoshone settlement award now exceeds $80 million and is increasing steadily—raises further questions as to their motivations.[45]

Quite possibly, a hallowed U.S. psuedophilosophy, extended from the nineteenth century doctrine of "Manifest Destiny" and holding that Indians are by definition "disentitled" from retaining substantial quantities of real property, has a certain bearing in this connection.[46] Most probably, concern that a significant Newe land recovery might serve to establish a legal precedent upon which other indigenous nations could accomplish similar feats also plays a role.[47] Another part of the answer can probably be glimpsed in the July 1996 purchase of a 48,437 acre ranch in Cresecent Valley by the Oro Nevada Mining Company.[48]

Oro Nevada Mining, which also holds mineral rights to an additional 46,606 acres of "public lands" in the area, is a subsibiary of the Canadian transnational, Oro Nevada Resources, Ltd.[49] The parent corporation has been heavily involved in the mining boom which has recently afflicted the Innu and Inuit peoples of Labrador, around Voisey's Bay, and in Nitassinan, along the north shore of the St. Lawrence in Québec.[50] Another subsidiary, Bre-X, was created to explore and develop gold deposits for the Suharto régime in Indonesia.[51]

In Crescent Valley, it is believed that Oro is preparing to enter into a collaborative arrangement with Placer Dome/Kennecott subsidiary Cortez Gold, which already operates mines on the Pipeline and Pipeline South gold deposits further north, to extract the mineral from areas immediately adjoining the Dann Ranch.[52] Indeed, there has been talk throughout the mining industry that Crescent Valley may well turn out to be the scene of the next big gold rush. To some extent self-fulfilling prophecies, such rumors have in turn prompted corporations from as far away as Australia to begin acquiring speculative leases.[53]

Even more to the point, however, is the fact that federal usurpation of Newe land rights since 1945 has devolved upon converting their "remote" and "uninhabited" territory into a sprawling complex of nuclear weapons testing facilities. In addition to the experimental detonations conducted in the Marshall Islands during the 1950s, and a handful of tests in the Aleutians a few years later, more than 900 U.S. nuclear test blasts have thus far occurred at the Energy Resource and Development Administration's Nevada Test Site located within the military's huge Nellis Gunnery Range in southern Nevada.[54] At least as recently as July 2, 1997, a "subcritical" plutonium device was detonated there.[55]

This largely secret circumstance has made Newe Segobia an area of vital strategic interest to the United States and, although the Shoshones have never understood themselves to be at war with the United States, it has afforded their homeland the dubious distinction of becoming by a decisive margin "the most bombed country in the world."[56] The devastation and radioactive contamination of an appreciable portion of Newe property is presently coupled with a plan to locate what will perhaps be the primary permanent storage facility for nuclear waste at Yucca Mountain, a site well within the affected area.[57] Moreover, the Pentagon has long since demonstrated a clear desire, evidenced in a series of plans to locate its MX missile system there, for most of the remaining Newe treaty territory, that vast and "vacant" geography lying north of the present testing grounds.

The latter situation, which involved bringing approximately 20,000 additional non-Indians onto Newe land, creating another 10,000 miles of paved roads, and drawing down 3.15 billion gallons of water from an already overtaxed water table in order to install a mobile missile system accommodating some two hundred nuclear warheads, provoked what may have been the first concerted Shoshone response to military appropriation of their rights.[58] As Corbin Harney put it at a mass meeting on the matter convened in October 1979, after the Carter administration had made its version of the MX program public, "Now we are witnessing the real reason why we are being forced to accept money for lands."[59]

At the same meeting, Glenn Holley articulated the implications of the MX project to the Newes. "Water is life," he said, "and the MX system will consume our water resources altogether. Another thing the MX will destroy is the natural vegetation: the herbs like the badeba, doza, sagebrush, chaparral, Indian tea… [N]ot only the herbs but other medicines like the lizard in the south, which we use to heal the mentally sick and arthritis. There will also be electric fences, nerve gas, and security people all over our lands. It will affect the eagles and the hawks, the rock chuck, ground squirrel, rabbit, deer, sage grouse, and rattlesnake. If this MX goes through, it will mean the total destruction of the Shoshone people, our spiritual beliefs and our ways of life."[60]

On this basis, overt Newe opposition to nuclear militarism became both pronounced and integral to assertion of their land claims. As the matter was framed in a resolution first published by the Sacred Lands Association during the early 1980s, "The Western Shoshone Nation is calling upon citizens of the United States, as well as the world community of nations, to demand that the United States terminate its invasion of our lands for the evil purpose of testing nuclear bombs and other weapons of war."[61]

This stance, in turn, attracted attention and increasing support from various sectors of the non-Indian environmental, freeze and antiwar movements, all of which are prone to engaging in largescale demonstrations against U.S. nuclear testing and related activities. Organizations such as SANE, Clergy and Laity Concerned, Earth First!, and the Sierra Club were represented at the 1979 mass meeting. Their loose relationship to the Shoshone land claim struggle has been solidified through the work of Newe activists like the late Joe Sanchez, and reinforced by the participation of groups like Friends of the Earth, the Environmental Defense Fund, the Great Basin Greens Alliance, the American Peace Test and the Global Anti-Nuclear Alliance.[62]

As Mander puts it, "[In this regard], there have been some positive developments. Many of the peace groups have belatedly recognized the Indian issue and now request permission from the Western Shoshone Nation to demonstrate on their land. The Indians, in turn, have been issuing the demonstrators 'safe passage' permits and have agreed to speak at rallies. The Western Shoshone National Council has called the nuclear testing facility 'an absolute violation of the Treaty of Ruby Valley and the laws of the United States'... Peace activists are instructed that if they are confronted or arrested by U.S. government officials while on Shoshone land, they should show their Shoshone permits and demand to continue their activities. Furthermore, in case of trial, the defendants should include in their defense that they had legal rights to be on the land, as granted by the landowners."[63]

Looking Forward

It is in this last connection that the greatest current potential may be found, not only for the Newes in their struggle to retain (or regain) their homeland, but for (re)assertion of indigenous land rights more generally, and for the struggles of non-Indians who seek genuinely positive alternatives to the North American status quo. In the combination of forces presently coalescing in the Nevada desert lie the seeds of a new sort of communication, understanding, respect, and the growing promise of mutually beneficial joint action between native and non-native peoples in this hemisphere.

For the Shoshones, the attraction of a broad—and broadening—base of popular support for their rights offers far and away the best possibility of bringing to bear the kind and degree of pressure necessary to compel the federal government to restore all, or at least some sizable portion, of their territory. For the non-Indian individuals and organizations involved, the incipient unity they have achieved with the Newes represents both a conceptual breakthrough and a seminal practical experience of the fact that active support of native land rights can tangibly further their own interests and agendas. For many American Indians, particularly those of traditionalist persuasion, the emerging collaboration of non-Indian groups in the defense of Western Shoshone lands has come to symbolize the possibility that there are elements of the dominant population that have finally arrived at a position in which native rights are not automatically discounted as irrelevancies or presumed to be subordinate to their own. On such bases, bona fide alliances can be built.

Herein lies what may be the most important lesson to be learned by those attempting to forge a truly American radical vision, and what may ultimately translate that vision into concrete reality: Native Americans cannot hope to achieve restoration of the lands and liberty which are legitimately theirs without the support and assistance of non-Indians, while non-Indian activists cannot hope to effect any transformation of the existing social order which is not fundamentally imperialistic, and thus doomed to replicate some of the most negative aspects of the present system, unless they accept the necessity of liberating indigenous land and lives as a matter of first priority.

Both sides of the equation are at this point bound together in all but symbiotic fashion by virtue of a shared continental habitat, a common oppressor, and an increasingly interactive history. There is thus no viable option but to go forward together, figuratively joining hands to ensure our collective well-being, and that of our children, and our children's children.

It is perhaps ironic, but undoubtedly appropriate, that Newe Segobia, long thought by the invading culture to have been one of the most useless regions in all of North America, and therefore one of the last areas to be functionally incorporated into its domain, should be the locale in which this lesson is first realized in meaningful terms. Yet, in its way, because it so plainly emblemizes much that has been worst in the historical nature of Indian/white relations, the Western Shoshone resistance and the outside support it has come to attract offers us a veritable relief map of the road we must all traverse if we are to attain a future which separates itself finally and irrevocably from the colonialism, genocide, and ecocide which have come before.

Notes

1. The full text of the Ruby Valley Treaty (18 Stat. 689) will be found in Charles J. Kappler, ed., *Indian Treaties, 1778-1883* (New York: Interland, 1973) pp. 851-3.

2. Rudolph C. Ryser, *Newe Segobia and the United States of America* (Kenmore, WA: Center for World Indigenous Studies, 1985). Also see Peter Matthiessen, *Indian Country*, (New York: Viking, 1984) pp. 261-89.

3. Actually, under U.S. law, a specific Act of Congress is required to extinguish aboriginal title; *United States ex rel. Hualapi Indians v. Santa Fe Railroad*, 314, U.S. 339, 354 (1941). On Newe use of the land during this period, see Richard O. Clemmer, "Land Use Patterns and Aboriginal Rights: Northern and Eastern Nevada, 1858-1971," *The Indian Historian,* Vol 7, No. 1 (1974) pp. 24-41, 47-49.

4. Ryser, *Newe Segobia*, op. cit., pp. 15-6.

5. Wilkinson had already entered into negotiations to represent the Temoak before the Claims Commission Act was passed; ibid., p. 13, n. 1.

6. The Temoaks have said consistently that Wilkinson always represented the claim to them as being for land rather than money. The firm is known to have run the same scam on other Indian clients; ibid., pp. 16-7.

7. Ibid., p. 16. Also see Robert T. Coulter, "The Denial of Legal Remedies to Indian Nations Under U.S. Law," *American Indian Law Journal,* Vol. 9, No. 3 (1977) pp. 5-9; Robert T. Coulter and Steven M. Tullberg, "Indian Land Rights," in Sandra L. Cadwalader and Vine Deloria, Jr., eds., *The Aggressions of Civilization: Federal Indian Policy Since the 1880s* (Philadelphia: Temple University Press, 1984) pp. 185-213, quote at pp. 190-1.

8. Glenn T. Morris, "The Battle for Newe Segobia: The Western Shoshone Land Rights Struggle," in my *Critical Issues in Native North America, Vol. II* (Copenhagen: International Work Group for Indigenous Affairs, 1990) pp. 86-98.

9. Quoted in Jerry Mander, *In Absence of the Sacred: The Failure of Technology and the Survival of the Indian Nations* (San Francisco: Sierra Club Books, 1991) pp. 307-8.

10. Ibid., p. 309.

11. Quoted in ibid., p. 310.

12. Ibid., p. 308.

13. Quoted in ibid., p. 310.

14. Quoted in ibid., p. 309.

15. Ibid., p. 308.

16. Morris, "Battle for Newe Segobia," op. cit., p. 90. The case is *Western Shoshone Identifiable Group v. United States*, 11 Ind. Cl. Comm. 387, 416 (1962). The whole issue is well covered in Jack D. Forbes, "The 'Public Domain' in Nevada and Its Relationship to Indian Property Rights," *Nevada State Bar Journal*, No. 30 (1965) pp. 16-47.

17. The first award amount appears in *Western Shoshone Identifiable Group v. United States*, 29 Ind. Cl. Comm. 5 (1972) p. 124. The second award appears in *Western Shoshone Identifiable Group v. United States*, 40 Ind. Cl. Comm. 305 (1977).

18. The final Court of Claims order for Wilkinson's retention in *Western Shoshone Identifiable Group v. United States*, 593 F.2d 994 (1979). Also see "Excerpts from a Memorandum from the Duckwater Shoshone Tribe, Battle Mountain Indian Community, and the Western Shoshone Sacred Lands Association in Opposition to the Motion and Petition for Attorney Fees and Expenses, July 15, 1980," in National Lawyers Guild, Committee on Indian Struggles, *Rethinking Indian Law*, (New Haven, CT: Advocate Press, 1982) pp. 68-9.

19. *Western Shoshone Identifiable Group v. United States*, 40 Ind. Cl. Comm. 311 (1977). The final award valued the Shoshone land at $1.05 per acre. The land in question brings about $250 per acre on the open market at present.

20. Ryser, *Newe Segobia*, op. cit., p. 8, n. 4.

21. Ibid, p. 20.

22. Quoted in Mander, *Absence of the Sacred*, op. cit., p. 301.

23. Quoted in ibid., pp. 308-9.

24. Ibid., p. 311.

25. Quoted in ibid., p. 302.

26. *United States v. Dann*, 572 F.2d 222 (1978). For reaction, see Kristine L. Foot, "*United States v. Dann*: What It Portends for Ownership of Millions of Acres in the Western United States," *Public Land Law Review*, No. 5, 1984, pp. 183–91.

27. Quoted in Mander, *Absence of the Sacred*, op. cit., p. 312.

28. Ibid.

29. *United States v. Dann*, Civ. No. R–74-60, April 25, 1980.

30. *United States v. Dann*, 706 F.2d 919, 926 (1983).

31. Morris, "Battle for Newe Segobia," op. cit., p. 94.

32. Quoted in Mander, *Absence of the Sacred*, op. cit., p. 318.

33. Ibid., pp. 316-17.

34. Angela, Ursula and Alessandra, WSDP Activists, "U.S. Jails Clifford Dan," *Western Shoshone Defense Project Newsletter*, Vol. 1, No. 4, 1993. One of the problems experienced in this case was the intervention of Canadian attorney Bruce Clark, who counseled Clifford Dann to adopt a strict "sovereignty defense" in simply rejecting U.S. jurisidiction at trial. While Clark's position was techincally correct, it would have been pertinent—as Colorado AIM leader Glenn Morris, himself an attorney, pointed out at the time—to have *also* observed that Dann happened to be entirely innocent of the charges against him. For his part, presiding judge Bill McKibben imposed an especially harsh sentence because, he said, he wanted to "make an example that U.S. law cannot be ignored."

35. Mander, *Absence of the Sacred*, op. cit., p. 317.

36. The Inter-American Commission is the organ mandated by the Charter of the OAS with the task of promoting the observance of human rights among OAS member states, including the United States. As a member of the OAS, the U.S. is legally bound to uphold the organization's human rights principles. The Commission's action was taken in response to a petition filed by Mary and Carrie Dann on Feb. 19, 1998; "Inter-American Commission on Human Rights Requests United States to Stay Action Against Western Shoshone Sisters," Indian Law Resource Center Press Release, Apr. 7, 1988. Also see "Inter-American Commission on Human Rights Considers the Danns' Case Against the United States," *Western Shoshone Defense Project Newsletter*, Vol. 5, No. 1, 1997.

37. Quoted in Mander, *Absence of the Sacred*, op. cit., p. 313.

38. Ibid.

39. Quoted in ibid., p. 316.

40. Conversation with Raymond Yowell, Reno Nevada, April 1991.

41. Quoted in Mander, *Absence of the Sacred*, op. cit., p. 314.

42. Ibid.

43. Quoted in ibid., p. 315.

44. Ibid.

45. Estimate provided by Raymond Yowell.

46. Anders Stephanson, *Manifest Destiny: American Expansion and the Empire of Right* (New York: Hill & Wang, 1995).

47. This, of course, was precisely the situation the entire Indian Claims Commission process of paying compensation rather than effecting land restorations was designed to avert. See Leonard A. Carlson, "What Was It Worth? Economic and Historical Aspects of Determining Awards in Indian Land Claims Cases," in Imre Sutton, ed., *Irredeemable America: The Indians' Estate and Land Claims* (Albuquerque: University of New Mexico Press, 1985) pp. 87–110.

48. Christopher Sewall, "Oro Nevada Mining Company: The Trojan Horse," *Western Shoshone Defense Project Newsletter*, Vol. 5, No.1, 1997.

49. Ibid.

50. "In 1995, Canadian company Diamond Field Resources discovered the world's richest nickel deposit at Voisey's Bay. Since then, over 300,000 mining claims have been filed by hundreds of companies and individuals on land that has never been ceded or sold by its original occupants. While currently pushing forward with their land claims, the Innu and Inuit were recently informed by the provincial government of Newfoundland that the land on which the mineral deposit is located will not be part of any land claims negotiations... On the southern portion of Innu territory (known as Nitassinan), along the north shore of the St. Lawrence River in Québec, a similar mining rush has occurred"; ibid., p. 9.

51. Suharto, whose military provides direct security for Bre-X's operations, has an especially bloody history. In 1965, he led the coup against Indonesian president Sukarno that left as many as a million people dead; Noam Chomsky and Edward S. Herman, *The Political Economy of Human Rights, Vol. 1: The Washington Connection and Third World Fascism* (Boston: South End Press, 1979) pp. 205-9. More recently, he has overseen the genocidal pacification of East Timor; John G. Taylor, *Indonesia's Forgotten War: The Hidden History of East Timor* (London: Pluto Press, 1991). The royalties paid by Bre-X, which claims to have discovered Indonesia's richest gold deposit, stand not only to reinforce this ghastly régime, but to augment the personal fortune Suharto—currently estimated at some $60 *billion*—has already siphoned off from his generally impoverished people.

52. On Nov. 10, 1997, Oro Resources Vice President for Government Affairs Tibeau Piquet announced the "Hand Me Down Project" to secure partners in opening mines in Crescent Valley. The Vancouver-based Placer Dome Corporation, a subsibary of Kennecott, was most prominently spotlighted as a possibility, probably because of its existing mines in the area. Others mentioned were the Toronto-based Barrick Gold Corporation and Denver's Newmont Mining; "Oro Nevada Action Alert, Letters Needed!" *Western Shoshone Defense Project Newsletter*, Vol. 5, No. 2, 1997. On Cortez Gold, see Chris Sewall, "Cortez, The Conquest Continues," *Western Shoshone Defense Project Newsletter*, Vol. 3, No. 1, 1995. On the Pipeline Mine, see Christopher Sewall, "Pipeline's Dirty Little Secrets: Placer Dome's new mine in Crescent Valley experiencing problems," *Western Shoshone Defense Project Newsletter*, Vol. 5, No. 2, 1997. On South Pipeline, see Christopher Sewall, "South Pipeline: We Told You So!," *Western Shoshone Defense Project Newsletter*, Vol. 5, No. 1, 1997. In addition to Pipeline and Pipeline South, another sixteen mines are operating in the area and a seventeenth, Echo Bay Mining's planned pit at Twin Creeks, has recently been okayed; Tom Myers, "Twin Creeks Mine Approved by BLM," *Western Shoshone Defense Project Newsletter*, Vol. 5, No. 1, 1997.

53. Christopher Sewall, "Australian Mining Giant, [Western Mining Corporation], Has Eyes On Western Shoshone Land," *Western Shoshone Defense Project Newsletter*, Vol. 5, No. 1, 1997. Aside from WMC, other corporations with speculative interests in the area include Amax Gold, Independence Mining, Royal Gold, Battle Mountain Gold, Homestake Mining and Uranez; "Oro Action Alert," op. cit.

54. On testing in Micronesia, see Jason Clay, "Militarization and Indigenous Peoples, Part I: The Americas and the Pacific," *Cultural Survival Quarterly*, No. 3, 1987. On testing in Nevada, see Dagmar Thorpe's *Newe Segobia: The Western Shoshone People and Land* (Lee, NV: Western Shoshone Sacred Lands Association, 1982) and the essay "Cold War Impacts on Native North America: The Political Economy of Radioactive Colonization," in my *A Little Matter of Genocide: Holocaust and Denial in the Americas, 1492 to the Present* (San Francisco/Winnipeg: City Lights/Arbeiter Ring, 1997) esp. pp. 324-32.

55. Ian Zabarte, "Western Shoshone National Sovereignty Violated by Subcritical Nuclear Weapons Test," *Western Shoshone Defense Project Newsletter*, Vol. 5, No. 2, 1997.

56. Bernard Nietschmann and William Le Bon, "Nuclear States and Fourth World Nations," *Cultural Survival Quarterly*, Vol. 11, No. 4, 1988, pp. 4-7.

57. The Yucca Mountain plan is probably best-handled in Gerald Jacob's *Site Unseen: The Politics of Siting a Nuclear Repository* (Pittsburg: University of Pittsburg Press, 1990) and Valerie L. Kuletz's *The Tainted Desert: Environmental and Social Ruin in the American West* (New York: Routledge, 1998). Also see *To Protect Mother Earth*, a documentary film directed by Joel Freedman (New York: Cinnamon Productions, 1990).

58. Martha C. Knack, "MX Issues for Native American Communities," in Francis Hartigan, ed., *MX in Nevada: A Humanistic Perspective* (Reno: Nevada Humanities Press, 1980) pp. 59-66.

59. Quoted in Mander, *Absence of the Sacred*, op. cit., p. 313.

60. Quoted in ibid., pp. 312-13.

61. Quoted in Nietschmann and Le Bon, "Nuclear States," op. cit., p. 7.

62. Sanchez, an organizer with the Seventh Generation Fund, died of leukemia on June 30, 1993. He was 37 years old; Mary Lee Dazey and Dedee Sanchez, "Remembering Joe Sanchez," *Western Shoshone Defence Project Newsletter*, Vol. 1, No. 5, 1993.

63. Mander, *Absence of the Sacred*, op. cit., p. 316.

189

LAST STAND AT LUBICON LAKE
Genocide and Ecocide in the Canadian North

> We've been pushed as far as we can go. This is where we make our stand.
>
> —Chief Bernard Ominayak, 1989

OFTEN the situation of even the smallest of peoples can provide considerable insight into the likely fate of much broader groups, the outcomes of their seemingly particularized circumstances becoming indicative of far more general problems. Such a case is the ongoing struggle of the Lubicon Lake Band of Cree in northern Alberta to preserve their ancestral landbase, their way of life and their very identity as a people. The methods which have been and are being used by a consortium of Canadian governmental and corporate entities to deny such things to the people of Lubicon Lake, and the reasons underpinning this governmental/corporate behavior, add up to a prospectus for all the indigenous peoples in the Anglo-dominated portion of this hemisphere.

The whole thing began in 1899 when a delegation from the Canadian government traveled through northern Alberta to secure the signatures of representatives from various aboriginal groups in the area upon an international document titled Treaty 8. The purpose of this instrument, as had been the case of each of the other Canadian-Indian treaties (a legal process begun in 1781), was to gain "clear title" to as much native land as possible for the British Crown. In exchange, under provisions of Treaty 8, each Indian band was to retain a formally acknowledged ("reserved") area within its traditional domain for its own exclusive use and occupancy, as well as hunting, fishing, and trapping rights within much larger contiguous territories. Additionally, each band was to receive a small monetary settlement for lands lost, and each individual band member was to receive, in perpetuity, an annual cash stipend.[1]

It was well understood in Ottawa at the time that the treaty commissioners had failed to contact, or secure agreement to the terms and conditions of Treaty 8, from many of the small bands scattered across the vast area affected by the document. The Canadian government nonetheless chose to view these bands as being equally bound by the treaty and relied upon the Indians' "moccasin telegraph" to eventually spread the word. An improvised arrangement was established wherein members of previously unnotified bands might simply show up at agencies serving the signatory groups in order to receive annual per capita payments. Little or no thought appears to have been devoted by the government to deciding how to keep such intermingling sorted out for record-keeping purposes, or how Canada might go about meeting its obligation to demarcate acceptable reserved areas for each late-notice band as it was identified.[2]

As it turned out, members of the Lubicon Lake Band did not receive word of Treaty 8 until sometime around 1910. At that point, nothing much changed for them other than that band members gradually began to make an annual trek to Whitefish Lake, the location of the agency serving another Cree group, in order to receive their annuities. The local Indian agent, following government guidelines, simply recorded their names on his pay list and went on about his business. For their part, the Lubicons continued to live where and how they had, very much unconcerned with what went on in Ottawa, or even at Whitefish Lake. The situation remained unchanged for about a quarter of a century.[3]

At some point in 1935, however, the residents of Lubicon Lake were informed that, given the appearance of their names on the list of Whitefish Lake payees, they were considered by Canada to be part of that more southerly band. It was suggested that they were therefore living in a location well outside "their" reserved area and should accordingly relocate to a place nearer the Whitefish Lake agency. Those at Lubicon Lake, of course, protested this misidentification and for the first time requested the establishment of a reserve of their own.[4] This led, in 1939, to a visit from C.P. Schmidt, the Alberta Inspector of Indian Agents, for purposes of investigating their claim. This resulted in a report by Schmidt to Ottawa stipulating that he had concluded the people at Lubicon Lake were in fact a band distinct from the people at Whitefish Lake, and that they were thus entitled to a reserve.[5]

The government initially accepted Schmidt's recommendation, as well as his census fixing the Lubicon population at 127 persons. This number was multiplied by the 128 acres per person the government felt was a sufficient domain for Indians, and it was thereby decided that the Lubicon Lake Reserve should be composed of some twenty-five square miles of territory. An aerial survey was conducted, and in 1940 the lines of the new reserve boundaries were tentatively drawn on the map. All seemed to be going quite well, with the only remaining formality being a ground survey by which to set the boundaries definitively. But Canada, enmeshed in World War II at this time and qualified surveyors being correspondingly scarce, decided to delay finalization of the process until hostilities had ceased.[6]

Things began to get sticky during the summer of 1942 when a man named Malcom McCrimmon was sent to Alberta to see that the province's annuity pay lists were in order. McCrimmon's stated concern, as part of a broader desire to "put all of Canada's resources behind the war effort," was to ensure that "these Indians are not getting something for nothing." To this end, he arbitrarily rewrote the rules pertaining to eligibility for per capita payments so that all who had been added to the Treaty 8 pay lists after 1912 were eliminated out-of-hand. He then went on to require that "an individual must furnish acceptable proof that his male ancestors were of pure Indian blood."

Given that only written birth records were posited as constituting such proof, and that Indians traditionally maintained no such records, the latter clause can be viewed as an attempt not only to limit the number of native people recognized as such (and therefore receiving annuities), but to eliminate them altogether. In any event, McCrimmon quickly removed the names of more than 700 northern Alberta Indians—including ninety of the 154 then belonging to the Lubicon Lake Band—from the pay lists. He also specifically recommended against establishing the Lubicon Lake Reserve because there were no longer "enough eligible Indians to warrant" such action. Hence, the earlier "postponement" of the reserve's actualization assumed an aura of permanence.[7]

Enter the Oil Companies

On April 17, 1952, the director of the Technical Division of (Alberta's) Provincial Lands and Forests Department wrote to the federal Department of the Interior in Ottawa that: "Due to the fact that there are considerable inquiries regarding the minerals in the [Lubicon Lake] area, and also the fact that there is a request to establish a mission at this point, we are naturally anxious to clear our records of this provisional reserve if the land is not required by this Band of Indians." Alberta followed up shortly thereafter by informing Ottawa that the Lubicon Lake site seemed "too isolated" to be effectively administered as a permanent reserve and that:

It is recommended that the twenty-four sections of land set aside for a reserve at Lubicon lake be exchanged for [a more convenient site]... [The Deputy Minister for Provincial Lands and Forests had] no objections to the transfer though there is no assurance that the mineral rights could be included [with the "more convenient" site ... If the reserve at Lubicon is retained, the Band would have the mineral rights... *[We] recommend the exchange be made even if mineral rights cannot be guaranteed* (emphasis added).[8]

The initiative embodied in this flurry of correspondence from Alberta was capped off on October 22, 1953, when the province handed the federal government a virtual ultimatum: "It is some years now since [the Lubicon Lake site was provisionally reserved, and] it would be appreciated if you would confirm that the proposal to establish this reservation has been abandoned. *If no reply has been received within 30 days, it will be assumed that the reservation has been struck from the records* (emphasis added)."[9]

For its part, the Department of the Interior opted for inaction concerning its acknowledged obligations to the Lubicon Lake Cree, allowing the province of Alberta to play the heavy in what amounted to an emerging and fully national policy of energy development in the Canadian north. The matter was rather clearly admitted in a February 25, 1954, letter from the Alberta regional Supervisor for Indian Affairs to the Indian agent within whose area of responsibility the Lubicons fell.

As you are no doubt aware, the Deputy Minister [for Provincial Lands and Forests] had from time to time asked when our Department [of the Interior] was likely to make a decision as to whether or not to take up [the Lubicon Lake] Reserve. *There were so many inquiries from oil companies to explore the area that it was becoming embarrassing to state that it could not be entered.* That situation existed when our Branch [Indian Affairs] was advised that unless the Department gave a definite answer before the end of 1953 the Provincial Authorities were disposed to cancel the reservation and return it to Crown Lands which then could be explored.... This was discussed when I was in Ottawa last October. *I was of the opinion that our Branch had taken no action and that the block [of land at Lubicon Lake] would automatically return to Alberta* (emphasis added).

The supervisor then went on to explain that the federal government was very well aware of the implications of this line of action, instructing his agent to collaborate directly in effecting the expropriation of Lubicon resources: "In approaching the subject with the Indians, *I think it would be well to keep in mind that the mineral rights [at Lubicon Lake] may be very much more valuable than anything else…If this Block [of land at Lubicon] was given up, then it is very unlikely that mineral rights would be made available with the surface rights of any other reserve that might be picked up* (emphasis added)."[10]

The minerals with which the government correspondence was primarily concerned at the time mostly consisted of oil and natural gas, rich deposits of which had earlier been determined by Petro-Canada, Ottawa's own energy corporation, to underlie the entire Peace River region. Petro-Canada had already enlisted a consortium of ten transnational energy giants—including Royal Dutch Shell, Shell Canada, Exxon, Gulf, and Standard Oil of California—to become involved in "exploration and development" of the area. Both the federal and provincial governments stood to reap a considerable profit on the bargain, with only the rights of a few small groups of Indians standing in the way. The obvious "solution," under such conditions, was simply to deny native rights within the intended development zone, setting the stage for the removal of all Indians from the area.

Even at that, there appears to have been substantial official resistance (especially within the Alberta government) to the idea of providing *any* acreage with which to establish substitute or "replacement" reserves for those Indians targeted for coerced relocation. As concerns the Lubicons in particular, the focus of governmental discourse had shifted to the vernacular of outright liquidation by early 1955, a matter readily evidenced in an instruction issued by the federal Superintendent of Reserves and Trusts to his staff.

> Consult the appropriate files and advise whether action was taken by the Department to officially establish [the Lubicon Lake Band] as a Band, for at that time any such action appears rather short-sighted, and if this group was not established as an official Band, *it will serve our purposes very well at the present time* (emphasis added).[11]

In another memo, the Alberta Regional Supervisor for Indian Affairs clarified the government's intent in denying the Lubicons' existence: "[T]he Whitefish Lake Band have no objection to [the Lubicon Lake people] being transferred…to their Band and I am suggesting [the local Indian agent] contact those members [of the Lubicon Lake Band] who are at present residing at Whitefish Lake and Grouard and ascertain if they wish to file applications for transfer. If they all wish to transfer it would reduce the Lubicon Lake Band membership to approximately thirty."[12] Elsewhere, the supervisor observed that:

It is quite possible that the seven families [who had been approached and said they'd accept enfranchisement in another band if they could not have a reserve at Lubicon Lake itself] will make application for enfranchisement in the near future... Should they do so I would recommend that enfranchisement be granted... The few remaining members of the [Lubicon Lake] Band could no doubt be absorbed into some other band.[13]

In the interests of oil extraction and attending profit potentials, then, the Lubicons finished the decade of the 1950s with the gains they had seemed to make in their relationship to the Canadian government during the 1930s and early '40s largely erased and confronted instead by the spectre of their complete administrative elimination as an identifiable human group.[14]

Development Begins

Things no doubt proceeded more slowly than Ottawa and Alberta originally intended. The abundant availability and low cost of oil during the 1960s created a situation in which Petro-Canada's transnational partners deemed it cost-prohibitive to underwrite the infrastructure necessary to allow production in the Canadian hinterland, and it was not until the OPEC-induced "energy crisis" of the early 1970s that this assessment of economic reality was altered. Thus, it was not until 1973 that investments were finally secured with which to begin the building of an all-weather road from Edmonton through the Lubicon Lake area.[15]

In the interim, the Lubicons had had ample opportunity to overcome their initial confusion concerning the government's various ploys, and had all but unanimously rejected the notion that they should be merged with the rolls of other bands. At about the same time the road construction project commenced to the south, the traditional governing council at Lubicon Lake met to reaffirm the existence—and right to *continuing* existence—of the band. They also decided that, since Ottawa had done nothing positive to solve the "question" of who in fact belonged to the band, the band would exercise its sovereign right of determining this for itself, independent of federal concerns and criteria. Most of those who had been placed on the rolls of other bands thereupon resumed their identification as Lubicons.

For approximately five years a rough stasis was maintained, as road work dragged on and on. The Lubicons continued to live and conduct their affairs very much as they had throughout the twentieth century, despite the persistent federal and provincial policy controversies their existence had sparked. Then, in 1978, as the road reached the Lubicon Lake region, there was a sudden upsurge in seismic and other forms of oil and gas exploration. While outsiders poured into the area, setting dynamite charges, bulldozing access roads and marking cut-lines, the true dimension of what was happening began to emerge. With their entire way of life plainly in jeopardy, the Lubicons could no longer simply ignore the government.[16] As they explained it in a 1983 presentation in Ottawa:

> Until about 10 years ago the questions of land, Band membership, mineral rights and rights generally were essentially academic. Our area was relatively isolated and inaccessible by road. We had little contact with outsiders, including Government officials. We were left pretty much alone. We were allowed to live our lives, raise our families, and pursue our traditional way of life without much interference. [But] about 10 years ago the Provincial Government started construction of an all-weather road into our area. The purpose of the road is clearly to facilitate development of our area. The road was completed about five years ago... Faced with the prospect of an influx of outsiders into our traditional area, we tried to file a caveat with the Provincial Government, the effect of which would have been to formally serve notice on all outsiders of our unextinguished, aboriginal claim to the area.[17]

Alberta refused to accept the caveat, and the Lubicons attempted to force the matter in federal court.

> The Provincial Government asked the court to postpone hearing the case until another being tried in the Northwest Territories was decided. The case in the Territories went against the Indians; however, the decision read that the court there would have found for the Indians, had the law been written as it was in Alberta and Saskatchewan... The Province then went back to court and asked for another postponement, during which they rewrote the relevant Provincial legislation, making the changes retroactive to before the time we tried to file our caveat... In light of the rewritten, retroactive Provincial legislation, the [federal] judge dismissed our case as no longer having any basis in law... It is noteworthy that the Federal Government chose to exercise its trust responsibility [to the Indians] during the caveat case by filing a brief *in behalf of the Provincial Government* (emphasis added).[18]

The Lubicons then petitioned Ottawa under conventional Canadian trust provisions to allocate them financial support with which to seek injunctive relief through the courts and to appoint a special land claims commissioner to attempt to resolve land title issues in the Peace River region. These ideas were rejected by the government in 1980. Instead, during the summer of 1981: "[T]he Provincial Government declared [the Lubicon] community to be a Provincial hamlet, surveyed it, divided it up into little 2-acre plots, and tried to force our people to either lease these plots, or accept them as 'gifts' from the Province. People who supported the Provincial Government's Hamlet and Land Tenure Program were promised services and security. People who opposed the program faced all kinds of consequences…"[19]

Fearing that acceptance of the Provincial Hamlet and Land Tenure Program would jeopardize their land rights, the band then asked the province to delay implementation of the program until its effect could be determined.

> They refused, stating that they had checked the legal implications of the program and had been assured that there was "no relationship between land claims and land tenure." When we continued to question the effect implementation of their program would have on our land rights, they resorted to a legalistic form of deception. One old woman, who can neither read nor write, signed a program application form after being told that she was signing for free firewood. Another was told that she was signing for an Alberta Housing trailer. A third was told she was signing a census form.[20]

The real relationship between Alberta's Hamlet and Land Tenure Program on the one hand, and the Lubicons' aboriginal rights on the other, was amply revealed the following year. "When it became absolutely and unavoidably clear that we would not get anywhere with the Provincial Government," the Lubicons recounted in their 1983 presentation, "we appealed to the Federal Minister [for Indian Affairs]. He responded by sending the Province a telex requesting a six-month delay in the implementation of the Provincial land tenure program, during which time, he said, he hoped to resolve the question of our land rights.… The Provincial Minister of Municipal Affairs responded to the Federal Minister's telex with a letter, questioning the very existence of our Band, and stating that *our community could not be part of a land claim anyway, since it was now a Provincial Hamlet, and was no longer classed as unoccupied Crown land…* (emphasis added)."[21]

Legal Stalemate

The federal minister concerned, E. Davie "Jim" Fulton, appears to have been something of a maverick in governmental circles and was unconvinced by Alberta's argument. Further, he actually sat down and talked with the

Lubicon leadership, reaching the conclusion that the band's position was not unreasonable and could be accommodated in some fashion by both Ottawa and the province. He therefore convened a meeting between representatives of his own federal Indian ministry and the provincial government of Alberta during January of 1982, intending to negotiate a resolution to the Lubicon land issue "agreeable to all parties concerned" (typically, the Indians themselves were entirely excluded when it came to such high-level deliberations over their rights and fate). To the minister's undoubted astonishment, negotiations broke down almost immediately.

> During the meeting between Federal and Provincial officials, the Province rejected out-of-hand most if not all of the points discussed between Federal officials and officials of the Band. Provincial officials refused to consider the question of land entitlement until they were satisfied as to the "merits" of that entitlement. They refused to agree to a timetable for determining the merits of that entitlement. They refused to consider the land which had been originally selected or which included our traditional community of Little Buffalo Lake. They refused to include mineral rights. They refused to consider any compensation whatsoever. They even refused to meet with any representatives of the Band.[22]

In the wake of the January meeting, the Lubicons once again requested financial assistance from the Indian ministry with which to litigate their land claims. Implausibly under the circumstances, Fulton denied the request on the basis that "the negotiating route has not been exhausted."[23] At a council meeting, the Lubicons then resolved, in view of the expressed intransigence of Alberta authorities and the bad faith evident in their continuing pursuit of the Hamlet and Land Tenure Program, to suspend all further dealings with the provincial government. It was also decided to pursue legal remedies despite Fulton's default on federal trust obligations, on the basis of the limited band resources and whatever external support might be obtained. Consequently, a second legal action was entered by the Lubicon Lake Cree before the Alberta Court of the Queen's Bench in February, 1982.[24]

> In the second legal action we asked the court for a declaration that we retain aboriginal rights over our traditional lands, that these rights include mineral rights, that these rights are under exclusive Federal jurisdiction, and that the oil and gas leases granted by the Province [on Lubicon land] are null, void and unconstitutional, or at least subject to Indian rights. We also asked the court to grant an immediate injunction preventing the oil companies from undertaking further development activities in our area.[25]

Attorneys for Alberta and for the various corporations involved argued

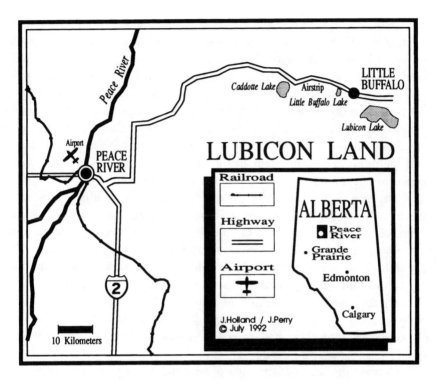

heatedly that the province itself enjoyed immunity from the desired injunctive relief, and that the corporations (including Petro-Canada, a purely federal entity)—as contractual agents of the province—were sheltered under the same mantle of immunity. To its credit, the court ruled in favor of the Lubicons on this outrageous thesis. But it then closeted itself to consider a range of procedural issues raised by the province and corporations concerning why the injunctive matter should not be heard, even though the Indians were entitled to bring it before the bench.

> Ultimately, we beat back all of these procedural challenges, but not in time to stop much of the damage that we'd hoped to stop. Concluding arguments on the procedural points were heard on December 2, 1982. In Alberta, such procedural points are usually decided very fast. However, in this case, a decision was not brought down until March 2, 1983, exactly three months to the day from the time concluding arguments were heard. These three months coincided exactly with the oil companies' winter season, which is of course the period of most intense development activity, since the ground at this time of year is frozen, allowing for the relatively easy transport of heavy equipment.[26]

Thus, the court was able to arrive at a judicially sound conclusion, avoiding the entry of a disastrously contaminating precedent into Canadian law, or risking being overturned upon review by a higher court, while simultaneously allowing those it was preparing to rule against to complete their objectionable activities prior to entry of its ruling. All the oil companies had to do was accelerate their exploration operations so as to be able to complete them in one winter rather than the two or three which had been remaining on their various schedules. The Lubicons were then presented with the opportunity to obtain an injunction suspending governmental and corporate operations which had already been completed.

This was the limit of the Lubicons' legal "success." With the most environmentally damaging aspects of the oil extraction process largely completed, the court was free to rule that pumping operations could proceed insofar as they—in themselves—presented "no real threat" to the Cree way of life. No attempt was made to determine whether the sheer infusion of outsiders into the formerly isolated Lubicon territory might not have precisely this effect. As a result of the court's de facto nonintervention in oil exploitation, the value of the petroleum being pumped from the immediate area of the Lubicon claim had exceeded $1 million in U.S. dollars per day by mid-1987 and was rising rapidly.[27]

Concerning the broader issues of land rights and jurisdiction, the court held that it could not resolve the issues because, as Bill McKnight, Fulton's replacement as federal Indian Minister, would later put it, the band "attempted to follow two mutually exclusive processes—a settlement under Treaty 8 and a settlement in aboriginal title." The court made no comment at all on the fact that it had been the government itself which had barred exercise of Lubicon rights under the treaty while simultaneously holding that they were covered by the document, at least for purposes of extinguishing their aboriginal title. Further, no hint was offered as to what in the court's view might be a correct course for the band to pursue in effecting a settlement under Crown Law.

The Lubicons, of course, took the matter to the Alberta Court of Appeal, which upheld the lower, Queen's Court in January 1985. In March, and again in May of the same year, the Supreme Court of Canada refused to hear the case.[28] Although the Lubicons have continued to pursue legal remedies in Canadian courts since then, the weight of their efforts to achieve a real solution has shifted heavily into other areas of endeavor.

Assertion of Lubicon Sovereignty

In 1982, under the leadership of Chief Bernard Ominayak, the people of Lubicon Lake, defining themselves at this point as being some 250 individuals, began to express ever more strongly their traditional rights as a wholly sovereign people.[29] Following this logic, they increasingly de-emphasized their entitlement, always resisted by the Alberta government, to the 25.4 square mile reserve provisionally demarcated in 1940. Instead, reasoning that since they'd never signed a treaty of cession they'd ceded no land at all, the Lubicons began to articulate their land rights in terms of the territory historically used by their ancestors for purposes of hunting, fishing, trapping, occupancy and trading purposes.

In total, this amounts to about a thousand times the area involved in the reserve Alberta had so resolutely attempted to cheat them of (but which they might well have accepted, had the government met its obligation to convey title to them during World War II). The 25,000 square mile tract of land claimed by aboriginal right comprises about a quarter of the entire province of Alberta. In addition, the Lubicons stipulated that they were due some $900 million in U.S. dollars for damages done to their territory during the period of illegal Canadian occupancy.[30]

The official response was initially to scoff at such "presumptuousness." The Lubicons, meanwhile, rather than continuing to argue their case in the courts, launched a public outreach and education campaign to secure popular support. To the government's surprise and consternation, the response to this effort was so generally favorable that steps were necessary to contain the situation. This assumed the form of an "independent investigation" undertaken in 1984 by the Reverend Dr. Randall Ivany, Ombudsman of Alberta, who dutifully went through the motions of examining the Lubicon claims before releasing a report entitled *Complaints of the Lubicon Lake Band of Indians*. Predictably, the document concluded that there was "no substance" to the Lubicons' allegations and "no factual basis" to their charge that various layers of Canadian government were engaged in committing cultural genocide against them.[31]

While Ivany's report was intended to undercut the rising tide of public sentiment favoring the Lubicons, its very transparency generated an altogether opposite dynamic. Capitalizing on this PR windfall, Chief Ominayak and other Lubicon leaders shortly began to issue statements to the effect that they were considering conducting a boycott, largescale demonstrations and other disruptions of the 1988 Winter Olympics, scheduled for Calgary, Alberta.

In something of a panic, both Alberta and Ottawa quickly resorted to what each must have felt were "extraordinary measures" in a mutual effort to avert an international embarrassment and scrutiny of what they had been doing to indigenous peoples under the guise of "domestic affairs." Ivany's sham investigation was quickly supplanted by another, this one functioning under auspices of McKnight's Department of Indian and Northern Affairs but chaired by the minister's predecessor, Jim Fulton (who, having been removed from office for not being sufficiently hardline, was now industriously hyped as a "friend of the Indian").[32]

The first tangible result of this official change in attitude was an offer, made on December 10, 1985, and recommended by Fulton, of the 1940 reserve area, complete with the mineral rights which had appeared so problematic to Canadian policymakers only a year before.[33] This overture was rejected on the same day by the Lubicons, with Chief Ominayak pointing out that it was the government's own greed and deviousness which had blocked establishment of the reserve for nearly half a century, forcing the Indians to pursue the full extent of their aboriginal rights in the first place. The Lubicons, he said, would be prepared to enter into any serious negotiations concerning Canadian recognition of their sovereignty and the real scope of their territory.[34]

After a quick huddle, Ottawa officials returned in January 1986 with the offer of an *ex gratia* award—which they'd previously refused to do on two separate occasions—of $1.5 million in Canadian dollars to cover the cost of Lubicon litigation for reserved land rights, to date. The Lubicons accepted the payment and then filed suit in April for that amount *plus* an additional $750,000 Canadian dollars to cover future costs of litigation; in November of 1986, the suit was amended to encompass $1.4 million in past litigation costs and $2 million in projected legal fees.[35] In the latter month, the Lubicons also stepped up their campaign to organize actions around the Olympics, undertaking their first truly mass mailing on the subject and sending a delegation to Europe to rally support.[36]

Meanwhile, in June, Fulton was replaced again, this time by Roger Tasse, a former Minister of Justice, who was charged with pushing through a "negotiated settlement" in which the band might drop its protest plans and assertion of broader land rights in exchange for clear title to a tract approximately the size of the 1940 reserve. Chief Ominayak agreed to meet with federal officials, but only on condition that the government of Alberta would be completely excluded from the proceedings. In July, after preliminary discussions, the Lubicons broke off negotiations when it became clear that Ottawa was not yet prepared to take up the matter of their aboriginal land rights in any meaningful way.[37]

This was followed in January 1987 by an announcement by the Lubicons that they had determined in council that the band was now comprised of 458 individuals, some 250 of whom did not appear on federal Indian registration lists, and that they were prepared to accept a ninety square mile reserve centering on the community of Little Buffalo, over which they would exercise full control. Additionally, they asserted undisturbed hunting, fishing and trapping rights over an area of approximately four thousand square miles and insisted that, in order for these rights to have meaning, the Lubicon band would require a voice equal to those of other governments in determining corporate licensing and the development policy impacting their region. Chief Ominayak also stated that the band would henceforth begin, by force if necessary, to evict corporate work crews within the reserve proper and elsewhere as need be. In March, the size of reserve area was amended to read "92 square miles/236 square kilometers" in a motion filed with the Court of Queen's Bench in Alberta.[38]

May of 1987 saw delegations of Lubicons in both the United States and Europe explaining the band's position, mustering support for the proposed Olympic boycott, and preparing an intervention on their case for submission in July to the United Nations Working Group on Indigenous Populations (a subpart of ECOSOC, the U.N. Economic and Social Council, reporting to the Human Rights Commission).[39] Another item on the delegates' agenda was a partially successful effort to convince various museums not to lend objects to "The Spirit Sings," a government-sponsored exhibition of native artifacts scheduled for display in conjunction with the Olympics in Calgary.[40] Such outreach efforts continued to achieve very positive results.[41]

In the face of mounting international pressure, both Ottawa and Alberta appointed formal negotiators—Brian Malone for the federal government, Jim Horseman for the province—in October 1987. The federal government simultaneously released *The Fulton Report*, a plan prepared by the former Indian minister calling for tripartite meetings between Ottawa, Alberta and the Lubicons to resolve the land rights and sovereignty issues "equitably and permanently."[42] The Lubicon leadership rejected the idea, pointing to the outcome of a similar tripartite negotiating arrangement signed on December 23, 1986, between Ottawa, Alberta and the thousand-member Fort Chippewyan Band of Cree, in which the Indians' traditional territory had been reduced into a mere twenty square mile reserve divided into nine separate parcels.

Chief Ominayak stated that his people hardly considered this to be the "productive result of negotiations" touted by Alberta, at least not from the indigenous perspective. He followed up on January 23, 1988, by releasing through the *Calgary Herald* the information that the Lubicons had entered into a formal alliance with other bands and many whites in the north country, and that these "Indians and non-Indians in Alberta, Saskatchewan and Québec have agreed to set up a resident army on Lubicon territory." Provincial fish and wildlife officials would "be subject to arrest and trial," he said, in the event they attempted to interfere with the exercise of Lubicon sovereignty anywhere within the unceded area.[43]

Such warnings carried a tangible ring of authority. As analyst John Goddard has observed, "It is hard to imagine an Indian band better prepared" to pursue its national rights "than the Lubicon Lake band of early 1988."

> By the time the Olympic Games opened in Calgary, the Lubicon people...commanded international support and the means to convert that support into political power. They had prevailed in disputes with Union Oil and all the other dozens of other oil companies that had gone from posting "No Trespassing" signs to asking the band's permission to work in Lubicon territory... Band members controlled the ninety square miles they had identified as [their] reserve. Plans for a new community were ready for tender... Essentially, the Lubicon Lake Cree remained a cohesive Indian society led by purposeful elders and a gifted chief. [44]

Faced with the prospect of an outright armed confrontation, Alberta Premier Don Getty at last began to give bits of ground, offering in March to immediately place the 1940 acre reserve area claimed by Alberta under Lubicon control, and to align with the Indians in negotiating for additional acreage from Ottawa. Chief Ominayak declined the transfer, but accepted the latter proposal, joining with Getty in calling for establishment of a three-member tribunal to hear and effect a binding resolution upon the

Lubicon claims against both the province and the central government.[45] McKnight, however, stonewalled the idea, countering that if "Alberta wishes to be bound by a tribunal in providing Alberta land to the Lubicons, that is Alberta's right," and that he expected the province to provide a 45 square mile parcel "in full satisfaction of *all* Lubicon claims," thus exempting Ottawa from any responsibility in the situation whatsoever.[46] On May 17, he filed suit to compel Getty to accede to his demands.

Confrontation

There followed several months of legal maneuvering in which McKnight thwarted all efforts to achieve a reasonable compromise. Finally, on October 6, 1988, James O'Reilly, the Lubicons' head litigator, appeared before the Alberta Court of Appeal at Calgary to read a statement prepared by his clients suspending further involvement in the Canadian judicial process. "This effort has been in vain," it stated. "From this day, we will no longer participate in any court proceedings in which the Lubicons are presently a party, whether in this court, the Court of Queen's Bench of Alberta, the Federal Court of Appeal or the Federal Court of Canada." Instead, it continued, by October 15, "the Lubicon Nation intends to assert and enforce its aboriginal rights and its sovereign jurisdiction as an independent Nation, with its own law enforcement and court systems."[47]

> The plan was to erect checkpoints on the four main roads into Lubicon territory. As of October 15, 1988, band members would stop all vehicles. Anybody wishing to work in the area would have to buy permits from the band office at the same rates as those paid to the Alberta government. All payments would be due in advance. Companies would have to submit copies of existing provincial authorizations to the band and post copies of approved Lubicon permits at all work sites…Oil-company employees refusing to acknowledge the band's authority would be turned back at the checkpoints. Officially, band members would be unarmed. But they had prepared spiked boards to throw across the road in an emergency, and some members hinted broadly that guns would also be at hand. [48]

"We don't have any choice," Chief Ominayak informed reporters shortly after O'Reilly had read the Lubicon statement. "It's time we protect what is ours. As of 1:00 P.M. on October 15, anybody who wants to come on our land will have to deal with us and recognize this land is ours."[49] "After fifty years of trying to get their own home recognized as their home, and their own land, and a fair deal," O'Reilly observed as the roadblocks went up, "and of being thrown from federal broken promise to federal broken promise and nothing happening, and nothing on the horizon, and their way of life being destroyed, and the United Nations having reproached Canada to do something about it and Canada saying basically, 'We don't care what you say,' and flouting international law—enough is enough! The Lubicons intend to make this literally their last stand."[50]

By the afternoon of the 15th, all oil company activity on Lubicon land had ceased, a matter which was variously estimated to cost the corporations from $260,000 to $430,000 (Canadian) per day.[51] By then, Getty had upped the provincial settlement offer from 25.4 to 79 square miles.[52] The Lubicons responded that recent births had expanded their population to a total of 478 people; using the standard multiplier of 128 acres per Indian which pertained across Canada, they therefore computed their minimum entitlement as being 95.6 square miles. They also asserted a claim to a ten percent royalty applicable to all resources illegally extracted from their territory during the previous half-century (a sum Getty admitted would be "in excess of $100 million," meaning that total oil and gas revenues derived from Lubicon land had been over $5 billion at that point).[53]

On October 21, the Royal Canadian Mounted Police staged a "raid" to dismantle the Lubicon checkpoints. They were met with no resistance, given that Getty was already promising that such "law enforcement" would be mostly symbolic, that the 27 Lubicons arrested would be immediately released, and that the gesture would inaugurate a new round of negotiations designed to resolve the Alberta/Lubicon conflict once and for all.[54] Chief Ominayak stipulated that, should the province deviate from this script, the roadblocks would be instantly reinstated and maintained indefinitely. In this, he received pledges of physical support from the Treaty 8 chiefs who vowed to replace, on a "body for body" basis, anyone hauled away by the RCMP.[55]

Eugene Steinhauer of Saddle Lake, a former president of the Indian Association and one of Alberta's best-known Indian leaders, left a hospital bed to be there. Chiefs from other bands around Alberta could be seen, including Lawrence Courtoreille, vice-president for Alberta of the Assembly of First Nations, and leaders such as Mohawk Chief Billy Two Rivers of Kahnewake near Montréal. Members of the Committee Against Racism from Calgary held placards saying "Support the Lubicon." News reporters and photographers were out in force, representing the national television networks, the radio networks, the Southam and Canadian Press news services, an Italian wire service and dozens of Alberta print and broadcast outlets... A group of clergy led by Peter Hamel of the Anglican Church of Canada joined the ranks. A

Dutch member of the European Parliament, Herman Verbeek, arrived separately, telling reporters, "It is important that Canadians be aware that people in Europe and all over the world know what is happening here"…Radio talk shows focused on the issue. "Do you recognize the Lubicon nation as sovereign?" asked the moderator of CBC Edmonton's "Phone Forum." Responses ran 80 per cent in the band's favor.[56]

In terms of more direct actions:

> The protest spread to other parts of the country. In Montréal, the Mohawks of Kahnewake slowed traffic on the Mercier Bridge [for two days] to distribute 10,000 Lubicon support flyers. In Brantford, Ontario, fifteen members of the Six Nations Mohawk reserve blocked highway traffic briefly in a similar show of solidarity. In Labrador, partly emboldened by the Lubicon move, a community of Innu Indians camped at the end of a military runway at Goose Bay to protest low-level military flights over their caribou lands. More than 150 people were arrested, then released.[57]

Under these conditions, Getty flew to the town of Grimshaw, near the Lubicon land, to meet with Chief Ominayak on October 22. By nightfall, an agreement had been hammered out wherein 95 square miles of land would be transferred to the Lubicons. Of this, Alberta committed to providing 79 square miles outright, with full subsurface rights. The remaining sixteen square miles were to be purchased from the province for the Indians by Ottawa, with Alberta retaining subsurface rights subject to Lubicon veto power over any provincial development scheme(s).[58] Both sides agreed to begin negotiations concerning cooperative administration of entities devoted to environmental oversight and wildlife management, and to jointly propose a more complete resolution package, including financial compensation and economic development support for the Lubicons, to the central government.[59]

> What an enormous victory the Grimshaw Agreement was. More had been accomplished in a week of confrontation than in a decade of official meetings and court appearances. Getty had [been forced to] develop an appreciation of how badly the Lubicon people had been treated over the years, telling Ominayak privately that he felt "ashamed" to have been part of the earlier government…For band members, the agreement vindicated a long-term strategy to build power and use it. The victory seemed to show that even the smallest and most remote of Canadian native societies, by holding together and working hard, could develop enough muscle to prevail over legal and political inequities.[60]

As Chief Ominayak put it the same evening, "We've done something today that could have been done years ago in a very short time compared with the forty-eight years we've been waiting…I hope we have shown today that if we put up a united front, there is not too much they can do to stop us...And with that, I thank all the community members, and say, 'Federal government—the Lubicons are coming at you.'"[61]

Federal Subversion

For its part, Ottawa reacted to the changed situation with a certain initial confusion when negotiations began on November 29, 1988. The immediate response of McKnight and his aides was to retreat, conceding that the Lubicon band membership should total 506 people, and that the land agreement worked out at Grimshaw was therefore quite reasonable. By the end of the second week of talks, the government had committed itself to providing $34 million to construct housing, roads, sewers, electrification, and public buildings on the reserve. A $5 million trust from which the Lubicons could draw annual interest to use as a lever to engage in economic development was also offered. This left only the issue of compensation for prior resource exploitation hanging when the talks were recessed for the Christmas/New Year holidays. Things appeared to be going very well.[62]

When negotiations resumed, however, it seemed the federal team had utilized the break to regroup itself in order to adopt an entirely different posture. The change was capped on January 24, 1989, when Ottawa spokesperson Brian Malone tabled what he called "a final, take-it-or-leave-it settlement offer." The terms of the proposal included only $30 million in "infrastructural development funding." It accepted the Lubicon membership rolls as a "working figure only," leaving actual band membership subject to approval of low-level functionaries (acting registrar Jim Allen had already gone behind the December agreement and was demanding "documentation" of the genealogy of scores of band members); this obviously held implications as to the quantity of land which would ultimately end up in Lubicon possession. Finally, it sought to void both the Lubicons' rights to compensation and their international efforts to secure support.

> Nothing in the written offer suggests that the band [would be] free to sue the federal government for compensation. The current wording obliges the band to "cede, release and surrender" all aboriginal claims and rights to current and future legal actions related to aboriginal rights. Under the provisions, the band must also agree to withdraw its complaints from the United Nations Human Rights Committee, "to acknowledge settlement of its grievance against Canada," before the compensation issue is settled...[Worse], nothing in the offer is binding, unlike the original treaties,

which are guaranteed in the Canadian constitution. "Any agreement arising out of this offer...will be subject to parliamentary appropriations during the applicable fiscal year," the text of the Lubicon offer states. If parliament failed for any reason to advance enough money to fulfill the agreement from year to year, implementation would be suspended.[63]

The reason for Ottawa's reassertion of a hard line, rejected categorically by the Lubicons the day it was tabled, quickly became apparent. In February 1989, Pierre Cadieux, bearing with him a whole new strategy with which to undermine and destroy the Lubicons, replaced William McKnight as head of Aboriginal Affairs.[64] Cadieux's concept was drawn from the classic vernacular of divide and conquer.

> First, the federal unit tried to identify a dissident faction within the Lubicon ranks that might be used to overthrow Ominayak. When such a faction proved nonexistent, federal players tried to create one, aiming to overthrow Ominayak or, alternatively, split the band. When that attempt also failed, federal players recruited native people from all over northern Alberta to create a new band designed to lay claim to Lubicon territory and accept the federal offer. The idea was cynical and brutal, but it provided the mechanism by which federal authorities could impose a settlement, ward off the United Nations Human Rights Committee, scotch the Grimshaw Agreement, and divide native people in the interior against each other so that the Lubicon people could never again mount an effective aboriginal-rights challenge.[65]

A part of the maneuver was to convince individual Indians who were not Lubicons, or who had no desire to live in Lubicon territory, to enroll in the band and then accept "land in severalty" elsewhere.[66] In this fashion, both the sense of unity evidenced by the band, and the basis of its assertion of collectivity in its land claims might be severely undercut. The tactic, of course, placed the government, which had been actively seeking to diminish or eliminate Lubicon membership altogether for nearly a century, in the position of suddenly and completely reversing itself, expanding the rolls willy-nilly over the protests of the Indians.

Within weeks, Cadieux claimed to have received a petition submitted by "182 people who are unhappy with the leadership of Bernard Ominayak...and who wish to receive their own 160 acre parcels of land in severalty."[67] Cadieux's representatives, while adamantly refusing to provide copies of the document, contended that "60 or 70" of the people signing the petition were "names familiar to those who are familiar with the [Lubicon] band list."[68] Cadieux promptly offered federal resources for the signatories— whom he dubbed "the disenfranchised Lubicons"—to retain an attorney,

Bob Young, while pursuing registration as status Indians and attending land claims, each award of which was to be deducted from the 95 square mile Lubicon settlement offer.[69]

In the end, the petition turned out to be forged, and to have contained the names of no enrolled Lubicons at all. By then, however, the effort to depose Ominayak—who had himself called for an election when rumors of "factionalism" had first surfaced—had failed when he was *unanimously* continued in office by a band poll conducted in late May. The government, meanwhile, had shifted gears.

> On August 28, 1989—eight months after the Ottawa talks—Pierre Cadieux constituted the newly registered Indians as an official band. The Woodland Cree band, he called it, using a generic term for the Cree of the northern woodlands. Not since the early treaty days had a band been formalized so quickly—within twelve weeks of Young's application, and ahead of about seventy aboriginal societies across the country who had been waiting up to fifty years for band status...Woodland members registering as status Indians had also jumped queue on thousands of native people waiting to regain status lost through marriage. Registration can often take years; some of Young's clients were processed in a week.[70]

On July 5, 1990, the ersatz band—of "300," "350," or "700" members, federal officials contradicted one another on the number, and kept the actual membership list secret—voted to fulfill its end of the bargain by signing an "accord" in which they received a reserve of 71 square miles to the west of Lubicon Lake, all of it without subsurface rights. It was arranged that sixteen square miles of this would be "sold back" to the government for $512,000 ($50 per acre) even before transfer occurred. Infrastructural development monies of $29 million were allocated. Another $19 million in "economic development funds," were also allotted to underwrite a series of unspecified projects. Each Woodland band member was paid $50 in federal funds to cast an "aye" vote in the referendum conducted to approve the "settlement." Each voter was also promised a check in the amount of $1,000 as "compensation for past losses" once the measure was passed.[71]

Later, they were informed that both the $50 and $1,000 payments were to be deducted from future welfare payments. In addition, the total amount of "compensation" paid—$713,400—would be charged against the monies due as payment for the sixteen square mile parcel acquired by Ottawa, as well as infrustructural and economic development funds.[72] Hence, the Woodland Band "owed" the federal government approximately $153,000 before its first member ever set foot on the new reserve. Before this travesty became public knowledge, the government let its other shoe drop. On July 7, Brian Malone announced during a speech at Cambridge, England, that Cadieux's office was organizing yet another instant band, this one at Loon Lake, about forty miles northeast of Lubicon. The group was said to be composed of 172 people represented by an assistant to Young. They wanted, Malone claimed stated smugly, a "good deal," one "comparable to that extended to the people of the Woodland Cree Reserve."[73]

> With the Woodland agreement to the west and an impending Loon Lake agreement to the northeast, Lubicon society was slowly being pulled apart. Exactly how many Lubicon members had defected was not certain. Malone told his Cambridge audience that 180 had gone to Woodland and 80 to Loon Lake, although representatives for the two groups put the numbers at "about 100" and "fewer than 25" respectively. Whatever the figures, the damage was enormous. People signing their names to the new band lists were following a course logical to anybody living in a world where the law is arbitrary, and where rewards and punishments are distributed at random; but almost everybody seemed to be paying a price. In some Lubicon families, one spouse had joined the Woodland group, the other had not. [In others], several children had joined...the others had not.[74]

Like the Lubicons' legal offensive of the early 1980s, their diplomatic initiatives had clearly foundered by 1991. Chief Ominayak and the rest of the Lubicon leadership, badly frayed by years of continuous effort, were thus placed in the position of needing to come up with a fresh approach while convincing their equally weary people to pick up and start anew amidst an increasingly confused situation. Nor was this the end of their problems.

The Daishowa Connection

On February 8, 1988, Premier Getty and his forestry minister, LeRoy Fjordbotten, announced that the government of Alberta had entered into an agreement with the Japanese forestry corporation, Daishowa, to construct a pulp mill and launch a timbering operation approximately sixty-five miles south of Little Buffalo.[75]

> The new pulp mill will be the largest hardwood pulp mill in Canada. It will employ about 600 people, 300 to take down and transport trees to the new mill, 300 to turn the trees into pulp. It will "produce" 1,000 metric tons of pulp per day, 340,000 metric tons per year. It will consume trees at the rate of about ... 4 million per year. The trees will come from a timber lease which covers an area of over 29,000 sq. kilometers,

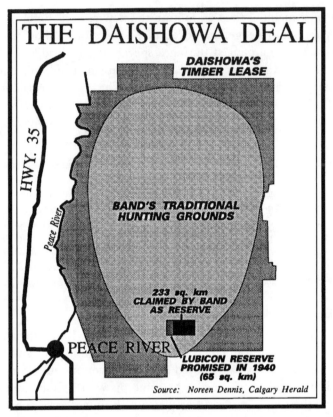

THE DAISHOWA DEAL

DAISHOWA'S
TIMBER LEASE

HWY. 35

Peace River

BAND'S TRADITIONAL
HUNTING GROUNDS

233 sq. km
CLAIMED BY BAND
AS RESERVE

PEACE RIVER

LUBICON RESERVE
PROMISED IN 1940
(65 sq. km)

Source: Noreen Dennis, Calgary Herald

more than 11,000 square miles. *The timber lease to supply the new pulp mill completely covers the entire Lubicon traditional area* (emphasis in original).[76]

The move was astute, insofar as it forced a certain reconciliation of the Ottawa and Alberta positions.

The new pulp mill will...cost more than 500 million dollars, including 75 million in Federal and Provincial Government grants. 9.5 million of the Government subsidy is being provided by Federal Indian Affairs Minister Bill McKnight, in his capacity as Minister responsible for the so-called Western Diversification Program. The Western Diversification Program is a political slush fund set up by the Federal Government to try and prop up its faltering political fortunes in western Canada. In his capacity as Indian Affairs Minister, Mr. McKnight is of course also supposedly responsible for ensuring that the constitutionally recognized rights of aboriginal people in Canada are respected.[77]

In addition, as Fjordbotten put it, "The Alberta government will be building rail and road access and other infrastructure to cost $65.2 million over the next five years, a necessary requirement to proceed in this relatively remote location. Lack of such access has long been an impediment to development of the forest industry in Northern Alberta."[78] In other words, the province intended to go for the Lubicon jugular. The announcements led Assembly of First Nations National Chief George Erasmus to demand that Prime Minister Brian Mulroney fire McKnight for conflict of interest.[79]

For his part, Chief Ominayak went on the Canadian Broadcasting Corporation radio station in Edmonton on February 9 to warn that "we're not going to allow anybody to come in and cut down our trees within our traditional lands." When asked by talk show hostess Ruth Anderson "how far he would go" to prevent the logging, he replied that it "just depends on how hard the other side is going to push. We basically decided that we're going to start asserting our own jurisdiction. Now they announce this pulp mill and also that they're going to be leasing all the timber rights on trees that are going to be needed for the pulp mill that we have on our traditional lands."

The exchange continued, with Anderson asking whether the Lubicons would "resort to violence to stop this latest assault on what you claim is your land?" Chief Ominayak replied that "our preference would be to not get into violence. But again, it all depends on how forceful the other side wants to be. But whatever it takes, that's what we're going to do." Elsewhere, the chief observed that the Lubicons are preparing to make a "last stand" on their land, and on their rights: "We're not threatening, we're not bluffing...and we would like to keep it as peaceful as possible. I just don't know how much longer we can go on like this."[80]

A breakthrough appeared to be in the offing when, on March 2, 1988, Daishowa's Vice President for North American Operations, Koichi Kitigawa, phoned Chief Ominayak, stating that "the corporation had not fully understood the extent of Lubicon claims" when it entered into its arrangement with the Alberta government. Kitigawa asked for a meeting with Ominayak "in Peace River, Little Buffalo or any place else."[81] This occurred five days later at the corporation's main offices in Vancouver, with the result that "senior Daishowa officials including Mr. Kitigawa agreed to stay out of the entire traditional Lubicon territory until there was a settlement of Lubicon land rights and an agreement negotiated with the Lubicon people respecting...environmental concerns."[82]

Although the Lubicons responded by suspending nationwide protests against it, "Daishowa officials started dissembling and backtracking on [the] March 7th agreement almost immediately after the meeting was over."[83] As early as March 25, for example, Kitigawa committed to writing an "understanding" that environmental safeguards *rather than* land rights were the crux of the issue and that the logging would commence as soon as a Forest Management Agreement could be hammered out with the provincial government.[84] Despite a prompt written reply by Chief Ominayak correcting Kitigawa's "misimpression," the corporation persisted.

> Starting in the fall of 1990 Daishowa officials have variously misrepresented [the] March 7th agreement saying first that it didn't cover Daishowa subcontractors and a wholly owned Daishowa subsidiary named Brewster Construction...then saying that it covered only a proposed reserve area (the boundaries of which were in fact not even delineated until October of 1988), then saying that it pertained only to so-called "new areas" not previously logged (nor in fact previously mentioned), and finally denying that there had ever been any agreement or commitment by Daishowa to stay out of the unceded Lubicon territory...[85]

On March 26, 1990, the United Nations Committee on Human Rights wrapped up a six-year investigation of the situation at Lubicon Lake with a report finding that Canada was violating Lubicon rights under Article 27 of the International Covenant on Civil and Political Rights. "Historical and more recent developments threaten the way of life and culture of the Lubicon Lake Band," the committee concluded, "and [will] constitute a violation of Article 27 so long as they continue."[86]

Nonetheless, on August 31, Daishowa spokesperson Wayne Crouse announced that Brewster Construction and three subcontractors would "be logging in the area that is claimed to be the traditional [Lubicon] hunting and trapping areas this winter." During a September 24 meeting requested by the Lubicons to clarify the corporations' intentions, Brewster Construction representative Doug Atikat contended that although his company was owned outright by Daishowa it constituted a "separate body" and was therefore not bound by any agreement between its parent and the Lubicons. Daishowa officials Wayne Thorp and Stu Dornbrierer not only concurred but went further, arguing in effect that no entity other than Daishowa itself, which they claimed was "respecting the agreement," was bound to comply with it.[87]

This was followed, in late October 1990, by the establishment of logging camps in the unceded territory by Brewster and two of the three subcontractors. The Lubicons responded on November 8 by issuing a warning that all such facilities would henceforth be subject to immediate "removal without notice."[88] When it became clear the admonition would not be heeded, direct action was called for and on November 24 equipment belonging to one of the subcontractors, Buchanan Logging Company, was torched. Although nobody was injured in the incident, thirteen Lubicons now face charges which could net them as much as fifty years apiece in Canadian prisons.[89]

Despite its potentially high cost to the individuals allegedly involved, and consequently to the Band as a whole, the raid accomplished its short-term objective. On December 7, even as other Daishowa representatives were publicly denying the existence of any agreement with the Lubicons, the corporation's Woodlands Operations Manager Barry Heinen announced that "The agreement still stands. We won't log within [the unceded territory] until the dispute is settled."[90] At about the same time, corporate spokesperson Allan Wahlstrom conceded for the first time that Daishowa actually *did* control the operations of Brewster, Buchanan and its other subordinates. It followed that Heinen's "we" might be understood as encompassing them as well as the parent corporation.[91]

Over the longer haul, however, things looked far less promising. On April 12, 1991, responding to a letter of inquiry concerning Daishowa's ultimate intentions on Lubicon land, corporate official Jim Morrison wrote that "Daishowa cannot indefinitely postpone the timber harvest to which it is entitled... After all, Daishowa's $580 million dollar investment in the Peace River Pulp Mill was premised on having a secure supply and eventually it will be needed." In the same missive, Morrison also restored the corporation to its posture of denying the terms of the March 7, 1988 agreement: "Daishowa at no time made a commitment to the Lubicon Band that involved their 'traditional territory.'"[92]

Friends of the Lubicon

Casting about for a nonviolent alternative with which to counter the threat posed by Daishowa, the Lubicons settled during the summer of 1991 on a strategy of organizing a comprehensive boycott of the corporation's paper products. Their hope was that lost sales revenues might offset or surpass whatever profits Daishowa anticipated in clearcutting the unceded land and that this, in turn, might compel the corporation to honor the 1988 agreement. The vehicle selected for accomplishing the task was "Friends of the Lubicon" (FOL), a Toronto-based non-Indian organization nominally headed by Kevin Thomas, Ed Bianchi and Stephen Kenda.[93]

Meanwhile, Morrison telegraphed Daishowa's next move in an August 27 letter to a Lubicon supporter in Québec named Vilhelmo Vanlenho. In it, Morrison asserted that "Daishowa Canada, Peace River Pulp Division, has purchased and is legally obligated to purchase salvage aspen from independent sawmillers, farmers and loggers...within [the unceded territory]." Moreover, he stated that, while Brewster Construction had "modified its logging plans" for the winter of 1990-91 "in hopes that talks [with the Lubicons] would be restarted," further "delays are no longer possible." In effect, Morrison had announced the corporation's intent to engage in fullscale logging operations on Lubicon land over the winter of 1991-92.[94]

Hence, with a sense of extreme urgency, Friends of the Lubicon launched the boycott on November 6, 1991, sending letters to officials of several major restaurant chains—Ho-Lee Chow, Cultures, and Pizza Pizza—each of which relied primarily (or exclusively) on Daishowa for paper bags, napkins and similar products. A letter was also sent to the Knechtel's chain of food stores, another major outlet for the corporation. The missives began as follows:

> As soon as the ground freezes in northern Alberta, Daishowa will begin clear cutting Lubicon land. This as well as previous destruction of their land by government sponsored oil and gas development, will result in the cultural genocide of the Lubicon people.[95]

Each executive was then asked to suspend his/her firm's purchase of Daishowa paper products until the corporation publicly agreed not to acquire pulp taken from Lubicon territory. The request was punctuated by a press release issued on November 14 under the heading "STOP THE GENOCIDE!" It read in part, "The Lubicon see the impending destruction of their forest as the final stage of a genocidal process that began with government-backed oil and gas development in the late seventies."[96] Three days later, a demonstration was conducted outside Daishowa's Bay Street offices in Toronto during which a leaflet was handed out explaining that the "Lubicon see [the corporation's planned operations] as an act of genocide against their Nation."[97]

By November 20, having garnered significant press attention, the FOL was prepared to send a second letter to the target companies, this one pointing out that "[c]hanging paper suppliers is little to ask when the alternative involves the genocide of an aboriginal community."[98] This was followed, on November 26, with another press release, captioned "STOP THE GENOCIDE, BOYCOTT DIASHOWA!"[99] On November 28, in conjunction with demonstrations outside Daishowa's world headquarters in Tokyo, the FOL began picketing Pizza Pizza restaurants—the only one of the four firms originally approached which had not already changed suppliers—in Toronto.[100] Their efforts were endorsed by the National Association of Japanese Canadians (NAJC) the same day.

> This position reflects the grave concern that the NAJC has over the environmental consequences that [Daishowa's] clear cutting operations represent. But of even greater importance is the concern of the NAJC about the long-term destructive effects that such action will have on the Lubicons themselves, and their very existence as a people.[101]

Undoubtedly surprised at the degree of success attained so quickly by the boycotters, Daishowa—which appears to have simply ignored a warning letter sent by Kevin Thomas on November 6—shortly began to backpedal on its plans to begin clearcutting.[102] These were soon to be postponed indefinitely, as the FOL gained momentum.

> The results of the Friends' campaign against Daishowa from 1991 to 1994 were, in a word, stunning. Approximately fifty companies using paper products (mostly paper bags) from Daishowa were approached by the Friends. The list of these companies reads like a Who's Who of the retail and fast food industries in Ontario—Pizza Pizza, the Liquor Control Board of Ontario, Cultures, Country Style Donuts, Mr. Submarine, Bootlegger, A&W, Kentucky Fried Chicken, Woolworth's, Roots, Club Monaco, Movenpeck Restaurants and Holt Renfrew, to name but a few. *Every one* of the companies approached by the Friends joined the boycott of Daishowa products. All but two did so...before their stores were picketed... Pizza Pizza was subjected to picketing outside its store on two occasions; Woolworth's had a single store picketed on two occasions... Both Pizza Pizza and Woolworth's joined the boycott.[103]

Although the corporation's in-house spin doctors tried their best to offset the FOL information blitz, they were plainly losing ground at a steady rate.[104] Finally, on January 11, 1995, Daishowa filed a SLAPP suit against Thomas, Bianchi and Kenda, as well as "John Doe, Jane Doe and Persons Unknown" in the Ontario Court of Justice. Citing millions of dollars in lost sales and an increasing erosion of its client base, Daishowa alleged that the

FOL leaders and their "co-conspirators" had engaged in "unlawful interference with Daishowa's contractual and economic relationships through the use of unlawful means such as threats, intimidation and coercion, misinformation and defamatory statements and the threat of secondary picketing and secondary boycott of Daishowa's customers."[105]

Before Thomas and his colleagues even had an opportunity to file their joint Statement of Defense, an interim injunction was issued to restrain them from engaging in boycott activities of any sort for a period of ninety days.[106] On May 19, just as the temporary restraining order expired, Daishowa's attorneys requested an interlocutory injunction which would last for the duration of legal proceedings. The matter was heard by Judge Frances Kiteley who "substantially dismissed" the motion, restraining the defendants only from referencing the March 7, 1988 agreement until such time as its nature was judicially clarified, and from employing the word "genocide" in their organizing materials until a judicial determination had been made as to whether such usage was defamatory.[107]

Daishowa immediately appealed this ruling to the Ontario Divisional Court, where it was overturned in a split decision.[108] All of the corporation's requests were thereupon granted and eventually expanded to include a prohibition against the defendants, their attorney and even an expert witness— University of Victoria law professor Chris Tollefson, a leading authority on SLAPP suits—from publicly discussing the case.[109] Both the Ontario Court of Appeal and Canada's Supreme Court subsequently declined without explanation to review the lower court's decision(s).[110]

In the end, after a 28-day trial marked by an extended recess to decide whether Daishowa was bound to disclose relevant financial records to the defendants, the appearance of 28 witnesses and submission of 82 exhibits containing more than a thousand documents,[111] the court produced a verdict which essentially reinstated Judge Kiteley's earlier ruling, purportedly "resolving" the issues she'd left hanging and thereby rendering its effects permanent.

In his opinion, released on April 14, 1998, the presiding judge, J.C. MacPherson, rejected Daishowa's argument that Thomas, Bianchi and Kenda had organized "illegal secondary picketing" insofar as the whole concept, nebulous at best, relates to labor disputes rather than consumer boycotts, especially those imbued with a broader "educational" purpose.[112] "The question which must be considered in this trial," the judge observed, "is whether the reasons in favour of the prohibition against secondary picketing in a labour relations context support a prohibition against picketing in a consumer boycott context. In my view, they do not."[113] He then went on to elaborate his reasoning in considerable detail.

> The fact that freedom of expression is protected in the *Charter of Rights and Freedoms*, coupled with the absence of any economic rights, except for mobility to pursue the gaining of a livelihood, is a clear indication that free speech is near the top of the values that Canadians hold dear… The plight of the Lubicon is precisely the type of issue that should generate widespread public discussion [in such a setting]. Moreover, there is not one penny of economic self-interest in the Friends' campaign… Rather, the economic component of the Friends' message is anchored in the same foundation as all its activities, namely to focus public attention on a public issue, the plight of the Lubicon, and Daishowa's alleged connection to that issue… [A]n important part of the Friends' message, and certainly the most effective part, is the attempt through speech in a picketing context to enlist consumers in a boycott of Daishowa products.[114]

"Is there anything unlawful about such a consumer boycott?" MacPherson queried in his finding on the issue. "And do those who conceive and organize it violate any law? I think not."[115] On the contrary, he concluded that "the manner in which the Friends have performed their picketing and boycott activities is a model of how such activities should be conducted in a democratic society."[116]

From there, it was a relatively easy matter for the judge to dispense with Daishowa's various torts. With respect to the corporation's allegation that the FOL had unlawfully interfered with its economic interests, he observed that since he had "already decided that none of the means used by the Friends in their campaign, including picketing, was unlawful, it follows that the plaintiff cannot succeed in its claim against the defendants."[117] Much the same language was used in rejecting allegations that Thomas, Bianchi, Kenda or anyone else associated with the FOL had "induced breach of contract," relied upon "intimidation" or "conspired to injure" the corporation.[118]

That Little Matter of Genocide

Having thus replicated Judge Kiteley's "substantial dismissal" of Daishowa's case, MacPherson concomitantly entered a glowingly categorical affirmation of the FOL's *formal* right to utilize the tactics of boycott and picketing in pursuit of its goals. From this noble-sounding position, however, he then proceeded to finalize the temporary restraints she'd imposed upon the defendants in her interlocutory order, thereby gutting their *practical* ability to exercise that right.

The first such maneuver came with MacPherson's assessment of the validity of the 1988 "no logging" agreement. Completely disregarding the obvious—that is, Chief Ominayak's testimony that "we would never have agreed to call off the growing nationwide protest [in March 1988] if Daishowa had not agreed to stay out of our unceded traditional territory until there was a settlement of Lubicon land rights"[119]—the judge announced that there was simply "no credible evidence" suggesting such an agreement had ever been reached. Even the earlier-quoted statements of Daishowa's senior management and other "relatively low-level employees" were summarily discounted as "mistaken" whenever they conflicted with what the judge described as his own "common sense" interpretation of events.[120]

Such findings of "fact" allowed the court to conclude that "the statements by the Friends to the effect that Daishowa made, and then broke, an agreement with the Lubicon on March 7, 1988 are false" and to permanently enjoin not only the defendants but the public at large "from asserting that Daishowa and the Lubicon Cree reached an agreement…concerning Daishowa's exercise of its logging rights" within unceded Lubicon territory.[121] This was because, as MacPherson himself noted, "Without question, the publication of [such] statements in letters and leaflets would tend to lower Daishowa's reputation in the community" and therefore comprise one of the FOL's more effective means of organizing its boycott.[122]

More egregious still was the court's handling of the FOL's employment of the terms "genocide" and "genocidal" in describing the anticipated impact of Daishowa's activities upon the Lubicons. This, MacPherson pronounced not only to be defamatory but "bordering on the grotesque," before enjoining both the defendants and everyone else from characterizing the corporation's conduct, past, present or projected, in such fashion.[123] In order to arrive at this assessment, however, it was necessary for him to advance what is, for a jurist, a rather interesting definition of the term.

> In my view, the plain and ordinary meaning of the word "genocide" is the intentional killing of a group of people. "Genocide" is defined by *Webster's Dictionary* (Seventh College Edition) as the "deliberate and systematic destruction of a racial, political or cultural group," by the *Shorter Oxford English Dictionary* (Third Edition, 1991 Reprint) as "annihilation of a race," and by the *Oxford English Dictionary* (Second Edition, 1989) as the "deliberate and systematic extermination of an ethnic or national group."[124]

One may perhaps be forgiven for believing that a judge might be more properly concerned with both the legal and the actual meanings of words than with their "plain and ordinary" connotations. This remains true despite MacPherson's reference to R.E. Brown's dictum that "defamatory meaning must be one which would be understood by reference to an ordinary and reasonable person."[125] The problem with Brown's postulation, of course, is that the meanings popularly assigned to things are often just plain wrong. The average person, upon hearing the words "punk" and "gunsel," for example, would typically understand them to mean "hoodlum" and "gunman." These are the popular misusages, now entered into the very dictionaries MacPherson cites. Yet, as Dashiell Hammett was wont to point out, both terms are actually pejoratives referring to young homosexuals.[126]

Surely, one of the most basic responsibilities of any "educational" entity—and, as was noted above, the judge acknowledged that the FOL embodies an educational dimension—is to correct such "plain and ordinary" misconstruals in order that more accurate understandings take hold among the public.[127] In the alternative, once-popular notions that time began only 3,000 years ago, that the earth is flat and that the universe revolves around it would likely continue to prevail, and the judiciary might find itself conducting endless retrials of the "Scopes Evolution Case."[128]

Ironically, even MacPherson readily admits to the existence of legal and other definitions of the term genocide which are radically at odds with his own "everyman" version. In some ways the most important is that contained in international law, specifically the second article of the United Nations Convention on Prevention and Punishment of the Crime of Genocide.[129] The judge bothered to quote it verbatim, and it is worth doing so here.

> In the present Convention, genocide means any of the following acts committed with intent to destroy, in whole or in part, a national, ethnical, racial or religious group, as such:
>
> (a) Killing members of the group;
>
> (b) Causing serious bodily or mental harm to members of the group;
>
> (c) Deliberately inflicting on the group conditions of life calculated to bring about its physical destruction in whole or in part;

(d)   Imposing measures intended to prevent births within the group;

(e)   Forcibly transferring children of the group to another group.

Exactly how MacPherson manages to equate "intentionally killing a group of people," as he put it, to "causing [them] serious...mental harm," or "serious bodily harm" for that matter, is left unstated. Equally mysterious is the reasoning he employs in deciding that "preventing births" or "transferring children" are somehow the same as mass killing. Conversely, he offers no advice as to how, if we were to accept his supposedly "reasonable" definition, we might avoid classifying *all* incidents of mass murder—the St. Valentine's Day Massacre, for instance—as "genocide."

Even when he broadens his horizons a bit to hold that "the essence of the meaning of the word 'genocide' is the *physical* destruction of a group identified on a racial, political, ethnic or cultural basis (his emphasis),"[130] the judge provides no explanation as to how the inflicting of "mental harm" or the "transferring [of] children...to another group" might be made to fit within his tightly drawn parameters. These are not matters of "opinion," it must be stressed, but matters of *law*. Plainly, MacPherson's "interpretation," if it may be called that, constrains the U.N.'s legal definition to a mere twenty percent—forty percent at best—of its actual content.

To be fair about it, the judge's deficiency in this respect may in part derive from Canadian law itself. Ottawa's statute implementing the Genocide Convention, which it purportedly ratified in 1952, was mysteriously drafted in such a way as to omit the Convention's prohibitions on transferring children and inflicting serious psychological or bodily harm, and, in 1985, was further revised to delete the prohibition of preventing births as well.[131] MacPherson juxtaposes his country's statutory language to that of the Convention without commenting on what might be implied by the glaring discrepancies between them, although he is obviously groping for some means of making them appear to reconcile.[132]

In any event, things deteriorate even further from there. While trying to make himself appear conversant with the full range of nuances associated with the neologism at issue, MacPherson quotes briefly from Raphaël Lemkin, the Polish jurist who coined it in 1944.[133] From this fragment, he concludes that "the Friends cannot even bring themselves within a fair reading of Professor Lemkin's definition."[134] Had the judge actually troubled himself to read the book from which he quotes, however, it would have been impossible for him to honestly evade the reality that the FOL's use of the term conforms *precisely* with Lemkin's. This is readily evidenced in an exchange between Daishowa attorney Peter Jervis and defendant Kevin Thomas.

Jervis: You were aware that genocide is understood as meaning the death of people.

Thomas: The death of…

Jervis: The word genocide means killing people, destroying people.

Thomas: I would have to refer you probably to other people's Affidavits and the definitions of genocide. As we understand the issue of genocide, it has to do with the destruction of a culture, an entire distinct society. It doesn't mean that you go in shooting people. It can also mean you are destroying a distinct society as a way of life. That is how I understand the definition of genocide.[135]

The truth is that, contra MacPherson's insistence, Lemkin defined genocide in primarily and explicitly *non*-lethal terms. In fact, in the very passage from which the judge extracts phrases so selectively, Lemkin states that, "Generally speaking, genocide does *not* mean the [physical] destruction of a nation, *except* when accomplished by mass killings… (emphasis added)."[136] On same page, another passage, completely unmentioned by MacPherson, reads:

Genocide has two phases: one, destruction of the national pattern of the oppressed group; the other, imposition of the national pattern of the oppressor. This imposition, in turn, may be made upon the oppressed population which is allowed to remain, or upon the territory alone, after removal of the population and colonization of the area by the oppressor's own nationals.[137]

Killing the members of an "oppressed group" is certainly one method of "removing" it from its territory. But it is, as Lemkin observed, an extreme and historically exceptional one. Correspondingly, well over half the proliferation of examples he deployed as illustrations of genocidal policies and processes do *not* involve killing, either directly or indirectly.[138] The core of Lemkin's idea, as Canadian analysts Robert Davis and Mark Zannis pointed out a quarter-century hence, has to do with the creation of conditions which lead to the dissolution/extinguishment of identifiable human groups as such, even if *every* individual member were to survive.[139]

It follows that when he was retained by the United Nations Secretariat to produce a draft Genocide Convention in 1947, Lemkin placed the greatest weight upon the article in which he delineated what is referred to as "Cultural Genocide."[140] Even in the article devoted to "Physical Genocide," a greater emphasis was accorded, *not* to direct killing but to what he called "slow death measures." These include "deprivation of the means of livelihood by confiscation of property, looting, curtailment of work, and the denial...of proper housing, clothing, food, hygiene and medical care."[141]

In substance, Lemkin's conception of genocide encompasses not only "the destruction of a group" but actions or policies "preventing its preservation and development."[142] Moreover, to borrow from the Saudi delegate who helped in preparing the final draft instrument in 1948, it involves not only the "planned disintegration of the political, social or economic structure of a group or nation" but the "systematic...debasement of a group, people or nation."[143]

Such is the definitional background against which the Genocide Convention must be read if it is to be understood. If it does not provide an accurate and appropriate description of the overall pattern of historical relations between Canada and the Lubicons, a context in which Daishowa is now very much an integral part, then *nothing* does. Indeed, MacPherson himself comes very close to saying this at one point.

> The essential subject matter of everything the Friends say and do is the plight of the Lubicon Cree... There can be little doubt that their plight, especially in recent years, is a tragic, indeed a desperate one. The compelling testimony of Chief Bernard Ominayak painted a vivid picture of the disintegration of a proud people who had lived successfully and prospered, on their own terms, for centuries. The loss of a traditional economy of hunting, trapping and gathering, the negative effect of industrial development on a people spiritually anchored in nature, the disintegration of a social structure grounded in families led by successful hunters and trappers, alcoholism, serious community health problems such as tuberculosis, and poor relations with governments and corporations engaged in oil and gas and forest operations on land the Lubicon regard as theirs—all of these have contributed to a current state of affairs for the Lubicon Cree which deserves the adjectives tragic, desperate and intolerable.[144]

It may well be that the judge, in common with most domestic jurists, lacked the competence in international human rights law to appreciate that what he was describing is a process of genocide, both cultural *and* physical. It is also likely that, his pretensions to having attained a sort of "instant expertise" notwithstanding, he lacked an inclination to delve very deeply into the relevant body of theory during the trial itself. The fact is, however, that he needed neither the specific competence nor the desire to attain it in order to arrive at something resembling an appropriate conclusion. Connecting the dots in such respects is, after all, the purpose of expert witnesses. Here, an ample base was laid by the FOL, while *none* was offered by Daishowa.

Among the authorities cited was the late Dr. James J.E. Smith, Curator of North American Ethnography for the Museum of the American Indian/ Heye Foundation, who, after eight years of studying the situation, concluded in 1990 that the Canadian government, in concert with corporations such as Daishowa, was engaged in activities which are "leading to the social and cultural genocide of the Lubicon Lake [Cree]."[145] Another was the McGill University Law Faculty (as a whole), who, in their publication *Quid Novi*, described the Lubicon situation as "Modern Genocide," and explained although "it is difficult for the average Canadian to believe that genocide still exists in our country," it does and is "not done by conventional military methods, but by legislation and corporate power."[146]

I myself provided additional testimony at trial, both written and oral, with regard to the legal, sociological and other definitions of genocide.[147] Both written and oral testimony was also provided by Dr. Joan Ryan, professor emeritus in anthropology at the University of Calgary, who, having studied conditions "on the ground" since 1980, concluded that "if Daishowa is permitted to proceed with cutting before settlement of the land claim, the Lubicon people will cease to exist as a viable Band [and] the genocidal destruction of Lubicon Cree society will be completed."[148] Dr. Ryan went on to observe that:

> The term "genocide" is not used lightly here, and it predictably evokes strong aversive reactions… However, it is important to use the term because it is accurate, and the reactions to it are important to deal with. I use the term "genocide" as defined by Webster (*New Encyclopedic Dictionary*, BD & L (New York: 1993)), that is, "the deliberate and systematic destruction of a racial, political, or cultural group" [and] I have tried to document the nature of the destruction of the Lubicon people, their way of life and their culture over the past 15 years in which I have known them. Further, I believe that such destruction has been deliberate and systematic.[149]

In sum, *every* bona fide expert, regardless of academic specialization, angle of approach or research methodology, arrived unerringly at the same conclusion: what is happening to the Lubicons is genocidal, nothing less. So how, in the face of such consensus, could Judge MacPherson have found the exact opposite to be true? Simple. Just as he'd earlier discounted all statements to the contrary by corporate officials in deciding there'd never been a "no cut" agreement for Daishowa to violate, he ignored altogether every inconvenient submission on the matter of genocide. Not one word of expert witness testimony is so much as mentioned in the verdict.

Having thus carefully distorted and trimmed the available evidence into seeming conformity with his own logically/factually untenable viewpoint, MacPherson positioned himself to denounce as an "enormous injustice…cavalier and grossly unfair to Daishowa" the FOL's entirely accurate characterization of the corporation's plans, attitudes and activities vis-à-vis the Lubicons.[150] Then, not content merely to brand the defendants' word usage as defamatory, he went on to "reject…on the merits" their contention that it "was nonetheless 'fair comment' on an important political and social issue."[151]

The Future

The preceding synopsis begs the question as to why a jurist of J.C. MacPherson's undeniable stature might have opted to comport himself in such an utterly squalid fashion. The answer is as fundamental as it is structural. The judge is part, and an élite part at that, of the very system he was called upon in this case to oppose. His position, its attendant comfort, privileges and whatever prestige he enjoys all depend upon that system's continuing to function in the smoothest possible manner. At base, then, systemic requirements and MacPherson's—or *any* judge's—perceptions of self-interest must inevitably coincide. The result is that the judicial function, irrespective of the judiciary's sanctimony about its role being to administer and dispense "justice," amounts to little more than the rationalizing of business as usual.[152]

When confronted with the issues and evidence in the FOL case, there were really only three hypothetical options MacPherson might have exercised by way of response.

- First, he could have concurred that the Lubicons are in fact suffering genocide by any reasonable definition and that the FOL's use of the term was therefore justified. In this instance, he might also have entered an emergency decree enjoining Daishowa from further activities pending judicial review in a more appropriate forum (i.e., a criminal court).[153]

- Second, he might have entered an opinion holding that although the FOL's usage of the term genocide conforms to a wide range definitions, including those found in international law, it failed to mesh with the much narrower definition embodied in Canadian law. On that basis he might have enjoined them from employing such characterizations of Daishowa in the future.[154]

- Third, there was the option he selected: to deny that anything remotely approximating genocide was occurring and then to wax indignant that the FOL had been so "irresponsible" as to suggest otherwise.

In actuality, the first two choices were foreclosed before the trial began. Leaving aside the fact that his verdict would have been instantly overruled by a higher court, had MacPherson accepted the international legal definition of genocide as binding and responded accordingly, the precedent would have opened the door to a virtually total destabilization and eventual collapse of the Canadian system. Daishowa, after all is not unique. Consider the bevy of oil corporations already operating on and systematically degrading unceded Lubicon land.

The reality is that, without exception, every corporation doing "developmental" business in Canada does so at the direct expense of and often with comparable impacts upon the ability of indigenous peoples to sustain themselves.[155] The Canadian state itself exists on the basis of the expropriation of native land and resources, the subordination of native polities.[156] And then there are such matters as whether the residential school system imposed for so long and with such catastrophic effects didn't constitute a "forced transfer of children" within the meaning of the Genocide Convention.[157] One need not be Einstein to see how the dominoes would fall on this one.

Reliance upon the second option would have been in many ways as bad. To openly admit not only that a genocide is occurring but that it is *permissible* for it to occur under the domestic laws of one's own country is something not even the most unabashed of nazi officials were prepared to do. Public response to the FOL's rather less than official argument to the same effect being what it was, one can only imagine the popular reaction to an official verdict first pronouncing them correct in their assessment and then ordering them to shut up about it. To call the likely result "destabilizing" is to wildly understate the possibilities. Again, one need not be Einstein...

This leaves denial. And so began MacPherson's contorted semantic odyssey, a journey leaving him—no doubt uncomfortably, a matter accounting perhaps for the peculiar belligerence with which his rhetoric on the topic is laced—sharing intellectual space with the likes of James Keegstra, Ernst Zundel, Steven Katz and other such deniers of genocides past.[158] As for the government he represents, the judge's performance places it firmly in league with those of Paraguay and Brazil, the judiciaries of which employed similar stratagems when rejoining allegations that native peoples within their borders were being subjected to genocide.[159]

Genocide denied, however, remains genocide, no matter how out of the sight and mind of polite society it may be rendered in the denial. How is it that the Lubicons are expected to respond now that their best hope of a "peaceful" resolution—the boycott—has been rendered ineffectual by MacPherson's subtextual pronouncement that the economic interests of the Canadian system outweigh their right to survive as a people?[160] Obviously, they cannot be expected to, as they put it, "lie down in a ditch and die."[161] On the contrary, the Lubicons are obliged to defend themselves by what Malcolm X called "any means necessary," and, to paraphrase Dr. Martin Luther King, Jr., those, like J.C. MacPherson, who would make the successful employment of peaceful methods impossible simply make reliance upon violent methods inevitable.[162]

Notes

1. John Goddard, "Last Stand of the Lubicon," *Equinox* (Nov. 1987) pp. 71-72. For further background, see George F.G. Stanley, *The Birth of Western Canada* (Toronto: University of Toronto Press, 1975).

2. *Lubicon Lake Band Presentation to the Standing Committee on Aboriginal Affairs and Northern Development: General History*, House of Commons, Ottawa (Canada), May 18, 1953, pp. 1-2 (hereinafter referred to as *Lubicon Presentation*). For background, see George Brown and Ron McGuire, *Indian Treaties in Historical Perspective* (Ottawa: Research Branch, Indian and Northern Affairs Ministry, 1979); Richard Price, ed., *The Spirit of the Alberta Indian Treaties* (Montréal: Institute for Research on Public Policy, 1980); Dennis F.K. Madill, *Treaty Research Report: Treaty Eight* (Ottawa: Treaties and Historical Research Centre, Indian and Northern Affairs Ministry, 1986).

3. Goddard, "last Stand," op. cit., p. 72.

4. Ibid.

5. *Lubicon Presentation*, op. cit., p. 3. Also see Richard Daniel, *Land Rights of Isolated Communities in Northern Alberta* (Edmonton: Isolated Communities Advisory Board, 1975).

6. Goddard, "Last Stand," op. cit.

7. Ibid.

8. Letter, Alberta Regional Supervisor of Aboriginal Affairs to the Minister of Aboriginal Affairs, May 19, 1953.

9. Letter, Director of the Technical Division of (Alberta) Lands and Forests to the Minister of Aboriginal Affairs, Oct. 22, 1953.

10. Letter, Alberta Regional Supervisor of Aboriginal Affairs to the Minister of Aboriginal Affairs, Feb. 25, 1954.

11. Directive, Superintendent of Reserves and Trusts to Lubicon Lake Indian agent, Feb. 9, 1955.

12. Letter, Alberta Supervisor of Aboriginal Affairs to Lubicon Lake Indian agent, Jan. 23, 1955.

13. Letter, Alberta Supervisor of Aboriginal Affairs to Lubicon Lake Indian agent, Jan. 21, 1955.

14. Such outcomes are standard throughout the world, a matter which is well-document by John Bodley in his *Victims of Progress* (Palo Alto, CA: Mayfield, [2nd ed.] 1983). Of particular interest in the Lubicon connection, see the section entitled "Big Oil Invades the Ecuadorian Amazon Rainforest" in Al Gedicks' *The New Resource Wars: Native and Environmental Struggles Against Multinational Corporations* (Boston: South End Press, 1993) pp. 33-8.

15. *Lubicon Presentation,* op. cit., p. 15.

16. Goddard, "Last Stand," op. cit., p. 68.

17. *Lubicon Presentation*, op. cit., pp. 14-5.

18. Ibid., pp. 15-6.

19. Ibid., pp. 17-8.

20. Ibid., p. 18.

21. Ibid., pp. 19-20.

22. Ibid., pp. 20-1.

23. Ibid., p. 21.

24. Ibid.

25. Ibid., p. 22.

26. Ibid., p. 23. Also see *Facts About the Lubicon Lake Indian Band Land Claims*, Government of Alberta, Feb. 10, 1988, p. 2 (hereinafter referred to as *Lubicon Land Claims*).

27. CBC radio broadcast, Feb. 2, 1988; the CBC contends "about 100" oil companies now have interest in the Lubicon land.

28. *Lubicon Land Claims*, op. cit.

29. Ibid.

30. Ibid.

31. Ibid.

32. Ibid.

33. Ibid.

34. Statement of Chief Bernard Ominayak, Edmonton, Alberta, Dec. 11, 1985.

35. *Lubicon Land Claims*, op. cit.

36. "Indians Vow to Boycott Olympics," *Calgary Herald*, Nov. 19, 1986. Also see Allen Connery, "Why Lubicons are Protesting," *Calgary Herald*, Jan. 27, 1988.

37. *Lubicon Land Claims*, op. cit.

38. Ibid.

39. Ibid., p. 3.

40. Ibid. Also see Paul Ogresko, "Sharing the Blame: Boycott Hits Olympic Museum," *Calgary Sunday Sun*, Jan. 31, 1988; Steve Hume, "The Spirit Weeps: Power, Genius and Hypocrisy at Glenbow Exhibit," *Edmonton Journal*, Feb. 14, 1988.

41. Among the long-term relationships established during this period were those with the European Assembly of North American Indian Support Groups. Links were also forged with Kalahui Hawai'i, the Maori sovereignty movement in New Zealand and numerous other indigenous rights organizations around the world; Mark Lowey and Kathy Kerr, "Lubicon Support on the Rise," *Calgary Herald*, Feb. 25, 1988.

42. E. Davie Fulton, *Lubicon Lake Indian Band Inquiry: Discussion Paper* (Ottawa: Office of the Minister for Indian Affairs, 1986).

43. *Lubicon Land Claims*, op. cit.

44. John Goddard, *Last Stand of the Lubicon Cree* (Vancouver/Toronto: Douglas and McIntyre, 1991) p. 159.

45. "Getty emerging from the shadows," *Calgary Herald*, Mar. 17, 1988. Also see "Getty calls play," *Edmonton Journal*, Mar. 17, 1988.

46. Quoted in Goddard, *Last Stand*, op. cit., p. 167. Also see "Indian Affairs may sue Alberta over Lubicons," *Ottawa Citizen*, Feb. 2, 1988; Graham Fraser, "McKnight condemns Alberta for move on land claimed by Lubicons," *Globe and Mail*, Feb. 11, 1988.

47. Ibid., p. 170.

48. Ibid., p. 171.

49. Quoted in ibid., p. 170.

50. Quoted in ibid., pp. 172-3.

51. Ibid., p. 185.

52. Ibid., p. 179.

53. See ibid.: on population and land, p. 185; on royalties, p. 181.

55. Ibid., pp. 188-91.

55. Press Release, Council of Treaty Eight Chiefs, Calgary, October 21, 1988.

56. Goddard, *Last Stand*, op. cit., pp. 173, 180-1.

57. Ibid., p. 186.

58. Chief Ominayak specified that one square mile would be located at a Bison Lake burial ground, one square mile at Haig Lake, and the balance at Lubicon Lake; ibid., p. 193.

59. The basic terms and provisions of the "Grimshaw Agreement" are covered in ibid., pp. 192-3.

60. Ibid., p. 195.

61. Quoted in ibid., p. 194.

62. The negotiations are covered in ibid., pp. 196-8.

63. Ibid., p. 200. Among other things, the "offer" also rejects outright a $16 million agricultural development project proposed by the Lubicons, and a $2.6 million vocational education center and maintenance shop. Instead, $100,000 would be provided to afford "training opportunities."

64. "Cadieux to head Indian Affairs," *Globe and Mail*, Feb. 14, 1989.

65. Goddard, *Last Stand*, op. cit., p. 203.

66. For analysis of the implications of this move, see Indian Association of Alberta, *Statement on the Indian Title to Lands Surveyed "In Severalty" Under Treaty Number Eight* (Ottawa: Treaty and Aboriginal Rights and Research Center, 1981).

67. Quoted in Goddard, *Last Stand*, op. cit., p. 206.

68. Ibid.

69. Discussion with Sharon Venne, Alfred, NY, Nov. 1990 (tape on file). As Goddard puts it, "After

years of accusing Ominayak of 'jacking up' membership figures to get more land, federal authorities were now accusing him of cutting members out."

70. Goddard, *Last Stand*, op. cit., p. 209. On the generic nature of the term employed, see James G.E. Smith, "Western Woods Cree," in *Handbook of North American Indians, Vol. 6: Subarctic* (Washington, D.C.: Smithsonian Institution, 1981). Cadieux claimed authority to do what he did under provision of Article 17 of the Indian Act: "The Minister may, whenever he considers it desirable, constitute new Bands and establish new Band Lists with respect thereto from existing Band Lists, or from the Indian Register, if requested to do so by persons proposing to form new Bands." "No protest can be made," the article concludes. See *Indian Acts and Amendments*, op. cit.

71. Discussed in Goddard, *Last Stand*, op. cit., pp. 211. The numerical discrepancies are apparently accounted for in the fact that the government wished to portray the Woodland Cree as a larger and more substantial group than the Lubicons for public relations purposes while simultaneously minimizing their numbers for purposes of computing their land entitlement. Hence a number of Métis and non-status Indians were lumped into the band roll, inflating the number to "700" for public consumption. Meanwhile, the land apportionment was based against only the 355 status Indians who were enrolled. In the end, 713 persons—the government claimed this was 87 percent of eligible voters—were paid to endorse the federally proposed settlement package. 98.5 percent complied by voting "aye."

72. Ibid., p. 212.

73. Quoted in ibid., p. 213.

74. Ibid.

75. Lubicon Press Release, Feb. 18, 1988.

76. Ibid.

77. Ibid., p. 2.

78. Government of Alberta, Press Release N.R. 055, Feb. 8, 1988, p. 1. Also see Karen Booth and David Holehouse, "Horseman to bypass band," *Edmonton Journal*, Feb. 16, 1988.

79. Letter, National Chief Georges Erasmus, Council of First Nations, to the Right Honorable Brian Mulroney, Prime Minister of Canada, Feb. 16, 1988.

80. Karen Booth, "Lubicon Prepare for 'Last Stand' on Land Claim," *The Edmonton Journal*, Jan. 25, 1988.

81. *Daishowa Inc. v. Friends of the Lubicon*, Ontario Court of Justice (Gen. Div.), File No. 95-CQ-59707, Affidavit of Bernard Ominayak (03/21/95) at p. 13.

82. Ibid., at p. 15. Chief Ominayak's interpretation of the agreement is supported by the statements of Kitigawa and other Daishowa officials as reported in the media on Mar. 7-8, 1988; attached to the affidavit as Exhibit 9.

83. Ibid., at p. 14.

84. Ibid., Exhibit 10.

85. Letter from Bernard Ominayak to Koichi Kitigawa, Apr. 2, 1988; ibid., Exhibit 10.

86. Ibid., Exhibit 3. According to Article 27 of the Covenant (U.N.G.A. Res. 2200 (XXI), 21 U.N. GAOR, Supp. (No. 16) 52, U.N. Doc. A/6316 (1967), "In States in which ethnic, religious or linguistic minorities exist, persons belonging to such minorities shall not be denied the right, in community with other members of their group, to enjoy their own culture, to profess and practise their own religion, or to use their own language"; Ian Brownlie, ed., *Basic Documents on Human Rights* (Oxford, UK: Clarendon Press, [3rd ed.] 1992) p. 134.

87. Ominayak Affidavit, op. cit., Exhibits 14, 15.

88. Ibid., Exhibit 18.

89. Ibid., Exhibit 19.

90. On Nov. 27, 1990, corporate representative Jim Morrison asserted unequivocally to Amy Santoro, a reporter for the newspaper *Windspeaker*, that there "was no agreement made between Daishowa and the Lubicons in 1988." He repeated the statement to reporters from *Alberta Native News* a few days later. Heinen's announcement, made to Santoro for *Windspeaker*, obviously admits the opposite; Ominayak Affidavit, op. cit., Exhibits 19, 21.

91. On Nov. 20, 1990, in an interview with *Edmonton Sun* reporter Gord Bannerman, Jim Morrison carefully distinguished between Daishowa itself, which he said would "not be logging on the east side of the Peace River this year," and Brewster Construction, which he acknowledged would

"commence logging [in the disputed area] tomorrow." Because of this illusory distinction, Morrison implied, Daishowa was honoring an agreement he officially declined to admit existed, even as its subparts openly violated it; ibid., Exhibit 19.

92. The letter of inquiry was sent in December 1990 by David Hallman, chair of the Taskforce on the Churches and Corporate Responsibility. Morrison's reply is attached to the Ominayak Affidavit (op. cit.) as Exhibit 24.

93. Ibid., pp. 24-5. *Daishowa Inc. v. Friends of the Lubicon*, Ontario Court of Justice (Gen. Div.), File No. 95-CQ-59707, Affidavit of Kevin Thomas (12/04/95).

94. Ominayak Affidavit, op. cit., pp. 25,26; Exhibit 25.

95. Quoted in FOL briefing paper provided by Sierra Legal Defense Fund, 1996 (copy on file).

96. Ibid.

97. Ibid.

98. Ibid.

99. Ibid.

100. Ibid. Photos in the Japanese press on Jan. 30, 1992, show the Tokyo demonstrators carrying placards reading "STOP THE LUBICON GENOCIDE!"

101. NAJC press release, Nov. 28, 1992; quoted in FOL briefing paper, op. cit. In a letter to Canadian Prime Minister Brian Mulroney dated Jan. 24, 1992, NAJC President Arthur Miki followed up by observing that his organization believed "genocide is not too strong a word" to describe what implementation of Daishowa's plans would mean for the Lubicons, and that the NAJC found this to be "completely unacceptable"; quoted in ibid.

102. "We expect from you a clear, firm and public commitment to not cut and not to purchase any wood cut on unceded Lubicon territory until after a settlement of Lubicon land rights and negotiation of a harvesting agreement with the Lubicon people that takes into account Lubicon wildlife and environmental concerns. Until such time we are initiating a public boycott campaign of Daishowa products. This campaign will encompass all Daishowa products which reach the public, including all paper products and chip board. We are currently negotiating with many of your clients who…are reconsidering their contracts with Daishowa"; quoted in *Daishowa Inc. v. Friends of the Lubicon*, Ontario Court of Justice (Gen. Div.), File No. 95-CQ-59707, Verdict of Judge J. MacPherson (Apr. 14, 1998) p. 9.

103. Ibid., pp. 21-2.

104. As Judge MacPherson put it, "Daishowa did not stand idly by while all this was happening from 1991 to 1994. Daishowa Inc., the company that made the paper products in its Winnipeg plant, employed its senior management and its Ontario sales people in efforts to persuade stores not to sever their relationship with Daishowa. Moreover, throughout these years, the senior management and public relations personnel of the parent company, Daishowa Forest Products Ltd., were deeply involved in trying to communicate Daishowa's position with a view to persuading customers to continue their economic relationship with Daishowa"; Verdict, op. cit., pp. 20-1.

105. Ibid., pp. 22-3. Also see Thomas Claridge, "Judge to rule May 19 on Lubicon boycott: Daishowa says $3-million in annual sales lost," *Globe and Mail*, May 1, 1995; Christopher Genovali, "Multinational Pulp Company SLAPPs Suit Against Activist Group," *Alternatives Journal*, Vol. 22, No. 3, 1996.

106. The interim injunction was granted on consent by Judge Wright on February 6, 1995. The defendants filed their statement on March 20; Verdict, op. cit., p. 22.

107. *Daishowa Inc. v. Friends of the Lubicon* (1995), 30 C.R.R. (2d) 26 (Gen. Div.).

108. *Daishowa Inc. v. Friends of the Lubicon* (1996), 27 O.R. (3d) 215 (Civ. Ct.). Judges Corbett and McRae concurred, while Judge O'Leary dissented.

109. Although Tollefson's academic work was proscribed by her ruling, Judge Kiteley refused to allow his attorney, Craig Flood, to make representations in his client's behalf during ensuing hearings. Cumulatively, Daishowa's various legal maneuvers to prevent exposure of its business practices qualified it for the *Multinational Monitor*'s list of the "Ten Worst Corporations of 1996"; Christopher Genovali, "Daishowa Tries to Gag Critics," *Alternatives Journal*, Vol. 23, No. 2, 1997.

110. "[T]he Ontario Court of Appeal simply refused to hear the case [on April 24, 1996], no reasons given… [T]he Supreme Court of Canada also refuse to hear the case [on June 19, 1997]—no reasons given"; Peter Mortinston, "Corporate Bully, Canadian Activists in Showdown," *Overview*, No. 63,

Aug. 1997.

111.Verdict, op. cit., p. 29.

112. "In [*Ontario (Attorney General) v.*] *Dielman* [(1994), 117 D.L.R. (4th) 449 (Gen. Div.)], Adams J., said that political protesters 'will often have multiple targets for their messages because of their multiple purposes' (p. 678). The Friends have multiple purposes in their campaign in support of the Lubicon Cree—they try to educate the public, persuade governments to change their policies, and dissuade Daishowa from logging on land the Lubicons believe belongs to them. With respect to this last purpose, the Friends speak directly to Daishowa. However, since the Friends are themselves consumers of Daishowa products they also take their message to their fellow consumers, both corporate (e.g., Pizza Pizza) and individual (e.g., fellow purchasers of Pizza Pizza products placed in Daishowa bags). In doing this, the Friends' message is not: we are engaged in a personal economic dispute with Daishowa, please help us. Rather, the essence of their message is: we, like you, are consumers of Daishowa products; on an important social issue Daishowa has taken a position that is detrimental to some of the poorest citizens in Canada; please join us in communicating to Daishowa that we will not continue as customers if it does not change its position"; Verdict, op. cit., pp. 39-40.

113. Ibid., p. 37. The "prohibition against secondary picketing" at issue is essentially a holdover from early twentieth century antisyndicalist legislation, the ongoing appropriateness of which the judge expresses doubts about even in a labor relations context; ibid., p. 40.

114. Ibid., pp. 40-1, 48, 46.

115. Ibid., p. 46.

116. Ibid., p. 50.

117. Ibid., p. 51.

118. In rejecting Daishowa's breach of contract claim, MacPherson followed the lead of the corporation's own clients, several of whom were called to testify during the trial, in observing that there were in fact no contracts to be breached. As Pizza Pizza CEO Michael Overs put it, "We did not breach any contract; there was no contract." Others who testified to this effect were representatives of Woolworth's, Movenpick restaurants, Country Style Donuts, Progress Packaging, Holt Renfrew, and Bowring's. In fact, Marc Robitaille, CEO of Omniplast (a primary distributor of Daishowa products) testified that *none* of the companies supplied by his firm were contractually bound to accept items produced by Daishowa; ibid., pp. 52-3. It should be noted that the corporate practice of leveling such vacuous charges against activist opponents in hopes that the latter will be bankrupted or otherwise "neutralized" in the course of mounting a legal defense is the very essence of the SLAPP suit phenomenon. Such manipulation of the legal system is now outlawed in a dozen U.S. states; Genovali, "Daishowa Tries to Gag Its Critics," op. cit.

119. Ominayak Affidavit, op. cit., p. 12.

120.Verdict, op. cit., pp. 67-8.

121. Ibid., pp. 68, 79. Concerning the public at large, MacPherson ruled that restraints should apply "to anyone who has notice of this decision and the court order which will effect it. The style of cause, which lists Jane Doe, John Doe and Persons Unknown as defendants, is a proper foundation to permit Daishowa to seek this relief, and it is appropriate on its merits to grant it"; ibid., p. 80.

122. Ibid., p. 68.

123. Ibid., pp. 75, 79, 80.

124. Ibid., p. 71. It should be noted that, aside from differing among themselves, each of these truncated dictionary definitions departs sharply from that framed in black letter international law. Religious groups, for example, are left unmentioned although they are among the legally protected categories or "classes." Political groups *are* mentioned, on the other hand, although they, along with "economic aggregates," were expressly deleted from the list of protected classes in 1948.

125. At pp. 70-1 of the Verdict, MacPherson quotes from R.E. Brown's *The Law of Defamation in Canada* (2nd ed.,Vol. 1, p. 52).

126. Hammett, the consumate wordsmith, was of course preoccupied with such matters of linguistic precision. See, e.g., Diane Johnson, *Dashiell Hammett: A Life* (New York: Random House, 1983).

127. Indeed, one might hope—with obvious futility in this case—that the courts would find themselves sharing a sense of educational responsibility.

128. This was the celebrated 1923 "Monkey Trial" of a young Dayton, Tennessee school teacher,

John T. Scopes, charged with violating the state's anti-evolution statute for teaching Darwin rather than Genesis in the classroom; Edward J. Larson, *Summer for the Gods: The Scopes Trial and America's Continuing Debate Over Science and Religion* (New York: Basic Books, 1997).

129. The full text of the Convention (U.N. GAOR Res. 260A (III), 9 Dec. 1948; U.S.T._____, T.I.A.S. No._____, 78 U.N.T.S. (1951)) will be found in Brownlie, *Basic Documents*, op. cit., pp. 31-4.

130. Verdict, op. cit., p. 71.

131. The mystery of how this came to be can be solved right here and now. In the parliamentary debates on ratifying the Genocide Convention conducted in May 1952, organizations like the Canadian Civil Liberties Association pointed out in "blunt language," as MacPherson would call it, that policies like imposing integrated education on Indian children could be construed as genocidal under existing international legal definition; Canada Civil Liberties Association, "Brief to Senate Standing Committee on Legal and Constitutional Affairs on Hate Propaganda," Apr. 22, 1969, p. 6. Parliament did nothing to alter the offending policies. Rather, it simply wrote its own version of the law—and thereby attempted to redefine the crime—so as to exempt itself from compliance. For details on Canada's efforts to constrict and otherwise subvert the meaning and intent of the Genocide Convention during the U.N. drafting process, see External Affairs Canada, *Canada and the United Nations* (Ottawa: Dept. of External Affairs, 1948) esp. p. 191. Canada's current statute on genocide will be found in the Criminal Code, R.S.C. 1985, c. C-46.

132. Verdict, op. cit., p. 72.

133. Ibid., p. 73.

134. Ibid., p. 75.

135. Thomas Affidavit, op. cit., p. 187.

136. Raphaël Lemkin, *Axis Rule in Occupied Europe* (Washington, D.C.: Carnegie Endowment for World Peace, 1944) p. 79.

137. Ibid. Lemkin's reference to colonization laid the groundwork for Sartre's famous equation of colonialism to genocide 24 years later, a conceptual innovation which would make Canada's relationship to all aboriginal peoples within its borders genocidal *by definition*; Jean-Paul Sartre, "On Genocide," *Ramparts*, Feb. 1968.

138. Lemkin's examples include such things as the repression of French language and legitimation of illegitimate children with German fathers in Luxembourg; ibid., pp. 196-7. His sophisticated analysis is obviously light years away from MacPherson's crude preoccupation with sheer butchery, but virtually interchangeable with the understanding expressed by Kevin Thomas and others in the FOL.

139. Robert Davis and Mark Zannis, *The Genocide Machine in Canada: The Pacification of the North* (Montréal: Black Rose Books, 1973) p. 18.

140. Lemkin's material is usually referred to as the "Secretariat's Draft" (U.N. Doc. A/362 (1947)); it is reproduced in Nehemiah Robinson, *The Genocide Convention: A Commentary* (New York: Institute for Jewish Affairs, 1960) pp. 122-30. For further background, see M. Lippman, "The Drafting of the 1948 Convention on Punishment and Prevention of the Crime of Genocide," *Boston University International Law Journal*, No. 3, 1984.

141. Davis and Zannis, *Genocide Machine*, op. cit., p. 19.

142. Secretariat's Draft, op. cit., Preamble.

143. U.N. Economic and Social Council, 6th Part (1948), quoted in Davis and Zannis, *Genocide Machine*, op. cit., p. 19.

144. Verdict, op. cit., pp. 42-3.

145. Dr. Smith's assessment was made in a letter to Prime Minister Brian Mulroney drafted immediately prior to the noted ethnographer's death. It was submitted to the court as Exhibit 4 attached to the Ominayak Affidavit, op. cit.

146. "Modern Genocide," *Quid Novi*, Nov. 30, 1987; submitted as Exhibit 30, Thomas Affidavit, op. cit.

147. Daishowa's attorneys objected strenuously to the introduction of *any* definitional material aside from dictionaries into evidence, especially my testifying, but declined to cross examine or otherwise challenge what I had to say on the stand. I was, however, constrained at Daishowa's request from making any direct reference to the Lubicon situation, ostensibly because I'd never conducted a site visit at Little Buffalo; my reply that I'd never visited Auschwitz in 1943 either, but that this hardly disqualified me from

concluding on the evidence that conditions there were genocidal, seemed to fall on deaf ears.

148. *Daishowa Inc. v. Friends of the Lubicon*, Ontario Court of Justice (Gen. Div.), File No. 95-CQ-59707, Affidavit of Joan Ryan (Mar. 20, 1995) p. 15.

149. Ibid., p. 8.

150. Verdict, op. cit., pp. 72, 76.

151. Ibid., p. 76.

152. For explication, see, e.g., Isaac Balbus, *The Dialectic of Legal Repression* (New York: Russell Sage Foundation, 1973).

153. Actually, had he arrived at this conclusion, MacPherson would have been *required* to enter such a decree pursuant to the principles elaborated under the "Nuremberg Doctrine," which Canada duly endorsed by signing the United Nations Affirmation of the Principles of International Law Recognized by the Charter of the Nuremberg Tribunal (U.N.G.A. Res. 95(I), U.N. Doc. A/236 (1946)) on Dec. 11, 1946. For text, see Burns H. Weston, Richard A. Falk and Anthony D'Amato, eds., *Basic Documents in International Law and World Order* (St. Paul, MN: West Publishing, 1990) p. 140.

154. Resort to this option might well have been subject to legal challenge in that while Canada's ratification of the Genocide Convention was accomplished by treaty, it's domestic implementing statute fails to fully conform with the Convention's provisions. This is impermissible under the Vienna Convention on the Law of Treaties (U.N. Doc. A/CONF.39/27 at 289 (1969), 1155 U.N.T.S. 331 reprinted in 8 I.L.M. 679 (1969)), Article 27 of which stipulates that "a party may not invoke the provisions of its internal law as justification for its failure to perform a treaty"; see generally, Sir Ian Sinclair, *The Vienna Convention on the Law of Treaties* (Manchester, UK: Manchester University Press, [2nd ed.] 1984). Moreover, genocide "is a crime under customary international law. The International Court of Justice (ICJ) said as much in an advisory opinion in connection with reservations some states have made upon ratifying the [Genocide] Convention"; Lawrence J. LeBlanc, *The United States and the Genocide Convention* (Durham, NC: Duke University Press, 1991) p. 3. The Genocide Convention is thus binding on Canada, irrespective of Canada's truncated statutory enunciation of it, or even if Canada had never ratified it in an form at all; International Court of Justice, *Reports of Judgments, Advisory Opinions and Orders: Reservations to the Convention on the Prevention and Punishment of the Crime of Genocide* (The Hague: ICJ, 1951) pp. 15–69.

155. See, e.g., Davis and Zannis, *Genocide Machine*, op. cit.; Boyce Richardson, *Strangers Devour the Land* (New York: Alfred A. Knopf, 1976); Miles Goldstick, *Wolleston: People Resisting Genocide* (Montréal: Black Rose Books, 1987); Terrance Nelson, *Genocide in Canada* (Ginew, Man.: Rouseau River First Nation, 1997).

156. Menno Boldt, *Surviving as Indians: The Challenge of Self-Government* (Toronto: University of Toronto Press, 1993).

157. J.R. Miller, *Shingwauk's Vision: A History of Native Residential Schools* (Toronto: University of Toronto Press, 1996).

158. Keegtra and Zundel are both notorious Canadian neonazi Holocaust deniers; Alan T. Davies, "The Queen versus James Keegstra: Reflections on Christian Antisemitism in Canada," *American Journal of Theology and Philosophy*, Vol. 9, Nos. 1-2, 1988; Leonidas E. Hill, "The Trial of Ernst Zundel: Revisionism and the Law in Canada," *Simon Wiesenthal Annual*, 1989. Katz is a Jewish scholar who argues that no "true" genocide *other than* the Holocaust has ever occurred. Among his more interesting forays has been to claim that the 1637-38 extermination of the Pequots wasn't "really" genocide since, in his estimation, "the number killed probably totaled less than half the tribe"; Steven T. Katz, "The Pequot War Considered," *New England Quarterly*, No. 64, 1991. For further analysis, and a wealth of similar illustrations, see the essays entitled "Assaults on Truth and Memory: Holocaust Denial in Context" and "Lie for Lie: Linkages between Holocaust Deniers and Proponents of the 'Uniqueness of the Jewish Experience in World War II," in my *A Little Matter of Genocide: Holocaust and Denial in the Americas, 1492 to the Present* (San Francisco/Winnipeg: City Lights/Arbeiter Ring, 1997). Also see David E. Stannard, "The Politics of Holocaust Scholarship: Uniqueness as Denial," in Alan S. Rosenbaum, *Is the Holocaust Unique? Perspectives in Comparative Genocide* (Boulder, CO: Westview Press, 1996).

159. Paraguay's 1974 response to notification by the U.N. Secretariat that it had been formally charged by the International League for the Rights of Man and other organizations with perpetrating genocide against the Aché Indians was that although "there are victims and victimizer, there is not the

third element necessary to establish the crime of genocide—that is 'intent.' As there is no 'intent' one cannot speak of 'genocide'"; quoted in Norman Lewis, "The Camp at Ceclio Baez," in Richard Arens, ed., *Genocide in Paraguay* (Philadelphia: Temple University Press, 1976) pp. 62-3. As for Brazil, its officially stated contention is that "crimes against the Brazilian indigenous population cannot be characterized as genocide, since the criminal parties involved never eliminated the Indians as an ethnic or cultural group. Hence there was lacking the special malice or motivation necessary to characterize the occurrence of genocide. The crimes in question were committed for exclusively economic reasons, the perpetrators having acted solely to take possession of the lands of the victims"; United Nations, Human Rights Communication No. 478, Sept. 29, 1969.

160. Use of the term "peaceful" in this context is highly problematic, implying as it does that so long as the victims of aggression do not "resort to violence" in responding, "peace" somehow prevails. This is nonsense. As was observed after an April 1994 site visit to Little Buffalo by Marilia Schuller, Executive Director of the World Council of Churches Program to Combat Racism, the Canadian state and collaborating corporations have long since begun to wage what amounts to low-intensity warfare against the Lubicons. It follows that nothing will be peaceful, regardless of what the Lubicons do, until Canadian/corporate aggression is ended; Schuller is quoted in FOL Briefing Document, op. cit.

161. Unidentified Lubicons quoted in Thomas Affidavit, op. cit., p. 24.

162. See Ward Churchill with Mike Ryan, *Pacifism as Pathology: Reflections on the Role of Armed Struggle in North America* (Winnipeg: Arbeiter Ring, 1998).

PART III: OTHER FRONTS

Industrial Slave
capitalist and communist
    imperialists
smiling with false faces
beckoning us
with their lies about progress
wanting us to enjoy
    the rape of the Earth
    and our minds

Industrial Slave
forked tongue legalistic contract
chains
turning our visions into tech no logical
dreams
national security war makers
desecrating the natural world
and god still trying to get over
what you done to his boy

Industrial Slave
material bound
law and ORDER
religious salvation
individually alone
Industrial Slave.

—John Trudell
from *Living in Reality*

GEOGRAPHIES OF SACRIFICE

The Radioactive Colonization of Native North America

> Our defeat was always implicit in the history of others; our wealth has always generated our poverty by nourishing the prosperity of others, the empires and their native overseers... In the colonial and neocolonial alchemy, gold changes to scrap metal and food into poison... [We] have become painfully aware of the mortality of wealth which nature bestows and imperialism appropriates.
>
> —Eduardo Galeano,
> *Open Veins of Latin America*

THE unstated rationales guiding the federal governments of both the United States and Canada in their contemporary handling of native peoples and territories are straightforward. It is not considered geopolitically expedient to allow a scattering of small, mostly landlocked nations to exercise anything resembling real sovereignty within their own borders. Moreover, it has been discovered that, perhaps ironically, the barren, residual landbase left to Indians in the twentieth century is extremely rich in resources: some sixty percent of all known U.S. "domestic" uranium reserves and a quarter of its low-sulfur coal lie under Indian land. In addition, as much as a fifth of the oil and natural gas are in reservation areas. Substantial assets of commercial and strategic minerals such as gold, silver, copper, bauxite, molybdenum and zeolites are at issue, as are water in the arid West and other "renewable resources" like timber.[1] The pattern of resource distribution in Canada is comparable.[2]

With such holdings, it would seem logical that the several million people indigenous to North America—a population officially acknowledged as consisting of approximately 1.9 million in the United States and perhaps as many more in Canada—should be among the continent's wealthiest residents.[3] As even the governments' own figures reveal, however, we receive the lowest per capita income of any population group and evidence every standard indicator of dire poverty: the highest rates of malnutrition, plague disease, death by exposure, infant mortality, teen suicide and so on.[4]

The U.S. government in particular has found that by keeping native assets pooled in reserved areas under its "trust" authority, it is able to channel them at very low rates to preferred corporations, using a "tribal" administrative apparatus it established during the late 1930s as a medium for leasing purposes.[5] Thus, as of 1984, stateside Indians were receiving only an average of 3.4 percent of the market value for uranium extracted from their land, 1.6 percent for our oil, 1.3 percent for natural gas, and a little under two percent for coal. These figures run as much as 85 percent below the royalty rates paid to non-Indians for the same items.[6]

This boon to the U.S. and Canadian economies has been enhanced by the governments' utilization of a self-proclaimed "plenary" power over Indians and Indian land to relax or dispense with environmental protection standards and job safety regulations, further lowering extraction and production costs while allowing certain of the more odious forms of production and waste disposal associated with advanced industrial technologies to be conveniently located—out of sight and mind of the mainstream public—in areas occupied primarily by native people.[7] In substance, we have been consigned to a status of "expendability" by federal, state and corporate economic planners in both Canada and the United States.[8]

From the perspective of North America's social, political and economic élites, the advantages of maintaining discrete Indian territories under trust control thus greatly outweigh any potential benefit accruing from final absorption of these residual areas.[9] The history of conquest, militarily or otherwise, which has always marked the U.S./Canadian relationship to Native North America, has correspondingly transformed itself into a process of colonization, albeit of an "internal" variety peculiar to highly evolved settler-states (Australia, New Zealand, Northern Ireland and Israel are other prime examples of this phenomenon).[10] The impacts of this system on American Indian environments and the people who inhabit them are in many ways best demonstrated through examination of the effects engendered by the uranium industry since 1950.

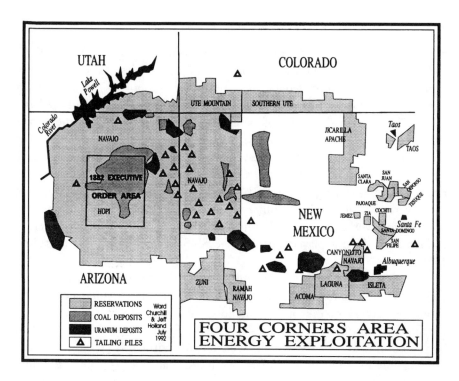

The following text appears within the map image:

UTAH   COLORADO

Lake Powell

Colorado River

UTE MOUNTAIN   SOUTHERN UTE

JICARILLA APACHE

Taos

TAOS

NAVAJO

SANTA CLARA   SAN JUAN   SAN ILDEFONSO   TESUQUE

1882 EXECUTIVE

NAVAJO

ORDER AREA

POJOAQUE

HOPI

JEMEZ   ZIA   COCHITI

NEW MEXICO

SANTA DOMINGO

Santa Fe

SAN FELIPE

CANYONCITO NAVAJO

Albuquerque

ARIZONA

ZUNI   RAMAH NAVAJO

LAGUNA   ISLETA

ACOMA

RESERVATIONS   Ward Churchill & Jeff Holland July 1992

COAL DEPOSITS

URANIUM DEPOSITS

▲ TAILING PILES

FOUR CORNERS AREA
ENERGY EXPLOITATION

The Four Corners Region

Although only about two-thirds of U.S. uranium deposits lie within reservation boundaries, over ninety percent of the country's mining and milling have been undertaken on or immediately adjacent to Indian land since the mineral became a profitable commodity during the early 1950s.[11] The bulk of this activity has occurred in the Grants Uranium Belt of the Colorado Plateau, the so-called "Four Corners" region, where the boundaries of Utah, Arizona, Colorado and New Mexico intersect. The Four Corners is home to the greatest concentration of landbased indigenous population remaining in North America: the Diné (Navajo), Southern Ute, Ute Mountain, Zuni, Laguna, Acoma, and several other Puebloan nations all reside there. Since by far the most extensive activity has occurred on the Navajo and Laguna Reservations, it will be useful to consider the situation of each in turn.

In 1952, the U.S. Interior Department's Bureau of Indian Affairs (BIA) awarded the Kerr–McGee Corporation the first contract—duly rubberstamped by the federally-created and -supported Navajo Tribal Council—to mine uranium on Diné land, employing about a hundred Indian miners at two-thirds the off-reservation pay scale.[12] In the same year, a federal inspector at the corporation's mine near the reservation town of Shiprock, New Mexico, found the ventilation fans in the facility's main shaft were not functioning.[13] When the same inspector returned in 1955, the fans ran out of fuel during his visit. By 1959, radiation levels in the Shiprock mine were estimated as being ninety-to-a-hundred times the maximum permissible for worker safety.[14] Nothing was done about the situation before the uranium deposit played out and the Shiprock operation was closed in 1970.[15]

At that point, Kerr–McGee simply abandoned the site, leaving the local community to contend with seventy acres of uranium tailings containing about 85 percent of the original radioactivity found in raw uranium ore, much of it continuously emitted in clouds of radon and thoron gas. The huge mounds of waste, which will remain virulently mutogenic and carcinogenic for thousands of years, begin less than sixty feet from the only significant surface water in the Shiprock area, the San Juan River.[16] It was shortly discovered that the BIA had "overlooked" inclusion of a clause requiring the corporation to engage in any sort of postoperational cleanup.[17] Richard O. Clemmer has explained the problem quite succinctly.

> [R]adon and thoron gases, while themselves inert, readily combine with the molecular structure of human cells and decay into radioactive thorium and [polonium]. Radon and thoron gases, if inhaled, irradiate cells in the lining of the respiratory tract, causing cancer. The millions of gallons of radioactive water [released by the uranium industry also] carry deadly selesium, cadmium, and lead that are easily absorbed into the local food chain, as well as emitting alpha and beta particles and gamma rays. Human ingestion of radioactive water can result in alpha particles recurrently bombarding human tissue and eventually tearing apart the cells comprising that tissue. Uranium-bearing tailings are constantly decaying into more stable elements and therefore emit radiation, as do particles of dust that blow with the wind and truck travel on dirt roads.[18]

The Bureau had also neglected to include much in the way of followup health care. Of the 150-odd Navajo miners who worked underground at the Shiprock facility over the years, eighteen had died of radiation-induced lung cancer by 1975.[19] By 1980, an additional twenty were dead of the same disease, while 95 more had contracted serious respiratory ailments and cancers.[20] The incidence of cleft palate and other birth defects linked to radiation exposure had also risen dramatically, both at Shiprock and at downstream communities drinking water contaminated by the uranium tailings.[21] The same could be said for Downes Syndrome, previously unknown among Diné.[22] Around the Kerr–McGee mine at Red Rock, where the most basic safety standards had also gone unenforced by federal inspectors, a similar pattern prevailed.

> The AEC [Atomic Energy Commission] claimed that it did not possess information about the health problems of uranium miners [or communities adjacent to uranium mines]. Unions and the Public Health Service physicians disagreed. Dr. Victor Archer at NIOSH [National Institute for Occupational Safety and Health] claimed that European physicians had noted a high incidence of lung cancer in uranium miners prior to 1940; the National Commission on Radiation Protection and the International Commission on Radiation Protection were aware of the potential hazards from radon gas by the early 1940s... Given that it had known that some cancers develop only ten to 20 years after initial exposure, it is inexcusable that the AEC had not analyzed the literature on radiation-related deaths in the mining industry. As far back as the 1950s, it was widely known that 70 percent of German and Czech pitch-blend and uranium miners who worked in the industries from the 1920s and earlier had died of lung cancer.[23]

Dr. Joseph Wagoner, director of epidemiological research at NIOSH, stated that both the cancer deaths and apparent mutogenic effects of Kerr–McGee's operations at Shiprock and Red Rock "present serious medical and ethical questions about the responsibility of [the corporation and] the federal government, which was the sole purchaser of uranium during the early uranium period."[24]

In 1979, eleven Red Rock miners suffering from lung cancer and/or fibrosis of the lungs, their families and the families of fifteen miners who had already died of the respiratory maladies filed what was to be an unsuccessful damage suit against the AEC and Kerr–McGee.[25]

> Several Navajos who worked in the uranium mills in the 1950s and 1960s [and who were] also afflicted with lung cancer or pulmonary diseases...joined the uranium miners in suing the federal government and uranium companies for compensation. Conditions in the mills were deplorable. An abandoned Shiprock mill was found to have $100,000 worth of yellowcake [pure, milled uranium] between two layers of

roofing, while workers tell of stirring yellowcake in open, steam-heated floor pans.[26]

The evidence continued to mount. Yet, by 1982—amidst ongoing federal assurances that there was really "no particular health hazard," and that resulting revenues would lead eventually to "economic self-sufficiency" and "jobs galore" for the impoverished Diné—42 more major mines and seven new mills were operating on Navajo land, while another fifteen major uranium projects were on the drawing board.[27] A substantial part of the Diné economy, both existing and projected, was being quite deliberately distorted to conform to the demands of the uranium industry, regardless of the effects on the Indians. The degree of confluence between governmental and corporate interests, as well as the intensity with which uranium development at Navajo was being pursued during this period, is indicated in a 1977 article in *Business Week*:

> Currently, 3,200 miners work underground and 900 more are in open pit operations. By 1990, the industry will need 18,400 underground miners and 4,000 above ground.... Once on the job, Kerr-McGee estimates that it costs $80,000 per miner in training, salary and benefits, as well as the costs for the trainees who quit. Kerr-McGee is now operating a training program at the Church Rock mine on the Navajo Reservation. The $2 million program is financed by the U.S. Labor Department. Labor Department sponsors hope the program will help alleviate the tribe's chronic unemployment.[28]

Kerr-McGee remained the major corporate player but had been joined by United Nuclear Corporation and Exxon. The rate of exploitation had grown frenzied. "Kerr-McGee's Church Rock No. 1 mine went into production early in 1976," analyst W.D. Armstrong observed the same year, "and it is estimated that production of uranium ore will reach...nearly 1 million tons per year by 1978. If Church Rock No. 2 and No. 3 mines come on stream in 1980 and 1983 respectively, annual production would approach 3 million tons per year."[29]

As the pace of such activities accelerated, so too did the environmental and human costs. On July 16, 1979, the United Nuclear uranium mill at Church Rock, New Mexico, was the site of the largest radioactive spill in U.S. history. A mill pond dam broke under pressure and released more than a hundred-million gallons of highly contaminated water into the Río Puerco. As has been observed elsewhere, despite "the greater publicity surrounding the Three Mile Island nuclear plant accident in March 1979, Church Rock resulted in the nation's worst release of radioactivity [until federal dumping at the government's Hanford weapons plant was revealed in 1990; see below]."[30]

Navajos herding their horses and sheep along the banks said the water looked putrid yellow, like battery acid. A Navajo woman and several animals that waded through the river that morning developed sores on their legs and later died. For a year the state told the Navajos not to eat their mutton, and butchers would not buy it. Friends and relatives shunned the Río Puerco people, refusing to shake their hands [for fear of contamination]. A decade later the residents still could not use local water supplies, partly because of the spill and partly because of several mines in the area.[31]

About 1,700 Navajo were immediately affected, their single source of water irradiated beyond any conceivable limit. Sheep and other livestock were also found to be heavily contaminated from drinking river water in the aftermath, yet United Nuclear refused to supply adequate emergency water and food supplies; a corporate official was quoted as saying in response to local Diné requests for assistance that "This is not a free lunch."[32] Rather than trying to offset the damage, the corporation stonewalled for nearly five years before agreeing to pay a minimal $525,000 out-of-court settlement to its victims.[33] United Nuclear was greatly aided in achieving this, for it, favorable outcome by an official finding that downstream Diné had suffered "little or no damage" as a result of the spill.[34]

Government officials at both the federal and state levels were later shown to have actively colluded with the corporation, both before and after the disaster. According to the Southwest Research and Information Center, an Albuquerque-based environmental organization, the whole thing was readily avoidable. United Nuclear, the group demonstrated, had known about cracks in the dam structure at least two months before the break. No costly repairs were made, however, because "political pressure was brought to bear."[35]

Even more striking, given the magnitude of what had so recently occurred, "New Mexico Governor Bruce King in 1981 told the New Mexico Environmental Improvement Agency to allow [United Nuclear] to *continue* an illegal water discharge [from its Church Rock mine], which the staff had been attempting to control for over a year (emphasis added)."[36] Similarly, the Kerr-McGee mine at Church Rock was allowed, quite illegally, to continue discharging upwards of 80,000 gallons of contaminated fluid per day— "dewatering" its primary shaft—into the local supply of surface water.[37] In actuality, this steady emission of effluents by the United Nuclear and Kerr-McGee mines has caused far more serious contamination of the Church Rock area than the 1979 spill.[38]

Such circumstances are hardly unique. When the Navajo Ranchers Association around Crownpoint, seeking to prevent what had occurred at Church Rock from happening to them, filed suit in federal court in 1978 to block Mobil Oil from launching a pilot uranium project in the Dalton Pass area, the judge ruled that the corporation's activities would have "insufficient impact" to necessitate so much as an environmental impact study.[39] In 1979, he refused to allow the plaintiffs to cancel Mobil's leases to their land, which the BIA had approved over their objections.[40] When the Diné plaintiffs argued in 1980 that their pastoral way of life would be destroyed by the plans of Mobil, Gulf, Kerr-McGee, Exxon and a dozen other energy corporations that had by then queued up to mine uranium near Dalton Pass, the judge responded that he could not understand why they would want to continue it anyway, given the "opportunity" for them to become miners and millers.[41] Such thinking was upheld by the Ninth U.S. Circuit Court, and this matter, too, was eventually "settled" on terms entirely acceptable to the corporations.[42]

Things are no better with regard to cleanup. Despite passage of the much-touted Uranium Mine Tailings Radiation Control Act in 1978,[43] the first attempt to address the question of radioactive wastes on Navajo land—tailings abandoned around the Foote Mineral Company mill near Shiprock in 1968—was not completed until 1986. This project was finished in such "timely" fashion only because Harold Tso, head of the Navajo Environmental Protection Administration, had himself convinced the tribal government to begin expending royalty monies on the effort as early as 1973.[44] The next three such operations affecting the Navajo—clearing tailings piles at long-abandoned mill sites in Monument Valley and Tuba City, Arizona (Rare Metals Corporation), and Mexican Hat, Utah (Texas Zink Corporation)—are all under exclusive federal control. Scheduled for completion in late 1991, none were finished by mid-decade.[45] Virtually nothing has been done with mill tailings around Church Rock or at several other comparable locations on the reservation.[46]

Nor is this the end of it. A 1983 study by the federal Environmental Protection Agency (EPA) concluded there were nearly a thousand additional "significant" nuclear waste sites surrounding the proliferation of abandoned mines, large and small, scattered about Diné territory. Cleanup of these locations was and is not required by any law, and they were designated by the EPA as "too remote" to be of "sufficient national concern" to warrant the expense of attempting their rehabilitation.[47] And so there remain, from White Mesa in the east to Tuba City in the west, hundreds upon hundreds of radioactive "sandpiles" still played upon by Diné youngsters and swept by the wind across the land.[48] Such is the fate of the largest indigenous nation—in terms of both landbase and population—in the United States.

Laguna Pueblo

At the neighboring Laguna Pueblo in New Mexico, the situation is perhaps worse. In 1952, the Anaconda Copper Company, a subsidiary of the Atlantic-Richfield Corporation, was issued a lease by the BIA to 7,500 acres of Laguna land on which to undertake open pit uranium mining and an adjoining milling operation. By 1980, the resulting Jackpile-Paguate Mine was the largest in the world, encompassing some 2,800 acres. It has been estimated that it would take 400 million tons of earth—enough to cover the entire District of Columbia 45 feet deep—to fill it in.[49] Of the earth removed, approximately eighty million tons were good grade uranium ore.[50] By the time the facility closed in 1982, Anaconda had realized about $600 million in profits from its operation at Laguna.[51]

In the process, the corporation, in collaboration with federal "development officers," virtually wrecked the traditional Laguna economy, recruiting hundreds of the small community's young people into wage jobs even as their environment was being gobbled up and contaminated.[52]

[Anaconda's] mining techniques require "dewatering," i.e., the pumping of water contaminated by radioactive materials to facilitate ore extraction. Since 1972, the Jackpile Mine has wasted more than 119 gallons per minute through this dewatering procedure. Altogether more than 500 million gallons of radioactive water have been discharged. This water, already radioactive from contact with uranium ore underground, is pumped over the 260 acre tailings pile comprised of overburden and processed ore sitting on soft, porous rock. From the tailings pond, this radioactive water either sinks back into the aquifer, evaporates, or seeps out of the tailings pond into the arroyos and drainage channels of the tiny Río Mequino stream that is fed by a natural spring near the tailings dam.[53]

Concerning milling:

At the Bluewater Mill, 18 miles west of the Laguna Reservation [on the western

247

boundary of the adjoining Acoma Pueblo, a 30 mile trip by rail, with raw ore hauled in open gondolas] near the bed of the San Jose River, Anaconda has added a 107-acre pond and a 159-acre pile comprising 13,500,000 tons of "active" tailings and 765,033 tons of "inactive" residues.[54]

Nor were Anaconda's the only such operation. Among the others were the Sohio-Reserve mill at Cebolleta, about a mile from the Laguna boundary, processing 1,500 tons of uranium ore per day. The Cebolleta mill's tailings pond covered fifty acres, its tailings pile having reached a height of 350 feet by 1980. Near Marquez, about fifteen miles northeast of Laguna, the Bokum Minerals Corporation had opened a shaft mine, and Kerr-McGee announced plans in 1979 to open a second.[54] Other projects were also in the works.

"Near Mount Taylor and San Mateo, twenty miles north of the Laguna and Acoma Reservations, six different companies have drilled exploration holes in eight different areas," Clemmer recounted at the time. "Gulf is sinking a deep underground shaft into the Navajos' and Acomas' sacred Mount Taylor, and mining has already changed the configuration of life in the area. Although Gulf acknowledges no responsibility, water supplies have become so contaminated with Bentonite from drilling mud that the National Guard have trucked water into San Mateo for residents' home use, and Gulf has drilled a new community well. Radon gas vents from Gulf's mine were situated so close to the school that the New Mexico EID has forced the school to close."[56]

Unsurprisingly, given all this, the Environmental Protection Agency informed the Lagunas in 1973, and again in 1977, that their only substantial source of surface water, the Río Paguate, was seriously contaminated with Radium-226 and other heavy metals.[57] In 1979, the General Accounting Office revealed that the groundwater underlying the whole of the Grants Uranium Belt, into which Laguna's wells are tapped, was also highly irradiated.[58] By then, it had become known that Anaconda had used low-grade uranium ore, well pulverized, as the gravel with which it had "improved" and expanded the Laguna road network. Soon, it was discovered that comparable material had been used in the construction of the tribal council building, community center and newly constructed Jackpile Housing complex, all supposed "benefits" of the uranium boom.[59]

In 1977, the tribal council belatedly began efforts to negotiate an arrangement by which Anaconda might be required to correct the situation.

As with the Navajo, however, it was quickly discovered that the BIA had failed to make postoperational cleanup a part of the contract it had signed on the Indians "behalf."[60] When the Jackpile-Paguate Mine was closed in 1982, the corporation provided only a $175,000 public relations grant designated to help with "retraining" the suddenly unemployed Laguna work force.[61]

The EPA explained that the Indians had "nothing to worry about" concerning the irradiation of their homes and other buildings since radiation levels therein, while "higher than normal," were still at a "reasonably low level." No mention was made of the fact that a "U.S. Public Health Service physician [had already] suggested that small doses of radiation exposure may actually promote more disease than larger doses because cells are damaged, rather than destroyed outright. Irradiated sex cells in parents can result in birth defects."[62]

Negotiations continued, nonetheless. From the Laguna side this was obviously because of the environmental devastation with which they had been left. After 1983, the federal government began to actually encourage this, as the extent of the damage began to attract public attention and generate pressure in nearby Albuquerque and among non-Indian environmental organizations. Meanwhile, the Indian position was simple enough:

> The Lagunas [asked] only to be able to graze their livestock, use the water safely, and breathe the air without worrying about lung cancer. Unlike [some] uranium mines, which lie in remote, unpopulated areas, one pit lay just 1,000 feet away from the Pueblo community of Paguate. Without proper protection of the groundwater, the mine pit area would remain covered with toxic, saline wastelands, according to the Interior Department. The DOI predicted that without reclamation, 95 to 243 additional radiation-induced cancer deaths could be expected within 50 miles of the mine.[63]

Anaconda was recalcitrant, rejecting the Laguna position as "unrealistic" and denouncing the government's data as "inaccurate" by as much as a factor of 100.[64] In 1985, the corporation threatened to sue both its native victims and the Department of the Interior as a means of "clarifying" that neither held a "legitimate right" to compel cleanup of the Jackpile site.[65]

During the second half of the '80s, however, the corporation's posture began to soften. This was apparently due in part to general public relations concerns and in another respect because it had become interested in a longrange prospect of returning to its operations on the reservation. In 1986,

Anaconda stipulated that it believed reclamation of its wastes would cost a total of $17 million and that it might, given options on renewing its mineral leases, be prepared to underwrite this expense. The Lagunas countered that the figure was far too low, with the result that the corporation agreed to fund an Indian-staffed "environmental rehabilitation program in the amount of $43.6 million over a ten-year period, beginning in 1988.[66]

Even if upgraded and extended further, however, the program won't necessarily make a lot of difference. After an extensive study of the difficulties and expense inherent to rehabilitation of land and water contaminated by uranium mining and milling, the Los Alamos Scientific Laboratory, the premier U.S. nuclear research center, figuratively threw up its hands. "Perhaps the solution to the radon problem," its team of scientists concluded in the laboratory's 1978 *Mini-Report*, "is to zone uranium mining and milling districts so as to forbid human habitation."[67] This recommendation dovetailed quite nicely with a suggestion made somewhat earlier by the National Academy of Science, which was incorporated into the Federal Energy Department's "Project Independence" in 1974. The idea was that locales such as the Four Corners region be designated "National Sacrifice Areas" in the interests of U.S. economic stability and energy consumption.[68]

Since both Anaconda and the government facilitators involved in hatching the Laguna "reclamation" deal were surely aware of these recommendations, it seems probable that the whole thing will turn out to be just one more charade, an elaborate ruse to forestall popular resistance to far greater levels of uranium production in the area during the early part of the next century. If so, the ploy has worked to a frightening extent.

Certainly, the emergent public concern over what was happening at Laguna, the Navajo Reservation and elsewhere in the Four Corners, so evident during the early 1980s, has largely dissipated over the past fifteen years. The way to wholesale geographical sacrifice looks wide open, given only an appropriate economic climate in which to foster it. Such a prospectus conforms very well with the government's 1989 refusal to adopt any sort of uniform standards for rehabilitation of uranium mining and milling zones.[69]

Of course, as American Indian Movement (AIM) leader Russell Means has pointed out, given the landlinked nature of indigenous societies, the sacrifice of any geographic region means the sacrifice of all native peoples residing within it.[70] Unlike the transient, extractive corporations doing business on their land, and the broader consumer society, landlinked peoples cannot simply pick up and leave whenever a given piece of real estate is "used up." To do so would be to engage in an act of utter self-destruction in terms of their identity and sociocultural integrity, in effect, of their cultural survival itself.[71]

On the other hand, staying put in the face of the sorts of "development" previewed with the Laguna and Navajo points clearly to rapid physical eradication. Hence, the obvious correspondence of the density of native population around the Grants Uranium Belt and the concept of National Sacrifice Areas has led Means and others to conclude that U.S. energy policy, especially as regards uranium mining and milling, amounts to "genocide...no more, no less."[72]

The Black Hills Region

A second region designated for potential national sacrifice is that around the Black Hills, including portions of the states of South Dakota, Nebraska, Wyoming, Montana and North Dakota. Probably not coincidentally, the targeted locale contains the second largest concentration of landbased Indians in North America, including the entire "Sioux Complex" of reservations, the Shoshone and Arapaho peoples of Wind River, and the Crow and Northern Cheyenne nations along the Powder River. All told, more than forty energy corporations are vying for position within this extremely rich "resource belt." As of August 1979, some 5,163 uranium claims averaging twenty acres apiece were held in the Black Hills National Forest alone.[73]

"Overall, the plans for industrializing the hills are staggering," Harvey Wasserman reported a year later. "They include a giant energy park featuring more than a score of 10,000 megawatt coal-fired plants, a dozen nuclear reactors, huge coal slurry pipelines designed to use millions of gallons of water to move crushed coal thousands of miles, and at least 14 major uranium mines."[74] Although, to date, the only significant uranium mining/milling enterprise undertaken in the area has been that begun in 1954 by the AEC at an abandoned army ordinance depot called Igloo near the southern Hills town of Edgemont, South Dakota (about twenty miles west of the Pine Ridge Reservation), its record snaps the implications of the broader schemes for regional "development" into sharp focus.

On June 11, 1962, an estimated 200 of the approximately 3.5 million tons of uranium tailings which resulted from the Igloo Operation, most of it piled along the Cottonwood Creek in downtown Edgemont, gave way under heavy rains. Once in the creek, they washed downstream a few hundred yards to the Cheyenne River, the major source of surface water for the western half of Pine Ridge.[75] Meanwhile, other tailings piles were also leaching into the Madison Formation, the shallow aquifer which is the primary groundwater source for the reservation, and deeper, into the underlying Oglala Aquifer.

By June 1980, the Indian Health Service announced that well water in the village of Slim Buttes, in the affected Red Shirt Table portion of the reservation, was testing at radiation levels three times the national safety standard; a new well tested at 14 times the "safe" level.[76] As the U.S. Department of the Interior summed up the situation in a 1979 report, "Contamination is well beyond the safe limit for animals. Escape by infiltration into the water table or by breakout to stream drainages could cause contamination by dangerous levels of radioactivity. Stock or humans using water from wells down gradient from tailing ponds would be exposed. Plants and animals encountering contaminated flows or contaminated sediments deposited in drainage channels would be exposed. Increasing the danger is the nondegradable and accumulative nature of this type of contamination."[77]

Under the circumstances, Tribal President Stanley Looking Elk requested that $175,000 of a $200,000 federal allocation for reservation water management be devoted to obtaining uncontaminated water supplies for the inhabitants of Slim Buttes and surrounding areas. The request was approved, but in a manner entirely reminiscent of the United Nuclear posture at Church Rock, the BIA stipulated it could be used *only for cattle*.[78] At the same time, studies indicated a Shiprock-like pattern in which stillbirths, infant deformities such as cleft palate and cancer deaths had all increased markedly in the affected area since 1970.[79] Government spokespersons adamantly insisted, as they had from the outset, that there was "no public health hazard" in its uranium operations (which had been by then closed down).[80]

Officials were still saying this in 1982, when they also began to admit that the Igloo/Edgemont locale was so contaminated it would make an ideal spot for a national nuclear waste dump.[81] Their unsuccessful drive to win public endorsement of this idea—which they claimed involved only a

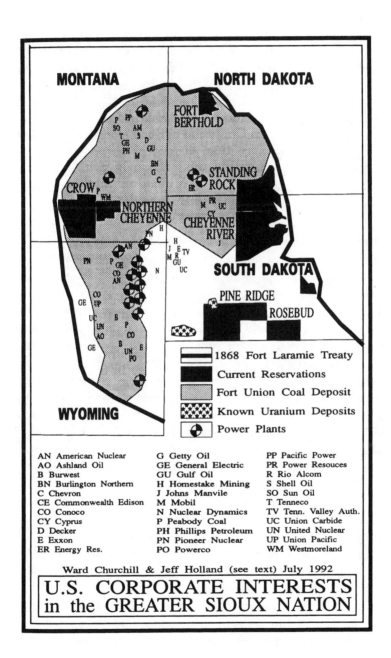

MONTANA

NORTH DAKOTA

FORT
BERTHOLD

CROW

STANDING
ROCK

NORTHERN
CHEYENNE

CHEYENNE
RIVER

SOUTH DAKOTA

PINE RIDGE

ROSEBUD

WYOMING

- 1868 Fort Laramie Treaty
- Current Reservations
- Fort Union Coal Deposit
- Known Uranium Deposits
- Power Plants

AN American Nuclear	G Getty Oil	PP Pacific Power
AO Ashland Oil	GE General Electric	PR Power Resouces
B Burwest	GU Gulf Oil	R Rio Alcom
BN Burlington Northern	H Homestake Mining	S Shell Oil
C Chevron	J Johns Manvile	SO Sun Oil
CE Commonwealth Edison	M Mobil	T Tenneco
CO Conoco	N Nuclear Dynamics	TV Tenn. Valley Auth.
CY Cyprus	P Peabody Coal	UC Union Carbide
D Decker	PH Phillips Petroleum	UN United Nuclear
E Exxon	PN Pioneer Nuclear	UP Union Pacific
ER Energy Res.	PO Powerco	WM Westmoreland

Ward Churchill & Jeff Holland (see text) July 1992

U.S. CORPORATE INTERESTS
in the GREATER SIOUX NATION

"minimal health risk"—included a "concession" to the sensibilities of the nearby Oglala Lakotas of Pine Ridge: During the period 1985-87, the government finally "fixed" the problem of surface water pollution.[82] By this, it is meant that federal contractors removed the mass of tailings from the banks of Cottonwood Creek, moved it a few miles *closer* to the reservation and dumped it on a barren plateau. There, it is now "secured" by a chainlink and razor wire fence labeled with small metal signs emblazoned with nuclear symbols and bearing the caption "Hazardous Wastes." As of this writing, the contaminants are still blowing freely in the wind.[83]

Such fences had, by this point, also made their appearance on Pine Ridge itself, demarcating a section of what was called the "Gunnery Range." A bleak 382,000 acre area located on the Red Shirt Table around Sheep Mountain and encompassing the northwestern eighth of the reservation, the land had been "borrowed" by the U.S. War Department in 1942 as a practice range for the training of aerial gunners. It was, by agreement, to be returned to the Oglalas at the conclusion of World War II. Instead, it was retained by the government in a vague "trust" status for the next quarter-century.[84] During the early 1970s, as part of a broader agenda to recover land in the region, the people of Pine Ridge ended the long limbo which had prevailed in the matter by mounting an effort to regain control over their property (*see* "The Black Hills Are Not For Sale" in this volume).

All things being equal, they might well have been successful. Unbeknownst to them, however, a secret experiment in satellite mapping undertaken jointly in 1970 by the National Aeronautics and Space Administration (NASA) and the National Uranium Research and Evaluation Institute (NURE, a component of the U.S. Geological Survey) had revealed a rich deposit of intermixed uranium and molybdenum underlying the Sheep Mountain locale.[85] Far from being willing to restore the land to the Oglalas, the government had therefore quietly made plans for permanent transfer of the Gunnery Range to itself. When the Indians physically resisted this idea, bringing in AIM to assist, an outright low intensity war was launched against them in 1973. Three years later, with at least 69 "insurgents" dead on Pine Ridge and another 340 having suffered serious physical assaults, federal authorities felt it was safe to proceed.[86]

On January 2, 1976, outgoing Tribal President Dick Wilson, who had actively collaborated in the counterinsurgency campaign conducted against his own ostensible constituents, signed an illegal agreement with the Interior

Department wherein title to the disputed area was formally passed from the Oglalas to the National Park Service which, in turn, added it to the existing Badlands National Monument.[87] Congress consummated the arrangement in 1977 by passing Public Law 90-468, an act stipulating that the Indians might recover surface use of the Gunnery Range at any time they expressed a desire to do so (by referendum), but that all mineral rights would forever belong to the United States.[88]

By 1979, it appears that this supposed addition to the "public domain" was serving other purposes as well. "The Air Force retained an area" and fenced it off in much the same fashion as the DoE site outside Edgemont, researcher Amelia Irvin discovered, "near which residents have sighted large containers being flown by helicopter. These reports have raised strong suspicions that the Gunnery Range was being used as a dump for high-level military nuclear waste, which may be leaking radioactivity into the aquifer. In the same area, the rate of stillborn or deformed calves has skyrocketed."[89]

Even as all this was going on, it was discovered that tailings at the Susquehanna-Western mill site—on the Wind River Reservation, near Riverton, Wyoming—was causing serious groundwater contamination on the west side of the Hills. Following the usual procedure, the corporation had simply walked away when it was finished with the facility in 1967.[90] "Because it was located on non-Indian land within reservation boundaries, the [Department of Energy] did not consider it an Indian site" and therefore ranked it as a high priority for cleanup.[91] The government's idea, vociferously rejected by Wind River's Arapahos and Shoshones, was to move the wastes a few miles, onto reservation land proper. Only when the State of Wyoming sided with the Indians in 1986, insisting that it wanted the material dumped nowhere within its borders, did the DoE alter its position.[92] As in the Edgemont example, however, most of the tailings remain on or near their original location at present.[93]

In the end, all that appears to have so far averted uranium development in and around the Black Hills of the scope evident along the Grants Belt was the same set of factors which interrupted its continuation in the Four Corners. Reaction to the Three Mile Island nuclear accident of March 1979, in combination with the AEC's having met by 1981 the ore-buying quotas established for it in the 1950s (and revised upward during the early '70s), brought about a precipitous decline in uranium prices.[94] A pound of yellowcake, which had brought $43 in the former year, garnered only $15 by the latter.[95] By 1982, virtually all U.S. uranium production had been suspended in favor of importing cheaper material from abroad. The spectacular "boom" cycle in the U.S. domestic uranium market therefore entered a continuing "bust" phase.

Other U.S. Locations

Although the Four Corners and Black Hills regions were the scenes of by far the most intensive uranium development during the boom period, they were not alone. In 1964, on the Spokane Reservation in Washington State, the BIA arranged a mining/milling lease on behalf of the Dawn Mining Company, partly owned by the much larger Newmont Mining Corporation. The Bureau's postoperational land reclamation clause to the contract specifically exempted the company from responsibility for any environmental damage resulting from "ordinary wear and tear and unavoidable accidents in their normal use." Dawn was required to post only a $15,000 bond to ensure cleanup whenever it completed its business on Spokane land. This occurred in 1981 and 1982 for the mining and milling operations respectively.[96] By then, the contours of disaster were emerging.

In 1977 BIA geologist Jim LeBret, a Spokane tribal member, "discovered dangerous toxic wastes trickling from the mine at Blue Creek, a favorite camping and picnic spot for tribal members before uranium mining had begun. He was accompanied by his father and uncle, who had discovered uranium on the reservation and previously owned interests in Dawn Mining. They left in tears after seeing the canary-yellow trickle of waste water and the destruction it had caused."[97] The BIA's only response was to order Dawn to build a dam, which contained the toxic wastes for several years (until after the company had pulled out).[98] This stopgap was obviously inadequate to address the problem.

> Even more serious contamination occurred after mining had stopped and the trickle had grown to a 75 to 400 gallons per minute stream of wastes. The Indian Health Service said in 1983 that the heavy metal and acid contamination was "appalling" and recommended the BIA "prevent livestock and humans from consuming the water in question by whatever means necessary." When the EPA tested the "seepage" [in 1984], the radiological chemist in Las Vegas said he had never seen such radioactive mine waste water before (Uranium-238 levels were *4,000 times* the area's natural level, forty times the EPA's maximum "safe" limit).[99]

What Anaconda had threatened to do with regard to the Jackpile-Paguate mine Dawn actually did at Spokane, filing suit against the Department of the Interior in 1982 as a defense against being compelled to underwrite any part of restoring the Blue Creek environment, an effort estimated to require a minimum of $10 million. Despite Dawn's having gleaned about $45 million in profits from the Spokane operation over the years, the company's president, Marcel DeGuire, pled poverty, claiming his firm's only assets were the abandoned mill and mine. He also asserted, but could not substantiate, that Dawn had already spent $4 million "restoring" the environment.[100]

"It was not until 1987 that the EPA [finally] forced the company to stop the discharge," one analyst noted. This was "six years after the mining stopped and ten years after the LeBrets noticed the discharge. By then it was too late for the reservation stream, Blue Creek, which previously had provided habitat for about thirteen thousand rainbow trout. In the spring of 1988 only five or six adults returned to spawn. [The] EPA admitted that if the mine had not been on Indian land, it would probably have come to someone's attention sooner."[101]

As of mid-1998, virtually nothing has been done to repair the damage to Blue Creek, and cleanup of the tailings piles surrounding Dawn's mill site have not even been scheduled for federal action.[102] A somewhat better result has been obtained with regard to the Western Nuclear Corporation's Sherwood mine and mill, also on the Spokane Reservation. Not built until 1978, neither facility had time to cause great environmental impact before being closed in 1982. In 1989, largely for public relations and tax reasons, the corporation transferred ownership of both facilities to the Spokane people and provided $4.4 million in reclamation funds.[103] Cleanup at these sites is nearly complete.[104]

Nor are mining and milling the only activities involved in the radioactive colonization of Native North America. Just east of the Four Corners area, near Santa Fe, New Mexico, is the Los Alamos Scientific Laboratory, author of a portion of the "National Sacrifice" thesis and birthplace of the atomic bomb.

> Between 1944 and 1952, the University of California's Los Alamos Scientific Laboratory (LASL), now operated on contract by the [Department of Energy], dumped liquid and solid wastes from its bomb-manufacturing projects into three nearby canyons. Since 1952, solid and liquid radioactive wastes have been treated at

one of two ion-exchange plants. Solid, radioactive waste is buried in 60-foot-deep, asphalt-lined shafts or in 55-gallon drums at several sites. Within the 56 acres encompassed by LASL's boundaries, there are about 300,000 tons of solid wastes, including 20 pounds of plutonium.... About 25,000 gallons of liquid radioactive wastes are pumped daily into nearby canyons. The canyon streams feed into the Río Grande six miles southeast at Otowi Bridge [on land belonging to the San Ildefonso Pueblo]. A 1978 report assured the public that "no migration of radioactive contaminants away from disposal sites has been observed by the continuing monitoring program." But officials now admit the inaccuracy of the report ... Sediments on San Ildefonso sacred lands have revealed plutonium levels 10 times higher than concentration attributed to fallout, although LASL maintains that these concentrations are "well below...guides established to protect human health."[105]

In addition to plutonium, tritium, "a radioactive gas or water vapor that is virtually impossible to control because it combines readily with oxygen and can be incorporated into the organic molecules in the human body and in nature," has been found in concentrations two to five times normal levels in area mule deer, ravens and other birds in the area. Cesium-137 has been found in mule deer at levels up to thirty-five times the norm.[106] Public opposition to such contamination has been constrained by the fact that north-central New Mexico is part of one of the country's more chronically depressed areas, and LASL provides some 8,650 jobs, more than $150 million in income to area residents (including people not only from San Ildefonso, but from the nearby San Juan and Santa Clara Pueblos).[107] Although the San Ildefonso governing council has passed several resolutions of concern about pollution from LASL, it has, under the circumstances, often professed an abiding sense of helplessness to attempt anything more. "What can we do?" one council member has been quoted as asking. "We have no say up there."[108]

A similar, though more extravagant, example is that of the Hanford nuclear weapons manufacturing facility, located in Washington State, about thirty miles upstream from the Yakima Reservation and operated by the AEC on behalf of the military from 1944 until its closure in 1989. Officials at the plant consistently utilized a "Top Secret" classification covering their procedures—much about what was really done at Hanford is still classified and may remain so for decades—as a shield behind which to pretend that "nothing adverse to the public welfare" was occurring.

It was not until well after the fact, in mid-1990, that citizens began to learn that the government had "cut costs" by ignoring even the most rudimentary public safety precautions. By 1991, it was known that, since 1945, plant managers had ordered that more than 440 *billion* gallons of water heavily laced with everything from plutonium to ruthenium be poured into shafts drilled into the earth for "disposal" purposes.[109] In addition, anywhere from 700,000 to 900,000 gallons of extraordinarily contaminated fluids are known to have leaked from a 177-unit underground "tank farm" in which wastes were stored.[110] The local aquifer has long since been reached by these virulent contaminants, as has the nearby Columbia River.[111]

"Not only has the Hanford plant been discharging and leaking radiation into the river for fifty years," Dr. Helen Caldicott discovered, "but serious accidents have occurred at the reactors. One could perhaps excuse the accidental release of radiation, but on several occasions huge clouds of isotopes were created knowingly and willfully. In December [1952], about 7,800 curies of radioactive Iodine 131 were deliberately released in an experiment designed to detect military reactors in the Soviet Union [only 15 to 24 curies of Iodine 131 escaped at Three Mile Island in 1979]."[112]

The true extent of environmental degradation around Hanford, while unknown—and steadfastly denied by "responsible officials"—is certain to be considerable and quite widespread.[113] One strong piece of evidence of this occurred as early as 1962 in a Hanford worker who had a dinner of oysters caught hundreds of miles downstream at the mouth of the Columbia River. When he went to work the next day, the contents of his stomach set off the radiation alarm at the Hanford plant.[114]

More generally, as Calidicott recounts, "Abnormally high incidence[s] of thyroid tumors and cancers have been observed in populations living downwind from Hanford. Strontium-90, Cesium-137, and Plutonium-239 have been [atmospherically] released in large quantities, as was, between 1952 and 1967, Ruthenium-106. People in adjacent neighborhoods were kept uninformed about these releases—before, during, and after—and none were warned that they were at risk for subsequent development of cancer. (Some experts have estimated that downwind farms and families received radiation doses ten times higher than those that reached Soviet people living near Chernobyl in 1986)."[115]

Another indicator of extensive contamination is that, following the pattern it established at Edgemont, the government began in 1984 to pursue a vigorous initiative to situate a major nuclear waste dump on or very close to Yakima land (alternatively, officials selected the Umatilla Reservation, also in Washington State, and the Nez Percé Reservation, in northern Idaho, as preferred dumpsites).[116] The plan was narrowly averted in 1988, mainly because of a sustained intertribal/intercultural opposition organized and spearheaded by Yakima leader Russell Jim.[117] Under provision of the 1982 Nuclear Waste Policy Act, the Yakimas have also been able to secure $12.8 million in federal funding—the State of Washington has received another $11.2 million—to study the degree and effects of nuclear contamination already present in their environment.[118]

Western Shoshone and Mescalero

A few hundred miles south-southeast of Hanford, deep in the Nevada desert, lies the Nellis Air Force Test Range. Consisting entirely of territory appropriated from the Western Shoshone (Newe) people in contravention of the 1863 Treaty of Ruby Valley, Nellis contains the Nevada Test Site (see "The Struggle for Newe Segobia," in this volume).[119] Here, the devices manufactured to the north, on Yakima land, have been tested: nearly a thousand nuclear detonations over the past half-century, 96 of them above ground, the last conducted during the summer of 1997.[120] The result has been a globally unparalleled irradiation of the Newe homeland.

As Howard Ball has observed in his book *Justice Downwind*, "The deadly atomic sunburst over Hiroshima, in 1945, produced 13 kilotons of murderous heat and radioactive fallout. At least 27 of the 96 above-ground bombs detonated between 1951 and 1958 at the Nevada Test Site produced a total of over 620 kilotons of radioactive debris that fell on downwinders. The radioactive isotopes mixed with scooped-up rocks and earth of the southwestern desert lands and 'lay down a swath of radioactive fallout' over Utah, Arizona and Nevada."[121] The great bulk of the estimated 12 billion curies of radioactivity thus released into the atmosphere settled on Shoshone land, of course, where it will remain actively carcinogenic and mutogenic for the next quarter-million years.[122]

The fallout situation is exacerbated, to say the least, by the effects of the more than 900 underground detonations which have been conducted at the test site over the years, a process which has left area groundwater contaminated with plutonium, tritium and other such substances at levels up to 3,000 times maximum "safe" limits.[123] The aquifir in question is the only dependable watersource available for the three remaining Western Shoshone reservations—Duckwater, Yomba and Timbisha—as well as the Las Legas

Source: Jay M. Gould, *The Enemy Within: The High Cost of Living Near Nuclear Reactors* (New York: Four Walls Eight Windows, 1996) p.46.

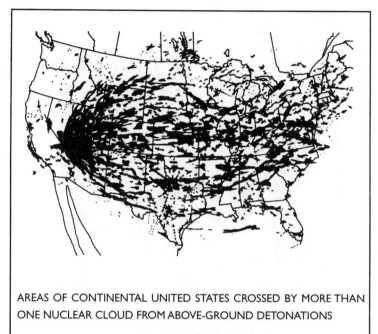

AREAS OF CONTINENTAL UNITED STATES CROSSED BY MORE THAN ONE NUCLEAR CLOUD FROM ABOVE-GROUND DETONATIONS

Paiute Colony and the Pahrump Paiute, Goshute and Moapa Paiute reservations.[124]

While the government has been adamant in its refusal to devulge the results of epidemiology studies conducted in the sparsely populated region, especially with respect to indigenous peoples, it has been credibly estimated that several hundred persons had already died of radiation-induced cancers by 1981.[125] The data concerning area rates of infant mortality, birth defects, childhood leukemias and so on have also been kept deliberately murky, although there are indicators that, like cancer deaths, they are running several times the U.S. national average.[126]

So thoroughly contaminated is the environment on and around the Nevada Test Site that, as was the case at both Hanford and Edgemont, the government has determined it would be an ideal locale in which to situate a nuclear waste dump. Indeed, it has decided to put *three* in the general vicinity: one at Yucca Mountain, in the southwestern corner of the test site itself; a second in California's Ward Valley, just south of the test site; the third on

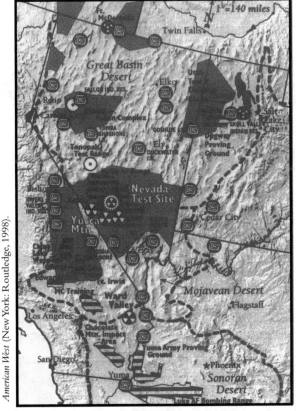

The Nuclear Landscape
Shaded areas here designate military airspace and military operations areas. Such areas extend the zone of military operations far beyond land holdings.

Source: Valerie L. Kuletz, *The Tainted Desert: Environmental and Social Ruin in the American West* (New York: Routledge, 1998).

the Skull Valley Goshute Reservation, a couple hundred miles to the north-east, across the Utah state line near the Air Force's Dugway Proving Grounds and Toole Ordnance Depot. A backup site for Skull Valley has been designated on the Fort McDermitt Paiute-Shoshone Reservation, along the border of Nevada and Oregon.[127]

Yucca Mountain, which opened in mid-1997, is slated to be the largest of the three repositories. It is of a "deep vault" type construction, built at a cost of $15 billion to accommodate about 70,000 tons of high-level waste stored in 55-gallon drums. It is also located in one of the least geologically stable parts of North America.

> Thirty-two earthquake fault lines lie in the vicinty of the mountain; there is evidence of recent volcanic activity in the area; and scientists have raised the possibility that all that waste, buried together in one place, might go "critical," erupting "in a [gigantic] nuclear explosion, scattering radioactivity to the winds or into the groundwater or both."[128]

At Ward Valley, the plan is to bury another several thousand tons of low-level waste in a series shallow trenches about 200 meters long. From there, radioactivity is virtually guranteed to leach steadily into the groundwater underlying a cluster of three small reservations—Fort Mojave, Colorado River and Chemhuevi—by which the site is flanked to its east.[129] For its part, Skull Valley is considered by many of its residents to already be so contaminated, not only by nuclear waste but by everything from nerve gas to biological warfare agents, that the siting of a dump there no longer really matters.[130]

Much the same can be said of the Mescalero Apaches, whose reservation adjoins the 4,000 square mile White Sands Test Range in southern New Mexico. Formerly known as the Alamagordo Bombing Range, White Sands was the scene of world's first experimental nuclear detonation, that of the so-called "Trinity Bomb," in 1945.[131] Since then, the testing of everything from depleted uranium ammunition to laser weaponry has occurred there, the virulently toxic byproducts drifting steadily into the Mescalero habitat.[132] Compounding the situation, the Pentagon announced during the mid-80s that it would shortly begin experimenting with the "permanent storage" of military-generated high-level nuclear waste in the depths of the nearby Carlsbad Caverns as rapidly as possible.[133]

Scheduled to open in 1998 despite bitter opposition, not only by the Mescaleros and allied environmental groups but from the State of New Mexico itself, this "Waste Isolation Pilot Project" (WIPP) promises to be merely the beginning of a much larger and extraordinarily dangerous process.[134] Thus trapped between White Sands to their east and the WIPP to their west, the Mescaleros opted to accept an above-ground storage facility within the boundaries of their reservation.[135] As analyst Valerie Kuletz has noted, "The logic is tragically sound: Because the reservation residents already have a massive deep-geologic nuclear-waste repository going in virtually next door (WIPP is some sixty miles distant as the crow flies), they may as well make some money storing nuclear waste themselves."[136]

Northern Saskatchewan

Although Australian, Namibian and Canadian ores all contributed to undermining the viability of U.S. uranium production during the early '80s, those of Canada were probably most decisive.[137] This is mainly due to the existence of several deposits of uranium in the northern portion of the province of Saskatchewan, first mapped during the 1960s, which are unrivaled in their richness by sources elsewhere on the planet.

"Uranium ore normally contains only a few tenths of a percent uranium," explains analyst Miles Goldstick. "In contrast, several large deposits in northern Saskatchewan contain ore grading in the tens of percent. Further, most of the rich deposits are close to the surface, which lowers the cost of getting the ore out of the ground. Many of these deposits are more than 100 times richer than the competing mines in the rest of the world. For example, the average grade of the Eliot Lake, Ontario, uranium deposits is .1% while the Cigar Lake deposit in Saskatchewan has an average grade of 15%... In 1979 when pockets of 45% ore were being mined at Cluff Lake, the owners bragged that in one day they took out over $9 million [Canadian] worth of uranium. It is so profitable to mine uranium in Saskatchewan that the province is known in industry circles as 'the Saudi Arabia of the uranium industry.'"[138]

While the proportion of uranium to tailings material contained in these ores has made it possible to realize a markedly greater margin of profit in northern Saskatchewan production than elsewhere, even while noticeably undercutting the price of competitors, it also means that the waste byproducts of mining and milling in the province are much "hotter" than anywhere else in the world. Specifically, since the residual radioactivity contained in tailings is directly proportionate to the percentage of uranium contained in the original ore, wastes in northern Saskatchewan are up to a hundred times more potent than those found in, say, the Four Corners region of the United States.[139] Put another way, only one one-hundredth the quantity of mining and milling would be necessary in northern Saskatchewan to produce the same qualitative impact on the people and environment evident at Laguna or Navajo. In actuality, much more than this has already been done.

"The large volume of...solid radioactive wastes produced by a uranium mill is hard to comprehend," Goldstick continues. "The 4 million [metric] tonnes of radioactive mill wastes produced by the Rabbit Lake mine alone is enough to cover almost knee deep a two-lane highway 800 kilometers long.... In January 1987 production of solid uranium wastes reached at least 130 million [metric] tonnes—about 110 million in Ontario and 20 in Saskatchewan. This amount represents a volume easily capable of covering a two lane highway a metre deep all the way from Vancouver to Halifax, coast to coast."[140]

Solid Radioactive Uranium Mill Wastes In Northern Saskatchewan – Present and Prospective

Mine	Quantity (metric tonnes)	Years Of Operation
Uranium City Area:		
Beaverlodge	6,000,000	1952-82
Gunnar	5,500,000	1955-64
Lorado	360,000	1957-60
Rabbit Lake	4,000,000	1975-85
Collin's Bay	1,930,000	1985-91
Cluff Lake		
Phase I	84,000	1981-84
Phase II	2,700,000	1984-95
Key Lake	4,500,000	1982-2000
Total	25,074,000	

Goldstick has produced the accompanying chart, indicating the antici-pated quantity of tailings from each northern Saskatchewan mill through the end of the century. Further, the aggregate discharge of liquid wastes, which have a greater and more immediate environmental impact than solid wastes, have been approximately twice as large by volume. The Rabbit Lake mill alone pumped about 7.7 million liters of of radioactive effluent into the habitat each day from 1975 until it closed down in 1985.[141] In addition to its radioactive toxicity, the waste water emitted by this and other mills contains high concentrations of lead, arsenic, zinc, manganese, cadmium and other deadly pollutants.[142] Small wonder that, as in the United States, the affected locales have come to be referred to as "sacrifice areas."[143]

Another thing similar to the U.S. experience is that creation of the situation has been marked by extensive governmental and corporate collu-sion. In fact, both the federal government in Ottawa and the provincial gov-ernment of Saskatchewan established their own profit-making firms in order to benefit from the anticipated uranium bonanza (Ottawa dubbed its corpo-ration Eldorado Nuclear Ltd., while the provincial administration selected Saskatchewan Mining Development Corporation as the name to describe its firm). Also like the U.S. scenario, the Canadian government created a mechanism through which to coopt or confuse the resistance of the indigenous people on whose land the mining would be done. This assumed the form of what is called the "Saskatchewan Indian Nations Corporation" (SINCO), which ensures that "native preference" will be exercised when hiring is done for such menial occupations as driving trucks and guarding mining and milling facilities.[144]

Throughout the 1970s, the provincial government busily utilized tax revenues to create an infrastructure necessary only to the uranium industry, including thousands of kilometers of roadways connecting projected mining sites in the north to the planned distribution center in Saskatoon, located far to the south.[145] The private beneficiaries of this massive expenditure of public funds were, of course, always intended to be such private concerns as the U.S.-owned Gulf Minerals Corporation and the Japanese utility, Kyushu Ltd., to which Saskatchewan Mining and Eldorado Nuclear jointly pledged delivery of 12.7 million kilograms of low cost uranium concentrate over a thirteen-year period beginning in 1987.[146] The "constellation of transnational resource corporations now active in northern Saskatchewan includes French, German, American and Japanese interests."[147]

Development

In truth, governmental mining and milling of good- to high-grade uranium has been going on in northwestern Saskatchewan at a relatively moderate pace since 1952, beginning with the first of what were eventually to be 25 open pit and underground mines around an ersatz town called "Uranium City." Before the greater profitability of higher-grade mines elsewhere caused it to be phased out in 1982, Eldorado Nuclear had spent fully thirty years "keeping overhead down" at the Uranium City complex by dumping both liquid and solid wastes directly into Lake Athabasca, from whence considerable contamination continues to flow down the Slave River to the Mackenzie and then into the Arctic Ocean.[148]

"The 'town' itself existed solely to serve the uranium industry," Goldstick observes, "Before the mines, no one lived there; after the mines, the population sank from its high of more than 4,000 in 1979 to fewer than 200 in 1983." A good thing, too, because, as in the Anaconda/Laguna example, it was found that the corporation had cut costs, this time by building everything from the street to the hospital from uranium tailings. In 1977, for instance, "it was discovered that classrooms in the local CANDU High

Uranium Mining Activity In
Northern Saskatchewan

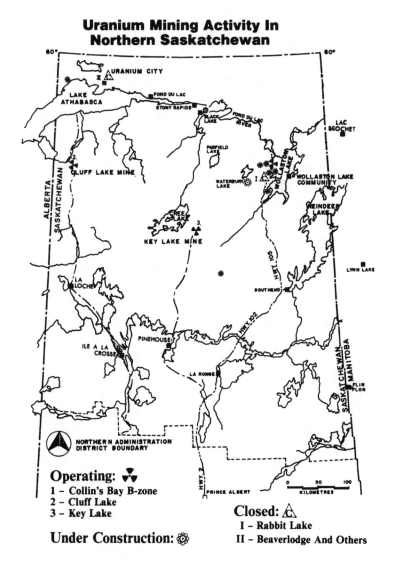

Operating: ☢
1 – Collin's Bay B-zone
2 – Cluff Lake
3 – Key Lake

Under Construction: ✦

Closed: ⚠
I – Rabbit Lake
II – Beaverlodge And Others

Brian Goldstick, *Wollaston.*

School—governmentally named to commemorate Canada's first on-line nuclear reactor—evidenced radon levels sixty times higher than the allowable limit; the school was nonetheless used for another five years."[149]

By the mid-70s, what became a government-sponsored boom was beginning to materialize. In 1975, Eldorado opened the Rabbit Lake Mine, in the northeastern portion of Saskatchewan, digging into an ore deposit ranging from .3 to three percent in purity. An open pit about 550 yards wide and 150 deep was created before the most profitable ore played out and the mine was closed in 1984. Eldorado, in collaboration with Gulf Minerals, had built the largest uranium mill in northern Canada—producing some $100 million (Canadian) per year in yellowcake—to service its Rabbit Lake endeavor, but it was not closed when the mine shut down.[150] Instead, beginning in 1982, the mill was expanded to accommodate the even greater volume of ore of a much higher grade expected from a new mine the corporation was opening at nearby Collin's Bay, on Wollaston Lake.[151]

"The Collin's Bay open pit mine is especially dangerous because the uranium is actually under the bottom of Wollaston Lake," says Goldstick. "In order to get at the uranium, part of the lake was diked off and drained in 1984. Mining below the bottom of the lake began in the spring of 1985. The pit is separated from the rest of the lake by a thin dike of steel that extends only about one metre above the water level, and may not be able to withstand strong waves which are a common occurrence on the lake. After the projected six years of mining [then extended to eight] the dike will be destroyed, allowing the further spread of contamination [in the lake, and then along various outflows]."[152]

Such activity is unquestionably intended to continue in the Wollaston Lake area until some point well into the twenty-first century, given a 1985 statement by Eldorado: "When the Collin's Bay deposit is eventually depleted, ore will be mined from several deposits within a twelve kilometre distance."[153] Wollaston is, however, hardly the only place in northern Saskatchewan afflicted in this fashion.

At Cluff Lake, southward across Lake Athabasca from Uranium City, preparation for mining and milling of extremely high grade ore began in 1978. Although the "Cluff Lake Mining Corporation" (a combination of Eldorado and Saskatchewan Mining) proudly announced when it began operations in 1980 that it was employing "new technology"—actually only huge concrete containers—for storing liquid wastes, the first major spill had occurred by 1982. This involved two tons of radium and raised the radiation level of a nearby stream to an incredible *600,000 times* the maximum limit.[154]

By 1986, it was discovered that at least 200 containers had cracked— they were being stacked two deep for reasons of "economy and convenience"—and had leaked another two-and-a-half tons of comparable contamination into the environment.[155] The corporation then announced it would accept a subsidy from Saskatchewan Mining to "solve" the problem by building yet another facility in 1987, this one to refine the radium waste itself in collaboration with a French consortium, AMOK.[156]

The Key Lake Mine in central Saskatchewan is the most southerly of all such operations in the province. It is now the largest open pit in the world. The mine, opened in 1983 by an international consortium including Saskatchewan Mining, Eldorado Nuclear and Uranez (a German firm) and calling itself the "Key Lake Mining Corporation," is estimated to contain more than 84 million kilograms of uranium in an average ore grade of 2.5 percent. The attendant mill capacity of 5.5 million kilos per year makes up about twelve percent of "Free World" yellowcake output.[157]

> Much to the embarrassment of [Key Lake Mining], within the first three months of operation at least 12 major spills of radioactive wastes occurred. The largest was in January, 1984 when over 100 million litres of radioactive liquid with radiation levels 20 times the regulation level spilled over the retaining walls of a holding pond.[158]

In many ways, all of this was simply a prelude to what will undoubtedly be the most dangerous operation of all: the mining of an ore pocket at Cigar Lake, discovered in 1981 but kept secret from the Canadian public until 1984, after "business details" had been worked out among governments and corporations in several countries.

> The most significant uranium deposit ever discovered is at Cigar Lake adjacent to Waterbury Lake. It is located 115 kilometres northeast of the Key Lake mine and 55 kilometres west-southwest of the Rabbit Lake mine. The Cigar Lake ore body is the world's largest [super] high-grade deposit. It contains over 100 million kilos of uranium at an average grade of 15%, with pockets as high as 60%. This is twice as big and 6 times as rich as the Key Lake "monster deposit." In addition, potential reserves at Cigar Lake are estimated to contain a further 50 million kilos at a grade of 4.7%.[159]

The international consortium quietly assembled to comprise the "Cigar Lake Mining Corporation" included not only Saskatchewan Mining and Eldorado Nuclear, but also Cogema Canada Ltd. (a Montréal-based subsidiary of the French Commisariat de l'Energie Atomique), Idemitsu Uranium Exploration Corporation Ltd. (a Japanese firm based in Calgary) and the Corona Grande Corporation. Mining startup at Cigar Lake has been delayed for several years because of certain "technical difficulties."

Although the huge deposit is well-concentrated in a 2,000 by 100 meter area, it is located more than 400 meters below ground, a factor which necessitates shaft mining. Given the richness of the ore and the depth of the shafts required, it is considered impossible, or at least cost prohibitive, to ventilate the mine sufficiently to create anything resembling survivable much less "safe" conditions for miners. Hence, more than $50 million (Canadian) has been expended in development of appropriate robotics with which to extract the ore. As is standard practice, the government has not bothered itself to conduct public hearings on the matter of what will happen to resulting "superwaste" once mining operations begin.[160]

Impacts

There are some 30,000 people resident to the mining region of northern Saskatchewan, more than 20,000 of them native Dene (Chipewyan) and Métis. As in the United States, these indigenous people are among the very poorest population sector in North America. And like their U.S. counterparts in the uranium mining zones, "Treaty Indians are hospitalized 61% more often than the average Saskatchewan resident. Since 1975, hospitalization for cancer, birth defects and circulatory illnesses have increased dramatically (between 123 and 600% in the northern population aged 15 to 64—the entire labor force). At the same time, there is a large increase in hospitalizations among young children for digestive disorders and birth anomalies."[161]

Unlike their southern cousins, however, the native people of Saskatchewan have never been concentrated on reservations. To the contrary, they are scattered across the entire northerly expanse of the province in thirty-five towns and villages, availing themselves of hunting, fishing and trapping rights over broad areas. Concomitantly, they subsist to a much higher degree on a traditional diet, taken from the land, than do Indians in the lower 48 states.[162] That they are suffering much the same signs of general health deterioration as U.S. Indians forced to live in constant close proximity to uranium production sites is indicative of the extent to which the entire northern Saskatchewan ecology has already been contaminated by the uranium industry.

The environment downstream from Eldorado Nuclear's Beaverlodge mine and mill at Uranium City, for example, has been extensively studied over the past twenty years. As early as 1977, a survey found that about a quarter of the lake chub in waters contaminated by tailings runoff suffered eye mutations, including pupil deformities and lense cataracts. "There was no evidence of infection or parasitic encystment within the eye," researchers concluded, "Cataracts may result from genetic makeup, nutritional deficiency, environmental effects, or a combination of the three. Certain factors such as high radiation, parasitic infection, or the presence of specific chemicals can contribute to cataract formation."[163]

The incidence of such deformities among suckers and other fish which feed along the bottom of waterbeds, where radioactive sediments quickly settle, was even higher. While native people in the area do not usually consume bottomfeeders, they do eat lake whitefish and other species which eat them and which thereby acquire an appreciable portion of the bottomfeeders' contamination. Fish collected from lakes downstream from the Beaverlodge facility in a 1979 study demonstrated as much as one hundred times more radioactivity in their tissue than fish collected from uncontaminated lakes.[164] Another study, conducted downstream from the Dubyna Mine at Uranium City, revealed northern pike with radiation counts averaging 6,500 times normal in the flesh, up to 11,000 times normal in the bone; lake trout were also found to have much greater than normal concentrations of uranium, thorium and Lead–210, while northern pike showed the greatest concentration of radium.[165]

In the area known as "Effluent Creek," downstream from the Rabbit Lake complex, which runs into Wollaston Lake's Hidden Bay, a 1978 study found ammonia concentrations so extreme that there was "a complete absence of benthic invertebrates in bottom samples along the entire length of the creek [and] there was at least localized impact in Hidden Bay in the vicinity of the Effluent Creek mouth."[166]

In terms of impact on fish, the study documents that toxicity tests of the Rabbit Lake waste discharge "on several occasions found the tailings effluent acutely lethal to rainbow trout." Laboratory tests from March 1977 to January 1979 putting rainbow trout in precipitation pond effluent, found that all fish died in 96 hours, even when the effluent concentration was only 10%. In July 1978 tests were conducted putting sucker fry collected from Collins Bay into plastic containers submerged for 56 hours in Effluent Creek, the inlet to Horseshoe Lake, and precipitation pond effluent. The water was found to be acutely lethal in all but the Effluent Creek sample.[167]

Downstream from the Dubyna mine, three aquatic plants—waterlilly, millfoil and sedge—were studied. Waterlilly consistently revealed concentrations of radium 11,000 times greater than normal; millfoil showed an average 14,000 times the normal level of uranium; sedge collected 13,000 times the normal level of Lead-210.[168]

> In 1983 a researcher from the Department of Biology at the University of Saskatchewan determined quantities of [Lead-210 and Polonium-210] in vegetation at two sites in the Rabbit Lake area, Collin's Creek and Hidden Bay, and for comparison purposes, two sites near the Churchill River, Birch Hill and Otter Rapids. The Rabbit Lake sites showed significantly greater accumulation in four of the ten species analyzed: blueberry, labrador tea, green alder, and black spruce. Collin's Creek was found to be a "hot spot" for all species except dry-land cranberry. A different study in another area looking at uranium levels in trees found the greatest amount in the growing tips of twigs, followed by the bark, leaves and wood.[169]

The study, conducted by Dr. Stella M. Swanson, concluded that radio-nuclides are collected by plant life in the following descending order: lichen, moss, shrubs and trees. Lichens and moss accumulate radioactivity at a rate five to ten times greater than shrubs and trees, respectively. Moss and lichens absorb contamination from the atmosphere while "higher" plant forms tend to take it in through the roots, making their contamination a somewhat more localized phenomenon than with "lower" forms.[170]

Humans, of course, directly consume some of these plants and thereby ingest contaminants. Blueberry, for instance, is the greatest radionuclide collector among shrubs and is an integral part of the northern native diet at certain times of the year. Moreover, vegetation composes the *whole* diet of virtually every bird and mammal which, along with fish, comprise more than two-thirds of the traditional Indian larder in the upper reaches of Saskatchewan. Caribou, to name one example, subsist primarily on moss and lichens. Moose and deer consider the young tips of shrubs and trees to be a high delicacy. Water fowl consume shoots from each of the three aquatic plants studied.[171]

> In the Canadian context, only a few studies examine accumulation of radioactivity in mammals. This area warrants more attention as there have been two reports of a cow

moose carrying a two-headed fetus being shot near Wollaston Lake. Further, Wollaston residents have often shot moose from the Rabbit Creek area, and people have seen moose drinking from the tailings ponds.[172]

Even fewer investigations have been conducted with regard to contamination of the indigenous people affected. Probably the closest was a study conducted from 1965 to 1969 with regard to the effects of mining and milling much lower-grade ore in Ontario upon twenty-five relatively proximate Inuit communities in the Northwest Territories. The results showed levels of soft tissue and bone irradiation as much as a hundred times normal, at times exceeding even the maximum limits established by the notoriously lax International Commission on Radiation Protection.[173]

To date, neither the government of Canada nor of Saskatchewan has offered any sort of realistic plan to dispose of the rapidly proliferating wastes being generated. Nor have the array of transnational corporations with which the two governments are involved. Rather, they have combined to offer what are, at best, utterly cosmetic "remedies" such as "revegetating" tailings piles. While prettying up thousands of acres of lethal waste—turning it all into "nice moose pastures," as one Eldorado official has put it—cannot be said to accomplish anything at all to combat the pollution, it might possibly make the effects even *worse*.[174]

> It is important to realize that plant growth on top of a tailings area does not mean the spread of contamination is stopped. Limited plant growth has been achieved with massive fertilizer application and natural plants have regrown along the edges. But plant growth can actually increase the quantity of radon gas escaping from wastes. This is because radium travels up through the roots and is distributed in the leaves. Thus the surface area available for radon release is greatly increased… In addition, root penetration allows water to seep through [any] protective soil cover and into tailings, allowing ground water to be polluted. As well, the plants themselves become contaminated through uptake of toxic materials, which pose a danger to animals eating them.[175]

None of this can be new or especially mysterious information to the governments and corporations pursuing such "rehabilitation" schemes, given that the Los Alamos Scientific Laboratory reached precisely the same conclusions concerning the "disutility" of revegetation twenty or more years ago.[176] Overall, then, "paranoid" assessments by Indians and allied non-Indian "radicals" that northern Saskatchewan is being quietly but steadily written off as a gigantic National Sacrifice Area take on considerable substance.[177] And, as with similar plans in the United States, the people of the land will necessarily be sacrificed along with the land itself.

Back in the U.S.A.

During the 1970s, it was a standard slogan among environmental activists, a truth apparently now forgotten, that "radioactive contamination is forever." Today, it has become something of a commonplace among North American progressives, including important sectors of the environmental movement, to consider nuclear issues "passé," a thing of the past, as if they had—or could have—gone away.[178] Some, like Barry Commoner, have taken things so far as to adopt a smug and self-congratulatory tone, pointing to an imagined "collapse of the nuclear industry" as evidence of a "grassroots victory over big business and big government."

> In one major area of production—nuclear power—public intervention has already had a powerful effect: In the United States it has brought the industry to an ignominious halt. The nuclear power industry is paralyzed because intense public opposition has made the industry pay its environmental bill, most dramatically by forcing the abandonment of the $5.3 billion plant at Shoreham, Long Island.[179]

While much of the "credit" for temporarily consolidating public sentiment against the nuclear industry must go to the spectacular nature of the 1986 Chernobyl disaster rather than to organizing, it *is* true that the antinuke movement posted some impressive tactical wins.[180] Popular opposition *did* have much to do with what happened at Shoreham, as well as the cancelling of reactor construction at other locations such as Seabrook, New Hampshire, and Point Conception and Diablo Canyon in California, well before Chernobyl.[181] Similarly, well-focused activism played a role in bringing about the closure of existing reactors like that at Fort St. Vrain, Colorado, and several military-use facilities.[182]

> As of [May 1992], reactors at Hanford, WA, and at Savannah River, SC, are out of commission (the K-Reactor at Savannah River was restarted in December, 1991, but shut down within days because it leaked radioactive tritium into streams); the uranium production plant at Fernald, OH, is closed permanently; uranium enrichment facilities at Portsmouth, OH, and Paducah, KY, are halted temporarily; and [plutonium] production at Rocky Flats [Colorado] has ended.[183]

Hopeful as these achievements are, however, what is occurring in northern Saskatchewan should be enough to disabuse *anyone* of the notion that the nuclear industry is somehow resultingly "dead." Even Commoner admits that, in 1982, there were only seventy-two operational nuclear reactors in the United States, whereas there are now 110.[184] These figures undoubtedly represent a slowing in the pace of reactor construction—ninety-five facilities were under construction in the United States in 1980, less than a dozen today—but hardly a "stoppage."[185]

Careful observers will also have noticed a marked upsurge in the propaganda (also known as "advertising") of the U.S. nuclear industry's "Big Four"—the Westinghouse, Babcock & Wilcox, Bechtel and Combustion Engineering corporations—and their subsidiaries, reintroducing the alleged benefits of the "peaceful atom" during the early-90s.[186] Perhaps even more to the point, the energy policy announced by George Bush in 1991 was about as diametrically opposed to Commoner's pleasant script as it is possible to be: the president's plan called for the building of *several hundred more* reactors within twenty years, at a cost of between $390 billion and $1.3 *trillion.*[187] Only the 1992 election of Bill Clinton and Al Gore appears to have staved off implementation, however temporary.[188]

Other signs of an impending resurgence in the U.S. nuclear industry also exist. Anaconda, for example, has indicated an interest in reopening its Jackpile-Paguate Mine at Laguna at some point early in the next century.[189] Marjane Ambler, a leading apologist for this sort of activity on Indian land, has predicted that mining and milling will not only resume at Navajo, Spokane and Wind River, but on the Ute Mountain Reservation in Colorado; the Cañoncito Reservation and Zuni, Acoma, Zia and Jemez pueblos in New Mexico, and the Hualapai Reservation in Arizona.[190] Unmentioned in her scenario are significant uranium deposits under the Crow and Northern Cheyenne Reservations in Montana and the Gunnery Range deposit at Pine Ridge.[191] Such wholesale development would, of course, dwarf the degree of radioactive colonization evident in Indian Country between 1950 and 1980.

The mechanism through which this can be accomplished is also present in a much more coherent form than was the case thirty years ago. Beginning in 1977, at the very height of the last U.S. uranium boom, the Federal Energy Administration provided $250,000 in "seed money"—an amount increased to $24 million annually in 1979 by the DoE—to create an entity capable of both coordinating and creating a more plausible facade of "Indian consent" to such exploitation.[192] Dubbed the "Council of Energy

Resource Tribes" (CERT), the new organization was composed of the chairs of the federally-created and -maintained tribal councils on what were already known to be the 25 most mineral-rich reservations in the country (the number of "participating tribes" has since grown to 43).[193]

The first task assigned CERT was to assemble a comprehensive inventory of energy assets in U.S. Indian Country as a whole, called a "Sears and Roebuck catalog of reservation resources" by critics.[194] Its second task was to assist in conceiving and implementing a plan by which more efficient corporate penetration might be accomplished.[195] This last placed CERT—over strong objections by a majority of those whose interests it supposedly represented—in a position of serving as central broker and liaison in virtually all Indian energy resource transactions, a matter which quickly attracted millions in ongoing corporate funding.[196]

Although the uranium bust of the 1980s affected CERT as it did sponsoring companies, the organization simply devoted more attention to fossil fuel extraction and to smoothing the way for the placement of nuclear waste dumps on Indian land, such as those approved at Mescalero and Skull Valley.[197] It has also moved itself into a position to reconcile environmental conflicts in Indian Country more generally.

> By 1984 the number of tribal requests for CERT's environmental technical assistance had mushroomed… In that year the EPA awarded CERT $125,000 to study wastes on twenty-five pilot reservations. Later, the EPA provided $90,000 to establish an environmental information base and provided other, relatively small contracts for regional meetings… To increase tribal support the CERT board created the CERT Technical Services Corporation, which was designed to market [such] technical assistance.[198]

In sum, CERT is now *ideally* situated to facilitate a fullscale resumption of uranium mining and milling in Indian Country. Further, it is well placed to bring about construction of many, perhaps all, of the reactors called for in the 1991 Bush plan in the same locale. Not only would such a strategy represent a genuine consummation of the National Sacrifice Area concept of the 1970s—with all the implied advantages of subsequent unrestricted use of sacrificed areas this entails—it would carry the added attraction of going virtually unnoticed by the general public until well after the fact. When questioned on the matter, governmental and corporate spokespersons could simply deny that the facilities themselves were being constructed. After all, they had no particular difficulty in masking the reality of what was going on in Indian Country the first time around, at least until the process was almost completed.

Even in a non-Indian setting like Cincinnati, the DoE, in collaboration with the Department of Defense, was able to pass off its Fernald, Ohio, uranium mill as a "pet food factory" for 37 years, during which time it quietly dumped at least 167,000 pounds of radionuclides into the Great Miami River, another 298,000 pounds into the atmosphere, and still another 12.7 million pounds into leaking earthen pits.[199] The same combination of players was able to hide the release of more than two million pounds of radioactive mercury from its Oak Ridge, Kentucky plant until 1988.[200] Until the same year, they were able to deny that the Rockwell International's operation of the Rocky Flats weapons facility—just west of Denver, Colorado—had resulted in extensive plutonium contamination of both water and landscape in a broad arc extending from Broomfield in the north to Golden in the south.[201] How much more easily and effectively might the government, businesses, and a "cooperating agency" like CERT be able to disguise what was underway in the "Great American Outback" where only a relative handful of Indians reside?

Fighting Back

The question points in important ways to what has been a crucial defect in the U.S. antinuclear movement—and the broader environmental movement of which it was and is mostly a part—all along. From the Clamshell and Abalone Alliances of the 1970s to the Freeze Movement of the 1980s, non-Indian activists have focused all but exclusively on the very final stages of the nuclear cycle.[202] In other words, they have inevitably concentrated on the reactors and weapons composed of byproducts eventually refined from the yellowcake uranium mined and milled at the front end of the cycle, on Indian land. Hence, their victories, however satisfying in an immediate sense, have always been tactical, never strategic. Put another way, whenever they have been successful in closing or preventing a reactor in one place, their opponents have simply built another (or two) somewhere else; whenever they have caused weaponry to be removed from one location, it has merely been shifted to another.[203]

If the specter of rampant nuclearism is ever to be truly abolished, such approaches must be changed, and drastically so. The key to a strategic vision for antinuclear activism is and has always been in finding ways to sever nuclear weapons and reactors from their roots. This means, first and foremost, that non-Indians cast off the blinders which have led them to the sort of narrow "not in my back yard" sensibility voiced by Barry Commoner and his erstwhile vice presidential running mate, LaDonna Harris (a Comanche and founding member of CERT).[204]

Rather than endlessly combating the end-products of the nuclear industry, the movement as a whole must shift its emphasis to preventing uranium from being taken out of the ground in the first place. This, in turn, means focusing everyone's primary energy and attention, not on places like Seabrook and Diablo Canyon, inhabited as they may be by "important" population sectors (i.e., Euroamericans), but upon places peopled by "Mere Indians": Key Lake and Cigar Lake in Canada, for example, or Navajo, Laguna and other reservations in the United States.[205]

Ultimately, stopping the processes of uranium extraction in Indian Country and consequent nuclear proliferation elsewhere will be impossible so long as the structure of colonial domination on the reservations is maintained. This means that coordinative and brokering organizations like CERT and the prevailing system of "tribal governance" must be opposed right along with the non-Indian governments and corporations which invented and sustain them. A top priority—probably *the* first priority—for the antinuclear movement, the broader environmental movement, and for North American progressivism in general, *must* be the decolonization of Native North America. To accomplish this, those representing indigenous liberation struggles must be accorded a central role in setting the agenda for and defining the priorities of radical social change on this continent.[206]

The alternative, if it may be called that, is at best only the prospect of what the French commentator André Gorz, in examining his own country's nuclear industry, once termed "electric fascism."[207] More likely, in North America, the radioactive colonization of Indian Country will go on and on, until—like some proverbial miner's canary sent first into shafts to detect with their lungs the presence of lethal gas—Indians die of the contaminants to which their "betters" have forcibly subjected them.[208] Unlike the canary, however, Indians can by their deaths provide no early warning of an avoidable fate about to befall those who sacrifice them in this fashion. This is true because, unlike miners who rely upon canaries, those who sacrifice Indians have no place to turn for safe haven once their victims have died.

The ecological effects of radioactive colonization know no boundaries. Radon gas and windblown radioactive particles do not know they are intended to stop when they reach non-Indian territory. Contaminated water does not know it is supposed to pool itself only under Indian wells. Irradiated flora and fauna are unaware they are meant only for consumption by indigenous "expendables." The effects of such things are just as fatal to non-Indians as they are to Indians; the longevity of radionuclides is still just as "forever" now as it was twenty years ago; nothing has really changed in these respects since John Gofman and Arthur Tamplin first published *Poisoned Power* in 1971.[209] Neither genocide nor ecocide can be "contained" when accomplished by nuclear means. The radioactive colonization of Native North America therefore threatens not only Indians, but the survival of the human species itself.

The tools for fighting back against any threat begin, it is said, with a precise understanding of the danger and, from there, the best means by which to counter it. In this instance, the situation is simple enough: Like it or not, we are all—Indian and non-Indian alike—finally in the same boat. At last there is no more room for non-Indians to maneuver, to evade, to find more "significant" issues with which to preoccupy themselves. Either the saving of indigenous lives becomes a matter of preeminent concern, or *no* lives will be saved. Either Native North America will be liberated, or liberation will be foreclosed for *everyone*, once and for all. The fight will either be waged on Indian land, for Indian lives, or it will be lost before it really begins. We must take our stand together. And we are *all* running out of time in which to finally come to grips with this fact.

Notes

1. U.S. Department of the Interior, Bureau of Indian Affairs, *Indian Lands Map: Oil, Gas, and Minerals on Indian Reservations* (Washington, D.C.: U.S. Government Printing Office, 1978).

2. Robert Page, *Northern Development: The Canadian Dilemma* (Toronto: McClelland and Stewart, 1986).

3. On the size of the U.S. Indian population, see Lenore A. Stiffarm and Phil Lane, Jr., "The Demography of Native North America: A Question of American Indian Survival," in M. Annette Jaimes, ed., *The State of Native America: Genocide, Colonization, and Resistance* (Boston: South End Press, 1992) pp. 23-54. On the numbers in Canada, see Olive Patricia Dickenson, *Canada's First Nations: A History of Founding Peoples from Earliest Times* (Norman: University of Oklahoma Press, 1992) p. 418.

4. U.S. Bureau of the Census, Population Division, Racial Statistics Branch, *A Statistical Portrait of the American Indian Population* (Washington, D.C.: U.S. Government Printing Office, 1984); U.S. Department of Health and Human Services, *Chart Series Book* (Washington, D.C.: Public Health Service 1988).

5. This refers to the so-called Indian Reorganization Act (48 Stat. 948), passed in 1934 and implemented throughout the remainder of the decade; see Vine Deloria, Jr., and Clifford M. Lytle, *The Nations Within: The Past and Future of American Indian Sovereignty* (New York: Pantheon, 1984).

6. Joseph G. Jorgenson, "The Political Economy of the Native American Energy Business," in Joseph G. Jorgenson, ed., *Native Americans and Energy Development, II* (Cambridge: Anthropology Resource Center/Seventh Generation Fund, 1984) pp. 9-20. It is noteworthy that Congress supposedly "fixed" the problem legislatively during the early 1980s, but without actually changing anything; "Congress Approves Royalty Management Bill without Royalty Increase," *Federal Lands*, Dec. 27, 1982.

7. Lorraine Turner Ruffing, "The Role of Federal Policy in American Indian Mineral Development," Roxanne Dunbar Ortiz, ed., *American Indian Energy Resources and Development* (Albuquerque: University of New Mexico Institute for Native American Development, 1980) pp. 9-38; Klara B. Kelly, "Federal Indian Land Policy and Economic Development in the United States," in Roxanne Dunbar Ortiz and Larry Emerson, eds., *Economic Development in American Indian Reservations* (Albuquerque: University of New Mexico Institute for Native American Development, 1979) pp. 129-35.

8. Kenneth Coates and Judith Powell, *The Modern North: People, Politics, and the Rejection of Colonialism* (Toronto: James Lorimer, 1989).

9. Michael Garrity, "The U.S. Colonial Empire Is as Close as the Nearest Reservation," in Holly Sklar, ed., *Trilateralism: Elite Planning for World Management* (Boston: South End Press, 1980) pp. 238-68.

10. For the original application of this concept to the Native North American context, see Robert K. Thomas, "Colonialism: Classic and Internal," *New University Thought*, Vol 4, No. 4, Winter 1966-67. Interestingly, the basic premise at issue here has been officially admitted by the U.S. government; see U.S. Dept. of Justice, Commission on Civil Rights, *The Navajo Nation: An American Colony* (Washington, D.C.: U.S. Government Printing Office, 1975). On Canada, see Menno Boldt, "Social Correlates of Nationalism: A Study of Native Indian Leaders in a Canadian Internal Colony," *Comparative Political Studies*, Vol. 14, No. 2, Summer 1981, pp. 205-31.

11. This is true despite the racist and utterly misleading emphasis placed by some analysts on the handful of mines and mills north of the Navajo Reservation, on the Colorado Plateau. A prime example is Raye C. Ringholz's *Uranium Frenzy: Boom and Bust on the Colorado Plateau* (Albuquerque: University of New Mexico Press, 1989), which manages to miss the matter of uranium mining in Indian Country altogether. For much more accurate views, see Richard Hoppe, "A Stretch of Desert Along Route 66—The Grants Belt—Is Chief Locale for U.S. Uranium," *Engineering and Mining Journal*, Vol. 79, No. 11, 1978, pp. 79-93; Winona LaDuke, "A History of Uranium Mining," *Black Hills/Paha Sapa Report*, Vol. 1, No. 1, 1979; Richard Nafziger, "Transnational Energy Corporations and American Indian Development," in Roxanne Dunbar Ortiz, ed., *American Indian Energy Resources and Development*, (Albuquerque: University of New Mexico Institute for Native American Development, 1980) pp. 9-38.

12. In addition to the Navajos employed as underground miners by Kerr-McGee during this period, somewhere between 300 and 500 were involved in "independent" Small Business Administration-

supported operations mining shallow (50 feet or less) deposits of uranium ore. The proceeds were sold in small lots to the AEC's ore-buying station, located at the Kerr-McGee milling plant near Shiprock. These miners left behind between one and two hundred open shafts, all emitting radon gas into the atmosphere; Harold Tso and Lora Mangum Shields, "Navajo Mining Operations: Early Hazards and Recent Interventions," *New Mexico Journal of Science*, Vol. 12, No. 1, 1980.

13. J. B. Sorenson, *Radiation Issues: Government Decision Making and Uranium Expansion in Northern New Mexico* (Albuquerque: San Juan Regional Uranium Study Working Paper 14, 1978) p. 2.

14. Ibid. Also see Jessica S. Pearson, *A Sociological Analysis of the Reduction of Hazardous Radiation in Uranium Mines* (Washington, D.C.: National Institute for Occupational Safety and Health, National Health Service, 1975).

15. It is estimated that well over 2.5 million tons of uranium ore were extracted before the mine closed; Phil Reno, *Navajo Resources and Economic Development* (Albuquerque: University of New Mexico Press, 1981) p. 138.

16. Author's measurement. As Tso and Shields note in their article ("Navajo Mining Operations," op. cit.): "This tailings pile is also within one mile of a day care center, the public schools...the Shiprock business district and cultivated farm lands."

17. This was standard Bureau practice; Justas Bavarskis, "Uranium: The West Mines, Mills and Worships Radioactive Fuel," *High Country News*, Mar. 10, 1978. He is relying in part on U.S. Environmental Protection Agency, *Radiological Quality of the Environment in the United States, 1977* (Washington, D.C.: U.S. Government Printing Office, 1977) pp. 58-67. Also see Tom Barry, "The BIA and Mineral Leases," *Navajo Times*, Nov. 2, 1978.

18. Richard O. Clemmer, "The Energy Economy and Pueblo Peoples," in *Native Americans and Energy Development, II*, op. cit., pp. 101-2.

19. M. J. Samet, et al., "Uranium Mining and Lung Cancer Among Navajo Men," *New England Journal of Medicine*, No. 310, 1984, pp. 1481-4; Anthony S. Schwagin and Thomas Hollbacher, "Lung Cancer Among Uranium Miners," in *The Nuclear Fuel Cycle* (Cambridge: Union of Concerned Scientists, 1973).

20. Richard Nafzinger, "Uranium Profits and Perils," in *Red Paper* (Albuquerque: Americans for Indian Opportunity, 1976). Also see Christopher McCleod, "Uranium Mines and Mills May Have Caused Birth Defects Among Navajo Indians," *High Country News*, Feb. 4, 1985.

21. Lora Mangum Shields and Alan B. Goodman, "Outcome of 13,300 Navajo Births from 1964–1981 in the Shiprock Uranium Mining Area" (unpublished paper delivered at the American Association of Atomic Scientists Symposium, New York, May 25, 1984).

22. *Radiological Quality of the Environment in the United States, 1977*, op. cit., pp. 62-6.

23. Lynn A. Robbins, "Energy Development and the Navajo Nation: An Update," in *Native Americans and Energy Development, II*, op. cit., p. 119. Actually, the astronomical rate of lung cancer among uranium miners was being reported in Europe from 1879 onward, and analyzed in the medical literature after 1902. The German-Czech experience was also being reported and analyzed in U.S. medical literature at least as early as 1942, when Wilhelm Huper devoted an entire chapter of a book to the topic (*Occupational Tumors and Allied Diseases* [Springfield, IL: Charles C. Thomas]). In 1944, Egon Lorenz published an essay entitled "Radioactivity and Lung Cancer" in the *Journal of the National Cancer Institute*. It concluded that "the radioactivity of the ore and radon content of the air in the mines are generally considered to be the primary cause" of lung cancer among uranium miners. Beyond reasonable doubt, then, the AEC *did* know that uranium mining equalled virtually certain death within twenty years of entering improperly ventilated shafts, and elected for its own reasons to send the Navajos in anyway. See generally, Robert N. Proctor, "Censorship of American Uranium Mine Epidemiology in the 1950s," in Marjorie Garber and Rebecca L. Walkowitz, eds., *Secret Agents: The Rosenberg Case, MacCarthyism and Fifties America* (New York: Routledge, 1995) pp. 59-75.

24. Quoted in Tom Barry, "The Deaths Still Go On: How Agencies Ignored Uranium Danger," *Navajo Times*, Aug. 31, 1978.

25. "Claims Filed for Red Rock Miners," *Navajo Times*, July 26, 1979; Tom Barry, "Bury My Lungs at Red Rock," *The Progressive*, Oct. 1976, pp. 25-7.

26. Robbins, "Energy Development," op. cit., p. 121. Marjane Ambler, "Uranium Millworkers Seek Compensation," *APF Reporter*, Sept. 1980.

27. Winona LaDuke, "How Much Development?" *Akwesasne Notes*, Vol. 11, No. 1, 1979.

28. "Manpower Gap in the Uranium Mines," *Business Week*, Nov. 1, 1977. For context, see Nancy J. Owens, "Can Tribes Control Energy Development?" in Joseph G. Jorgenson, ed., *Native Americans and Energy Development* (Cambridge: Anthropology Resource Center, 1978).

29. W. D. Armstrong, *A Report on Mineral Revenues and Tribal Economy* (Window Rock, AZ: Navajo Office of Minerals Development, June 1976).

30. Marjane Ambler, *Breaking the Iron Bonds: Indian Control of Energy Development* (Lawrence: University Press of Kansas, 1990) p. 175. Also see Janet Siskind, "A Beautiful River That Turned Sour," *Mine Talk*, Summer/Fall 1982, pp. 37-59.

31. Ambler, *Iron Bonds*, op. cit., pp. 174-5. Also see LaDuke, "A History of Uranium Mining," op. cit. In this article, LaDuke quotes a New Mexico Environmental Improvement Agency report dated earlier the same year that was leaked to the Southwest Research and Information Center. In this document, it is acknowledged that spill-area livestock exhibited "higher than normal levels of Lead 210, Polonium 210, Thorium 230, and Radium 236." The state recommended the Diné not eat mutton thus contaminated. Indian Health Service Area Director William Mohler nonetheless suggested they go ahead and eat their animals, cautioning only that they should "perhaps" avoid eating organ tissues, where radioactive toxins might be expected to concentrate most heavily. Mohler agreed, however, that the meat was probably "inappropriate" for commercial sale. In other words, he deemed the animals "safe enough" for consumption by mere Indians, but not by non-Indians in New York or London; J. W. Schomisch, "EID Lifts Ban on Eating Church Rock Cattle," *Gallup Independent*, May 22, 1980.

32. Quoted in Dan Liefgreen, "Church Rock Chapter Upset at UNC," *Navajo Times*, May 8, 1980.

33. Frank Pitman, "Navajos-UNC Settle Tailings Spill Lawsuits," *Nuclear Fuel*, Apr. 22, 1985.

34. "EID Finds That Church Rock Dam Break Had Little or No Effect on Residents," *Nuclear Fuel*, Mar. 14, 1983.

35. Chris Shuey, "The Puerco River: Where Did the Water Go?" *The Workbook*, No. 11, 1988, pp. 1-10; Steve Hinschman, "Rebottling the Nuclear Genie," *High Country News*, Jan. 19, 1987.

36. Ambler, *Iron Bonds*, op. cit., p. 175. The instruction was delivered by memo, from Governor King to Thomas E. Baca of the Environmental Improvement Agency on January 9, 1981 (copy on file). For context, see "Mine Dewatering Operation in New Mexico Seen Violating Arizona Water Standards," *Nuclear Fuel*, Mar. 1, 1982.

37. The laws violated by the United Nuclear and Kerr-McGee dewatering procedures are the Public Law 92-500 (the "Clean Water Act of 1972," 86 Stat. 816) and P.L. 93-523 (the "Safe Drinking Water Act of 1974," 88 Stat. 1660). Although they are federal statutes, enforcement is left to individual states. They are often suspended altogether on Indian reservations; Christopher McCleod, "Kerr-McGee's Last Stand," *Mother Jones*, Dec. 1980.

38. Ambler, *Iron Bonds*, op. cit., p. 175.

39. *Walter H. Peshlakai, et al. v. James R. Schlesinger, et al.*, V.S.D.C. for the District of Columbia, Civ. No. 78-2416 (1978). For analysis, see Tom Barry, "Navajo Legal Services and Friends of the Earth Sue Six Federal Agencies over Alleged Careless Mining Policies," *American Indian Journal*, Feb. 1979, pp. 5-7.

40. "Judge Reviewing Request to Stop Mobil Project," *Navajo Times*, July 19, 1979.

41. Quoted in Hansley Hadley, "Between Sacred Mountains," *Navajo Times*, Dec. 7, 1983.

42. *Peshlakai v. Duncan*, 476 F.Supp. 1247, 1261 (1978).

43. Public Law 95-604 (92 Stat. 3021). For analysis, see Bob Rankin, "Congress Debates Cleanup of Uranium Mill Wastes," *Congressional Quarterly*, Aug. 19, 1978, p. 2180.

44. The role of Harold Tso and his agency in getting things rolling—at *Indian* expense—is mentioned in Ford, Bacon & Davis Utah, *A Summary of the Phase II: Title I Engineering Assessment of Inactive Uranium Mill Tailings, Shiprock Site, N.M.* (Salt Lake City: Ford, Bacon & Davis Utah Engineering Consultants, 1977) p. 65.

45. Ambler, *Iron Bonds*, op. cit., p. 179. Present state of incompletion verified through site inspection by the author.

46. Site inspections by the author.

47. U.S. Department of Energy Environmental Protection Agency, *Potential Health and Environmental Hazards of Uranium Mine Wastes* (Washington, D.C.: U.S. Government Printing Office, 1983) pp. 1-23. It should be noted that the Navajo Environmental Protection Administration has again

tried to address the situation, this time by diverting federal funds designated for the reclamation of abandoned coal mines on their land for use in cleaning up some of the worst uranium mine sites. Such monies are, however, greatly insufficient to the task; "Congress Unlocks $30 Million Mine Land Funds," *Navajo Times,* July 10, 1987.

48. Haunting sequences of Diné children playing in the proliferation of abandoned tailings piles around Tuba City are contained in Christopher McCleod's film *Four Corners: A National Sacrifice Area?* (San Francisco: Earth Image Films, 1981).

49. The Jackpile-Paguate Mine was supplanted for the dubious distinction of the world's largest by Namibia's Rossing Mine only after the former's closure in 1982; Dan Jackson, "Mine Development on U.S. Indian Lands," *Engineering and Mining Journal,* Jan. 1980; John Aloysius Farrel, "The New Indian Wars," *Denver Post,* Nov. 20-27, 1983.

50. Clemmer, "Energy Economy," op. cit., pp. 98-9.

51. Ambler, *Iron Bonds,* op. cit., p. 181.

52. Clemmer ("Energy Economy,"op. cit.) estimates on p. 99 that this involved some 450 others, or about "roughly three-quarters of the Laguna work force." Another 160 Acomas were also employed, mainly at the Bluewater mill. Also see Employment Security Commission of New Mexico, *Major Employers in New Mexico by County, 1976* (Santa Fe: mimeo, 1976).

53. Clemmer, "Energy Economy," op. cit., p. 99.

54. Ibid., pp. 97-8. Also see Hope Aldrich, "Problems Pile Up at Uranium Mills," *Santa Fe Reporter,* Nov. 13, 1980.

55. Clemmer, "Energy Economy," op. cit., pp. 97-8; Hope Aldrich, "The Politics of Uranium," *Santa Fe Reporter,* Dec. 7, 1978.

56. Clemmer, "Energy Economy," op. cit., p. 98. Also see Lynda Taylor and G. Theodore Davis, "Uranium Mining and Milling: The Human Costs," unpublished paper presented at the New Mexico Physicians for Social Responsibility Conference, Albuquerque, Mar. 10, 1980.

57. Radium-226 levels were calculated as being 30 times the "safe" levels; U.S. Environmental Protection Agency, unpublished report, number deleted (unauthorized copy filed with the Southwest Research and Information Center, Albuquerque, June 1973).

58. Comptroller General of the United States, "EPA Needs to Improve the Navajo Safe Water Drinking Program" (Washington, D.C.: General Accounting Office, Sept. 10, 1980).

59. Report by Johnny Sanders (Chief, Environmental Health Services Branch), T. J. Harwood (Director, Albuquerque Area Indian Health Service) and Mala L. Beard (ACL Hospital District Sanitarian) to the Governor of the Laguna Pueblo, Aug. 11, 1978; copy on file with the Southwest Research and Information Center, Albuquerque.

60. Gerald F. Seib, "Indians Awaken to Their Lands' Energy Riches and Seek to Wrest Control from Companies," *Wall Street Journal,* Sept. 20, 1979.

61. Ambler, *Iron Bonds,* op. cit., p. 181.

62. Taylor and Davis, "Uranium Mining and Milling," op. cit., quoting Dr. Joseph Wagoner.

63. Ambler, *Iron Bonds,* op. cit., p. 182.

64. Marjane Ambler, "Lagunas Face Fifth Delay of Uranium Cleanup," *Navajo Times Today,* Feb. 4, 1986.

65. The threatened litigation is mentioned in U.S. Department of the Interior, Bureau of Land Management, *Jackpile-Paguate Uranium Mine Reclamation Project Environmental Impact Statement* (Albuquerque: Bureau of Land Management, Oct. 1986) p. 1.

66. "Agreement Signed for Reclamation of Jackpile Mine in New Mexico" (Washington, D.C.: Department of the Interior News Release, Dec. 12, 1986).

67. D. R. Dreeson, "Uranium Mill Tailings: Environmental Implications," *Los Alamos National Scientific Laboratory Mini-Report,* Feb. 1978, pp. 1-4.

68. The term "National Sacrifice Area" accrues from Thadias Box, et al., *Rehabilitation Potential for Western Coal Lands* (Cambridge: Ballinger, 1974), the published version of a study commissioned by the National Academy of Science and submitted to the Nixon administration for potential implementation as federal policy in 1972. Policy extrapolation occurs in the U.S. Department of Energy, Federal Energy Administration, Office of Strategic Analysis report, *Project Independence: A Summary* (Washington, D.C.: U.S. Government Printing Office, Nov. 1, 1974). The theme is also taken up by the Office of Technology

Assessment in a report to Congress entitled *Strategic Minerals: Technologies to Reduce U.S. Import Vulnerability* (Washington, D.C.: U.S. Government Printing Office, 1985).

69. Ambler, *Iron Bonds*, op. cit., p. 183.

70. Russell Means, "The Same Old Song," in my *Marxism and Native Americans* (Boston: South End Press, 1983) p. 25.

71. The matter has been well-studied, and the conclusion is inescapable. See, e.g., Thayer Scudder, et al., *No Place to Go: Effects of Compulsory Relocation on Navajos* (Philadelphia: Institute for the Study of Human Issues, 1982).

72. Means, "Same Old Song," op. cit.

73. Amelia Irvin, "Energy Development and the Effects of Mining on the Lakota Nation," *Journal of Ethnic Studies*, Vol. 10, No. 2, 1982.

74. Harvey Wasserman, "The Sioux's Last Fight for the Black Hills," *Rocky Mountain News*, Aug. 24, 1980.

75. Peter Matthiessen, *Indian Country* (New York: Viking, 1984) pp. 203-18.

76. Madonna Gilbert (Thunderhawk), "Radioactive Water Contamination on the Red Shirt Table, Pine Ridge Reservation, South Dakota" (Porcupine, SD: Women of All Red Nations, unpublished report, Mar. 1980).

77. Quoted in Women of All Red Nations (WARN), "Radiation: Dangerous to Pine Ridge Women," *Akwesasne Notes*, Vol. 12, No. 1, 1980. Also see Patricia J. Linthrop and J. Rotblat, "Radiation Pollution in the Environment," *Bulletin of Atomic Scientists*, Sept. 1981, esp. p. 18.

78. WARN, "Radiation: Dangerous to Pine Ridge Women," op. cit.

79. Ibid. Such results are consistent with findings in broader, nonreservation settings; Earl E. Reynolds, "Irradiation and Human Evolution," in his *The Process of Ongoing Human Evolution* (Detroit: Wayne State University Press, 1960), esp. p. 92. Also see Arthur R. Tamplin and John W. Gofman, *Population Control Through Nuclear Pollution* (Chicago: Nelson-Hall, 1971).

80. The Igloo operation was suspended in 1972. Like Kerr-McGee on Navajo, and Anaconda at Laguna, the government made no effort to clean up the radioactive wastes it had generated; Matthiessen, *Indian Country*, op. cit.

81. "Nuclear Waste Facility Proposed Near Edgemont," *Rapid City Journal*, Nov. 19, 1982.

82. "Edgemont Waste Facility No Health Hazard Says Chem-Nuclear Corporation," *Rapid City Journal*, Dec. 10, 1982.

83. Site visit by author. Photos of the new tailings piles, fence and signs, taken by Cynthia Martinez, appear in my *Critical Issues in Native North America, Vol. II* (Copenhagen: International Work Group on Indigenous Affairs, 1991) pp. 39, 41.

84. Jaqueline Huber, et al., *The Gunnery Range Report* (Pine Ridge, SD: Office of the President, Oglala Sioux Tribe, 1981).

85. On the NASA/NURE collaboration, see Peter Matthiessen, *In the Spirit of Crazy Horse* (New York: Viking, [2nd ed.] 1991) p. 417. On disposition of minerals discovered thereby, see J. P. Gries, *BIA Report 12: Status of Mineral Resource Information on the Pine Ridge Reservation, South Dakota* (Washington, D.C.: U.S. Department of the Interior, 1976).

86. A list of the dead, as well as the dates and causes of death, is contained in my and Jim Vander Wall's *The COINTELPRO Papers: Documents from the FBI's Secret Wars Against Dissent in the United States* (Boston: South End Press, 1990) pp. 393-5;. For reproduction of an official document describing the Indian resistance as "insurgents"—rather than as "radicals" or "political extremists"—see p. 271. For further details of the way in which the war was waged, see my and Vander Wall's *Agents of Repression: The FBI's Secret Wars Against the Black Panther Party and the American Indian Movement* (Boston: South End Press, 1988).

87. U.S. National Park Service, "Memorandum of Agreement Between the Oglala Sioux Tribe of South Dakota and the National Park Service of the Department of [the] Interior to Facilitate Establishment, Development, Administration, and Public Use of the Oglala Sioux Tribal Lands, Badlands National Monument" (Washington, D.C.: U.S. Department of the Interior, Jan. 2, 1976). The transfer was illegal insofar as the still-binding 1868 Fort Laramie Treaty requires the express consent of three-quarters of *all* adult, male Lakotas before any Lakota land cession can be considered legally valid; the clause was designed specifically to *prevent* maneuvers such as those between Wilson and his federal sponsors. For

more on Wilson and the treaty, see Rex Wyler, *Blood of the Land: The U.S. Government and Corporate War Against the American Indian Movement* (Philadelphia: New Society, [2nd ed.] 1992).

88. U.S. Department of Interior National Park Service, *Master Plan: Badlands National Monument* (Denver: Rocky Mountain Regional Office, Feb. 1978). The clause allowing recovery of surface rights to the land by the Lakotas completely inverts the treaty requirement that such a referendum must be conducted before a land *cession* can be considered valid.

89. Irvin, "Energy Development," op. cit., p. 99.

90. Marjane Ambler, "Wyoming to Study Tailings Issue," *Denver Post*, Feb. 5, 1984.

91. Ambler, *Iron Bonds*, op. cit., p. 179.

92. U.S. Department of Energy, *Environmental Assessment on Remedial Action at the Riverton Uranium Mill Tailings Site, Riverton, Wyoming* (Albuquerque: Department of Energy Western Regional Office, June 1987).

93. Site visit by the author.

94. "GRI Projects 1% Annual Growth Rate in U.S. Energy Use Through 2010," *Inside Energy*, Aug. 15, 1988.

95. John D. Smillie, "Whatever Happened to the Energy Crisis?" *The Plains Truth*, Apr. 1986. Actually, the 1979 price of yellowcake was probably greatly and illegally inflated, having risen from $6 per pound in 1972 to $41 in 1977. In the latter year, Westinghouse Corporation, the largest commercial buyer in the U.S., filed a price-fixing suit against nearly every uranium producing company in the world. The suit was rendered moot by the market bust before it could be decided; Ambler, *Iron Bonds*, op. cit., p. 78.

96. The history is contained in *Dawn Mining Company v. Clark*, Civ. No. 82-974JLQ, District Court for Eastern Washington (1982).

97. Ambler, *Iron Bonds*, op. cit., p. 176.

98. Ibid.

99. Ibid. Ambler is relying on a letter from Paul B. Hahn, Chief of the Evaluation Branch, EPA Office of Radiation Programs, Las Vegas Facility, to Richard Parkin, Chief of the Water Compliance Section, EPA Region 10, dated Feb. 18, 1987.

100. *Dawn Mining Company v. Clark*, op. cit.

101. Ambler, *Iron Bonds*, op. cit., pp. 176-7.

102. Site visit by the author.

103. On the startup of the Sherwood facility, see Stan Dayton, "Washington's Sherwood Project: A Newcomer in an Orphan District," *Engineering and Mining Journal*, Nov. 1978. On the extent of environmental degradation at Sherwood, see U.S. Department of the Interior, Bureau of Indian Affairs, *Sherwood Uranium Project, Spokane Indian Reservation: Final Environmental Statement* (Portland, OR: Bureau of Indian Affairs Area Office, Aug. 19, 1976). On Western Nuclear's transfer of both mine and mill to the Spokanes, see U.S. Department of the Interior, Bureau of Indian Affairs, "Mineral Resource Facilities Maintenance Contract for the Sherwood Mine-Mill Complex" (Portland, OR: Bureau of Indian Affairs Area Office, Dec. 1989).

104. Site visit by the author.

105. Clemmer, "Energy Economy," op. cit., p. 103.

106. Ibid., p. 104.

107. Employment Security Commission of New Mexico, op. cit.

108. Clemmer, "Energy Economy," op. cit., p. 104.

109. Elouise Schumacher, "440 Billion Gallons: Hanford Wastes Would Fill 900 King Domes," *Seattle Times*, Apr. 13, 1991. No one need worry about this, however, given that the EPA has recently discovered that tobacco smoking (*rather than* such radioactive pollution by the government and major corporations) is the "primary environmental hazard" in the United States. Correspondingly, as the author discovered during a 1989 visit to Hanford, the many near-abandoned buildings at the plant—situated directly atop the greatest known release of carcinogenic waste in human history—have been designated by law as no smoking zones. One will incur a $2,500 fine—imposed by the very entity which is solely responsible for what has happened at Hanford—for lighting up one cigarette on a U.S. airliner while those who dumped a near half-billion gallons of radioactive toxins into the public water supply waltz off merrily, without so much as a slap on the wrist. Such are the present priorities of environmental

consciousness in the U.S., implicitly endorsed even by a wide spectrum of those describing themselves as "progressive" or "politically conscious."

110. Kenneth B. Noble, "The U.S. for Decades Let Uranium Leak at Weapon Plant," *New York Times*, Oct. 15, 1988; Martha Odom, "Tanks That Leak, Tanks That Explode…Tanks Alot DOE," *Portland Free Press*, May 1989.

111. Matthew L. Wald, "Wider Peril Seen in Nuclear Waste from Bomb Making," *New York Times*, Mar. 28, 1991.

112. Helen Caldicott, M.D., *If You Love This Planet: A Plan to Heal the Earth* (New York: W. W. Norton, 1992) p. 89.

113. At one point, plant officials even attempted to "lose" key documents concerning what it had done at Hanford; Larry Lang, "Missing Hanford Documents Probed by Energy Department," *Seattle Post-Intelligencer*, Sept. 20, 1991.

114. Caldicott, *Planet*, op. cit., p. 89. Also see Susan Wyndham, "Death in the Air," *Australian Magazine*, Sept. 29-30, 1990.

115. Caldicott, *Planet*, op. cit., p. 90. Also see Keith Schneider, "Seeking Victims of Radiation Near Weapon Plant," *New York Times*, Oct. 17, 1988. Overviews of the Hanford disaster will also be found in Michele Stenehjem Gerber's *On the Home Front: The Cold War Legacy of the Hanford Nuclear Site* (Lincoln: University of Nebraska Press, 1992) and Michael D'Antonio's *Atomic Harvest: Hanford and the Lethal Toll of America's Nuclear Arsenal* (New York: Crown, 1993).

116. Marjane Ambler, "Nuke Waste Sites Border Indian Lands," *Navajo Times*, Oct. 8, 1984. Also see Warner Reeser, *Inventory of Hazardous Waste Generators and Sites on Selected Indian Reservations* (Denver: Council of Energy Resource Tribes, 1985).

117. Marjane Ambler, "Law Recognizes Tribal Concerns: DOE Ignores Them, Says 3 Tribes," *Navajo Times Today*, Apr. 29, 1985; "Russell Jim is Pro-Safety, Not Anti-Nuclear," *High Country News*, July 7, 1988. The 1988 congressional decision to build the waste facility at Yucca Mountain, Nevada, rather than in Washington or Idaho, is mentioned in *Breaking the Iron Bonds*, op. cit., p. 234.

118. Public Law 97-425 (96 Stat. 2201).

119. Nellis, consisting of approximately 3.5 million acres of what were called "unappropriated public domain lands," was created in 1940 under Executive Order 8578. In 1952, 435,000 acres in the Yucca Flats area of the facility were set aside for the exclusive purpose of testing nuclear weaponry. Another 318,000 acres were added to this "Nevada Test Site" in 1961; David Loomis, *Combat Zoning: Military Land Use in Nevada* (Las Vegas: University of Nevada Press, 1994) pp. 9-10.

120. U.S. Department of Energy, *Announced U.S. Nuclear Tests July 1945 through December 1991* (Washington, D.C.: U.S. Government Printing Office, 1992). On an additional 204 "unannounced" tests, see *New York Times*, Dec. 8, 1992. On the July 2, 1997, experiment, see Ian Zabarte, "Western Shoshone National Sovereignty Violated by Subcritical Nuclear Weapons Test," *Western Shoshone Defense Project Newsletter*, Vol. 5, No. 2, Fall/Winter 1997.

121. Howard Ball, *Justice Downwind: America's Atomic Testing Program in the 1950s* (New York: Oxford University Press, 1986) p. 85.

122. This is the half-life of plutonium. It should be noted that a single pound of plutonium, dispersed evenly throughout the earth's atmosphere, would be sufficient to cause lung cancer in every human being now alive; Dr. Helen Caldicott, quoted in Leslie J. Freeman, *Nuclear Witnesses: Insiders Speak Out* (New York: W.W. Norton, 1982) p. 294.

123. Valerie Kuletz, *The Tainted Desert: Environmental and Social Ruin in the American West* (New York: Routledge, 1998) p. 70.

124. See, e.g., Dagmar Thorpe, *Newe Segobia: The Western Shoshone Land and People* (Lee, NV: Western Shoshone Sacred Lands Association, 1982).

125. On withholding of data, see "Feds Snub Tribe's Radiation Exposure," *Reno Gazette-Journal*, June 7, 1994. On death toll, see James W. Hulse, *Forty Years in the Wilderness* (Reno: University of Nevada Press, 1986) p. 61.

126. On data suppression, see Bill Curry, "A-Test Officials Feared Outcry After Health Study," *Washington Post*, Apr. 17, 1979. For general background, see Melin R. Sikov and D. Dennis Mahlum, eds., *Radiation Biology of the Fetal and Juvenile Mammal: Proceedings of the Ninth Annual Hanford Biology Symposium at Richland, Washington, 5-8 May, 1969* (Springfield, VA: Clearinghouse for Federal Scientific

and Technical Information, 1969). More specifically, see Ernest J. Sternglass, "Cancer: Relation of Prenatal Radiation to Development of Disease in Childhood," *Science,* June 7, 1963; "Infant Mortality and Nuclear Tests," *Bulletin of Atomic Scientists,* Apr. 1969; "Can the Children Survive?" *Bulletin of Atomic Scientists,* June 1969.

127. Kuletz, *Tainted Desert,* op. cit., pp. 102-16.

128. Ibid., p. 102. Kuletz is quoting an article entitled "Scientists Fear Atomic Explosion of Buried Waste," *New York Times,* Mar. 5, 1995. More technically, see Jacque Emel, Roger Kasperson, Robert Gable and Otwin Renn, *Post-closure Risks at the Proposed Yucca Mountain Repository: A Review of Methodological and Technical Issues* (Reno: State of Nevada Nuclear Waste Project Office, 1988).

129. Philip M. Klasky, "The Eagles's View of Ward Valley: Environmentalists and Native American Tribes Fight Proposed Nuclear Dump in the Mojave Desert," *Wild Earth,* Spring 1994.

130. As tribal member Leon Bear put it, "People have to understand that this whole area is already considered a waste zone by the federal government, the state of Utah, and the country... Toole Depot, a military site, stores 40% of the nation's nerve gas and other hazardous gas only 40 miles away from us. Dugway Proving Grounds...is only 14 miles away, and it experiments with viruses like plague and tuberculosis... From all directions, north south, east and west, we're surrounded by the waste of Toole County, the state of Utah, and U.S. society"; quoted in Randal D. Hansen, "Nuclear Agreement Continues U.S. Policy of Dumping on Goshutes," *The Circle,* Oct. 1995.

131. On creation and growth of Alamagordo, see Tad Bartimus and Scott MacCartney, *Trinity's Children: Living Along America's Nuclear Highway* (Albuquerque: University of New Mexico Press, 1991) p. 11.

132. Ibid., pp. 32, 40. For context, see William Thomas, *Scorched Earth: The Military's Assault on the Environment* (Philadelphia: New Society, 1995).

133. The original idea appears to have arisen during the mid-70s when a nearly defunct potash mining company near Carlsbad recommended to the AEC that its abandoned mineshafts be used for such purposes; Charles C. Reith and N. Timothy Fischer, "Transuranic Waste Disposal: The WIPP Project," in their edited volume, *Deserts as Dumps? The Disposal of Hazardous Materials in Arid Ecosystems* (Albuquerque: University of New Mexico Press, 1992) p. 314.

134. As it stands, WIPP is to accommodate only such military waste as was generated after 1970. A further quarter million cubic meters of waste from the Manhattan Project alone remains to be permanently disposed of; Debra Rosenthal, *At the Heart of the Bomb: The Dangerous Allure of Nuclear Weapons* (Menlo Park, CA: Addison-Wesley, 1990) p. 195. However much plutonium-laced material is ultimately stored there will be subjected to the Carlsbad Caverns' continuous seepage of highly corrosive brine. Whatever leaks from the steel containers in which waste is stored will likely flow through rock fissures into the underlying aquifir; Scientists Review Panel on WIPP, *Evaluation of the Waste Isolation Pilot Project (WIPP) as a Water-Saturated Nuclear Waster Repository* (Albuquerque: New Mexico Concerned Scientists, 1988). As at Yucca Mountain, the material also has a potential to reach critical mass and detonate (see note 128).

135. Winifred E. Frick, "Native Americans Approve Nuclear Waste Dump on Tribal Lands," *City on a Hill Press,* Mar. 16, 1995. There has, however, been considerable resistance among at least some sectors of the reservation population; Beth Enson, "The Nuclear Struggle Continues on the Mescalero Apache Reservation," *The Workbook,* Vol. 20, No. 1, Spring 1995.

136. Kuletz, *Tainted Desert,* op. cit., p. 101. Also see Randel D. Hansen, "Mescalero: The Privatization of Genocide," *The Circle,* Jan. 1995.

137. A. D. Owen, "The World Uranium Industry," *Raw Materials Report,* Vol. 2, No. 1, 1983.

138. Miles Goldstick, *Wollaston: People Resisting Genocide* (Toronto: Black Rose Books, 1987) pp. 74-5.

139. Actually, the problem may be even more severe, given that the greater proportion of non-radioactive material in the byproducts of lower grade ore may serve to some extent in retarding radon and thoron emissions. If so, then the effect is exponential; both the "quality" and quantity of radioactive contamination in northern Saskatchewan would be higher than at comparable U.S. sites; John Moelaert, "This Dust Is Making Me Sick," *The Energy File,* Apr. 1979.

140. Goldstick, *Wollaston,* op. cit., p. 107.

141. *Annual Report, 1984* (Ottawa: Eldorado Nuclear, Ltd., Mar. 7, 1985).

142. National Research Council of Canada, Associate Committee on Scientific Criteria for Environmental Quality, *Lead in the Canadian Environment* (Ottawa: NRCC Publications, Dec. 1973). Also see Canadian Atomic Energy Control Board, Advisory Panel on Uranium Tailings, *The Management of Uranium Tailings: An Appraisal of Current Practices* (Ottawa: AECB Report 1196, Sept. 1978) p. 13.

143. For use of the term, see Goldstick, *Wollaston*, op. cit., p. 74.

144. Ibid., pp. 75-7.

145. David McArthur, "Surface Leases and Socio-Economic Considerations of Uranium Mining" (Ottawa: Mining Law Institute Occasional Papers, June 1983).

146. Jim Harding, "Saskatchewan: The Eye of the Uranium Controversy," *Briarpatch*, Apr. 1985.

147. Goldstick, *Wollaston*, op. cit., p. 78. Also see Bud Jorgensen, "Easing of Uranium Export Rules Urged for Canada," *Globe and Mail*, May 4, 1986.

148. Atomic Energy Control Board, *Uranium Tailings*, op. cit., p. 3.

149. Goldstick, *Wollaston*, op. cit., pp. 79-80; Moelaert, "This Dust…" op. cit.

150. Although Eldorado Nuclear, as a wholly government-created entity, is ostensibly owned "by the people of Canada," it has been far less forthcoming with its financial information than many private concerns. Goldstick has calculated the profitability of the Rabbit Lake operation based on Eldorado's 1984 report that its operation had produced more than 1.6 million kilograms of yellowcake during its lifetime, and then multiplying by the average $62.50 (Canadian) price per kilo which prevailed during the same period.

151. Milling at the Rabbit Lake facility did not stop while the building involved in its expansion was going on, of course. When construction workers sought to reveal the safety hazards which resulted and to unionize in self-defense, Eldorado summarily fired them and then cancelled its contract with their employer, Enerpet Construction Ltd., of Calgary. Scab labor—apparently willing to risk a high degree of irradiation in exchange for a government paycheck—was used to complete the project; "Men Say Fired for Unionizing," *The Star Phoenix* (Saskatoon) Jan. 24, 1984.

152. Goldstick, *Wollaston*, op. cit., pp. 81-2.

153. Quoted in ibid., p. 82.

154. Terry Pugh, "Garbage Never Looked So Good," *Briarpatch*, Sept. 1986.

155. A total of 2,916 such containers had stacked up by 1983, when mining of the first Cluff Lake ore pocket was completed. Three years later, the number was thought to have tripled, and by now there may be more than 20,000. Under the best of conditions, the containers are expected to last only 100 years, while the half-life of much of the material within them is as long as 80,000 years. Neither the corporation nor the government has explained what is supposed to happen to the wastes after the end of its first century of storage; ibid.

156. The Saskatchewan investment was $2.3 million (Canadian). Cluff Lake Mining estimated that it could produce 56,700 kilograms of yellowcake and 283,000 grams of gold—at an aggregate value of $4.5 million—just from the radium wastes "on hand." AMOK, one-third of which is owned by the French government's Commisariat de l'Energie Atomique (which builds and tests France's nuclear weapons) committed to buy the bulk of the yellowcake; "AMOK Solves Problem of Radioactive Waste," *Globe and Mail*, Aug. 16, 1986.

157. Goldstick, *Wollaston*, op. cit., p. 84; Jorgenson, "Political Economy," op. cit.

158. Goldstick, *Wollaston*, op. cit., p. 85.

159. Ibid.

160. Ibid., pp. 85-6.

161. Diana Ralph, "Faulty Prescription for Northern Native People: Health-Damaging Development and Little Care" (unpublished paper completed, Feb. 1984; quoted by Goldstick, *Wollaston*, op. cit., p. 24).

162. Murray Dobbin, ed., *Economic Options for Northern Saskatchewan* (Saskatoon: Northern Saskatchewan Economic Options Conference, 1984) p. 11.

163. R. G. Ruggles and W. J. Rowley, *A Study of Water Pollution in the Vicinity of the Eldorado Nuclear Ltd., Beaverlodge Operation, 1976 and 1977* (Edmonton: Environmental Protection Service, 1978).

164. Stella M. Swanson, "Levels of Ra226, Pb210, and Utotal in Fish Near a Saskatchewan Uranium Mine and Mill," *Health Physics*, Vol. 45, No. 1, July 1983, pp. 67-80.

165. Saskatchewan Research Council, Chemistry and Biology Division, *Environmental Overview*

Assessment for the Dubyna 31-Zone Uranium Production Program for United Nuclear Ltd. (Saskatoon: Saskatchewan Research Council, Dec. 13, 1978) p. 71.

166. D. J. Robinson, F. G. Ruggles and A. Zaida, *A Study of Water Pollution in the Vicinity of Gulf Minerals Rabbit Lake Uranium Mine, 1978* (Regina: Environment Canada Surveillance Report EPS-5-W and NR-83-1, 1978) pp. i, 11.

167. Ibid., p. i, quoted and paraphrased in Goldstick, *Wollaston*, op. cit., p. 116.

168. Saskatchewan Research Council, *Environmental Overview*, op. cit., p. 44.

169. Goldstick, *Wollaston*, op. cit., p. 116.

170. Swanson, "Levels in Fish," op. cit., p. 10.

171. Ibid., p. 19.

172. Goldstick, *Wollaston*, op. cit., p. 110.

173. R. B. Holtzman, "Ra266 and the Natural Airborne Nuclides Pb210 and Po210 in Arctic Biota," in William Snyder, ed. *Radiation Protection,* (Oxford: Pergamon Press, 1968) pp. 1,087-96.

174. Quoted in Goldstick, *Wollaston*, op. cit., p. 121.

175. Ibid.

176. Dreeson, "Uranium Mill Tailings," op. cit.

177. See, e.g., the opening paragraph in the introduction to Goldstick (*Wollaston*, op. cit., p. 12): "The uranium industry is more active in northern Saskatchewan than any other place in the western world. For the native people of the area it is the dominant force continuing the destructive momentum built up over 300 years of colonialism. If the present trend continues, the result will be genocide."

178. Witness a veteran activist literally shouting at me during a presentation I made at the 1998 CHOICES conference in Winnipeg: "We've *done* plutonium! Now we're concentrating on tobacco smoking!"

179. Barry Commoner, *Making Peace with the Planet* (New York: New Press, [5th ed.] 1992) pp. 103-4.

180. On the context of Chernobyl and its effects, see World Commission on Environment and Development, *Our Common Future* (New York: Oxford University Press, 1987).

181. On Seabrook and Diablo Canyon, see Harvey Wasserman, *Energy War: Reports from the Front* (Westport, CT: Lawrence Hill, 1979). On Point Conception, see Matthiessen, *Indian Country*, op. cit.

182. Two reactors in the U.S.—those at Fort St. Vrain and Hanford—were based on the same defective gas-cooled design as the Soviet reactor at Chernobyl, using "hoppers of boronated steel balls which fall into holes in the graphite moderator block if the current to magnetic latches is interrupted"; Amory B. Lovins and L. Hunter Lovins, *Brittle Power: Energy Strategy for National Security* (Andover, MA: Brick House, 1982) p. 197.

183. Marcia Klotz, et al., *Citizen's Guide to Rocky Flats: Colorado's Bomb Factory* (Boulder, CO: Rocky Mountain Peace Center, 1992) p. 6.

184. Commoner, *Peace*, op. cit., pp. 87-8.

185. Ibid., p. 88.

186. Caldicott, *Planet*, op. cit., pp. 36-7, 65, 152. Ironically but predictably, the nuclear industry has purported to adopt as its own the environmental movement's new top priorities: greenhouse gases and the global warming produced thereby. Only atomic energy, the story goes, can offer a "clean, safe and reliable alternative" to the huge level of gaseous emission produced by coal- and oil-fired electrical generators.

187. U.S. Department of Energy, Nuclear Information and Resource Service, *Nuclear Power and National Energy Strategy* (Washington, D.C.: U.S. Government Printing Office, Apr. 1991).

188. Opposing the proliferation of nuclear reactors was a centerpiece in the Clinton/Gore effort to make themselves appear as an "environmentally friendly" alternative to Bush during the 1992 U.S. general election, with Gore going so far as putting his name to a tract on the topic of "sustainable development"; Albert E. Gore, *Earth in the Balance* (New York: Houghton-Mifflin, 1992). Once in office, the pair have maintained this posture, although they've done nothing to dismantle the already-existing complex of reactors, end the military's reliance upon depleted uranium ammunition, terminate subcritical testing or prevent upgrading of the military's arsenal of nuclear warheads. Rather, they appear to have used the tissue-thin image as "liberal ecologists" they gained by not allowing construction of new reactors as a medium through which to divert public attention away from the gigantic systemic problem

of plutonium contamination, focusing it instead on such comparatively irrelevant "issues" as tobacco smoking by individuals.

189. Preliminary work appears already to have begun; site visit by author, June 1995.

190. Ambler, *Iron Bonds*, op. cit., p. 173.

191. See map of Crow resources, ibid., p. 36.

192. On "seed money," see ibid., p. 95; on 1979 DoE funding level, p. 100. Overall, see Winona LaDuke, "The Council of Energy Resource Tribes," in Jorgenson, *Native Americans and Energy Development, II*, op. cit., pp. 58-70.

193. Ambler, *Iron Bonds*, op. cit., p. 95. The 1988 member councils were those at Ute Mountain and Southern Ute, Florida Seminole, Navajo, Nez Percé, Yakima, Oklahoma Cherokee, Jicarilla Apache, Pine Ridge Sioux, Standing Rock Sioux, Cheyenne River Sioux, Rosebud Sioux, Blackfeet, Spokane, Tulé River, Turtle Mountain Chippewa, Uintah and Ouray Ute, Chemeheuvi, Cour d'Alene, Cheyenne-Arapaho, Northern Cheyenne, Walker River, Pawnee, Shoshone-Bannock, Umatilla, Penobscot, Kalispel, Muckleshoot, Saginaw Chippewa, Ponca, Rocky Boy Chippewa-Cree, Crow, Flathead, Fort Belknap, Fort Berthold, Fort Peck, Hopi, Hualapai, and the Acoma, Jemez, Santa Ana, Zia and Laguna Pueblos.

194. Geoffrey O'Gara, "Canny CERT Gets Money, Respect, Problems," *High Country News*, Dec. 14, 1979. Also see Winona LaDuke, "CERT: An Outsider's View In," *Akwesasne Notes*, Vol. 12, No. 2, 1980.

195. Ambler, *Iron Bonds*, op. cit., pp. 95-100. It should be noted that, although CERT deliberately fostered a bare-knuckled image of itself as an "Indian OPEC" during its early days, it was always explicitly accommodationist. Founding director Peter McDonald obtained federal funding by first pledging unequivocal support to the government and promising that the organization's members were "posed to make a massive contribution to the national effort [to achieve energy self-sufficiency]"; O'Gara, "CERT," op. cit. It should also be mentioned that the individual hired by McDonald to head up CERT's resource development policy and its implementation, Ahmed Kooros, was former oil minister for the Shah of Iran; Mike Meyers, "Ahmed Kooros: A Discussion," *Akwesasne Notes*, Vol. 12, No. 1, 1980.

196. Probably the best overall Indian critique of CERT offered during this period was Philip "Sam" Deloria's "CERT: It's Time for an Evaluation," *American Indian Law Newsletter*, Sept./Oct. 1982. Also see Ken Peres and Fran Swan, "The New Indian Elite: Bureaucratic Entrepreneurs," *Akwesasne Notes*, Vol. 12, No. 1, 1980.

197. CERT was a prime mover in seeking to convince either the Yakimas, the Umatillas, or the Nez Percés to accept a high-level dump during the second half of the 1980s; U.S. Environmental Protection Agency, *EPA Policy for the Administration of Environmental Programs on Indian Reservations* (Washington, D.C.: U.S. Government Printing Office, Nov. 8, 1984). Its role at Mescalero was equally prominent; Hansen, "Mesalero," op. cit.; Frick, "Native Americans Approve Waste Dump," op. cit. On Skull Valley, see Hansen, "Nuclear Agreement," op. cit. Overall, see Grace Thorp, "Radioactive Racism? Native Americans and the Nuclear Waste Legacy," *The Circle*, Apr. 1995.

198. Ambler, *Iron Bonds*, op. cit., p. 115. She quotes DoE official Marie Monsen as describing EPA as CERT's new "glamor girl" by 1990.

199. Caldicott, *Planet*, op. cit., p. 90; Klotz, *Citizen's Guide to Rocky Flats*, op. cit., p. 6.

200. Oak Ridge Environmental Peace Alliance, *A Citizen's Guide to Oak Ridge* (Knoxville, KY: OREPA Publications, 1989).

201. On water contamination, see Joan Lowy and Janet Day, "Flats Water Threat Cited," *Rocky Mountain News*, Dec. 7, 1988. On extent of ground contamination, see Nicholas Lenssen, *Nuclear Waste: The Problem That Won't Go Away* (Washington, D.C.: Worldwatch Institute Paper 106, Dec. 1991) pp. 34-5).

202. On the Clamshell and Abalone Alliances, see Wasserman, *Energy War*, op. cit. On the Freeze Movement, see Michael Albert and David Dellinger, eds., *Beyond Survival: New Directions for the Disarmament Movement* (Boston: South End Press, 1983); despite the suggestion that "new directions" are involved, there is *no* discussion of possibly decolonizing the source(s) of uranium, thus severing nuclear weapons structure from its root.

203. In fact, a good case can be made that the capacity for U.S. nuclear weaponry has actually gone *up* since George Bush announced "cuts" in such weapons in September 1991 and January 1992; Klotz, *Citizen's Guide to Rocky Flats*, op. cit., p. 11.

204. On LaDonna Harris' role in founding CERT, as well as serving as Commoner's Citizen Party running mate in 1980, Ambler, *Iron Bonds*, op. cit., pp. 93-4, 101-2.

205. This is a variation of the "Mere Gook Rule" articulated by Noam Chomsky and others to explain the callousness with which U.S. policymakers view the suffering they inflict upon nonwhite peoples at home and abroad while pursuing the "national interest;" Edward S. Herman, *Beyond Hypocrisy: Decoding the News in an Age of Propaganda* (Boston: South End Press, 1992) pp. 54-6. That Euroamerican progressivism might be tinged with a touch of the same perspective tends to speak for itself.

206. Much can be learned from the Australian antinuclear movement, which made aboriginal rights a centerpiece of its strategy, and which has therefore been much more effective than its U.S. and Canadian counterparts in halting front end nuclear activities in their country; see, e.g., C. Tatz, *Aboriginies & Uranium and Other Essays* (Victoria: Heineman, 1982).

207. André Gorz, *Ecology as Politics* (Boston: South End Press, 1980) pp. 102-14.

208. Felix Cohen, "Dean of American Indian Law," coined the Indian's miner's canary analogy to describe certain juridical and policy phenomena in the U.S. Winona LaDuke and other native rights activists have since applied it in the more physical manner used here; Felix S. Cohen, "The Erosion of Indian Rights, 1950-53: A Case Study in Bureaucracy," *Yale Law Journal*, No. 62, 1953, p. 390.

209. John W. Gofman (Ph.D., M.D.) and Arthur R. Tamplin (Ph.D.), *Poisoned Power: The Case Before and After Three Mile Island* (Emmaus, PA: Rodale Press, [2nd. edition] 1979). For a much more recent iteration of this theme, see Jay M. Gould, *The Enemy Within: The High Cost of Living Near Nuclear Reactors* (New York: Four Walls Eight Windows, 1996).

THE WATER PLOT
Hydrological Rape in Northern Canada

> There are strange things
> done in the midnight sun
> By the men who toil for gold;
> The Arctic Trails have
> their secret tales
> That would make your
> blood run cold...

—Robert Service

I N northern Canada, a water diversion scheme far larger than anything yet undertaken in the United States has been planned, piloted and awaits only the right climate of public opinion.[1] The idea is to divert Canada's hydro-electricity and clean, fresh waters to support the growing demand of the lower forty-eight U.S. states. According to proponents of the plan, Canada would earn a great deal of foreign exchange, and would profit considerably from the employment created by construction of the required dams, dikes, canals, tunnels and pumping stations. Little is said about what will happen once these works are built. As will be seen, what little benefit might actually accrue to the citizens of Canada will be vastly outweighed by the costs of adverse economic, human and environmental consequences.

Land that Supports Its People

In the Canadian northlands, the indigenous Dene, Cree, Inuit and Ojibwe populations live primarily by time-honored methods of hunting, trapping and fishing, affording these occupations not only practical but central spiritual significance.[2] Those who hold wage jobs do so mainly in the three industries which support the resident non-Indian population: mining, forestry and tourism.[3] Each of these economies must be considered in any assessment of the overall impacts attending the projected hydrological rape of the Subarctic.

As developments in northern Québec over the past quarter-century have amply demonstrated, massive water diversion is utterly devastating to the ecosystems upon which indigenous economies depend. The habitat of furbearing animals, without which there can be no trapping, is flooded out when freeflowing waters are dammed.[4] Similarly, much of the bottomland on which large mammals graze becomes submerged, killing or driving the animals away and destroying the basis for commercial or even subsistence hunting. Aquatic life is also disrupted by damming. Many of the varieties of fish native to northern Canada require a current in which to thrive; they disappear quickly once their rivers and streams have been converted into relatively motionless reservoirs.[5] The flooding caused by dams also tends to cause mercury contamination and other forms of water pollution which renders poisonous to consume even those types of fish which are able to adapt.[6]

If the grand plan for water diversion in the Subarctic is consummated, the impact upon indigenous peoples there will be catastrophic. It is certain to destroy their present economic self-sufficiency and, as will be seen below, will foreclose on every economic alternative supposedly available to them. The net result may well be their rapid disappearance *as peoples*. In this sense, the effect of the "Water Plot" carries implications of genocide as well as ecocide.[7]

Permanent Deforestation

Although northern Canada is abundantly wooded, it takes more dollars' worth of equipment to generate a penny's worth of profit from the pulp and paper industry than nearly any other business in the world. Because trees in the Subarctic grow comparatively slowly, each paper mill must draw on a broad forest area in order to ensure that the large capital investment involved receives a perpetual supply of raw materials.[8]

In northwestern Ontario, for example, timber limits are now almost fully allocated throughout the "harvesting" area south of Highway 11 and north of Lake Nipagon. Reservoirs already cover tens of thousands of square miles of former woodlands in the region, and it is easy to see that further hydrological "improvements" can only be accomplished through destabilization of the forestry industry.[9] If the Water Plot were to achieve full fruition, forests and forestry, not only in Ontario, but elsewhere in the north, would become relics of the past. Reduction of forestry would deny the indigenous people of the area not only a primary source of what limited cash they now receive, but also one of the major alternatives to their traditional economy that the dominant culture has always espoused.[10]

The Mining Industry

There is an estimated billion dollars worth of nickel in the new Inco mine on Shebandowan Lake, in Ontario. The entrance to the mine shaft is barely twenty feet above the natural level of the lake. Shebandowan is but one of many similar sites, all of them yielding rich mineral ores, including not only nickle, but copper, bauxite, manganese, uranium, iron, silver and, of course, gold.[11] Each of the mines is similarly located, at or very near lake level. Projected areas of flooding if the Water Plot is consummated show that all of these will disappear beneath the waves, as will a number of Indian and non-Indian communities.

Planners explain that construction of an elaborate system of cofferdams, causeways and pumping facilities will be sufficient to save many existing mine sites. They are silent, however, concerning the expense involved; there are no estimates of the increase in costs of Canadian ores needed to pay the tab. In all likelihood, mining in much of northern Canada will be priced out of the market and correspondingly gutted. Further, planners have little to say about how their scheme would affect exploration and mining of presently undiscovered mineral deposits which will be buried not tens, but often hundreds of feet under water.[12] Water diversion of the sort now envisioned would thus demolish the second supposed alternative to traditional native economies.

Tourism

Tourism, the third and final basis for an indigenous cash economy in the northlands, is also threatened. For more than forty years, a solid business of sport fishing and hunting, camping and the like has developed and provides a cash supplement to the subsistence activities of many native people.[13] This will be completely ruined if fast-moving pike streams, as well as pickerel lakes, are converted into huge, largely stagnant inland seas in which only carp can live, and upon which one can barely cast a line without snagging the rotting remains of once proud pine forests. As is readily demonstrated behind the sprawling Bennett Dam in British Columbia, even where water still flows navigation will be severely impaired by floating timber and land-

294

ings will have to be made on mudflats, amidst the skeletal remains of miles upon miles of drowned trees.[14] The tourist industry in most of northern Canada will be obliterated if the Water Plot is realized. And with it would go the last hope of survival for the region's indigenous peoples.

Genocide as "National Sacrifice"

Once the dams and attendant paraphernalia are put in place, the entire developed area will quite literally be gone, leaving nothing by which a population, indigenous or otherwise, can support itself. Northern Canada will have become what in the United States has been described as a "National Sacrifice Area." It follows that the human beings who reside there will have been simultaneously converted into what American Indian Movement leader Russell Means has termed "national sacrifice *peoples*."[15]

As the dimension of this incipient disaster has dawned on people throughout Canada, and to a lesser extent in the United States, questions have been raised. The response of the Canadian government and of various provincial governments, has been to become increasingly secretive about their water diversion and hydroelectric projects. Largescale, detailed maps of the targeted locales, on which it might be possible to decipher the likely extent of flooding, have been withdrawn from circulation. Even general information and smallscale maps have become quite difficult to obtain in many instances.[16]

Apparently, the government intends to deny the public's right to know what is being done to them and "their" resources until the dams have been erected and the damage done.[17] But, contrary to Ottawa's wishes, or the wishes of the cliques inhabiting a number of corporate board rooms and provincial capitals, such information is the property of the people, and not just of North America. Genocide is, after all, a crime against all humanity.[18] The same is true of ecocide. As will be shown, existing and planned projects in the Canadian northlands entail significant negative implications for the biosphere of the entire planet.

The James Bay Projects

It all began early in the twentieth century, when the "first hydroelectric plants were built at those rare sites where large amounts of electric power could be generated, and where there were nearby cities to which it could be shipped, or the power so abundant and cheap that electricity-consuming industries could be enticed to build new plants near where it was generated."[19] Such endeavors were not especially disruptive of the environment, and remained concentrated in the heavily populated southeastern corridor of Canada. By the late 1930s, however:

> English-speaking capitalists and engineers [had] built the first major powerhouses in [Québec], harnessing the Saint Lawrence River at rapids near Montréal, as well as tributaries of the Saint Lawrence where they tumbled off the central plateau of the Québec-Labrador Peninsula. Montreal Light, Heat and Power Consolidated, for instance, supplied the large and growing market of Montréal with power generated nearby. It grew into one of the largest privately owned electrical utilities in the world and made Irish-born financier Henry Holt exceedingly wealthy. Shawnigan Water and Power Company, launched by American entrepreneurs, generated cheap and abundant electricity at Shawnigan Falls on the Saint Maurice River, a tributary of the Saint Lawrence. The company attracted aluminum refineries, pulp and paper mills, and other electricity-hungry industries to locate in what had been wilderness, and the surplus power flowed through North America's first long distance high-voltage transmission line to Montréal. On the Saguenay River, another tributary of the Saint Lawrence, a subsidiary of the Aluminum Company of America—a subsidiary which later became the multinational firm Alcan—built its own hydroelectric plants to power its aluminum refineries.[20]

Toward the end of World War II, in April 1944, the provincial government began to lay the groundwork for a vast expansion of Québec's hydroelectrical generation by nationalizing Montreal Light, Heat and Power. The resulting public utility, dubbed Hydro-Québec, began a rapid program of building "ever-bigger hydro projects on rivers ever-farther from the centres of population and industry, running transmission lines at ever-higher voltages over ever-greater distances."[21]

The new utility doubled in size, and then doubled again. By 1963, it had become the largest employer in Québec, and a source of pride among the province's large nationalist population. It had also begun to export a considerable portion of its electrical output to the United States and was eyeing schemes of development which transcended provincial boundaries altogether. It was in this context that the Liberal administration of Jean Lesage had swept into power, quickly increasing Québec's debt by $600 million in order to absorb all private utilities remaining within its borders.[22] By 1967,

Québécois watched with pride [as an] army of workers and fleets of trucks [built] a dam—a giant, graceful structure of arched concrete—on the Manicougan River, some 700 kilometers away [from Montréal]. Technology usually advances in small steps, but to transmit power from the distant Manic hydroelectric complex, Hydro-Québec made a large extrapolation; it more than doubled the standard voltage used for high voltage distance power transmission, and developed the first 735-kilovolt transmission line.[23]

Next came the majestic falls of the Churchill River, more than a thousand kilometers distant. Hydro-Québec did not develop Churchill Falls, which is in Labrador, the mainland portion of the province of Newfoundland and Labrador. But Hydro-Québec was its only potential customer. After marathon negotiations, Hydro-Québec signed a deal with Brinco, the company developing the hydroelectric project. In return for securing the loans which paid for construction of the Churchill Falls hydroelectric plant, Hydro-Québec, for sixty-five years, got almost all its enormous output at what turns out to be extremely low rates: about one-fiftieth of those it charged when it sold power in the United States.[24]

With the election of Robert Bourassa as Premier of Québec in April 1970, the pace of development increased exponentially. Having campaigned on a promise of delivering 100,000 new jobs in short order, the new premier demanded an immediate startup of a massive project to dam three major rivers—the Nottaway, Broadback and Rupert—all of them draining into James Bay, an adjunct at the southern extreme of Hudson Bay.[25] Hydro-Québec initially resisted the idea, which it had been exploring since at least as early as 1965, on the basis that anticipated expenses would be too great ($6 billion, at a minimum) and that demand for the quantity of power generation which would result did not yet exist.[26]

Bourassa, however, quickly overcame the financial objection by arranging an initial $300 million loan through David Rockefeller of the Chase Manhattan Bank. Consumption concerns were then partially addressed via assurances from the banker's brother, New York Governor Nelson Rockefeller. The good governor, it should be noted, was in an excellent position to give such guarantees since he served simultaneously as president of Consolidated Edison, which supplies power to New York City.[27] As a result of these maneuverings, a new subsidiary of Hydro-Québec, the Société d'energie de la Baie James (James Bay Energy Corporation) was established in 1971 to move things along.[28]

James Bay I

By the time construction actually began in 1972, the scope of the project had been expanded to include a complex on the La Grande River. It was there that Canadian Bechtel, a subsidiary of the huge Bechtel International construction corporation, was contracted to engage in "phase one" building, ultimately moving enough earth to recreate the Great Pyramid of Cheops eighty times over.[29] In the process, Bechtel also pushed through a network of roads where none had previously existed, installed airports and housing to accommodate 5,000 workers and began generally to "open up" the previously pristine James Bay wilderness to the ravages of "civilization."[30] And, as analyst Sean McCutcheon has pointed out, after such a dynamic is set in motion, it becomes almost impossible to stop: "Once having paid a relatively fixed sum for infrastructure, then the more dams Hydro-Québec builds, the lower the cost per kilowatt generated tends to be. Thus economies of scale encourage building on a large scale."[31]

The developers, however, encountered intense and unexpectedly effective opposition early on from the Mistissini Cree people indigenous to the area, a group the Bourassa administration had casually dismissed as "squalid savages."[32] Beginning in February 1972, a pair of young men, Philip Awashish and Billy Diamond, alerted by newspaper articles summarizing the government's plans, began a village by village campaign to organize a cohesive Indian resistance to the James Bay Project. By April, they had retained James O'Reilly, a specialist in environmental and Canadian Indian law, and filed a motion with the Superior Court of Québec to enjoin all building pending the outcome of an independent environmental impact study they themselves had commissioned (an earlier provincial study had been a sham, extrapolating from studies conducted in connection with the Aswan Dam in Egypt to give the James Bay plan a clean bill of health, and containing virtually no information related to subarctic conditions).[33]

After a number of site visits, a team of fifteen scientists were prepared to take the stand in October and November of the same year and testify that not only would the proposed dams, roads and transmission lines precipitate an environmental catastrophe of the first magnitude, but its impact upon the Cree and more northerly Inuits would be "culturally genocidal."[34] Einar

Skinnarland, who had been a ranking engineer in the Churchill Falls endeavor, testified that he was having "second thoughts" about such projects, "especially [those involving] wholesale river diversions," which he described as being "the most disastrous decisions we can make." He termed the economic and energy rationales underlying construction "baloney."[35] More than sixty native people also took the stand, once their attorney had convinced the court that even under Canadian law they held a range of rights with regard to their lives and land.[36]

> Carefully coached by O'Reilly, speaking for the most part through translators, they explained themselves to the urban world which many of them had never before visited. They talked about fishing, hunting and trapping, about their reverence for the land, about their reliance upon it for what they call country food: for bear, beaver, caribou, moose, rabbit, seal, and whale; for geese and ptarmigan; for Arctic char, pike, salmon, sturgeon, trout, walleye, and whitefish.[37]

The defendants named in the action—Hydro-Québec, the James Bay Development Corporation and the James Bay Energy Corporation—"could not find a scientist in Canada to testify on their behalf and were astounded by the 'emotional fervour' of the opponents of the project." In the end, they were reduced to countering that: A) the Indians and Inuits had "no right" to oppose destruction of their cultures by the dams because their cultures would "inevitably" be destroyed anyway; B) that the threat to both people and environment was being greatly overstated because the initial phases of the project would flood "only" three percent of the affected portion of the province; and C) halting the project would be "inconvenient" to the non-native majority of Québec's population.[38] The court was plainly unconvinced by such arguments.

In November 1973, Superior Court Judge Albert Malouf, who had spent the summer and fall crafting his opinion, ruled in favor of the plaintiffs, holding in effect that Bechtel and other developers were trespassing on native land. He then ordered all construction to be halted until a hearing on a permanent injunction could be held.[39] A week later, the Québec Court of Appeal overturned Malouf's decision, not on the basis of law, but because, it said, the interests of the "greater society" compelled it to do so. The appeals court, however, stipulated that the Crees and Inuits held a right to sue for damages, a circumstance which contained the prospect of dramatically increasing the costs of doing developmental business in the James Bay area.[40]

Fearing a legal impasse, which in turn might give investors in the hydroelectric project cold feet, Bourassa had to settle with the natives. He offered a treaty, the terms of which included, among other things, payment of a hundred million dollars. In March 1974, Cree hunting families were flown out of bush camps to vote on this offer and flatly rejected it. "The Indian lands are not for sale, not for millions and millions of dollars," said Billy Diamond.[41]

Ottawa then entered the fray, providing funding with which to form an entity called the "Grand Council of the Crees of Quebec," composed largely of representatives deemed acceptable to the government; Billy Diamond himself was co-opted into becoming Grand Chief.[42] A comparable group, the Northern Inuit Association of Quebec, headed by Charlie Watts, was created to "represent" that people.[43] The purpose was to negotiate an out-of-court settlement of some sort which would clear the way for a project completion unhampered by extensive litigation or other "obstructionist" acts by the natives. After eight months of intensive negotiation, what was called the "James Bay and Northern Quebec Agreement," strongly opposed by the bulk of grassroots Crees and Inuits, was signed in November 1975.[44]

> The Agreement divided just over one million square kilometers of land—not just the James Bay territory, but all of Québec north of the 49th parallel, that is, two-thirds of the whole province—into three categories. About one percent of the land, in blocks around villages, is essentially Native-owned. The only resource of interest in this land is wildlife; before the Natives could select land in this category, the provincial government subtracted those areas with known hydroelectric or mineral potential, as well as land it would need for roads and power lines. About fourteen percent is shared land; only Natives can hunt, trap, and fish here, but Québec can develop mines, hydroelectric projects, and the like. The remaining 85 percent of the land is public, though certain species of wildlife are reserved for the Natives.[45]

Indian control over schools, health and social services and other government-funded programs was conceded, and members of the Cree Grand Council/Northern Inuit Association were placed on a range of environmental oversight boards. In addition, the Cree communities were awarded a total of $135 million, to be paid over twenty years, as compensation; Inuit communities were awarded $90 million. A minimum annual income was guaranteed to the hunters of both groups, and additional funds were committed to underwrite the relocation of any village or band forced to move because of flooding or related factors. Altogether, the package came to some $500 million in payments and guarantees. In exchange, the native people had only to formally relinquish aboriginal rights to their homeland and, for the first time, accept ultimate federal and provincial authority over their affairs.[46]

The government could well afford its "generosity" in the deal. In attaining native sanction, or an appearance of it, for its consolidation of power over indigenous territory, Canada and Québec had finally placed themselves in a lawful position to renege on any portion of the agreement. All that was juridically required was that one or the other resort to such "domestic" or "internal" expedients as the exercise of "imminent domain" over native property.[47] Meanwhile, construction was proceeding full tilt at not one, but *four* sites along the La Grande.

At its peak, during 1978-79, the project employed more than 22,000 people working nearly around the clock. By the time it was completed in 1984, it had cost approximately $20 billion, fifteen times the per capita expenditure of U.S. citizens in sending the Apollo space craft to the moon, more than three times what the Bourassa administration had originally predicted.[48] The La Grande, third largest river in Québec, as well as two of its main tributaries, the Eastmain and the Caniapiscau, had been effectively "killed," transformed from freeflowing currents into a series of stagnant lakes and ponds incapable of supporting most lifeforms.[49]

Ironically, the huge cost overruns associated with James Bay I were in part responsible for Bourassa's defeat in the 1976 provincial election and René Lévesque's rise to power as leader of the Parti Québécois, just as the project began to show a return.[50] In 1978, Hydro-Québec completed its first interconnection with the New York Power Authority and, by October 1979, was exporting electrical current equivalent to that which could be produced by burning 150,000 barrels of oil per day. By 1985, with James Bay I complete, the utility's aggregate production had outstripped total provincial usage even during the peak mid-winter months of consumption by at least 7,000 kilowatts.[51] The grid capacity for exporting overages of such magnitude to the United States not yet being available, Hydro-Québec began aggressively pursuing the development of electrically-intensive—and environmentally devastating—industries such as aluminum refining in the southern portion of the province itself.

Electrical charges strong enough to erase credit cards, stop digital watches or pull a wrench from someone's hands are what separate pure aluminum from its ore. An aluminum smelter uses as much power as a small city. So much electricity is used in making it that aluminum can be thought of as congealed electricity; the multinational firms who produce aluminum build their billion dollar smelters not where the ore is mined, but where they can be assured of getting abundant, cheap electricity. Hydro-Québec offered rates low enough to induce several of these firms, notably Reynolds and Péchiney, to build or expand smelters in the Saint Lawrence Valley, and to induce other firms to build a magnesium smelter as well as pulp and paper mills. All these plants use enormous quantities of electricity and, since their products are mainly exported, they are, in effect, exporting Québec's electricity.[52]

Even as this was occurring, however, the grid "problem" was being resolved. In March of 1982, Hydro-Québec had entered into another long-term contract to provide greatly increased power to the New York Power Authority and, in 1984, the conduit was completed through which to fulfill its commitment. In 1983, the utility also signed the first of a two-part package with the New England Power Pool, an arrangement which committed it to providing a direct line to New Hampshire. The second part of the agreement, signed in 1985, called for erecting a 2,500 kilometer line, directly from the La Grande generating facility to a point just outside Boston. A separate deal was negotiated in 1984 through which Hydro-Québec would supply year-round power to Vermont.[53] By the early nineties, James Bay was suppling approximately ten percent of the electricity consumed in the northeastern U.S. states.[54]

None of this, of course, was sufficient to offset the huge debt incurred in the process of constructing James Bay I, much less render it profitable for the taxpayers who, in the final analysis, were its real investors.[55] On the other hand, it "proved the viability" of projects on the scale conceived by Bourassa and his colleagues, and appealed to nationalist sensibilities of those who reveled in the idea, pushed hard by provincial and utility propagandists alike, that by becoming the "sole provider" of a "crucial commodity" to Canada's powerful southerly neighbor they had accomplished something "independent" of the Anglocentric government in Ottawa on behalf of Québécois culture.[56] As Ojibwe activist Winona LaDuke, who spent several years at James Bay, puts it:

> These things take on a life of their own. Once you've gone in debt to start one, the only way to stay abreast of the debt service is to go even further in debt, borrowing more and more so you can build more and more and more, no matter what the consequences to land and people. You lose control of your destiny. In this sense, Canada is no different than most Third World countries. It owes its soul to U.S. corporate and financial élites, and so it must sacrifice everything it has, everything it is or claims to be,

to satisfying the demands of those élites. For the power structure of Canada, especially in Quebec, there is no longer a way out of the trap it laid for itself thirty years ago. Canada is now little more than a U.S. satellite, an energy colony.[57]

Hence, even before James Bay I was finished, the groundwork was laid for undertaking James Bay II, a far more ambitious, and therefore more destructive, project.

James Bay II

In 1986, Robert Bourassa returned to power in Québec, bringing with him a plan to generate 12,000 megawatts of power to the northeastern United States by the turn of the century.[58] To this end, he almost immediately oversaw a revision of provincial legal codes in such a way that restrictions limiting sales of electricity to short-term contracts were eliminated. This allowed negotiation of contracts for "firm" provision of large blocks of hydroelectric current over periods ranging from fifteen to thirty years rather than the one-to-five-year packages previously offered.

As a result, by early 1988 Hydro-Québec had signed agreements with Central Maine Power and Vermont Joint Owners, a utilities consortium in those states. A year later, the largest export contract ever, a deal to sell another thousand megawatts to the New York Power Authority every year for twenty-one years, was finalized.[59] Bourassa announced at about the same time that, in order to meet the requirements of these new contracts, as well as to accommodate burgeoning industrialization in the Saint Lawrence Valley, Québec would need to possess a generating capacity of some twelve thousand megawatts by 1998.[60] The amount was nearly triple the total Hydro-Québec could muster, even considering its portion of Labrador's generation at Churchill Falls.

To acquire the necessary generating capacity, Bourassa stated, it would be necessary to move forward with a new three-stage project which made James Bay I seem tiny by comparison. The first stage, to begin immediately, was to construct two additional generating facilities in the existing La Grande River Complex. The second stage, to begin in 1991, would be to build a new complex involving five major dams along the Great Whale River (Grande rivière de la Baleine) about 160 kilometers north of the La Grande; another 4,400 square kilometers would be flooded at a projected construction cost of $12.6 billion. The third stage, by far the most extravagant, was set to begin not later than 1993. It was a return to the original

303

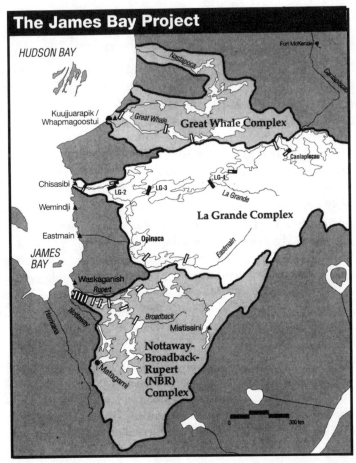

The James Bay Project

HUDSON BAY

Fort McKenzie

Nastapoca

Caniapiscau

Kuujjuarapik /
Whapmagoostui

Great Whale

Great Whale Complex

Caniapiscau

Chisasibi

LG-2 LG-3 LG-4

Wemindji

La Grande

La Grande Complex

Eastmain

Opinaca

JAMES
BAY

Eastmain

Waskaganish

Rupert

Harricana

Nottaway

Broadback

Mistissini

**Nottaway-
Broadback-
Rupert
(NBR)
Complex**

Matagami

0   300 km

concept of diverting the Nottaway and Rupert Rivers into the Broadback
through construction of at least eleven major dams. No predictions were offered as to how much territory would be flooded in this, but construction
costs were projected at $44 billion (U.S.).[61] Together, the three complexes
which would be in place when James Bay II was complete would effect a
"replumbing" of virtually all of northern Québec (see Map I).

For funding, Bourassa had already returned to New York in 1985,
meeting with John Dyson, former president of the New York Power Authority, and James Schlesinger, U.S. Energy Secretary under Jimmy Carter
and at the time a vice president in the Lehman Brothers investment banking
firm. The latter, in exchange for a 1.7 percent commission, organized the

underwriting by an array of U.S. investment firms of an estimated $50 billion in bond issues over ten years in order to guarantee Hydro-Québec's "solvency" during construction of the megaproject.[62]

In 1989, Bourassa informed his public of these astronomical figures through resort to the usual nostrums of "progress": such expenditures would, he claimed, create forty thousand new jobs for Québec and "generate $40 billion in annual revenues by the year 2000."[63] By then, however, both the degree of error embodied in the government's earlier cost, profit and employment estimates, and the actual environmental and cultural consequences of James Bay I, were becoming well-known.[64]

The environmental portrait is indeed bleak, the La Grande Complex having ultimately inundated about 12,000 square kilometers of forest land, including some 83,000 linear kilometers of shoreline.[65] As at Bennett Dam, "the rims of [the La Grande] reservoirs do not, and can not, replace any of the lost wetland habitat; they are broad, lifeless banks of mud, rock and dead trees."[66] In substance, the populations of aquatic mammals along the La Grande, Eastmain and Caniapiscau—beaver, muskrat, snowshoe hare, mink and otter, among others, all of which had still been abundant during the mid-seventies—had been exterminated.[67] Submerged wood and floating debris, as well as silt, have destroyed the water's capacity to oxygenate and have clogged spawning grounds, decimating most varieties of fish.[68]

> Millions of plants—mainly the pioneering, colonizing species, jack pine, willow and alder—have been planted in an effort to reforest zones stripped by construction, as well as to reduce erosion on sections of the banks of dissecated rivers. This has been done, however, in only a fraction of damaged areas, those along the most well-used roads and around the most-visited installations. It will take a long time before the scattered plants reseed the barren spaces between them.[69]

Many Crees assert unequivocally that the damage has been terrible, much worse than anything they were led to expect: "There are fewer and fewer ducks and geese each year; the climate is changing; animals are confused because their migration routes have been disrupted."[70] The last claim was amply born out by a spectacular instance in late September 1984 when an estimated 10,000 caribou drowned during a single attempt by a large herd to cross the newly-transformed Caniapiscau.[71]

Among the native people themselves, the permanent neurological damage caused by eating mercury-contaminated fish has become a substantial problem.[72] Fear of this, along with a steady diminishment in available game animals, has led to a marked alteration in diet: an increase in the sugars and starches indicative of "civilized" consumption. Compounded by the increasingly sedentary way of life imposed upon them by the disappearance of traplines and decreased hunting and fishing, all of which kept them physically active, this has led to a sudden appearance of diabetes, heart disease and obesity, maladies unknown in Cree communities until the 1980s.

As traditional life has quickly disintegrated along the La Grande, social decay has come to be manifested in spiraling rates of alcoholism, glue-sniffing among young people and other forms of substance abuse. Concomitantly, domestic violence, child abandonment and suicide, all of them virtually unheard of among the Cree until recently, have made their ugly appearances.[73] Like the habitat itself, the indigenous society impacted by James Bay I is plainly dying. Moreover, the sort of native participation in environmental oversight guaranteed in the James Bay and Northern Québec Agreement of 1975, participation which might be used to favorably alter such an outcome, has proven illusory.

> Native leaders complain that they have not been able to exercise any significant control over decisions affecting their region. The mechanisms, such as joint committees, which were to give them power to participate actively in economic development of their land—not just as beneficiaries, but as controllers—do not work. For instance, the Crees have not been able to stop the loggers who, with Québec's permission, are now clear-cutting most of the harvestable timber in the southern portion of the Cree homeland (including lands which Hydro-Québec hopes to flood in the Nottaway-Broadback-Rupert complex).[74]

Under these conditions, Cree opposition to James Bay II was instantaneous and far more profound than was the case with the James Bay I proposals of the early seventies. In 1987, they decided to put the Grand Council, originally designed by the government to serve as a vehicle of cooptation, to work in forging a unified resistance to what was planned along the Great Whale and in the "tri-river" area.[75] A young Mistissini named Matthew Coon-Come was elected to head this effort, and even Billy Diamond resumed his "radical" stance long enough to describe the agreement he himself had signed a dozen years earlier as "a trail of broken promises."[76]

The bulk of the Inuits north of the project zone also renounced representation by the Northern Inuit Association and the "leadership" of Charlie Watts, by then a member of the Canadian Senate and called "Megawatts" by his ostensible constituents, and joined the Crees in opposing all further construction.[77] Both peoples flatly refused to negotiate with Hydro-Québec about James Bay II, despite a billion dollar offer introduced by the utility in 1989 if they would endorse an updated version of the 1975 "understanding."[78]

This time they were not alone, a matter reflecting increased sophistication on the part of Coon-Come and others in the ways of attracting non-Indian support in both Canada and the United States, as well as heightened sensitivity among many non-Indians with regard to native and environmental issues. In Montréal, longtime environmental activist Hélène Lajambe and Gordon Edwards, head of the Canadian Coalition for Nuclear Responsibility, utilized the 1989 conference of the Canadian Greens to establish what may have been the first anti-James Bay II organization outside of Indian Country.[79]

This was soon followed by demands for a moratorium on construction by the Coalition for Public Debate on Energy, an organization in Québec City claiming membership of one-sixth of the provincial population. The Arctic Resources Committee and Cultural Survival (Canada), both based in Ottawa, joined in, as did a new entity in Québec, Prudent Residents Opposed To Electrical Cable Transmission (PROTECT).[80] Things developed similarly south of the border:

> In Vermont, for example, Jim Higgins, a social worker who has canoed in the James Bay area, helped found the New England Energy Efficiency Coalition. In New York City, Jeff Wollack of the Solidarity Foundation—which puts royalties earned by the Irish rock group U2 to work in defense of Native peoples—helped found the James Bay Defense Coalition, which comprises some 20 organizations, and began lobbying to cancel the New York Power Authority contracts. Major international environmental organizations became involved. In July 1989 the New York-based National Audubon Society publicized, in Québec, its concerns that water resource developments would harm the large numbers of migratory birds that use the James Bay coast, and called for full, public environmental hearings. The Sierra Club created an umbrella organization, the James Bay and Northern Quebec Task Force [Mouvement au Courant], and channeled funds through a think-tank founded by Hélène Lajambe, the Centre d'analyse des politiques énergétiques, to establish an office in Montréal. The large organizations have not swallowed up the grassroots movement. There are at least 30 anti-James Bay II groups on college campuses throughout New York State, and more elsewhere in the Northeast.[81]

The building of such a serious, multiethnic and multinational opposition movement had almost immediate effect. In January 1989, a group calling itself No Thank Q Hydro-Québec was successful in convincing the Maine Public Utilities Commission to deny approval of the Central Maine Power contract.[82] In New York, the Sierra Club, PROTECT, the Cree Grand Council and other groups joined in a suit against the New York Power Authority, arguing that it is required to ensure that all electricity it imports is generated under conditions conforming to the state's own environmental protection standards.

Although the legal action was unsuccessful, it was helpful in bringing pressure to bear on Governor Mario Cuomo and New York City Mayor David Dinkins. Consequently, in June of 1991, the state announced it was delaying ratification of its 1,000-megawatt contract with Hydro-Québec for one year while the environmental implications of James Bay II were studied by New York's own experts.[83] In Vermont, the most recalcitrant of New England states, opponents also scored a partial victory in October; the state utilities board voted to approve 340 of the 450 megawatts called for in the Vermont Joint Owners contract with Hydro-Québec, but only if the latter could guarantee that none of the electricity imported was generated at James Bay II facilities.[84]

Under these circumstances, Bourassa had little alternative but to postpone the beginning of construction for a year, until the summer of 1992. In April of that year, however, New York canceled its major contract altogether and announced it was reviewing its previous arrangements with Hydro-Québec as well. Left seriously in the lurch—the province was already guaranteeing $30 billion in long-term debt for its utility, which needed another $500 million in short-term funds to stay solvent—Bourassa was forced to announce a second year's postponement.[85] Meanwhile, public opinion polls showed that support in Québec for further development had plummeted for the first time.[86] Coon-Come and other Cree leaders reinforced this decline in support by stating that they would meet any attempt to get building underway with physical resistance; the credibility of their warning was dramatically underscored by an armed confrontation between Mohawks, provincial police and the Canadian army at the town of Oka, near Montréal, in 1990.[87]

In April 1990, responding to rumblings from Bourassa and his energy minister, Lise Bacon, concerning use of the power of imminent domain to force the issue, O'Reilly and other attorneys for the Crees filed suit in the

Queen's Court challenging the provision of the James Bay and Northern Quebec Agreement whereby their clients allegedly relinquished aboriginal rights to their land both north and south of the La Grande. After much governmental maneuvering, including repeated motions by Québec that the case be dismissed, it was finally docketed for April 1992.[88]

Even as these actions were unfolding, in June 1991, Crees prevented an Inuit delegation aligned with Charlie Watts from leaving the Great Whale Airport to participate in a provincially sponsored environmental impact hearing intended to secure some measure of native "ratification" for the James Bay II plan. Instead, the Grand Council filed another suit in Queen's Court, this one to compel the federal review process stipulated in the 1975 agreement, but never actualized. Judge Paul Rouleau upheld the Crees' position in August and, although Québec filed an appeal, federal oversight hearings were again ordered, a process which would have taken as long as two years once it began.[89] By 1996, the province had had enough, and Premier Jacques Parizeau shelved James Bay II indefinately.[90]

Other Water Diversion Schemes

Despite this major (if possibly transient) victory against the Water Plot in northern Québec, the balance of Canada remains in many ways up for grabs. This is readily evidenced by the damming of the Saint John River in New Brunswick, despite serious and sustained "protests by local residents that the benefits of this 'development' were vastly overrated, and that irreparable environmental damage was being done."[91]

There are other illustrations, but the extent of the situation is nowhere better revealed than in an official document of the Ottawa government entitled *Water Diversion Proposals of North America*.[92] Summarized therein are eight major scenarios—the James Bay Projects account for only two—in which Canada's water and/or hydroelectricity are to be exported to the United States. The most grandiose of these, the Great Recycling and Northern Development (GRAND) Project and the North American Water and Power Alliance (NAWAPA), if combined would turn literally the whole subarctic west of Québec into a single, interconnected "plumbing system." The purpose of this would be primarily to provide truly gargantuan quantities of fresh water to the arid and semiarid western plains and southwestern desert regions of the United States. These plans can be traced back to the

Canada-U.S. Free Trade Agreement of 1989; the subsequent North American Free Trade Agreement (NAFTA), which includes Mexico, means that the water will likely reach areas as far south as that country, after the creation of "agribusiness zones" in Sonora and Chihuahua. Secondarily, planners suggest "adjustment" of water levels in the Great Lakes system as a means of flushing industrial pollutants into the Atlantic Ocean, hydroelectric generation (as much as six times that which would be yielded by James Bay I and II combined) and provision of emergency water during droughts to the U.S. midwestern corn and industrial belts. Each of these gigantic projects is worthy of being examined in turn.

The GRAND Project

The GRAND Project, which is concentrated in northern Ontario, calls for construction of some 160 kilometers of dikes across James Bay to create a fresh water reservoir the size of Lake Superior. The water would be drawn off through the major rivers west of the bay—the Moose, Ogoki, Albany, Kenogami, Ramskau, Attawapiskat and Skwaw—each of which would be extensively dammed in order to control water flow and afford a "fringe benefit" of allowing hydroelectric generation. To the north, along Ontario's portion of Hudson Bay's western shore, a comparable damming of major rivers—the Winisk, Severn, Sachigo and Duck—would occur. Canals would join the northern complex to its southern counterpart by traversing the distance between Trout Lake and the Attawapiskat. From there, the joint flow would be diverted into Lake Nipigon and thence into Lake Superior.

The scope of the hydrological (re)engineering involved encompasses *all* of northern Ontario (see Map II). A minimum of fifty major dams, including at least three "megadams," are called for if the scheme is to work. More than 250 kilometers of lined canal will be needed, not to mention thousands of kilometers of all-weather road, airports, housing for as many as 100,000 workers, scores of pumping facilities, hydroelectric plants and so on. No cost estimates of what would be required to complete the GRAND Project have been released, but a conservative projection might be twice the aggregate expenditure calculated for both James Bay Projects, or about $150 billion (U.S.). Moreover, little has been said with regard to what the environmental consequences of such an extravagant rearrangement of the natural order might be, although, where James Bay I destroyed the ecology of an area approximately the size of West Germany, the GRAND Project would

THE WATER PLOT IN NORTHERN ONTARIO

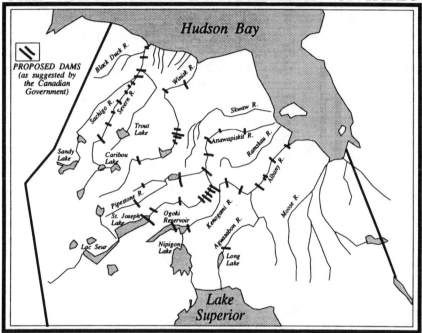

PROPOSED DAMS
(as suggested by
the Canadian
Government)

Hudson Bay

Black Duck R.
Winisk R.
Sachigo R.
Severn R.
Skwaw R.
Trout Lake
Attawapiskit R.
Ramskau R.
Sandy Lake
Caribou Lake
Albany R.
Pipestone R.
Moose R.
St. Joseph Lake
Ogoki Reservoir
Kenogami R.
Aquasabon R.
Lac Seur
Nipigon Lake
Long Lake
Lake Superior

flood about three times as much territory (at a minimum). The implications for the area's indigenous Ojibwe, Waswanipi Cree and Inuit populations are stark.[93]

Actually, the GRAND concept is not new. To the contrary, its origins may be discovered in some of the earliest largescale water projects in Canada. North of Lake Superior, two diversions from the James Bay watershed into the Great Lakes were carried out during World War II. The headwaters of the Ogoki River were converted into a lake and now flow into Ombabika Bay on Lake Nipagon. The Long Lake watershed, which formerly drained north via the Kenogami River, was diverted into Lake Superior through the Aquasaubon River at Terrace Bay. The Ogoki diversion was implemented in 1940 to permit Ontario Hydro to increase the capacity of its Niagara River generating plants to meet wartime demand. The purpose of the Long Lake diversion was to supply power to the U.S.-owned Kimberly-Clark paper mill at Terrace Bay. At the time of these diversions, the United States was not yet at war and refused to reduce the quantity of hydro power Ottawa had committed to supply, or to allow Canada to withdraw more than its prewar "share" of Niagara River water.[94]

Serious planning for realization of something along the lines of the present GRAND Project can be traced back at least a quarter-century, to October 1965, when, "the Prime Minister of Canada and the Premier of Ontario announced that the governments of Canada and Ontario had agreed to undertake a series of coordinated studies on Ontario's northern water resources and related economic developments. Most of the work is being done in five river basins draining to Hudson Bay and James Bay. These are the Severn, Winisk, Attawapiskat, Albany and Moose River Basins."[95]

A coordinating committee was then formed for purposes of liaison and oversight of investigations to be carried out by agencies of the two governments with "respect to waters draining into James Bay and Hudson Bay in Ontario, to assess the quantity and quality of water resources for all purposes; to determine present and future requirements for such waters; and to assess alternative possibilities for utilization of such waters locally or elsewhere through diversion."[96]

Thereafter, the "Federal Surveys and Mapping Branch...completed preliminary mapping of a possible diversion route between the Attawapiskat and Albany Rivers... A potential diversion route between Winisk Lake and the Attawapiskat River were [sic] also mapped by the [Engineering] Division."[97] In the process:

> Approximately four miles of leveling was carried out south of the Pipestone River to the north boundary of the Ogoki River and interconnecting structure sites along the Aguta glacial moraine. These sites were investigated in 1967 in connection with an engineering study of a scheme for using the Aguta Moraine as a diversion barrier. A topographic survey by the transit-stadia method was completed for a dam site on the Ogoki River at Whiteclay Lake to investigate the feasibility of providing additional storage required to regulate increased diversion flow to the Great Lakes. In addition, work described below was carried out in connection with engineering feasibility studies of power development on the Albany River from streams further north.[98]

Federal and provincial agencies and private consulting engineering firms known to be actively involved in the Ontario development project are known to include Canada's Department of Mines, Energy and Resources (Inland Waters Branch); Geological Survey of Canada (Policy and Planning Branch); Canada Department of Transport (Meteorology Branch); Water

Survey of Canada (Federal Surveys and Mapping Branch); Federal Engineering Division; Ontario Water Resources Commission (Division of Water Resources, Hydrologic Branch and Surveys and Projects Branch); Ontario Department of Economics (Applied Economics Branch); Ontario Department of the Treasury (Economic Planning Branch); Ontario Department of Lands and Forests; Ontario Department of Mines; Ontario Hydro-Electric Power Commission; Gibb, Underwood and McClellan (a U.S. engineering firm); James F. McLaren (a U.S. engineer); J. W. Livvy (an Idaho engineer with a branch office in Vancouver, B.C.); J. D. Mollard (a Regina engineer); and Ripley, Klohn and Leonoff (a Winnipeg engineering firm).[99] The U.S. Army Corps of Engineers has also been directly involved at least once, conducting an "ice survey" during the period 1967-69.[100]

These agencies, particularly the branches of the Water Resources Commission and Energy, Mines and Resources Department, have steadily collected data on stream flow, snow course, rainfall, water levels, chemical analyses of water, bathymetric contours of lakes and geological mapping. They have also conducted considerable core inspection and hydraulic testing of bore holes drilled along the Albany River, have levelled large areas, and have conducted feasibility studies of alternative diversion routes to those mentioned in the government documents quoted above, and have even gone to the lengths of making anthropological/sociological studies of the likely effects of development upon the region's native peoples.[101]

The initial field work in Ontario appears to have begun in 1966, and to have accelerated steadily after 1969. Construction itself had actually begun somewhat earlier, and with predictable results.

> In 1958, hydro dams flooded almost 1,600 hectares of the Whitedog reserve, damaging traplines at Whitedog and the nearby Grassy Narrows reserve in northern Ontario. Then, from 1962 to 1970, a pulp mill pumped 9,000 kilograms of mercury into the English-Wabigoon River system, poisoning the fish. Dozens of Ojibways at Grassy Narrows who relied on fish as their staple diet, ended up with dangerous levels of mercury in their blood and symptoms of mercury poisoning such as tremors, tunnel vision, impaired hearing, and slow reflexes. For years, politicians assured the Indians that their fears were exaggerated. The provincial government suppressed the results of the mercury tests. Warning signs were pulled down. But the Indians were eventually forced to stop fishing, and their commercial fishery was wiped out.[102]

"Alcoholism and crime, which had been minor problems at Grassy Narrows in the early 1960s, soon reached epidemic proportions," observes analyst Geoffrey York. "By the late 1970s, a survey found that two-thirds of the adults on the reserve were heavy drinkers, and half of the children in Grade 2 and Grade 3 sere sniffing gasoline regularly. The suicide rate soared, and three-quarters of all deaths were caused by violence. Not until 1985 were the Ojibways compensated for the destruction of their way of life. The owners of the pulp mill agreed to pay $11.75 million in [damages], while the federal and provincial governments provided $4.92 million, and Ontario Hydro gave $1.5 million to the Whitedog band to compensate for the flooding." [103] But by then it was far too late.

NAWAPA

NAWAPA, once described by *Newsweek* magazine as "the greatest, most colossal, stupendous, supersplendificent public works project in history,"[104] was conceived by the Ralph M. Parsons engineering firm during the 1960s "to divert 36 trillion gallons of water [per year] from the Yukon River in Alaska [through the Great Bear and Great Slave Lakes southward] to thirty-three states, several Canadian provinces, and northern Mexico."[105] Under its provisions, the Yukon River, Rocky Mountain Trench, Peace River, Great Bear, Great Slave and Lesser Slave Lakes, Athabasca River, North Saskatchewan River, Fraser River, Nelson River, Qu'Appelle River, Columbia River and Lake Winnipeg, as well as many tributaries, would all be tied together. From Lake Winnipeg, a portion of the proceeds would be channeled into the western end of Lake Superior, the remainder into the dry zone of the United States west of the Mississippi River (see Map III).

As with the GRAND Project, there are signs that motions are being made toward fulfillment of the NAWAPA "vision." NAWAPA takes as its focus the western provinces of British Columbia, Saskatchewan, Alberta, Manitoba, the Yukon and the Northwest Territories. Beginning in British Columbia, where horror stories concerning the effects of the W.A.C. Bennett Dam and its attendant Columbia River Treaty are well known, a Canadian Broadcasting Corporation (CBC) television program aired on the night of January 18, 1972, revealed plans to dam the Fraser River.[106] Nothing further was heard on the matter, and it was all but forgotten. This was a mistake.

> A second dam, completed at Moran Canyon on the Fraser River in 1976, backed up water into a 170 mile "lake." Since then, another score of dams have been built along the Columbia River, and twenty-five more along the Fraser. Another thirteen have

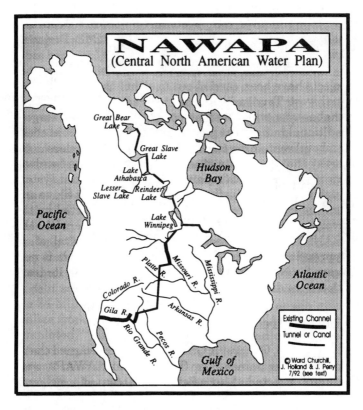

NAWAPA
(Central North American Water Plan)

Great Bear Lake

Great Slave Lake

Lake Athabasca

Lesser Slave Lake / Reindeer Lake

Lake Winnipeg

Hudson Bay

Pacific Ocean

Platte R.
Missouri R.
Mississippi R.
Colorado R.
Gila R.
Arkansas R.
Rio Grande R.
Pecos R.

Atlantic Ocean

Gulf of Mexico

Existing Channel
Tunnel or Canal

© Ward Churchill, J. Holland & J. Perry 7/92 (see text)

been built along the Thompson River, and as many as thirty more are are either in progress or planned in the immediate future.[107]

The consequences for native people were nothing less than catastrophic, replicating in all essential respects the experience of the Sekani in northern B.C. when a dozen of their villages were submerged under eighty meters of water behind the Bennett Dam.

> The federal government transferred the Sekani reserve to the province... Although the province made arrangements to help the white farmers who would be affected by the flooding, it ignored the 125 families of the Sekani band... The Sekani houses were burned down, the villages bulldozed, and most of the Sekani were dumped onto the territory of another Indian band. In the late 1960s, after several years of misery, the [Sekanis] migrated back to Ingenaki Point, the only remaining habitable corner of their homeland. Because they did not officially have a reserve, the federal government gave them virtually nothing. They lived in one-room shacks made of logs salvaged

from the hydro reservoir and carried buckets of water up a steep hill from the reservoir. The water soon became contaminated with salmonella.[108]

It was not until 1987 that, under pressure from the media, a provincial cabinet minister finally consented to even visit Ingenika Point. Forced to admit that the living conditions there were—and had been for twenty years—the "worst he'd ever seen in British Columbia," he arranged a morsel of compensation: the province underwrote repairs on the makeshift houses and paid for the drilling of a deepwater well.[109]

To the east, in the Prairie Provinces, the *Winnipeg Free Press* has reported that Manitoba Hydro intends to regulate water levels in Lake Winnipeg as part of its Nelson River Power Development Project, before going ahead with a planned diversion of South Indian Lake. According to CBC filmmaker Dick Bocking, some water will be diverted directly to the United States, and the Kettle Lake Dam and South Indian Lake hydro plant will, in combination, produce far more electricity than can possibly be used by Winnipeg. Barring construction of environmentally devastating industries such as the aluminium smelters installed in Québec—and no such plans have been announced—the excess hydroelectric output is plainly slated for export southward. Because of the expense of the Manitoba endeavor, comparable diversions in Alberta and Saskatchewan—part of the so-called PRIME Project—have been postponed, but not abandoned.[110]

As in Ontario and Québec, the impacts of such developments upon native people are already starkly apparent in Manitoba. At Moose Lake and Chemawawin, in the lush Saskatchewan River Delta, once considered to be among the most peaceful and self-sufficient reserves in Canada, Manitoba Hydro's massive Grand Rapids Dam—it required eighty million kilos of concrete, stands twenty meters high and includes dikes extending a dozen kilometers in each direction to create the fourth largest lake in the entire province (2,200 square kilometers of the delta were flooded)—has wrought havoc.[111]

At Moose Lake, whose residents received a total of only $10,000 in compensation, "cattle and muskrat ranches were wiped out, the crops and gardens were destroyed, and the supply of moose fell sharply."[112] Crime and alcoholism, both of which had been virtually nonexistant on the reserve in 1960, began to rise dramatically after the flooding occurred in 1964. Elias Martin, a drug and alcoholism counselor for the band estimated that upwards of ninety percent of all adults were addicted to one or both by 1978, a symptom of their compulsion to anesthetize themselves against the "stress, anxiety and fear" attending the loss of their way of life and consequent destitution.[113] "The impact of the flooding was even worse among the Cree people at Chemewawin, who lived nearby on the shores of Cedar Lake," observes Geoffrey York.[114]

> Before the Grand Rapids hydro dam was built, they enjoyed the same abundant resources as the Moose Lake band and had a prosperous economy of hunting, trapping and fishing. Alcohol abuse was rare and crime was virtually unknown. "There are no apparent community problems," a provincial official reported in 1963. Another official said that the "thriving economy" was "the most striking aspect" of the reserve at Cedar Lake... But all that was radically altered by the Grand Rapids hydro project and flooding. In the end, nearly the whole reserve disappeared under water, and the Cree were forced to relocate to a vastly inferior site [Easterville, known as "The Rockpile"] about sixty kilometers southeast, on the opposite shore of Cedar Lake... The federal government made no effort to help the band. Using its powers under the Indian Act, the government simply expropriated the Chemawawin reserve and transferred the land to the province.[115]

As a result of the flooding, Cedar Lake was shortly choked with logs and debris, and the water level often fluctuated so that it became dangerous to fish on the lake. The result was a 93 percent reduction in the Chemawawins' annual fish harvest, while even the remnant was rendered dubious by mercury contamination. Their hunting and trapping economies also collapsed as moose and furbearing animals disappeared. To top things off, it was shortly discovered that untreated sewage at Easterville had seriously contaminated the band's supply of potable water.[116]

By 1966—even as Manitoba Hydro publicly described the relocation as a "huge success"—a federal study quietly concluded that it constituted a "social disaster," noting that the Crees were "desperate," alcohol abuse was spreading rapidly, vandalism had become commonplace and that children were often neglected for the first time in the band's history. A decade and a half later, it was reported that some ninety percent of all Chemawawins were subsisting on welfare and that "mental depression" had become an endemic condition on the reserve. In 1986, E.E. Hobbs and Associates, a consulting firm retained to assess the impact of the Grand Rapids project upon the Indians, concluded that there was "certainly no evidence that the Chemewawin [had] recovered from the trauma of their move, the loss of their treaty lands and their resource base."[117]

> Whatever the wider benefits the Grand Rapids hydro project may have brought for Manitoba, for the Chemawawin Cree it has meant the destruction of their way of life.

317

Today, the band has no viable economic base, few prospects for the future, a wide range of accelerating social problems and a diminished level of confidence and self-esteem, the inevitable consequence of the decline in the band's fortunes since the flooding. [118]

Sometimes, the results have been even more drastic. "In the 1980s, the Cree bands at Cross Lake and Norway House in northern Manitoba," for example, "were hit by suicide epidemics after their traditional economy of hunting and fishing was severely damaged by hydro flooding. Because of the hydro projects, water levels in some northern Manitoba lakes and rivers have fluctuated wildly, dropping by as much as 2.5 meters every summer. Weeds, rocks, and mud flats made it almost impossible for the Cree to continue fishing. Hunting and trapping became difficult because thousands of animals were drowned."[119]

[With their] pride and self-reliance stripped away…[f]rom 1985 to 1987, there were 126 suicide attempts at Cross Lake, and 20 band members killed themselves in one eight-month period… At the same time, there were as many as fifteen suicide attempts each month by the Cree at Norway House [as] for the first time in centuries, band members realized there is no point in teaching their children the traditions of hunting and fishing. "I cannot pass on what was passed on to me, I can't pass it on to my kids and they won't be able to pass it on to their kids," one band member said.[120]

There can be no question that not only corporate but governmental officials were fully aware of the genocidal implications of the hydro projects before undertaking them. In 1960, it was predicted in a study made by Indian Affairs Canada that construction of the Grand Rapids Dam would precipitate the economic collapse of the Chemawawin and Moose Lake bands almost as fast as it was completed. Provincial officials were also predicting that the dam's impact on the indigenous economy would, "no doubt, be greater than any compensation."[121]

Later, a senior provincial official admitted that he had seen a tragedy brewing as early as 1962, two years before the flooding. An environmental impact study, commissioned by the Manitoba government, confirmed that the flooding would cause serious damage—but its results were kept secret. In a confidential memo, a federal official warned Ottawa that "many of the resources from which the [native] people derived a livelihood…will be lost or seriously depleted for a number of years and in some cases, possibly forever."[122]

No recommendations were forthcoming in any of these documents as to how such culturally destructive and potentially lethal impacts might be offset or even significantly mitigated. Moreover, even as Ottawa was transfer-ring title to the reserves for purposes of moving the project forward, all par-ties sought to forestall "controversy" by directly and deliberately misleading the incipient victims as to the anticipated results. In a letter written in 1964, for instance, Manitoba Premier Duff Roblin assured the anxious Crees that they would "in fact be able to earn as good a living as before and, we hope, a better living."[123]

Small wonder, given the nature and magnitude of such betrayals, that the "suicide epidemics at Cross Lake and Norway House were just two examples of the frightening trend toward self-annihilation in native commu-nities... A study of Manitoba suicides from 1971 to 1982 found that the suicide rate for native teenagers was eleven times higher than the rate among white teenagers. According the the study, native males were 'by far the highest risk group' in Manitoba."[124]

> For Canada as a whole, the suicide rate for Indians under the age of twenty-five is about six times higher than the rate for non-natives in the same age group. One-third of all suicides. Each year, Indians lose almost five thousand potential years of life because of suicide. As shocking as these figures are, they may be underestimates. Violent deaths account for 36 percent of all Indian deaths, and a large portion of these are believed to be unreported suicides. Often an apparent suicide is officially recorded as an accident because the victim was intoxicated and the coroner is reluctant to record that the victim took his own life. Many drownings and car crashes may also be hidden suicides. Researchers believe the true rate of Indian suicides may be twelve times the national average.[125]

In fact, experts like University of Lethbridge sociologist Menno Boldt contend that the suicide rate among Canadian Indians may well be the highest of any group in the world. Boldt is joined by University of Manitoba professor Michael Moffat, who argues that the destruction of their traditional culture combines with the absense of any viable replacement in-duces an endemic sense of despair among aboriginal youth.[126] "It's one thing to say they should find meaning in their lives by struggling to reclaim their homelands and traditions," observes veteran Ojibwe activist Terrance Nelson, "but how are they supposed to do that when the homeland itself is under eighty meters of water? What we're talking about here is permanent destruction, both of the environment and of ways of life that go with it, a combination of ecocide and genocide."[127]

It is true that, to date, no major water diversion projects have been carried out in either the Yukon or the Northwest Territories, home to traditional Inuits and Dene, who together comprise one of the largest remaining traditional indigenous groups (by territory, if not by sheer numbers) on the planet. It is nonetheless noteworthy that feasibility studies on damming the headwaters of the Yukon River, and assembly of a canal system which would carry its fluids into first the Great Slave and then the Great Bear Lakes, *have* been conducted by the government and assorted contractors.[128] As with the GRAND Project, it seems that only the arrival of an "appropriate climate" of public opinion in Canada is necessary for NAWAPA to begin this final phase of its transition from drawing board to reality.

The Future of the North is Ours

In 1966, General A. G. L. McNaughton warned that if plans such as James Bay, GRAND and NAWAPA were actually effected, "Jurisdiction and control…although nominally international, would in reality be dominated by [the United States, which] would thereby acquire a formidable vested interest in the national waters of Canada. It is obvious that if we make a bargain to divert water to the United States, we cannot ever discontinue or we shall face force to compel compliance." He therefore concluded that ideas like those underlying each of the megaprojects represented "a monstrous concept, a diabolical thesis."[129]

Indeed, even without use of its military power, the United States has proven itself increasingly able to impose its will upon Canada as water diversion has increased since 1970. As has been noted, Québec has been forced to saddle itself with an astronomical debt load, much of it secretively assumed and virtually all of it held by Wall Street firms, since beginning its pursuit of "economic independence" at James Bay. This, in turn, has compelled provincial authorities to solicit an influx of "productive facilities" on terms favorable to the foreign corporations holding the reigns rather than to Canada; "by such deals, Québec is locking itself into an almost Third World condition as a supplier of subsidized energy to an enormous, global, extractive industry."[130]

During the same year that General McNaughton issued his warning, the Parsons Company of Los Angeles, author of the NAWAPA plan, announced that Canada would need to invest a minimum of $40 billion as "its part" in funding the project. It was noted that it would be necessary to borrow virtually all of this sum in the United States at a nominal interest rate of eight percent, or $3.2 billion per year in debt service. The latter figure should be compared to the four billion dollars per year Parsons estimated Canada might realize from export of hydroelectricity if NAWAPA were completed.[131] And, of course, inflation and other factors have conspired to drive the figure up by at least 400 percent over the subsequent quarter-century; the minimum price tag which could now be associated with just the "Canadian portion" of NAWAPA is somewhere around $160 billion, with annual debt service of about $14 billion.[132]

Between James Bay, the GRAND Project and NAWAPA, an array of "development interests" are moving along with plans which would incumber the Canadian public with about a third of a *trillion* dollars in debt, nearly $30 billion yearly in interest alone. This, in the context of a seriously deteriorating world economy and with the bulk of the profits flowing, one way or the other, to points south of the U.S./Canadian border.[133] Yet both Ottawa and the provincial régimes appear to be proceeding, full speed ahead, despite a range of consequences which should long since have become obvious to anyone who cared to examine the matter; history has yet to offer a single instance in which the patterns of debt assumption and external investment which have emerged in Canada turned out to have benefitted the "host" country, either economically or in terms of sociopolitical self-determination.[134]

Environmentally, the prospects are even worse. Jan Beyea of the Audubon Society has compared James Bay to the Brazilian rainforest in terms of its importance to the ecological equilibrium of the world, placing the James Bay Projects in a perspective never hinted at by developers.[135]

> Québec is not alone in disturbing this maritime ecosystem. Manitoba and Ontario, the provinces which share the western coasts of James Bay and Hudson Bay, are planning hydroelectric projects which will amplify the impacts of James Bay II. When the dams are built, far more fresh water will flow into James Bay in the winter than it did before, and far less in the spring. How will this affect the algae that grow under ice in the winter and bloom in the spring, and that form one of the bottom layers of a food pyramid whose upper layers include birds, seals, beluga [whales], and humans? How will the changes in salinity affect the dense beds of eelgrass on which the Brant geese feed, and which seem to require brackish conditions to flourish? Can the food-producing processes in this linked system of marshes, each with its own mix of plants and its own pattern of varying salinity over the year, adapt to alterations in the seasonal rhythm with which rivers have been pouring fresh water into salt water ever since the

last Ice Age? How will the mercury injected into this ecosystem affect its creatures? Will ocean currents carry repercussions of disruptions in James Bay to Hudson Straight, the channel connecting Hudson Bay to the Atlantic, one of the most productive areas of the Arctic; will effects be felt to the south, on the Grand Banks of Newfoundland?[136]

And what of the ecologies of the river basins and intervening territory across the entire subarctic expanse of northern Canada? Shall they all go the way of the La Grande? If so, then what? As the matter has been framed elsewhere, "What must be understood is that the Canadian North—like the Antarctic, the Amazon Basin in Brazil, and a few other portions of the globe—is absolutely essential to ecological survival. If it is destroyed, eventually everything else will be destroyed. We are all running out of 'alternatives' and places to hide from the grim reality which now stalks us, regardless of where and how we live."[137] In a very real sense, then, "The Crees [and other native peoples resisting the water plot] are not just defending their own cultures and environment; both in [Canada] and in the United States they and their advisers are challenging current energy and economic policies, and are proposing alternatives."[138]

In effect, by struggling to defend themselves against the ravages of genocide and ecocide, the indigenous peoples of the northlands have taken a position which could ultimately save their neighbouring colonizers from themselves being colonized by a more powerful neighbor. In doing so, they have taken the sole position which stands to save the vital subarctic ecology for all humanity. Theirs is thus a truly human position, perhaps the *only* genuinely human position to have emerged from the whole context of controversy and contention surrounding the Water Plot, and others are slowly but steadily waking up to the fact.

Non-Indians are at last discovering the truth Indians have known, insights about the relationship of humans and nature that native people have been trying to share all along.[139] This is why the Crees and others have "gained many supporters, on both sides of the border and around the world. The fundamental difference between the current dispute and that of twenty years ago is the extent to which thoughts and feelings that were dismissed a generation ago as the motley notions of counterculture cranks are now credible. Environmental concerns have moved from the margin towards the mainstream of politics. So, too, has sympathy with Native peoples."[140] In this new and evolving confluence of interest and understanding between Indian and non-Indian lie the seeds, not only of the demise of the Water Plot itself, but of many comparable enterprises underway in this "postmodern" age.

Herein, perhaps, lies the silver lining to the Water Plot's menacing cloud. In catalyzing an apprehension of the natural order antithetical to its own existence, it may well transcend itself, laying the groundwork for a widespread negation of the beliefs, attitudes and outlooks which ushered it into being in the first place. If so, it will have turned out to be a blessing rather than a curse, the cornerstone of a sustainable and radically better future not only for ourselves, but for all who come after us.

Notes

1. This is not to say that everything is "okay" in the United States. For a succinct treatment of the relevant issues in the "Lower Forty-Eight," see Daniel McCool's *Command of the Waters: Iron Triangles, Federal Water Development, and Indian Water* (Berkeley: University of California Press, 1987).

2. See, e.g., Adrian Tanner, *Bringing Home Animals: Religious Ideology and Mode of Production Among Mistassini Cree Hunters* (Memorial University of Newfoundland: Institute of Social and Economic Research, No. 23, 1979).

3. This is brought out clearly in Morris Zaslow's *The Northward Expansion of Canada, 1914-1967* (Toronto: McClelland and Stewart, 1988).

4. James VanStone, "Changing Patterns of Indian Trapping in the Canadian Subarctic," in William C. Wonders, ed., *Canada's Changing North* (Toronto: McClelland and Stewart, 1976) pp. 170-86.

5. There are a number of good studies which reach such conclusions, e.g., Peter Gorrie's "The James Bay Power Project," *Canadian Geographic*, Feb/Mar 1990, pp. 21-31; the relevant portions of Harold Cardinal's *The Unjust Society: The Tragedy of Canada's Indians* (Edmonton: Hurtig, 1969).

6. Robert Hecky, "Methylmercury Contamination in Northern Canada," *Northern Perspectives*, Oct. 1978, pp. 8-9. Also see George Hutchenson and Dick Wallace, *Grassy Narrows* (Toronto: Van Nostrand Reinhold, 1977). That the problem continues is readily evidenced in an article, "Indians Eating Contaminated Fish," published in the *Globe and Mail* on Nov. 5, 1990.

7. For a detailed elaboration of the way in which the term "genocide" is used herein, see the essay entitled "Defining the Unthinkable: Towards a Viable Understanding of Genocide," in my *A Little Matter of Genocide: Holocaust and Denial in the Americas, 1492 to the Present* (San Francisco: City Lights, 1997) pp. 399-444. On "ecocide," see Barry Weinberg, *Ecocide in Indochina: The Ecology of War* (San Francisco: Canfield Press, 1970).

8. Such considerations are covered in Zaslow, *Northward Expansion*, op. cit.

9. These and related issues are covered in Kenneth S. Coats and William K. Morrison, eds., *For Purposes of Dominion* (Toronto: Captus University, 1989).

10. Robert Paige, *Northern Development: The Canadian Dilemma* (Toronto: McClelland and Stewart, 1986). Also see William F. Sinclair, *Native Self-Reliance Through Resource Development* (Vancouver: Hemlock, 1984).

11. A good overview of the scale on which mineral resources are at issue in the subarctic may be found in Robert Davis and Mark Zannis, *The Genocide Machine in Canada: The Pacification of the North* (Montréal: Black Rose Books, 1973). Mining, of course, carries with it its own set of environmental problems, as well as constraints against the bona fide expression of indigenous sovereignty; see J. Rick Ponting, ed., *Arduous Journey: Canadian Indians and Decolonization* (Toronto: McClelland and Stewart, 1986). Also see "Geographies of Sacrifice," in this volume.

12. Paige, *Northern Development*, op. cit.

13. Sinclair, *Native Self-Reliance*, op. cit.

14. On the negative effects of the Bennett Dam, see Boyce Richardson, *Strangers Devour the Land: The Cree Hunters of the James Bay Area Versus Premier Bourassa and the James Bay Development Corporation* (Post Mills, VT: Chelsea Green, 1991) p. 148.

15. The term "national sacrifice area" accrues from Thadis Box, et al., *Rehabilitation Potential for Western Coal Lands* (Cambridge, MA: Ballinger Publishing Co., 1974). The book is the published version of a study commissioned by the National Academy of Science and submitted to the Nixon administration for potential implementation as federal policy in 1972. At the 1980 Black Hills International Survival Gathering, AIM leader Russell Means spelled out the implications of the concept by linking it to the sacrifice of entire peoples; see his "The Same Old Song," in my *Marxism and Native Americans* (Boston: South End Press, 1983) p. 25.

16. Damn the Dams Campaign and the Institute for Natural Progress, "The Water Plot: Hydrological Rape in Northern Canada," in my *Critical Issues in Native North America*, (Copenhagen: International Work Group on Indigenous, 1989) pp. 137-51.

17. This sort of governmental and corporate secrecy has long been endemic to northern Canadian water development initiatives in general; Boyce Richardson, *James Bay: The Plot to Drown the Northern*

Woods (San Francisco: Sierra Club Books, 1972).

18. Convention on Prevention and Punishment of the Crime of Genocide (U.S.T, T.I.A.S. No.____, 78 U.N.T.S. 277, Dec. 9, 1948); text contained in Ian Brownlie, ed., *Basic Documents on Human Rights* (Oxford: Clarendon, 1981) pp. 31-4.

19. Sean McCutcheon, *Electric Rivers: The Story of the James Bay Project* (Montréal: Black Rose Books, 1991) p. 15.

20. Ibid.

21. Ibid., p. 16. The impetus underlying this sort of rampant "infrastructural" expansion is detailed very well in Thomas P. Hughs, *Networks of Power: Electrification in Western Society, 1880-1930* (Baltimore: Johns Hopkins University Press, 1923).

22. See Graham Frasier, *PQ: René Lévesque and the Parti Québécois in Power* (Toronto: Macmillan, 1984); Jane Jacobs, *The Question of Separatism: Quebec and the Struggle Over Sovereignty* (New York: Random House, 1980).

23. McCutcheon, *Electric Rivers*, op. cit., p. 16. The Manicougan and Churchill Falls projects are covered in Daniel Deudney, *Rivers of Energy: The Hydroelectric Potential* (New York: Worldwatch Paper 44, June 1981).

24. Ibid., p. 17. Also see Philip Smith, *Brinco: The Story of Churchill Falls* (Toronto: McClelland and Stewart, 1975).

25. L. Ian McDonald, *From Bourassa to Bourassa: A Pivotal Decade in Canadian History* (Montréal: Harvest House, 1984). Bourassa, who opposed separatism, won against the Parti Québécois, which had taken to advocating nuclear rather than hydroelectric development; Roger Lecasse, *Baie James: une épopée* (Québec: Libre Expression, 1983) p. 129.

26. Ibid., p. 112-4. Also see Philippe Faucher and Johannes Bergeron, *Hydro-Québec: las société d l'heure de pointe* (Montréal: Les Presses del'Université de Montréal, 1986).

27. Alain Chanlat, with André Bolduc and Daniel Larouche, *Gestion et culture d'enterprise: le cheminement d'Hydro-Québec* (Québec: Québec/Amérique, 1984).

28. Société d'energie de la Baie James, *Le Complexe hydroélectrique de la Grande Rivière: réalisation de la première phase* (Québec: Les Éditions de la Chenelière, 1987).

29. The utility is extraordinarily proud of this feat; Hydro-Québec, *James Bay: Development, Environment and the Native People of Québec* (Montréal: Hydro-Québec, 1984) p. 22.

30. Hydro-Québec, *James Bay and the Environment: Hydro-Québec Development Plan, 1989-1991— Horizon 1998* (Montréal: Hydro-Québec, 1989) p. 3.

31. McCutcheon, *Electric Rivers*, op. cit., p. 35.

32. This view of native people is repeatedly expressed in so many words by Bourassa in his *James Bay* (Montréal: Harvest House, 1973). Such sentiments were also expressed by Gilles Massé, Minister of Natural Resources for Québec, in the *Montréal Gazette* (Nov. 8, 1972), and are are well matched to those of James Bay Energy Corporation CEO Robert Boyd, quoted in McCutcheon (*Electric Rivers*, op. cit., p. 45): "I know the Crees well... They're all lazy."

33. The organizing is covered in Richardson's *Strangers Devour the Land*, op. cit.

34. The team's findings were self-published by John and Gillian Spence as *Ecological Considerations of the James Bay Project* (Montréal, 1972). Also see Alan Penn's "Development of James Bay: The Role of Environmental Assessment in Determining the Legal Rights to an Interlocutory Injunction," *Journal of the Fisheries Research Board of Canada*, No. 32, 1975, pp. 136-60.

35. Quoted in McCutcheon, *Electric Rivers*, op. cit., pp. 50-1.

36. O'Reilly's legal argument was based primarily on the Indian Act, the provisions of which had not before really been applied to the indigenous peoples of the Hudson Bay region; Indian Affairs Canada, *Indian Acts and Amendments, 1868-1950* (Ottawa: Research Branch: Indian and Northern Affairs Ministry of Canada, 1981). Also see *Ancestral Lands, Alien Laws: Judicial Perspectives on Aboriginal Title* (Saskatoon: University of Saskatchewan Law Centre, 1983).

37. McCutcheon, *Electric Rivers*, op. cit., p. 50.

38. Ibid., p. 52.

39. Roger Lacasse, *Baie James, une épopée* (Québec: Libre expression, 1983).

40. Albert Malouf, *La Baie James indienne: text intégral du judgement du Judge Albert Malouf* (Québec: Éditions du Jour, 1973).

41. McCutcheon, *Electric Rivers*, op. cit., p. 55.

42. Although Diamond could never quite bring himself to admit the extent to which he was duped in the Grand Council scenario, he comes close in his "Aboriginal Rights: The James Bay Experience," in Menno Boldt and J. Anthony Long, eds., *Aboriginal Peoples and Aboriginal Rights* (Toronto: University of Toronto Press, 1985) pp. 265-85. For an apologetic assessment, see Roy McGregor, *Chief: The Fearless Vision of Billy Diamond* (New York: Viking, 1989).

43. Irwin Colin, "Lords of the Arctic, Wards of the State," *Northern Perspectives*, Jan.-Mar. 1989, pp. 2-20.

44. Harvey Feit, "Negotiating Recognition of Aboriginal Rights: History, Strategies and Reactions to the James Bay and Northern Quebec Agreement," *Canadian Journal of Anthropology*, Vol. 1, No. 2, Winter 1980, pp. 159-71; Colin Scott, "Ideology of Reciprocity Between the James Bay Cree and the Whiteman State," in Peter Skalník, ed., *Outwitting the State* (New Brunswick, NJ: Transaction, 1989).

45. McCutcheon, *Electric Rivers*, op. cit., p. 59.

46. Indian Affairs Canada, *James Bay and Northern Québec Agreement Implementation Act Review* (Ottawa: Ministry of Indian and Northern Affairs, 1982).

47. The principles underlying the government's strategy are laid out rather clearly in Indian Affairs Canada, *Under the Flag: Canadian Sovereignty and the Native People in Northern Canada* (Ottawa: Ministry of Indian and Northern Affairs, 1984). Also see Menno Boldt's analysis in his "Social Correlates of Nationalism: A Study of Native Indian Leaders in a Canadian Internal Colony," *Comparative Political Studies*, Vol. 14, No. 2, 1981, pp. 205-31.

48. Jean Morisset, *L'identité usurpée, Vol. 1: L'Amérique écartée* (Québec: Nouvelle optique, 1985) p. 151.

49. See Joyce Rosenthal and Jan Beyea, *Long-Term Threats to Canada's James Bay from Human Development* (New York: National Audubon Society Environmental Policy Analysis Department Report No. 29, July 1989).

50. Robert Bourassa, *Deux fois la Baie James* (Québec: Les Éditions La Presse, 1981).

51. Peter Haekle, "Power Politics," *Saturday Night*, June 1984, pp. 15-27. It should be noted that New York and New England generate their own electricity primarily by burning fuel oil.

52. McCutcheon, *Electric Rivers*, op. cit., p. 91.

53. Jane Kramer, "Power-ties Link Canada, United States," *Focus*, Vol. 4, No. 2, 1985, pp. 9-15. For much fuller details and context, see Amory Lovins, L. Hunter Lovins and Seth Zuckerman, *Energy Unbound: A Fable of America's Future* (San Francisco: Sierra Club Books, 1986); Richard Munson, *The Power Makers: The Inside Story of America's Biggest Business and Its Struggle to Control Tomorrow's Electricity* (Emmaus, PA: Rodale Press, 1985).

54. Barrie McKenna, "James Bay Plan: A Whale for the Killing?" *Globe and Mail*, Sept. 28, 1991.

55. The scale of loans and bonded indebtedness incurred during its construction, combined with a steady acceleration of normal operating and maintenance costs, suggests that James Bay I cannot under any circumstances become solvent in a conventional business sense for approximately 50 years. By then, aside from a need to replace major equipment components, the La Grande River dams will have become silted in to the point that they are of marginal or submarginal utility for power generation. In economic terms, the entire project can be seen only as a net loss to the general public, profitable only for the élite strata which engineered it; André Delisle, "Le Mirage des Hydro-Dollars," *Québec-Science*, Apr. 1982, pp. 42-7.

56. See, e.g., Hydro-Québec, *Hydro-Québec: Des premiers défis à l'aube de l'an 2000* (Québec: Forces/Libre expression, 1984); Robert Bourassa, *Power from the North* (Toronto: Prentice-Hall, 1985).

57. Winona LaDuke, lecture at the University of Colorado/Boulder, April 1992 (tape on file).

58. Bourassa, *Power from the North*, op. cit.

61. Jean-Marc Carpentier, "Electricity Exports in a Context of Complementarity," *Forces*, No. 89, 1990, pp. 40-2.

60. Gérard Belanger and Jean-Thomas Bernard, "Hydro-Québec et les aluminaries," *Les Devoir*, Oct. 20, 1989.

61. *Hydro-Québec Development Plan, 1989-1991*, op. cit.; McCutcheon *Electric Rivers*, op. cit., pp. 140-1.

62. Ibid., pp. 142-3. Also see Jean-Jaques Simard, "Contrepoint: Une perspective québécoise du

développement nordique," *Northern Perspectives*, Mar./Apr. 1988, pp. 22-32.

63. Quoted in McCutcheon, *Electric Rivers*, op. cit., pp. 138.

64. Using the approximate 300 percent cost multiplier which pertained with James Bay I, the expense embodied in the second and third stages of James Bay II would be $37.8 billion and $132 billion, respectively. Obviously, the public of Québec could never hope to see such costs recovered within the lifetime of the facilities created.

65. Fikret Berkes, "Some Environmental and Social Impacts of the James Bay Hydroelectric Project, Canada," *Journal of Environmental Management*, No. 12, 1981, pp. 157-72.

66. McCutcheon, *Electric Rivers*, op. cit., p. 98.

67. Fikret Berkes, "The Intrinsic Difficulty of Predicting Impacts: Lessons from the James Bay Hydro Project," *Environmental Impact Assessment Review*, No. 8, 1988, pp. 201-20.

68. For graphic illustrations of the scale of destruction, see Rolf Wittenborn and Claus Biegert, eds., *James Bay Project: A River Drowned by Water* (Montréal: Montréal Museum of Fine Art, 1981).

69. McCutcheon, *Electric Rivers*, op. cit., p. 100.

70. Ibid., p. 112.

71. Ted Williams, "Who Killed 10,000 Caribou?" *Audubon*, Mar 1985, pp. 12-7; Lawrence Jackson, "World's Largest Caribou Herd Mired in Quebec-Labrador Boundary Dispute," *Canadian Geographic*, June-July 1985, pp. 25-33.

72. Berkes, "Intrinsic Difficulty," op. cit.; Hecky, "Methylmercury Contamination," op. cit.

73. Harvey Feit, "Legitimation and Autonomy in James Bay Cree Responses to Hydro-Electric Development," in *Indigenous Peoples and the Nation-State: "Fourth World" Politics in Canada, Australia and Norway,* Noel Dyck, ed., *Indigenous Peoples* (St. John's: Memorial University of Newfoundland, 1985).

74. McCutcheon, *Electric Rivers*, op. cit., pp. 129-30.

75. Catherine Leconte, "L'entrevue du lundi: Matthew Coon-Come," *Le Devoir*, Sept. 23, 1991.

76. Billy Diamond, "Villages of the Dammed: The James Bay Agreement Leaves a Trail of Broken Promises," *Arctic Circle*, Nov./Dec. 1990, pp. 24-34.

77. Conversation with Dalee Sambo, Inuit Circumpolar Conference, Sept. 1988.

78. James O'Reilly, lead attorney for the Crees, responded on behalf of his clients that, because of the nature of breaches to the previous agreement, the utility and government already owed the Indians and Inuits more than $1 billion in damages (McCutcheon,*Electric Rivers*, op. cit., p. 155).

79. Lajambe had been involved in fighting against the James Bay projects almost since the outset. See her "D'une baie James à l'autre," *La Presse*, Mar. 23, 1987.

80. McCutcheon, *Electric Rivers*, op. cit., pp. 159-61.

81. Ibid., pp. 161-2.

82. Paul Wells, "Most Utilities Must Prove Their Proposal Is Cheapest," *Montréal Gazette*, July 24, 1991.

83. Stephen Hazell, "Battling Hydro: Taming Quebec's Runaway Corporate Beast Is a Herculean Task," *Arctic Circle*, July/Aug. 1991, pp. 40-1.

84. Richardson, *Strangers Devour the Land*, op. cit., p. 357.

85. WARN, "New York Cancels Contract with James Bay Project," *Women of All Red Nations*, June 1992.

86. Michelle Lalonde, "Soaring Price Tag Raises Serious Doubts About Great Whale," *Globe and Mail*, Apr. 30, 1991.

87. On the land dispute and other issues which led to the Oka confrontation, see Geoffrey York and Loreen Pindera, *People of the Pines: The Warriors and the Legacy of Oka* (Boston: Little, Brown, 1991).

88. McCutcheon, *Electric Rivers*, op. cit., p. 184.

89. *Cree Regional Authority et al. v. Attorney General of Quebec*, 42 FTR 168 (1991); affirmed by the Federal Court of Appeal (127 NR 52, 43 FTR 240 (1991)).

90. For further context, Richardson, *Strangers Devour the Land*, op. cit., pp. 328-61; Grand Council of the Crees (Eeyou Astchee), *Never Without Consent: The James Bay Crees' Stand Against Forcible Inclusionn Into an Independent Quebec* (Toronto: ECW Press, 1998) esp. pp. 117-9, 130-2, 174.

91. Dam the Dams and INP, "Water Plot," op. cit., p. 143.

92. Canadian Board of Resource Ministers, *Water Diversion Proposals of North America* (Edmonton: Alberta Department of Agriculture, Water Resources Division, Development Planning Branch, 1968);

hereinafter referenced as *Diversion Proposals*.

93. Conversation with Winona LaDuke, op. cit.

94. Dam the Dams and INP, "Water Plot," op. cit. For further background on the World War II period, see Richard Bocking, *Canada's Water for Sale* (Toronto: James Lewis and Samuel, 1972).

95. Ontario Water Resources Commission, *Data for Northern Ontario Water Resource Studies, 1966-68* (Toronto: Water Resources Bulletin 1-1, Gen. Series, 1969) p. 1; hereinafter referenced as *Data*.

96. Ibid., p. 2.

97. Co-ordinating Committee on Northern Ontario Water Resource Studies, *Seventh Progress Report to the Governments of Ontario and Canada* (Toronto: Ontario Water Resources Commission, 1969) pp. 8-9; hereinafter referenced as *Seventh Report*.

98. Co-ordinating Committee on Northern Ontario Water Resource Studies, *Sixth Progress Report to the Governments of Ontario and Canada* (Toronto: Ontario Water Resources Commission, 1968) pp. 6-7; hereinafter referenced as *Sixth Report*.

99. *Data*, op. cit., pp. 2, 10; *Sixth Report*, op. cit., pp. 3-6; *Seventh Report*, op. cit., p. 6.

100. *House of Commons Debates* (Ottawa: Queen's Publisher, 1967) p. 4007.

101. *Sixth Report*, op. cit., pp. 2, 6; *Seventh Report*, op. cit., pp. 7-8.

102. Geoffry York, *The Dispossessed: Life and Death in Native Canada* (Boston: Little, Brown, 1992) p. 120.

103. Ibid. Also see Anastasia M. Shkilnyk, *A Poison Stronger Than Love: The Destruction of an Ojibwa Community* (New Haven, CT: Yale University Press, 1985).

104. *Newsweek*, Feb. 22, 1965, p. 53. In the same article, U.S. Secretary of Interior Stewart Udall is quoted as saying, "I'm for this type of thinking. I'm glad engineers talk so much about it."

105. McCool, *Command of the Waters*, op. cit. pp. 107-8.

106. On the Columbia River Treaty, see Donald Waterfield, *Continental Waterboy* (Toronto: Free North Press, 1970). Also see Bocking, *Canada's Water*, op. cit.

107. Mariana Guerrero, "American Indian Water Rights: The Blood of Life in Native North America," in M. Annette Jaimes, ed., *The State of Native America: Genocide, Colonization and Resistance* (Boston: South End Press, 1992) p. 210.

108. York, *Dispossessed*, op. cit., pp. 120-1.

109. Ibid., p. 121.

110. Dam the Dams and INP, "Water Plot," op. cit., pp. 143-4.

111. See generally, E.E. Hobbs & Associates, *The Grand Rapids Hydro Development and the Devastation of the Cree: Final Report* (Winnipeg, 1986).

112. York, *Dispossessed*, op. cit., p. 109.

113. Quoted in ibid.

114. Ibid., p. 110.

115. Ibid.

116. Hobbs, *Devastation of the Cree*, op. cit., p. 15.

117. Ibid., pp. 15-19.

118. Ibid., p. 29.

119. York, *Dispossessed*, op. cit., p. 96.

120. Ibid., pp. 96-7.

121. Quoted in ibid., p. 111.

122. Ibid.

123. Quoted in ibid.

124. Ibid., p. 97.

125. Ibid.

126. Ibid.

127. Conversation with Terrance Nelson, Winnipeg, 1996.

128. *Diversion Proposals*, op. cit.

129. McNaughton's statements are contained in *Water Resources of Canada* (Ottawa: Royal Society of Canada, 1968). Further contextualization will be found in Michael Hart's *A North American Free Trade Agreement: The Strategich Implications for Canada* (Ottawa: Centre for Trade Policy and Law and the Institute for Research on Public Poicy, 1990) and Richard Gwyn's *Nationalism Without Walls: The Unbearable*

Lightness of Being Canadian (Toronto: McClelland and Stewart, 1995).

130. Richardson, *Strangers Devour the Land*, op. cit., p. 352. For detailed examination of the workings of the offending entities in other contexts, see Richard J. Barnett and Ronald E. Müller, *Global Reach: The Power of Multinational Corporations* (New York: Simon and Schuster, 1974). More specifically, see Tony Clark, *Silent Coup: Confronting the Big Business Takeover of Canada* (Toronto: Canadian Centre for Plocy Alternatives and James Lorimer, 1997).

131. *Diversion Proposals*, op. cit. A good related reading is G. Bruce Doern's and and Bruce W. Tomlin's *Faith and Fear: The Free Trade Story* (Toronto: Stoddard, 1991).

132. On some of these "other factors," see Robert Chodos, Rae Murphy and Eric Hamovich, *Canada and the Global Economy: Alternatives to the Corporate Strategy for Globalization* (Toronto: James Lorimer, 1993).

133. See, e.g., William K. Carroll, *Corporate Power and Canadian Capitalism* (Vancouver: University of British Columbia Press, 1986); Stephen McBride and John Shields, *Dismantling a Nation: The Transition to Corporate Rule in Canada* (Halifax, NS: Fernwood, 1997).

134. For succinct examinations of the theoretical bases for this result, see Samir Amin, *Unequal Development: An Essay on the Social Formation of Peripheral Capitalism* (New York: Monthly Review Press, 1976); Ian Roxborough, *Theories of Underdevelopment* (New York: Macmillan, 1979).

135. Beyea is quoted in Andrés Picard, "James Bay: A Power Play," *Toronto Globe and Mail*, Apr. 13-17, 1990.

136. McCutcheon, *Electric Rivers*, op. cit., pp. 165-6.

137. Dam the Dams and INP, "Water Plot," op. cit., p. 150.

138. McCutcheon, *Electric Rivers*, op. cit., p. 156. As concerns the sorts of alternatives being proposed, see Environmental Committee of the Sanikiluaq and Rawson Academy of Science, *Sustainable Development in the Hudson Bay/James Bay Bioregion: An Ecosystem Approach* (Toronto: Canadian Arctic Resources Committee, 1991).

139. A nice selection of statements along this line will be found in Virginia Irving Armstrong, ed., *I Have Spoken: American History Through the Voices of the Indians* (Athens, OH: Swallow Press, 1971).

140. McCutcheon, *Electric Rivers*, op. cit., p. 157.

LIKE SAND IN THE WIND

The Making of an American Indian Diaspora in the United States

> They are going away! With a visible reluctance which nothing has overcome but the stern necessity they feel impelling them, they have looked their last upon the graves of their sires—the scenes of their youth, and have taken up the slow toilsome march with their household goods among them to their new homes in a strange land. They leave names to many of our rivers, towns, and counties, and so long as our State remains the Choctaws who once owned most of her soil will be remembered.
>
> —*Vicksburg Daily Sentinel*, February 25, 1832

> We told them that we would rather die than leave our lands; but we could not help ourselves. They took us down. Many died on the road. Two of my children died. After we reached the new land, all my horses died. The water was very bad. All our cattle died; not one was left. I stayed till one hundred and fifty-eight of my people had died. Then I ran away...
>
> —Standing Bear, January 1876

WITHIN the arena of Diaspora Studies, the question of whether the field's analytical techniques might be usefully applied to the indigenous population of the United States is seldom raised. In large part, this appears to be due to an unstated presumption on the part of diaspora scholars that because the vast bulk of the native people of the U.S. remain inside the borders of that nation-state, no population dispersal comparable to that experienced by Afroamericans, Asian Americans, Latinos—or, for that matter, Euroamericans—is at issue. Upon even minimal reflection, however, the fallacy imbedded at the core of any such premise is quickly revealed.

To say that a Cherokee remains essentially "at home" so long as s/he resides within the continental territoriality claimed by the U.S. is equivalent to arguing that a Swede displaced to Italy, or a Vietnamese refugee in Korea, would be at home simply because they remain in Europe or Asia. Native Americans, no less than other peoples, can and should be understood as identified with the specific geographical settings by which they came to

330

identify themselves as peoples. Mohawks are native to the upstate New York/southern Québec region, not Florida or California. Chiricahua Apaches are indigenous to southern Arizona and northern Sonora, not Oklahoma or Oregon. The matter is not only cultural, although the dimension of culture is crucially important, but political and economic as well.

Struggles by native peoples to retain use and occupancy rights over their traditional territories, and Euroamerican efforts to supplant them, comprise the virtual entirety of U.S./Indian relations since the inception of the republic. All forty of the so-called "Indian Wars" recorded by the federal government were fought over land.[1] On more than 370 separate occasions between 1778 and 1871, the Senate of the United States ratified treaties with one or more indigenous peoples by which the latter ceded portions of its landbase to the U.S. In every instance, a fundamental quid pro quo was arrived at: Each indigenous nation formally recognized as such through a treaty ratification was simultaneously acknowledged as retaining a clearly demarcated national homeland within which it might maintain its sociopolitical cohesion and from which it could draw perpetual sustenance, both spiritually and materially.[2]

At least five succeeding generations of American Indians fought, suffered and died to preserve their peoples' residency in the portions of North America which had been theirs since "time immemorial." In this sense, the fundamental importance they attached to continuing their linkages to these areas seems unquestionable. By the same token, the extent to which their descendants have been dislocated from these defined, or definable, landbases is the extent to which it can be observed that the conditions of diaspora have been imposed upon the population of Native North America. In this respect, the situation is so unequivocal that a mere sample of statistics deriving from recent census data will be sufficient to tell the tale:

- By 1980, nearly half of all federally recognized American Indians lived in off-reservation locales, mostly cities. The largest concentration of indigenous people in the country—90,689—was in the Los Angeles Metro Area.[3] By 1990, the proportion of urban-based Indians is estimated to have swelled to approximately fifty-five percent.[4]

- All federally unrecognized Indians—a figure which may run several times that of the approximately 1.9 million the U.S. officially admits still exist within its borders—are effectively landless and scattered everywhere across the country.[5]

- Texas, the coast of which was once one of the more populous locales for indigenous people, reported a reservation-based Native American population of 859 in 1980.[6] The total Indian population of Texas was reported as being 39,740.[7] Even if this number included only members of peoples native to the area (which it does not), it would still represent a reduction from about 1.5 million at the point of first contact with Europeans.[8]

- A veritable vacuum in terms of American Indian reservations and population is now evidenced in most of the area east of the Mississippi River, another region once densely populated by indigenous people. Delaware, Illinois, Indiana, Kentucky, Maryland, New Hampshire, New Jersey, Ohio, Pennsylvania, Rhode Island, Tennessee, Vermont, Virginia, West Virginia show no reservations at all.[9] The total Indian population reported in Vermont in 1980 was 968. In New Hampshire, the figure was 1,297. In Delaware, it was 1,307; in West Virginia, 1,555. The reality is that a greater number of persons indigenous to the North American continent now live in Hawai'i, far out in the Pacific Ocean, than in any of these easterly states.[10]

The ways in which such deformities in the distribution of indigenous population in the U.S. have come to pass were anything but natural. To the contrary, the major causative factors have consistently derived from a series of official policies implemented over more than two centuries by the federal government of the United States. These have ranged from forced removal during the 1830s, to concentration and compulsory assimilation during the 1880s, to coerced relocation beginning in the late 1940s. Interspersed through it all have been periods of outright liquidation and dissolution, continuing into the present moment. The purpose of this essay is to explore these policies and their effects on the peoples targeted for such exercises in "social engineering."

The Postrevolutionary Period

During the period immediately following the American War of Independence, the newly formed United States was in a "desperate financial plight...[and] saw its salvation in the sale to settlers and land companies of western lands" lying outside the original thirteen colonies.[11] Indeed, the revolution had been fought in significant part in order to negate George III's

Proclamation of 1763, an edict restricting land acquisition by British subjects to the area east of the Appalachian Mountains and thereby voiding certain speculative real estate interests held by the U.S. Founding Fathers. During the war, loyalty of rank-and-file soldiers, as well as major creditors, had been maintained through warrants advanced by the Continental Congress with the promise that rebel debts would be retired through issuance of deeds to parcels of Indian land once the decolonization was achieved.[12] A substantial problem for the fledgling republic was that in the immediate aftermath, it possessed neither the legal nor the physical means to carry through on such commitments.

In the Treaty of Paris, signed on September 3, 1783, England quit-claimed its rights to all present U.S. territory east of the Mississippi. Contrary to subsequent Americana, this action conveyed no bona fide title to any of the Indian lands lying within the area.[13] Rather, it opened the way for the United States to replace Great Britain as the sole entity entitled under prevailing international law to *acquire* Indian land in the region through negotiation and purchase.[14] The U.S.—already an outlaw state by virtue of its armed rejection of lawful Crown authority—appears to have been emotionally prepared to seize native property through main force, thereby continuing its initial posture of gross illegality.[15] Confronted by the incipient indigenous alliance espoused by Tecumseh in the Ohio River Valley (known at the time as the "Northwest Territory") and to the south by the powerful Creek and Cherokee confederations, however, the U.S. found itself militarily stalemated all along its western frontier.[16]

The Indian position was considerably reinforced when England went back on certain provisions of the Treaty of Paris, refusing to abandon a line of military installations along the Ohio until the U.S. showed itself willing to comply with minimum standards of international legalism, "acknowledging the Indian right in the soil" long since recognized under the Doctrine of Discovery.[17] To the south, Spanish Florida also aligned itself with native nations as a means of holding the rapacious settler population of neighboring Georgia in check.[18] Frustrated, federal authorities had to content themselves with the final dispossession and banishment of such peoples as the Abenaki and Delaware (Lenni Lanape)—whose homelands fell within the original colonies, and who had been much weakened by more than a century of warfare—to points beyond the 1763 demarcation line. There, these early elements of a U.S. precipitated indigenous diaspora were taken in by stronger nations such as the Ottawa and Shawnee.[19]

Meanwhile, George Washington's initial vision of a rapid and wholesale expulsion of all Indians east of the Mississippi, expressed in June 1783,[20] was tempered to reflect a more sophisticated process of gradual encroachment explained by General Philip Schuyler of New York in a letter to Congress the following month:

> As our settlements approach their country, [the Indians] must, from the scarcity of game, which that approach will induce, retire farther back, and dispose of their lands, unless they dwindle to nothing, as all savages have done…when compelled to live in the vicinity of civilized people, and thus leave us the country without the expense of purchase, trifling as that will probably be.[21]

As Washington himself was to put it a short time later, "[P]olicy and economy point very strongly to the expediency of being on good terms with the Indians, and the propriety of purchasing their Lands in preference to attempting to drive them by force of arms out of their Country…The gradual extension of our Settlements will certainly cause the Savage as the Wolf to retire…In a word there is nothing to be gained by an Indian War but the Soil they live on and this can be had by purchase at less expense."[22] By 1787, the strategy had become so well-accepted that the U.S. was prepared to enact the Northwest Ordinance (1 Stat. 50), codifying a formal renunciation of what it had been calling its "Rights of Conquest" with respect to native peoples: "The utmost good faith shall always be observed towards the Indian; their land shall never be taken from them without their consent; and in their property, rights, and liberty, they shall never be invaded or disturbed—but laws founded in justice and humanity shall from time to time be made, for wrongs done to them, and for preserving peace and friendship with them."[23]

The Era of Removal

By the early years of the nineteenth century, the balance of power in North America had begun to shift. To a certain extent, this was due a burgeoning of the Angloamerican population, a circumstance actively fostered by government policy. In other respects, it was because of an increasing consolidation of the U.S. state and a generation-long erosion of indigenous strength resulting from the factors delineated in Schuyler's policy of gradual expansion.[24] By 1810, the government was ready to resume what Congress described as the "speedy provision of the extension of the territories of the United States" through means of outright force.[25] Already, in 1803, provision had been made through the Louisiana Purchase for the massive displacement of all eastern Indian nations into what was perceived as the "vast wasteland" west of the Mississippi.[26] The juridical groundwork was laid by the Supreme Court with Chief Justice John Marshall's opinion in *Fletcher v. Peck* (10 U.S. 87), a decision holding that the title of U.S. citizens to parcels of Indian property might be considered valid even though no Indian consent to cede the land had been obtained.[27]

With the defeat of Great Britain in the War of 1812, the subsequent defeat of Tecumseh's confederation in 1813, and General Andrew Jackson's defeat of the Creek Red Sticks in 1814, the "clearing" of the east began in earnest.[28] By 1819, the U.S. had wrested eastern Florida from Spain, consummating a process begun in 1810 with assaults upon the western ("panhandle") portion of the territory.[29] Simultaneously, the first of a pair of "Seminole Wars" was begun on the Florida peninsula to subdue an amalgamation of resident Miccosukees, "recalcitrant" Creek refugees, and runaway chattel slaves naturalized as free citizens of the indigenous nations.[30] In 1823, John Marshall reinforced the embryonic position articulated in *Peck* with *Johnson v. McIntosh* (21 U.S. (98 Wheat.) 543), an opinion inverting conventional understandings of indigenous status in international law by holding that U.S. sovereignty superseded that of native nations, even within their own territories. During the same year, President James Monroe promulgated his doctrine professing a unilateral U.S. "right" to circumscribe the sovereignty all other nations in the hemisphere.[31]

In this environment, a tentative policy of Indian "removal" was already underway by 1824, although not codified as law until the Indian Removal Act (ch. 148, 4 Stat. 411) was passed in 1830. This was followed by John Marshall's opinions, rendered in *Cherokee v. Georgia* (30 U.S. (5 Pet.) 1 (1831)) and *Worcester v. Georgia* (31 U.S. (6 Pet.) 551 (1832)), that Indians comprised "domestic dependent nations," the sovereignty of which was subject to the "higher authority" of the federal government.[32] At that point, the federal program of physically relocating entire nations of people from their eastern homelands to what was then called the "Permanent Indian Territory of Oklahoma" west of the Mississippi became full-fledged and forcible.[33] The primary targets were the prosperous "Five Civilized Tribes" of the Southeast: the Cherokee, Creek, Chickasaw, Choctaw and Seminole nations.

They were rounded up and interned by troops, concentrated in camps until their numbers were sufficient to make efficient their being force-marched at bayonet-point, typically without adequate food, shelter or medical attention, often in the dead of winter, as much as 1,500 miles to their new "homelands."[34]

There were, of course, still those who attempted to mount a military resistance to what was happening. Some, like the Sauk and Fox nations of Illinois, who fought what has come to be known as the "Black Hawk War" against those dispossessing them in 1832, were simply slaughtered *en mass*.[35] Others, such as the "hard core" of Seminoles who mounted the second war bearing their name in 1835, were forced from the terrain associated with their normal way of life. Once ensconced in forbidding locales like the Everglades, they became for all practical intents and purposes invincible—one group refused to make peace with the U.S. until the early 1960s—but progressively smaller and more diffuse in their demography.[36] In any event, by 1840 removal had been mostly accomplished (although it lingered as a policy until 1855), with only "the smallest, least offensive, and most thoroughly integrated tribes escaping the pressure to clear the eastern half of the continent of its original inhabitants."[37] The results of the policy were always catastrophic for the victims. For instance, of the approximately 17,000 Cherokees subjected to the removal process, about 8,000 died of disease, exposure and malnutrition along what they called the "Trail of Tears."[38] In addition:

> The Choctaws are said to have lost fifteen percent of their population, 6,000 out of 40,000; and the Chickasaw...surely suffered severe losses as well. By contrast the Creeks and Seminoles are said to have suffered about 50 percent mortality. For the Creeks, this came primarily in the period immediately after removal: for example, "of the 10,000 or more who were resettled in 1836–37...an incredible 3,500 died of 'bilious fevers.'"[39]

Nor was this the only cost. Like the Seminoles, portions of each of the targeted peoples managed through various means to avoid removal, remaining in their original territories until their existence was once again recognized by the U.S. during the twentieth century. One consequence was a permanent sociocultural and geographic fragmentation of formerly cohesive groups; while the bulk of the identified populations of these nations now live in and around Oklahoma, smaller segments reside on the tiny "Eastern Cherokee" Reservation in North Carolina (1980 population

4,844); "Mississippi Choctaw" Reservation in Mississippi (pop. 2,756); the Miccosukee and "Big Cypress," "Hollywood" and "Brighton" Seminole Reservations in Florida (pops. 213, 351, 416 and 323, respectively).[40]

An unknown but significant number of Cherokees also went beyond Oklahoma, following their leader, Sequoia, into Mexico in order to escape the reach of the U.S. altogether.[41] This established something of a precedent for other peoples such as the Kickapoos, a small Mexican "colony" of whom persists to this day.[42] Such dispersal was compounded by the fact that throughout the removal process varying numbers of Indians escaped at various points along the route of march, blending into the surrounding territory and later intermarrying with the incoming settler population. By-and-large, these people have simply slipped from the historical record, their descendants today inhabiting a long arc of mixed-blood communities extending from northern Georgia and Alabama, through Tennessee and Kentucky, and into the southernmost reaches of Illinois and Missouri.[43]

Worse was yet to come. At the outset of the removal era proper, Andrew Jackson—a leading proponent of the policy who had ridden into the White House on the public acclaim deriving from his role as commander of the 1814 massacre of the Red Sticks at Horseshoe Bend and a subsequent slaughter of noncombatants during the First Seminole War—offered a carrot as well as the stick he used to compel tribal "cooperation."[44] In 1829, he promised the Creeks that:

> Your father has provided a country large enough for all of you, and he advises you to remove to it. There your white brothers will not trouble you; they will have no claim to the land, and you can live upon it, you and all your children, as long as the grass grows or the water runs, in peace and plenty. It will be yours forever.[45]

Jackson was, to put it bluntly, lying through his teeth. Even as he spoke, he was aware that the Mississippi, that ostensible border between the U.S. and Permanent Indian Territory proclaimed by Thomas Jefferson and others, had already been breached by the rapidly consolidating states of Louisiana, Arkansas and Missouri in the south, Iowa, Wisconsin and Minnesota in the north.[46] Nor could Jackson have been unknowing that his close friend, Senator Thomas Hart Benton of Missouri, had stipulated as early as 1825 that the Rocky Mountains rather than the Mississippi should serve as an "everlasting boundary" of the U.S.[47] By the time the bulk of removal was completed a decade later, Angloamerican settlement was reaching well into

Kansas. Their cousins who had infiltrated the Mexican province of Texas had revolted, proclaimed themselves an independent republic, and were negotiating for statehood. The eyes of empire had also settled on all of Mexico north of the Río Grande, and the British portion of Oregon as well.[48]

Peoples such as the Shawnee and Potawatomi, Lenni Lanape and Wyandot, Peoria, Sac, Fox, and Kickapoo, already removed from their eastern homelands, were again compulsorily relocated as the western Indian Territory was steadily reduced in size.[49] This time, they were mostly shifted southward into an area eventually conforming to the boundaries of the present state of Oklahoma. Ultimately, sixty-seven separate nations (or parts of nations), only six of them in truly indigenous to the land at issue, were forced into this relatively small dumping ground.[50] When Oklahoma, too, became a state in 1907, most of the territorial compartments reserved for the various Indian groups were simply dissolved. Today, although Oklahoma continues to report the second largest native population of any state, only the Osage retain a reserved landbase which is nominally their own.[51]

Subjugation in the West

The U.S. "Winning of the West" which began around 1850—that is, immediately after the northern half of Mexico was taken in a brief war of conquest—was, if anything, more brutal that the clearing of the east.[52] Most of the U.S. wars against native people were waged during the following thirty-five years under what has been termed an official "rhetoric of extermination."[53] The means employed in militarily subjugating the indigenous nations of California and southern Oregon, the Great Plains, Great Basin, and northern region of the Sonora Desert devolved upon a lengthy series of wholesale massacres. Representative of these are the slaughter of about 150 Lakotas at Blue River (Nebraska) in 1854, some five hundred Shoshones at Bear River (Idaho) in 1863, as many as 250 Cheyennes and Arapahos at Sand Creek (Colorado) in 1864, perhaps three hundred Cheyennes on the Washita River (Oklahoma) in 1868, 175 Piegan noncombatants at the Marias River (Montana) in 1870, and at least a hundred Cheyennes at Camp Robinson (Nebraska) in 1878. The parade of official atrocities was capped off by the butchery of another three hundred unarmed Lakotas at Wounded Knee (South Dakota) in 1890.[54]

Other means employed by the government to reduce its native opponents to a state of what it hoped would be abject subordination included the four-year internment of the entire Navajo (Diné) Nation in a concentration camp at the Bosque Redondo, outside Fort Sumner, New Mexico, beginning in 1864. The Diné, who had been force-marched in what they called the "Long Walk," a three hundred mile trek from their Arizona homeland. They were then held under abysmal conditions, with neither adequate food nor shelter, and died like flies. Approximately half had perished before their release in 1868.[55] Similarly if less dramatically, food supplies were cut off to the Lakota Nation in 1877—militarily defeated the year before, the Lakotas were being held under army guard at the time—until starvation compelled its leaders to "cede" the Black Hills area to the U.S.[56] The assassination of resistance leaders such as the Lakotas' Crazy Horse (1877) and Sitting Bull (1890) was also a commonly used technique.[57] Other recalcitrant figures like Geronimo (Chiricahua) and Satanta (Kiowa) were separated from their people by being imprisoned in remote facilities like Fort Marion, Florida.[58]

In addition to these official actions, which the U.S. Census Bureau acknowledged in an 1894 summary as having caused a minimum of 45,000 native deaths, there was an even greater attrition resulting from what were described as "individual affairs."[59] These took the form of Angloamerican citizens at large killing Indians, often systematically, under a variety of quasi-official circumstances. In Dakota Territory, for example, a $200 bounty for Indian scalps was paid in the territorial capitol of Yankton during the 1860s; the local military commander, General Alfred Sully, is known to have privately contracted for a pair of Lakota skulls with which to adorn the city.[60] In Texas, first as a republic and then as a state, authorities also "placed a bounty upon the scalp of any Indian brought in to a government office— man, woman, or child, no matter what 'tribe'—no questions asked."[61] In California and Oregon, "the enormous decrease [in the native population of 1800] from about a quarter-million to less than 20,000 [in 1870 was] due chiefly to the cruelties and wholesale massacres perpetrated by the miners and early settlers."[62]

> Much of the killing in California and southern Oregon Territory resulted, directly and indirectly, from the discovery of gold in 1848 and the subsequent influx of miners and settlers. Newspaper accounts document the atrocities, as do oral histories of the California Indians today. It was not uncommon for small groups or villages to be attacked by immigrants...and virtually wiped out overnight.[63]

It has been estimated that Indian deaths resulting from this sort of direct violence may have run as high as a half-million by 1890.[64] All told, the indigenous population of the continental United States, which may still have been as great as two million when the country was founded, had been reduced to well under 250,000 by 1900.[65] As the noted demographer Sherburn F. Cook has observed, "The record speaks for itself. No further commentary is necessary."[66]

Under these conditions, the U.S. was able to shuffle native peoples around at will. The Northern Cheyennes and closely allied Arapahos, for instance, were shipped from their traditional territory in Montana's Powder River watershed to the reservation of their southern cousins in Oklahoma in 1877. After the Cheyenne remnants, more than a third of whom had died in barely a year of malaria and other diseases endemic to this alien environment, made a desperate attempt to return home in 1878, they were granted a reservation in the north country. But not before the bulk of them had been killed by army troops. Moreover, they were permanently separated from the Arapahos, who were "temporarily" assigned to the Wind River Reservation of their hereditary enemies, the Shoshone, in Wyoming.[67]

A faction of the Chiricahua Apaches who showed signs of continued "hostility" to U.S. domination by the 1880s were yanked from their habitat in southern Arizona and "resettled" around Fort Sill, Oklahoma.[68] Hinmaton Yalatkit (Chief Joseph) of the Nez Percé and other leaders of that people's legendary attempt to escape the army and flee to Canada were also deposited in Oklahoma, far from the Idaho valley they'd fought to retain.[69] Most of the Santee Dakotas of Minnesota's woodlands ended up on the windswept plains of Nebraska, while a handful of their relatives remained behind on tiny plots which are now called the "Upper" and "Lower Sioux" reservations.[70] A portion of the Oneidas, who had fought on the side of the rebels during the revolution, were moved to a small reservation near Green Bay, Wisconsin.[71] An even smaller reserve was provided in the same area for residual elements of Connecticut's Mahegans, Mohegans, and other peoples, all of them lumped together under the heading "Stockbridge-Munsee Indians."[72] On and on it went.

Allotment and Assimilation

With the native ability to militarily resist U.S. territorial ambitions finally quelled, the government moved first to structurally negate any meaningful residue of national status on the part of indigenous peoples, and then to dissolve them altogether. The opening round of this drive came in 1871, with the attachment of a rider to the annual Congressional Appropriations Act (ch. 120, 16 Stat. 544, 566) suspending any further treatymaking with Indians. This was followed, in 1885, with passage of the Major Crimes Act (ch. 341, 24 Stat. 362, 385), extending U.S. jurisdiction directly over reserved Indian territories for the first time. Beginning with seven felonies delineated in the initial statutory language, and combined with the Supreme Court's opinion in *U.S. v. Kagama* (118 U.S. 375 (1886)) that Congress possessed a unilateral and "incontrovertible right" to exercise its authority over Indians as it saw fit, the 1885 act opened the door to subsequent passage of the more than five thousand federal laws presently regulating every aspect of reservation life and affairs.[73]

In 1887, Congress passed the General Allotment Act (ch. 119, 24 Stat. 388), a measure designed expressly to destroy what was left of basic indigenous socioeconomic cohesion by eradicating traditional systems of collective landholding. Under provision of the statute, each Indian identified as such by demonstrating "one-half or more degree of Indian blood" was to be issued an individual deed to a specific parcel of land—160 acres per family head, eighty acres per orphan or single person over eighteen years of age, and forty acres per dependent child—within existing reservation boundaries. Each Indian was required to accept U.S. citizenship in order to receive his or her allotment. Those who refused, such as a substantial segment of the Cherokee "full-blood" population, were left landless.[74]

Generally speaking, those of mixed ancestry whose "blood quantum" fell below the the required level were summarily excluded from receiving allotments. In most cases, the requirement was construed by officials as meaning that an applicant's "blood" had to have accrued from a single people; persons who whose cumulative blood quantum derived from inter-marriage between several native peoples were thus often excluded as well. In other instances, arbitrary geographic criteria were also employed; all Chero-kees, Creeks and Choctaws living in Arkansas, for example, were not only excluded from allotment, but permanently denied recognition as members of their respective nations as well.[75] Once all eligible Indians had been as-signed their allotments within a given reservation—all of them from the worst land available therein—the remainder of the reserved territory was declared "surplus" and opened to non-Indian homesteaders, corporate acquisition, and conversion into federal or state parks and forests.[76]

Under the various allotment programs, the most valuable land was the first to go. Settlers went after the rich grasslands of Kansas, Nebraska, and the Dakotas; the dense black-soil forests of Minnesota and Wisconsin; and the wealthy oil and gas lands of Oklahoma. In 1887, for example, the Sisseton Sioux of South Dakota owned 918,000 acres of rich virgin land on their reservation. But since there were only two thousand of them, allotment left more than 600,000 acres for European American settlers... The Chippewas of Minnesota lost their rich timber lands; once each member had claimed [their] land, the government leased the rest to timber corporations. The Colvilles of northeastern Washington lost their lands to cattlemen, who fraudulently claimed mineral rights there. In Montana and Wyoming the Crows lost more than two million acres, and the Nez Percés had to cede communal grazing ranges in Idaho. All sixty-seven of the tribes in Indian Territory underwent allotment... On the Flathead Reservation [in Montana]—which included Flatheads, Pend Oreilles, Kutenais, and Spokanes...the federal government opened 1.1 million acres to settlers. A similar story prevailed throughout the country.[77]

By the time the allotment process had run its course in 1930, the residue of native land holdings in the U.S. had been reduced from approximately 150 million acres to a little over fifty million.[78] Of this, more than two-thirds consisted of arid or semiarid terrain deemed useless for agriculture, gazing, or other productive purposes. The remaining one-third had been leased at extraordinarily low rates to non-Indian farmers and ranchers by local Indian agents exercising "almost dictatorial powers" over remaining reservation property.[79]

Indians across the country were left in a state of extreme destitution as a result of allotment and attendant leasing practices. Worse, the situation was guaranteed to be exacerbated over succeeding generations insofar as what was left of the reservation landbase, already insufficient to support its occupants at a level of mere subsistence, could be foreseen to become steadily more so as the native population recovered from the genocide perpetrated against it during the nineteenth century.[80] A concomitant of allotment was thus an absolute certainty that ever-increasing numbers of Indians would be forced from what remained nominally their own land during the twentieth century, dispersed into the vastly more numerous American society-at-large. There, it was predictable (and often predicted) that they would be "digested," disappearing once and for all as anything distinctly Indian in terms of sociocultural, political, or even racial identity. The record shows that such outcomes were anything but unintentional.

The purpose of all this was "assimilation," as federal policymakers described their purpose, or—to put the matter more unabashedly—to bring about the destruction and disappearance of American Indian peoples as such. In the words of Francis E. Leupp, Commissioner of Indian Affairs from 1905 through 1909, the Allotment Act in particular should be viewed as a "mighty pulverizing engine for breaking up the tribal mass" which stood in the way of complete Euroamerican hegemony in North America. Or, to quote Indian Commissioner Charles Burke a decade later, "[I]t is not desirable or consistent with the general welfare to promote tribal characteristics and organization."[81]

The official stance was consecrated in the Supreme Court's determination in its 1903 *Lonewolf v. Hitchcock* opinion (187 U.S. 553)—extended from John Marshall's "domestic dependent nation" thesis of the early 1830s—that the U.S. possessed "plenary" (full) power over all matters involving Indian affairs. In part, this meant the federal government was unilaterally assigning itself perpetual "trust" prerogatives to administer or dispose of native assets, whether these were vested in land, minerals, cash, or any other from, regardless of Indian needs or desires.[82] Congress then consolidated its position with passage of the 1906 Burke Act (34 Stat. 182), designating the Secretary of Interior as permanent trustee over Indian Country. In 1924, a number of lose ends were cleaned up with passage of the Indian Citizenship Act (ch. 233, 43 Stat. 25) imposing U.S. citizenship upon all native people who had not otherwise been naturalized. The law was applied across-the-board to all Indians, whether they desired citizenship or not, and thus included those who had forgone allotments rather than accept it.[83]

Meanwhile, the more physical dimensions of assimilationist policy were coupled to a process of ideological conditioning designed to render native children susceptible to dislocation and absorption by the dominant society. In the main, this assumed the form of a compulsory boarding school system administered by the Interior Department's Bureau of Indian Affairs (BIA) wherein large numbers of indigenous children were taken, often forcibly, to facilities remote from their families and communities. Once there, the youngsters were were prevented from speaking their languages, practicing their religions, wearing their customary clothing or wearing their hair in traditional fashion, or in any other way overtly associating themselves with their own cultures and traditions. Instead, they were indoctrinated—typically for a decade or more—in Christian dogma and European values such as the "work ethic." During the summers, they were frequently "farmed out" to Euroamerican "foster homes" where they were further steeped in the dominant society's views of their peoples and themselves.[83]

Attendance was made compulsory [for all native children, aged five to eighteen] and the agent was made responsible for keeping the schools filled, by persuasion if possible, by withholding rations and annuities from the parents, and by other means if necessary... [Students] who were guilty of misbehavior might either receive corporal punishment or be imprisoned in the guardhouse [a special "reform school" was established to handle "incorrigible" students who clung to their traditions]... A sincere effort was made to develop the type of school that would destroy tribal ways.[84]

The intention of this was, according to the perpetrators and many of their victims alike, to create generations of American Indian youth who functioned intellectually as "little white people," facilitating the rapid dissolution of traditional native cultures desired by federal policymakers.[85] In combination with a program in which native children were put out for wholesale adoption by Euroamerican families, the effect upon indigenous peoples was devastating.[86] This systematic transfer of children not only served to accelerate the outflow of Indians from reservation and reservation-adjacent settings, but the return of individuals mentally conditioned to conduct themselves as non-Indians escalated the rate at which many native societies unraveled within the reservation contexts themselves.[87]

The effects of the government's allotment and assimilation programs are reflected in the demographic shifts evidenced throughout Indian Country from 1910 through 1950. In the former year, only 0.4 percent of all identified Indians lived in urban locales. By 1930, the total had grown to 9.9 percent. As of 1950, the total had grown to 13.4 percent. Simultaneously, the displacement of native people from reservations to off-reservation rural areas was continuing apace.[88] In 1900, this involved only about 3.5 percent of all Indians. By 1930, the total had swelled to around 12.5 percent and, by 1950, it had reached nearly eighteen percent.[89] Hence, in the latter year, nearly one-third of the federally recognized Indians in the United States had been dispersed to locales other than those the government had defined as being "theirs."

Reorganization and Colonization

It is likely, all things being equal, that the Indian policies with which the United States ushered in the twentieth century would have led inexorably to a complete eradication of the reservation system and corresponding disappearance of American Indians as distinct peoples by some point around 1950. There can be no question but that such a final consolidation of its internal landbase would have complemented the phase of transoceanic expansionism into which the U.S. entered quite unabashedly during the 1890s.[90] That things did not follow this course seems mainly due to a pair of ironies, one geological and the other unwittingly imbedded in the bizarre status of "quasi-sovereignty" increasingly imposed upon native nations by federal jurists and policymakers over the preceding hundred years.

As regards the first of these twin twists of fate, authorities were becoming increasingly aware by the late 1920s that the "worthless" residue of territory to which indigenous people were consigned was turning out to be extraordinarily endowed with mineral wealth. Already, in 1921, an exploratory team from Standard Oil had come upon what it took to be substantial fossil fuel deposits on the Navajo Reservation.[91] During the next three decades, it would be discovered that just how great a proportion of U.S. "domestic" resources lay within American Indian reservations.

> Western reservations in particular…possess vast amounts of coal, oil, shale oil, natural gas, timber, and uranium. More than 40 percent of the national reserves of low sulfur, strippable coal, 80 percent of the nation's uranium reserves, and billions of barrels of shale oil exist on reservation land. On the 15-million-acre Navajo Reservation, there are approximately 100 million barrels of oil, 25 trillion cubic feet of natural gas, 80 million pounds of uranium, and 50 billion tons of coal. The 440,000-acre Northern Cheyenne Reservation in Montana sits atop a 60-foot-thick layer of coal. In New Mexico, geologists estimate that the Jicarilla Apache Reservation possesses 2 trillion cubic feet of natural gas and as much as 154 million barrels of oil. [92]

This led directly to the second quirk. The more sophisticated federal officials, even then experiencing the results of opening up Oklahoma's lush oil fields to unrestrained corporate competition, realized the extent of the disequilibriums and inefficiencies involved in this line of action when weighed against the longer-term needs of U.S. industrial development.[93] Only by retaining its "trust authority" over reservation assets would the government be in a continuing position to dictate which resources would be exploited, in what quantities, by whom, at what cost, and for what purpose, allowing the North American political economy to evolve in ways preferred by the country's financial élite.[94] Consequently, it was quickly perceived as necessary that both Indians and Indian Country be preserved, at least to some extent, as a facade behind which the "socialistic" process of central economic planning might occur.

For the scenario to work in practice, it was vital that the reservations be made to appear "self-governing" enough to exempt themselves from the usual requirements of the U.S. "free market" system whenever this might be convenient to their federal "guardians." On the other hand, they could never become independent or autonomous enough to assume control over their own economic destinies, asserting demands that equitable royalty rates be paid for the extraction of its ores, for example, or that profiting corporations underwrite the expense of environmental clean-up once mining operations had been concluded.[95] In effect, the idea was that many indigenous nations should be maintained as outright internal colonies of the United States rather than being liquidated out-of-hand.[96] All that was needed to accomplish this was the creation of a mechanism through which the illusion of limited Indian self-rule might be extended.

The vehicle for this purpose materialized in 1934, with passage of the Indian Reorganization Act (ch. 576, 48 Stat. 948), or "IRA," as it is commonly known. Under provision of this statute, the traditional governing bodies of most indigenous nations were supplanted by "Tribal Councils," the structure of which were devised in Washington, D.C., functioning within parameters of formal constitutions written by BIA officials.[97] A democratic veneer was maintained by staging a referendum on each reservation prior to its being reorganized, but federal authorities simply manipulated the outcomes to achieve the desired results.[98] The newly installed IRA councils were patterned much more closely upon the model of corporate boards than of governments, and possessed little power other than to sign off on business agreements. Even at that, they were completely and "voluntarily" subordinated to U.S. interests: "All decisions of any consequence (in thirty-three separate areas of consideration) rendered by these 'tribal councils' were made 'subject to the approval of the Secretary of Interior or his delegate,' the Commissioner of Indian Affairs."[99]

One entirely predictable result of this arrangement has been that an inordinate amount of mining, particularly that related to "energy development," has occurred on Indian reservations since the late mid-to-late 1940s. Virtually *all* uranium mining and milling during the life of the U.S. Atomic Energy Commission's (AEC's) ore buying program (1954-1981) occurred on reservation land; Anaconda's Jackpile Mine, located at the Laguna Pueblo in New Mexico, was the largest open pit uranium extraction operation in the world until it was phased out in 1979.[100] Every year, enough power is generated by Arizona's Four Corners Power Plant alone—every bit of it from coal mined at Black Mesa, on the Navajo Reservation—to light the lights of Tucson and Phoenix for two decades, and present plans include a four-fold expansion of Navajo coal production.[101] Throughout the West, the story is the same.

On the face of it, the sheer volume of resource "development" in Indian Country over the past half-century should—even under disadvantageous terms—have translated into *some* sort of "material improvement" in the lot of indigenous people. Yet the mining leases offered to selected corporations by the BIA "in behalf of" their native "wards"—and duly endorsed by the IRA councils—have consistently paid such a meager fraction of prevailing market royalty rates that no such advancement has been discernable. Probably the best terms were those obtained by the Navajo Nation in 1976, a contract paying a royalty of fifty-five cents per ton for coal; this amounted to eight percent of market price at a time when Interior Secretary Cecil Andrus admitted the *minimum* rate paid for coal mined in off-reservation settings was 12.5 percent (more typically, it was upwards of fifteen percent).[102] Simultaneously, a 17.5 cents per ton royalty was being paid for coal on the Crow Reservation in Montana, a figure which was raised to forty cents—less than half the market rate—only after years of haggling.[103] What are at issue here are not profits, but the sort of "super-profits" usually associated with U.S. domination of economies in Latin America.[104]

Nor has the federally coordinated corporate exploitation of the reservations translated into wage income for Indians. As of 1989, the government's own data indicated that reservation unemployment nationwide still hovered in the mid-sixtieth percentile, with some locales running persistently running in the ninetieth.[105] Most steady jobs involved administering or enforcing the federal order, reservation by reservation. Such "business-related" employment as existed tended to be temporary, menial, and paid the minimum wage, a matter quite reflective of the sort of transient, extractive industry —which brings its cadre of permanent, skilled labor with it—the BIA had encouraged to set up shop in Indian Country.[106] Additionally, the impact of extensive mining and associated activities had done much to disrupt the basis for possible continuation of traditional self-sufficiency occupations, destroying considerable acreage which held potential as grazing or subsistence garden plots.[107] In this sense, U.S. governmental and corporate activities have "underdeveloped" Native North America in classic fashion.[108]

Overall, according to a federal study completed in 1988, reservation-based Indians experienced every indice of extreme impoverishment: by far the lowest annual and lifetime incomes of any North American population group, highest rate of infant mortality (7.5 times the national average), highest rates of death from plague disease, malnutrition and exposure, highest rate of teen suicide, and so on. The average life expectancy of a reservation-based Native American males is 44.6 years, that of females about three years longer.[109] The situation is much more indicative of a Third World context than of rural areas in a country that claims to be the world's "most advanced industrial state." Indeed, the poignant observation of many Latinos regarding their relationship to the U.S., that "your wealth is our poverty," is as appropriate to the archipelago of Indian reservations in North America itself as it is to the South American continent. By any estimation, the "open veins of Native America" created by the IRA have been an incalculable boon to the maturation of the U.S. economy, while Indians continue to pay the price by living in the most grinding sort of poverty.[110]

And there is worse. One of the means used by the government to maximize corporate profits in Indian Country over the years—again rubber-stamped by the IRA councils—has been to omit clauses requiring corporate reclamation of mined lands from leasing instruments. Similarly, the cost of doing business on reservations has been pared to the bone (and profitability driven up) by simply waiving environmental protection standards in most instances.[111] Such practices have spawned ecological catastrophe in many locales. As the impact of the Four Corners plant, one of a dozen coal-fired electrical generation facilities currently "on-line" on the Navajo reservation, has been described elsewhere:

> The five units of the 2,075 megawatt power plant has been churning out city-bound electricity and local pollution since 1969. The plant burns ten tons of coal per minute—five million tons per year—spewing three hundred tons of fly-ash and other waste particulates into the air each day. The black cloud hangs over ten thousand acres of the once-pristine San Juan River Valley. The deadly plume was the only visible evidence of human enterprise as seen from the Gemini-12 satellite which photographed the earth from 150 miles in space. Less visible, but equally devastating is the fact that since 1968 the coal mining operations and power plant requirements have been extracting 2,700 gallons from the Black Mesa water table each minute—60 million gallons per year—causing extreme desertification of the area, and even the sinking of some ground by as much as twelve feet.[112]

Corporations engaged in uranium mining and milling on the Navajo Reservation and at Laguna were also absolved by the BIA of responsibility for cleaning-up upon completion of their endeavors, with the result that hundreds of tailings piles were simply abandoned during the 1970s and eighties.[113] A fine sand retaining about 75 percent of the radioactive content of the original ore, the tailings constitute a massive source of windblown carcinogenic/mutogenic contaminants effecting all persons and livestock residing within a wide radius of each pile.[114] Both ground and surface water has also been heavily contaminated with radioactive byproducts throughout the Four Corners region.[115] In the Black Hills region, the situation is much the same.[116] At its Hanford nuclear weapons facility, located near the Yakima Reservation in Washington State, the AEC itself secretly discharged some 440 billion gallons of plutonium, strontium, celsium, tritium and other high level radioactive contaminants into the local aquifer between 1955 and 1989.[117]

Given that the half-life of the substances involved is as long as a quarter-million years, the magnitude of the disaster inflicted upon Native North America by IRA colonialism should not be underestimated. The Los Alamos National Scientific laboratory observed in its February 1978 *Mini-Report* that the only "solution" its staff could conceive to the problems presented by windblown radioactive contaminants would be "to zone the land into uranium mining and milling districts so as to forbid human habitation." Similarly:

> A National Academy of Science (NAS) report states bluntly that [reclamation after any sort of mining] cannot be done in areas with less than 10 inches of rainfall a year; the rainfall over most of the Navajo Nation [and many other western reservations] ranges from six to ten inches a year. The NAS suggests that such areas be spared development or honestly labeled "national sacrifice areas."[118]

Tellingly, the two areas considered most appropriate by the NAS for designation as "national sacrifices"—the Four Corners and Black Hills region—are those containing the Navajo and "Sioux Complex" of reservations, the largest remaining blocks of acknowledged Indian land and concentrations of landbased indigenous people in the U.S. For this reason, many American Indian activists have denounced both the NAS scheme, and the process of environmental destruction which led up to it, as involving not only National Sacrifice Areas, but "National Sacrifice Peoples" as well.[119] At the very least, having the last of their territory zoned "so as to forbid human habitation" would precipitate an ultimate dispersal of each impacted people, causing its disappearance as a "human group" per se.[120] As American Indian Movement leader Russell Means has put it, "It's genocide...no more, no less."[121]

Regardless of whether a policy of national sacrifice is ever implemented in the manner envisioned by the NAS, it seems fair to observe that the conditions of dire poverty and environmental degradation fostered on Indian reservations by IRA colonialism have contributed heavily to the making of the contemporary native diaspora in the United States. In combination with the constriction of the indigenous landbase brought about through earlier policies of removal, concentration, allotment and assimilation, they have created a strong and ever-increasing pressure upon reservation residents to "cooperate" with other modern federal programs meant to facilitate the outflow and dispersal of Indians from their residual landbase. Chief among these have been termination and relocation.

Termination and Relocation

As the IRA method of administering Indian Country took hold, the government returned to such tasks as "trimming the fat" from federal expenditures allocated to support Indians, largely through manipulation of the size and disposition of the recognized indigenous population.

> By 1940, the...system of colonial governance on American Indian reservations was largely in place. Only the outbreak of World War II slowed the pace of corporate exploitation, a matter that retarded initiation of maximal "development" activities until the early 1950s. By then, the questions concerning federal and corporate planners had become somewhat technical: what to do with those indigenous nations which had refused reorganization? How to remove the portion of Indian population on even the reorganized reservations whose sheer physical presence served as a barrier to wholesale strip mining and other profitable enterprises anticipated by the U.S. business community?[122]

The first means to this end was found in a partial resumption of nineteenth century assimilationist policies, focused this time on specific peoples, or parts of peoples, rather than upon Indians as a whole. On August 1, 1953, Congress approved House Resolution 108, a measure by which the federal legislature empowered itself to enact statutes "terminating" (i.e., withdrawing recognition from, and thus unilaterally dissolving) selected native peoples, typically those who had rejected reorganization, or who lacked the kind of resources necessitating their maintenance under the IRA.[123]

> Among the [nations] involved were the comparatively large and wealthy Menominee of Wisconsin and the Klamath of Oregon—both owners of extensive timber resources. Also passed were acts to terminate...the Indians of western Oregon, small Paiute bands

in Utah, and the mixed-bloods of the Uintah and Ouray Reservations. Approved, too, was legislation to transfer administrative responsibility for the Alabama and Coushatta Indians to the state of Texas... Early in the first session of the Eighty-Fourth Congress, bills were submitted to [terminate the] Wyandotte, Ottawa, and Peoria [nations] of Oklahoma. These were enacted early in August of 1956, a month after passage of legislation directing the Colville Confederated Tribes of Washington to come up with a termination plan of their own...During the second administration of President Dwight D. Eisenhower, Congress enacted three termination bills relating to...the Choctaw of Oklahoma, for whom the termination process was never completed, the Catawba of South Carolina, and the Indians of the southern California *rancherias*.[124]

It is instructive that the man chosen to implement the policy was Dillon S. Myer, an Indian Commissioner whose only apparent "job qualification" was in having headed up the internment program targeting Japanese Americans during the Second World War.[125] In total, 109 indigenous nations encompassing more than 35,000 people were terminated before the liquidation process had run its course during the early 1960s.[126] Only a handful, like the Menominee and the Siletz of Oregon, were ever "reinstated."[127] Suddenly landless, mostly poor and largely unemployed, those who were not mostly scattered like sand in the wind.[128] Even as they went, they were joined by a rapidly swelling exodus of people from unterminated reservations, a circumstance fostered by yet another federal program.

Passed in 1956, the "Relocation Act" (P.L. 959) was extended in the face of a steady diminishment throughout the first half of the decade in federal allocations to provide assistance to people living on reservations. The statute provided funding to underwrite the expenses of any Indian agreeing to move to an urban area, establish a residence, and undergo a brief period of job training. The quid pro quo was that each person applying for such relocation was required to sign an agreement that s/he would never return to his or her reservation to live. It was also specified that all federal support would be withdrawn after relocatees had spent a short period—often no more than six weeks—"adjusting" to city life.[129] Under the conditions of near-starvation on many reservations, there were many takers; nearly 35,000 people signed up to move to places like Los Angeles, Minneapolis, San Francisco, Chicago, Denver, Phoenix, Seattle and Boston during the period 1957-1959 alone.[130]

Although there was ample early indication that relocation was bearing disastrous fruit for those who underwent it—all that was happening was that relocatees were exchanging the familiar squalor of reservation life for that of the alien Indian ghettos that shortly emerged in most major cities—the government accelerated the program during the 1960s. Under the impact of termination and relocation during the fifties, the proportion of native people who had been "urbanized" rose dramatically, from 13.5 percent at the beginning of the decade to 27.9 percent at the end. During the sixties, relocation alone drove the figure upwards to 44.5 percent. During the 1970s, as the program began to be phased out, the rate of Indian urbanization decreased sharply, with the result that the proportion had risen to "only" forty-nine percent by 1980.[131] Even without a formal federal relocation effort on a national scale, the momentum of what had been set in motion over an entire generation carried the number into the mid-fiftieth percentile by 1990, and there is no firm indication the trend is abating.[132]

Despite much protestation to the contrary, those who "migrated" to the cities under the auspices of termination and relocation have already begun to join the legions of others, no longer recognized as Indians even by other Indians, who were previously discarded and forgotten along the tortuous route from 1776 to the present.[133] Cut off irrevocably from the centers of their sociocultural existence, they have increasingly adopted arbitrary and abstract methods to signify their "Indianness." Federally sanctioned "Certificates of Tribal Enrollment" have come to replace tangible participation in the political life of their nations as emblems of membership. Federally issued "Certificates of Degree of Indian Blood" have replaced discernable commitment to Indian interests as the ultimate determinant of identity.[134] In the end, by embracing such "standards," Indians are left knowing no more of being Indian than do non-Indians. The process is a cultural form of what, in the physical arena, has been termed "autogenocide."[135]

Looking Ahead

The Indian policies undertaken by the United States during the two centuries since its inception appear on the surface to have been varied, even at times contradictory. Openly genocidal at times, they have more often be garbed, however thinly, in the attire of "humanitarianism." In fact, as the matter was put by Alexis de Tocqueville, the great French commentator on the early American experience, it would occasionally have been "impossible to destroy men with more respect to the laws of humanity."[136] Always, however, there was and underlying consistency in the sentiments which begat policy: to bring about the total dispossession and disappearance of North America's indigenous population. It was this fundamental coherence in U.S. aims, invariably denied by "responsible scholars" and officials alike, which caused Adolf Hitler to ground his own notions of *lebensraumpolitik* (politics of living space) in the U.S. example.[137]

> Neither Spain nor Britain should be the models of German expansion, but the Nordics of North America, who had ruthlessly pushed aside an inferior race to win for themselves soil and territory for the future. To undertake this essential task, sometimes difficult, always cruel—this was Hitler's version of the White Man's Burden.[138]

As early as 1784, a British observer remarked that the intent of the fledgling United States with regard to American Indians was that of "extirpating them totally from the face of the earth, men, women and children."[139] In 1825, Secretary of State Henry Clay opined that U.S. Indian policy should be predicated in a presumption that the "Indian race" was "destined to extinction" in the face of persistent expansion by "superior" Anglo-Saxon "civilization."[140] During the 1870s, General of the Army Phil Sheridan is known to have called repeatedly the for "complete extermination" of targeted native groups as a means of making the West safe for repopulation by Euroamericans.[141] Subsequent assimilationists demanded the disappearance of any survivors through cultural and genetic absorption by their conquerors.[142] Well into the twentieth century, Euroamerica as a whole typically referred—often hopefully—to indigenous people as "the vanishing race," decimated and ultimately subsumed by the far greater number of invaders who had moved in upon their land.[143]

Many of the worst U.S. practices associated with these sensibilities have long since been suspended (arguably, because their goals were accomplished). Yet, largescale and deliberate dislocation of native people from their land is anything but an historical relic. Probably the most prominent current example is that of the Big Mountain Diné, perhaps the largest remaining enclave of traditionally oriented Indians in the United States. Situated astride an estimated twenty-four billion tons of the most accessible low sulfur coal in North America, the entire 13,000 person population of the Big Mountain area is even now being forcibly expelled to make way for the Peabody Coal Company's massive shovels. There being no place left on the remainder of the Navajo Reservation in which to accommodate their sheep-herding way of life, the refugees, many of them elderly, are being "resettled" in off-reservation towns like Flagstaff, Arizona.[144] Some have been sent to Phoenix,

Denver, and Los Angeles. All suffer extreme trauma and other maladies resulting from the destruction of their community and consequent "transition."[145]

Another salient illustration is that of the Western Shoshone. Mostly resident to a vast expanse of the Nevada desert secured by the ancestors in the 1863 Treaty of Ruby Valley, the Shoshones have suffered the fate of becoming the "most bombed nation on earth" by virtue of the U.S. having located the majority of its nuclear weapons testing facilities in the southern portion of their homeland since 1950. During the late seventies, despite its being unable to demonstrate that it had ever acquired valid title to the territory the Shoshones call Newe Segobia, the government began to move into the northern area as well, stating an intent to construct the MX missile system there. While the MX plan has by now been dropped, the Shoshones are still being pushed off their land, "freeing" it for use in such endeavors as nuclear waste dumps like the one recently opened at Yucca Mountain .[146]

In Alaska, where nearly two hundred indigenous peoples were instantly converted into "village corporations" by the 1971 Alaska Native Claims Settlement Act (85 Stat. 688), there is a distinct possibility that the entire native population of about 22,000 will be displaced by the demands of tourism, North Slope oil development, and other "developmental" enterprises by some point early in the twenty-first century. Already, their landbase has been constricted to a complex of tiny "townships" and their traditional economy mostly eradicated by the impacts of commercial fishing, whaling, and sealing, as well as the effects of increasing Arctic industrialization on regional caribou herds and other game animals.[147] Moreover, there is a plan—apparently conceived in all seriousness—to divert the waterflow of the Yukon River southward all the way to the Río Grande, an expedient to supporting continued non-Indian population growth in the arid regions of the lower forty-eight states and creating the agribusiness complex in the northern Mexican provinces of Sonora and Chihuahua envisioned in NAFTA.[148] It seems certain that no traditional indigenous society can be expected to stand up against such an environmental onslaught.

Eventually, if such processes are allowed to run their course, the probability is that a "Final Solution of the Indian Question" will be achieved. The key to this will rest, not in an official return to the pattern of nineteenth century massacres or emergence of some Auschwitz-style extermination center, but in the erosion of sociocultural integrity and confusion of identity afflicting any people subjected to conditions of diaspora. Like water flowing from a leaking bucket, the last self-consciously Indian people will pass into oblivion silently, unnoticed and unremarked. The deaths of cultures destroyed by such means usually occurs in this fashion, with a faint whimper rather than resistance and screams of agony.

Notes

1. U.S. Bureau of the Census, *Report on Indians Taxed and Indians Not Taxed in the United States (except Alaska) at the Eleventh United States Census: 1890* (Washington, D.C.: U.S. Government Printing Office, 1894) pp. 637-8.

2. Texts of 371 ratified treaties may be found in Charles J. Kappler, *Indian Treaties, 1778-1883* (New York: Interland, 1973).

3. U.S. Bureau of the Census, *1980 Census of the Population, Vol. I: Characteristics of the Population*, Table 69, "Persons by Race and Sex for Areas and Places: 1980" (Washington, D.C.: U.S. Government Printing Office, 1983) pp. 201-12.

4. National Congress of the American Indian (NCAI) *Briefing Paper* (Washington, D.C.: NCAI, April 1991).

5. Jack D. Forbes, "Undercounting Native Americans: The 1980 Census and Manipulation of Racial Identity in the United States," *Wicazo Sa Review*, Vol. VI, No. 1, Spring 1990, pp. 2-26.

6. U.S. Bureau of the Census, *1980 Census of the Population, Supplementary Report: American Indian Areas and Alaska Native Villages, 1980* (Washington, D.C.: U.S. Government Printing Office, 1984) p. 24.

7. Ibid., Table I, p. 14.

8. Henry F. Dobyns, *Their Numbers Become Thinned: Native American Population Dynamics in Eastern North America* (Knoxville: University of Tennessee Press, 1983) p. 41.

9. Francis Paul Prucha, *Atlas of American Indian Affairs* (Lincoln: University of Nebraska Press, 1990) pp. 151-7.

10. *1980 Census of the Population, Supplementary Report*, Table I, op. cit. The American Indian population reported for Hawai'i in 1980 was 2,655.

11. Reginald Horsman, *Expansion and American Indian Policy, 1783-1812* (Ann Arbor: University of Michigan Press, 1967) pp. 6-7.

12. Thomas Perkins Abernathy, *Western Lands and the American Revolution* (Albuquerque: University of New Mexico Press, 1979).

13. The complete text of the 1783 Treaty of Paris may be found in Hunter Miller, ed., *Treaties and Other International Acts of the United States of America* (Washington, D.C.: U.S. Government Printing Office, 1931) pp. 151-7.

14. This interpretation corresponds to conventional understandings of contemporaneous international law ("Discovery Doctrine"); see Robert A. Williams, Jr., *The American Indian in Western Legal Thought: The Discourses of Conquest* (New York: Oxford University Press, 1990).

15. Reflections on initial U.S. stature as a legal pariah are more fully developed in Vine Deloria, Jr.'s "Self-Determination and the Concept of Sovereignty," in Roxanne Dunbar Ortiz and Larry Emerson, eds., *Economic Development in American Indian Reservations* (Albuquerque: Native American Studies Center, University of New Mexico, 1979).

16. On the Northwest Territory, see Randolph C. Downes, *Council Fires on the Upper Ohio: A Narrative of Indian Affairs on the Upper Ohio until 1795* (Pittsburg: University of Pittsburg Press, 1940). On the situation further south, see R.S. Cotterill, *The Southern Indians: The Story of the Five Civilized Tribes Before Removal* (Norman: University of Oklahoma Press, 1954).

17. A.L. Burt, *The United States, Great Britain, and British North America, from the Revolution to the Establishment of Peace after the War of 1812* (New Haven: Yale University Press, 1940) pp. 82-105.

18. Arthur P. Whitaker, *The Spanish-American Frontier, 1783-1795* (Boston: Houghton-Mifflin, 1927). Also see John W. Caughey, *McGillivray of the Creeks* (Norman: University of Oklahoma Press, 1938).

19. David R. Edmunds, *Tecumseh and the Quest for American Indian Leadership* (Boston: Little, 1984).

20. Horsman, *Expansion and American Indian Policy*, op. cit., p. 7.

21. Letter from Schuyler to Congress, July 29, 1783, in *Papers of the Continental Congress, 1774-1789* (Washington, D.C.: National Archives, Item 153, III) pp. 601-7.

22. Letter from Washington to James Duane, September 7, 1783, in John C. Fitzpatrick, ed., *The Writings of George Washington from Original Manuscript Sources, 1745-1799* (Washington, D.C.: U.S. Government Printing Office, 1931-1944) Vol. XXVII, pp. 133-40.

23. In actuality, legitimate Conquest Rights never had bearing on the U.S. relationship to indigenous nations, exercise of such rights being restricted to the very confined parameters of what was at the time defined as being prosecution of a "Just War"; Williams, *American Indian in Western Legal Thought*, op. cit.

24. For analysis, see Bernard W. Sheehan, *Seeds of Extinction: Jeffersonian Philanthropy and the American Indian* (Chapel Hill: University of North Carolina Press, 1973).

25. Quoted from "Report and Resolutions of October 15, 1783," *Journals of the Continental Congress, Vol. XXV* (Washington, D.C.: U.S. Government Printing Office, no date) pp. 681-93.

26. The idea accords quite perfectly with George Washington's notion that all eastern Indians should be pushed into the "illimitable regions of the West," meaning what was then Spanish territory beyond the Mississippi (letter from Washington to Congress, June 17, 1783, in Fitzpatrick, *Writings of George Washington*, op. cit., pp. 17-8). In reality, however, the U.S. understood that it possessed no lawful right to unilaterally dispose of the territory in question in this or any other fashion. In purchasing the rights of France (which had gained them from Spain in 1800) to "Louisiana" in 1803, the U.S. plainly acknowledged indigenous land title in its pledge to Napoleon Bonaparte that it would would respect native "enjoyment of their liberty, property and religion they profess." Hence, the U.S. admitted it was not purchasing land from France, but rather a monopolistic French right within the region to acquire title over specific areas through the negotiated consent of individual Indian nations.

27. Further elaboration on the implications of the cases mentioned herein may be found in "The Tragedy and the Travesty," in *this volume*. It should be noted here, however, that Marshall was hardly a disinterested party in the issue he addressed in *Peck*. Both the Chief Justice and his father were holders of the deeds to 10,000 acre parcels in present-day West Virginia, awarded for services rendered during the revolution but falling within an area never ceded by its aboriginal owners; Leonard Baker, *John Marshall: A Life in Law* (New York: Macmillan, 1974) p. 80.

28. On the War of 1812, see Sidney Lens, *The Forging of the American Empire* (New York: Thomas Y. Crowell Co., 1971) pp. 40-61. On Tecumseh, see John Sugden, *Tecumseh's Last Stand* (Norman: University of Oklahoma Press, 1985). On the Red Sticks, see Joel W. Martin, *Sacred Revolt: The Muskogees' Struggle for a New World* (Boston: Beacon Press, 1991).

29. C.C. Griffin, *The United States and the Disruption of the Spanish Empire, 1810-1822* (New York: Columbia University Press, 1937).

30. Edwin C. McReynolds, *The Seminoles* (Norman: University of Oklahoma Press, 1957).

31. Frederick Merk, *The Monroe Doctrine and American Expansionism* (New York: Alfred A. Knopf, 1967); Albert K. Weinberg, *Manifest Destiny* (Chicago: Quadrangle Books, 1963) pp. 73-89.

32. This was the ultimate in playing both ends against the judicial middle. Thereafter, Indians could always be construed as sovereign for purposes of alienating their lands to the United States, thus validating U.S. title to territory it desired, but never sovereign enough to refuse federal demands; Vine Deloria, Jr., and Clifford M. Lytle, *American Indians, American Justice* (Austin: University of Texas Press, 1983).

33. See generally, Grant Foreman, *Advancing the Frontier, 1830-1860* (Norman: University of Oklahoma Press, 1933).

34. Gloria Jahoda, *The Trail of Tears: The Story of the American Indian Removals, 1813-1855* (New York: Holt, Rinehart and Winston, 1975). Also see Grant Foreman, *Indian Removal: The Immigration of the Five Civilized Tribes* (Norman: University of Oklahoma Press, 1953).

35. Driven from Illinois, the main body of Sauks were trapped and massacred—men, women and children alike—at the juncture of the Bad Axe and Mississippi Rivers in Wisconsin; Cecil Eby, *"That Disgraceful Affair": The Black Hawk War* (New York: W.W. Norton, 1973) pp. 243-61.

36. In many ways, the Seminole "hold-outs" were the best guerrilla fighters the U.S. ever faced. The commitment of 30,000 troops for several years was insufficient to subdue them. Ultimately, the U.S. broke off the conflict, which was stalemated, and in which it was costing several thousand dollars for each Indian killed; Fairfax Downey, *Indian Wars of the United States Army, 1776-1865* (New York: Doubleday, 1963) pp. 116-7.

37. Wilcomb E. Washburn, *The Indian in America* (New York: Harper Torchbooks, 1975) p. 169.

38. Russell Thornton, "Cherokee Losses During the Trail of Tears: A New Perspective and a New Estimate," *Ethnohistory*, No. 31, 1984, pp. 289-300.

39. Ibid., p. 293.

40. *1980 Census of the Population, Supplementary Report*, op. cit.

41. Duane H. King, *The Cherokee Nation: A Troubled History* (Knoxville: University of Tennessee Press, 1979) pp. 103-9.

42. Angie Debo, *A History of the Indians of the United States* (Norman: University of Oklahoma Press, 1977) p. 157.

43. Very little work has been done to document this proliferation of communities, although their existence has been increasingly admitted since the 1960s.

44. Marquis James, *Andrew Jackson: Border Ruffian* (New York: Grossett and Dunlap, 1933). Jackson's stated goal was not simply to defeat the Red Sticks, but to "exterminate" them. At least 557 Indians, many of them noncombatants, were killed after being surrounded at the Horseshoe Bend of the Tallapoosa River, in northern Alabama.

45. The text of Jackson's talk of March 23, 1829 was originally published in *Documents and Proceedings relating to the Formation and Progress of a Board in the City of New York, for the Emigration, Preservation, and Improvement of the Aborigines of America* (New York: Indian Board for the Emigration, Preservation and Improvement of the Aborigines of America, 1829) p. 5.

46. Frederick Merk, *Manifest Destiny and Mission in American History* (New York: Alfred A. Knopf, 1963).

47. Quoted in Lens, *Forging of the American Empire*, op. cit., p. 100.

48. Actually, this transcontinental gallop represents a rather reserved script. As early as 1820, Luis de Onis, former Spanish governor of Florida, observed that, "The Americans...believe that their dominion is destined to extend, now to the Isthmus of Panama, and hereafter over all the regions of the New World...They consider themselves superior to the rest of mankind, and look upon their republic as the only establishment upon earth founded on a grand and solid basis, embellished by wisdom, and destined one day to become the sublime colossus of human power, and the wonder of the universe (quoted in Lens, *Forging of the American Empire*, op. cit., pp. 94-5). It is a matter of record that William Henry Seward, Secretary of State under Lincoln and Johnson in the 1860s, advanced a serious plan to annex all of Canada west of Ontario, but was ultimately forced to content himself with acquiring Alaska Territory. See R. W. Van Alstyne, *The Rising American Empire* (New York: Oxford University Press, 1960).

49. A map delineating the "permanent" territories assigned these peoples after removal is contained in Jack D. Forbes, *Atlas of Native History* (Davis, CA: D-Q University Press, no date).

50. The federal government recognizes less than half (32) of these nations as still existing; see John W. Morris, Charles R. Goins, and Edward C. McReynolds, *Historical Atlas of Oklahoma* (Norman: University of Oklahoma Press, [3rd ed.] 1986) Map 76.

51. According to *1980 Census of the Population, Supplementary Report* (Table I, op. cit.) Oklahoma's Indian population of 169,292 is second only to California's 198,275. The Osage Reservation evidences a population of 4,749 Indians, 12.1 percent of its 39,327 total inhabitants (ibid., p. 22).

52. On the War with Mexico, see George Pierce Garrison, *Westward Expansion, 1841-1850* (New York: Harper, 1937).

53. David Svaldi, *Sand Creek and the Rhetoric of Extermination: A Case-Study in Indian-White Relations*, (Washington, D.C.: University Press of America, 1989).

54. Much of this is covered in Ralph K. Andrist, *The Long Death: The Last Days of the Plains Indians* (New York: Collier Books, 1964). Also see Paul Andrew Hutton, *Phil Sheridan and His Army* (Lincoln: University of Nebraska Press, 1985).

55. L.R. Bailey, *The Long Walk: A History of the Navajo Wars, 1846-68* (Pasadena, CA: Westernlore Publications, 1978).

56. This episode is covered adequately in Edward Lazarus, *Black Hills, White Justice: The Sioux Nation versus the United States, 1775 to the Present* (New York: HarperCollins, 1991) pp. 71-95.

57. See Robert Clark, ed., *The Killing of Chief Crazy Horse* (Lincoln: University of Nebraska Press, 1976), and the concluding chapter of Stanley Vestal's *Sitting Bull: Champion of the Sioux* (Norman: University of Oklahoma Press, 1957).

58. The imprisonment program is described in some detail in the memoirs of the commandant of Marion Prison, later superintendent of the Carlisle Indian School; Richard Henry Pratt, *Battlefield and Classroom: Four Decades with the American Indian, 1867-1904* (New Haven: Yale University Press, [reprint] 1964).

59. *Report on Indians Taxed and Indians Not Taxed*, op. cit., pp. 637-8.

60. Lazarus, *Black Hills, White Justice*, op. cit., p. 29. It should be noted that, contrary to myth, scalping was a practice introduced to the Americas by Europeans, not native people. It was imported by the British—who had previously used it against the Irish—during the seventeenth century; Nicholis P. Canny, "The Ideology of English Colonialism: From Ireland to America," *William and Mary Quarterly*, 3rd Series, XXX, 1973, pp. 575-98.

61. Lenore A. Stiffarm and Phil Lane, Jr., "The Demography of Native North America: A Question of American Indian Survival," in M. Annette Jaimes, ed., *The State of Native America: Genocide, Colonization and Resistance* (Boston: South End Press, 1992) p. 35. It is instructive that the Texas state legislature framed its Indian policy as follows: "We recognize no title in the Indian tribes resident within the limits of the state to any portion of the soil thereof; and…we recognize no right of the Government of the United States to make any treaty of limits with the said Indian tribes without the consent of the Government of this state" (quoted in Washburn, *The Indian in America,* op. cit., p. 174). In other words, extermination was intended to be total.

62. James M. Mooney, "Population," in Frederick W. Dodge, ed., *Handbook of the Indians North of Mexico, Vol. 2* (Washington, D.C.: Bureau of American Ethnology, Bulletin No. 30, Smithsonian Institution, 1910) pp. 286-7.

63. Sherburn F. Cook, *The Conflict Between the California Indian and White Civilization* (Berkeley: University of California Press, 1976) pp. 282-4.

64. Russell Thornton, *American Indian Holocaust and Survival: A Population History Since 1492* (Norman: University of Oklahoma Press, 1987) p. 49.

65. Thornton estimates the aboriginal North American population to have been about 12.5 million, most of it within what is now the continental U.S. Dobyns (*Numbers Become Thinned*, op. cit.) estimates it as having been as high as 18.5 million. Kirkpatrick Sale, in his *The Conquest of Paradise: Christopher Columbus and the Columbian Legacy* (New York: Alfred A. Knopf, 1990) splits the difference, placing the figure at 15 million. Extreme attrition due to disease and colonial warfare had already occurred prior to the American War of Independence. Something on the order of two million survivors in 1776 therefore seems a reasonable estimate. Whatever the exact number in that year, it had been reduced to 237,196 according to U.S. census data for 1900; U.S. Bureau of the Census, *Fifteenth Census of the United States, 1930: The Indian Population of the United States and Alaska,* Table 2, "Indian Population by State, 1890-1930" (Washington, D.C.: U.S. Government Printing Office, 1937) p. 3.

66. Cook, *Conflict*, op. cit. p. 284.

67. Donald J. Berthrong, *The Cheyenne and Arapaho Ordeal: Reservation and Agency Life in the Indian Territory, 1875-1907* (Norman: University of Oklahoma Press, 1976). Also see Mari Sandoz, *Cheyenne Autumn* (New York: Avon, 1964).

68. Dan L. Thrapp, *The Conquest of Apacheria* (Norman: University of Oklahoma Press, 1967).

69. Merril Beal, *I Will Fight No More Forever: Chief Joseph and the Nez Percé War* (Seattle: University of Washington Press, 1963).

70. Kenneth Carley, *The Sioux Uprising of 1862* (St. Paul: Minnesota Historical Society, 1961).

71. Edmund Wilson, *Apology to the Iroquois* (New York: Farrar, Strauss, and Cudahy, 1960).

72. As of 1980, a grand total of 582 members of these amalgamated peoples were reported as living on the Stockbridge Reservation; *1980 Census of the Population, Supplementary Report,* Table I, op. cit.

73. The next major leap in this direction was passage of the Assimilative Crimes Act (30 Stat. 717) in 1898, applying state, territorial, and district criminal codes to "federal enclaves" such as Indian reservations; Robert N. Clinton, "Development of Criminal Jurisdiction on Reservations: A Journey Through a Jurisdictional Maze," *Arizona Law Review,* Vol. 18, No. 3, 1976, pp. 503-83.

74. Overall, see Janet A. McDonnell, *The Dispossession of the American Indian, 1887-1934* (Bloomington: Indiana University Press, 1991).

75. As is stated in the current procedures for enrollment provided by the Cherokee Nation of Oklahoma, "Many descendants of the Cherokee Indians can neither be certified nor qualify for tribal membership in the Cherokee Nation because their ancestors were not enrolled during the final enrollment [during allotment, 1899-1906]. Unfortunately, these ancestors did not meet the [federal] requirements for the final enrollment. The requirements at the time were…having a permanent residence within the Cherokee Nation (now the fourteen northeastern counties of Oklahoma). If the ancestors

had...settled in the states of Arkansas, Kansas, Missouri, or Texas, they lost their citizenship within the Cherokee Nation at that time."

76. D.S. Otis, *The Dawes Act and the Allotment of Indian Land* (Norman: University of Oklahoma Press, 1973).

77. James S. Olson and Raymond Wilson, *Native Americans in the Twentieth Century* (Urbana: University of Illinois Press, 1984) pp. 82-3.

78. Kirk Kicking Bird and Karen Ducheneaux, *One Hundred Million Acres* (New York: Macmillan, 1973).

79. The powers of individual agents in this regard accrued from an amendment (26 Stat. 794) made in 1891. The descriptive language comes from Deloria and Lytle, *American Indians, American Justice*, op. cit., p. 10.

80. This is known as the "Heirship Problem," meaning that if a family head with four children began with a 160 acre parcel of marginal land in 1900, his/her heirs would each inherit forty acres somewhere around 1920. If each of these heirs, in turn, had four children, then their heirs would inherit ten acres, circa 1940. Following the same formula, their heirs would have inherited 2.5 acres each in 1960, and their heirs would have received about one-half acre each in 1980. In actuality, many twentieth century families have been much larger during the twentieth century—as is common among peoples recovering from genocide—and contemporary descendants of the original allottees often find themselves measuring their "holdings" in square inches. For a fuller discussion of the issue, see Ethel J. Williams, "Too Little Land, Too Many Heirs: The Indian Heirship Problem," *Washington Law Review*, No. 46, 1971.

81. Rebecca L. Robbins, "Self-Determination and Subordination: The Past, Present and Future of American Indian Governance," in *State of Native America*, op. cit., p. 93. The quote from Leupp comes from his book, *The Indian and His Problem* (New York: Scribner, 1910) p. 93; that from Burke from a letter to William Williamson on Sept. 16, 1921 (William Williamson Papers, Box 2, File—Indian Matters, Misc., I.D. Weeks Library, University of South Dakota).

82. Among other things, the decision meant that the U.S. had decided it could unilaterally absolve itself of any obligation or responsibility it had incurred under provision of any treaty with any indigenous nation while simultaneously considering the Indians to still be bound by *their* treaty commitments. See Ann Laquer Estin, "*Lonewolf v. Hitchcock*: The Long Shadow," in Sandra L. Cadwallader and Vine Deloria, Jr., eds., *The Aggressions of Civilization: Federal Indian Policy Since the 1880s* (Philadelphia: Temple University Press, 1984) pp. 215-45. This was an utterly illegitimate posture under international custom and convention at the time, a matter amply reflected in contemporary international black letter law. See Sir Ian Sinclair, *The Vienna Convention on the Law of Treaties* (Manchester: Manchester University Press, [2nd ed.] 1984).

83. Much of this is covered—proudly—in Pratt, *Battlefield to Classroom*, op. cit. Also see David Wallace Adams, *Education for Extinction: American Indians and the Boarding School Experience, 1875-1928* (Lawrence: University Press of Kansas, 1995)..

84. Evelyn C. Adams, *American Indian Education: Government Schools and Economic Progress* (Morningside Heights, NY: King's Crown Press, 1946) pp. 55-6, 70.

85. The phrase used was picked up by the author in a 1979 conversation with Floyd Westerman, a Sisseton Dakota who was sent to a boarding school at age six. For a broader statement of the same theme, see Vine Deloria, Jr., "Education and Imperialism," *Integrateducation*, Vol. XIX, Nos. 1-2, January 1982, pp. 58-63. For ample citation of the federal view, see J.U. Ogbu, "Cultural Discontinuities and Schooling," *Anthropology and Education Quarterly*, Vol. 12, No. 4, 1982, pp. 1-10.

86. On adoption policies, including those pertaining to so-called "blind" adoptions (where children are prevented by law from ever learning their parents' or tribe's identities), see Tillie Blackbear Walker, "American Indian Children: Foster Care and Adoptions," in U.S. Office of Education, Office of Educational Research and Development, National Institute of Education, *Conference on Educational and Occupational Needs of American Indian Women* (Washington, D.C.: U.S. Dept. of Education, 1980) pp. 185-210.

87. The entire program involving forced transfer of Indian children is contrary to Article II (d) of the United Nations 1948 Convention on Punishment and Prevention of the Crime of Genocide; Ian Brownlie, *Basic Documents on Human Rights* (Oxford: Clarendon Press, [3rd ed.] 1992) p. 31.

88. Thornton, *American Indian Holocaust and Survival*, op. cit., p. 227.

89. These estimates have been arrived at by deducting the reservation population totals from the overall census figures deployed in Prucha (*Atlas*), and then subtracting the urban population totals used by Russell Thornton (see Note 88, above).

90. The U.S., as is well known, undertook the Spanish-American War in 1898 primarily to acquire overseas colonies, notably the Philippines and Cuba (for which Puerto Rico was substituted at the last moment). It also took the opportunity to usurp the government of Hawai'i, about which it had been expressing ambitions since 1867, and to obtain a piece of Samoa in 1899. This opened the door to its assuming "protectorate" responsibility over Guam and other German colonies after World War I, and many of the Micronesian possessions of Japan after World War II. See Julius Pratt, *The Expansionists of 1898* (Baltimore: Johns Hopkins University Press, 1936); Richard O'Connor, *Pacific Destiny: An Informal History of the U.S. in the Far East, 1776-1968* (Boston: Little, Brown, 1969).

91. Anita Parlow, *Cry, Sacred Ground: Big Mountain, USA* (Washington, D.C.: Christic Institute, 1988) p. 30.

92. Olson and Wilson, *Native Americans in the Twentieth Century*, op. cit., p. 181.

93. For a good overview, see Craig H. Miner, *The Corporation and the Indian: Tribal Sovereignty and Industrial Civilization in Indian Territory, 1865-1907* (Columbia: University of Missouri Press, 1976).

94. This is brought out in thinly veiled fashion in official studies commissioned at the time. See, for example, U.S. House of Representatives, Committee of One Hundred, *The Indian Problem: Resolution of the Committee of One Hundred Appointed by the Secretary of Interior and Review of the Indian Problem* (Washington, D.C.: H.Doc. 149, Ser. 8392, 68th Cong., 1st Sess., 1925). Also see Lewis Meriam, et al., *The Problem of Indian Administration* (Baltimore: Johns Hopkins University Press, 1928).

95. This was standard colonialist practice during the same period. See Mark Frank Lindsey, *The Acquisition and Government of Backward Territory in International Law* (London: Longmans Green, 1926).

96. For what may be the first application of the term "internal colonies" to analysis of the situation of American Indians in the U.S., see Robert K. Thomas, "Colonialism: Classic and Internal," *New University Thought*, Vol. 4, No. 4, Winter 1966-67.

97. For the best account of how the IRA "package" was assembled, see the relevant chapters of Deloria and Lytle, *Nations Within*, op. cit.

98. The classic example of this occurred at the Hopi Reservation, where some 85 percent of all eligible voters actively boycotted the IRA referendum in 1936. Indian Commissioner John Collier then counted these abstentions as "aye" votes, making it appear as if the Hopis had been nearly unanimous in affirming reorganization rather than overwhelmingly rejecting it. See Oliver LaFarge, *Running Narrative of the Organization of the Hopi Tribe of Indians* (unpublished manuscript in the LaFarge Collection, University of Texas at Austin). In general, the IRA referendum process was similar to—and served essentially the same purpose as—those more recently orchestrated abroad by the State Department and CIA; see Edward S. Herman and Frank Brodhead, *Demonstration Elections: U.S.-Staged Elections in the Dominican Republic, Vietnam, and El Salvador* (Boston: South End Press, 1984).

99. Robbins, "Self-Determination and Subordination," op. cit., p. 95.

100. See generally, my and Winona LaDuke's "Native North America: The Political Economy of Radioactive Colonization," in *State of Native America*, op. cit., pp. 241-66.

101. Alvin Josephy, "Murder of the Southwest," *Audubon Magazine*, Sept. 1971, p. 42.

102. Bruce Johansen and Roberto Maestas, *Wasi'chu: The Continuing Indian Wars* (New York: Monthly Review Press, 1979) p. 162. The minimum rate was established by the Federal Coal Leasing Act of 1975, applicable everywhere in the U.S. except Indian reservations.

103. Olson and Wilson, *Native Americans in the Twentieth Century*, op. cit., p. 200.

104. The term "super-profits" is used in the manner defined by Richard J. Barnet and Ronald E. Müller in their *Global Reach: The Power of the Multinational Corporations* (New York: Touchstone, 1974).

105. U.S. Department of Interior, Bureau of Indian Affairs, *Indian Service Population and Labor Force Estimates* (Washington, D.C.: U.S. Government Printing Office, 1989). The study shows one-third of the 635,000 reservation-based Indians survey had an annual income of less than $7,000.

106. U.S. Senate, Committee on Labor and Human Resources, *Guaranteed Job Opportunity Act: Hearing on S. 777* (Washington, D.C.: 100th Cong., 1st Sess., Mar. 23 1987, Appendix A).

107. The classic image of this is that of Emma Yazzie, an elderly and very traditional Diné who subsists on her flock of sheep, standing forlornly before a gigantic Peabody coal shovel which is digging

up her scrubby grazing land on Black Mesa. The coal is to produce electricity for Phoenix and Las Vegas, but Yazzie has never had electricity (or running water) in her home. She gains nothing from the enterprise. To the contrary, her very way of life is being destroyed before her eyes. See Johansen and Maestas, *Wasi'chu*, op. cit., p. 141.

108. The term "underdevelopment" is used in the sense defined by Andre Gunder Frank in his *Capitalism and Underdevelopment in Latin America* (New York: Monthly Review Press, 1967).

109. U.S. Bureau of the Census, *A Statistical Profile of the American Indian Population* (Washington, D.C.: U.S. Government Printing Office, 1984). Also see U.S. Department of Health and Human Services, *Chart Series Book* (Washington, D.C.: Public Health Service, 1988).

110. The terminology accrues from Eduardo Galeano, *The Open Veins of Latin America: Five Centuries of the Pillage of a Continent* (New York: Monthly Review Press, 1973).

111. Thus far, the only people which has been able to turn this around have been the Northern Cheyenne, which won a 1976 lawsuit to have Class I environment protection standards applied to their reservation, thereby halting construction of two coal-fired generating plants before it began. The BIA had already waived such protections in the Cheyennes' "behalf." See Johansen and Maestas, *Wasi'chu*, op. cit., p. 174.

112. Rex Weyler, *Blood of the Land: The U.S. Government and Corporate War Against the American Indian Movement* (New York: Everest House, 1982) pp. 154-5.

113. Tom Barry, "Bury My Lungs at Red Rock," *The Progressive*, Feb. 1979.

114. On tailings and associated problems such as radon gas emissions, see J.B. Sorenson, *Radiation Issues: Government Decision Making and Uranium Expansion in Northern New Mexico* (Albuquerque: San Juan Regional Study Group, Working Paper 14, 1978). On carcinogenic/mutogenic effects, see J.M. Samet, et al., "Uranium Mining and Lung Cancer in Navajo Men," *New England Journal of Medicine*, No. 310, 1984, pp. 1481-4; Harold Tso and Laura Mangum Shields, "Navajo Mining Operations: Early Hazards and Recent Interventions," *New Mexico Journal of Science*, Vol. 20, No. 1, June 1980.

115. Richard Hoppe, "A stretch of desert along Route 66—the Grants Belt—is chief locale for U.S. uranium," *Engineering and Mining Journal*, Nov. 1978. Also see Nancy J. Owens, "Can Tribes Control Energy Development?" in Joseph Jorgenson, ed., *American Indians and Energy Development* (Cambridge, MA: Anthropology Resource Center, 1978).

116. Amelia Irvin, "Energy Development and the Effects of Mining on the Lakota Nation," *Journal of Ethnic Studies*, Vol. 10, No. 2, Spring 1982.

117. Elouise Schumacher, "440 billion gallons: Hanford wastes would fill 900 King Domes," *Seattle Times*, Apr. 13, 1991.

118. Johansen and Maestas, *Wasi'chu*, op. cit., p. 154. They are referring to Thadis Box, et al., *Rehabilitation Potential for Western Coal Lands* (Cambridge, MA: Ballinger, 1974). The book is the published version of a study commissioned by the National Academy of Science and submitted to the Nixon administration in 1972.

119. Russell Means, "Fighting Words on the Future of Mother Earth," *Mother Jones*, Dec. 1980, p. 27.

120. Bringing about the destruction of an identifiable "human racial, ethnical or racial group" as such, is and always has been the defining criterion of genocide. As the matter was framed by Raphaël Lemkin, who coined the term: "Generally speaking, genocide does not necessarily mean the immediate destruction of a nation, *except when* accomplished by mass killing of all the members of a nation. It is intended rather to signify a coordinated plan of different actions aimed at destruction of the essential foundations of the life of national groups, with the aim of annihilating the groups themselves. The objective of such a plan would be disintegration of the political and and social institutions, of culture, language, national feelings, religion, and the economic existence of national groups, and the destruction of personal security, liberty, health, dignity, and the lives of individuals belonging to such groups. Genocide is the destruction of the national group as an entity, and the actions involved are directed against individuals, not in their individual capacity but as members of the national group (emphasis added)." Raphaël Lemkin, *Axis Rule in Occupied Europe* (Washington, D.C.: Carnegie Endowment for International Peace, 1944) p. 79. The view is reflected in the 1948 Convention on Punishment and Prevention of the Crime of Genocide.

121. Means, "Fighting Words," op. cit.

122. Robbins, "Self-Determination and Subordination," op. cit., p. 97.

123. The complete text of House Resolution 108 appears in Part II of Edward H. Spicer's *A Short History of the United States* (New York: Van Nostrum, 1968).

124. James E. Officer, "Termination as Federal Policy: An Overview," in Kenneth R. Philp, ed., *Indian Self-Rule: First-Hand Accounts of Indian-White Relations from Roosevelt to Reagan* (Salt Lake City: Howe Bros., 1986) p. 125.

125. Richard Drinnon, *Keeper of Concentration Camps: Dillon S. Myer and American Racism* (Berkeley: University of California Press, 1987).

126. Raymond V. Butler, "The Bureau of Indian Affairs Activities Since 1945," *Annals of the Academy of American Academy of Political and Social Science*, No. 436, 1978, pp. 50-60. The last dissolution, that of the Oklahoma Ponca, was delayed in committee and was not consummated until 1966.

127. See generally, Nicholas Peroff, *Menominee DRUMS: Tribal Termination and Restoration, 1954-1974* (Norman: University of Oklahoma Press, 1982).

128. Oliver LaFarge, "Termination of Federal Supervision: Disintegration and the American Indian," *Annals of the American Academy of Political and Social Science*, No. 311, May 1975, pp. 56-70.

129. See generally, Donald L. Fixico, *Termination and Relocation: Federal Indian Policy, 1945-1960* (Albuquerque: University of New Mexico Press, 1986).

130. Sharon O'Brien, *American Indian Tribal Governments* (Norman: University of Oklahoma Press, 1989) p. 86.

131. U.S. Bureau of the Census, *General Social and Economic Characteristics: United States Summary* (Washington, D.C.: U.S. Government Printing Office, 1983) p. 92. Also see Thornton, *American Indian Holocaust and Survival*, op. cit., p. 227.

132. NCAI *Briefing Paper*, op. cit.

133. For use of the term "migration" to describe the effects of termination and relocation, see James H. Gundlach, Nelson P. Reid and Alden E. Roberts, "Native American Migration and Relocation," *Pacific Sociological Review*, No. 21, 1978, pp. 117-27. On the "discarded and forgotten," see American Indian Policy Review Commission, Task Force Ten, *Report on Terminated and Nonfederally Recognized Tribes* (Washington, D.C.: U.S. Government Printing Office, 1976).

134. Alan L. Sokin, *The Urban American Indian* (Lexington, MA: Lexington Books, 1978).

135. The term was coined in the mid-1970s to describe the self-destructive behavior exhibited by the Khmer Rouge régime in Kampuchea (Cambodia) in response to genocidal policies earlier extended against that country by the United States. For analysis, see Noam Chomsky and Edward S. Herman, *After the Cataclysm: Postwar Indochina and the Reconstruction of Imperial Ideology* (Boston: South End Press, 1979).

136. Alexis de Tocqueville, *Democracy in America* (New York: Harper & Row, 1966) p. 312.

137. "Hitler's concept of concentration camps as well as the practicality of genocide owed much, so he claimed, to his studies of British and United States history. He admired the camps for Boer prisoners in South Africa and for the Indians in the wild West; and often praised to his inner circle the efficiency of America's extermination—by starvation and uneven combat—of the red savages who could not be tamed by captivity"; John Toland, *Adolf Hitler* (New York: Doubleday, 1976) p. 802.

138. Norman Rich, *Hitler's War Aims: Ideology, the Nazi State, and the Course of Expansion* (New York: W.W. Norton, 1973) p. 8. Rich is relying primarily on the secret but nonetheless official policy position articulated by Hitler during a meeting on November 5, 1937 and recorded by his adjutant, Freidrich Hössbach. The "Hössbach Memorandum" is contained in *Trial of the Major War Criminals before the International Military Tribunal, Proceedings and Documents, Vol. 25* (Nuremberg: 1947-1949) pp. 402-6.

139. John F.D. Smyth, *A Tour of the United States of America* (London: Privately Published, 1784) p. 346.

140. Quoted in Reginald Horsman, *Race and Manifest Destiny: The Origins of Racial Anglo-Saxonism* (Cambridge, MA: Harvard University Press, 1981) p. 198.

141. See the various quotes in Hutton, *Phil Sheridan* , op. cit.

142. Henry E. Fritz, *The Movement for Indian Assimilation, 1860-1890* (Philadelphia: University of Pennsylvania Press, 1963).

143. The classic articulation, of course, is Joseph K. Dixon's 1913 *The Vanishing Race*, recently reprinted by Bonanza Books, New York. An excellent examination of the phenomenon may be found in Stan Steiner's *The Vanishing White Man* (Norman: University of Oklahoma Press, 1976).

144. Parlow, *Cry, Sacred Land*, op. cit. Also see Jerry Kammer, *The Second Long Walk: The Navajo-Hopi Land Dispute* (Albuquerque: University of New Mexico Press, 1980).

145. Thayer Scudder, et al., *No Place to Go: Effects of Compulsory Relocation on Navajos* (Philadelphia: Institute for the Study of Human Issues, 1982).

146. Dagmar Thorpe, *Newe Segobia: The Western Shoshone People and Land* (Battle Mountain, NV: Western Shoshone Sacred Lands Association, 1981). Also see Glenn T. Morris, "The Battle for Newe Segobia: The Western Shoshone Land Rights Struggle," in Ward Churchill, ed., *Critical Issues in Native North America, Vol. II* (Copenhagen: IWGIA Doc. 68, 1991) pp. 86-98.

147. M.C. Barry, *The Alaska Pipeline: The Politics of Oil and Native Land Claims* (Bloomington: Indiana University Press, 1975). Also see Thomas R. Berger, *Village Journey: The Report of the Alaska Native Review Commission* (New York: Hill and Wang, 1985).

148. The plan is known by the title of its sponsoring organization, the North American Water and Power Association (NAWAPA). It is covered in Mark Reisner's *Cadillac Desert: The American West and Its Disappearing Water* (New York: Viking, 1986). Also see "The Water Plot," in this volume.

PART IV: AN ALTERNATIVE

This time I almost wanted to believe you
when you said it would be alright
you wanted to end the suffering;
And the deliberateness of the wrongs
were only in my imagination
This time I almost wanted
to believe you
when you implied
      the times of sorrow
          were buried in the past
              never would we
                  have to worry
                      about shadows and
                          memories clinging
                            and draining
                              the strength
                  from our souls

This time I almost wanted
to believe you
when you spoke
      of peace and love
      and caring and duty
      and God and destiny
But somehow the
           death in your eyes
              and your bombs
              and your taxes
              and your greed
told me
this time
I cannot afford
to believe you.

—John Trudell
from *Living in Reality*

I AM INDIGENIST

Notes on the Ideology of the Fourth World

> The growth of ethnic consciousness and the consequent mobilization of Indian communities in the Western hemisphere since the early 1960s have been welcomed neither by government forces nor by opposition parties and revolutionary movements. The "Indian Question" has been an almost forbidden subject of debate throughout the entire political spectrum, although racism, discrimination and exploitation are roundly denounced on all sides.
>
> —Roxanne Dunbar Ortiz
> *Indians of the Americas*

VERY often in my writings and lectures, I have identified myself as being "indigenist" in outlook. By this, I mean that I am one who not only takes the rights of indigenous peoples as the highest priority of my political life, but who draws upon the traditions—the bodies of knowledge and corresponding codes of value—evolved over many thousands of years by native peoples the world over. This is the basis upon which I not only advance critiques of, but conceptualize alternatives to the present social, political, economic, and philosophical status quo. In turn, this gives shape not only to the sorts of goals and objectives I pursue, but the kinds of strategy and tactics I advocate, the variety of struggles I tend to support, the nature of the alliances I am inclined to enter into, and so on.

Let me say, before I go any further, that I am hardly unique or alone in adopting this perspective. It is a complex of ideas, sentiments, and understandings which motivates the whole of the American Indian Movement, broadly defined, here in North America. This is true whether you call it AIM, or Indians of All Tribes (as was done during the 1969 occupation of Alcatraz), the Warriors Society (as was the case with the Mohawk rebellion at Oka in 1990), Women of All Red Nations, or whatever.[1]

It is the spirit of resistance that shapes the struggles of traditional Indian people on the land, whether the struggle is down at Big Mountain, in the Black Hills, or up at James Bay, in the Nevada desert or out along the

Columbia River in what is now called Washington State.[2] In the sense that I use the term, indigenism is also, I think, the outlook that guided our great leaders of the past: King Philip and Pontiac, Tecumseh and Creek Mary and Osceola, Black Hawk, Nancy Ward and Satanta, Lone Wolf and Red Cloud, Satank and Quannah Parker, Left Hand and Crazy Horse, Dull Knife and Chief Joseph, Sitting Bull, Roman Nose and Captain Jack, Louis Ríel and Poundmaker and Geronimo, Cochise and Mangus, Victorio, Chief Seattle, and on and on.[3]

In my view, those, Indian and non-Indian alike, who do not recognize these names and what they represent have no sense of the true history—the reality—of North America. They have no sense of where they've come from or where they are and thus can have no genuine sense of who or what they are. By not looking at where they've come from, they cannot know where they are going or where it is they *should* go. It follows that they cannot understand what it is they are to do, how to do it, or why. In their confusion, they identify with the wrong people, the wrong things, the wrong tradition. They therefore inevitably pursue the wrong goals and objectives, putting last things first and often forgetting the first things altogether, perpetuating the very structures of oppression and degradation they think they oppose. Obviously, if things are to be changed for the better in this world, then this particular problem must itself be changed as a matter of first priority.

In any event, all of this is not to say that I think I am one of the significant people I have named, or the host of others, equally worthy, who've gone unnamed. I have no "New Age" conception of myself as the reincarnation of someone who has come before. But it *is* to say that I take these ancestors as my inspiration, as the only historical examples of proper attitude and comportment on this continent, this place, this land on which I live and of which I am a part. I embrace them as my heritage, my role models, the standard by which I must measure myself. I try always to be worthy of the battles they fought, the sacrifices they made. For the record, I have always found myself wanting in this regard, but I subscribe to the notion that one is obligated to speak the truth, even if one cannot live up to or fully practice it. As Chief Dan George once put it, I "endeavor to persevere," and I suppose this is a circumstance which is shared more-or-less equally by everyone presently involved in what I refer to as "indigenism."

Others whose writings and speeches and actions may be familiar, and who fit the definition of indigenist—or "Fourth Worlder," as we are sometimes called—include Winona LaDuke and John Trudell, Simon Ortiz, Russell Means and Leonard Peltier, Glenn Morris and Leslie Silko, Jimmie Durham, John Mohawk and Oren Lyons, Bob Robideau and Dino Butler, Ingrid Washinawatok and Dagmar Thorpe. There are scholars and attorneys like Vine Deloria, Don Grinde, Pam Colorado, Sharon Venne, George Tinker, Bob Thomas, Jack Forbes, Rob Williams and Hank Adams. There are poets like Wendy Rose, Adrian Louis, Dian Million, Chrystos, Elizabeth Woody and Barnie Bush.

There are also many grassroots warriors in the contemporary world, people like the Dann sisters, Bernard Ominayak, Art Montour and Buddy Lamont, Madonna Thunderhawk, Anna Mae Aquash, Kenny Kane and Joe Stuntz, Minnie Garrow and Bobby Garcia, Dallas Thundershield, Phyllis Young, Andrea Smith and Richard Oaks, Margo Thunderbird, Tina Trudell and Roque Duenas. And, of course, there are the elders, those who have given, and continue to give, continuity and direction to indigenist expression; I am referring to people like Chief Fools Crow and Matthew King, Henry Crow Dog and Grampa David Sohappy, David Monongye and Janet McCloud and Thomas Banyacya, Roberta Blackgoat and Katherine Smith and Pauline Whitesinger, Marie Leggo and Phillip Deer and Ellen Moves Camp, Raymond Yowell and Nellie Red Owl.[4]

Like the historical figures I mentioned earlier, these are names representing positions, struggles, and aspirations which should be well-known to every socially-conscious person in North America. They embody the absolute antithesis of the order represented by the "Four Georges"—George Washington, George Custer, George Patton and George Bush—emblemizing the sweep of "American" history as it is conventionally taught in that system of indoctrination the United States passes off as "education." They also stand as the negation of that long stream of "Vichy Indians"[5] spawned and deemed "respectable" by the process of predation, colonialism, and genocide the Four Georges signify.

The names I have listed cannot be associated with the legacy of the "Hang Around the Fort" Indians, broken, disempowered, and intimidated by their conquerors, or with the sellouts who undermined the integrity of their own cultures, appointed by the United States to sign away their peoples' homelands in exchange for trinkets, sugar, and alcohol. They are not the figurative descendants of those who participated in the assassination of people like Crazy Horse and Sitting Bull, and who filled the ranks of the colonial police to enforce an illegitimate and alien order against their own. They are not among those who have queued up to roster the régimes installed by the U.S. to administer Indian Country from the 1930s onward, the craven puppets who to this day cling to and promote the "lawful authority" of federal force as a means of protecting their positions of petty privilege, imagined prestige, and often their very identities as native people. No, indigenists and indigenism have nothing to do with the sorts of Quisling impulses driving the Ross Swimmers, Dickie Wilsons, Webster Two Hawks, Peter McDonalds, Vernon Bellecourts and David Bradleys of this world.[6]

Instead, indigenism offers an antidote, a vision of how things might be that is based in how things have been since time immemorial, and how things must be once again if the human species, and perhaps the planet itself, is to survive much longer. Predicated on a synthesis of the wisdom attained over thousands of years by indigenous, landbased peoples around the globe—the Fourth World or, as Winona LaDuke puts it, "The Host World upon which the first, second and third worlds all sit at the present time"—indigenism stands in diametrical opposition to the totality of what might be termed "Eurocentric business as usual."[7]

Indigenism

The manifestation of indigenism in North America has much in common with the articulation of what in Latin America is called *indigenismo*. One of the major proponents of this, the Mexican anthropologist/activist Guillermo Bonfil Batalla, has framed its precepts this way: "[I]n America there exists only one unitary Indian civilization. All the Indian peoples participate in this civilization. The diversity of cultures and languages is not an obstacle to affirmation of the unity of this civilization. It is a fact that all civilizations, including Western civilization, have these sorts of internal differences. But the level of unity—the civilization—is more profound than the level of specificity (the cultures, the languages, the communities). The civilizing dimension transcends the concrete diversity."[8]

> The differences between the diverse peoples (or ethnic groups) have been accentuated by the colonizers as part of the strategy of domination. There have been attempts by some to fragment the Indian peoples…by establishing frontiers, deepening differences and provoking rivalries. This strategy follows a principle objective: domination, to which end it is attempted ideologically to demonstrate that in America, Western civilization is confronted by a magnitude of atomized peoples, differing from one

another (every day more and more languages are "discovered"). Thus, in consequence, such peoples are believed incapable of forging a future of their own. In contrast to this, the Indian thinking affirms the existence of one—a unique and different—Indian civilization, from which extend as particular expressions the cultures of diverse peoples. Thus, the identification and solidarity among Indians. Their "Indianness" is not a simple tactic postulated, but rather the necessary expression of an historical unity, based in common civilization, which the colonizer has wanted to hide. Their Indianness, furthermore, is reinforced by the common experience of almost five centuries of [Eurocentric] domination.[9]

"The past is also unifying," Bonfil Batalla continues. "The achievements of the classic Mayas, for instance, can be reclaimed as part of the Quechua foundation [in present-day Guatemala], much the same as the French affirm their Greek past. And even beyond the remote past which is shared, and beyond the colonial experience that makes all Indians similar, Indian peoples also have a common historic project for the future. The legitimacy of that project rests precisely in the existence of an Indian civilization, within which framework it could be realized, once the 'chapter of colonialism ends.' One's own civilization signifies the right and the possibility to create one's own future, a different future, not Western."[10]

As has been noted elsewhere, the "new" indigenist movement Bonfil Batalla describes equates "colonialism/imperialism with the West; in opposing the West...[adherents] view themselves as anti-imperialist. Socialism, or Marxism, is viewed as just another Western manifestation."[11] A query is thus posed:

> What, then, distinguishes Indian from Western civilization? Fundamentally, the difference can be summed up in terms of [humanity's] relationship with the natural world. For the West ... the concept of nature is that of an enemy to be overcome, with man as boss on a cosmic scale. Man in the West believes he must dominate everything, including other [individuals]. The converse is true in Indian civilization, where [humans are] part of an indivisible cosmos and fully aware of [their] harmonious relationship with the universal order of nature. [S]he neither dominates nor tries to dominate. On the contrary, she exists within nature as a moment of it....Traditionalism thus constitutes a potent weapon in the [indigenous] civilization's struggle for survival against colonial domination.[12]

Bonfil Batalla contends that the nature of the indigenist impulse is essentially socialist, insofar as socialism, or what Karl Marx described as "primitive communism," was and remains the primary mode of indigenous social organization in the Americas.[13] Within this framework, he remarks that there are "six fundamental demands identified with the Indian movement," all of them associated with sociopolitical, cultural, and economic autonomy (or sovereignty) and self-determination:

> First there is land. There are demands for occupied ancestral territories...demands for control of the use of the land and subsoil; and struggles against the invasion of...commercial interests. Defense of land held and recuperation of land lost are the central demands. Second, the demand for recognition of the ethnic and cultural specificity of the Indian is identified. All [indigenist] organizations reaffirm the right to be distinct in culture, language and institutions, and to increase the value of their own technological, social and ideological practices. Third is the demand for [parity] of political rights in relation to the state... Fourth, there is a call for the end of repression and violence, particularly that against the leaders, activists and followers of the Indians' new political organizations. Fifth, Indians demand the end of family planning programmes which have brought widespread sterilization of Indian women and men. Finally, tourism and folklore are rejected, and there is a demand for true Indian cultural expression to be respected. The commercialization of Indian music and dance are often mentioned...and there is a particular dislike for the exploitation of those that have sacred content and purpose for Indians. An end to the exploitation of Indian culture in general is [demanded].[14]

In North America, these *indigenista* demands have been adopted virtually intact and have been conceived as encompassing basic needs of native peoples wherever they have been subsumed by the sweep of Western expansionism. This is the idea of the Fourth World explained by Cree author George Manuel, founding president of the World Council of Indigenous Peoples:

> The 4th World is the name given to indigenous peoples descended from a country's aboriginal population and who today are completely or partly deprived of their own territory and its riches. The peoples of the 4th World have only limited influence or none at all in the nation state [in which they are now encapsulated]. The peoples to whom we refer are the Indians of North and South America, the Inuit (Eskimos), the Sami people [of northern Scandinavia], the Australian aborigines, as well as the various indigenous populations of Africa, Asia and Oceana.[15]

Manuel might well have included segments of the European population itself, as is evidenced by the ongoing struggles of the Irish, Welsh, Basques and others to free themselves from the yoke of settler-state oppression imposed upon them as long as 800 years ago.[16] In such areas of Europe, as well as in "the Americas and [large portions of] Africa, the goal is not the creation of a state, but the expulsion of alien rule and the reconstruction of societies."[17]

That such efforts are entirely serious is readily evidenced in the fact that, in a global survey conducted by University of California cultural geographer Bernard Neitschmann from 1985 to 1987, it was discovered that of the more than 100 armed conflicts then underway, some 85 percent were being waged by indigenous peoples against the state or states which had laid claim to and occupied their territories.[18] As Theo van Boven, former director of the United Nations Division (now Center) for Human Rights, put it in 1981, the circumstances precipitating armed struggle "may be seen with particular poignancy in relation to the indigenous peoples of the world, who have been described somewhat imaginatively—and perhaps not without justification—as representing the fourth world: the world on the margin, on the periphery."[19]

The Issue of Land in North America

What must be understood about the context of the Americas north of the Río Grande is that neither of the nation-states, the United States and Canada, which claim sovereignty over the territory involved has any legitimate basis at all in which to anchor its absorption of huge portions of that territory. I am going to restrict my remarks in this connection mostly to the United States, mainly because that is what I know best, but also because both the United States and Canada have evolved on the basis of the Anglo-Saxon common law tradition.[20] So, I think much of what can be said about the United States bears a certain utility in terms of understanding the situation in Canada. Certain of the principles, of course, also extend to the situation in Latin America, but there you have an evolution of nation-states based on the Iberian legal tradition, so a greater transposition in terms is required.[21] The shape of things down south was summarized eloquently enough by the Peruvian freedom fighter Hugo Blanco with his slogan, "Land or Death!"[22]

The United States, during the first ninety-odd years of its existence, entered into and ratified more than 370 separate treaties with the peoples indigenous to the area now known as the 48 contiguous states.[23] There are a number of important dimensions to this, but two aspects will do for our purposes here. First, by customary international law and provision of the U.S. Constitution itself, each treaty ratification represented a formal recognition by the federal government that the other parties to the treaties—the native peoples involved—were fully sovereign nations in their own right.[24] Second, the purpose of the treaties, from the U.S. point of view, was to serve as real estate documents through which the United States acquired legal title to specified portions of North America from the indigenous nations it was thereby acknowledging already owned it.

From the viewpoint of the indigenous nations, of course, these treaties served other purposes: the securing of permanently guaranteed borders to what remained of their national territories, assurance of the continuation of their ongoing self-governance, trade and military alliances, and so forth. The treaty relationships were invariably reciprocal in nature: Indians ceded certain portions of their land to the United States, and the United States incurred certain obligations in exchange.[25] Even at that, there were seldom any outright sales of land by Indian nations to the United States. Rather, the federal obligations incurred were usually couched in terms of perpetuity. The arrangements were set up by the Indians so that, as long as the United States honored its end of the bargains, it would have the right to occupy and use defined portions of Indian land. In this sense, the treaties more nearly resemble rental or leasing instruments than actual deeds. And what happens under Anglo-Saxon common law when a tenant violates the provisions of a rental agreement?

The point here is that the United States has long since defaulted on its responsibilities under every single treaty obligation it ever incurred with regard to Indians. There is really no dispute about this. In fact, there is even a Supreme Court opinion, the 1903 *Lonewolf* case, in which the good "Justices" held that the United States enjoyed a "right" to disregard any treaty obligation to Indians it found inconvenient, but that the remaining treaty provisions continued to be binding upon the Indians. This was, the high court said, because the United States was the stronger of the nations involved and thus wielded "plenary" power—this simply means *full* power—over the affairs of the weaker indigenous nations. Therefore, the court felt itself free to unilaterally "interpret" each treaty as a bill of sale rather than a rental agreement.[26]

Stripped of its fancy legal language, the Supreme Court's position was (and remains) astonishingly crude. There is an old adage that "possession is nine-tenths of the law." Well, in this case the court went a bit further, arguing that possession was *all* of the law. Further, the highest court in the land went on record boldly arguing that, where Indian property rights are concerned, might, and might alone, makes right. The United States held the power to simply take Indian land, they said, and therefore it had the "right" to do so. This is precisely what the nazis argued only thirty years later, and the United States had the unmitigated audacity to profess outrage and shock that Germany was so blatantly transgressing against elementary standards of international law and the most basic requirements of human decency.[27]

For that matter, this is all that Sadam Hussein stood for when he took Kuwait—indeed, Iraq had a far stronger claim to rights over Kuwait than the United States has ever had with regard to Indian Country—with the result that George Bush began to babble about fighting a "Just War" to "roll back naked aggression," "free occupied territory," and "reinstate a legitimate government." If he were in any way serious about that proposition, he would have had to call air strikes in on himself instead of ordering the bombing of Baghdad.[28]

Be that as it may, there are a couple of other significant problems with the treaty constructions by which the United States allegedly assumed title over its landbase. On the one hand, a number of the ratified treaties can be shown to be fraudulent or coerced, and thus invalid. The nature of the coercion is fairly well known; perhaps a third of the ratified treaties involved direct coercion. Now comes the matter of fraud, which assumes the form of everything from the deliberate misinterpretation of proposed treaty provisions to the Senate's alteration of treaty language after the fact and without the knowledge of the Indian signatories.

On a number of occasions, the United States appointed its own preferred Indian "leaders" to represent their nations in treaty negotiations.[29] In at least one instance, the 1861 Treaty of Fort Wise, U.S. negotiators appear to have forged the signatures of various Cheyenne and Arapaho leaders.[30] Additionally, there are about 400 treaties which were never ratified by the senate and were therefore never legally binding, but upon which the United States now asserts its claims concerning lawful use and occupancy rights to, and jurisdiction over, appreciable portions of North America.[31]

When all is said and done, however, even these extremely dubious bases for U.S. title are insufficient to cover the gross territoriality at issue. The federal government itself tacitly admitted as much during the 1970s in the findings of the so-called Indian Claims Commission, an entity created in 1946 to make "quiet" title to all illegally taken Indian land within the lower 48 states.[32] What the commission did over the ensuing thirty-five years was in significant part to research the ostensible documentary basis for U.S. title to literally every square foot of its claimed territory. It found, among other things, that the United States had no legal basis whatsoever—no treaty, no agreement, not even an arbitrary act of Congress—to fully one-third of the area within its boundaries.[33]

At the same time, the data revealed that the reserved areas still nominally possessed by Indians had been reduced to about 2.5 percent of the same area.[34] What this means in plain English is that the United States cannot pretend to have even a shred of legitimacy in its occupancy and control of upwards of thirty percent of its "home" territory. And, lest such matters be totally lost in the shuffle, I should note that it has even less legal basis for its claims to the land in Alaska and Hawai'i.[35] Beyond that, its "right" to assert dominion over Puerto Rico, the "U.S." Virgin Islands, "American" Samoa, Guam, and the Marshall Islands tends to speak for itself.

Indian Land Recovery in the United States?

Leaving aside questions concerning the validity of various treaties, the beginning point for any indigenist endeavor in the United States centers, logically enough, in efforts to restore direct Indian control over the huge portion of the continental United States that was plainly never ceded by native nations. Upon the bedrock of this foundation, a number of other problems integral to the present configuration of power and privilege in North American society can be resolved, not just for Indians, but for everyone else as well. It is probably impossible to solve, or even to begin meaningfully addressing, certain of these problems in any other way. But still, it is, as they say, "no easy sell" to convince anyone outside the more conscious sectors of the American Indian population itself of the truth of this very simple fact.

In part, uncomfortable as it may be to admit, this is because even the most progressive elements of the North American immigrant population share a perceived commonality of interest with the more reactionary segments. This takes the form of a mutual insistence upon an imagined "right" to possess native property, merely because they are here, and because they desire it. The Great Fear is, within any settler-state, that if indigenous land rights are ever openly acknowledged, and native people therefore begin to recover some significant portion of their land, the immigrants will correspondingly be dispossessed of that which they have come to consider "theirs" (most notably, individual homes, small farms, ranches and the like).

Tellingly, every major Indian land recovery initiative in the United States during the second half of the twentieth century—the Western Shoshone, those in Maine, the Black Hills, the Oneida claims in New York State are prime examples—has been met by a propaganda barrage from right-wing organizations ranging from the Ku Klux Klan to the John Birch Society to the Republican Party warning individual non-Indian property holders of exactly this "peril."[36]

I will debunk some of this nonsense in a moment, but first I want to take up the posture of self-proclaimed leftist radicals in the same connection. And I will do so on the basis of principle, because justice is supposed to matter more to progressives than to rightist hacks. Let me say that the pervasive and near-total silence of the left in this connection has been quite illuminating. Non-Indian activists, with only a handful of exceptions, persistently plead that they cannot really take a coherent position on the matter of Indian land rights because, "unfortunately," they are "not really conversant with the issues" (as if these are tremendously complex).

Meanwhile, they do virtually nothing, generation after generation, to inform themselves on the topic of who actually owns the ground they are standing on. The record can be played only so many times before it wears out and becomes just another variation of "hear no evil, see no evil." At this point, it does not take Einstein to figure out that the left does not know much about such things because it has never *wanted* to know, or that this is so because it has always had its own plans for utilizing land it has no more right to than does the status quo it claims to oppose.

The usual technique for explaining this away has always been a sort of pro forma acknowledgment that Indian land rights are of course "really important stuff" (yawn), but that one "really does not have a lot of time" to get into it (I'll buy your book, though, and keep it on my shelf even if I never read it). Reason? Well, one is just "overwhelmingly preoccupied" with working on "*other* important issues" (meaning, what they consider to be *more* important things). Typically enumerated are sexism, racism, homophobia, class inequities, militarism, the environment, or some combination. It is a pretty good evasion, all in all. Certainly, there is no denying any of these issues their due; they *are* all important, obviously so. But more important than the question of land rights? There are some serious problems of primacy and priority imbedded in the orthodox script.

377

To frame things clearly in this regard, let us hypothesize for a moment that all of the various non-Indian movements concentrating on each of these issues were suddenly successful in accomplishing their objectives. Let us imagine that the United States as a whole were somehow transformed into an entity defined by the parity of its race, class and gender relations, its embrace of unrestricted sexual preference, its rejection of militarism in all forms and its abiding concern with environmental protection (I know, I know, this is a sheer impossibility, but that is my point).

When all is said and done, the society resulting from this scenario is *still*, first and foremost, a colonialist society, an imperialist society in the most fundamental sense and with all that this implies. This is true because the scenario does nothing at all to address the fact that whatever happens is on someone else's land, not only without their consent, but with an adamant disregard for their rights to the land. Hence, all it means is that the immigrant or invading population has rearranged its affairs in such a way as to make itself more comfortable at the continuing expense of indigenous people. The colonial equation remains intact and may even be reinforced by a greater degree of participation and vested interest in maintenance of the colonial order among the settler population at large.[37]

The dynamic here is not very different from that evident in the American Revolution of the late eighteenth century, is it? And we all know very well where that led. Should we therefore begin to refer to socialist imperialism, feminist imperialism, gay and lesbian imperialism, environmentalist imperialism, Afroamerican and la Raza imperialism? I would hope not.[38] I would hope this is all just a matter of confusion, of muddled priorities among people who really do mean well and who would like to do better. If so, then all that is necessary to correct the situation is a basic rethinking of what it is that must be done, and in what order. Here, I would advance the straightforward premise that the land rights of "First Americans" should be a priority for anyone seriously committed to accomplishing positive change in North America.

But before I suggest everyone jump up and adopt this priority, I suppose it is only fair that I investigate the converse of the proposition: If making things like class inequity and sexism the preeminent focus of progressive action in North America inevitably perpetuates the internal colonial structure of the United States, does the reverse hold true? I will state unequivocally that it does not.

There is no indication whatsoever that a restoration of indigenous sovereignty in Indian Country would foster class stratification anywhere, least of all in Indian Country. In fact, all indications are that when left to their own devices, indigenous peoples have consistently organized their societies in the most class-free manner. Look to the Haudenosaunee (Six Nations Iroquois Confederacy) for an example. Look to the Muscogee (Creek) Confederacy. Look to the confederations of the Yaqui and the Lakota, and those pursued and nearly perfected by Pontiac and Tecumseh. They represent the very essence of enlightened egalitarianism and democracy. Every imagined example to the contrary brought forth by even the most arcane anthropologist can be readily offset by a couple of dozen other illustrations along the lines of those I just mentioned.[39]

Would sexism be perpetuated? Ask the Haudenosaunee clan mothers, who continue to assert political leadership in their societies through the present day. Ask Wilma Mankiller, recent head of the Cherokee Nation, a people who were traditionally led by what were called "Beloved Women." Ask a Lakota woman—or man, for that matter—about who owned all real property in traditional society, and what that meant in terms of parity in gender relations. Ask a traditional Navajo grandmother about her social and political role among her people. Women in most traditional native societies not only enjoyed political, social, and economic parity with men, but they also often held a preponderance of power in one or more of these spheres.

Homophobia? Homosexuals of both genders were, and in many settings still are, deeply revered as special or extraordinary, and therefore spiritually significant, within most indigenous North American cultures. The extent to which these realities do not now pertain in native societies is exactly the extent to which Indians have been subordinated to the morés of the invading, dominating culture. Insofar as restoration of Indian land rights is tied directly to the reconstitution of traditional indigenous social, political, and economic modes, one can see where this leads; the Indian arrangements of sex and sexuality accord rather well with the aspirations of feminism and gay rights activism.[40]

How about a restoration of native land rights precipitating some sort of "environmental holocaust?" Let us get at least a little bit realistic here. If one is not addicted to the fabrications of Smithsonian anthropologists about how Indians lived,[41] or George Weurthner's eurosupremicist *Earth First!* fantasies about how we beat all the woolly mammoths and mastodons and sabertoothed cats to death with sticks,[42] then this question is not even on the board. I know it has become fashionable among *Washington Post* editorialists to make snide references to native people "strewing refuse in their wake" as they "wandered nomadically" about the "prehistoric" North American landscape.[43] What is this supposed to imply? That we, who were mostly "sedentary agriculturalists" in any event, were dropping plastic and aluminum cans as we went?

As I said, let us get real. Read the accounts of early European invaders about what they encountered: North America was invariably described as being a "pristine wilderness" at the point of European arrival, despite the fact that it had been occupied by fifteen or twenty million people enjoying a remarkably high standard of living for nobody knows how long. 40,000 years? 50,000 years?[44] Longer? Now contrast that reality to what has been done to this continent over the past couple of hundred years by the culture Weurthner, the Smithsonian and the *Post* represent, and you tell *me* about environmental devastation.[45]

That leaves militarism and racism. Taking the last first, there really is no indication of racism in traditional indigenous societies. To the contrary, the record reveals that Indians habitually intermarried between groups and frequently adopted both children and adults from other groups. This occurred in precontact times between Indians, and the practice was broadened to include those of both African and European origin, and ultimately Asian origin as well, once contact occurred. Those who were naturalized by marriage or adoption were considered members of the group, pure and simple. This was always the native view.[46]

The Europeans and subsequent Euroamerican settlers viewed things rather differently, however, and foisted off the notion that Indian identity should be determined primarily by "blood quantum," an outright eugenics code similar to those developed in places like nazi Germany and apartheid South Africa. Now, *that* is a racist construction if there ever was one. Unfortunately, a lot of Indians have been conned into buying into this anti-Indian absurdity, and that is something to be overcome. But there is also solid indication that quite a number of native people continue to strongly resist such things as the quantum system.[47]

As to militarism, no one will deny that Indians fought wars among themselves both before and after the European invasion began. Probably half of all indigenous peoples in North America maintained permanent warrior societies. This could perhaps be reasonably construed as "militarism." But not, I think, with the sense the term conveys within the European/ Euroamerican tradition. There were never, so far as anyone can demonstrate, wars of annihilation fought in this hemisphere prior to the Columbian arrival. None. In fact, it seems that it was a more-or-less firm principle of indigenous warfare *not* to kill, the object being to demonstrate personal bravery, something that could be done only against a *live* opponent. There is no honor to be had in killing another person, because a dead person cannot hurt you. There is no risk.

This is not to say that nobody ever died or was seriously injured in the fighting. They were, just as they are in full-contact contemporary sports like football and boxing. Actually, these kinds of Euroamerican games are what I would take to be the closest modern parallels to traditional Indian warfare. For us, it was a way of burning excess testosterone out of young males and not much more. So, militarism in the way the term is used today is as alien to native tradition as smallpox and atomic bombs.[48]

Not only is it perfectly reasonable to assert that a restoration of native control over unceded lands within the United States would do nothing to perpetuate such problems as sexism and classism, but the reconstitution of indigenous social standards that this would entail stands to free the affected portions of North America from such maladies altogether. Moreover, it can be said that the process should have a tangible impact in terms of diminishing such things elsewhere. The principle is this: Sexism, racism, and all the rest arose here as a concomitant to the emergence and consolidation of the eurocentric nation-state form of sociopolitical and economic organization. Everything the state does, everything it can do, is entirely contingent upon its maintaining internal cohesion, a cohesion signified above all by its pretended territorial integrity, its ongoing domination of Indian Country.

Given this, it seems obvious that the literal dismemberment of the nation-state necessary for Indian land recovery correspondingly reduces the ability of the state to sustain the imposition of objectionable policies within itself. It follows that realization of indigenous land rights serves to undermine or destroy the ability of the status quo to continue imposing a racist, sexist, classist, homophobic, militaristic order upon *non*-Indians.

A brief aside: Anyone with doubts as to whether it is possible to bring about the dismemberment from within of a superpower state in this day and age, ought to sit down and have a long talk with a guy named Mikhail

Gorbechev. It would be better yet if one could chew the fat with Leonid Breznev, a man who we can be sure would have replied in all sincerity, only twenty years ago, that this was the most outlandish idea he'd ever heard. Well, look on a map today, and see if you can find the Union of Soviet Socialist Republics. It ain't there, folks. Instead, you are seeing—and you will see it more and more—the reemergence of the very nations Léon Trotsky and his colleagues consigned to the "dustbin of history" clear back at the beginning of the century. These megastates are not immutable. They can be taken apart. They can be destroyed. But first we have to decide that we can do it and that we *will* do it.

So, all things considered, when indigenist movements like AIM advance slogans like "U.S. Out of North America," non-Indian radicals should not react defensively. They should cheer. They should see what they might do to help. When they respond defensively to sentiments like those expressed by AIM, what they are ultimately defending is the very government, the very order they claim to oppose so resolutely. And if they manifest this contradiction often enough, consistently enough, pathologically enough, then we have no alternative but to take them at their word: that they really are at some deep level or another aligned, all protestations to the contrary notwithstanding, with the mentality that endorses our permanent dispossession and disenfranchisement, our continuing oppression, our ultimate genocidal obliteration as self-defining and self-determining peoples. In other words, they make themselves part of the problem rather than becoming part of the solution.

Toward a North American Union of Indigenous Nations

There are certain implications to Indian control over Indian land that need to be clarified, beginning with a debunking of the "Great Fear," the reactionary myth that any substantive native land recovery would automatically lead to the mass dispossession and eviction of individual non-Indian home owners. Maybe in the process I can reassure a couple of radicals that it is okay to be on the right side of this issue, that they will not have to give something up in order to part company with Pat Buchanan on this. It is hard, frankly, to take this up without giggling, because of some of the images it inspires. I mean, what *are* people worried about here? Do all of you really foresee Indians standing out on the piers of Boston and New York City, issu-

382

ing sets of waterwings to long lines of non-Indians so they can all swim back to the Old World? Gimme a break.

Seriously, one can search high and low, and never find an instance in which Indians have advocated that small property owners be pushed off the land in order to satisfy land claims. The thrust in every single case has been to recover land within national and state parks and forests, grasslands, military reservations and the like. In some instances, major corporate holdings have also been targeted. A couple of times, as in the Black Hills, a sort of joint jurisdiction between Indians and the existing non-Indian government has been discussed with regard to an entire treaty area.[49] But even in the most hardline of the indigenous positions concerning the Black Hills—that advanced by Russell Means in his TREATY Program, where resumption of exclusively Lakota jurisdiction is demanded—there is no mention of dispossessing or evicting non-Indians.[50] Instead, other alternatives, which I will take up later, were carefully spelled out.

In the meantime, though, I would like to share with you something the right-wing propagandists never mention when they are busily whipping up non-Indian sentiment against Indian rights. Recall that I said that the quantity of unceded land within the continental United States makes up about one-third of the landmass? Let's just round this off to thirty percent, because there is the matter of 2.5 percent of the overall landbase still set aside as Indian reservations. Now juxtapose that thirty percent to the approximately 35 percent of the same landmass the federal government presently holds in various kinds of trust status. Add the ten or twelve percent of the land the individual states hold in trust. That adds up to a thirty-percent Indian claim against a 45 to 47 percent *governmental* holding.[51] Never mind the percentage of the land held by major corporations. Conclusion? It is, and always has been, quite possible to accomplish the return of every square inch of unceded Indian Country in the United States without tossing a single non-Indian homeowner off the land on which they live.

Critics—that is the amazingly charitable self-description employed by those who ultimately oppose the assertion of indigenous rights in any form and as a matter of principle—are always quick to point out that the problem with this arithmetic is that the boundaries of the government trust areas do not necessarily conform in all cases to the boundaries of unceded areas. That is true enough, although I would just as quickly point out that more often than not they *do* correspond. This "problem" is nowhere near as big as it is made out to be. And there is nothing intrinsic to the boundary question which could not be negotiated once non-Indian America acknowledges that Indians have an absolute moral and legal right to the quantity of territory which was never ceded. Boundaries can be adjusted, often in ways which can be beneficial to both sides involved in the negotiation.[52]

Let me give you an example. Along about 1980, two Rutgers University professors, Frank and Deborah Popper, undertook a comprehensive study of land-use patterns and economy in the Great Plains region. What they discovered is that 110 counties—one quarter of all the counties in the entire Plains region falling within the western portions of the states of North and South Dakota, Nebraska, Kansas, Oklahoma, and Texas, as well as eastern Montana, Wyoming, Colorado, and New Mexico—have been fiscally insolvent since the moment they were taken from native people a century or more ago.

This is an area of about 140,000 square miles, inhabited by a widely dispersed non-Indian population of only around 400,000 attempting to maintain school districts, police and fire departments, road beds and all the other basic accoutrements of "modern life" on the negligible incomes which can be eked from cattle grazing and wheat farming on land which is patently unsuited for both enterprises. The Poppers found that without considerable federal subsidy each and every year none of these counties would ever have been "viable." Nor, on the face of it, will any of them ever be. Bluntly put, the pretense of bringing Euroamerican "civilization" to the Plains represents nothing more than a massive economic burden on the rest of the United States.

What the Poppers proposed on the basis of these findings is that the government cut its perpetual losses by buying out the individual landholdings within the target counties and converting them into open space wildlife sanctuaries known as "Buffalo Commons." The whole area would in effect be turned back to the bison which were very nearly exterminated by Phil Sheridan's buffalo hunters back in the nineteenth century as a means of starving "recalcitrant" Indians into submission. The result would, they argue, be both environmentally and economically beneficial to the nation as a whole.

It is instructive that such thinking has gained increasing credibility and support from Indians and non-Indians alike, beginning in the second half of the 1980s. Another chuckle here: Indians have been trying to tell non-Indi-

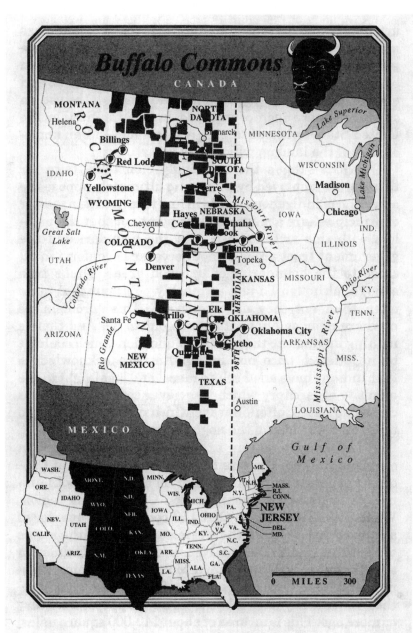

Buffalo Commons

Anne Matthews, *Where the Buffalo Roam.*

ans that this would be the outcome of fencing in the Plains ever since 1850 or so, but some folks have a real hard time catching on. Anyway, it is entirely possible that we will see some actual motion in this direction over the next few years.[53]

So, let us take the Poppers' idea to its next logical step. There are another hundred or so economically marginal counties adjoining the "perpetual red ink" counties already identified. These do not represent an actual drain on the U.S. economy, but they do not contribute much either. They could be "written off" and lumped into the Buffalo Commons with no one feeling any ill effects whatsoever. Now add in adjacent areas like the national grasslands in Wyoming, the national forest and parklands in the Black Hills, extraneous military reservations like Ellsworth Air Force Base, and existing Indian reservations. This would be a huge territory lying east of Denver, west of Lawrence, Kansas, and extending from the Canadian border to southern Texas, all of it "outside the loop" of U.S. business as usual.

The bulk of this area is unceded territory owned by the Lakota, Pawnee, Arikara, Hidatsa, Crow, Shoshone, Assiniboine, Cheyenne, Arapaho, Kiowa, Comanche, Jicarilla and Mescalero Apache nations. There would be little cost to the United States, and virtually no arbitrary dispossession or dislocation of non-Indians if the entire Commons were restored to these peoples. Further, it would establish a concrete basis from which genuine expressions of indigenous self-determination could begin to reemerge on this continent, allowing the indigenous nations involved to begin the process of reconstituting themselves socially and politically and to recreate their traditional economies in ways that make contemporary sense. This would provide alternative socioeconomic models for possible adaptation by non-Indians and alleviate a range of considerable costs to the public treasury incurred by keeping the Indians in question in a state of abject and permanent dependency.

Critics will undoubtedly pounce upon the fact that an appreciable portion of the Buffalo Commons area I have sketched out—perhaps a million acres or so—lies outside the boundaries of unceded territory. That is the basis for the sorts of multilateral negotiations between the United States and indigenous nations I mentioned earlier. This land will need to be "charged off" in some fashion against unceded land elsewhere and in such a way as to bring other native peoples into the mix. The Poncas, Omahas, and Osages, whose traditional territories fall within the area in question, come immediately to mind, but this would extend as well to all native peoples willing to exchange land claims somewhere else for actual acreage in this locale. The idea is to consolidate a distinct indigenous territory while providing a definable landbase to as many different Indian nations as possible in the process.

From there, the principle of the Buffalo Commons *cum* Indian Territory could be extended westward into areas that adjoin or are at least immediately proximate to the Commons area itself. The fact is that vast areas of the Great Basin and Sonoran Desert regions of the United States are even more sparsely populated and economically insolvent than the Plains. A great deal of the area is also held in federal trust.

Hence, it is reasonable, in my view at least, to expand the Commons territory to include most of Utah and Nevada, northern Montana and Idaho, quite a lot of eastern Washington and Oregon, most of the rest of New Mexico, and the lion's share of Arizona. This would encompass the unceded lands of the Blackfeet and Gros Ventre, Salish, Kutenai, Nez Percé, Yakima, Western Shoshone, Goshutes and Utes, Paiutes, Navajo, Hopi and other Pueblos, Mescalero and Chiricahua Apache, Havasupi, Yavapai and O'odam. It would also set the stage for further exchange negotiations to consolidate this additional territory in order to establish a landbase for a number of other indigenous nations.

At this point, we have arrived at an area comprising roughly one-third of the continental United States, a territory that, regardless of the internal political and geographical subdivisions effected by the array of native peoples within it, could be defined as a sort of "North American Union of Indigenous Nations." Such an entity would be in a position to assist other indigenous nations outside its borders but still within the remaining territorial corpus of the United States to resolve land claim issues accruing from fraudulent or coerced treaties of cession (another fifteen or twenty percent of the present 48 states).

It would also be in a position to facilitate an accommodation of the needs of untreatied peoples within the United States, the Abenaki of Vermont, for example, and the Hawaiian and Alaskan natives. Similarly, it would be able to help secure the self-determination of U.S. colonies like Puerto Rico. One can see the direction the dominoes would begin to fall.

Nor does this end with the United States. Any sort of indigenous union of the kind I have described would be as eligible for admission as a fully participating member of the United Nations as, say, Croatia and the

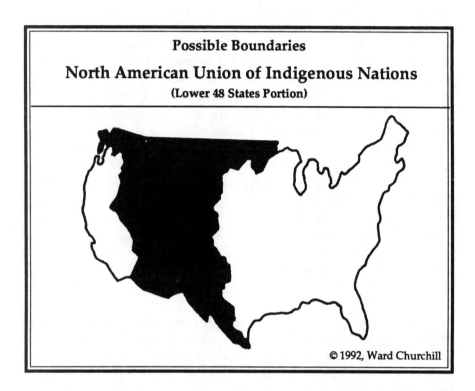

Possible Boundaries

North American Union of Indigenous Nations
(Lower 48 States Portion)

© 1992, Ward Churchill

Ukraine have recently shown themselves to be. This would set a very important precedent, insofar as there has never been an American Indian entity of any sort accorded such political status on the world stage.

The precedent could serve to pave the way for comparable recognition and attainments by other Native American nations, notably the confederation of Incan peoples of the Andean highlands and the Mayans of present-day Guatemala and southern Mexico (Indians are the majority population, decisively so, in both locales), and from there, other indigenous nations elsewhere around the world. Again, one can see the direction the dominoes would fall. If we are going to have a "New World Order," let us make it something just a bit different from what George Bush and his friends had in mind. Right?

Sharing the Land

There are several closely related matters that should be touched upon before wrapping this up. One has to do with the idea of self-determination or what is meant when indigenists demand the unrestricted right for native peoples. Most non-Indians, and even a lot of Indians, seem confused by this and want to know whether it is not the same as complete separation from the United States, Canada, or whatever the colonizing power may be. The answer is "not necessarily."

The unqualified acknowledgment of the right of the colonized to total separation ("secession") from the colonizer is the necessary point of departure before any exercise of self-determination can occur. Decolonization means the colonized can then exercise the right to total separation in whole or in part, as they see fit, in accordance with their own customs and traditions, and their own appreciation of their needs. They decide for themselves what degree of autonomy they wish to enjoy and thus the nature of their political and economic relationship(s), not only with their former colonizers, but with all other nations as well.[54]

My own inclination, which is in some ways an emotional preference, tends to run toward complete sovereign independence, but this is not the point. I have no more right to impose my preferences on indigenous nations than do the colonizing powers; each indigenous nation will choose for itself the exact manner and extent to which it expresses its autonomy, its sovereignty. To be honest, I suspect very few would be inclined to adopt my sort of "go it alone" approach (and, actually, I must also admit that part of my own insistence upon it often has more to do with forcing concession of the right from those who seek to deny it than it does with putting it into practice). In any event, I expect there would be the hammering out of a number of sets of international relations in the "free association" vein, a welter of variations of commonwealth and home rule governance.[55]

The intent here is not, no matter how much it may be deserved in an abstract sense, to visit some sort of retribution, real or symbolic, upon the colonizing or former colonizing powers. It is to arrive at new sets of relationships between peoples that effectively put an end to the era of international domination. The need is to gradually replace the existing world order with one that is predicated in collaboration and cooperation between nations. The only way to ever really accomplish this is to physically disassemble the gigantic state structures—structures that are literally grounded on systematic intergroup domination; they cannot in any sense exist without it—which are still evolving in this neoimperialist era. A concomitant of this disassembly is the inculcation of voluntary, consensual interdependence between formerly dominated and dominating nations and a redefinition of the word "nation" itself to conform to its original meaning: bodies of people bound together by their bioregional and other natural cultural affinities.[56]

This last point is, it seems to me, crucially important. Partly, this is because of the persistent question of who gets to remain in Indian Country once land restoration and consolidation have occurred. The answer, I think, is, up to a point, anyone who wants to. By "anyone who wants to" I mean anyone who wishes to apply for formal citizenship within an indigenous nation, thereby accepting the idea that s/he is placing him/herself under unrestricted Indian jurisdiction and will thus be required to abide by native law.[57]

Funny thing—I hear a lot of non-Indians asserting that they reject nearly every aspect of U.S. law, but the idea of placing themselves under anyone else's jurisdiction still leaves them pretty queasy. I have no idea how many non-Indians might actually opt for citizenship in an indigenous nation, but I expect there will be some. And I suspect some native people have been so indoctrinated by the dominant society that they will elect to remain within it rather than availing themselves of their own citizenship. So there will be a bit of a trade-off in this respect.

Now, there is the matter of the process working only "up to a point." This point is very real. It is defined not by political or racial considerations but by the carrying capacity of the land. The population of indigenous nations everywhere has always been determined by the number of people that could be sustained in a given environment or bioregion without overpowering and thereby destroying it.[58] A very carefully calculated balance, one that was calibrated to the fact that in order to enjoy certain sorts of material comfort human population must be kept at some level below saturation, was always maintained between the number of humans and the rest of the habitat. In order to accomplish this, native peoples have always incorporated into the very core of our spiritual traditions the concept that all life forms and the earth itself possess rights equal to those enjoyed by humans.

Rephrased, this means it would be a fundamental violation of traditional native law to supplant or eradicate another species, whether animal or plant, in order to make way for some greater number of humans or to increase the level of material comfort available to those who already exist. Conversely, it is a fundamental requirement of traditional law that each human accept his or her primary responsibility of maintaining the balance and harmony of the natural order *as it is encountered*.[59]

One is essentially free to do anything one wants in an indigenous society so long as this cardinal rule is adhered to. The bottom line with regard to the maximum population limit of Indian Country as it has been sketched in this presentation is some very finite number. My best guess is that a couple of million people would be pushing things right through the roof. Whatever. Citizens can be admitted until that point has been reached, and no more. And the population cannot increase beyond that number over time, no matter at what rate. Carrying capacity is a fairly constant reality; it tends to take thousands of years to change, if it changes at all.

Population and Environment

What I am going to say next will probably startle a few people (as if what has been said already has not). I think this principle of population restraint is the single most important example Native North America can set for the rest of humanity. It is *the* thing that is most crucial for others to emulate. Check it out. I just read that Japan, a small island nation that has so many people they are literally tumbling into the sea, and that has exported about half again as many people as live on the home islands, is expressing "official concern" that its birth rate has declined very slightly over the last few years. The worry is that in thirty years there will be fewer workers available to "produce" and then to "consume" whatever is produced.[60]

Ever ask yourself what is used in "producing" something? Or what is being "consumed"? Yeah. You got it. Nature is being consumed and with it the ingredients that allow ongoing human existence. While it is true that nature can replenish some of what is consumed, this can only be done at a certain rate. This rate has been vastly exceeded, and the excess is intensifying by the moment. An overburgeoning humanity is killing the natural world, and thus itself. It is no more complicated than that.[61] Here we are in the midst of a rapidly worsening environmental crisis of truly global portions, every last bit of it attributable to a wildly accelerating human consumption of the planetary habitat, and we have one of the world's major offenders expressing grave concern that the rate at which it is able to consume might actually drop a notch or two. *Think* about it. I suggest that this attitude signifies nothing so much as stark, staring madness. It is insane, suicidally, homicidally, and ecocidally insane.

And, no, I am not being rhetorical. I mean these terms in a clinically precise fashion. But I do not want to convey the impression that I am singling out the Japanese. I only used them as an illustration of a far broader pathology called "industrialism"—or, more lately, "postindustrialism"—a sickness centered in an utterly obsessive drive to dominate and destroy the natural order (words like "production," "consumption," "development," and "progress" are no more than code words masking this reality).[62]

It is not only the industrialized countries that are afflicted with this dis–ease. One by-product of the past five centuries of European expansionism and the resulting hegemony of eurocentric ideology is that the latter has been drummed into the consciousness of *most* peoples to the point where it is now subconsciously internalized. Everywhere, you find people thinking it "natural" to view themselves as the incarnation of god on earth ("created in the image of God") and thus duty-bound to "exercise dominion over nature" in order to "multiply, grow plentiful, and populate the land" in ever increasing "abundance."[63]

The legacy of the forced labor of the *latifundia* and inculcation of Catholicism in Latin America is a tremendous overburden of population who devoutly believe that "wealth" can be achieved (or is defined) by having ever *more* children.[64] The legacy of Mao's implementation of a "reverse technology" policy—the official encouragement of breakneck childbearing rates in his already overpopulated country, solely as a means to deploy massive labor power to offset capitalism's "technological advantage" in production—resulted in a tripling of China's population in only two generations.[65] And then there is India...

Make absolutely no mistake about it. The planet was never designed to accommodate six billion human beings, much less the *ten* billion predicted to be here a mere forty years hence.[66] If we are to turn power relations around between people and between groups of people, we must also turn around the relationship between people and the rest of the natural order. If we do not, we will die out as a species, just like any other species that irrevocably overshoots its habitat. The sheer number of humans on this planet needs to come down to about one quarter of what it is today, or maybe less, and the plain fact is that the bulk of these numbers are in the Third World.[67] So, I will say this clearly: not only must the birth rate in the Third World come down, but the population levels of Asia, Latin America, and Africa *must* be reduced over the next few generations, beginning right now.

Of course, there is another dimension to the population issue, one that is in some ways even more important, and I want to get into it in a minute. But first I have to say something else. This is that I do not want a bunch of Third Worlders jumping up in my face screaming that I am advocating "genocide." Bullshit. It is genocide when some centralized state or some colonizing power imposes sterilization or abortion on target groups. It is not genocide at all to recognize that we have a problem and take the logical steps *ourselves* to solve it. Voluntary sterilization is not a part of genocide. Voluntary abortion is not a part of genocide. And, most importantly, educating ourselves and our respective peoples to bring our birth rates under control through conscious resort to birth control measures is not a part of genocide.[68]

What it *is* is taking responsibility for ourselves again; it is taking responsibility for our destiny and our children's destiny. It is about rooting the ghost of the Vatican out of our collective psyches, along with the ghosts of Adam Smith and Karl Marx. It is about getting back in touch with our *own* ways, our *own* traditions, our *own* knowledge, and it is long past time that we got out of our own way in this respect. We have an awful lot to unlearn and an awful lot to relearn, and not much time in which we can afford the luxury of avoidance. We need to get on with it.

The other aspect of population I want to take up is that there is another way of counting. One way, the way I just did it, and the one that is conventionally done, is to simply point to the number of bodies or "people units." That is valid enough as far as it goes, but it does not really go far enough. This brings up the second method, which is to count by relative rate of resource consumption per body—the relative degree of environmental impact per individual—and to extrapolate this into people units.

Using this method, which is actually more accurate in ecological terms, we arrive at conclusions that are a little different than the usual notion that the most overpopulated regions on earth are in the Third World. The average resident of the United States, for example, consumes about thirty times the resources of the average Ugandan or Laotian. Since a lot of poor folk reside in the United States, this translates into the average yuppie consuming about seventy times the resources of an average Third Worlder.[69] Every yuppie born counts as much as another seventy Chinese.

Lay *that* one on the next soccer mom who approaches you with a baby stroller and an outraged look, demanding that you to put your cigarette out, eh? It is plainly absurd for any American to complain about smoking when you consider the context of the damage done by overall U.S. consumption patterns. Tell 'em you'll put the butt out when they snuff the kid and not a moment before. Better yet, tell 'em they should snuff themselves, as well as the kid, and do the planet a *real* favor. Just "kidding" (heh-heh).

Returning to the topic at hand: multiply the U.S. population by a factor of thirty—a noticeably higher ratio than either western Europe or Japan—in order to figure out how many Third Worlders it would take to have the same environmental impact. I make that to be 7.5 *billion* U.S. people units. I think I can thus safely say the most overpopulated portion of the globe is the United States.

Either the consumption rates really have to be cut in this country, especially in the more privileged social sectors, or the number of people must be drastically reduced, or both. I advocate both. How much? That is a bit subjective, but I will tentatively accept the calculations of William Catton, a respected ecologist and demographer. He estimated that North America was thoroughly saturated with humans by 1840.[70] So we need to get both population and consumption levels down to what they were in that year or preferably a little earlier. Alternatively, we need to bring population down to an even lower level in order to sustain a correspondingly higher level of consumption.

Here is where I think the reconstitution of indigenous territoriality and sovereignty in the West can be useful with regard to population. You see, land is not just land; it is also the resources within the land, things like coal, oil, natural gas, uranium, and maybe most important, water. How does that bear on U.S. overpopulation? Simple. Much of the population expansion in this country over the past quarter-century has been into the southwestern desert region. How many people have they got living in the valley down there at Phoenix, a place that might be reasonably expected to support 500?

Look at LA: twenty million people where there ought to be maybe a few thousand. How do they accomplish this? Well, for one thing, they have diverted the entire Colorado River from its natural purposes. They are siphoning off the Columbia River and piping it south. They have even got a project underway to divert the Yukon River all the way down from Alaska to support southwestern urban growth and to irrigate a proposed U.S. agribusiness penetration of northern Sonora and Chihuahua. Whole regions of our ecosphere are being destabilized in the process.

Okay, in the scenario I have described, the entire Colorado watershed would be in Indian Country, under Indian control. So would the source of the Columbia. And diversion of the Yukon would have to go right through Indian Country. Now, here's the deal. No more use of water to fill swimming pools and sprinkle golf courses in Phoenix and LA. No more watering Kentucky bluegrass lawns out on the yucca flats. No more drive-thru car washes in Tucumcari. No more "Big Surf" amusement parks in the middle of the desert. Drinking water and such for the whole population, yes. Indians should deliver that. But water for this other insanity? No way. I guarantee that will stop the inflow of population cold. Hell, I will guarantee it will start a pretty substantial outflow. Most of these folks never wanted to live in the desert anyway. That's why they keep trying to make it look like Florida (another delicate ecosystem which is buckling under the weight of population increases).[71]

And we can help move things along in other ways as well. Virtually all the electrical power for the southwestern urban sprawls comes from a combination of hydroelectric and coal-fired generation in the Four Corners area. This is smack dab in the middle of Indian Country, along with all the uranium with which a "friendly atom" alternative might be attempted and most of the low sulfur coal. Goodbye to the neon glitter of Las Vegas and San Diego. Adios to air conditioners in every room. Sorry about your hundred-mile expanses of formerly streetlit expressway. Basic needs will be met, and that's it.

This means we can also start saying goodbye to western rivers being backed up like so many sewage lagoons behind massive dams. The Glen Canyon and Hoover dams are coming down, boys and girls. And we can begin to experience things like a reduction in the acidity of southwestern rain water as facilities like the Four Corners Power Plant are cut back in generating time and eventually eliminated altogether. What I'm saying probably sounds extraordinarily cruel to a lot of people, particularly those imbued with the belief that they have a "God-given right" to play a round of golf on

395

the well-watered green beneath the imported palm trees outside an air-conditioned casino at the base of the Superstition Mountains. Tough. Those days can be ended without hesitation or apology.

A much more legitimate concern rests in the fact that a lot of people who have drifted into the southwest have no place to go to. The places they came from are crammed. In many cases, that's why they left. To them, I say there's no need to panic; no one will abruptly pull the plug on you or leave you to die of thirst. Nothing like that. But quantities of both water and power will be set at minimal levels. In order to have a surplus, you will have to bring your number down to a certain level over a certain period. At that point, the levels will again be reduced, necessitating another population reduction. Things can be phased in over an extended period—several generations, if need be.[72]

Provision of key items such as western water and coal should probably be negotiated on the basis of reductions in population and consumption by the United States as a whole rather than simply the region served. This would prevent population shifts being substituted for actual reductions.[73] Any such negotiated arrangement should also include an agreement to alter the U.S. distribution of food surpluses and the like, so as to ease the transition to a lower population and a correspondingly greater self-sufficiency in hardpressed Third World areas.

The objective inherent in every aspect of this process should be, and can be, to let everyone down as gently as possible from the long and intoxicating high that has beset so much of the human species in its hallucination that it, and it alone, is the only thing of value and importance in the universe. In doing so, and I believe *only* in doing so, can we fulfill our obligation to bequeath our grandchildren, and our grandchildren's grandchildren, a world that is fit (or even possible) to live in.[74]

I Am Indigenist

There are any number of other matters that should be discussed, but they will of necessity have to await another occasion. What has been presented here has been only the barest outline, a glimpse of what might be called an "indigenist vision." I hope that it provides enough shape and clarity to allow anyone who wishes to pursue the thinking further to fill in at least some of the gaps I have not had the time to address, and to arrive at insights and conclusions of their own. Once the main tenets have been advanced, and I think to some extent that has been accomplished here, the perspective of indigenism is neither mystical nor mysterious.

In closing, I would like to turn again to the critics, the skeptics, those who will decry what has been said here as being "unrealistic" or even "crazy." On the former score, my reply is that as long as we define realism, or reality itself, in conventional terms—the terms imposed by the order of understanding in which we now live—we will be doomed to remain locked forever into the present trajectory. We will never break free, because any order, any structure, defines reality only in terms of itself. Consequently, allow me to echo a sentiment expressed during the French student revolt of 1968: "Be realistic; demand the impossible!"[75] If you read through a volume of American Indian oratory, and there are several available, you will find that native people have been saying the same thing all along.[76]

As to my being crazy, I would like to say thanks for the compliment. Again, I follow my elders and my ancestors—and R. D. Laing, for that matter—in believing that when confronted with a society as obviously insane as this one, the only sane posture one can adopt is what that society would automatically designate as crazy.[77]

I mean, Indians were not the ones who turned birthing into a religious fetish while butchering off a couple hundred million people with weapons of mass destruction and systematically starving another billion or so to death. Indians never had a Grand Inquisition, and we never came up with a plumbing plan to reroute the water flow on the entire continent. Nor did we ever produce "leaders" of the caliber of Ronald Reagan, Jean Kirkpatrick and Ross Perot. Hell, we never even figured out that turning prison construction into a major growth industry was an indication of social progress and enlightenment. Maybe we were never so much crazy as we were congenitally retarded.

Whatever the reason—and please excuse me for suspecting it might be something other than craziness or retardation—I am indescribably thankful that our cultures turned out to be so different, no matter how much abuse and sacrifice it entailed. I am proud to stand inside the heritage of native struggle. I am proud to say I am an unreconstructable indigenist. For me, there is no other reasonable or realistic way to look at the world. And I invite anyone who shares that viewpoint to come aboard, regardless of your race, creed, or national origin.

Maybe Chief Seattle said it best back in 1854: "Tribe follows tribe, and nation follows nation, like the waves of the sea. Your time of decay may be distant, but it will surely come, for even the white man whose god walked with him and talked with him as friend with friend, cannot be exempt from the common destiny. We may be brothers after all. We will see."[78]

Notes

1. For what is probably the best available account of AIM, IAT, and WARN, see Peter Matthiessen's *In the Spirit of Crazy Horse* (New York: Viking, [2nd ed.] 1991). On Oka, see Linda Pertusati, *In Defense of Mohawk Land: Ethnopolitical Conflict in Native North America* (Albany: State University of New York Press, 1997).

2. On James Bay, see Boyce Richardson's *Strangers Devour the Land* (Post Mills, VT: Chelsea Green, [2nd ed.] 1991).

3. While it is hardly complete, a good point of departure for learning about many of the individuals named would be Alvin M. Josephy's *The Patriot Chiefs* (New York: Viking, 1961).

4. The bulk of those mentioned, and a number of others as well, appear in *The Indigenous Voice: Visions and Realities*, 2 Vols. (London: Zed Books, 1988).

5. The term "Vichy Indians" comes from Russell Means. See his "The Same Old Song," in my *Marxism and Native Americans* (Boston: South End Press, [2nd ed.] 1989) pp. 19-33.

6. Ross Swimmer is an alleged Cherokee and former Philips Petroleum executive who served as head of the U.S. Bureau of Indian Affairs under Ronald Reagan and argued for suspension of federal obligations to Indians as a means of teaching native people "self-reliance." Dickie Wilson was head of the federal puppet government on Pine Ridge Reservation during the early 1970s, and while in this position, he formed an entity, called the GOONs, to physically assault and frequently kill members and supporters of AIM. Webster Two Hawks was head of the National Tribal Chairman's Association funded by the Nixon administration. He used his federally-sponsored position to denounce Indian liberation struggles. Peter McDonald—often referred to as "McDollar" in Indian Country—utilized his position as head of the puppet government at Navajo to sell his people's interests to various mining corporations during the 1970s and '80s, greatly enriching himself in the process. Vernon Bellecourt is a former Denver wig stylist who moved to Minneapolis and became CEO of a state-chartered corporation funded by federal authorities to impersonate the American Indian Movement. David Bradley is a no-talent painter living in Santa Fe whose main claim to fame is in having made a successful bid to have the federal government enforce "identification standards" against other Indian artists; he has subsequently set himself up as a self-anointed "Identity Police," a matter which, thankfully, leaves him little time to produce his typical graphic schlock. To hear them tell it, of course, each of these individuals acted in the service of "Indian sovereignty."

7. See Winona LaDuke's "Natural to Synthetic and Back Again," the preface to *Marxism and Native Americans*, op. cit., pp. i-viii.

8. Guillermo Bonfil Batalla, *Utopía y Revolución: El Pensamiento Político Contemporáneo de los Indios en América Latina* (Mexico City: Editorial Nueva Imagen, 1981) p. 37; translation by Roxanne Dunbar Ortiz.

9. Ibid., pp. 37-8.

10. Ibid. p. 38.

11. Roxanne Dunbar Ortiz, *Indians of the Americas: Human Rights and Self-Determination* (London: Zed Books, 1984) p. 83.

12. Ibid. p. 84.

13. For an excellent overview on the implications of Marx's thinking in this regard, see the first couple of chapters in Walker Connor's *The National Question in Marxist-Leninist Theory and Strategy* (Princeton, NJ: Princeton University Press, 1984).

14. Dunbar Ortiz, *Indians of the Americas*, op. cit., p. 85.

15. George Manuel and Michael Posluns, *The Fourth World: An Indian Reality* (New York: Free Press, 1974).

16. On the Irish and Welsh struggles, see Peter Berresford Ellis, *The Celtic Revolution: A Study in Anti-Imperialism* (Talybont: Wales: Y Lolfa, 1985). On the Basques, see Kenneth Medhurst, *The Basques and Catalans* (London: Minority Rights Group Report No. 9, Sept 1977).

17. Dunbar Ortiz, *Indians of the Americas*, op. cit., p. 89.

18. Bernard Neitschmann, "The Third World War," *Cultural Survival Quarterly*, Vol. 11, No. 3 (1987).

19. Geneva Offices of the United Nations, Press Release, Aug. 17, 1981 (Hr/1080).

20. For an excellent analysis of this tradition from an indigenist perspective, see Robert A. Williams, Jr., *The American Indian in Western Legal Thought: The Discourses of Conquest* (New York: Oxford University Press, 1990).

21. On the Iberian legal tradition, see James Brown Scott, *The Spanish Origin of International Law* (Oxford: Clarendon Press, 1934).

22. Hugo Blanco, *Land or Death: The Peasant Struggle in Peru* (New York: Pathfinder, 1972). Blanco was a marxist, and thus sought to pervert indigenous issues through rigid class analysis—defining Indians as "peasants" rather than by nationality—but his identification of land as the central issue was and is nonetheless valid.

23. The complete texts of 371 of these ratified treaties can be found in Charles J. Kappler, ed., *American Indian Treaties, 1778-1883* (New York: Interland, 1973). The Lakota scholar Vine Deloria, Jr., has also collected the texts of several more ratified treaties which do not appear in Kappler, but which will be published in a forthcoming collection.

24. The constitutional provision comes at Article I, Section 10. Codification of customary international law in this connection is explained in Sir Ian Sinclair, *The Vienna Convention on the Law of Treaties* (Manchester: Manchester University Press, [2nd ed.] 1984).

25. See generally, Vine Deloria, Jr., and Clifford E. Lytle, *American Indians, American Justice* (Austin: University of Texas Press, 1983).

26. *Lonewolf v. Hitchcock*, 187 U.S. 553 (1903). For analysis, see Ann Laquer Estin, "*Lonewolf v. Hitchcock*: The Long Shadow," in Sandra L. Cawallader and Vine Deloria, Jr., eds., *The Aggressions of Civilization: Federal Indian Policy Since the 1880s* (Philadelphia: Temple University Press, 1984) pp. 215-45.

27. Probably the best exposition of the legal principles articulated by the U.S. as being violated by the nazis may be found in Bradley F. Smith, *The Road to Nuremberg* (New York: Basic Books, 1981).

28. A fuller enunciation of this thesis may be found in my "On Gaining 'Moral High Ground': An Ode to George Bush and the 'New World Order,'" in Cynthia Peters, ed., *Collateral Damage: The "New World Order" at Home and Abroad* (Boston: South End Press, 1992) pp. 359-72.

29. For the origins of such practices, see Dorothy V. Jones, *License for Empire: Colonialism by Treaty in Early America* (Chicago: University of Chicago Press, 1982). A good survey of U.S. adaptations will be found in Donald Worcester, ed., *Forked Tongues and Broken Treaties* (Caldwell, ID: Caxton, 1975).

30. The travesty at Fort Wise is adequately covered in Stan Hoig's *The Sand Creek Massacre* (Norman: University of Oklahoma Press, 1961) pp. 13-7.

31. Deloria compilation, forthcoming.

32. On the purpose of the commission, see Harvey D. Rosenthal, "Indian Claims and the American Conscience: A Brief History of the Indian Claims Commission," in Imre Sutton, ed., *Irredeemable America: The Indians' Estate and Land* (Albuquerque: University of New Mexico Press, 1985, pp. 35-86). One must read between the lines a bit.

33. Russel Barsh, "Indian Land Claims Policy in the United States," *North Dakota Law Review*, No. 58 (1982) pp. 1-82.

34. The percentage is arrived at by juxtaposing the approximately fifty million acres within the current reservation landbase to the more than two *billion* acres of the lower 48 states. According to the Indian Claims Commission findings, Indians actually retain unfettered legal title to about 750 million acres of the continental U.S.

35. Concerning Alaska, see M. C. Berry, *The Alaska Pipeline: The Politics of Oil and Native Land Claims* (Bloomington: Indiana University Press, 1975). On Hawai'i, see the Haunani-Kay Trask, *From a Native Daughter: Colonialism and Sovereignty in Hawai'i* (Monroe, ME: Common Courage Press, 1993).

36. A good exposition on this phenomenon may be found in Paul Brodeur, *Restitution: The Land Claims of the Mashpee, Passamaquoddy, and Penobscot Indians of New England* (Boston: Northeastern University Press, 1985).

37. The problem is partially but insightfully examined in Ronald Weitzer, *Transforming Settler States: Communal Conflict and Internal Security in Zimbabwe and Northern Ireland* (Berkeley: University of California Press, 1992).

38. It is entirely possible to extend a logical analysis in this direction. See, for instance, J. Sakai, *Settlers: The Mythology of the White Proletariat* (Chicago: Morningstar Press, 1983).

39. Sharon O'Brien, *American Indian Tribal Governments* (Norman: University of Oklahoma Press, 1989).

40. These matters are covered quite well in Janet Silman, ed., *Enough Is Enough: Aboriginal Women Speak Out* (Toronto: Women's Press, 1987).

41. The Smithsonian view of Indians has been adopted even by some of the more self-consciously "revolutionary" organizations in the United States. For a classic example, see Revolutionary Communist Party, USA, "Searching for the Second Harvest," in *Marxism and Native Americans*, op. cit., pp. 35-58.

42. The thesis is, no kidding, that Indians were the first "environmental pillagers," and it took the invasion of enlightened Europeans like the author of the piece to save the American ecosphere from total destruction by its indigenous inhabitants; George Weurthner, "An Ecological View of the Indian," *Earth First!* Vol. 7, No. 7, Aug. 1987.

43. Paul W. Valentine, "Dances with Myths," *Arizona Republic*, Apr. 7, 1991 (Valentine is syndicated, but is on staff at the *Washington Post*).

44. A fine selection of such early colonialist impressions can be found in the first few chapters of Richard Drinnon's *Facing West: The Metaphysics of Indian Hating and Empire Building* (New York: Schoken, 1980). On the length of indigenous occupancy in the Americas, see George F. Carter, *Earlier Than You Think: A Personal View of Man in America* (College Station: Texas A&M University Press, 1980). On precontact population, see Henry F. Dobyns, *Their Number Become Thinned: Native American Population Dynamics in Eastern North America* (Knoxville: University of Tennessee Press, 1983).

45. For a succinct but reasonably comprehensive survey of actual precontact indigenous material and intellectual realities, see Jack Weatherford, *Indian Givers: How the Indians of the Americas Transformed the World* (New York: Fawcett Columbine, 1988).

46. Jack D. Forbes, *Black Africans and Native Americans: Race, Color and Caste in the Evolution of Red-Black Peoples* (New York: Oxford University Press, 1988).

47. On federal quantum policy, see my essay, "The Crucible of American Indian Identity: Native Tradition versus Colonial Imposition in Postconquest North America," *American Indian Culture and Research Journal*, Vol. 22, No. 2, 1998.

48. Probably the best examination of Indian warfare and "militaristic" tradition is Tom Holm's "Patriots and Pawns: State Use of American Indians in the Military and the Process of Nativization in the United States," in M. Annette Jaimes, ed., *The State of Native America: Genocide, Colonization and Resistance* (Boston: South End Press, 1992) pp. 345-70.

49. Referred to here is the so-called "Bradley Bill" (S.1453), introduced before the Senate by Bill Bradley in 1987. For analysis, *see* the special issue of *Wicazo Sa Review* (Vol. XIV, No. 1, Spring 1988) devoted to the topic. Also see "The Black Hills Are Not For Sale," in this volume.

50. Russell Means and Ward Churchill, *TREATY: A Platform For Nationhood* (Porcupine, S.D.: TREATY Campaign, 1982); appended to the present volume.

51. Barsh, "Indian Land Claims," op. cit.

52. A number of examples may be found in Mark Frank Lindley's *The Acquisition and Government of Backward Country in International Law: A Treatise on the Law and Practice Relating to Colonial Expansion* (London: Longmans Green, 1926).

53. Probably the only accessible material to date on the Buffalo Commons idea is unfortunately a rather frothy little volume. Anne Matthews, *Where the Buffalo Roam: The Storm Over the Revolutionary Plan to Restore America's Great Plains* (New York: Grove Weidenfeld, 1992).

54. For one of the best elaborations of these principles, see Zed Nanda, "Self-Determination in International Law: Validity of Claims to Secede," *Case Western Reserve Journal of International Law*, No. 13, 1981.

55. A prototype for this sort of arrangement exists between Greenland (populated mainly by Inuits) and Denmark; Gudmundur Alfredsson, "Greenland and the Law of Political Decolonization," *German Yearbook on International Law*, No. 25 (1982).

56. Although my argument comes at it from a very different angle, the conclusion here is essentially the same as that reached by Richard Falk in his *The End of World Order: Essays in Normative International Relations* (New York: Holmes & Meier, 1983).

57. This is the basic idea set forth in *TREATY*, op. cit.

58. The concepts at issue here are brought out very well in William R. Catton, Jr., *Overshoot: The Ecological Basis of Revolutionary Change* (Urbana: University of Illinois Press, 1982).

59. For further elaboration, see Vine Deloria, Jr., *God Is Red* (New York: Delta, 1973). The ideas

have even caught on, at least as questions, among some Euroamerican legal practitioners; see Christopher D. Stone, *Should Trees Have Standing? Towards Legal Rights for Natural Objects* (Los Altos, CA: William Kaufman, 1972).

60. CNN "Dollars and Cents" reportage, May 27, 1992.

61. The idea is developed in detail in Jeremy Rifkin's *Entropy: A New World View* (New York: Viking, 1980). It should be noted, however, that the world view in question is hardly new; indigenous peoples have held it all along.

62. One good summary of this, utilizing extensive native sources—albeit many of them go unattributed—is Jerry Mander's *In the Absence of the Sacred: The Failure of Technology and the Survival of Indian Nations* (San Francisco: Sierra Club Books, 1991).

63. If this sounds a bit scriptural, it is meant to. A number of us see a direct line of continuity from the core imperatives of Judeo-Christian theology, through the capitalist secularization of church doctrine and its alleged marxian antithesis, right on through to the burgeoning technotopianism of today. This is a major conceptual cornerstone of what indigenists view as eurocentrism (a virulently anthropocentric outlook in its essence).

64. The information is in André Gunder Frank's book, but the conclusion is avoided; André Gunder Frank, *Capitalism and Underdevelopment in Latin America: Historical Studies of Chile and Brazil* (New York: Monthly Review, 1967).

65. See Jerome Ch'en, *Mao and the Chinese Revolution* (New York: Oxford University Press, 1967).

66. Paul R. Ehrlich and Anne H. Ehrlich, *The Population Explosion* (New York: Simon and Schuster, 1990).

67. Extrapolating from the calculations of Catton in *Overshoot*, op. cit.

68. Sound arguments to this effect are advanced in Paul R. Ehrlich and Anne H. Ehrlich, *Population/Resources/Environment* (San Francisco: W. H. Freeman, 1970).

69. Paul R. Ehrlich and Anne H. Ehrlich, from their book *Healing the Earth*, quoted in CNN series *The Population Bomb*, May 1992.

70. This would be about fifty million, or less than one-fifth the present U.S. population; Catton, *Overshoot*, op. cit., p. 53.

71. This is essentially the same argument, without ever quite arriving at the obvious conclusion, advanced by Marc Reisner in his *Cadillac Desert* (New York: Penguin, 1986).

72. A good deal of the impact could also be offset by implementing the ideas contained in John Todd and George Tukel, *Reinhabiting Cities and Towns: Designing for Sustainability* (San Francisco: Planet Drum Foundation, 1981).

73. For purposes of comparison, see *Funding Ecological and Social Destruction: The World Bank and International Monetary Fund* (Washington, D.C.: Bank Information Center, 1990). By contrast, the concept described in the text might be dubbed "Struggling for Ecological and Social Preservation."

74. Many indigenous peoples take the position that all social policies should be entered into only after consideration of their likely implications, both environmentally and culturally, for descendants seven generations in the future. Consequently, a number of seemingly good ideas for solving short-run problems are never entered into because no one can reasonably predict their longer term effects. See Sylvester M. Morey, ed., *Can the Red Man Help the White Man? A Denver Conference with Indian Elders* (New York: Myrin Institute, 1970).

75. Allan Priaulx and Sanford J. Ungar, *The Almost Revolution: France, 1968* (New York: Dell, 1969).

76. See, for example, Virginia Irving Armstrong, ed., *I Have Spoken: American History Through the Voices of the Indians* (Chicago: Swallow Press, 1971).

77. R. D. Laing, *The Politics of Experience* (New York: Ballantine, 1967).

78. Armstrong, *I Have Spoken*, op. cit., p. 79.

APPENDIX: IN STRUGGLE FOR EARTH

I was listening
to the voices of life
chanting in unison
carry on the struggle
the generations surge
together
in resistance
to meet
the reality of power

Mother Earth
embraces her children
In natural beauty
to last beyond
oppressor's brutality

As the butterfly
floats into life
We are the spirit
of natural life
Which is forever

The power of understanding
real connections to Spirit
is meaning
our resistance
our struggle
is not sacrifice
lost
It is
natural energy
properly used.

—John Trudell
from *Living in Reality*

TREATY

The Platform of Russell Means' Campaign for President of the Oglala Lakota People, 1982

Publisher's Note:

The following is the complete text of the position paper drafted by Ward Churchill in 1981 for use by Russell Means in constructing the platform upon which he would bid to become "Tribal President" on the Pine Ridge Reservation, South Dakota, the following year. All subsequent campaign literature was derived therefrom, and the points/reasoning articulated therein resonated so favorably with grassroots Oglala Lakotas on the reservation that the U.S. Bureau of Indian Affairs, working in concert with the existing tribal government, manufactured by federal authorities under the 1934 Indian Reorganization Act, were ultimately compelled to nullify Means' candidacy in order to prevent his probable election.

Tellingly, the pretext used for this purpose was that Means had been previously convicted of a felony, albeit not under the laws of the people he sought to lead. Instead, he had been convicted and imprisoned in 1978 under the laws of South Dakota and the United States for having engaged in what those dubious entities considered to be "criminal syndicalism." The basis of this allegation rested exclusively in his actions and pronouncements as a leader of the American Indian Movement in rejecting contentions that either the state or federal governments possessed the least legitimate authority in Lakota territory. Of this charge, he has proudly stated that he was "guilty as sin," observing that it should have served to underscore his standing as an Oglala Lakota patriot rather than disqualifying him from running for and holding office.

In any event, while such intervention by the colonizing power precluded whatever success Means might have had in realizing the TREATY program—and graphically demonstrated the limitations of electoral politics in the process—the document itself continues to stand as one of the better elaborations of the radical alternative to business as usual in Indian Country. Long unavailable to interested parties, it is provided here for whatever utility it may afford to those desiring to develop similarly comprehensive rebuttals to the status quo.

405

115 Years of the BIA, 50 Years the IRA: What Have We Lost?

> The white man made us many promises, but he kept only one. He promised to take our land and he took it.
>
> —Mahpiya Luta (Red Cloud), 1882

AS is shown in the accompanying sequence of maps, the Lakota people have lost more than ninety percent of the landbase which the United States solemnly agreed to respect "forever." *None* of the missing territory has been willingly given up by the Lakota Nation. The three-quarters express consent of adult male Lakotas required in order for alienation of Lakota land title to be legal, as is stipulated unequivocally in the 1868 Fort Laramie Treaty, has *never* been obtained. This fact in itself makes any transfer of Lakota lands to non-Lakota "owners" since 1868 *illegal*. Even the U.S. Supreme Court has said so.

Almost the entirety of our homeland has been taken illegally—*stolen*—by agents of the U.S. Bureau of Indian Affairs (BIA) and, since 1934, by the web of processes and procedures which fall under the so-called "Indian Reorganization Act" (IRA).

It should be understood that even the extent of theft depicted in the maps does not reveal the desperation of our true situation. They show only major blocks of territory stripped from legitimate Lakota ownership and control. What is not and can not be accurately reflected is the fact that even the remaining pittance of reservation land is "checkerboarded," that is, given over to non-Indian use and control by unscrupulous BIA/IRA leasing arrangements. Nor can the maps demonstrate that land not overtly leased in this way is "held in trust" by the federal government through the BIA.

In effect, it is both fair and accurate to say that *all* of the Lakota landbase has been stolen since 1868. We are quite aware that the Indian Reorganization Act has meant the organization of Indians off our land. By the same token, the BIA is an agency devoted to eliminating the affairs of the people it is ostensibly meant to serve.

It is clear. Our ancestors reserved land for the undisturbed use and occupancy of the Lakota people because without a landbase there can be no people. The actions of the BIA and the intent of the IRA have therefore been to destroy us, not to help us.

The following program is put forth by the TREATY (**T**rue **R**evolution for **E**lders, **A**ncestors, **T**reaties and **Y**outh). It is offered as the platform of

406

Russell Means in his candidacy to become President of the Oglala Lakota people in 1982, and will be shared by all others who run under the TREATY banner.

By supporting the TREATY Program, we believe it is possible for the Lakotas to reassert our true sovereignty, reversing the effects we've suffered under the BIA and the IRA, recovering what is rightfully ours and rejoining the community of nations as a full and equal partner. This *can* and *should be* the legacy we bequeath to our posterity.

Each point of the Program is detailed in the sections below.

Water

The Fort Laramie Treaty of 1868 places the eastern boundary of the "Great Sioux Nation" on he *east* bank of the Missouri River. Almost the entirety of the aquifer known as the Madison Formation lies within the boundaries of our territory, as defined by the Treaty. This means that *all* the water in the Missouri and its western watershed, as well as the groundwater in western South Dakota, belong to the Lakota people. Our rights to it were guaranteed forever by the United States at Fort Laramie.

In this way, our ancestors saw to it that the people would have ample water with which to flourish within our homeland, generation after generation. Even after the Paha Sapa [Black Hills] and "Unceded Indian Territory" were stolen in 1877, the Missouri River water and much of the aquifer remained within Lakota holdings. The U.S. was interested in gold in those days. Water was not an issue for it, and so water was left in Indian hands.

But during the period of the Allotment and Homestead Acts, when so much of what was then called the "Great Sioux Reservation" was taken, water became a major issue. The wasi'chus [whites] became interested in farming and ranching as well as mining, and suddenly, as if by magic, the *west* bank of the Missouri River became the eastern boundary of our remaining lands.

Overnight, with no authorization from the Lakota people at all, the federal government decided that the water in the Missouri River did not belong to us. And, while the size of our reserved territories have been steadily diminished since passage of the IRA in 1934, our right to aquifer water is said to have "passed" along with the land.

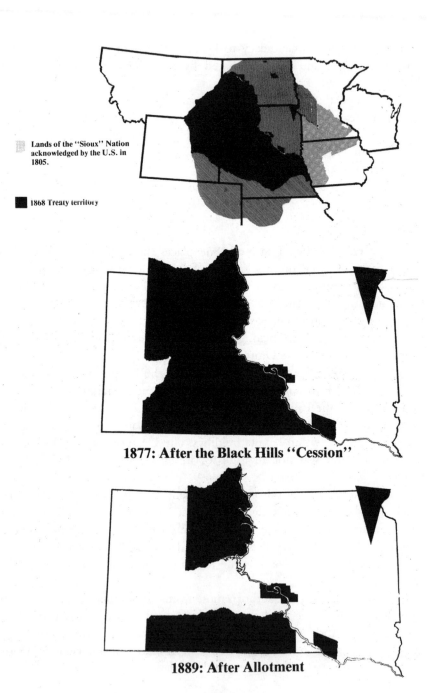

Lands of the "Sioux" Nation acknowledged by the U.S. in 1805.

1868 Treaty territory

1877: After the Black Hills "Cession"

1889: After Allotment

The Pine Ridge Reservation after breakup of "The Great Sioux Reservation" circa 1900.

In 1960, after 25% of Pine Ridge was stolen by "referendum" to form Bennett County. The shaded area is the "gunnery range" supposedly "borrowed" by the U.S. government in 1942.

In 1975, after the gunnery range was signed over "officially, to become a permanent part of the Badlands National Monument."

Today, after Washabaugh County was created from the 25% of reservation land lying north of Bennett County, less than 40% of the reservation remains under tribal jurisdiction.

Today, almost nothing remains of the water rights our ancestors fought so hard to preserve for us. Oahe and other major dams along the Missouri divert massive amounts of water to exclusively non-Indian use. What little groundwater remains available is being increasingly contaminated by mining and other industrial processes. Plans are on the board right now to drain the entire aquifer through ETSI and other corporate projects. If such plans succeed, the very basis for life itself will be gone from the whole Black Hills Region.

Given the situation, the administration of U.S. President Jimmy Carter was correct in designating the Black Hills a "National Sacrifice Area." And you can be sure that the official outlook has not changed for the better now that it is to be voiced by the Reagan Administration's Interior Secretary, James Watt.

Such realities were clearly foreseen by our ancestors in the terms of the Treaty they established for protection of *their* unborn. It is our responsibility to conduct ourselves in the same manner, extending similar protection over *our* unborn. If we do not offer water to our future generations, we offer nothing at all.

Sovereignty

Within the understandings of international law, it is the right of *all* sovereign nations to enter into treaty relationships with other sovereign nations. Conversely, *only* sovereign nations are entitled to enter into such relationships. Individuals and other entities imbued with a standing subordinate to nations—such as states or provinces, cities, counties and the like—do not have the legal right to make treaties.

Article 1 of the United States Constitution reflects this fact. The Article states unambiguously that subordinate entities may *not* enter into treaties. It follows that the federal government can enter into treaties *only* with other sovereign nations. For the government to conduct itself otherwise would be an illegal act under *both* U.S. and international law.

The United States government, which we can only presume was and is aware of its own laws, chose to enter into treaties with the Lakota Nation in 1805, 1847, 1851 and 1868. Not once, but *four* times did the United States, by definition of its own Constitution, acknowledge what our ancestors already knew: that the Lakota people were, and therefore *are*, sovereign in the precisely same sense as the United States itself. This principle has been recognized in legal doctrine from before the time of Chief Justice John Marshall in the early nineteenth century.

A nation which enters into a treaty relationship with another has both a moral and a legal obligation to carry out its responsibilities under the terms and provisions enshrined in the treaty document. The Lakota Nation has always done so, not only with respect to the United States but with all other nations.

The United States, on the other hand—as was shown in the sections on land and water, and as will be shown in the sections which follow—has patently failed (or refused) to do so with respect to the Lakota.

The immoral and illegal actions of the United States in this regard thus represent a clear infringement upon Lakota sovereignty. By international legal definition, this amounts to "Acts of War" continuing to this very day. In effect, the United States, which proposed and ratified four separate "treaties of peace and friendship" with the Lakota Nation, has never stopped waging what amounts to an undeclared war against us.

There is a definition of this sort of behavior by nations, a definition advanced by the U.S. itself in describing the illegal conduct of the nazi régime during its prosecution at Nuremberg after World War II. The definition is this: A nation which willingly and intentionally violates the sovereignty of another for purposes of territorial or other gain is guilty of the *crime* of "Waging Aggressive War."

The U.S. assumed a leading role in trying and executing or imprisoning the nazi leaders deemed responsible for waging aggressive war during the 1930s and '40s, yet it is equally guilty, where the Lakota Nation is concerned, of waging exactly the same kind of war.

And there is more. The reason treaties are so important in international affairs is that they are the *primary* mechanism through which major understandings between nations can be reached short of war, or to end existing wars. They are voluntary arrangements entered into by all parties expressly as a means to *prevent violence*. The violation of any treaty is therefore an inherently violent act. Similarly, the blocking of treaty agreements is an inherently violent act, as it prevents peaceful solutions to international problems.

Since treaties are voluntary, any sovereign nation has a right to decline to be involved in one (or many). The United States exercised this right in 1871, when it declined to become involved in any further treaties with indigenous nations, including the Lakotas. There was a snag, however. The U.S. had earlier reached an understanding with these same nations wherein it had reserved unto itself the *exclusive* prerogative of making treaties with them.

The matter cannot be had both ways. A nation cannot monopolize the right to treat with other nations and then refuse to negotiate treaties with them. Not only does this serve to undermine the sovereignty of these other nations, it destabilizes the whole delicate structure by which nonviolent international problem solving is meant to be accomplished. Hence, it is fair to say that aggressive war and violent usurpation of sovereignty have been built into the U.S. relationship to the Lakota and other indigenous nations since at least 1871.

Such a situation obviously cannot be allowed to continue. Either the United States must end its aggressive war against the Lakota Nation by honoring its existing treaties with us, and by indicating its willingness to negotiate new treaties which are mutually acceptable, or the Lakota Nation must enter, by treaty, into new international relationships designed to guarantee Lakota sovereignty both now and in the future.

To be sure, our ancestors would expect no less.

Self-Determination

According to the United Nations Charter and other elements of international law, *all* peoples possess an inherent right to self-determination. That is, we have an absolute right to our own form of government, our own legal system, our own methods of organizing our communities, control over our economy, our own means of determining who is/is not a citizen, our own manner to defining our relationship to other peoples, and so on. In substance, it is recognized in black letter law that we are inalienably a nation and entitled to determine for ourselves the form of our socioeconomic and political life.

Unquestionably, the United States, in cynical disregard of this fundamental standard of international comportment and legality, has acted to systematically deny the right of self-determination to the Lakota people. This is true not only where land, water and treaties are concerned, but in other important ways as well.

Government

The Lakota Nation has, and has always had, its own form of government. Traditionally, this has been constituted in the Councils of Elders ("Chiefs"). The United States unequivocally recognized the validity of our traditional government when it entered into its treaty relationship with us. Indeed, the right of our government to continue its functioning is permanently guaranteed in the 1868 Fort Laramie Treaty and elsewhere.

Nonetheless, in 1936, on the basis of the IRA, the U.S. intervened massively in our internal affairs. Central to this externally dictated "reorganization" of our national life was the imposition of a thoroughly alien type of government. This took the form of an elected "president" and "tribal council" operating on the basis of a written "constitution" formulated not by Lakotas, but by BIA officials in Washington, D.C.

It should be self-evident that any people subjected to such a process by another nation has been denied the right of self-determination at the most basic level. Denial of the right of self-determination with respect to the form of one's government is to be denied the right of participation in the genuine political life of one's country. It's that simple.

Jurisdiction

The key to any legal system is the question of where it holds jurisdiction. Our ancestors reserved the authority of the Lakota legal system over our territory through the 1868 Treaty. The U.S. agreed, guaranteeing us this right forever.

Yet, in 1885 the United States unilaterally extended its own jurisdiction over our territory through what it called the "Seven Major Crimes Act." After that, the scope of U.S. jurisdictional usurpation was broadened, year after year, law after law. With each expansion of U.S. jurisdiction, Lakota authority suffered a corresponding loss. The process was/is one in which the alien legal system quite literally shoved the Lakota legal system aside.

Today, Lakota jurisdiction, and thus the Lakota legal system itself, has been reduced to sheer meaninglessness. It holds no real power over either Lakotas or non-Lakotas living within our reservations.

Instead, the U.S. government wields absolute police and judicial power over Lakota territory, as is readily evidenced by the manner in which the FBI and Federal Marshals Service have recently conducted themselves on our reservations and the number of Lakotas currently serving time in federal prisons for "crimes" committed on Lakota land.

The true magnitude of this violation of our self-determining rights may be fully appreciated only if one considers the implications of the United States authorizing itself to assert a comparable "authority" over Canada, France or Japan. While the latter prospect is instantly perceived as being not only absurd but criminal, such U.S. conduct vis-à-vis the Lakota Nation is, legally speaking, no less so.

Tiospayes

The Lakota people have, and have always had, the means by which to organize ourselves into communities. A number of such forms have been traditionally enjoyed, and have long since proven themselves effective, whether organization was/is along family/clan lines, around seasonal needs, or in reflection of specific tasks/responsibilities undertaken by the group living as a community (or, in Lakota, "Tiospaye").

Another aspect of traditional Lakota community organization has always been the direct interaction of the various Tiospayes in comprising a multifaceted, multilevel national governing structure. In effect, Lakota society has always been organized in a manner sometimes described by Euroamerican political theorists as a "participatory democracy."

Yet, despite the fact that the traditional Tiospaye form of social organization amply met the needs of the Lakota people, the United States intervened to impair or nullify it. This was accomplished mainly through the BIA's exercise of a federally self-assigned "trust authority," beginning in the late-1880s, to manipulate Lakota landholdings, cash and other assets in such ways as to make it impossible for traditional Lakota communities to retain their cohesion.

In doing this, the BIA has not simply engaged in a policy of inducing severe social disruption, but has acted to reduce and redefine Lakota governance mechanisms to a single dimension. Where there was once a functioning interpenetration of an array of community forms there is now the single governmental edifice allowed by the IRA. Participation of the entire people in the governing process, even to the extent evident in the surrounding non-Indian society of South Dakota, is thereby prevented within the Lakota Nation.

Once again, this is a clear violation of our self-determining rights.

Economics

Since time immemorial, the Lakota people have demonstrated complete economic self-sufficiency. At the same time, we have been able to live in harmony with our environment, demonstrating respect for all natural relations, human and non-human alike. In sum, it is accurate to observe that not only have we always possessed our own mode of economy, but one which has proven itself to be remarkably efficient and durable in terms of meeting the full range of our material and other needs for sustenance.

The Lakota economy, of course, has always been synonymous with our landbase and attendant sources of water. As the United States has steadily stolen Lakota land and usurped our water rights, it has consciously acted to destroy our traditional economy. Further, the U.S. has moved quite deliberately to replace the Lakota economy with its own.

In the process, the U.S. has sought to convert what remains of Lakota territory, as well as our supplies of water, into mere "resources." Those who have imposed this situation, which the BIA refers to as "resource development," have promised that the Lakota people would benefit by being equally "developed"—thus becoming resources *themselves*—as workers profitably employed in various corporate enterprises.

Plainly, there are some very serious questions that need to be asked about the wisdom of entering into a process by which all people and places are commodified and thereby converted into mere *things*.

But, leaving such issues aside, the fact is that the promise has been a total lie. Today, real unemployment and corresponding poverty among Lakotas is over 90 percent. The level of self-sufficiency evidenced among even those who have somehow managed to cling to a few acres of land is nearly zero. *This* among a people who have *always* been productively occupied in the past, and who have *never* been truly impoverished.

Meanwhile, the wealth of our land, our water, our very habitat itself is being stripped away, inch by inch, pound by pound, all for the use and profit of others.

And the price we pay for this "progress"? It cannot be measured only in the depths of our destitution. Besides the obvious costs, there is the radioactive and chemical contamination of what little water remains to us, a matter which has led to spiraling rates of cancer, stillbirth and genetic mutations like cleft palate. Every new stripmine, uranium mill, power generating plant and production facility serves to up the ante of the consequences we endure.

The situation is already bad, and it promises to become much worse in coming years. Lakota territory is extraordinarily rich in minerals, and both the federal government and its corporate partners are once again offering "jobs, income and prosperity" to those foolish enough to grant them easy access.

What happens when the "resources" are gone? Look around you. The conditions currently prevailing at Pine Ridge are but a small taste of what is to come.

The example of Laguna Pueblo, which placed its faith in uranium mining, is very much to the point. Only a few years ago [i.e., 1977], Laguna had the highest per capita income and lowest unemployment of any reservation in North America. Then the uranium played out, and with it went the jobs and royalties which had made Laguna "prosper."

Now the corporate sugar daddy is gone, the water is radioactively contaminated, and so are the foundations of homes and community buildings, the roadbeds and the farmland. The old economy of Laguna cannot be reconstructed, the new economy is bust, and the chances are that the people will not even be able to remain on their homeland because of the contamination.

The people of Laguna are rapidly being reduced to absolute dependence upon unemployment compensation, welfare, ADC, commodities distribution, the Indian Health Service and "Christian charity." So are the Lakota people. The only difference between them and us is that their situation is likely permanent, and ours doesn't have to be.

But it could be. If we follow their lead, if we allow the trend of industrial "progress" to continue, our present situation will *not* be temporary. It *will* be permanent. There will be *no way* to regain self-sufficiency in terms acceptable to our own Lakota tradition.

Insofar as the United States and its corporate allies are presently seeking to leave us no alternative but to accept such a fate, they are guilty of denying Lakota self-determination in the most egregious manner imaginable.

Defining Citizens

All sovereign nations hold the right to determine for themselves, according to their own perceptions of need and interest, the composition of their own citizenry. Consequently, every country in the world has methods by which it defines the basis of citizenship. The United States certainly does. The Lakota Nation has the same right.

Traditionally, the Lakota people have always had ways through which we've established the parameters of our membership, including criteria allowing for the acceptance of non-Lakotas into our society. Similarly, we've always possessed understandings of when and to what extent it was appropriate to enter into alliances and other relationships which in certain instances led to forms of joint or mutual citizenship.

Today, the situation is rather different. The United States has taken it upon itself to decide for us who is and is not Lakota. The basis upon which the U.S. determines such matters? Through a system of "blood quantum" as crude and vicious as the race codes by which the nazis determined who was Jewish, Gypsy, etc. This, and the *place* of birth.

Membership/citizenship in the Lakota Nation, which is rightly decided upon a whole range of factors including knowledge of/allegiance to Lakota tradition, has thereby been reduced to an essentially racial proposition by outsiders.

Further, by unilaterally imposing its own citizenship upon all Lakotas, the United States has presumed to decide for us that we are to be permanently allied with it in the most intimate sort of way. We never had a choice as to whether we would be permanent allies with and citizens of the United States. This was simply forced down our throats as a people.

Of course there are those who will say that "dual citizenship" —i.e., holding both Lakota and U.S. citizenship at the same time—is a good thing, or at least that it does us no harm. To them, the following question must be asked: If dual citizenship does no harm, why does the federal government actively prevent us from making anyone we wish a Lakota citizen? To put it another way, if dual citizenship is so good, why isn't our naturalization of new citizens considered to be in *everybody's* interest?

The answer is that dual citizenship, as it is used by the U.S., is and always has been a means of confusing and diluting the sociopolitical integrity of the Lakota Nation. By insisting that a people which is suffering a war of aggression at the hands of a given nation are simultaneously citizens of the aggressor nation, the aggressor can keep its victims psychologically off balance, their spirit of resistance radically diminished. This renders the victims vulnerable, a much "softer" target than would otherwise be the case.

Conversely, the last thing any aggressor power would want or allow to happen is for any appreciable part of its own population to come to view itself as citizens of the victim nation, with all the feelings of kinship, empathy and solidarity this entails.

Also, in addition to confusing all too many Lakota people about where their real interests and loyalties should lie, the dual citizenship policy employed by the United States serves to dilute the Lakota Nation *physically*. By combining dual citizenship with blood quantum, the U.S. government has actually been able to create new citizens for itself at the direct expense of the Lakotas.

In other words, the child of any dual citizen whose blood quantum falls below the U.S.-approved minimum automatically becomes *only* a U.S. citizen, *never* a Lakota citizen. By defining Lakota identity in terms of genetic "standards," the U.S. government is able to effectively regulate the size of the Lakota population in accordance with its own rather than our perception of needs and interests.

All in all, the assumption of U.S. control over the definition of Lakota citizenship, and the imposition of its own citizenship upon all Lakotas, are two more blatant denials of the Lakota right to self-determination.

U.S. Internal Colonialism, A Crime Against Humanity

The result of all this—and the list could have been made *much* longer—is a feeling of total powerlessness among most Lakota people at the present time. This is entirely natural in a situation where the average citizen possesses no influence or control over his/her community affairs, day-to-day personal affairs, employment situation and the like, never mind regional and national policies and politics. This is especially true when the terms of one's life are defined by an outside force strictly on the basis of race, rather than by one's self on the basis of outlook and interest.

In sum, the combination of all these factors points directly to a certain harsh reality: The Lakota Nation exists today as a colony of the United States. And, since the Lakota Nation is landlocked, surrounded by the United States, it may be said to constitute an *internal* U.S. colony. The symptoms of disempowerment and lack of influence over those situations which most effect us are shared by the Lakota people with colonized peoples the world over.

The Lakotas, and American Indian peoples in general, also suffer a number of other things in common with colonized peoples everywhere. Our lack of power and influence over our own affairs is *real*, not imagined, and this is borne out in certain physical "proofs." For example, because of the fact that colonized peoples are deprived by their colonizers, for profit, of the self-determining ability to act in their own interests they may be expected to be markedly poorer than citizens of the colonizing powers.

Sure enough, American Indians, overall, have, by a decided margin, the lowest per capita income of any sector of the North American population.

Colonized people, because of our enforced poverty, may be expected to be hungry more often than others. Sure enough, American Indians evidence the highest rates of malnutrition of any population group in both the U.S. and Canada.

Colonized people should, in light of this, suffer diseases at rates far higher than our colonizers. True to form, American Indians suffer the highest per capita incidence of all manner of readily preventable/curable diseases. We are also burdened with the highest rates of infant mortality, teen suicide, death by exposure and by far the shortest lifespan of any group in North America.

These are some of the human consequences of the colonial relationship imposed by the United States upon the Lakota Nation. When the nazis adopted similar policies against the peoples of eastern Europe during the Second World War, the U.S. stood at the forefront in charging the German leadership with "Crimes Against Humanity." At Nuremberg in 1946, the United States took a leading role in convicting and either executing or imprisoning the nazi potentates guilty of such crimes, just as it did concerning charges that the Germans had waged an aggressive war against their neighbors.

Obviously, as the defendants argued during the Nuremberg trials, the United States neither practices the lofty form of enlightened humanitarianism it preaches, nor does it adhere to the "standards" of legal comportment it so sanctimoniously imposes on others. It didn't then, and it doesn't now. Indeed, it never has.

Alcoholism and Substance Abuse

Before proceeding to lay out the TREATY Program for changing things, it seems appropriate that we stop and examine in some depth another of the more virulent by-products of the ubiquitous sense of powerlessness and despair induced by U.S. colonialism among Lakotas.

What we will look at is alcoholism, because it is a truly devastating disease, unknown to our ancestors, which now pervades every nook, cranny and dimension of our society. Moreover, we will look at alcoholism in particular because, of all the maladies with which we are presently afflicted, it demonstrates most clearly how two different aspects of colonization, the mental and the physical, interact in their impact upon the colonized as individuals, and how this serves to destroy our families, our communities and, ultimately, our society as a whole.

It is a bitter fact that alcoholism is rampant on Pine Ridge. There are no communities, and very few homes, in which it is not a problem. More deaths on the highway and from exposure, more cases of child abuse and domestic violence, and more cases of the dereliction of basic human decency are caused by alcohol than all other reasons combined. Money which is desperately needed to offset malnutrition and other horrible conditions, especially among children, goes to drinking alcohol, day in and day out.

Psychologically, this is in large part an understandable situation. People who feel powerless to effect their lives and living conditions, and who find such feelings reinforced at every turn, lose hope. People who lose hope begin to look for ways to escape the realities which make them feel hopeless.

Alcohol, which is always available in off-reservation towns like Scenic [South Dakota] and White Clay [Nebraska], offers a way to gain this escape through sheer oblivion. It works so well that it has become a potential moneymaker on the reservation and there are therefore those who advocate that Pine Ridge be opened up to liquor sales.

In any event, the psychological motivation to drink alcohol created by colonial domination is more than sufficient to provide the basis for chronic alcoholism on the reservation. That in itself would warrant serious concern and action on the part of anyone, or any group, committed to the wellbeing of the Lakota people.

But there is more to the problem than just psychology. With Lakotas, there is also a problem feeding the mental compulsion to drink with a more tangible physical craving. This has nothing to do with genetics, a supposedly innate "Indian" disposition towards alcoholism, but with day-to-day reality of another sort: the very food we are forced to eat.

This is not meant as a joke.

The typical Lakota diet today consists of starches: potatoes, white flour, white rice, beans, grits, etc. Such foods are both relatively cheap when bought "on the market" and constitute the great bulk of what the federal government provides as commodity provisions. They thereby comprise our basic (affordable) staples. Obviously, a high-starch diet is not balanced as it should be, and, when consumed over a sustained period, this has significant consequences.

The first thing any competent dietitian will tell you is that a diet which is unbalanced towards starches will cause an abnormal blood sugar content in the body, and certain critical vitamin and mineral deficiencies as well. This last means that a person subsisting on a high-starch diet is suffering from malnutrition even though s/he is eating large amounts of food.

It may sound strange, but basing a diet on starch means, among other things, that a person can be very overweight and literally starving to death *at the same time.*

The blood sugar problem caused by the typical Lakota high-starch diet is even trickier. In simplest terms, what it means is that the body chemistry is "tuned" in such a way that when a person takes a drink of alcohol, very likely for the psychological reasons mentioned above, the alcohol reacts in the person's imbalanced blood to create a physical craving.

In other words, if you've subsisted on a high-starch for a while and then drink some alcohol, you will experience addiction to alcohol. The longer you've been on such a diet, the more you drink; the more you drink, the stronger your addiction. It's not heroin, but it's the same principle.

Thus, most Lakotas who drink not only "need" alcohol for psychological reasons, because they feel beaten and depressed and wish to mentally escape these feelings, but, once they've begun drinking, because of a very real physical addiction as well. The mental and the physical go hand in hand. So the problem must be dealt with on both levels if it is to be dealt with at all. This is all the more true when one considers that a major by-product of the combination of poor diet and alcohol consumption we are discussing is diabetes, a leading killer of adult Lakotas and perhaps the single most prominent disease in the inventory of what ails us as a people.

Plainly, there is plenty of reason to deal with the problem, a conclusion based simply in the fact that so many Lakotas now suffer from alcoholism and related maladies. Worse, it is equally plain that the problem affects not only our present generation, but our future generations as well.

An unborn child carried in the womb of his/her mother is totally dependent on the diet of the mother for the nutrients s/he takes in. If the mother is subsisting on a high-starch diet, and especially if the mother is drinking as well, the child will be born with a chemical predisposition to become an alcoholic, or will actually *be* an alcohol from the first moment.

If the child is born with its body already addicted to alcohol, it will have to go through withdrawal—"DTs" and all—from the instant of birth. If the child is born with a predisposition towards alcoholism rather than alcoholism per se, he or she will retain this predisposition so long a s/he is forced to remain on a high-starch diet.

At still another level, when the mother engages in heavy and/or extended drinking during pregnancy, the unborn are impacted in other ways as well. This is through the so-called "Fetal Alcohol Syndrome" (FAS) in which the quantity of alcohol toxicity transmitted through the mother's blood to her unborn child is sufficient to cause mental retardation, physical deformity or both. Such effects are irreversible and are evident in increasing numbers of Lakota children today.

In the traditional Lakota way, it is our responsibility to protect the unborn as a matter of highest priority. And, with something like alcoholism, the only means of providing such protection is by eliminating the condition of colonialism which produces both the physical and psychological circumstances underlying the disease.

It cannot really be questioned that colonialism is at the root of the alcoholism problem among our people. After all, we *never* used alcohol in any form before the United States forced its "trust authority" upon us. It is from such an understanding of our situation and what is necessary to change it for the better that the TREATY Program came into being.

The TREATY Program

Since the TREATY views U.S. colonialism as the source of the kinds of problems experienced on Pine Ridge and throughout the rest of the Lakota Nation—for *all* the reasons stated above and *many* more—it views a comprehensive *anti colonialist program* as the *only* reasonable plan to offer. What follows is an overview of the ways and means by which the TREATY intends to begin turning its program into reality, its positions into a policy of self-sufficiency for the Oglala Lakota people.

It must be understood that this overview is not an in-depth articulation of our plan. Far too much space would be required for us to go into all the details and complexities involved. Instead, our intention is merely to give people a clear idea of the direction in which we are headed, and some of the major methods we will use in accomplishing our goals.

Government

Upon election, the TREATY will *immediately* alter the structure of the Oglala Lakota government in the following ways:

- First, legislative power—the power to determine policy for the Oglala people—will be returned to the Councils of Elders, traditional chiefs and other traditional Lakota governmental bodies.

- Second, the elected governing body—the tribal president and council—will serve primarily as a buffer between the traditionals and the federal bureaucracy. It will also hold the responsibility of implementing the policy decisions of the traditionals.

From its first moment, the TREATY will thus serve merely the executive branch of government, a branch which—in contrast to the mutation which has occurred in the U.S. government—is rightly subordinate to the traditional, legislative branch.

Over the longer term, even this function of the tribal president/council should be viewed as temporary and transitional since the ultimate intention of the TREATY is to dissolve this IRA form of governance as rapidly as the traditional Lakota form can be fully reconstituted. This means that the current IRA-imposed constitution must be revised to serve as a provisional document reflecting the new legislative/executive arrangement and mandating a complete revitalization of traditional Lakota government at the earliest possible date.

Tiospayes

As one means of accomplishing this, the TREATY administration will work under direction of the traditionals to establish functioning local governments in every community on the reservation within the first six months to one year of its tenure. Further, the TREATY administration will work under direction of both the traditionals and the newly (re)constituted local governments during its second year to establish functioning regional governments representing several communities simultaneously, on whatever basis the people decide.

In this way, the overall traditional Lakota form of governance, multifaceted and multileveled, can be rebuilt to its fullest natural extent in the most rapid possible fashion.

A portion of the TREATY position in this connection will be the immediate reversal of current policies using housing and development funds to restructure existing communities. Funds will be channeled *directly* to community members *where they are*, or where the *choose* to be.

In cases such as cluster housing programs, where people have already been coerced into physical relocation, funds will be devoted to undoing the damage done. People will be supported in moving back to their original communities if they so desire. In substance, existing and naturally—rather than "efficiently"—formed Lakota communities will be nurtured at all costs.

While this transitional program of physical readjustment is being carried out, the TREATY will also conduct a study to determine what sorts of structures—residences, community buildings, schools, etc.—are most appropriate in terms of meeting the stated needs of each reservation community. Additional tribal development monies will then go directly to meeting these real needs rather than the "needs" of some planning agency in Washington, D.C.

Jurisdiction

The TREATY will immediately redefine and reconfigure the roles and functions of the tribal police and courts.

- First, the tribal courts will be dissolved in the form they have been constituted under the IRA. Judicial authority will be handed over immediately to the traditionals who comprise the *proper* authorities among our people. The prevailing code of criminal laws and penalties will be suspended and/or phased out, replaced as quickly as possible by that of the traditional Lakota (among other things, this means *no jails*).

- Second, the tribal police will be viewed as a transitional agency operating under traditional Lakota law and answering, through the tribal president, to the traditionals. This situation will be maintained until such time as the traditional Akicita (warriors' societies) can be effectively reconstituted. The Akicita will then replace the current BIA/IRA-imposed police apparatus as *the* enforcement mechanism of governance within Oglala territory.

Current members of the tribal police may or may not ultimately become members of the Akicita, depending on the decision of the traditional government in each individual instance.

In the interim, the tribal police will be instructed to enforce Oglala jurisdiction over Oglala territory. Their authority will encompass both Lakota and non-Lakota individuals within this area. Non-Lakotas who do not wish to live under sovereign Lakota jurisdiction, and in accordance with the traditional Lakota code of legality, will be free to leave the reservation immediately.

Similarly, attempts by non-Lakota law enforcement agencies to assert jurisdiction within Oglala territory will be considered as criminal acts under both Lakota and international law. Offenders will be dealt with in ways deemed appropriate by the traditional government, whether this be a matter of simple expulsion from Lakota territory, expulsion accompanied by impoundment of weapons and vehicles, or by some other means.

The "arrest" of a Lakota national by representatives of non-Lakota police agencies will be treated as kidnapping in the event it occurs within Oglala territory.

Tribal police personnel unprepared to implement such a policy will be free to resign immediately. In the alternative, they will be fired. In either event, they will be replaced with individuals prepared to act in behalf of the people rather than on behalf of outside interests such as the FBI, State of South Dakota and the U.S. government.

The TREATY administration will also establish, as a matter of Lakota *national* priority, a "Center for International Law" staffed by Lakota and allied legal experts, the sole purpose of which will be to utilize all international legal means to recover every square inch of Lakota treaty territory.

As land is recovered, it will be placed under Lakota jurisdiction in the manner described above.

Sovereignty

Each of the preceding three categories of activity has obviously been aimed at the exercise of Lakota *sovereignty* within the internationally understood and accepted meaning of that term.

A primary responsibility of the TREATY administration will be to work with the Center for International Law, Lakota Treaty Council, International Indian Treaty Council and other appropriate bodies to attain renewed international recognition of the sovereign Lakota Nation.

Success in this area will be signaled by a formal declaration of recognition coming from a United Nations member-state *other than the United States*.

This is both extremely important and entirely possible to achieve. By being formally recognized by other governments around the world, the Lakota Nation immediately gains access to the U.N. and other international agencies capable of applying considerable pressure upon the U.S. government to end its war against the Lakota and honor its treaty commitments.

We will also gain entree to the International Court of Justice ("World Court") located in the Hague (Netherlands). This will allow us to take the U.S. to court before the other nations of the world rather than merely in the rigged/closed system of the United States itself.

The advantages of this in terms of our ability to effectively sue for restoration of our property and other rights should be obvious. Plainly, it is high time that the judges determining the legitimacy of our claims were not representatives of the opposing party.

Finally, through such recognition the Lakota Nation would be able once again to exercise its rights to enter into treaties and other international agreements (e.g., trade agreements) with governments other than that of the U.S.

If the United States does not wish to enter into such relationships with us, fine. That is its right. *But*, this in no way prevents an internationally recognized Lakota government from entering into relationships with *other* countries, including other indigenous nations within the United States itself.

Given all this, you can bet that international recognition will bring about a rapid and positive change in U.S./Lakota intergovernmental relations, *especially* in terms of the U.S. honoring its existing treaty obligations.

Economics

The TREATY economic program is tied directly to the land and to the traditional Lakota view of the people's relationship to our overall environment. From this, certain things automatically follow.

- First of all, all mining and other corporate leases within Lakota territory will be immediately canceled. As the experience of the Lagunas, Navajos and others have abundantly shown, temporary jobs and royalties from mining are of no benefit when the environment is destroyed as a result. This rule will apply to all treaty lands recovered as well as to the current reservation area.

- Second, agricultural and grazing leases let by the BIA to non-Lakotas within Lakota territory will be suspended pending a comprehensive investigation of the manner in which they were negotiated, as well as the terms and conditions they entail. All leases found to have been processed by the BIA without consent of the Lakota landowners will be canceled outright.

In the event the true landowners wish to utilize their property—and they will be encouraged to do so either directly or through tribal enterprises—they will assume immediate control over their land. In the event they do not, a consenting and equitable leasing arrangement will be constructed, either by the individuals concerned or by the Lakota Nation itself.

In the event that leases were entered into in a basically consenting fashion, but were negotiated at inordinately low rates by the BIA in its self-assigned "trust" capacity, the Lakota landowner(s) will have the option either to recover their land by canceling the lease or to renegotiate the lease to reflect equitable terms.

The TREATY administration will also establish a "Center for Individual Land Recovery" which will be devoted to research and the filing of Forced Fee Patents and other actions designed to recover "off-reservation" lands illegally taken from the Lakota people in areas such as Bennett County.

Meanwhile, all fences serving as boundary markers and the like shall be removed within the entire Oglala Lakota territory at the earliest possible date. The open range that results will be consigned to the (re)establishment of herds of buffalo, antelope, sheep, certain varieties of cattle and other animals naturally adaptable to the region's semiarid climate.

Tribal income will be committed to developing this "resource base" as rapidly as is feasible within the natural constraints of the landbase, and to extending it to dairy operations at the earliest possible date.

Fencing will be restricted to agricultural purposes, to keep livestock living on the open range from destroying gardens and small fields. Crop selection will be determined by the types of plant most naturally compatible with the climate and soil conditions natural to the area. Location of agricultural plots will be determined by the natural availability of water from place to place. Hence, it seems likely that relatively few areas will be fenced under the TREATY Program.

Realization of the TREATY economic program is of course contingent upon several major factors discussed below.

Land

Implementation of a full-fledged economic program is based upon our previously mentioned plan to recover treaty land. The 1868 Treaty Territory is more than sufficient to allow the Lakota Nation to rebuild a viable economy around the traditional forms of animal hunting/raising and limited agriculture. This traditional economic mode can be recreated without our engaging in the transitory and environmentally devastating processes of mining and industrialization. The key is to force the restoration of a national landbase sufficient to support our economy.

Water

Recovery of our landbase will bring with it control over the water reserved for *our* use by our ancestors. The best agricultural and grazing lands within the 1868 Treaty Territory—that is to say, the lands with the best water sourcing—now lie outside of reservation boundaries. We must recover it.

In the meantime, we must demand the fullest application of our right to water with the current reservation landbase because it is the springboard upon which both our economic recovery and broader land recovery initiatives must be launched.

As a means of actualizing our water rights, the TREATY administration will immediately establish a "Center for Water Rights Litigation" similar to the above-mentioned Centers for International Law and Individual Land Recovery.

In terms of water, land recovery will eventually mean that locales which have come under U.S. Bureau of Reclamation and Army Corps of Engineers "development" will have to be considered. This is true especially within the western Missouri, Niobrara and North Platte watershed areas.

Such "water control" construction will have to be investigated on a case by case basis to determine its overall environmental impact. Structures found to be destructive of the environment, such as those which deplete our aquifer faster than it replenishes itself, will be dismantled. Those found to yield no irreparable damage will be retained.

All water coming under Lakota control will be assigned a first use priority of meeting the needs of Lakota citizens. Water surpluses, if any, will go to development of a revitalized Lakota economy.

Electrification

One of the "benefits of technology" to which most Lakotas have become accustomed during the 20th century is electricity. A return to our traditional economy does not mean the elimination of electrical power. It does, however, draw into question the sources of such power and the sorts of technology used to generate it.

The TREATY is committed not only to *maintaining* electrical power within Lakota territory, but to *improving* its availability, dependability and method of generation.

- An immediate priority for the TREATY administration will be to establish an "Oglala Lakota Electrical Power Commission." The purpose of this commission will be to disentangle Pine Ridge from its current sources of electrical power, making the Oglala people completely self-administering in this regard.

- Second, the TREATY administration will initiate a program to construct alternative electrical generation units, ultimately to be built by a tribal manufacturing facility, to replace the sorts of technology presently used to generate our electrical power.

- We live with an all but unused and non-depletable natural resource: the wind. It is possible to construct generators relying entirely on the wind to generate electricity. Total reliance upon wind power in meeting Lakota electrical needs is a firm goal of the TREATY, a goal it is entirely possible to meet over a very short period of time.

This plan will encompass each sector of the 1868 Treaty Territory as it is recovered. Eventually, there will be no coal-fired or nuclear power plants within the entire Black Hills Region (and possibly no hydroelectric generating facilities either). Wind power, which is essentially cost-free beyond construction outlays, is more than ample to meet the needs of the entire Lakota Nation.

Electrical rates within the Lakota Nation can therefore be projected. To the extent that they are charged at all, resulting funds will go into equipment maintenance and investment in the overall economic development of the Lakota Nation.

In sum, electrical power may well be the first area in which the Lakota Nation becomes *entirely* self-sufficient.

Additionally, there is every probability that the output of the Lakota national wind generation system, when complete, will be greater than needed by the people. Surplus electricity may then be sold at equitable rates to areas adjoining the Lakota Nation. All profits realized from such sales will be invested in economic development and other programs benefitting the people as a whole.

Lakota/U.S. Relations

The TREATY is committed to the position that not one square inch of Lakota territory is for sale. It is thus clearly *not* part of the TREATY economic program that revenues will be generated by land sales or "settlements."

As part of its land recovery program, however, the TREATY intends to conduct in-depth studies concerning the type and extent of damage inflicted upon the Lakota landbase and the scale of profits accruing to the U.S. economy by virtue of the illegal and protracted U.S. occupation of the 1868 Treaty Territory.

The Homestake Mining Company, to take but one prominent example, has extracted an estimated $14-to-16 *billion* in gold from the Black Hills over the past century. Homestake itself will of course be nationalized once the land it occupies has been recovered. It will also be closed immediately, thereby ending its cyanide contamination of water as far downstream as the Gulf of Mexico.

But the gold already stolen *still* belongs to the Lakota Nation. The same principle holds true with respect to other mining enterprises—the uranium extracted from pits near the town of Edgemont, for instance—as well as timbering and other corporate activities.

Use fees must be retroactively charged against federal installations such as Ellsworth Air Force Base, Fort Meade, the Hot Springs VA Hospital, Igloo Army Ordinance Depot, and so forth, even though each such facility will be immediately shut down upon recovery of our landbase.

Then there are charges which must be levied in connection with environmental destruction and the costs of repairing it (where possible). The permanent defacing of Mount Rushmore is a case in point, as is the destruction of another entire mountain for purposes of creating what is ostensibly a gigantic sculptural likeness of Crazy Horse for the edification of non-Indian tourists.

In some ways more important, however, are the expenses which can be readily projected with respect to dismantling Bureau of Reclamation and Army Corps of Engineers projects, reclaiming mined or otherwise devastated areas, cleaning up uranium tailings and other nuclear wastes, and similar matters. Reparations are due across the board.

A block payment of indemnity is also due the Lakota people as a whole for the pain, suffering and material/spiritual degradation we have collectively experienced by being denied the benefit of our landbase over an extended period.

And, finally, the United States has a legal obligation to make direct payment to the Lakota Nation for its continued use of all lands outside the 1868 Treaty Area which still belong by both unrelinquished aboriginal right as well as by treaty right to the Lakota people.

Of particular interest in this regard are those areas encompassed by the terms of the 1851 Treaty of Fort Laramie. Here, a fair "rent," plus interest, accruing from the date(s) of illegal taking seem an appropriate remedy, at least until such time as a new international compact can be hammered out.

It is of course difficult at this point to calculate with any degree of precision the aggregate amount owed by the United States to the Lakota Nation. A final tally must therefore be deferred until such time as the abovementioned studies have been completed. The following very conservative estimates will thus serve as preliminary figures.

1) Expropriated profits, plus interest.............................. $100 billion
2) Use fees (government installations)........................... $ 25 billion
3) Environmental damage...$250 billion
4) Back rent, plus interest... $ 50 billion
5) Block indemnity.. $100 billion

Total $525 billion

The Lakota Nation, unlike its imperialist counterpart, the United States, is not economically unreasonable. We are therefore prepared to waive punitive damages and to negotiate a long-term payment plan through which the U.S. can begin to reintegrate itself among the ranks of civilized nations by retiring its debt in compensatory damages to the Lakota people in a relatively painless manner.

The TREATY suggests that discussions begin with the idea of a $50 billion initial lump payment, the balance to be paid over a 50 year period. We believe that an interest rate of 10 percent, compounded annually, should be considered quite reasonable in view of the rates set by the U.S.-controlled World Bank and comparable institutions.

In addition, the U.S. should be prepared to pay $2.5 billion annually in rent for its extended leases of unceded Lakota land within the 1851 Treaty Territory and other such areas. This arrangement will continue until final disposition of these matters is negotiated through an appropriate international instrument.

The TREATY further recommends that the Lakota Nation waive any further financial or "trust" obligations on the part of the United States, whether real or self-assigned, within the 1868 Treaty Territory. This waiver should be considered effective so long as the above-described annual payments by the U.S. are made in a regular and timely fashion.

It seems self-evident that anything resembling the financial base sketched herein would allow all phases of the TREATY Program to be implemented.

Moreover, it is to be anticipated that long before the 50-year payment schedule has run its course, the Lakota Nation will have fully regained its rightful position as a sovereign, self-determining, self-sufficient and self-perpetuating relative within the family of nations.

Other International Relations

It should be expected that the United States, given its lengthy history of international misconduct, may prove reluctant either to return stolen Lakota land or to provide appropriate compensation for its presently ongoing expropriation of Lakota resources.

In the event that such expectations are borne out, the TREATY Program calls for the solicitation of non-U.S. developmental aid with which to undertake the necessary legal and other actions necessary to eventually compel U.S. compliance with the rule of law, to initiate service programs critically needed by the people, and to establish an increasingly viable economic base for the Lakota Nation *despite* U.S. preferences.

The negotiation of relevant international agreements will be conducted by the traditional government with the TREATY administration serving as a diplomatic/executive arm.

Other Initiatives

Clearly, the main thrust of the TREATY Program as outlined above is to reassert Lakota sovereignty, self-determination and economic self-sufficiency. Our goal is to bring about the complete decolonization of the Lakota Nation. Put another way, this means booting the U.S. *out* of Lakota territory, *all* Lakota territory.

This will in itself solve our problems over the long run. But conditions on the reservation today are such that other, shorter-run initiatives must be undertaken immediately, before things like economic development are very far along. Some of the major areas in which this is true are the following.

Nutrition

It is an immediate objective of the TREATY to begin a nutrition program designed to replace the current federal commodity program. The TREATY nutrition program will be focused primarily on providing a balanced diet *directly* to Lakota youth, but it will also include the entire reservation population.

The TREATY firmly maintains that until the pervasive condition of malnutrition so evident among Lakotas is corrected, *nothing* else can be truly accomplished.

Consequently, as a transitional program on the way to self-sufficiency, the TREATY administration will negotiate with a wide array of non-governmental agencies, both in the U.S. and elsewhere in the international arena, to secure meat, poultry and dairy products, produce, whole grain products and vitamin supplements sufficient to provide an adequate diet to all Oglala Lakotas.

Commitments will be sought from the sponsoring agencies to continue their support for a period of 10 years, if need be.

Health

The great majority of diseases chronically suffered by Lakotas are directly related to poor nutrition. In providing a balanced diet to the people, the TREATY will have taken a significant step towards solving our problem of ill health. Nonetheless, more than a nutrition program is necessary.

The TREATY plans to construct, as a matter of national priority, at least four solar-powered water purification facilities on Pine Ridge. These facilities will provide *pure* drinking water to all reservation residents within two years. This pure water, distribution of which will constitute a tribal enterprise, will replace the contaminated water supplies—which spread all manner of disease—now available.

The TREATY is also committed to the thoroughgoing reorganization of existing healthcare facilities, bringing in competent staff, opening fixed and/or mobile community clinics, and the initiation of a general inoculation program during the first year of our administration.

It is a fundamental goal of the TREATY to institute free comprehensive and continuous health care for all Oglalas within the first two years.

Alcoholism

As was noted earlier, alcoholism is a special problem among Lakotas today. The TREATY therefore has a special program with which to counteract it.

The first step is to permanently ban liquor sales on the reservation, and to undertake suits and other actions to end its sale in adjoining localities. The second step, which begins at the same time as the first, is to balance the Lakota diet, thereby eliminating the physical basis for continuing alcohol addiction among our people.

From that point, the TREATY will undertake a substantial psychological intervention program designed to combat alcohol dependency. This of course includes appropriate modes of counseling, but is geared more towards providing a concrete sense of empowerment among those who presently feel themselves to be disempowered.

The TREATY proceeds with an understanding that the reintroduction of pride and self-respect among the people is the only sure means of ending our rampaging alcoholism crisis. Thus, the longer-term TREATY programs for bringing about a restoration of our sovereignty, self-determination and self-sufficiency should be seen as the ultimate method of "curing" both mental and physical dependency upon alcohol and other such substances.

Education

The current BIA-run school system on Pine Ridge is plainly a total failure, at least if the education of our youth is or ever was its intention.

In response, the TREATY calls for the assumption of community control over each local school district within the first year of its administration.

Curricula will then be redesigned to provide accurate and comprehensive instruction in Lakota history and language, foreign languages such as English and Spanish, U.S. history and international affairs, economics (from our own perspective), traditional indigenous science and the "Three Rs."

Our children *will* learn to read in our schools, something that cannot be said of the BIA system.

Also integral to the Lakota educational model will be solid instruction in our traditional values and spirituality, practical skills such as animal husbandry and carpentry, as well as oratory. This last is perfectly in keeping with our oral tradition and lends itself as much to the "modern world" as to the world of our ancestors.

Further, the TREATY intends to designate each local school campus as a community center in order to facilitate the rapid (re)integration of the educational system with day-to-day community life and to bring our youth into more direct and regularized interaction with elders.

It is not, and has never been, the desire of the Lakota Nation to usurp individual non-Lakota landholders within our Treaty Territory. We are instead concerned mainly with (re)occupying and using foreign governmental and corporate holdings within the boundaries of our nation.

Hence, unless guilty of specific crimes against Lakotas or other indigenous peoples, individual homeowners, ranchers and the like who happen to be non-Lakota will be welcome to remain in the sovereign Lakota Nation. Nor is there any reason why, in doing so, they cannot retain their personal property up to, say, a limit of 160 acres.

There is of course a quid pro quo. Non-Lakotas opting to reside permanently in the Lakota Nation will be subject to all laws, rules and regulations prevailing within *Lakota* jurisdiction. Individuals unwilling to accept this arrangement will be free to leave Lakota territory in precisely the same manner they would leave any other country with which they are unsatisfied.

In other words, they will be entitled to take with them all personal effects *other than* land title.

Lakota citizenship will obviously prevail within the Lakota Nation. Individuals of non-Lakota origin who wish to reside permanently in our country will therefore be encouraged to apply to become Lakota citizens. If accepted, they will enjoy all the same rights and privileges, and incur the same responsibilities, as an other Lakota.

So-called "dual citizenship"—the holding of U.S. and Lakota citizenship simultaneously—will *not* be acceptable, however. A choice must be made to be *either* a U.S. citizen *or* a Lakota citizen. Becoming a Lakota citizen will thus entail the formal renunciation of U.S. citizenship.

Those of non-Lakota origin who wish remain in Lakota territory, under Lakota jurisdiction, but without relinquishing their U.S. citizenship, will be free to apply for status as "landed immigrants" (this will also pertain to those of other nationalities). If accepted, they will be able to stay on, retaining their land holdings.

Immigrant status, which is envisioned as being renewable, will be reviewed at 5-year intervals. Violation of Lakota law, however, will result in immediate deportation, the conditions of which will be determined by the nature of the crime (with possessions, without possessions, etc.).

Inheritance of any sort will not apply to immigrants. Ownership of

land and improvements will pass with the death or departure of each immigrant to the Lakota Nation.

Conclusion

This has been a summary of the major points of the TREATY Program. Although less than exhaustive in both scope and depth, it should prove
sufficient to provide a sound sense of the direction pursued by Russell
Means and all other candidates currently campaigning for election under the
TREATY banner. Watch for supplemental documents examining various aspects of the TREATY agenda in greater detail.

Index

439

Burke Charles: 343
Burke Act, *see* U.S. statutes
Bush, Barnie: 369
Bush, George: 275, 276, 289n188, 369, 375, 382;
    invocation of "Just War" principle by: 375;
    "New World Order" of: 389
Business Week (magazine): 244
Butler, Dino: 369

C

Cadieux, Pierre: 209-11
    invents "Loon Lake Cree Band": 211;
    invents "Woodland Cree Band": 210,
    231n70, 231n71
Caldicott, Helen: 259
Calgary Herald (newspaper): 204
California, genocide of Indians in: 339
Canada
    U.S. plan to invade: 75n64, 358n48
Canadian Broadcasting Corp. (CBC): 314
Canadian Civil Liberties Association: 234n131
Canadian Coalition for Nuclear Responsibility:
    307
Canadian Constitution
    Charter of Rights and Freedoms of: 219
Canadian court cases
    Bear Island (1984): 49, 62; *Calder* (1973): 49;
    Cardinal (1974): 49, 61-2; *Connolly v.
    Woolrich* (1867): 61
Canadian courts
    Court of Appeal (Alberta): 200, 205; Court
    of Appeal (Ontario): 218; Court of Appeal
    (Québec): 299; Court of Justice (Ontario):
    218; Court of the Queen's Bench (Alberta):
    198, 200, 203, 205; Court of the Queen's
    Bench (Québec): 309; Divisional Court
    (Ontario): 218; Superior Court (Québec):
    298, 299; Supreme Court of Canada: 200,
    218
Canadian government (federal)
    Court of Appeal: 205; Dept. of Indian and
    Northern Affairs: 197, 202, 318; Dept. of
    Interior: 192, 193; Dept. of Mines, Energy
    and Resources: 312, 313; Dept. of Transport:
    312; Federal Engineering Div.: 312; Federal
    Surveys and Mapping Branch: 312;
    Geological Survey of Canada: 312; Ministry
    of Justice: 203; Royal Canadian Mounted
    Police (RCMP): 206; Water Survey of
    Canada: 312
Canadian government (provincial)
    Dept. of Economics (Ontario): 313; Dept.
    of Lands and Forests (Ontario): 313; Dept.

of Mines (Ontario): 313; Dept. of the
    Treasury (Ontario): 313; Hamlet and Land
    Tenure Pgm. (Alberta): 197; Indian Affairs
    Branch (Alberta): 193, 194; Liquor Control
    Board (Ontario): 217; Municipal Affairs
    Dept. (Alberta): 197; Provincial Lands and
    Forests Dept. (Alberta): 192, 193;
    Superintendent of Reserves and Trusts
    (Alberta): 194; Water Resources Comm.
    (Ontario): 312, 313
Canadian Indian treaties: 41, 190
    Treaty 6: 82n138; Treaty 8 (1899): 190-1,
    192, 200
Canadian statutes
    Act for Extending Jurisdiction of the
    Courts of Justice in the Provinces of Upper
    and Lower Canada (1803): 71n25; Act for
    Regulating the Fur Trade (1824): 71n25;
    Act for the Gradual Enfranchisement of the
    Indians (1869): 83n161; Act to Amend and
    Consolidate the Laws Respecting Indians
    (1880): 83n161; Act to Amend the Indian
    Act (1932): 83n161; Act to Encourage the
    Gradual Civilization of the Indian Tribes
    (1857): 57; British North American Act
    (1867): 58, 79n100; Constitution Acts
    (1871, 1982): 58, 60, 83n161; Indian Acts
    (1876, 1880, 1906, 1920): 59, 231n70,
    325n36; Indian Advancement Act (1884):
    59, 83n161
Canadian Greens Party: 307
Captain Jack (Modoc leader): 368
Cardwell, Edward: 79n104
Carroll, Earl: 157, 170n89
Carson, Christopher ("Kit"): 135
Carter, Jimmy: 181, 184, 304, 410
Castaneda, Carlos: 18
Castillo, Bobby: 28
Catawbas
    extermination of: 53; termination of: 351
Catholicism and overpopulation: 392-3
Catton, William: 15, 394
Overshoot (book) of: 15
Cayugas: 93
    land claims of: 105-6; 1789 leasing
    agreement and: 95; 1838 expropriation of:
    97; 1980 lawsuit of: 104-5, 107, 112n60
Center for International Law: 426
Centerwall, Willard: 164n11
Central Maine Power Authority: 303, 308
Chemehuave Reservation: 263
Chase-Manhattan Bank: 297
Chemawawin Ojibwe Reserve: 316-8
    crime and alcoholism at: 317; impact of

Grenada, size of: 21, 55, 82n146
Grimshaw Agreement: 207–8, 209
Grinde, Don: 369
Gros Ventres: 387
Grotius, Hugo: 72n34
Guam
    U.S. acquisition of: 361n90, 376
Gulf Minerals Corp.: 140, 194
    collaboration with Eldorado Nuclear of: 268; interests in Saskatchewan uranium: 266; Mt. Taylor uranium mine of: 248
Gunnison Lake, armed confrontation at: 26
Gurwitz, Lew: 28, 155–6, 169n80, 170n81, 170n82, 170n87

H

Hale, Albert: 171n100
Hallman, David: 232n92
Hamel, Pete: 207
Hamilton, Clarence: 143, 149, 151
Hamley, Frederick: 164n13
Hammett, Dashiel: 221
Hanford nuclear weapons facility: 258–9, 261, 349; and AEC: 258; and public health impacts of: 259; deliberate releases of radioactive iodides from: 259; establishment of: 258; nuclear contamination by: 259–60, 285n109, 349; "Top Secret" classification of: 258
Harney, Corbin: 181, 184
Harris, LaDonna: 278
Haudenosaunee (Iroquois Confederacy): 27, 58, 83n158, 93–108, 379; and Allotment Act: 110n27; and Indian Claims Commission: 102; as military threat: 109n3; compensation offered to: 123; continuing sovereignty of: 108; influence on U.S. Constitution: 30n7; IRA and: 101; land claims of: 100–7; leases and: 94–5; political organization of: 16, 101, 102; Removal and: 98; traditional territory of: 94, 106; Treaty of Canandaiga and: 95; Treaties of Buffalo Creek and: 97–8, 100, 110n20; Treaty of Fort Harmar and: 94; Treaty of Fort Stanwix and: 93, 94; *U.S. v. Boylan* suit and: 110n31; *also see* Cayugas, Mohawks, Oneidas, Onondagas, Senecas, Tuscaroras
Havasupis: 387
Hawai'i/Hawaiians: 376, 387
    annexation of: 45, 75n61; right to decolonization of: 89n232; statehood imposed upon: 75n61; U.S.-supported *coup d'etat* in: 75n61

Hearst Corp.
Homestake Mine of: 128, 189n53, 431
Heinen, Barry: 215, 231n90
"Heirship Problem," the: 360n80
Hidatsas: 386
Higgins, Jim: 307
Hiroshima, U.S. nuclear bombing of: 260
Hitler, Adolf
    and Hössbach Memorandum: 363n138; *lebensraumpolitik* of: 353; on British policy towards Boers: 363n137; on U.S. genocide of American Indians: 363n137
Hohokam: 31n9
Holland, Jeff: 29
Holland Land Co.: 96, 97, 100
Holly, Glenn: 175, 178, 184
Holt, Henry: 296
Holt Renfrew restaurants: 217, 233m118
Ho-Lee Chow restaurants: 216
Hoover Dam: 395
Hopi/Hopis: 136–62
    and Mormonism: 136, 138–44, 163–4n11; Grazing District 6 and: 139–40, 141; *Hamilton v. Nakai* suit and: 141; Hotevilla village of: 137; impact of Navajo–Hopi Relocation Act upon: 148; Joint Use Area (JUA) and: 141–62; Kikmongwe form of government of: 137; Moenkopi village of: 136, 146, 167n39; partition lands ("HPL") of: 145, 148, 152; reorganization of: 59, 84n175, 137, 361n98; reservation boundaries of: 136; Tobacco Clan of: 136; traditional agriculture of: 136; Tribal Council of: 138–41; "Tribal Rangers" of: 144, 171n104
Horowitz, Irving Louis: 135
Horsman, Jim: 204
Horton, Frank: 105, 106
Horton, Robert Wilmot: 57
Howard, Edgar: 132n21
Hualapai Reservation: 275
Hussein, Saddam: 375
Hydro-Québec Power Commission: 296–8, 301–9; and aluminum industry: 301–2l; and Central Maine Power Authority: 303; and Churchill Falls hydro facility: 297, 303; and destruction of Eastman and Caniapiscau Rivers: 300; and La Grande River Project: 298, 301; and Manic hydro complex: 297; and New England Power Pool: 302; and New York Power Authority: 301, 302, 303; and State of Vermont: 302; and Vermont Joint Owners Power Corp.: 303, 308; contract cancellations and: 308; La Grande

II generating facility of: 302; Société d'energie de la Baie James subsidiary of: 298, 299; 1973 suit against: 299; *also see* James Bay I Project; James Bay II Project.

of: 327n64; Tri-River component of: 304;
opposed by Mistissini Cree and Inuits: 305–
9; planning of: 303–4; projected cost of:
303–4; suits filed against 308–9, 327n78
James Bay and Northern Quebec Agreement:
300, 306, 309
James Bay Defense Coalition: 307
Japan, overpopulation of: 391–2
Japanese Americans, internment of: 351
Jemez Pueblo: 275
Jenny Expedition: 115
Jervis, Peter: 223
Jicarilla Apaches: 386
mineral resources of: 345; reservation of:
345
Jim, Russell: 260
John Birch Society: 377
Johnson, Richard: 110n20
Journal of Ethnic Studies: 28
Just War, concept of: 51, 80n112

K

Kadenahe, Bahe: 155, 156
Kaiser Corp.: 165n20
Kalahui Hawai'i: 230n41
Kame'eleihiwa, Lilikala: 28
Kampuchea (Cambodia)
autogenocide in: 363n135
Kane, Kenny: 369
Katanga
Zaire's internal colonization of: 25
Katz, Steven: 228, 235n158
Katzenberger, Elaine: 29
Keegstra, James: 229, 235n158
Kelly, Fred: 28
Kelly, John Peter: 28
Kelly, Peter: 28
Kenda, Stephen: 216, 218, 219
Kennecott Copper Corp.: 165n17, 166n20
Cortez Gold subsidiary of: 182; Placer
Dome subsidiary of: 183, 189n52
Kennedy, John: 171n94
Kennedy, Edward ("Ted"): 169n60
Kentucky Fried Chicken (KFC) restaurants: 217
Kerr-McGee Corp.: 140, 242, 246, 248, 280n12
abandons uranium tailings: 242; BIA awards
initial contract to: 242; Church Rock No. 1
uranium mine of: 244, 245; Church Rock
No. 2 uranium mine of: 244; Church Rock
No. 3 uranium mine of: 244; job training
pgm. of: 244; lawsuits against: 243–4; legal
violations of: 282n37; lung cancer among
uranium miners of: 243; Redrock uranium

mine of: 243; Shiprock uranium mill of:
243–4, 281n12; Shiprock uranium mine of:
242, 243; worker safety violations of: 243-4
Key Lake (Saskatchewan)
uranium mining at: 269, 278
Khmer Rouge: 363n135
Kickapoos
Mexican Colony of: 337; removal to
Oklahoma of: 338
Kiersch, G.: 164n14
Kimberly-Clark Corp.: 311
King Philip (Metacom; Wampanoag leader): 368
King, Bruce: 245
King, Martin Luther Jr.: 228
King, Matthew: 29, 369
Kinne, Wisner: 105
Kiowas: 116, 386
Kirkpatrick, Jean: 397
Kitely, Francis: 218, 220, 232n109
Kitigawa, Kiochi: 213, 214
Klamaths
termination of: 54, 119, 350
Knechtel's food stores: 216
Knox, Henry: 40
Kohr, Leopold: 12
Kooros, Ahmed: 290n195
Korean War: 119
Kroeber, Alfred L.: 30n5, 54
Ku Klux Klan: 377
Kuletz, Valerie: 263
Kurlitz, Leo: 182
Kutenais
dispossession of: 342
Kuwait
Iraqi rights to: 375
Kyushu, Ltd.: 266

L

LaDuke, Winona: 28, 282n31, 291n208, 302, 369;
"Host World" concept of: 370
LaFarge, Oliver: 84n175, 137, 138
Laguna Pueblo: 140, 241, 247–50, 251, 265, 266,
275, 278, 346, 348, 416; and Anaconda
Copper Co.: 247–50, 346; and EPA: 248,
249; Jackpile Housing at: 248; Paguate
community of: 249; road network at: 248;
uranium contamination at: 247-9, 416;
uranium mining/milling at: 247-9
Laing, R.D.: 397
Lajambe, Hélène: 307
Lakota Times (newspaper): 130
Lakota Treaty Council: 426
Lakotas ("Sioux"): 27, 186n192, 186n193, 113–

Million, Dian: 369
Mi'kmaq
British expropriation of: 73-4n47
Mistissini Cree
  compensation to: 300; impact of James Bay
  I upon: 306; opposition to James Bay hydro
  projects: 298-309
Mobil Oil Corp.: 140, 246
Moffat, Michael: 319
Mohawk, John: 28, 369
Mohawk Warriors Society: 69n7, 367
Mohawks: 93, 107, 331
  and Ganiekeh confrontation: 102-3;
  Caughnawaga Reserve of: 102, 103; *James
  Deere* suit of: 101; Kanewake Reserve of:
  206, 207; Moss Lake Agreement and: 103;
  Oka community of: 26, 103, 108, 308, 367;
  St. Regis Reservation of: 101, 102, 103;
  support to Lubicon Cree of: 206, 207; 1789
  leasing agreement and: 96
Mohler, William: 282n31
Mollard, J.D.: 313
Monaco, size of: 20-1, 55
Monongye, David: 29, 149, 155, 369
Monroe, James: 335
Monroe Title and Abstract Co.: 105
Montour, Art: 369
Montoya, Joseph: 167n32, 167n39
Montreal Light, Heat and Power Consolidated:
  296
Moonan, Paul Sr.: 105
Mooney, James: 30n5
Moose Lake Ojibwe Reserve: 316-7, 318
  compensation to: 316; crime and alcoholism
  at: 316
Morgan, Thomas Jefferson: 52
Mormons/Mormonism: 136, 138-41, 165n17,
  168n48
Mormon Hopi faction, *see* Sekaquaptewa Faction
Morrall, Bill: 149
Morris, Chester: 154
Morris, Glenn T.: 28, 37, 86n192, 89n224,
  172n111, 176, 188n34, 369
Morrison, Jim: 215, 216, 231n90, 231-2n91
Morrison-Knudson Corp.: 165n20
Moskop, Wendy: 169n60
Movenpeck restaurants: 217, 233n118
Moves Camp, Ellen: 369
Mr. Submarine restaurants: 217
Mulroney, Brian: 213, 232n101
Museum of the American Indian/Heye
  Foundation: 225
My Lai Massacre: 145
MX missile program (U.S.): 184, 354

N

Nagaland
  India's internal colonization of: 25
Namibia
  Rossing uranium mine in: 283n49
Nash, Phileo: 154
National Academy of Science (NAS)
  "National Sacrifice Area" concept of: 162,
  172n114, 250-1, 265, 276, 283n68, 349-50
National Aeronautics and Space Administration
  (NASA): 254
National Association of Japanese Canadians
  (NAJC): 217, 232n101
National Audubon Society: 307, 321
National Lawyers Guild (NLG): 155-6, 170n81
Big Mountain Legal Defense/Offense
  Committee (BMLDOC) of: 155, 156, 157,
  169n80
National Liberation Movements, legal concept of:
  86-7n203
National Sacrifice Areas, concept of: 162,
  172n114, 250-1, 257, 265, 273, 276,
  283n68, 295, 349-50, 410; and "National
  Sacrifice Peoples": 295, 349
National Tribal Chairman's Association (NTCA):
  399n6
nations/nationality
  anthropological definition of: 20, 38-9; legal
  conceptualization of: 19-20, 41
Native Nevadan (newspaper): 176
Native North America: 331
  contemporary impoverishment of: 240;
  contemporary demography of: 331-2, 344,
  352, 358n51; contemporary population size
  of: 239, 331; employment data on: 347;
  diaspora of: 331-2, 350, 352; ecological
  understandings of: 17; economies of: 16;
  health data on: 240, 348; historical genocide
  of: 339-40; intellectual attainments of: 16;
  length of existence: 31n15, 380; low
  intensity warfare against: 38; material
  culture of: 15-6; medical practices of: 30n9;
  mineral resources of: 239, 345; mineral
  royalties received by: 240, 346, 347; oral
  traditions of: 16; political organization of:
  16-7; precolumbian population size of: 17,
  359n65, 380; precolumbian warfare of: 381;
  spiritual traditions of: 17; underdevelopment
  of: 347; world view of: 17
Natural World, concept of: 11-3
Navajo-Hopi Relocation Act (P.L. 93-531), *see*
  U.S. statures

Navajo-Hopi Relocation Commission: 146, 153, 158, 171n109; expenses associated with: 148
Navajo Power Plant: 165n17
Navajo Ranchers Association: 246
Navajo Nation: 265, 275, 278, 345, 348, 349
   Cañoncito Reservation of: 275;
   Environmental Protection Administration
   of: 246, 282-3n47; landbase of: 21; mineral
   resource base of: 20, 345; mineral royalties
   received by: 347 ;also see Diné
nazis/nazism: 40, 120, 375, 380, 411, 417, 418
Neitschmann, Bernard: 25, 373
Nellis Test Range: 183, 260, 286n119
   creation of: 286n119; Nevada Test Site area
   of: 183, 260, 261; Yucca Flats area of:
   286n119
Nelson, Emma: 154
Nelson, Terrance: 319
Neurath, Constantin von: 78n99
Nevada Power Co.: 165n20
"New Age," concept of: 18, 368
New England Energy Efficiency Coalition: 307
New England Power Pool: 302
New Hampshire, 1980 native population of: 332
New Mexico Environmental Protection Agency:
   245, 282n31
New York Genesee Co.: 95
New York Power Authority: 102, 301, 307, 308
   and Hydro-Québec: 301, 302, 303; Niagara
   Power Project of: 102
Newes/Newe Segobia: 173-86, 354, 377, 387
   alliances of: 184-5; and Indian Claims
   Commission: 174-6; and the IRA: 174, 175;
   Battle Mountain area of: 175; compensation
   offered to: 177, 179, 182; ecocide and: 186;
   Duckwater Reservation of: 181, 260;
   genocide and: 186; MX missile program
   and: 184, 354; National Council of: 185;
   nuclear testing and: 183, 260-1; resistance
   of: 178-86; restitution received by: 173;
   Temoak band of: 174, 175, 176, 187n6;
   Timisha Reservation of: 260; traditional
   territory of: 174; treaty territory of: 173,
   175, 176, 183, 354; Yomba Reservation of:
   260; Yucca Mountain nuclear waste facility
   and: 184, 261, 354
Newmont Mining Corp.: 165n20, 189n52
Blue Creek uranium contamination and: 256-7;
   Dawn Mining subsidiary of: 256; Spokane
   uranium mill of: 256-7
Newsweek (magazine): 314
Nez, Hosteen: 153
Nez, Miller: 154
Nez Percé/Nez Percé Reservation: 340

proposed as nuclear waste dump: 260,
   290n197; removal to Oklahoma of: 340;
   traditional territory of: 340
Nightgoose, Loughrienne: 170n84
Nixon, Richard M.: 283n68, 399n6
No Thank Q Hydro-Québec: 308
Norman Yoke, concept of: 46, 47, 75n66
North American Water and Power Alliance
   (NAWAPA): 309, 314-15, 320, 321,
   364n148; anticipated cost of: 320-1;
   geographic scope of: 314
Northern Inuit Association of Quebec: 300, 306
Northwest Ordinance, *see* U.S. statutes
Norway House Cree Reserve: 318-9
   impact of hydro flooding upon: 318; suicide
   rate at: 319; traditional economy of: 318
nuclear reactors: 274-5
   Chernobyl: 259, 274, 289n182; Diablo
   Canyon: 274, 277; Fort St.Vrain: 274,
   289n182; Hanford: 274, 289n182; Point
   Conception: 274; Savannah River: 274;
   Seabrook: 274, 277; Shoreham: 274; Three
   Mile Island: 244, 255, 259
Nuremberg Doctrine: 72n30, 235n153, 419
   Aggressive War construction of: 411; Crimes
   Against Humanity construction of: 121,
   295, 419; Crimes Against the Peace
   construction of: 121
Nuremberg Trials: 78n99, 411, 419

O

Oahe Dam: 410
Oaks, Richard: 369
O'Brien, Robert: 127
O'Connell, John: 178-9
O'Reilly, James: 205-6, 298, 299, 308, 325n36,
   327n78

Ogden, David A.: 96
Ogden Land Co.: 97, 98, 100
Oglala Aquifer
   contamination of: 252, 255
   Madison Formation of: 407
Ogoki Water Diversion Project (Ontario): 311
Ojibwes (Chippewas): 19, 292, 303, 310, 313-4;
   dispossession of: 342; *also see* Chemawawin
   Ojibwe Reserve; Grassy Narrows Ojibwe
   Reserve; Moose Lake Ojibwe Reserve;
   Whitedog Ojibwe Reserve
Oka
   armed confrontation at: 26, 103, 108, 308,
   367
Oklahoma

Sandinistas: 106, 169n80
SANE: 185
Santa Clara Pueblo: 258
Santoro, Amy: 231n90, 231-2n91
Sartre, Jean-Paul
colonialism equals genocide dictum of: 27, 33n43
Saskatchewan: 263-74
as "sacrifice area": 265, 273; radioactive effluent contamination in: 265, 269, 271-2; uranium mining in: 263-70; uranium mill wastes in: 264-5; *also see* Cigar Lake; Cluff Lake; Rabbit Lake; Wollaston Lake
Saskatchewan Indian Nations Development Corp.: 266
Saskatchewan Mining Development Corp.: 265, 266; collaboration with Eldorado Nuclear of: 268-9; collaboration with Uranez of: 269; interest in Cigar Lake Mining of: 270; Key Lake Mining subsidiary of: 269
Satank (Kiowa leader): 368
Satanta (Kiowa leader): 339, 368
Sauk and Fox
removal to Oklahoma of: 338; U.S. war against: 336
Save the Arizona Strip Association: 168n48
Saxifrage Publications Group: 29
scalp bounties: 339
scalping, origin of: 359n60
Scarth, Todd: 29
Schifter, Richard: 150
Schlesinger, James: 304
Schmidt, C.P.: 191
Schuller, Marilia: 236n160
Schuyler, Philip: 334
Scopes, John T.: 233n128
Scopes Evolution Case ("Scopes Monkey Trial"): 221, 233-4n128
Scots/Scotland
British internal colonization of: 25
Scudder, Thayer: 151
Secakuku, Ferrell: 160
secession, right of: 13, 389
Sekaquaptewa, Abbot: 138, 151, 158, 169n61
Sekaquaptewa, Emory: 138
Sekaquaptewa, Emory Jr.: 138
Sekaquaptewa, Helen: 167n33
Sekaquaptewa, Wayne: 138
Sekaquaptewa Faction: 158, 165n17, 166n29, 167n32; and Grazing District 6: 139-40, 164n11; and *Healing v. Jones* suit: 140; and Hopi reorganization: 138; and "Navajo-Hopi range dispute": 144; ascendancy in Hopi tribal Council: 138-9; controls Hopi

newspaper: 139; hires John Boyden: 140; monopolizes government contracts: 138-9; relationship to Sam Steiger: 144
Seminoles
Big Cypress Reservation of: 337; Brighton Reservation of: 337; ethnic composition of: 335; Hollywood Reservation of: 337; massacre of: 337; removal to Oklahoma of: 335-6; Trail of Tears attrition of: 336; wars of: 335, 336
Senecas: 93
Allegheny Band of: 101, 106-7; Alleghany Reservation of: 99, 100, 101, 102; and Salamanca lease: 101, 106-7, 110-1n38; and Seneca Nation Settlement Act: 107; Cattaraugus Reservation of: 99; Kinzua Dam and: 102; Tonawanda Band of: 98; *U.S. v. Forness* suit and: 100; 1789 expropriation of: 94; 1810 expropriation of: 96; 1838 land "cession" of: 96; 1905 lawsuit of: 98-9;
Seneca County Liberation Organization (SCLO): 105
Service, Robert: 292
settler-states
Australia: 25, 240; Canada: 37, 42, 240; Israel: 25, 240; New Zealand: 25, 240; Northern Ireland: 25, 240; Rhodesia: 25; South Africa: 25; U.S.: 37, 42, 240; *also see* colonialism
Sequoia (Cherokee leader): 337
Seventh Generation Fund: 175
Seward, William Henry: 358n48
Seymor, Frederick: 79n104
Shawnees: 333
defeat at Fallen Timbers (1794): 96; removal of: 338
Shawnigan Water and Power Co.: 296
Shay, Kee: 29
Shebandowan Lake (Ontario)
mineral resources around: 294; nickel mine at: 294
Sheridan, Philip: 82n151, 353, 384
Shoshones: 251, 386
and Arapahos: 340; Bear River Massacre of: 338; uranium mining/milling and: 255; Wind River Reservation of: 251, 275, 340
Sidney, Ivan: 158, 160
Sierra Club: 185, 307, 308
James Bay and Northern Québec Task Force of: 307
Siletz
termination/restoration of: 351
Silko, Leslie: 369
Simkin, William: 148, 167n40

University of Victoria: 218
Uranez Corp.: 189n53, 269
　　collaboration with Eldorado Nuclear and
　　Saskatchewan Mining of: 269; Key Lake
　　Mining subsidiary of: 269
uranium enrichment facilities: 274
　　Fernald: 274, 277; Paducah: 274;
　　Portsmouth: 274
U.S. Air Force: 262
　　Dugway Proving Grounds of: 262;
　　Ellsworth Air Base of: 386, 431; Toole
　　Ordnance Depot of: 262; also see Nellis Test
　　Range
U.S. Army
　　Alamagordo Bombing/White Sands Test
　　Range of: 263; Corps of Engineers of: 102,
　　313, 431; Igloo Ordnance Depot of: 252-3,
　　431; 7th Cavalry Rgt. of: 115-6
U.S. Constitution: 373, 410
　　Article I of: 20, 41, 72n36, 94, 400n24, 410;
　　Article II: 73n38; Article VI: 41; Commerce
　　Clause of: 94; First Amendment to: 127;
　　Haudenosaunee influence on: 30n7;
　　Supremacy Clause of: 73n36
U.S. Court of Claims: 120, 121, 122, 128, 177
U.S. Courts of Appeal
　　8th Circuit: 123, 170n88; 9th Circuit: 179,
　　246
U.S. Dept. of Energy: 250, 255, 257, 276, 277
　　as Atomic Energy Commission (AEC): 140,
　　243, 251, 281n12, 281n23, 346; Energy
　　Resource and Development Administration
　　of: 183, 275; Federal Power Commission of:
　　102; National Uranium Research and
　　Evaluation Institute (NURE) of: 254; Oak
　　Ridge facility of: 277; "Project
　　Independence" of: 250; also see Hanford
　　nuclear weapons facility; Los Alamos
　　Scientific Laboratory
U.S. Dept. of Health, Education and Welfare
　　(DHEW; now Dept. of Health and Human
　　Services): 243; National Commission on
　　Radiation Protection of: 243; National
　　Institute for Occupational Safety and
　　Health (NIOSH) of: 243; Public Health
　　Service (PHS) of: 243, 249;
U.S. Dept. of Interior: 167n35, 181, 182, 249, 252,
　　254-5, 257; Bureau of Indian Affairs (BIA)
　　of: 47, 101, 115, 137, 139, 151, 152, 155,
　　156, 158, 164n11, 164n14, 171n97, 175,
　　177, 242, 249, 252, 256, 343, 346, 347,
　　399n6, 405, 406, 414, 425, 435; Bureau of
　　Land Management (BLM) of: 146, 178, 181;
　　Bureau of Reclamation of: 165n17, 165n20,

429; Central Arizona Project of: 165n17,
165n20; Environmental Protection Agency
(EPA) of: 246-7, 248, 249, 256, 257, 276,
285n109; Forestry Service of: 124, 127,
164n11; Geological Survey of: 254;
National Park Service of: 255; Office of
Surface Mining (OSM) of: 161
U.S. Dept. of Justice: 100, 121, 123
　　Federal Bureau of Investigation (FBI) of:
　　127, 153, 413, 425; Marshals Service of: 127,
　　156, 413; U.S. v. Forness suit of: 101
U.S. Dept. of Labor: 244
U.S. Dept. of the Treasury: 177
U.S. Dept. of War ("Defense"): 115, 254
　　headquarters of ("Pentagon"): 184, 263;
　　Veterans Administration of: 431
U.S. General Accounting Office (GAO): 248
U.S. House of Representatives: 143, 146, 166n23;
　　Concurrent Resolution 108 of (1953): 54,
　　350; Interior and Insular Affairs Committee
　　of: 145, 159; passes Navajo-Hopi
　　Relocation Act: 146; Resolution 10337 of
　　(1974): 145, 167n33; Resolution 4281
　　(1986): 159; Resolution 1235 (1991): 159;
　　Subcommittee on Indian Affairs of: 150
U.S. Indian treaties: 41, 73n38, 331, 373, 411-13;
　　Fort Laramie Treaties (1851, 1868): 114,
　　115, 122, 124, 132n3, 284n87, 406, 413,
　　428, 430, 431, 432; Treaties of Buffalo
　　Creek (1838, 1842): 97, 98, 100, 110n20;
　　Treaty of Canandaiga (1794): 96, 100; Treaty
　　of Fort Harmar (1789): 94, 100; Treaty of
　　Fort Stanwix (1784): 93, 94, 96, 100, 102,
　　103, 104; Treaty of Fort Wise (1861): 375;
　　Treaty of Hopewell (???): 55; Treaty of
　　Ruby Valley (1863): 173, 176, 177, 185, 260,
　　354; Treaty with the Navajo (1868): 136;
　　Treaty with the Omahas (1854): 76n74
U.S. Senate: 143, 151, 166n23, 331
　　Interior Committee of: 150; passes Navajo-
　　Hopi Relocation Act: 146; treaty ratification
　　authority of: 73n38, 331
U.S. statutes
　　Alaska Native Claims Settlement Act
　　(1971): 354; American Indian Religious
　　Freedom Act (1978): 127; American Indian
　　Self-Determination and Educational
　　Assistance Act (1975): 64, 68; Assimilative
　　Crimes Act (1898): 359n73; Burke Act
　　(1906): 48, 77n83, 343; Clean Water Act
　　(1972): 282n37; Federal Coal Leasing Act
　　(1975): 361n102; General Allotment Act
　　("Dawes Act"; 1887): 47-8, 110n27, 118,
　　132n18, 133n27, 341-3, 407; Homestead